Properties of Matter & SHM

for JEE Main & Advanced

(Study Package for Physics)

Fully Solved

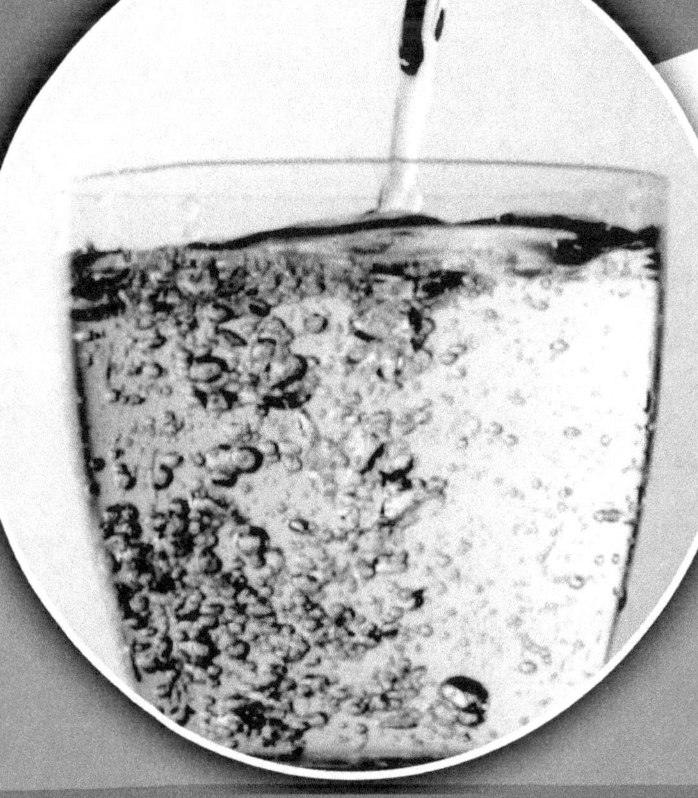

Includes Past JEE & KVPY Questions

Useful for Class 11, KVPY & Olympiads

- **Head Office :** B-32, Shivalik Main Road, Malviya Nagar, New Delhi-110017
- **Sales Office :** B-48, Shivalik Main Road, Malviya Nagar, New Delhi-110017
  Tel. : 011-26691021 / 26691713

Page Layout : Prakash Chandra Sahoo

Typeset by Disha DTP Team

Printed at : Repro Knowledgecast Limited, Thane

For further information about the books from DISHA,

Log on to **www.dishapublication.com** or email to **info@dishapublication.com**

STUDY PACKAGE IN PHYSICS FOR JEE MAIN & ADVANCED

Booklet No.	Title	Chapter Nos.	Page Nos.
1	Units, Measurements & Motion	Ch 0. Mathematics Used in Physics Ch 1. Units and Measurements Ch 2. Vectors Ch 3. Motion in a Straight Line Ch 4. Motion in a Plane	1-202
2	Laws of Motion and Circular Motion	Ch 5. Laws of Motion and Equilibrium Ch 6. Circular Motion	203-318
3	Work Energy, Power & Gravitation	Ch 7. Work, Energy and Power Ch 8. Collisions and Centre of Mass Ch 9. Gravitation	319-480
4	Rotational Motion	Ch 1. Rotational Mechanics	1-120
5	Properties of Matter & SHM	Ch 2. Properties of Matter Ch 3. Fluid Mechanics Ch 4. Simple Harmonic Motion	121-364
6	Heat & Thermodynamics	Ch 5. Thermometry, Expansion & Calorimetry Ch 6. Kinetic Theory of Gases Ch 7. Laws of Thermodynamics Ch 8. Heat Transfer	365-570
7	Waves	Ch 9. Wave – I Ch 10. Wave –II	571-698
8	Electrostatics	Ch 0. Mathematics Used in Physics Ch 1. Electrostatics Ch 2. Capacitance & Capacitors	1-216
9	Current Electricity	Ch 3. DC and DC circuits Ch 4. Thermal and Chemical effects of Current"	217-338
10	Magnetism, EMI & AC	Ch 5. Magnetic Force on Moving Charges & Conductor Ch 6. Magnetic Effects of Current Ch 7. Permanent Magnet & Magnetic Properties of Substance Ch 8. Electromagnetic Induction Ch 9. AC and EM Waves	339-618
11	Ray & Wave Optics	Ch 1. Reflection of Light Ch 2. Refraction and Dispersion Ch 3. Refraction at Spherical Surface, Lenses and Photometry Ch 4. Wave optics	1-244
12	Modern Physics	Ch 5. Electron, Photon, Atoms, Photoelectric Effect and X-rays Ch 6. Nuclear Physics Ch 7. Electronics & Communication	245-384

Contents

Study Package Booklet 5 - Properties of Matter & SHM

CHAPTER 2

Properties of Matter

(121- 186)

2.1 Deforming Force

When force is applied in such a way that the body has no translation motion, but molecules of body are forced to undergo a change in their relative position, is called deforming force. As a result of this force, the body may undergo a change in length, volume or shape. The force can be applied by the following ways :

(i)   When body is subjected to two equal and opposite forces.

(ii)   When one end of the body is connected to a fixed support and other end is subjected to a force. In this case there develops an equal amount of reaction force on the fixed end.

      In both the cases, the force on any section of the body will be $T - F = 0$ or $T = F$. It is not $2F$, not zero (*fig. 2.1*).

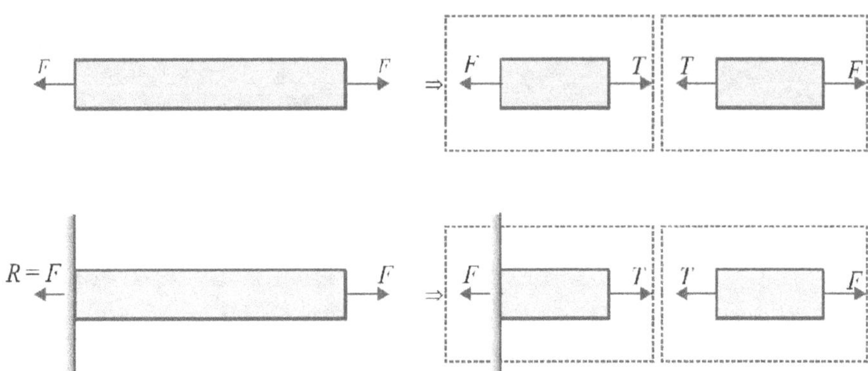

Fig. 2.1

(iii)   When force is applied at one end of the body, the inertia plays a significant role to stretch the body. Let a body of mass m is subjected to force F at its one end. The force T at any section can be calculated as :

$$\text{Acceleration} \qquad a = \frac{F}{m}$$

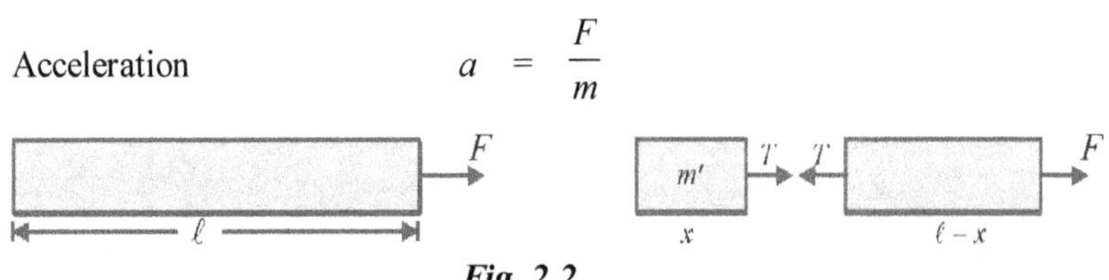

Fig. 2.2

Mass of the x length of the body

$$m' = \frac{m}{\ell}x$$

By Newton's second law for the mass m, we have

$$T = m'A$$
$$= \left(\frac{m}{\ell}x\right)\frac{F}{m} = \frac{Fx}{\ell}$$

For $\qquad x = 0,\ T = 0$

For $\qquad x = \dfrac{\ell}{2},\ T = \dfrac{F}{2}$

For $\qquad x = \ell,\ T = F$

2.2 ELASTICITY AND PLASTICITY

If a body regains its original size and shape after removal of deforming force, it is said to be elastic and the property is called **elasticity**. If body does not regain its original size and shape even after removal of deforming force, it is said to be plastic and property of the body is called **plasticity**. If a body regains its original size and shape completely and immediately after removal of force, it is said to be perfectly elastic body. If body does not show any tendency to regain its original size and shape after removal of the deforming force, it is said to be perfectly plastic. But in practice no body is perfectly elastic and no one perfectly plastic.

2.3 STRESS

When a body is deformed under a force, each section of the body is set-up an internal force which tends to bring the body into its original state. The internal restoring force set up per unit area of resisting area is called stress. As the restoring force is equal and opposite to the external deforming force, therefore

$$\text{Stress } (f) = \frac{\text{Applied force}}{\text{Area}} = \frac{F}{A}$$

The SI unit of stress is N/m^2. This is also called pascal, i.e., $1 N/m^2 = 1 Pa$.

2.4 STRAIN

When a deforming force acts on a body, the body undergoes a change in size and shape. So strain can be defined as :

$$\text{Strain(e)} = \frac{\text{Change in dimension}}{\text{Original dimension}}$$

Strain is a dimensionless quantity.

2.5 TYPES OF STRESSES AND STRAINS

Depending on the force applied on the body, there are three types of stresses and corresponding strains.

1. **Direct or longitudinal stress and strain**

   The force is applied along one direction of the body in such a way that its shape will not change. The force may be tensile force or it may be compressive force . Accordingly there are two types of direct stresses :

   (i) Tensile stress

   (ii) Compressive stress

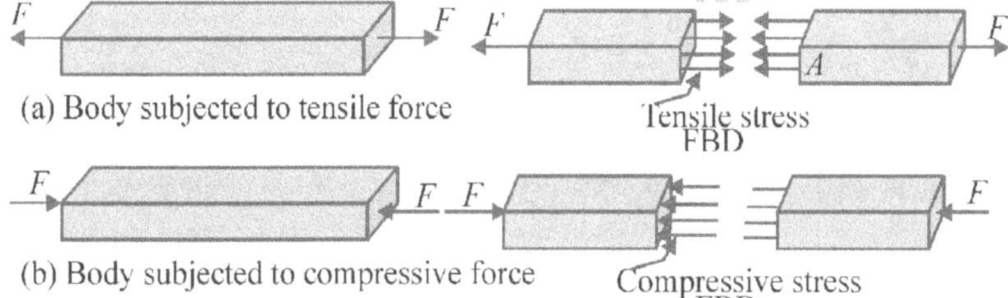

Fig. 2.3

$$\text{Direct stress} \qquad f = \frac{F}{A}$$

$$\text{Longitudinal strain} \qquad e = \frac{\Delta \ell}{\ell}$$

where $\Delta \ell$ is the change in length of the body and ℓ is the original length of the body.

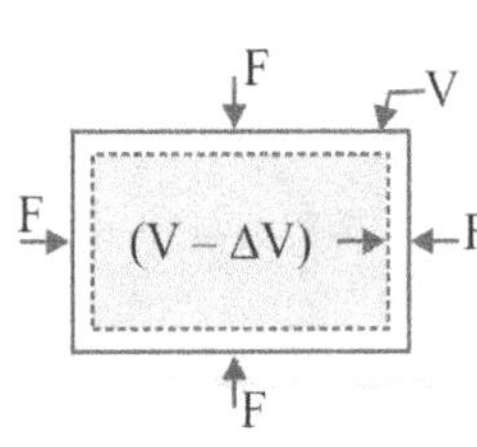

Fig. 2.4

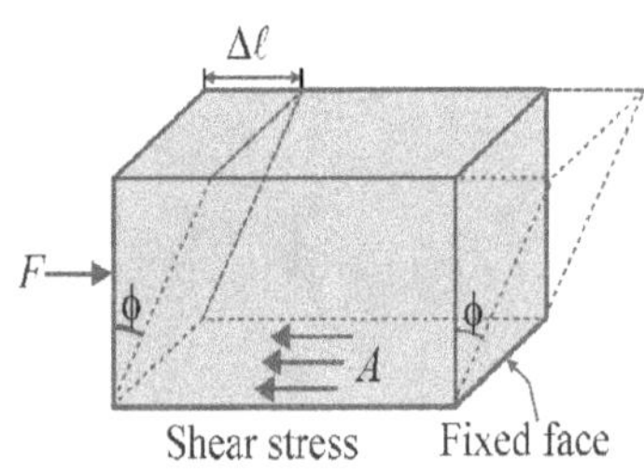

Shear stress   Fixed face

Fig. 2.5

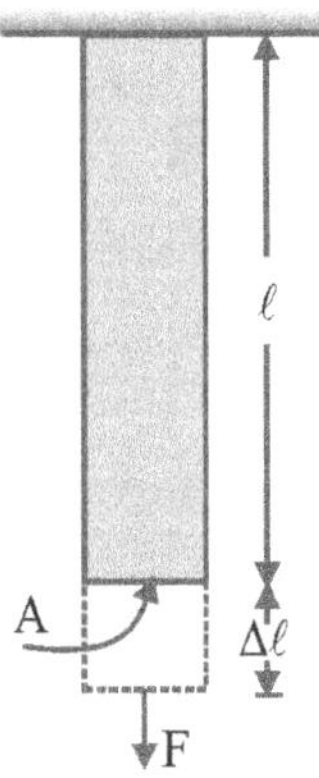

Fig. 2.6

2. Normal stress and volumetric strain

When body is subjected to a uniform force from all possible directions and shape of body does not change, then the corresponding stress is called normal stress. When body is placed inside fluid, it subjected to uniform pressure from all round.

Consider a body of volume V and surface area A. When it subjected to uniform force F from all sides, then

$$\text{Normal stress} \quad F = \frac{F}{A} = \text{pressure}(P)$$

$$\text{Volumetric strain} \quad e = \frac{\text{Change in volume}}{\text{Original volume}}$$

$$= \frac{\Delta V}{V}$$

3. Shear stress and shear strain

When a force acts in such a way that it changes the shape of the body, the corresponding stress is called shear stress.

$$\text{Shear stress} \quad f = \frac{F}{A}$$

$$\text{Shear strain,} \quad e = \phi \simeq \tan \phi = \frac{\Delta \ell}{\ell}$$

2.6 ELASTIC LIMIT

The maximum stress within which body can regains its original size and shape after removal of the deforming force is called **elastic limit.** If body exceed this limit, then it will not get initial size and shape completely, it will get permanent set and is said to be overstrained.

2.7 HOOKE'S LAW

It stated that within elastic limit, the stress is directly proportional to the strain . Thus

$$\text{Stress} \propto \text{Strain}$$

or
$$\text{Stress} = E \times \text{strain}$$

or
$$\frac{\text{Stress}}{\text{Strain}} = E$$

where E is a constant called modulus of elasticity or coefficient of elasticity. It is a material property which does not depend on size and shape of the body.

2.8 DIFFERENT TYPES OF MODULII OF ELASTICITY

Depending on three types of stresses and strains, there are three types of modulus of elasticity, viz; Young's modulus, bulk modulus and shear modulus.

1. Young's modulus of elasticity

It is defined as :
$$Y = \frac{\text{Longitudinal stress}}{\text{Longitudinal strain}}$$

Suppose a wire of length ℓ and cross-section area A is subjected to external force F, then Young's modulus

$$Y = \frac{f}{e} = \frac{F/A}{\Delta\ell/\ell}$$

or
$$Y = \frac{F\ell}{A\Delta\ell} \qquad \ldots(i)$$

Also
$$\Delta\ell = \frac{F\ell}{AY} \qquad \ldots(ii)$$

For a circular cross-section with a suspended load Mg, we have $F = Mg$ and $A = \pi r^2$.

$$\therefore \qquad Y = \frac{Mg\ell}{\pi r^2 \Delta\ell} \qquad \ldots(iii)$$

Note:

The above equation can be written as :

$$F = \frac{YA}{\ell}\Delta\ell$$

or, if $\dfrac{YA}{\ell}$ is replaced by a single constant k and elongation $\Delta\ell$ is represented by x, then

$$F = kx \quad \left[k = \frac{YA}{\ell} \right]$$

Hooke's law was originally stated in this form, rather than in terms of stress and strain.

2. Bulk modulus of elasticity

Consider a body of volume V. Suppose force F acts uniformly from each direction of the body. The pressure on the body in addition to existing pressure $P = \dfrac{F}{A}$.

The bulk modulus is defined as :

$$B = \frac{\text{Normal stress}}{\text{Volumetric strain}}$$

or
$$B = \frac{P}{\left(\Delta V/V\right)}$$

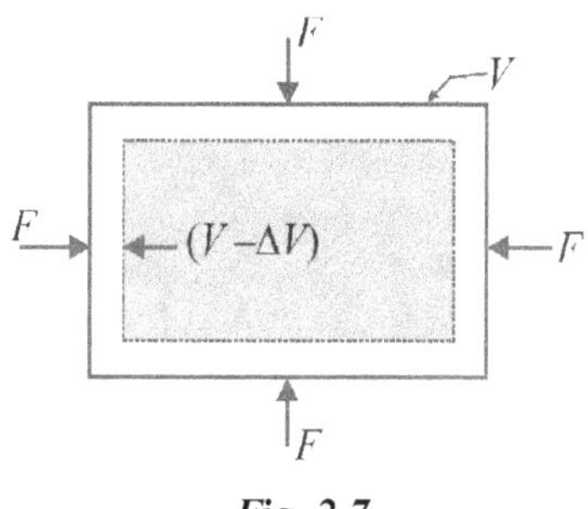

Fig. 2.7

Compressibility : It is the reciprocal of bulk modulus of the material of the body.

Thus compressibility
$$\kappa = \frac{1}{B}.$$

Note:

The bulk modulus in differential form can be written as

$$B = \frac{dP}{\left(-\dfrac{dV}{V}\right)}$$

Here negative sign indicates that with increase in pressure, the volume of body will decrease.

3. Shear modulus

It is defined as :

$$\eta = \frac{\text{Shear stress}}{\text{Shear strain}}$$

$$= \frac{(F/A)}{\phi} = \frac{F}{A\phi}$$

Here ϕ is the shear strain, which is equal to $\dfrac{\Delta\ell}{\ell}$.

$$\therefore \qquad \eta = \frac{F}{A} \cdot \frac{\ell}{\Delta\ell}$$

Important points

1. Solid possess all the three molulii of elasticity.
2. Liquids and gases possess only bulk modulus.
3. For a perfectly rigid body, strain produced will be zero and hence molulii of elasticity will be ∞.
4. Shear occurs in case of twisting, cutting, tearing.
5. Elasticity of the material get affected by the following :
   (i) Hammering and rolling - Increases.
   (ii) Annealing (formation of larger crystal) - Decreases.
   (iii) Presence of impurities - May increase or decrease, depending on the mixing material.
   (iv) With increase in temperature, elasticity of most of the material decreases.

2.9 STRESS-STRAIN CURVE FOR A METALLIC WIRE

Determination of Young's modulus by Searle's method

Experiment shows a metal wire is subjected to a gradually increasing load. It is found that the strain is directly proportional to the corresponding stress upto a certain limit only and beyond that the relation is non-linear. In investigating the mechanical properties of material beyond this limit, the relationship between the strain and corresponding stress is usually represented by tensile test diagram.

Explanation of different parts of stress-strain curve :

(i) **OA** : In this region, the stress is proportional to strain upto A and Hooke's law is obeyed. Point A is called proportional limit. Slope of line OA gives Young's modulus of material of wire.

(ii) **AB** : From A to B, strain is not proportional to stress, but if the load is removed at any point between O and B, the curve will be retraced and the material will return to its original length. In the region OB, the material is said to be elastic and the point B is called elastic limit. Upto point B, the elastic forces of the material are conservative; when the material returns to its original shape, work done in producing the deformation is recovered.

(iii) **Beyond B** : If the wire is loaded further, the strain increases rapidly than the corresponding stress. If the load is removed from any point beyond B (say C), the wire does not come back to its original length but traverses the dotted line CE as shown in *Fig. 2.9*. Even on reducing the stress zero, a small strain equal to OE is left in the wire, and the material is said to have a permanent set.

(iv) **Beyond C** : If the wire is loaded beyond C, a large increase in strain is observed until point D is reached at which fracture (failure) takes place. From B to D, the material is said to undergo plastic flow, which is irreversible. The stress corresponding to the fracture point is called ultimate or breaking strength.
Figure shows the stress-strain curves for different materials.

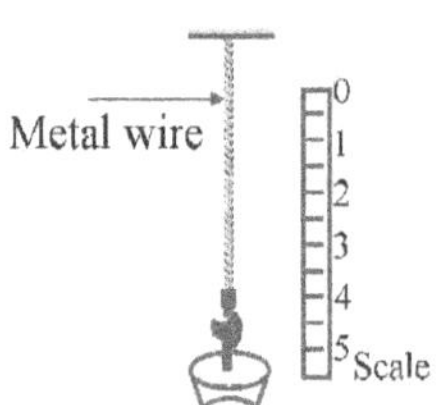

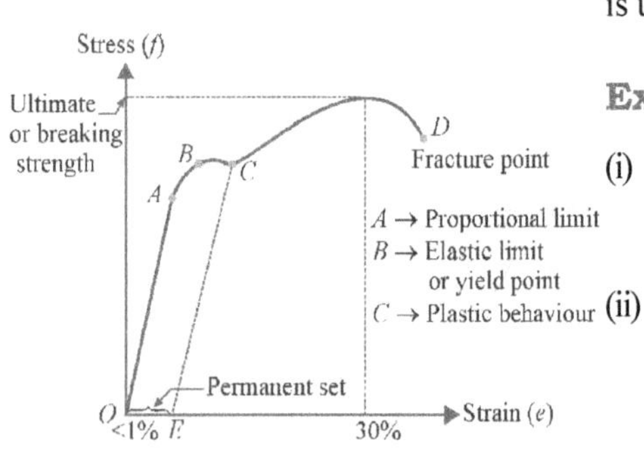

Fig. 2.8

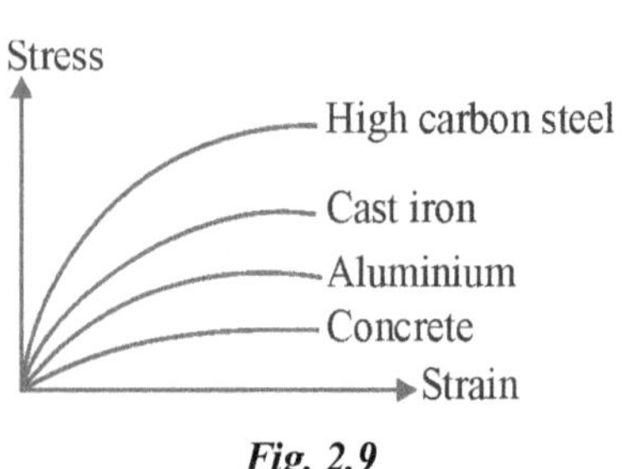

Fig. 2.9

Note:

1. For the hard material like high carbon steel, cast-iron, points A and B are indifferentiable.
2. The material with large region BD will be more ductile and small region of BD is called brittle material.

2.10 ELASTIC HYSTERESIS

Some materials like rubber can be stretched to over six to seven times its original length. These materials are called elastomers. When unloaded, the material is restored to its original length. But any stage of loading and unloading, strain is not proportional to stress. The fact that stress-strain curve is not retraced on unloading, is known as elastic hysteresis.

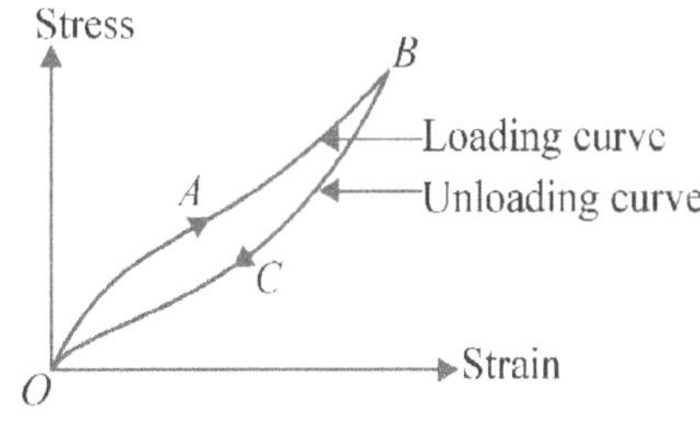

Fig. 2.10

Note:

1. Rubber possesses large amount of elasticity, but it does not obey Hooke's law.
2. The area of the loop $OABCO$ represents the energy lost as heat during the loading-unloading cycle.

Ex. 1 The stress-strain graphs for materials A and B are shown in *Fig. 2.11*.

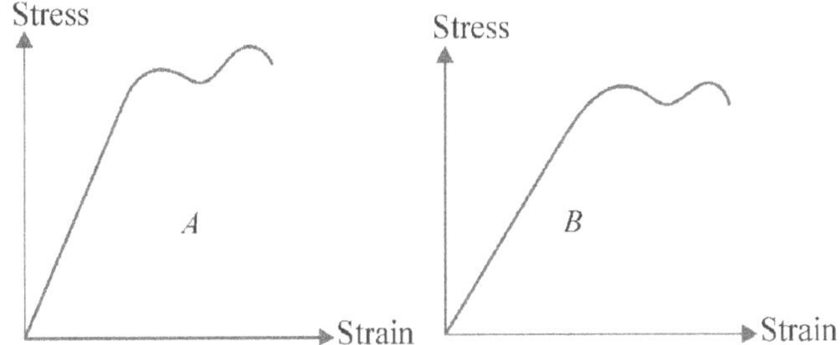

Fig. 2.11

The graphs are drawn to the same scale.

(a) Which of the material has greater Young's modulus ?

(b) Which material is more ductile?

(c) Which is more brittle ?

(d) Which of the two is stronger material ?

Sol.

(a) As the slope of stress-strain curve A is greater, so Young's modulus of material A will be greater than that of B.

(b) As plastic region for A is greater, so material A is more ductile.

(c) More ductile material will be brittle, so material A is less brittle.

(d) The breaking strength of material A is greater than material B, so material A is stronger than B.

Ex. 2 Two different types of rubber are found to have the stress-strain curves as shown in *Fig. 2.12*.

(a) A heavy machine is to be installed in a factory. To absorb the vibrations of the machine, a block of rubber, is placed between the machinary and the floor. Which of the two rubbers A and B would you prefer to use for this purpose ? Why?

(b) Which of the two rubber materials would you choose for a car tyres?

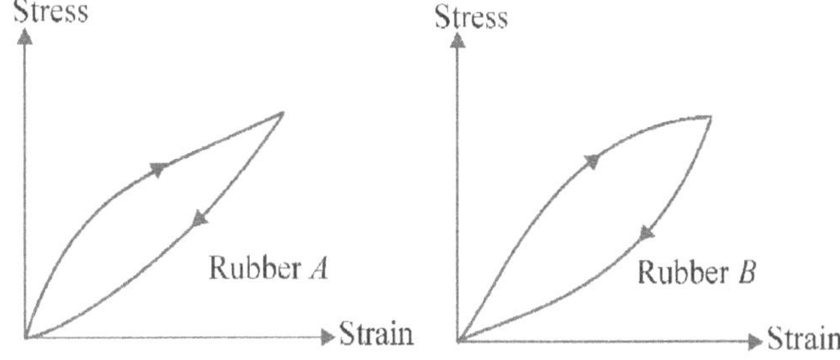

Fig. 2.12

Sol.

It is clear from the figures that area enclosed in hysteresis loop is larger for B than A. So rubber B will absorb more energy than A.

(a) In heavy machine, the energy of vibrations is quite large, so rubber B is suitable for the purpose.

(b) In a car tyre small energy is to be absorbed by tyres (more by air inside it) so rubber A is suitable for the purpose.

Ex. 3 (a) It is possible to double the length of a metallic wire by applying a force over it?

(b) Is elastic limit a property of the material of the wire?

(c) Which is more elastic : water or air?

(d) Why does a wire get heated when it is bent back and forth?

(e) The ratio stress/strain remains constant for a small deformation. What happens to this ratio if deformation is made very large?

(f) Why are electric / telephone poles given hollow structure?

Sol.

(a) No, because elastic limit strain is about 10^{-3} and wire actually break much before it is stretched to double length.

(b) No. It also depends on the radius of the wire.

(c) Water is more elastic than air. More strain is produced in air comparison to water for some amount of stress, so ratio stress/strain is small for air.

(d) When a wire is bent back and forth, its deformations are beyond elastic limit, so the work done against interatomic forces is no longer stored entirely in the elastic potential energy and some part of it will convert into heat.

(e) When the deforming force exceeds the elastic limit, the strain increases more rapidly than stress. Hence the ratio stress / strain decreases.

(f) Hollow poles have greater moment of inertia in comparison to solid poles made from the same amounts of material and so less deformation

Ex. 4 Read each of the statements below carefully and state, with reasons, if it is true or false.

(a) **The modulus of elasticity of rubber is greater than that of steel.**

(b) **The stretching of a coil is determined by its shear modulus.**

(c) **Elastic restoring forces are strictly conservative only, when Hooke's law is obeyed.**

Sol.

(a) False. When steel and rubber are subjected to same amount of deforming force, large amount of strain will be produced in rubber.

The ratio $\left[\dfrac{\text{stress}}{\text{strain}}\right]$ and hence Young's modulus will be smaller for rubber.

(b) True. When coil spring is subjected to a force, its shape will change.

(c) False. Elastic forces are conservative even material subjected to these forces does not obey Hooke's law.

Ex. 5 A bar of cross-section A is subjected to equal and opposite tensile forces at its ends. Consider a plane section of the bar whose normal makes an angle θ with the axis of the bar.

(a) **What is the tensile stress on this plane ?**

(b) **What is the shearing stress on this plane ?**

(c) **For what value of θ is the tensile stress maximum?**

(d) **For what value of θ is the shearing stress maximum?**

Sol.

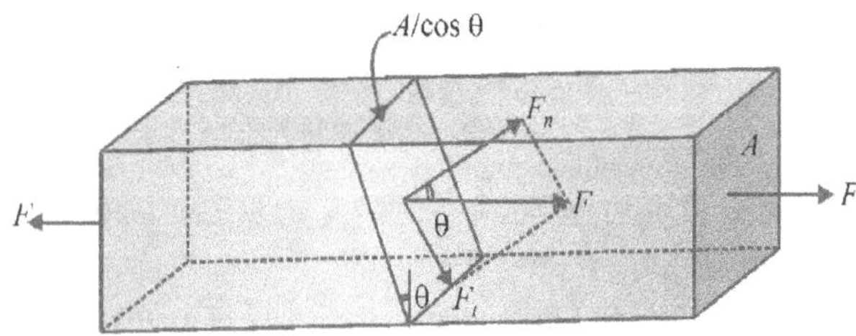

Fig. 2.13

The area of the given section $A' = \dfrac{A}{\cos\theta}$.

The tensile force F can be resolved into two perpendicular components, F_n and F_t, where $F_n = F\cos\theta$ and $F_t = F\sin\theta$.

(a) Tensile stress $= \dfrac{F_n}{A'} = \dfrac{F\cos\theta}{(A/\cos\theta)} = \dfrac{F}{A}\cos^2\theta$ *Ans.*

(b) Shearing stress $= \dfrac{F_t}{A'} = \dfrac{F\sin\theta}{(A/\cos\theta)} = \dfrac{F}{A}\sin\theta\cos\theta$

$\qquad = \dfrac{F}{2A}\sin 2\theta$ *Ans.*

(c) Tensile stress will be maximum when $\cos^2\theta$ is maximum, i.e., $\cos\theta = 1$ or $\theta = 0°$.   *Ans.*

(d) Shear stress will be maximum when $\sin 2\theta$ is maximum, i.e., $\sin 2\theta = 1$ or $2\theta = 90°$ or $\theta = 45°$ *Ans.*

Ex. 6 Two wires of diameter 0.25 cm, one made of steel and other made of brass are loaded as shown in *Fig. 2.14*. The unloaded length of the steel wire is 1.5 m and that of brass is 1.0 m. Young's modulus of steel is 2.0 × 10¹¹ Pa and that of brass is 0.91 × 10¹¹ Pa. Compute the elongations of steel and brass wires.

Sol.

For brass wire :

$$\ell = 1.0 \text{ m}, \ r = 0.125 \times 10^{-2} \text{ m}$$

$$F = 6 \times 9.8 \text{ N}, \ Y = 0.91 \times 10^{11} \text{ N/m}^2$$

We have,

$$\Delta\ell = \dfrac{F\ell}{AY}$$

$$= \dfrac{(6 \times 9.8) \times 1.0}{\pi(0.125 \times 10^{-2})^2 \times (0.91 \times 10^{11})}$$

$$= 1.32 \times 10^{-4} \text{ m} \qquad \textit{Ans.}$$

For steel wire :

$$\ell = 1.5 \text{ m}, \ r = 0.125 \times 10^{-2} \text{ m}$$

$$F = (6+4) \times 9.8 \text{ N} = 98 \text{ N},$$

$$Y = 2.0 \times 10^{11} \text{ N/m}^2$$

We have, $\quad \Delta\ell = \dfrac{F\ell}{AY}$

$$= \dfrac{98 \times 1.5}{\pi(0.125 \times 10^{-2})^2 \times (2.0 \times 10^{11})}$$

$$= 1.5 \times 10^4 \text{ m} \qquad \textit{Ans.}$$

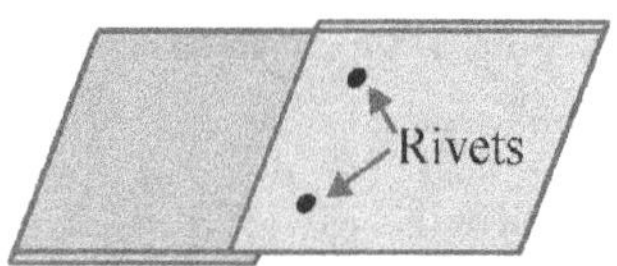

Fig. 2.14

Ex. 7 Two long metallic strips are joined together by two rivets each of radius 2.0 mm (*Fig. 2.15*). Each rivet can withstand a maximum shearing stress of 1.5 × 10⁹ Pa. What is the maximum tensile force that the strip can exert, assuming that each rivet shares the stretching load equally?

Sol.

The resisting area of each rivet = cross-sectional area of rivet

Fig. 2.15

or $\quad A = \pi r^2 = \pi(2 \times 10^{-3})^2$

$$= 4\pi \times 10^{-6} \text{ m}^2$$

The tensile force, that each rivet can withstand

$$F = fA = (1.5 \times 10^9) \times (4\pi \times 10^{-6})$$

$$= 18.86 \times 10^3 \text{ N}$$

The maximum tensile force the strip can withstand

$$= 2F = 2 \times 18.86 \times 10^3$$

$$= 3.77 \times 10^4 \text{ N} \qquad \textit{Ans.}$$

Ex. 8 Four identical hollow cylindrical columns of steel support a big structure of mass 50,000 kg. The inner and outer radii of each column are 30 cm and 40 cm respectively. Assuming the load distribution to be uniform, calculate the compressional strain of each column. The Young's modulus of steel is 2.0×10^{11} Pa.

Sol.

The load wear by each column $= \dfrac{50000 \times 9.8}{4} = 1.225 \times 10^5 \, N$

Resisting area of each column $= \pi(R^2 - r^2)$
$= \pi \left[(0.4)^2 - (0.3)^2\right] = 0.22 \, m^2$

Compressional strain

$= \dfrac{\text{Stress}}{\text{Young's modulus}}$

$= \dfrac{F/A}{Y} = \dfrac{F}{YA}$

$= \dfrac{1.225 \times 10^5}{(2.0 \times 10^{11}) \times (0.22)}$

$= 2.78 \times 10^{-6}$ *Ans.*

Extension due to self weight

Consider a specimen of length ℓ and cross-sectional area A. If density of its material is ρ, then weight of the specimen $W = \rho A \ell g$. The specimen is hanging from the rigid support. The specimen extends due to self weight.

Let us consider an element of thickness dx at a distance x from the free end.

The weight of the element $W' = x A \rho g$.

The extension of the element due to this loa

$$\delta \ell = \frac{W'(dx)}{AY}$$

$$= \frac{(xA\rho g)dx}{AY} = \frac{\rho g}{Y} x\, dx$$

The total extension

$$\Delta \ell = \int_0^\ell \delta \ell = \frac{\rho g}{Y} \int_0^\ell x\, dx$$

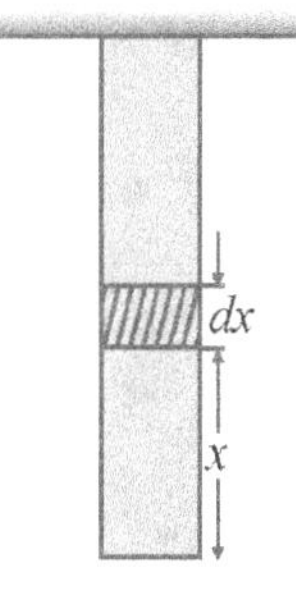

Fig. 2.16

or

$$\Delta \ell = \frac{\rho g \ell^2}{2Y}$$

Substituting $W = \rho A \ell g$ in the above equation, we get

$$\Delta \ell = \frac{W \ell}{2AY}$$

If the specimen is subjected to an external force in addition to its weight, then its total extension

$$\Delta \ell = \frac{F \ell}{AY} + \frac{W \ell}{2AY}$$

Thermal stress

Consider a specimen which is clamped between two rigid supports and subjected to change in temperature by ΔT. If the specimen is free to expand, its length will increase by $\ell \alpha \Delta T$.

The strain produced

$$e = \frac{\Delta \ell}{\ell} = \frac{\ell \alpha \Delta T}{\ell}$$

$$= \alpha \Delta T$$

This strain is prevented by the supports and therefore stress is induced in each section of the specimen.

Thus thermal stress

$$f_{th} = eY = \alpha \Delta T Y$$

or

$$f_{th} = Y \alpha \Delta T$$

The force exerted by the support

$$F = f_{th} A = Y A \alpha \Delta T.$$

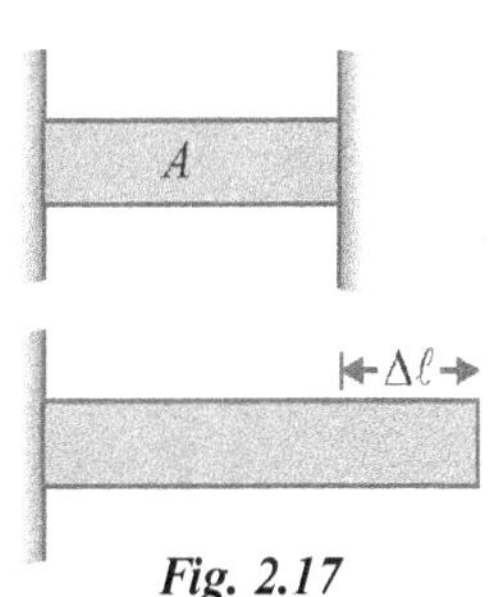

Fig. 2.17

Ex. 9   A steel wire of uniform cross-section 1 mm^2 is heated to 70°C and stretched by tying it two ends rigidly. Calculate the change in tension of the wire when the temperature falls from 70°C to 35°C. Coefficient of linear expansion of steel is 1.1×10^{-5}/°C and the Young's modulus is 2.0×10^{11} N/m^2.

Sol.

We know that thermal stress

$$f_{th} = Y\alpha\Delta T$$

here

$$\Delta T = 70 - 35 = 35°C$$

$$\therefore \quad f_{th} = 2.0 \times 10^{11} \times 1.1 \times 10^{-5} \times 35$$
$$= 7.7 \times 10^7 \text{ N/m}^2$$

The change in tension (decrease because temperature falls)

$$= f_{th}A = (7.7 \times 10^7) \times (1 \times 10^{-6})$$
$$= 77.0 \text{ N} \qquad\qquad \textbf{\textit{Ans.}}$$

2.11 POISSON'S RATIO

In the previous part of our study we have consider the change in dimension of the body in the direction of applied force. We have ignored the change in lateral direction of the body. When a force is applied along the length of the specimen, the longitudinal strain

$e = \dfrac{\Delta \ell}{\ell}$. If radius r is decreased by Δr, then

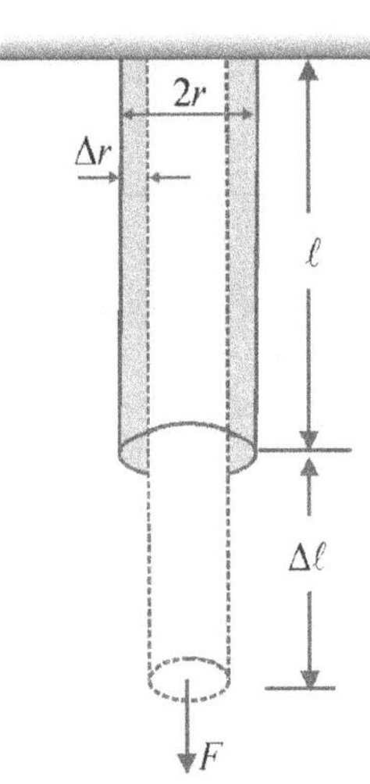

Fig. 2.18

Lateral strain $\qquad\qquad = \dfrac{-\Delta r}{r}$

Poisson's ratio $\qquad \sigma = \dfrac{\text{Lateral strain}}{\text{Longitudinal strain}}$

or $\qquad\qquad \sigma = \dfrac{-\Delta r / r}{\Delta \ell / \ell}$

The negative sign indicate that longitudinal and lateral strains are in opposite sense.

> **Note :**
>
> 1.   The theoretical value of σ lies between -1 to 0.5. But in practice, the value of σ lies between 0.2 to 0.5. The value of σ for rubber is 0.5.
>
> 2. $Y = 3B(1 - 2\sigma)$, $Y = 2\eta(1 + \sigma)$, $Y = \dfrac{9\eta B}{\eta + 3B}$

Change in volume

Consider a rod of circular cross-section of radius r and length ℓ. The volume of the rod

$$V = \pi r^2 \ell \qquad\qquad \ldots\text{(i)}$$

We can write

$$\frac{\Delta V}{V} = \frac{2\Delta r}{r} + \frac{\Delta \ell}{\ell} \qquad\qquad \ldots\text{(ii)}$$

We know that

$$\sigma = \frac{-\Delta r / r}{\Delta \ell / \ell}$$

$$\therefore \quad \frac{\Delta r}{r} = -\sigma \frac{\Delta \ell}{\ell}$$

Substituting this value in equation (ii), we get

$$\frac{\Delta V}{V} = 2\left(-\sigma \frac{\Delta \ell}{\ell}\right) + \frac{\Delta \ell}{\ell}$$

or

$$\frac{\Delta V}{V} = \frac{\Delta \ell}{\ell}(1 - 2\sigma)$$

For no change in volume of the rod, $\Delta V = 0$

$$\therefore \qquad \frac{\Delta \ell}{\ell}(1-2\sigma) = 0$$

or $\qquad\qquad \sigma = 0.5$

Thus a material having Poisson's ratio 0.5 suffers no change in volume when a force is applied on it.

Change in density

Consider a body of density ρ, is subjected to all round pressure P. Its initial density

$$\rho = \frac{M}{V} \qquad \text{...(i)}$$

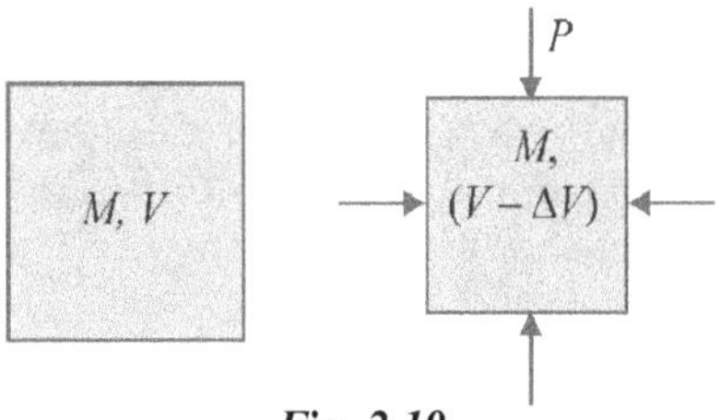

and final density $\qquad \rho' = \frac{M}{(V-\Delta V)} \qquad \text{...(ii)}$

We have $\qquad\qquad B = \dfrac{P}{\left(\dfrac{\Delta V}{V}\right)}$

$$\therefore \qquad \Delta V = \frac{PV}{B}$$

Substitute the value of ΔV in equation (ii), we have

$$\rho' = \frac{M}{\left(V-\dfrac{PV}{B}\right)} = \frac{M}{V\left(1-\dfrac{P}{B}\right)}$$

From equation (i), $\qquad \rho = \dfrac{M}{V}$

$$\therefore \qquad \rho' = \frac{\rho}{\left(1-\dfrac{P}{B}\right)}$$

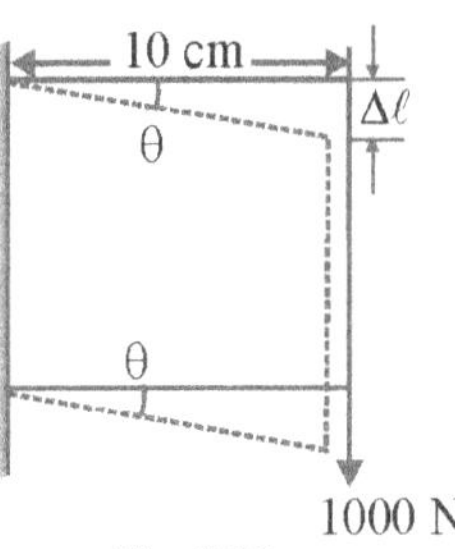

Fig. 2.19

If a body is inside water at a depth h, then $P = \rho_\omega g h$ and $\rho' = \dfrac{\rho}{\left(1-\dfrac{\rho_\omega g h}{B}\right)}$.

Ex. 10 Compute the bulk modulus of water from the following data : Initial volume = 100.0 litre, pressure increase = 100.0 atm, final volume = 100.5 litre (1 atm = 1.013 × 10⁵ N/m²).

Sol.

Given, increase in pressure $P = 100 \times 1.013 \times 10^5$ N/m²

Increase in volume $\quad \Delta V = V_f - V_i$

$$= (100.5 - 100) \times 10^{-3} \text{ m}^3$$
$$= 0.5 \times 10^{-3} \text{ m}^3$$

We know that bulk modulus

$$B = \frac{P}{\left(\dfrac{\Delta V}{V}\right)} = \frac{100 \times 1.013 \times 10^5}{\left(\dfrac{0.5 \times 10^{-3}}{100 \times 10^{-3}}\right)}$$

$$= 2.026 \times 10^9 \text{ N/m}^2 \qquad \textbf{\textit{Ans.}}$$

Ex. 11 The edge of an aluminium cube are 10 cm long. One face of the cube is firmly fixed to a vertical wall. A mass of 100 kg is then attached to the opposite face of the cube. The shear modulus of aluminium is 25GPa. What is the vertical deflection of this face?

Sol.

Shearing force $\quad F = 100g$

$$= 100 \times 10 = 1000 \text{ N}$$

Shear stress $\quad f = \dfrac{F}{A} = \dfrac{1000}{0.1^2}$

$$= 1 \times 10^5 \text{ N/m}^2$$

We know that, the shear modulus

$$\eta = \frac{f}{e}$$

Fig. 2.20

$$\therefore \qquad e = \frac{f}{\eta} = \frac{1 \times 10^5}{25 \times 10^9} = 4 \times 10^{-6}$$

If $\Delta\ell$ is the vertical deflection of the face, then

$$e = \frac{\Delta\ell}{\ell}$$

$$\therefore \qquad \Delta\ell = e\ell = (4 \times 10^{-6}) \times (0.10)$$
$$= 4 \times 10^{-7} \text{ m} \qquad \textit{Ans.}$$

Ex. 12 A wire of radius r stretched without tension along a straight line is lightly fixed at A and B. What is the tension in the wire, when it is pulled into the shape ACB?. Assume Young's modulus of material of the wire to be Y.

Sol.

Initial length of the wire $= 2\ell$

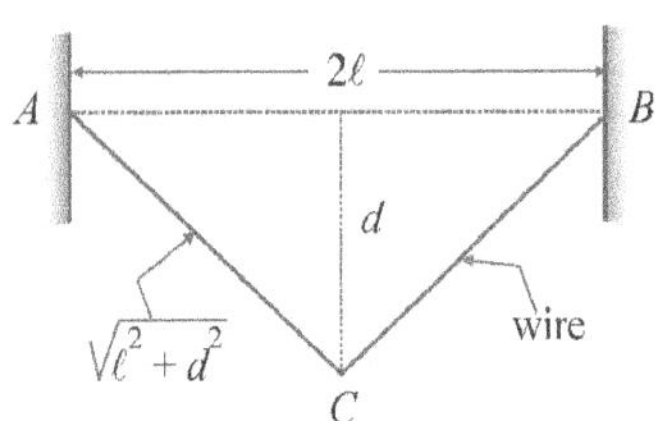

Fig. 2.21

Final length of the wire $= 2\sqrt{\ell^2 + d^2}$

$\therefore$ Strain produced in the wire

$$e = \frac{\Delta L}{L} = \frac{2(\ell^2 + d^2)^{1/2} - 2\ell}{2\ell}$$

$$= \frac{\ell\left(1 + \dfrac{d^2}{\ell^2}\right)^{1/2} - \ell}{\ell}$$

If $d \ll \ell$, then we can write $\left(1 + \dfrac{d^2}{\ell^2}\right)^{1/2} = \left(1 + \dfrac{d^2}{2\ell^2}\right)$

$$\therefore \qquad e = \left(1 + \frac{d^2}{2\ell^2}\right) - 1 = \frac{d^2}{2\ell^2}$$

If T is the tension in the wire, then stress corresponding to strain

$$f = \frac{T}{A} = \frac{T}{\pi r^2}.$$

We know that Young's modulus

$$y = \frac{f}{e}$$

$$\text{or} \qquad Y = \frac{T/\pi r^2}{d^2/2\ell^2}$$

$$\text{or} \qquad = \frac{\pi Y d^2 r^2}{2\ell^2} \qquad \textit{Ans.}$$

Ex. 13 A light rod of length 2.00 m is suspended from the ceiling horizontally by means of two vertical wires of equal length tied to its ends. One of the wires is made of steel and is of cross-section 10^{-3} m^2 and the other is of brass of cross-section 2×10^{-3}m^3. Find out the position along the rod at which a weight may be hung to produce;

(i) equal stresses in both wires,
(ii) equal strains in both wires.
    Young's modulus of brass $= 10^{11}$ N/m^2
    Young's modulus of steel $= 2 \times 10^{11}$ N/m^2

Sol.

Suppose a_1 and a_2 are the cross-section areas, and Y_1 and Y_2 are the Young's moduli of steel and brass wire respectively. Let T_1 and T_2 are the tensions in the steel and brass wires respectively.

Let x is the position of the hanging weight from the steel wire

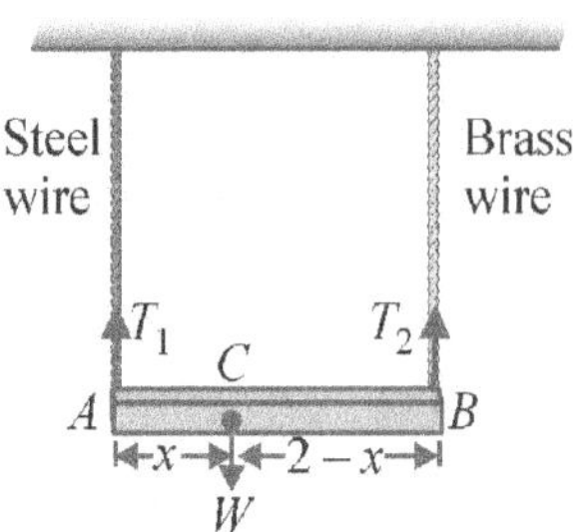

Fig. 2.22

(i) **First case :** For equal stresses in both wires, we have

$$\frac{T_1}{a_1} = \frac{T_2}{a_2}$$

$$\text{or} \qquad \frac{T_1}{10^{-3}} = \frac{T_2}{2 \times 10^{-3}}$$

$$\text{or} \qquad T_2 = 2T_1 \qquad \dots \text{(i)}$$

As the whole system is in equilibrium, so $\Sigma\vec{\tau} = 0$.

Taking moment of all the forces acting on the rod about C, we have

$$T_1 x - T_2(2 - x) = 0 \qquad \dots\text{(ii)}$$

Solving equations (i) and (ii), we get

$$x = \frac{4}{3} \text{m} \qquad \textit{Ans.}$$

(ii) **Second case :** For equal strains in both the wires

$$e_1 = e_2$$

$$\frac{f_1}{Y_1} = \frac{f_2}{Y_2}$$

$$\text{or} \qquad \frac{T_1/a_1}{Y_1} = \frac{T_2/a_2}{Y_2}$$

$$\text{or} \qquad \frac{T_1}{10^{-3} \times 2 \times 10^{11}} = \frac{T_2}{2 \times 10^{-3} \times 10^{11}}$$

$$\text{or} \qquad T_1 = T_2 \qquad \dots \text{(iii)}$$

From equations (ii) and (iii), we get

$$x = 1 \text{ m} \qquad \textit{Ans.}$$

Ex. 14 Two rods of equal cross-sections, one of copper and the other of steel are joined to form a composite rod of length 2.0 m at 20° C, the length of the copper rod is 0.5 m. When the temperature is raised to 120°C, the length of composite rod increases to 2.002 m. If the composite rod is fixed between two rigid walls and thus not allowed to expand, it is found that the length of the component rods also do not change with increase in temperature. Calculate the Young's modulus and the coefficient of linear expansion of steel. Given Young's modulus of copper = 1.3×10^{11} N/m², coefficient of linear expansion of copper $\alpha_c = 1.6 \times 10^{-5} /°C$.

Sol.

The change in length of copper rod due to change in temperature from 20°C to 120°C

$$\Delta \ell_1 = \ell_c \alpha_c \Delta T$$
$$= 0.5\alpha_c (120 - 20) = 50\alpha_c$$

For steel,
$$\Delta \ell_2 = \ell_s \alpha_s \Delta T$$
$$= 1.5\alpha_s (120 - 20) = 150\alpha_s$$

Total change in length
$$\Delta \ell = \Delta \ell_1 + \Delta \ell_2 = 50\alpha_c + 150\alpha_s$$

It is given that
$$\Delta \ell = 0.002 \text{m}$$

$$\therefore \quad 50\alpha_c + 150\alpha_s = 0.002$$

or
$$\alpha_s = \frac{0.002 - 50\alpha_c}{150}$$

$$= \frac{0.002 - 50 \times 1.6 \times 10^{-5}}{150}$$

$$= 0.8 \times 10^{-5} /°C \qquad \textit{Ans.}$$

If there is no change in the length of individual rod, then stress in both the rods must be equal. So

$$f_{\text{steel}} = f_{\text{copper}}$$

or
$$Y_s \alpha_s \Delta T = Y_c \alpha_c \Delta T$$

or
$$Y_s = \frac{Y_c \alpha_c}{\alpha_s}$$

$$= \frac{1.3 \times 10^{13} \times 1.6 \times 10^{-5}}{0.8 \times 10^{-5}}$$

$$= 2.6 \times 10^{15} \text{ N/m}^2 \qquad \textit{Ans.}$$

Ex. 15 1kg weight is suspended by a rubber cord 2.00 m long and of cross-section 0.5 cm². It is made to describe a horizontal circle of radius 50 cm in 4 times a second. Find the extension of the cord. (Young's modulus $Y = 5 \times 10^8$ N/m²).

Sol.

Given, frequency of rotation , $n = 4$ per second

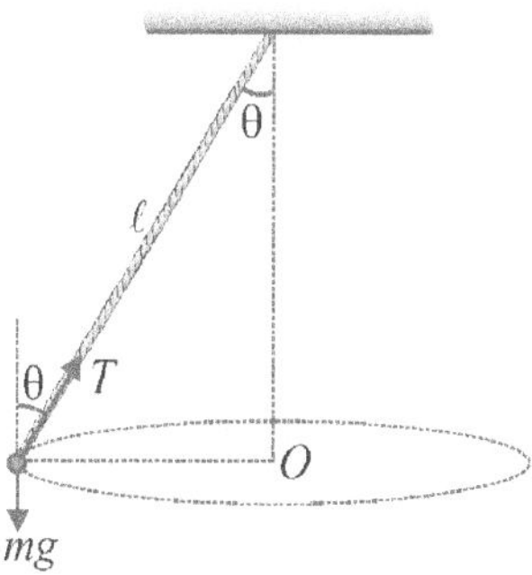

Fig. 2.23

$\therefore$ Angular frequency,
$$\omega = 2\pi n$$
$$= 2 \times \pi \times 4$$
$$= 8\pi \text{ rad/s}$$

If T is the tension in the cord and cord makes angle θ with the vertical, then by Newton's second law

$$T \sin\theta = m\omega^2 r1 \qquad \text{... (i)}$$

and
$$T \cos\theta = mg \qquad \text{... (ii)}$$

Squaring and adding above equations, we get

$$T = \sqrt{(m\omega^2 r)^2 + (mg)^2}$$

The extension of the cord due to tension force T,

$$\Delta \ell = \frac{T\ell}{AY}$$

$$= \frac{\sqrt{(m\omega^2 r)^2 + (mg)^2}}{AY} \times 2$$

$$=$$

$$= \frac{\sqrt{\{1 \times (8\pi)^2 \times (0.5)\}^2 + (1 \times 9.8)^2}}{(0.5 \times 10^{-4}) \times (5 \times 10^8)} \times 2$$

$$= 2.53 \times 10^{-2} \text{ m} \qquad \textit{Ans.}$$

2.12 Elastic Potential Energy of a Strained Body: Strain Energy

Suppose a wire of length ℓ and cross-section area A is fixed at one end and is stretched by an external force applied at the free end. The force is adjusted in such a way that it stretched slowly. When the extension is x, the wire under direct stress $\frac{F}{A}$ and strain $\frac{x}{\ell}$.

$$\therefore \qquad Y = \frac{f}{e} = \frac{F/A}{x/\ell}$$

or
$$F = \frac{AY}{\ell} x$$

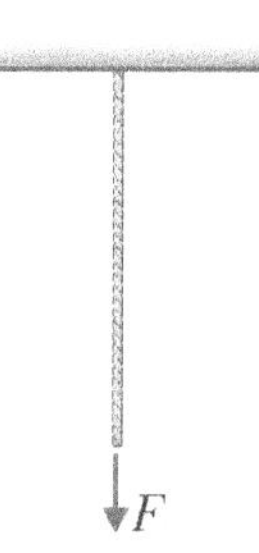

**Fig. 2.24

Work done by external force in further extension dx, is

$$dW = Fdx = \left(\frac{AYx}{\ell}\right)dx$$

The total work done by the external force in an extension from 0 to $\Delta\ell$, is

$$W = \int_0^{\Delta\ell}\left(\frac{AY}{\ell}x\right)dx = \frac{AY}{2\ell}\Delta\ell^2$$

This work is stored in its elastic potential energy.

$$\therefore \qquad U = \frac{AY}{2\ell}\Delta\ell^2$$

or

$$U = \frac{1}{2}\left(Y\frac{\Delta\ell}{\ell}\right)\times\left(\frac{\Delta\ell}{\ell}\right)\times(A\ell)$$

or

$$U = \frac{1}{2}\times \text{stress}\times \text{strain}\times \text{volume}$$

Note:

$$u = \frac{U}{\text{volume}} = \frac{1}{2}\times f\times e = \frac{f^2}{2Y} = \frac{e^2 Y}{2}.$$

Ex. 16 A 40 kg boy whose legs are 4 cm^2 in area and 50 cm long falls through a height of 2 m without breaking his leg bones. If the bones can withstand a stress of 0.9×10^8 N/m^2. Calculate the Young's modulus for the material of the bone.

Sol.

In the process of fall mechanical energy of the body remain constant. Thus

Loss in P.E. = Gain in elastic potential energy by both the legs

or
$$mgh = 2\times\left(\frac{1}{2}\times \text{stress}\times \text{strain}\times \text{volume}\right)$$

or
$$mgh = 2\times\frac{f^2}{2Y}\times(A\ell)$$

or
$$40\times 9.8\times 2 = \frac{(0.9\times 10^8)^2}{Y}\times(4\times 10^{-4}\times 0.50)$$

After solving, we get, $Y = 2.05\times 10^9$ N/m^2 *Ans.*

Ex. 17 A copper rod, 25 mm in diameter is encased in steel tube 30 mm diameter and 35 mm external diameter. The ends are rigidly attached. The composite bar is 500 mm long and is subjected to an axial pull of 30 kN. Find the stresses induced in the rod and tube. Take Y for steel $= 2\times 10^5$ N/mm^2 and Y for copper 1×10^5 N/mm^2.

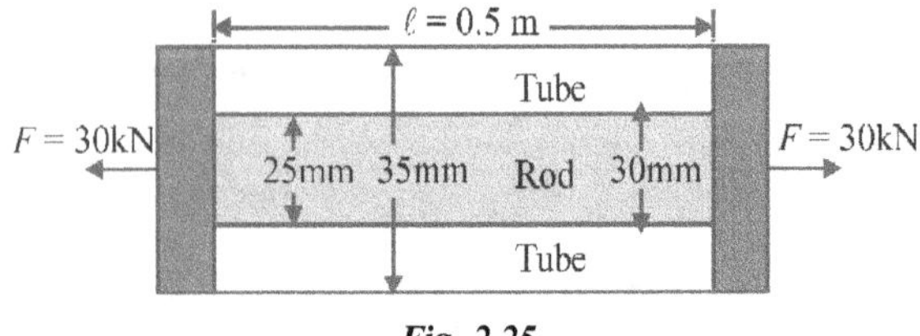

Fig. 2.25

Sol.

Let us use suffix 1 for copper rod and 2 for steel tube.

$$A_1 = \pi(12.5)^2 = 490.6 \text{ mm}^2$$
$$A_2 = \pi[17.5^2 - 15^2] = 255.1 \text{ mm}^2$$

If f_1 and f_2 are the stresses in the rod and tube respectively, then

$$f_1 A_1 + f_2 A_2 = F = 30000\text{N}$$

or $f_1(490.6) + f_2(255.1) = 3000$ ... (i)

As both rod and tube are joined together, so

$$\Delta\ell_1 = \Delta\ell_2$$

$$\frac{f_1\ell_1}{Y_1} = \frac{f_2\ell_2}{Y_2} \qquad (\text{As } \ell_1 = \ell_2)$$

or
$$f_1 = \frac{Y_1}{Y_2}f_2$$

or
$$f_1 = \frac{1\times 10^5}{2\times 10^5}f_2 = 0.5 f_2 \qquad ... (ii)$$

Solving (i) and (ii), we get

$$f_1 = 29.97 \text{ N/mm}^2$$

and
$$f_2 = 59.95 \text{ N/mm}^2 \qquad \textbf{\textit{Ans.}}$$

Bending of Beam

Beam is the structural member which can carry transverse load. A simply supported beam is supported at its ends. A cantilever beam is fixed at one end.

Deflection of beam : Deflection of beam at its centre due to load placed as shown in Fig. 2.26.

$$\delta = \frac{W\ell^3}{48YI} \quad \text{for simply supported beam}$$

and

$$\delta = \frac{W\ell^3}{3YI} \quad \text{for cantilever beam}$$

where I is called geometric moment of area.

(i) For rectangular cross-section

$$I = \frac{bd^3}{12}$$

(ii) For circular cross-section

$$I = \frac{\pi r^4}{4}$$

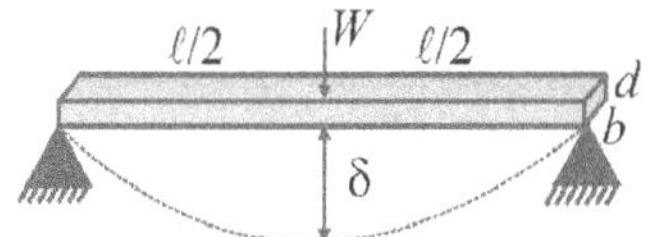
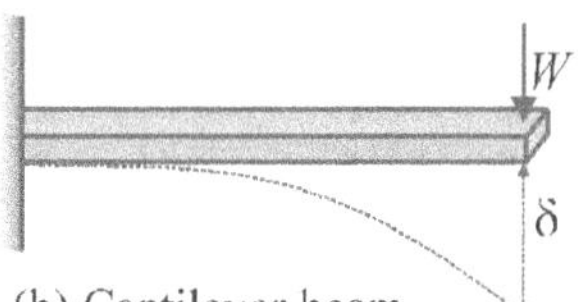

(a) Simply supported beam

(b) Cantilever beam

Fig. 2.26

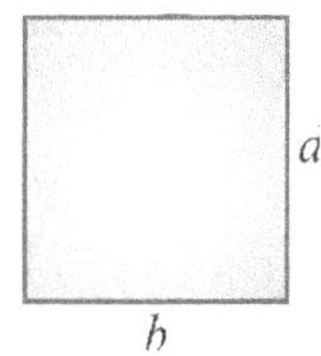

Fig. 2.27

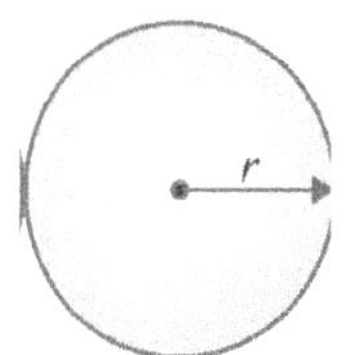

Fig. 2.28

Twisting of a shaft

Let us consider a shaft of length ℓ and radius r, whose one end is rigidly clamped and torque τ is applied at the free end. Because of this the free end is twisted by an angle θ. From the diagram, arc

$$s = r\theta = \ell\phi$$

where $\theta \rightarrow$ angle of twist and

$\phi \rightarrow$ angle of shear

Torsional rigidity of shaft

$$\frac{\tau}{\theta} = \frac{\pi\eta r^4}{2\ell}$$

where $\eta \rightarrow$ modulus of rigidity.

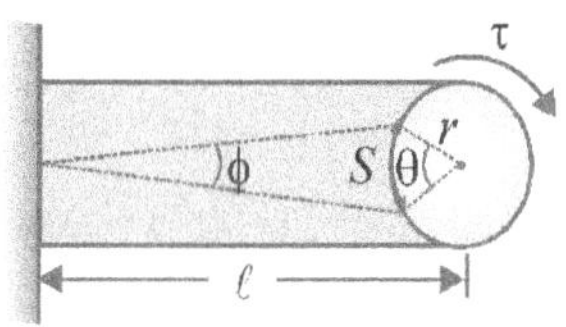

Fig. 2.29

Ex. 18 A uniform elastic plank moves over a smooth horizontal plane due to a constant force F_0 distributed uniformly over the end face. The surface of the end face is equal to A and Young's modulus of the material is Y. Find the compressive strain of the plank in the direction of the acting force.

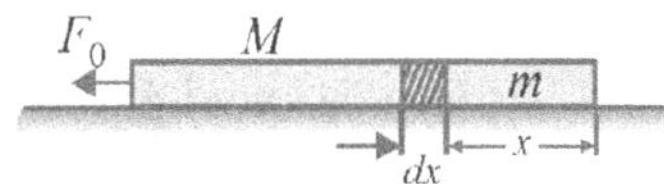

Fig. 2.30

Sol.

The force at any section is due to the inertia behind the section. The stress therefore increases from zero to maximum at the end where force is applied.

Consider a small element of length dx at a distance x from the free end. The force

Elongation of the element

$$F_x = ma$$

$$= \left(\frac{M}{L}x\right) \times \frac{F_0}{M} = \frac{F_0 x}{L}$$

Fig. 2.31

$$d\ell = \frac{F_x(dx)}{AY} = \frac{\left(\dfrac{F_0 x}{L}\right)dx}{AY}$$

Total elongation

$$d\ell = \int_0^L \frac{F_0}{ALY} x\,dx$$

$$= \frac{F_0}{2ALY}L^2$$

or

$$\Delta\ell = \frac{F_0 L}{2AY} \qquad \textit{Ans.}$$

Ex. 19 A slightly conical wire of length ℓ and radii r_1 and r_2 is stretched by two forces applied parallel to length in opposite directions and normal to end faces. If Y denotes the Young's modulus, then find the elongation of the wire.

Sol.

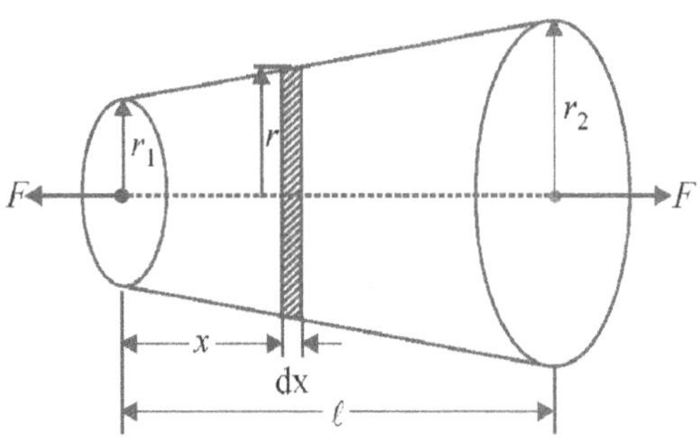

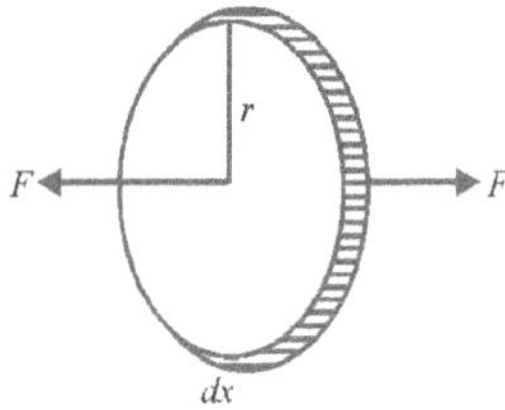

Fig. 2.32

Consider an element of length dx at distance x as shown in *Fig. 2.32*. The radius of the section

$$r_x = r_1 + \left(\frac{r_2 - r_1}{\ell}\right)x$$

The extension of the element

$$d\ell = \frac{F(dx)}{A_x Y}$$

$$= \frac{Fdx}{\pi r_x^2 Y}$$

Total extension

$$\Delta\ell = \int_0^\ell \frac{Fdx}{\pi\left[r_1 + \dfrac{r_2 - r_1}{\ell}x\right]^2 Y}$$

$$= \frac{F\ell}{\pi r_1 r_2 Y} \qquad \textit{Ans.}$$

Ex. 20 A horizontally oriented copper rod of length ℓ is rotated about a vertical axis passing through its middle. Calculate the rotated frequency at which the rod ruptures. Breaking or rupture strength of copper takes as σ and density of copper ρ.

Sol.

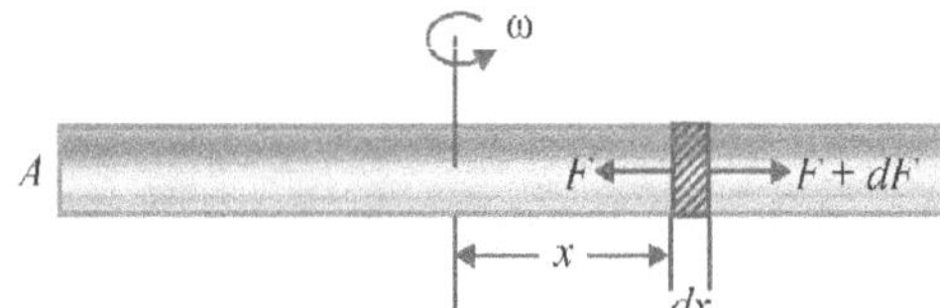

Fig. 2.33

The stresses are zero at the free end and maximum at the axis. Therefore the rod will ruptures at the middle.

Let us consider an element of rod at a distance x from the axis, the mass of element

$$dm = \rho A dx$$

Applying Newton's second law

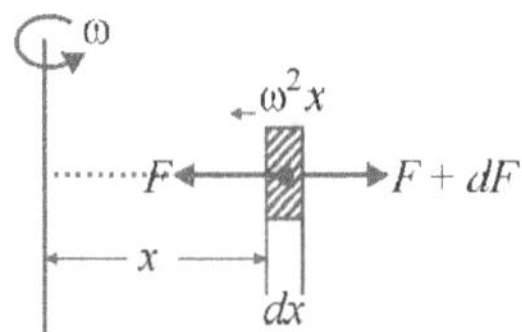

Fig. 2.34

$$F - (F + dF) = (dm)a_n$$

or

$$-dF = (\rho A dx)\omega^2 x$$

where ω is the rotation speed.

$$\therefore \qquad F = -\int dF = -\int(\rho A dx)\omega^2 x$$

$$= -\rho A\omega^2 \frac{x^2}{2} + C$$

at

$$x = \ell/2, F = 0$$

$$\therefore \qquad C = \frac{\rho A\omega^2 \ell^2}{8}$$

Now

$$F = \rho\frac{A\omega^2}{2}\left(\frac{\ell^2}{4} - x^2\right)$$

at $x = 0$, $F = \rho\dfrac{A\omega^2\ell^2}{8}$ and $f = \dfrac{F}{A} = \dfrac{\rho\omega^2\ell^2}{8}$

Rupture of rod will occur when $f = \sigma$

$$\therefore \qquad \frac{\rho\omega^2\ell^2}{8} = \sigma$$

$$\Rightarrow \qquad \omega = \sqrt{\frac{8\sigma}{\rho\ell^2}}$$

or

$$n = \frac{1}{2\pi}\sqrt{\frac{8\sigma}{\rho\ell^2}} \qquad \textit{Ans.}$$

Ex. 21 A ring of radius R made of lead wire breaking strength σ and density δ, is rotated about a stationary vertical axis passing through its centre and perpendicular to the plane of the ring. Calculate the number of rotation at which the ring ruptures.

Sol.

Due to rotation, each part of ring experiences an outward force (centrifugal force). Because of this force, the ring will rupture.

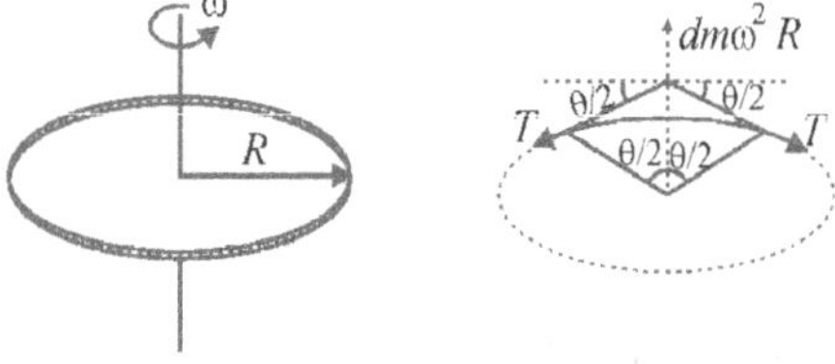

Fig. 2.35

Let us consider small part of ring, which subtend angle θ at the centre.

Mass of the element $(dm) = \delta dv = \delta(AR\theta)$

$$\therefore \qquad 2T\sin\theta/2 = (dm)\omega^2 R$$

When θ is small $\sin\theta/2 \simeq \theta/2$

$$\therefore \qquad 2T \times \theta/2 = (\delta AR\theta)\omega^2 R$$

$$\Rightarrow \qquad T = \delta A\omega^2 R^2$$

The stress at any section of the ring

Fig. 2.36

$$f = \frac{T}{A} = \frac{\delta A\omega^2 R^2}{A}$$

$$= \delta\omega^2 R^2$$

Rupture takes place when $f = \sigma$

$$\therefore \qquad \sigma = \delta\,\omega^2 R^2$$

$$\Rightarrow \qquad \omega = \sqrt{\frac{\sigma}{\delta R^2}}$$

$$\text{and} \qquad n = \frac{1}{2\pi}\sqrt{\frac{\sigma}{\delta R^2}} = \frac{1}{2\pi R}\sqrt{\frac{\sigma}{\delta}} \qquad \textit{Ans.}$$

Ex. 22 *Two beams are made of same material and having equal length are rest at their ends and subjected to same load at their centre. One beam square in cross-section other circular cross-section. If their cross-sectional area are equal, then calculate ratio of deflection at their centres.*

Sol.

$$\text{We have} \qquad \delta = \frac{W\ell^3}{48YI}$$

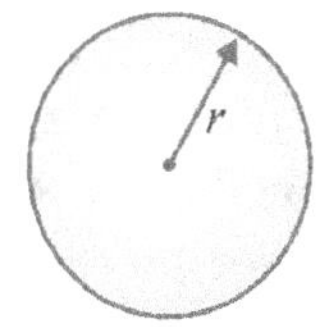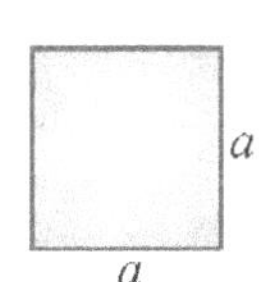

Fig. 2.37

$$\therefore \qquad \frac{\delta_{\text{square}}}{\delta_{\text{circular}}} = \frac{I_{\text{circular}}}{I_{\text{square}}} \qquad [\,\pi r^2 = a^2\,]$$

$$= \frac{\pi r^4/4}{\left(\dfrac{a^4}{12}\right)} = \frac{3\pi r^4}{a^4} = \frac{3\pi r^4}{(\pi r^2)^2} = \frac{3}{\pi}$$

Ans.

Ex. 23 Two cylinders A and B of the same material have same length, their radii being in the ratio $1:2$ respectively. The two are joined end to end as shown. One end of cylinder A is rigidly clamped while free end of cylinder B is twisted through an angle θ. Find the angle of twist of cylinder A.

Sol.

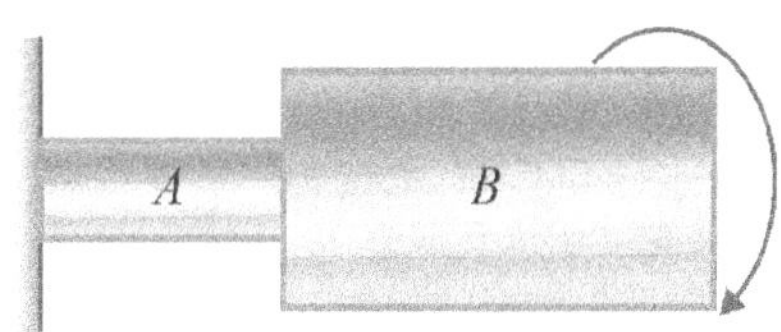

Fig. 2.38

Let θ_1 and θ_2 are the angle of twist produced in cylinders A and B respectively.

Given, $\qquad\qquad \theta_1 + \theta_2 = \theta \qquad\qquad$ ...(i)

On being in series, the torque acts at their free ends are equal.

$$\text{We have} \qquad \tau = \frac{\pi\eta r^4\theta}{2\ell}$$

$$\therefore \qquad \frac{\pi\eta r^4\theta_1}{2\ell} = \frac{\pi\eta(2r)^4\theta_2}{2\ell}$$

$$\Rightarrow \qquad \theta_1 = 16\theta_2 \qquad\qquad \text{...(ii)}$$

From (i) and (ii), we have

$$\theta_1 = \frac{16}{17}\theta \qquad\qquad \textit{Ans.}$$

Ex. 24 The length of a metal wire is ℓ_1 when the tension is T_1 and ℓ_2 when the tension is T_2. Find the unstretched length of the wire.

Sol.

Let ℓ is the unstretched length of the wire.

Using $F = kx$, we have

$T_1 = k\,(\ell_1 - \ell)$ and $T_2 = k(\ell_2 - \ell)$

After solving, we get $\quad \ell = (T_2\ell_1 - T_1\ell_2)/(T_2 - T_1)$. $\qquad$ *Ans.*

2.13 SURFACE TENSION

Cohesive and adhesive forces : The force of attraction between molecules of same substance is called cohesive force or cohesion.

The force of attraction between molecules of different substances is called adhesive force or adhesion.

These force are of electromagnetic nature. They vary with eight power of distance between the molecules.

These forces are responsible for surface tension.

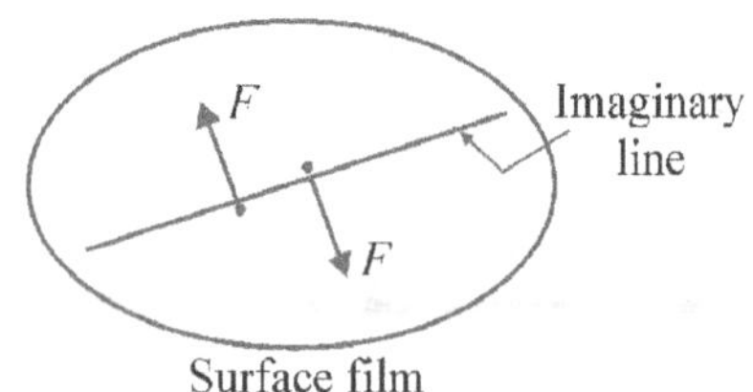

Surface film

Fig. 2.39

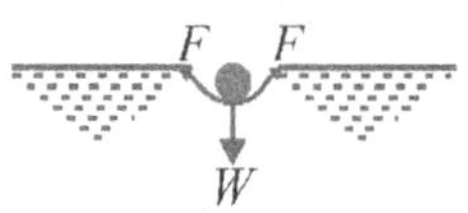

Fig. 2.40

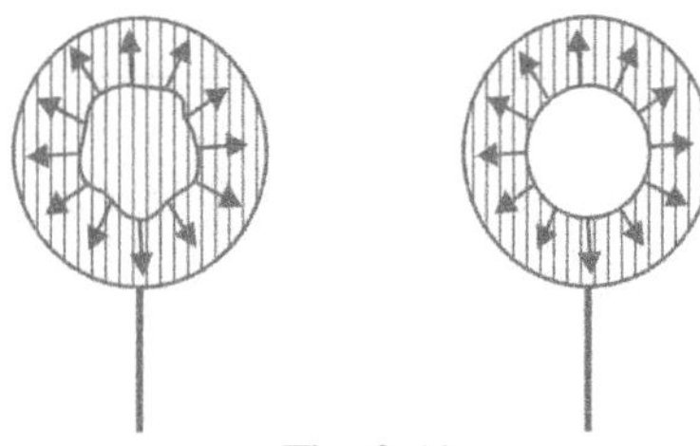

Fig. 2.41

A soap film in a circular wire frame

Fig. 2.42

Surface tension : The property of liquid by which liquid tends to acquire minimum surface area, is called surface tension.

Mathematically surface tension of liquid is the force acting on a unit length of an imaginary line drawn on free surface of the liquid. Thus if F be the total force acting on l length of the line, then surface tension

$$T = \frac{F}{\ell}$$

2.14 EXAMPLE BASED ON SURFACE TENSION

(i) Needle supported on water surface :

When a needle is placed gently on the water surface, it remain floating on it. The floating needle causes slight depression. The surface tension force F acts tangentially to the curved surface as shown in *Fig. 2.40*. The vertical components of the forces balances the weight of the needle.

(ii) Endless wet thread on a soap film :

Take a circular wire frame and dip it into soap solution, a thin soap film is formed on the frame.

If a wet endless thread loop is gently placed over the film, it takes any irregular shape. But when the film is pricked inside, the loop stretched outwards and takes a circular shape. This is because for a given length a circle has the maximum surface area and so the soap film tries to get maximum possible area due to surface tension.

(iii) Small mercury droplets are spherical :

Small mercury droplets are spherical because surface tension force tend to decrease their surface area to a minimum value and a sphere has minimum surface area for a given volume.

Larger mercury drops become flatted due to the large gravitational force on them. Here the shape of the droplets are such that the sum of the gravitational potential energy and the surface potential energy is minimum. To get this, centre of gravity of droplets moves down.

2.15 MOLECULAR THEORY OF SURFACE TENSION

The distance upto which the force of attraction between two molecules is considerable is called molecular range. It is $r_0 = 10^{-9}$ m.

To understand surface tension, let us consider a molecule which is completely inside the liquid. It is surrounded by molecules from all directions, so net force on the molecule is zero. On the other hand, a molecule on the free surface of liquid is surrounded by molecules on liquid side. Thus it experiences a net downward force. Because of it the surface of the liquid behave like a stretched membrane. If the molecules from liquid inside are shifted to free surface, work is to be done in the process.

And, therefore molecules on free surface possess an extra energy in comparison to the molecules inside the liquid. This extra energy is called surface energy.

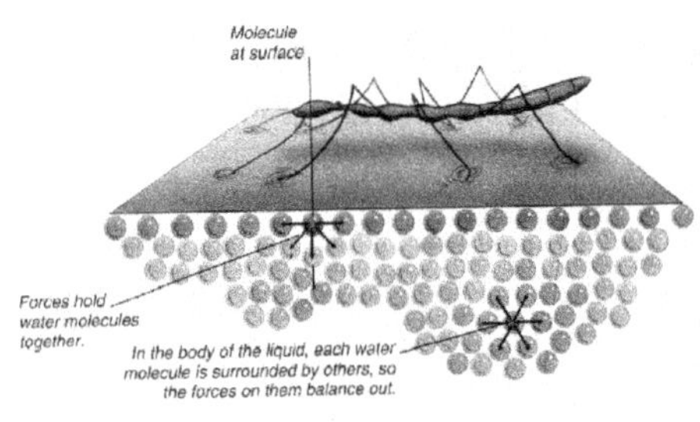

Fig. 2.43

2.16 SURFACE ENERGY AND SURFACE TENSION

The extra energy possessed by the molecules of the surface film in comparison to the energy of the molecules inside the liquid is called surface energy.

Surface tension can be defined as the work done in increasing the area of the surface film by unit amount. Thus surface tension

$$T = \frac{\text{Work done}}{\text{Increase in surface area}}$$

The SI unit of surface tension is J/m^2.

2.17 WORK DONE IN INCREASING THE AREA OF THE SURFACE FILM

Consider a wire frame $ABCD$ in which AB is movable. Dip the frame into soap solution. A thin film of soap solution is formed inside the frame. The surface tension force on the movable wire AB, $F = 2T\ell$. Here the factor 2 is taken because the soap film has two free surfaces.

Work done in displacing the wire from AB to $A'B'$

$$W = F \times x$$
$$= 2\,T\ell x = T(2\ell x)$$

or
$$W = T\Delta A$$

where ΔA is the effective increase in area of the film.

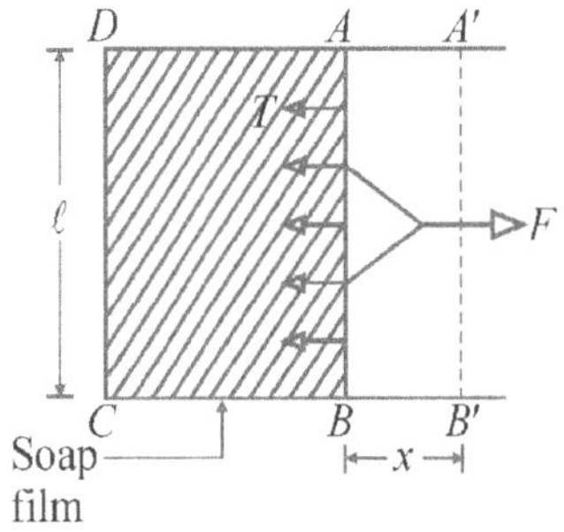

Fig. 2.44

Work done in breaking a liquid drop

Let a liquid drop of radius R breaks into n-identical drops. If r is the radius of each small drop, then

$$\frac{4}{3}\pi R^3 = n \times \frac{4}{3}\pi r^3$$

$$\Rightarrow \quad r = \frac{R}{n^{1/3}}$$

The increase in surface area

$$\Delta A = [n \times 4\pi r^2 - 4\pi R^2]$$

Work done
$$W = T\Delta A = T[n \times 4\pi r^2 - 4\pi R^2]$$

> **Note:**
>
> 1. If breaking of drop takes place in self process the energy of resulting drops will decrease and so the temperature of the drops decrease.
> 2. If number of small drops coalesce to form a big drop, the internal energy of resulting drop will increase and so its temperature increases.

Work done in blowing a soap bubble

A soap bubble of radius R is to be blown. The effective increase in surface area $\Delta A = 2 \times 4\pi R^2$.

Work done,
$$W = T\Delta A$$
$$= T \times 2(4\pi R^2)$$
$$= 8\,\pi T R^2$$

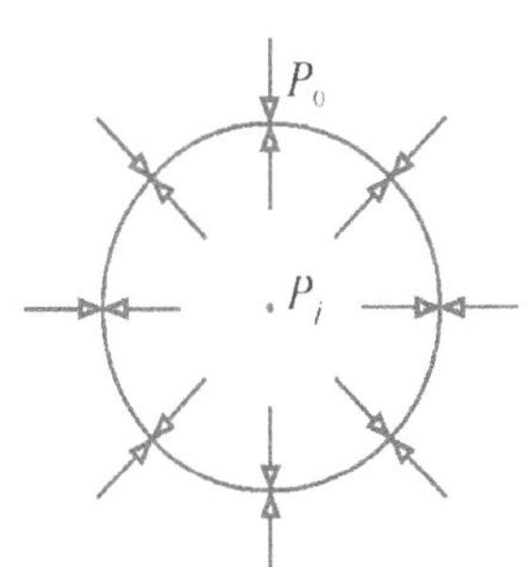

Fig. 2.45

2.18 PRESSURE DIFFERENCE

Liquid drop

Consider a liquid drop of radius R. Let P_i be the pressure inside the drop and P_0 be the pressure outside the drop. Consider the equilibrium of the half of the drop. The force due to pressure difference $(P_i - P_o)$ acts on the projected area in upward direction. The force due to surface tension acts all over the perimeter in downward direction.

The force due to pressure difference $= (P_i - P_o)\,\pi R^2$

The force due to surface tension $= T \times 2\pi R$

For the vertical equilibrium of the drop

$$(P_i - P_o)\pi R^2 = T \times 2\pi R$$

$$\Rightarrow \quad (P_i - P_o) = \frac{2T}{R}$$

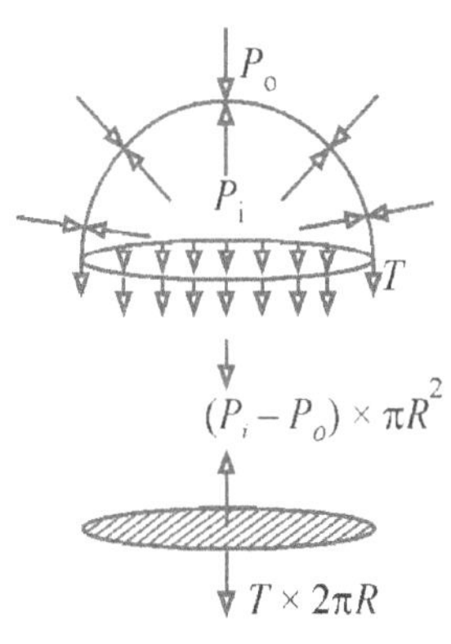

Fig. 2.46

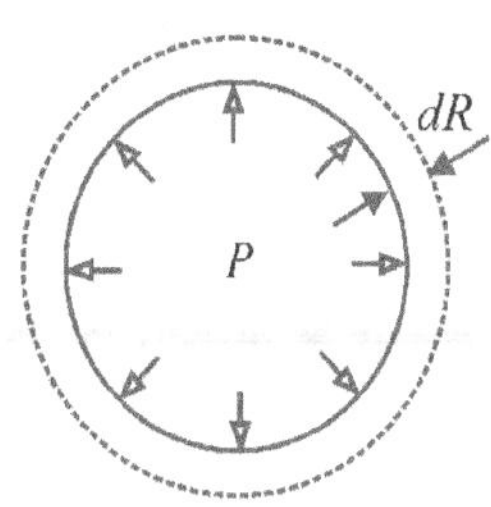

Fig. 2.47

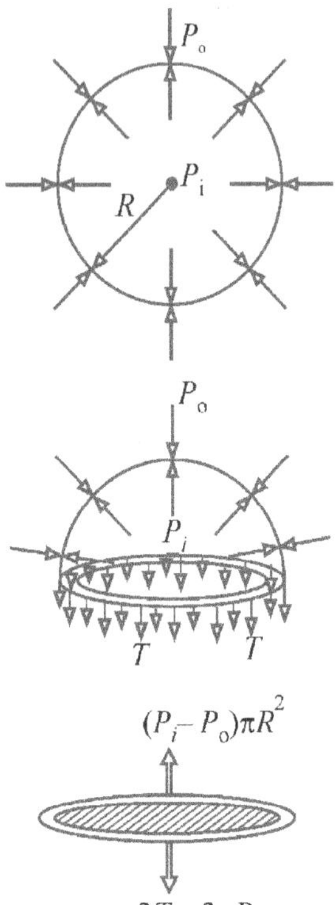

Fig. 2.48

Method II : Consider a spherical liquid drop of radius R. Let T be the surface tension of the liquid. Suppose P is an excess pressure inside the drop over that on outside, i.e., $P = P_i - P_o$. Let the radius of the drop increases from R to $(R + dR)$ due to the excess pressure P.

$$\text{Initial surface area} = 4\pi R^2$$
$$\text{Final surface area} = 4\pi(R + dR)^2$$
$$= 4\pi(R^2 + 2R\,dR + dR^2)$$

On being small dR^2 can be neglected

$$\therefore \qquad \text{Final surface area} = 4\pi R^2 + 8\pi R\,dR$$

$$\text{Increase in surface area} = (4\pi R^2 + 8\pi R\,dR) - 4\pi R^2 = 8\pi R\,dR$$

Work done in increasing the surface area $=$ Surface tension $\times$ increase in surface area

or $\qquad\qquad\qquad\qquad W = T \times 8\pi R\,dR$

But work done $\qquad\qquad\qquad W =$ Pressure $\times$ change in volume
$$= P \times 4\pi R^2 dR$$

Hence $\qquad (P \times 4\pi R^2)dR = T \times 8\pi R\,dR$

$$\therefore \qquad\qquad P = \frac{2T}{R}$$

Soap bubble

Consider a soap bubble of radius R. Let P_i be the pressure inside the bubble and P_o be the pressure outside the bubble. Consider the equilibrium of the half of the bubble. The force due to pressure difference $(P_i - P_o)$ acts on the projected area in upward direction. The force due to surface tension acts all over the perimeter and in downward direction.

The force due to pressure difference $= (P_i - P_o)\,\pi R^2$

The force due to surface tension force $= 2T \times 2\pi R$

Here the factor 2 is taken because soap film has two free surfaces.

Thus for the vertical equilibrium of the bubble

$$(P_i - P_o)\pi R^2 = 2T \times 2\pi R$$

$$\Rightarrow \qquad P_i - P_o = \frac{4T}{R}$$

Note:

Pressure difference in a film having one free surface is $P_i - P_0 = \dfrac{2T}{R}$. For a film having radii of curvatures R_1 and R_2 the pressure difference for one free surface is

$$P_i - P_o = T\left(\frac{1}{R_1} + \frac{1}{R_2}\right)$$

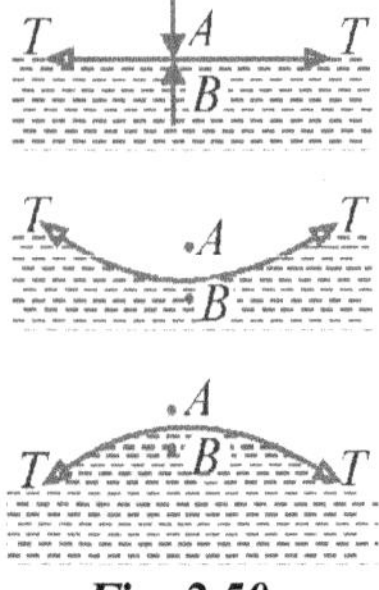

Fig. 2.50

Fig. 2.49

Pressure difference

$$P_A - P_B = 0$$

$$P_A - P_B = \frac{2T}{R}$$

$$P_B - P_A = \frac{2T}{R}$$

Air bubble inside water

Let an air bubble of radius R is at a depth h below the free surface of water. The pressure difference

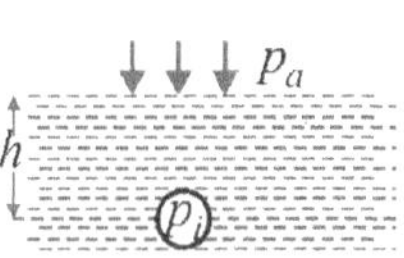
Fig. 2.51

$$P_i - P_o = \frac{2T}{R}$$

$$\Rightarrow \quad P_i = \frac{2T}{R} + P_o = \frac{2T}{R} + (\rho g h + P_a)$$

Ex. 25 A light open rigid paper frame as shown in *Fig. 2.52* floats on the surface of water.

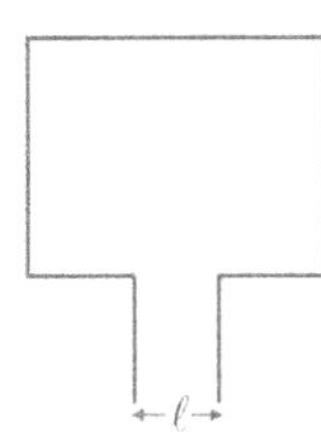
Fig. 2.52

What will happen to the frame if some soap solution is dropped inside it? What force will act on the frame and in what direction will it acts?

Sol.

If T_1 and T_2 be the surface tensions of the water and the soap film, then the frame will be acted with a force

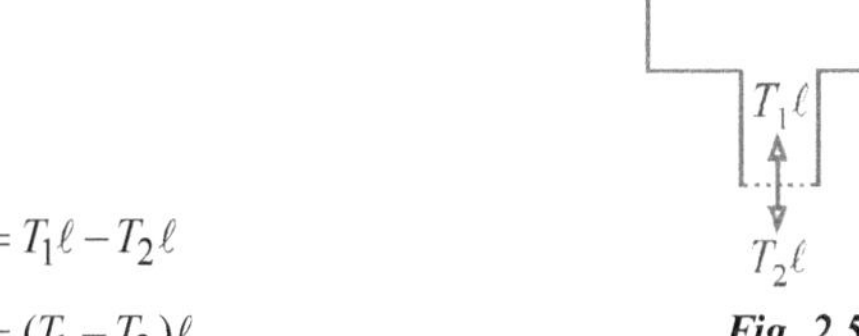
Fig. 2.53

$$F = T_1 \ell - T_2 \ell$$
$$= (T_1 - T_2)\ell$$

The frame will begin to move in the direction of the force F. **Ans.**

Surface tension force on different objects :

1. Wire or thin rod
$$F = 2T\ell$$

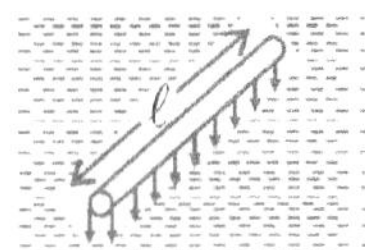
Fig. 2.54

2. Circular disc
$$F = 2\pi r T$$

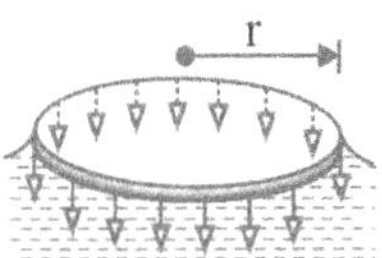
Fig. 2.55

3. Annular disc
$$r_i = r$$
$$r_o = R$$
$$F = 2\pi r T + 2\pi R T$$

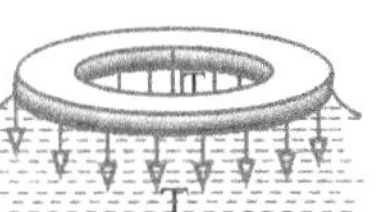
Fig. 2.56

4. Ring
$$F = 2\pi R T + 2\pi R T$$
$$= 4\pi R T$$

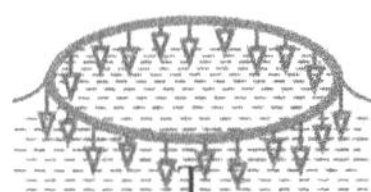
Fig. 2.57

5. Rectangular plate $(a \times b)$
$$F = T(2a + 2b)$$

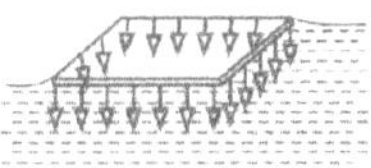
Fig. 2.58

6. Wire frame $(a \times b)$
$$F = T \times 2(2a + 2b)$$

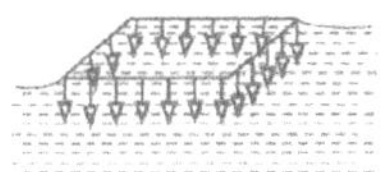
Fig. 2.59

Shape of meniscus

Shape of meniscus depends on the relative values of adhesive and cohesive forces.

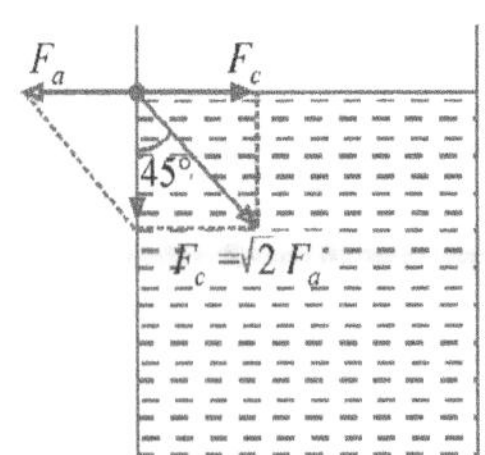

Fig. 2.60

1. If $F_c = \sqrt{2}F_a$, the net force acts vertically downward. The liquid meniscus is horizontal.

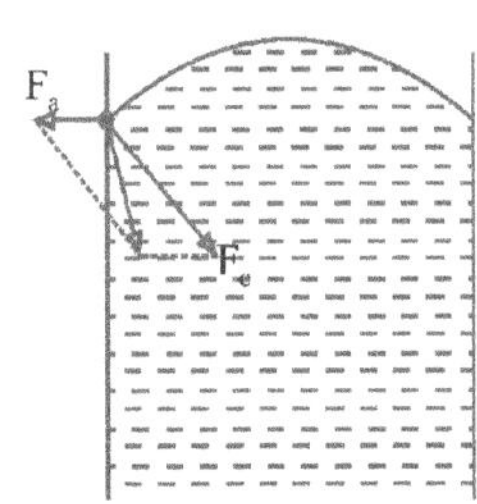

Fig. 2.61

2. If $F_c < \sqrt{2}F_a$, the net force directed outside the liquid. The liquid meniscus is concave upwards.

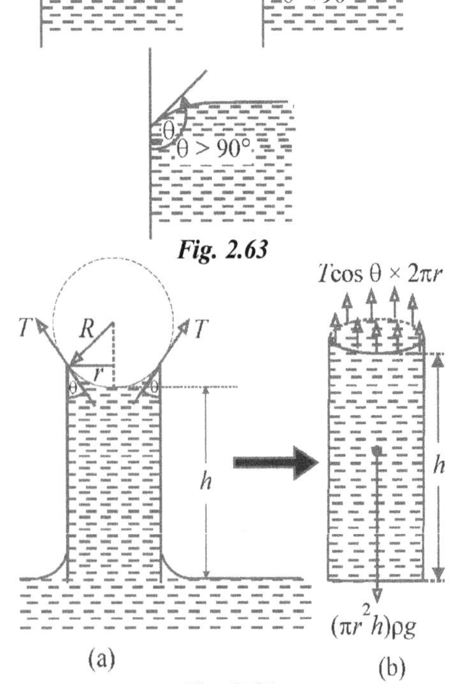

Fig. 2.62

3. If $F_c > \sqrt{2}F_a$, the net force directed inside the liquid. The meniscus is convex upward.

2.19 ANGLE OF CONTACT

It is defined as the angle between the tangent to the liquid surface at the point of contact to the solid surface inside liquid.

(i) Angle of contact is the property of the materials in contact.

(ii) It decreases with the increase in temperature.

(iii) It decreases with the addition of soluble impurities, like soap, detergent etc.

- Pure water in silver tube
- Mercury in glass tube ($\theta = 140°$)
- Liquid wets the solid surface

- Water in glass tube ($\theta = 8°$)
- Liquid does not wet the solid surface
- Liquid does not wet solid surface

Fig. 2.63

2.20 CAPILLARY RISE

When one end of a narrow tube (capillary) dipped into a liquid, the liquid rises or falls in the tube. This phenomenon is called **capillarity**.

Let us consider a tube of radius r whose one end is dipped into liquid of surface tension T. Surface tension force acts all over the perimeter of the tube at the meniscus in upward direction. Because of this force liquid will rise in the tube till the weight of the liquid in the tube is equal to the surface tension force.

Method I : By load balancing method

$$T \cos\theta \times 2\pi r = \pi r^2 h\rho g$$

or

$$h = \frac{2T\cos\theta}{r\rho g}$$

(a)   (b)

Fig. 2.64

If R is the radius of the meniscus, then

$$R = \frac{r}{\cos\theta}$$

$$\therefore \quad h = \frac{2T}{\left(\dfrac{r}{\cos\theta}\right)\rho g}$$

or

$$h = \frac{2T}{R\rho g}$$

Method II : By pressure balance method

In case of capillary rise the shape of meniscus is concave upward. The pressure just below the free surface of the liquid is less than the pressure at point A by an amount $\dfrac{2T}{R}$.

So to compensate this pressure difference, liquid will rise in the tube. From the figure

$$P_A = P_a$$

$$P_B = P_A - \frac{2T}{R}$$

Also

$$P_D = P_B + h\rho g$$

or

$$P_D = \left(P_A - \frac{2T}{R}\right) + h\rho g$$

Since $P_D = P_C = P_A = P_a$

$$\therefore \quad \frac{2T}{R} = h\rho g$$

or

$$h = \frac{2T}{R\rho g}$$

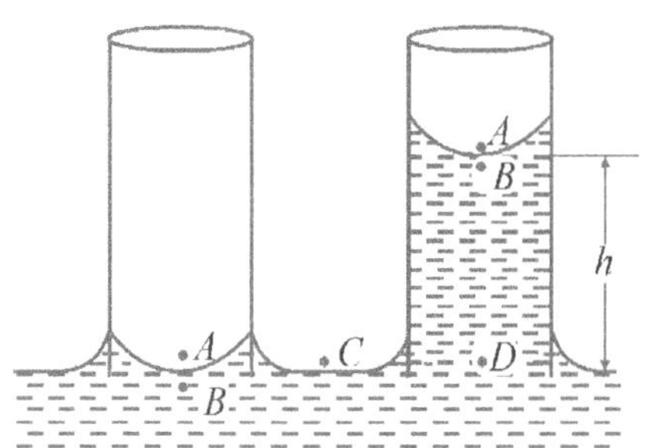

Fig. 2.65

Capillary tube of insufficient length

Theoretically the rise of liquid in the tube is $h = \dfrac{2T}{R\rho g}$. If the length of the tube above liquid is ℓ, if less than h, then the liquid will rise to full length of the tube and the free surface of the liquid will acquire larger radius of curvature in such a way, that the product $hR = \ell R'$.

We have,

$$h = \frac{2T}{R\rho g}$$

or

$$hR = \frac{2T}{\rho g} \quad \text{(constant)}$$

For the tube of length $\ell < h$, let radius of curvature be R' then $hR = \ell R'$

or

$$R' = \frac{hR}{\ell}$$

As $\ell < h, \therefore R' > R$.

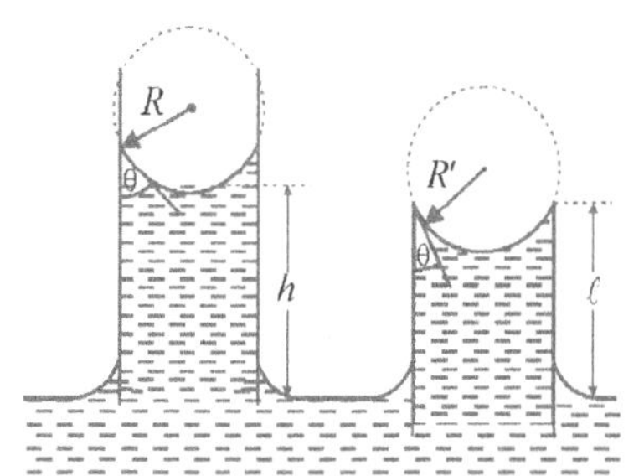

Fig. 2.66

Note:

1. The energy required to raise the liquid in the capillary tube is obtained from the surface energy of the air glass surface. In case when liquid (mercury) gets depressed inside it, below its level outside the tube, the glass-liquid surface decreases, whereas the air-glass surface increases by an equal amount, resulting in a net increase in the surface energy of the whole system. This energy is derived from the depression of the liquid in the tube. i.e., by decreasing gravitational potential energy by equal amount.

2. In deriving the formula of capillary rise, we have ignored the volume of the liquid in the shaded portion (see figure). If it is taken into account then :

Volume of shaded portion = Volume of cylinder of radius r and height r – volume of the hemisphere

$$= (\pi r^2)r - \frac{1}{2}\left(\frac{4}{3}\pi r^3\right) = \frac{\pi r^3}{3}$$

Thus, we write

$$T\cos\theta \times 2\pi r = (\pi r^2 h)\rho g + \left(\frac{\pi r^3}{3}\right)\rho g$$

or
$$h = \frac{2T\cos\theta}{r\rho g} - \frac{r}{3}$$

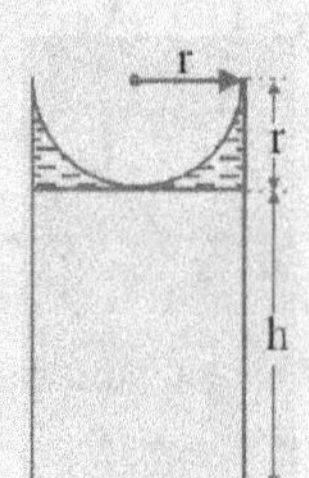

Fig. 2.67

3. Capillary rise in tube of square cross-section :
If a is the width of the tube, then

$$T\cos\theta \times (4a) = (a^2 h)\rho g$$

$$\therefore \qquad h = \frac{4T\cos\theta}{a\rho g}$$

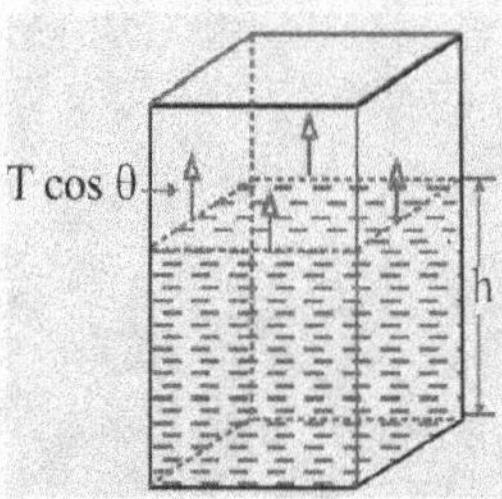

Fig. 2.68

Apparent angle of contact

We know that
$$h = \frac{2T\cos\theta}{r\rho g} \qquad \ldots(i)$$

For the tube of insufficient length $\ell < h$, so we have

$$\ell = \frac{2T\cos\theta'}{r\rho g} \qquad \ldots(ii)$$

Here θ' is the apparent angle of contact.
From equations (i) & (ii), we get

$$\cos\theta' = \frac{\ell}{h}\cos\theta$$

Note:

Since $\ell < h$, so the value of θ' will be greater than θ.

Tube inside liquid

The rise of liquid in the capillary tube does not depend on the portion of the tube inside liquid. But total length of the liquid remain depends on the length of the tube.

(i) Suppose ℓ length of the tube is inside the liquid, which is less than the rise of the liquid in the tube. When the tube is taken out of the liquid the length of liquid in the tube will be $(h + \ell)$.

(ii)   If length of the tube inside liquid is greater or equal to h, the length of the liquid remains in the tube will be $(h + h) = 2h$.

It can be explained as : The pressure at points A and B are :

$$P_A = P_a - \frac{2T}{R} \quad \text{and} \quad P_B = P_a + \frac{2T}{R}$$

Clearly

$$P_B = P_A + \rho g h'$$

or

$$\left(P_a + \frac{2T}{R}\right) = \left(P_a - \frac{2T}{R}\right) + \rho g h'$$

or

$$h' = \frac{4T}{\rho g R} = 2h$$

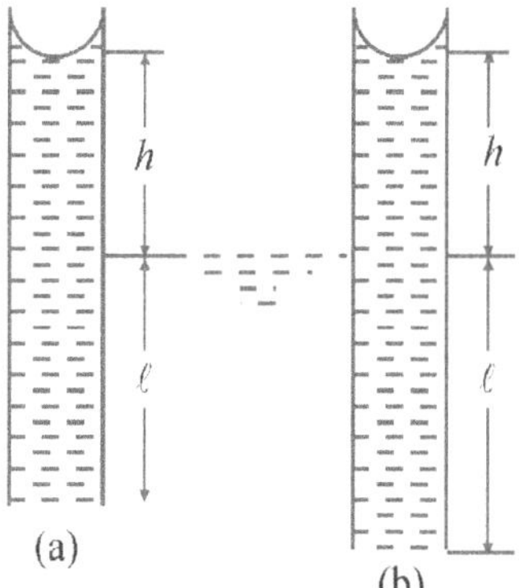
Fig. 2.69

Inclined tube

If the tube is inclined with the vertical, the rise of liquid in the tube will be same, but length of the liquid in the tube will increase.

If h is the rise of liquid, then length of liquid in the tube $\ell = \dfrac{h}{\cos \alpha}$.

Work done by surface tension force

In the process of rise of liquid in the tube, the liquid pressure at the wall of

the tube increase from zero to $\rho g h$. So average pressure, $P_{av} = \dfrac{\rho g h}{2}$

The change in volume of air

$$\Delta V = \pi r^2 h$$

Also

$$h = \frac{2T \cos \theta}{r \rho g}$$

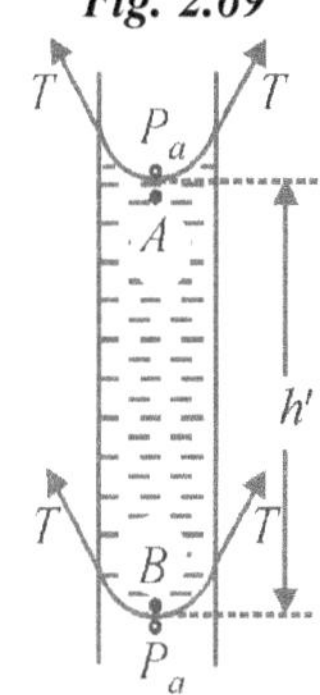
Fig. 2.70

Work done in increasing the glass-liquid surface (decreasing glass-air surface)

$$W = P_{av} \Delta V = \left(\frac{\rho g h}{2}\right)\left(\pi r^2 h\right)$$

$$= \frac{\pi}{2} \rho g r^2 h^2 = \frac{\pi \rho g r^2}{2}\left(\frac{2T \cos \theta}{r \rho g}\right)^2$$

$$= \frac{2T^2 \pi \cos^2 \theta}{\rho g}$$

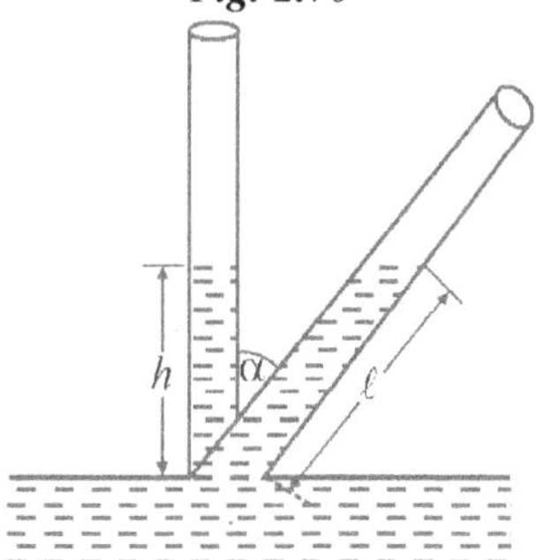
Fig. 2.71

Capillary tube of varying radius

Suppose radius of the tube varies from r_1 and r_2 in its total length ℓ. The radius at the position of meniscus

$$r = r_1 - \left(\frac{r_1 - r_2}{\ell}\right) h$$

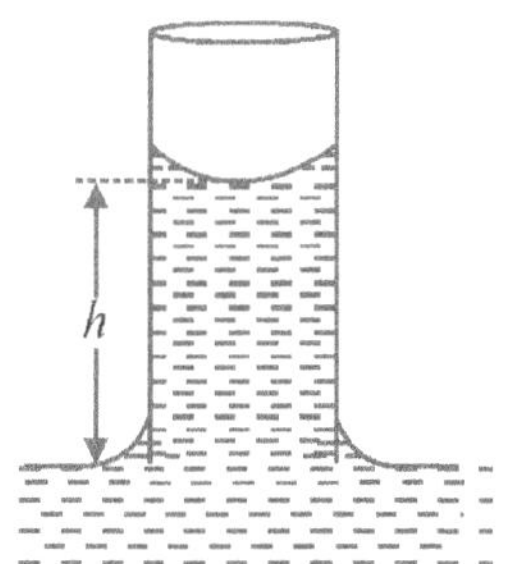
Fig. 2.72

The rise of the liquid in the tube can be obtained by the formula $h = \dfrac{2T \cos \theta}{r \rho g}$, by placing

the value of r in terms of r_1 and r_2.

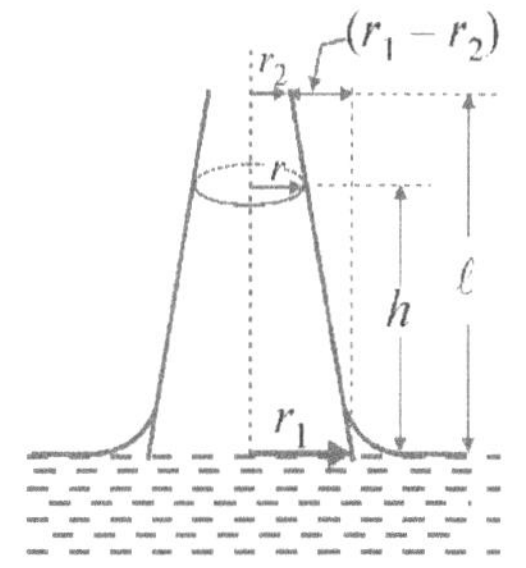
Fig. 2.73

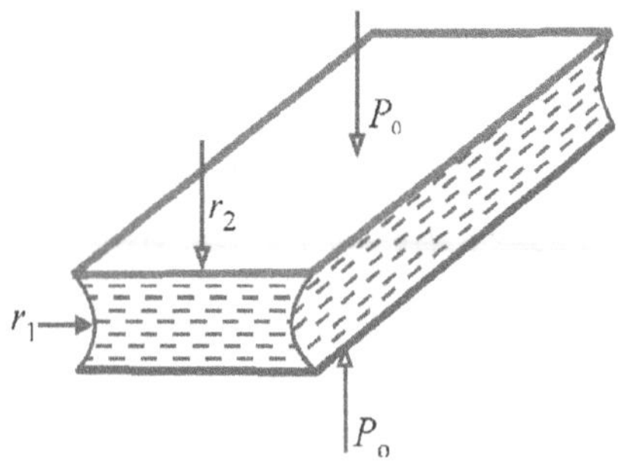

Fig. 2.74

Force required to separate the plates having some liquid between them

When some liquid is put between the plates, the pressure between the plates P_i becomes less than the outside pressure P_o. So an outwards force is required to separate them. Let d be the separation between the plates and r_1 and r_2 are the radii of curvatures of two sides of the surface film. The pressure difference

$$P_o - P_i = T\left(\frac{1}{r_1} + \frac{1}{r_2}\right)$$

Here $r_1 \simeq \dfrac{d}{2}$ also $r_2 \gg r_1$, so $\dfrac{1}{r_2} \ll \dfrac{1}{r_1}$

$$\therefore \qquad P_o - P_i = \frac{T}{r_1}$$

$$= \frac{T}{d/2} = \frac{2T}{d}$$

Force required

$$F = (P_o - P_i) \times \text{area of plate}$$

$$= \frac{2T}{d} \times A = \frac{2TA}{d}$$

Ex. 26 The following design of a perpetuum mobile has been suggested. A capillary tube of radius r is chosen which allows water to rise to a height h (see *Fig. 2.75*). At a height h_1, smaller than h, the capillary is bent and its upper end is made into a broad funnel as shown in the diagram. the surface tension is enough to raise the liquid to the height h_1 and introduce it into the funnel. The liquid in the broad part of the funnel detaches itself from its upper surface and flows down unimpeded. A water wheel can be installed in the path of the drops falling back into the vessel, thus providing a perpetuum mobile. Will this perpetuum mobile actually operate? Find the error in the reasoning above.

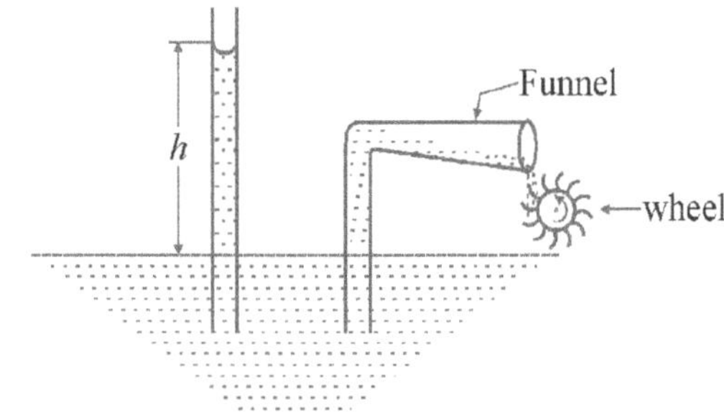

Fig. 2.75

Sol.

The perpetuum mobile will not operate and the water will not flow out of the funnel. As soon as the water enters into the funnel the radius of curvature of the meniscus will begin to increase and, correspondingly, the surface tension will gradually decrease. The water in the funnel will only reach the section with that radius R where the surface tension exactly equalizes the weight of the water of column h. If T be the surface tension of water, then

$$T(2\pi R) = \pi r^2 h\rho g$$

or $\qquad R = \dfrac{\rho g h r^2}{2T}$ *Ans.*

Ex. 27 Two soap bubbles of radii r_1 and r_2 coalesce to form a single bubble under isothermal condition. Find the radius of resulting bubble.

Sol.

As the process is isothermal, so by Boyle's law, we have

$$P_1 V_1 + P_2 V_2 = PV$$

If r is the radius of the resulting bubble, then

$$\left(\frac{4T}{r_1}\right) \times \frac{4}{3}\pi r_1^3 + \left(\frac{4T}{r_2}\right) \times \frac{4}{3}\pi r_2^3 = \left(\frac{4T}{r}\right) \times \frac{4}{3}\pi r^3$$

or $\qquad r_1^2 + r_2^2 = r^2$ *Ans.*

Ex. 28 Two soap bubbles come together to form a double bubble. Find the radius of curvature at the contact point.

Sol.

Pressure inside smaller bubble is greater, so curvature on this side will be concave.

Suppose two soap bubbles of radii r_1 and r_2 come in contact and r be the radius of contact point

$$P_1 = \left(\frac{4T}{r_1} + P_a\right) \text{ and } P_2 = \left(\frac{4T}{r_2} + P_a\right)$$

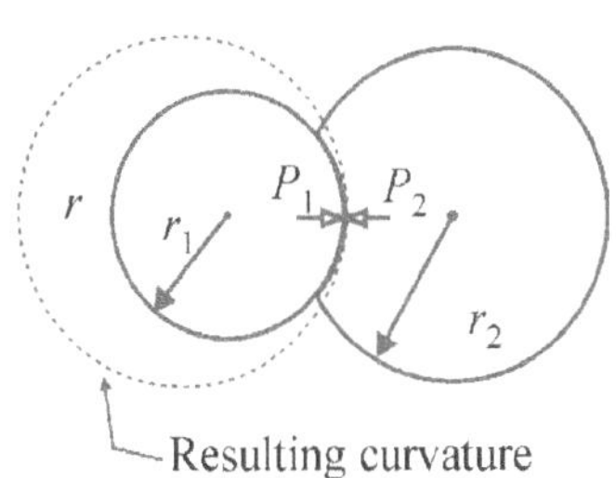

Fig. 2.76

For resulting curvature $P_1 - P_2 = P$

$$\text{or} \left(\frac{4T}{r_1} + P_a \right) - \left(\frac{4T}{r_2} + P_a \right) = \frac{4T}{r}$$

$$\text{or} \qquad \frac{1}{r_1} - \frac{1}{r_2} = \frac{1}{r}$$

$$\Rightarrow \qquad r = \frac{r_2 - r_1}{r_1 r_2} \qquad \textit{Ans.}$$

Ex. 29 A capillary tube of radius 0.50 mm is dipped vertically in a pot of water. Find the difference between the pressure of the water in the tube 5.0 cm below the surface and atmospheric pressure. Surface tension of water = 0.075 N/m.

Sol.

$$P_A = P_a$$

$$P_B = P_a - \frac{2T}{r}$$

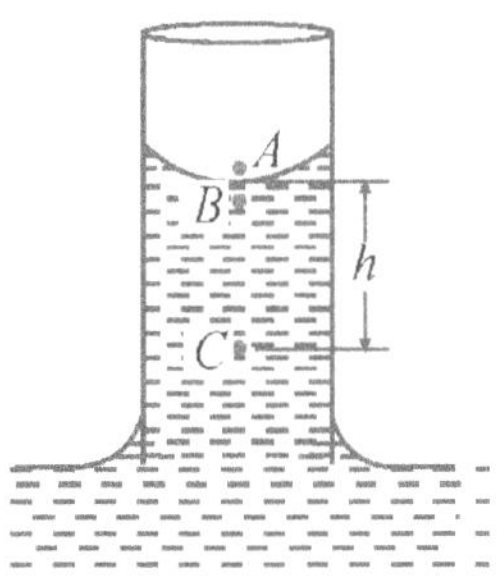

Fig. 2.77

$$\text{and} \qquad P_C = P_B + h\rho g$$

$$= \left(P_a - \frac{2T}{r} \right) + h\rho g$$

$$\therefore \qquad P_C - P_a = h\rho g - \frac{2T}{r}$$

$$= 0.05 \times 10^3 \times 9.8 - \frac{2 \times 0.075}{0.5 \times 10^{-3}}$$

$$= 190 \text{ N/m}^2 \qquad \textit{Ans.}$$

Ex. 30 A wire forming a loop is dipped in to soap solution and taken out so that a film of soap solution is formed. A loop of ℓ long thread is gently put on the film and the film is pricked with a needle inside the loop. The thread loop takes the shape of a circle. Find the tension in the thread. Surface tension of soap solution is T.

Sol.

If r the radius of the loop formed, then

$$\ell = 2\pi r$$

$$\Rightarrow \qquad r = \frac{\ell}{2\pi}$$

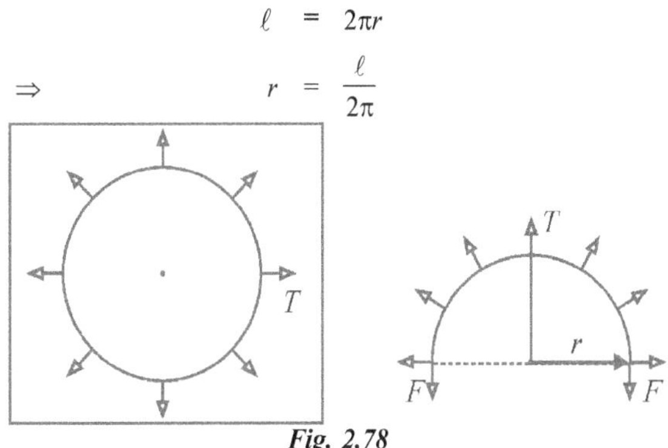

Fig. 2.78

Surface tension force on the half loop

$$= T \times \text{projected length of the loop}$$

$$= T \times 2r$$

Now consider the equilibrium of the half loop, we have

$$2F = T \times 2r$$

$$\Rightarrow \qquad F = Tr$$

$$\text{or} \qquad F = \frac{T\ell}{2\pi} \qquad \textit{Ans.}$$

Ex. 31 A soap bubble is being blown at the end of a very narrow tube of radius b. Air (density ρ) moves with a velocity v inside the tube and comes to rest inside the bubble. The surface tension of the soap solution is T. After some time the bubble, having grown to a radius r, separates from the tube. Find the value of r. Assume that $r \gg b$ so that you can consider the air to be falling normally on the bubble's surface.

Sol.

The bubble will separate from the tube when thrust force exerted by the air is equal to the force due to excess pressure.

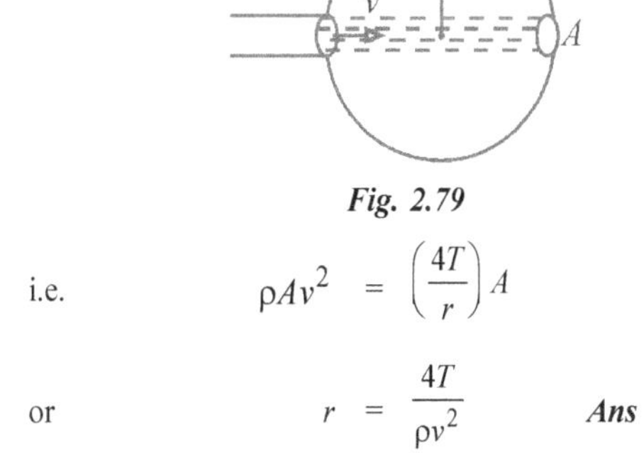

Fig. 2.79

$$\text{i.e.} \qquad \rho A v^2 = \left(\frac{4T}{r} \right) A$$

$$\text{or} \qquad r = \frac{4T}{\rho v^2} \qquad \textit{Ans}$$

Ex. 32 If a number of little droplets of water of surface tension T, all of the same radius r combine to form a single drop of radius R and the energy released is converted into kinetic energy, find the velocity acquired by the bigger drop.

Sol.

By conservation of volume

$$\frac{4}{3}\pi R^3 = n\frac{4}{3}\pi r^3$$

$$\text{or} \qquad n = \frac{R^3}{r^3}$$

Mass of the bigger drop, m = volume × density

$$= \frac{4}{3}\pi R^3 \times 1 \qquad [\text{density} = 1 \text{ g/cm}^3]$$

$$= \frac{4}{3}\pi R^3$$

Energy released in the process = Surface tension × decrease in surface area

$$= T \times 4\pi \,(nr^2 - R^2)$$

$$= 4\pi T\left[\frac{R^3}{r^3}r^2 - R^2\right]$$

$$= 4\pi TR^2\left[\frac{R}{r} - 1\right]$$

$$= 4\pi TR^2\left[\frac{R - r}{r}\right]$$

Increase in K.E. = Decrease in energy of the system

or

$$\frac{1}{2}mv^2 = 4\pi TR^2\left[\frac{R - r}{r}\right]$$

or

$$\frac{1}{2}\left(\frac{4}{3}\pi R^3\right)v^2 = 4\pi TR^2\left[\frac{R - r}{r}\right]$$

$$\therefore \qquad v = \sqrt{\frac{6T(R - r)}{Rr}} \qquad \textit{Ans.}$$

Here v will be in cm/s.

Ex. 33

A glass plate of length 10 cm, breadth 4 cm and thickness 0.4 cm, weighs 20 g in air. It is held vertically with long side horizontal and half the plate immersed in water. What will be its apparent weight? Surface tension of water = 70 dyne/cm.

Sol.

The force acting on the plate are :

(i)   Weight of the plate vertically downwards,
$$W = mg = 20 \text{ g-}f$$

(ii)   Buoyant force due to liquid, $F_b = V\rho_\ell g$

$$= \left(\frac{\ell b t}{2}\right)\rho_\ell g$$

$$= \left(\frac{10 \times 4 \times 0.4}{2}\right) \times 1 \text{ g-}f$$

$$= 8 \text{ g-}f$$

(iii)   Force due to surface tension, vertically downward
$$F = T \times \text{Perimeter of plate in contact with water}$$

$$= \frac{70}{980} \times 2(10 + 0.4)g - f$$

$$= 1.5 \text{ g} - f$$

Apparent weight of the plate

$$= (W + F) - F_b$$
$$= (20 + 1.5) - 8$$
$$= 13.5 \text{ g-f} \qquad \textit{Ans.}$$

Ex. 34

A glass U-tube is such that the diameter of one limb is 3.0 mm and that of the other is 6.00 mm. The tube is inverted vertically with the open ends below the surface of water in a beaker. What is the difference between the heights to which water rises in the two limbs? Surface tension of water is 0.07 N/m. Assume that the angle of contact between water and glass is 0°.

Sol.

Let P_A and P_B are the pressures at points A and B respectively. The pressure at point C,

$$P_C = P_A - \frac{2T}{R_1}$$

where

$$R_1 = \frac{r_1}{\cos 0°} = r_1$$

The pressure at point D, $\quad P_D = P_B - \frac{2T}{R_2}$

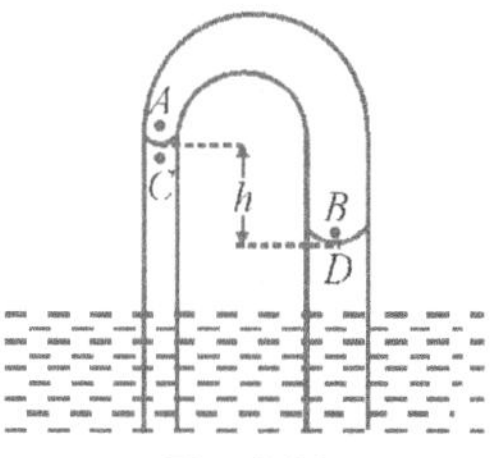

Fig. 2.80

where,

$$R_2 = \frac{r_2}{\cos 0°} = r_2$$

If h is the difference between heights rise in two limbs, then
$$P_D - P_C = h\rho g$$

or $\quad \left(P_B - \dfrac{2T}{R_2}\right) - \left(P_A - \dfrac{2T}{R_1}\right) = h\rho g$

As $P_A = P_B$ and $R_1 = r_1 = 1.5$ mm, $R_2 = r_2 = 3.0$ mm, so

$$2T\left(\frac{1}{r_1} - \frac{1}{r_2}\right) = h\rho g$$

$$0.2 \times 0.07\left(\frac{1}{1.5 \times 10^{-3}} - \frac{1}{3 \times 10^{-3}}\right) = h \times 1000 \times 9.8$$

After solving, we get
$$h = 4.76 \times 10^{-3} \text{ m} \qquad \textit{Ans.}$$

Ex. 35

A container of width $2a$ is filled with a liquid. A thin wire of weight per unit length λ is gently placed over the liquid surface in the middle of the surface as shown in *Fig. 2.81*. As a result the liquid surface is depressed by a distance y ($y \ll a$). Determine the surface tension of the liquid.

Sol.

Let ℓ be the length of the wire. As λ is the mass per unit length of the wire, so weight of the wire

$$W = \lambda \ell g$$

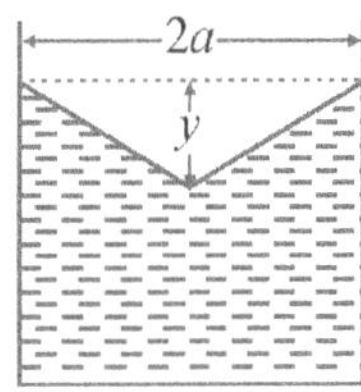

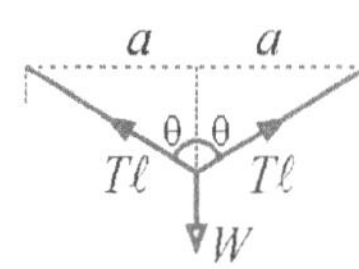

Fig. 2.81   *Fig. 2.82*

If T is the surface tension, then surface tension force $= T\ell$

The weight of the wire is balanced by the vertical component of the surface tension force $T\ell$, so

$$2T\ell\cos\theta = 0$$

$\therefore$
$$T = \frac{W}{2\ell\cos\theta} = \frac{\lambda\ell g}{2\ell\cos\theta} = \frac{\lambda g}{2\cos\theta}$$

From the figure

$$\cos\theta = \frac{y}{\sqrt{a^2+y^2}} = \frac{y}{a} \qquad (\text{As } y << a)$$

$\therefore$
$$T = \frac{\lambda g}{2(y/a)} = \frac{\lambda ga}{2y} \qquad \textit{Ans.}$$

Ex. 36

A capillary tube of radius r and height h is connected to a broad tube as shown in Fig. 2.83. The broad tube is gradually filled with drops of water falling at equal intervals. Plot the changes in the levels of water in both tubes with time and changes in the difference between these levels. Calculate the maximum water level in the broad tube and the maximum difference in the levels. The surface tension of water is T.

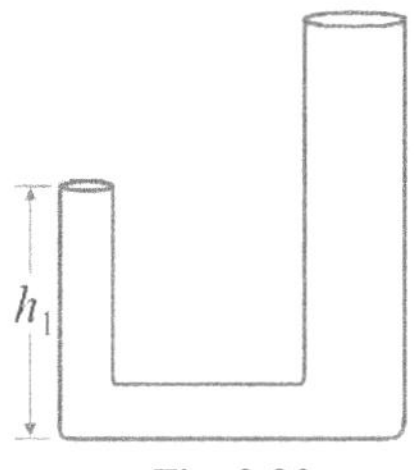

Fig. 2.83

Sol.

From the moment the filling begins to the moment of time A the water level will uniformly rise in the capillary tube (curve I) and remain at the same level in the broad tube (curve II). The difference in the levels will constantly increase. At the moment of time t_A the difference in the levels

will reach $h_0 = \dfrac{2T}{\rho gr}$.

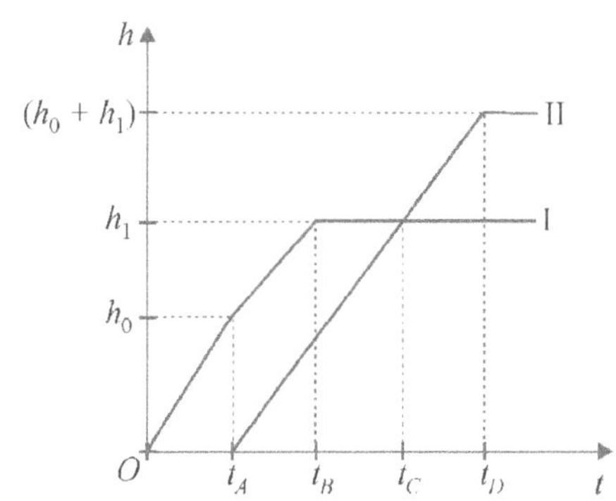

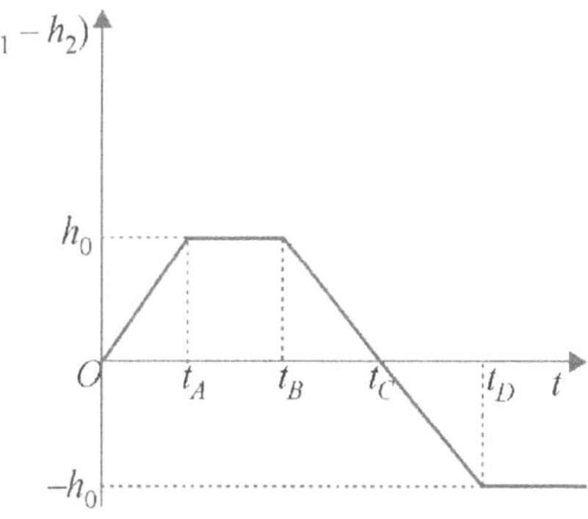

Fig. 2.84

From this moment up to the moment of time t_B the levels in the capillary and broad tube will rise with the same velocities while the difference in the levels will remain constant and equal to h_0. At the moment of time t_B the water level in the capillary tube will reach the end of the capillary and will stop at a height h_1. From the moment t_B to the moment t_D the water level will continuously rise in the broad tube. The water level in the capillary will remain constant but the meniscus will change its shape from concave to convex of same radius r at the moment t_D. The difference in the levels in the section BC will decrease to zero and in the section CD it will change its sign and will increase to h_0. At the moment t_D the water will begin to flow out of the capillary tube and from this moment onwards all the levels will be constant. The maximum height to which the water rises in the broad tube is $h_0 + h_1$. The maximum difference in the levels is h_0.

Ex. 37

Two spherical soap bubbles coalesce. If V is the consequence change in volume of the contained air and S the change in total surface area, show that
$$3PV + 4ST = 0,$$
where T is the surface tension of soap bubble and p is atmospheric pressure.

Sol.

Suppose a and b are the radii of the two soap bubbles and P_a, P_b are the pressures inside them. Let c be the radius and P_c the pressure inside the resulting bubble. Then

$$P_a = P + \frac{4T}{a}, \; P_b = P + \frac{4T}{b} \text{ and } P_c = P + \frac{4T}{c}$$

If V_a, V_b and V_c are the volumes of two soap bubbles and that of the resulting bubble, then by Boyle's law, we have

$$P_a V_a + P_b V_b = P_c V_c$$

or $\left(P + \dfrac{4T}{a}\right) \times \dfrac{4}{3}\pi a^3 + \left(P + \dfrac{4T}{b}\right) \times \dfrac{4}{3}\pi b^3 = \left(P + \dfrac{4T}{c}\right) \times \dfrac{4}{3}\pi c^3$

or $P\left(\dfrac{4}{3}\pi a^3 + \dfrac{4}{3}\pi b^3 - \dfrac{4}{3}\pi c^3\right) + \dfrac{4T}{3}\left(4\pi a^2 + 4\pi b^2 - 4\pi c^2\right) = 0$

But $\left(\dfrac{4}{3}\pi a^3 + \dfrac{4}{3}\pi b^3 - \dfrac{4}{3}\pi c^3\right) = V$ (change in volume)

and $(4\pi a^2 + 4\pi b^2 - 4\pi c^2) = S$ (change in surface)

On substituting these values in above equation, we get

$$PV + \frac{4T}{3}S = 0$$

or $\qquad 3PV + 4TS = 0 \qquad\qquad \textit{Proved}$

Ex. 38

Soapy water drips from a capillary. When the drop breaks away, the diameter of it neck is D. The mass of the drop is m. Find the surface tension of soapy water.

Sol.

When the drop breaks away from the capillary,

$$\text{weight of the drop} = \text{force of surface tension}$$

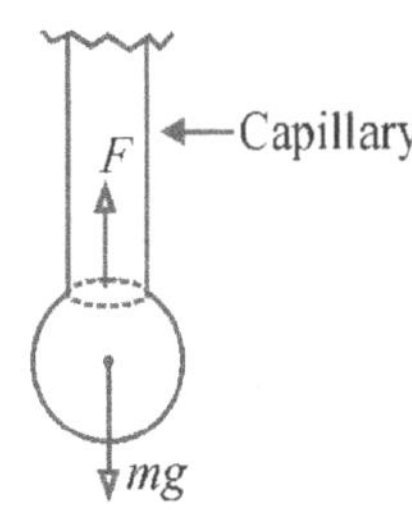

Fig. 2.85

or
$$mg = \pi D \times T$$

or
$$T = \frac{mg}{\pi D} \qquad \textbf{\textit{Ans.}}$$

Ex. 39

What is the pressure inside a drop of mercury of radius 3.00 mm of room temperature? Surface tension of mercury at that temperature (20°C) is 4.65×10^{-1} N/m. The atmospheric pressure is $1.01 \times 10^5 Pa$. Also give the excess pressure inside the drop.

Sol.

If P_i and P_o be the inside and outside pressures of the drop, then

$$P_i - P_o = \frac{2T}{R}$$

$$\therefore \qquad P_i = P_o + \frac{2T}{R}$$

$$= 1.01 \times 10^5 + \frac{2 \times 4.65 \times 10^{-1}}{3.00 \times 10^{-3}}$$

$$= 1.013 \times 10^5 \; Pa \qquad \textbf{\textit{Ans.}}$$

Ex. 40

A water drop falls in air with a uniform velocity. Find the difference between the curvature radii of the drop' surface at the upper and lower points of the drop separated by the distance $h = 2.3$ mm.

Sol.

Suppose R_1 and R_2 be the radii of curvatures at the upper point and lower point of the drop respectively. The pressure inside the drop at the upper end,

$$P_A = P_o + \frac{2T}{R_1}$$

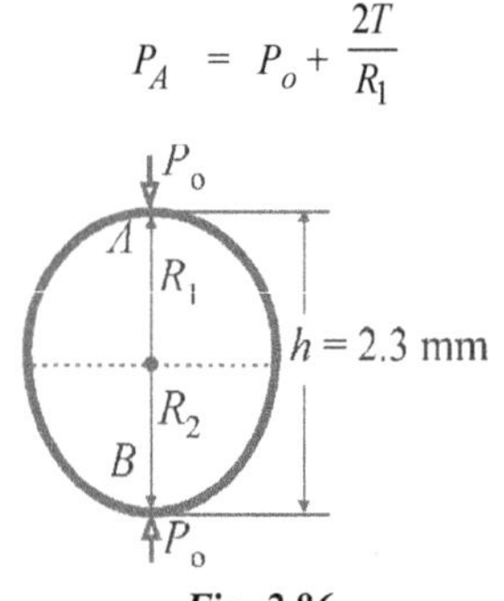

Fig. 2.86

and pressure at the lower end

$$P_B = P_o + \frac{2T}{R_2}$$

where P_o is the atmospheric pressure.

As the drop is falling with uniform velocity, so

$$P_B = P_A + \rho g h$$

or
$$P_o + \frac{2T}{R_2} = P_o + \frac{2T}{R_1} + \rho g h$$

or
$$2T\left(\frac{1}{R_2} - \frac{1}{R_1}\right) = \rho g h$$

or
$$2T\frac{(R_1 - R_2)}{R_1 R_2} = \rho g h$$

It can be assumed that $R \simeq R_2$ and $R_1 + R_2 = h$ so $R_1 = R_2 = h/2$. Therefore, we get

$$2T(R_1 - R_2) = (\rho g h) R_1 R_2$$

$$= \rho g h \times \left(\frac{h}{2} \times \frac{h}{2}\right)$$

$$\therefore \qquad R_1 - R_2 = \frac{\rho g h^3}{8T} \qquad \textbf{\textit{Ans.}}$$

Ex. 41

A mercury drop shaped as a round tablet of radius R and thickness h is located between two horizontal glass plates. Assuming that $h << R$, find the mass m of a weight which has to be placed on the copper plate to diminish the distance between the plates n-times. The contact angle equals θ. Calculate m if $R = 2.0$ cm, $h = 0.38$ mm, $n = 2.0$ and $\theta = 135°$.

Sol.

We know that pressure inside a film greater than outside pressure by an amount $T\left(\dfrac{1}{r_1} + \dfrac{1}{r_2}\right)$. If θ is the angle of contact then $h = 2r_1 \cos\theta$ or

$r_1 = \dfrac{h}{2\cos\theta}$. Since the tablet is between the plates, so $r_2 = R$. Thus pressure difference

$$= T\left(\frac{1}{r_1} + \frac{1}{r_2}\right) = T\left[\frac{1}{h/2\cos\theta} + \frac{1}{R}\right]$$

As h is small in comparison to R, so $\dfrac{1}{R} << \dfrac{1}{h}$, $\therefore P = \dfrac{2T\cos\theta}{h}$

The total force exerted by mercury drop on the upper glass plate is nearly

$$F = P \times \text{projected area of the drop}$$

$$= \left(\frac{2T\cos\theta}{h}\right) \times \pi R^2$$

$$= \frac{2\pi R^2 T \cos\theta}{h} \qquad \ldots (i)$$

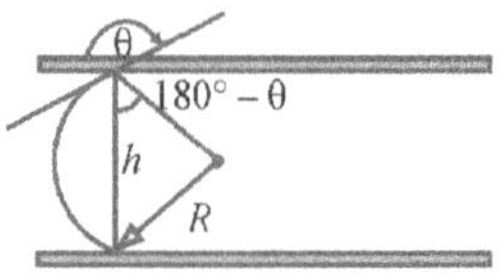

Fig. 2.87

Let R' becomes the new radius of curvature when the distance between the plates is decreased by n-times. Assuming mercury to be incompressible, we have

$$\pi R^2 h = \pi R'^2 \left(\frac{h}{n}\right)$$

$$\Rightarrow \quad R' = \sqrt{n}\,R$$

The force exerted by the mercury drop now becomes

$$F' = \frac{2T(\pi\sqrt{n}R)^2 T\cos\theta}{(h/n)}$$

$$= n^2 F \qquad \ldots \text{(ii)}$$

If mg be the weight placed on the upper plate then

$$F' = F + mg$$

$$\therefore \ m = \frac{F'-F}{g} = \frac{F(n^2-1)}{g} = \frac{2\pi R^2 T\cos\theta}{gh}(n^2-1) \quad \textbf{\textit{Ans.}}$$

Ex. 42

Find the life time of a soap bubble of radius R connected with the atmosphere through a capillary of length ℓ and inside radius r. The surface tension is T, the viscosity coefficient of the gas is η.

Sol.

Suppose at any time t, the radius of the bubble is x, then the pressure inside bubble is $\left(P_o + \dfrac{4T}{x}\right)$, where P_o is the atmospheric pressure. Using Poisullie's equation

$$Q = \frac{\pi\Delta P r^4}{8\eta\ell}$$

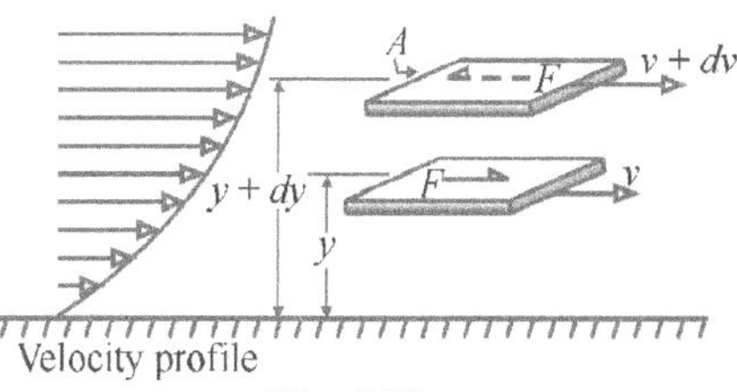

Fig. 2.88

where

$$\Delta P = (P_i - P_o)$$

$$= P_o + \frac{4T}{x} - P_o = \frac{4T}{x}$$

Thus we can write

$$\frac{\pi\left(\dfrac{4T}{x}\right)r^4}{8\eta\ell} = Q$$

$$= -\frac{dV}{dt} = -\frac{d}{dt}\left(\frac{4}{3}\pi x^3\right)$$

$$= -4\pi x^2 \frac{dx}{dt}$$

or

$$\frac{Tr^4}{8\eta\ell} = -x^3 \frac{dx}{dt}$$

or

$$\frac{Tr^4}{8\eta\ell}\int_0^t dt = -\int_R^0 x^3 dx$$

$$\frac{Tr^4}{8\eta\ell}t = \frac{R^4}{4}$$

$$\therefore \quad t = \frac{2\eta\ell R^4}{Tr^4} \qquad \textbf{\textit{Ans.}}$$

2.21 Viscosity

Viscosity is the property of fluid by virtue of which an internal force of friction comes into play in a moving fluid and which opposes the relative motion between the adjacent layers. This opposing force is called **viscous force** or viscous drag. Viscous force also acts between solid surface and liquid layers due to relative motion between them. Viscosity is primarily due to cohesion and molecular momentum exchange between fluid layers, and as flow occurs, these affects appear as shearing stresses between the moving layers of the fluid.

Consider a liquid moving over a stationary horizontal surface. The liquid can be assumed moving in the form of layers, one layer moves over the other. The layer in contact with the surface is at rest and the velocity of the every other layer increases upward. The velocity profile will be parabolic (see *Fig. 2.89*).

Fig. 2.89

Newton's law of viscosity

Consider two liquid layers at distances y and $y + dy$ from the stationary surface and moving with velocity v and $v + dv$ respectively. The change in velocity with the height of the liquid is $\dfrac{dv}{dy}$ and is called velocity gradient.

According to Newton, viscous force F acting tangentially between two layers is

(i)   proportional to the area A of the layer in contact

$$F \propto A$$

(ii)   proportional to the velocity gradient between the layers

$$F \propto \left(\frac{dv}{dy}\right)$$

$$\therefore \qquad F = -\eta A\left(\frac{dv}{dy}\right)$$

where η is the coefficient of viscosity of the liquid. Negative sign shows that the viscous force acts opposite to the motion of the liquid.

Units of coefficient of viscosity

(i)   The CGS unit of η is dyne-s/cm^2 and is called poise.

(ii)   The SI unit of η is N–s/m^2 = $Pa - s$ and 1 N-s/m^2 = 10 poise.

Ex. 43 A metal plate of area 0.10 m^2 is connected to a 0.01 kg mass via a string that passes over an ideal pulley (considered massless and frictionless), as shown in *Fig. 2.90*. A liquid with a film thickness of 0.3 mm is placed between the plate and the table. When released the plate moves to the right with a constant speed of 0.085 m/s. Find the coefficient of viscosity of the liquid.

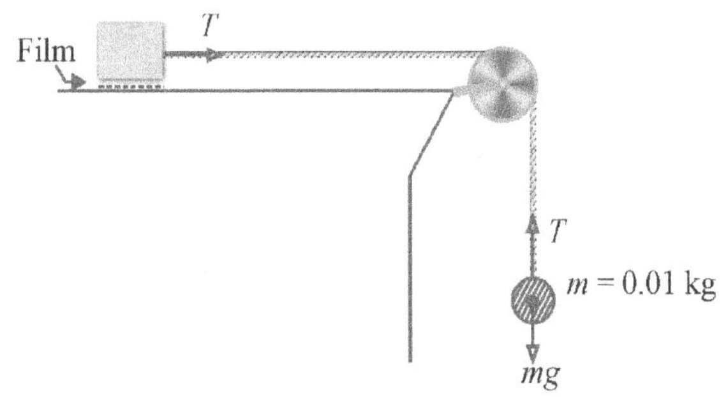

Fig. 2.90

Sol.

As the metal plate moves with constant velocity, so

$$mg - T = 0$$
$$\Rightarrow \qquad T = mg$$

If F is the viscous force on the plate, then

$$F = T$$
$$= mg = 0.01 \times 9.8 = 9.8 \times 10^{-2} \text{ N}$$

By Newton's law of viscosity

$$F = \eta A \frac{dv}{dy}$$

where

$$\frac{dv}{dy} = \frac{0.085}{0.3 \times 10^{-3}} = 28.3 / s$$

$$\therefore \qquad 9.8 \times 10^{-2} = \eta \times 0.10 \times 28.3$$

or

$$\eta = 3.4 \times 10^{-3} \text{ N - s/m}^2 \qquad \textit{Ans.}$$

2.22 FACTOR AFFECTING VISCOSITY

Temperature :

(i)   With the increase in the temperature of the liquid, cohesion between the liquid molecules decrease and hence viscosity of the liquid decreases.

      Stotle empirical formula for the variation of the viscosity of a liquid is given by

$$\eta_t = \frac{\eta_0}{1 + \alpha t + \beta t^2}$$

      where η_0 and η_t are the viscosity at 0°C and t°C respectively, and α and β are constants.

(ii)   Viscosity of the gases is due to the collisions between the molecules. With increase in temperature, collisions between the molecules of the gases increases and hence viscosity increases, $\eta \propto \sqrt{T}$.

Pressure:

(i)   Viscosity of liquids increase with increase in pressure. The viscosity of water decreases with increase in pressure.

(ii)   The viscosity of the gases do not depend on the pressure.

2.23 VISCOSITY VERSUS FRICTION

Viscous force	Friction
1. Viscous force is directly proportional to the area of layer.	1. Friction does not depend on area of contact.
2. It is directly proportional to the relative velocity between the layers.	2. It is almost independent on the velocity of the object.
3. It is independent on the normal reaction between the layers.	3. It is directly proportional to the normal reaction on the body.

2.24 POISEUILLE'S EQUATION

Consider a viscous liquid flowing in a horizontal pipe with constant velocity. Assuming a cylinder of liquid of radius r and length ℓ. It has outer surface $2\pi r\ell$. The viscous drag on the cylinder is

$$F_v = -\eta(2\pi r\ell)\frac{dv}{dr}$$

Since there is no acceleration, so this force is balanced by the force on the cylinder due to pressure difference. The pressure difference at input and output is $P_i - P_o = \Delta P$.

$$\therefore \quad -\eta(2\pi r\ell)\frac{dv}{dr} = \Delta P \times \pi r^2$$

$$\Rightarrow \quad dv = -\frac{\Delta P}{2\eta\ell}r\,dr$$

or

$$\int_v^0 dv = -\frac{\Delta P}{2\eta\ell}\int_r^R r\,dr$$

or

$$v = \frac{\Delta P}{4\eta\ell}(R^2 - r^2)$$

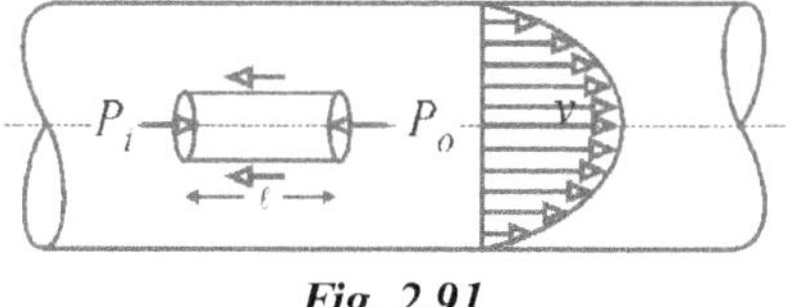

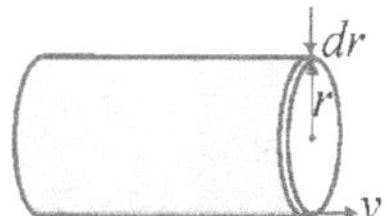

Rate of flow : Rate of flow in small element of cylinder,

$$dQ = v\,dA$$

$$= v \times 2\pi r\,dr$$

$$\therefore \quad Q = \int_0^R v \times 2\pi r\,dr$$

$$= \int_0^R \frac{\Delta P}{4\eta\ell}(R^2 - r^2) \times 2\pi r\,dr$$

or

$$Q = \frac{\pi\Delta P R^4}{8\eta\ell}$$

The above equation can be written as

$$Q = \frac{\Delta P}{R_F} = \frac{P_i - P_o}{R_F}$$

where R_F is the resistance of the pipe and is equal to,

$$R_F = \frac{8\eta\ell}{\pi R^4}.$$

Ex. 44 A liquid is flowing in a horizontal pipe of length ℓ under pressure difference $P_1 - P_2$. Calculate the pressure at a distance x from one end.

Sol.

Suppose P is the pressure at a distance x from left end. As the rate of flow is equal in each part of the pipe, so

$$\frac{P_1 - P}{R_1} = \frac{P - P_2}{R_2}$$

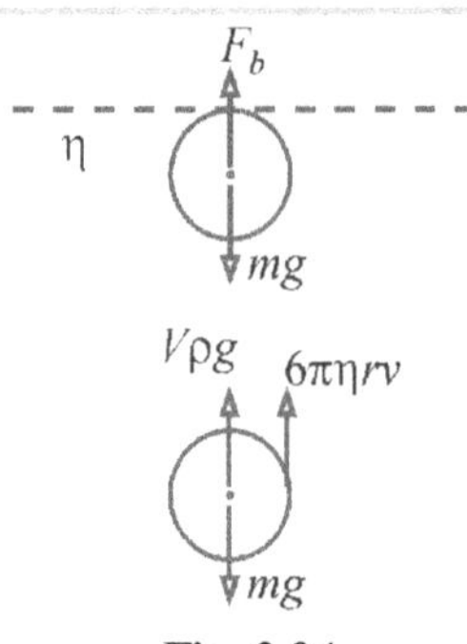

Fig. 2.93

where

$$R_1 = \frac{8\eta x}{\pi r^4}, \quad R_2 = \frac{8\eta(\ell - x)}{\pi r^4}$$

$\therefore$

$$\frac{P_1 - P}{\left(\dfrac{8\eta x}{\pi r^4}\right)} = \frac{P - P_2}{\dfrac{8\eta(\ell - x)}{\pi r^4}}$$

$$\frac{P_1 - P}{x} = \frac{P - P_2}{(\ell - x)}$$

or

$$P = \left[\frac{P_1(\ell - x) + P_2 x}{\ell}\right] \quad \textit{Ans.}$$

2.25 STOKE'S LAW

When any body moves in a viscous fluid, it experiences a viscous force or drag force, which is proportional to the velocity of the body.

Stoke experimentally found that, when a spherical body falls in a viscous liquid, it experiences a viscous force $6\pi\eta rv$ (this value is different from the value theoretically obtained from Newton's law).

Let us consider a spherical body of radius r is placed just inside liquid of density ρ. It experiences gravitational force (mg) and buoyant force both of constant values and viscous force of variable value. Because of the net downward force the body starts accelerating and viscous force starts increasing. At certain velocity the net force on the body becomes zero, and thereafter body moves with constant velocity, is called **terminal velocity**.

Thus

$$F_v + F_b = mg$$

or

$$6\pi\eta rv_t + V\rho g = V\sigma g$$

or

$$6\pi\eta rv_t + \frac{4}{3}\pi r^3 \rho g = \frac{4}{3}\pi r^3 \sigma g$$

$\therefore$

$$v_t = \frac{2}{9}r^2 \frac{(\sigma - \rho)}{\eta}g$$

Clearly terminal velocity does not depend on initial velocity of the body.

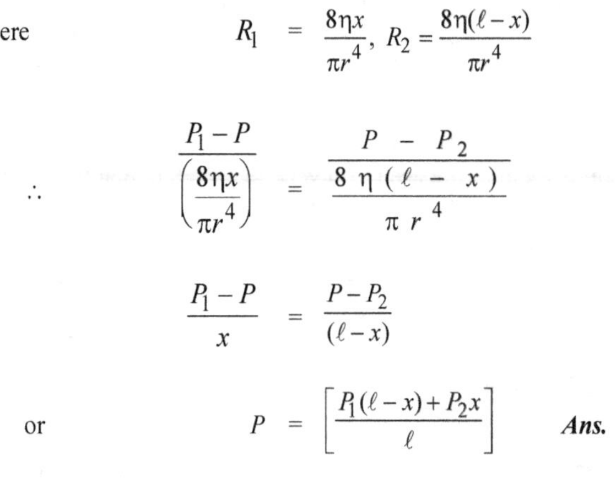

Fig. 2.94

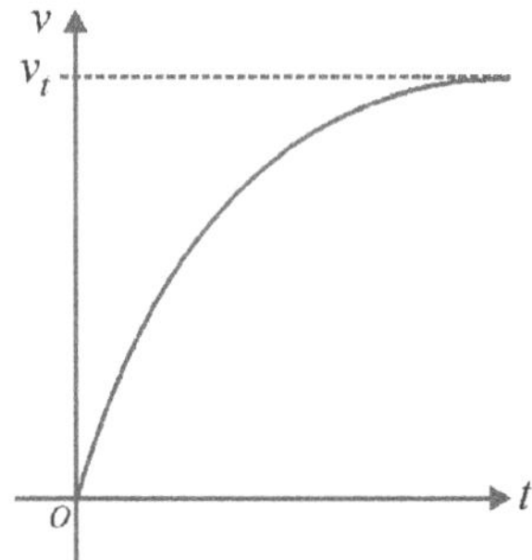

Fig. Variation of velocity of the body with time.

Fig. 2.95

Ex. 45 A sliding fit cylindrical body of mass of 1 kg drops vertically down at a constant velocity of 5 cm/s. Find the viscosity of the oil.

Sol. As the body moves with constant velocity

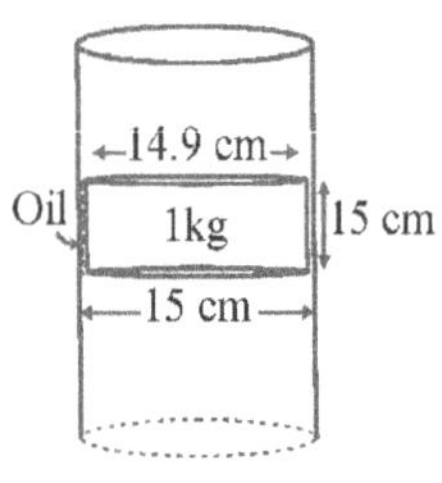

Fig. 2.96

$\therefore$

$$mg = F_v$$

or

$$1g = \eta A \frac{dv}{dy}$$

or

$$1g = \eta(2\pi r \ell)\frac{dv}{dy}$$

or $\quad 1g = \eta(2\pi \times 7.5 \times 10^{-2} \times 15 \times 10^{-2})\left(\dfrac{0.05 - 0}{0.05 \times 10^{-2}}\right)$

After solving, we get

$$\eta = 1.4\,\frac{\text{N--s}}{\text{m}^2} \quad \textit{Ans.}$$

Ex. 46
A powder comprising particles of various sizes is stirred up in a vessel filled to a height of 10 cm with water. Assuming the particles to be spherical, find the size of the largest particle that will remain in suspension after 1 hour. (Density of powder = 4 g/cm^3. Viscosity of water = 0.01 poise).

Sol.
Terminal velocity of the largest particle which is just about to settle at the bottom of the vessel

$$v_t = \frac{10 \times 10^{-2}}{3600} \text{ m/s}.$$

Let r be the radius of that particle, then

$$v_t = \frac{2}{9} r^2 \frac{(\sigma - \rho)}{\eta} g$$

where

$$\sigma = 4 \times 10^3 \text{ kg/m}^3$$

and

$$\eta = \frac{0.01}{10} \frac{\text{N}-\text{s}}{\text{m}^2}$$

After solving, we get $r = 2.0 \times 10^{-6}$ m **Ans.**

Ex. 47
Through a very narrow gap of height h, a thin plate of large extension is pulled at a velocity v on one side of the plate is oil of viscosity μ_1 and on the other side oil of viscosity μ_2. Calculate the position of the plate so that (i) the shear force on the two sides of the plate is equal (ii) the pull required to drag the plate is minimum.

Sol.
Let y is the distance of the plate from one of the surface.
(i)   Force per unit area of the upper surface of the plate

$$f_1 = \mu_1 \frac{dv}{dy} = \mu_1 \frac{v}{(h-y)}$$

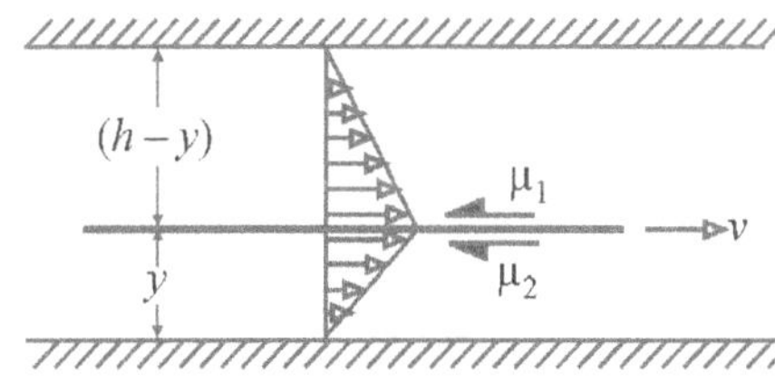

Fig. 2.97

and force per unit area on the bottom surface of the plate

$$f_2 = \mu_2 \frac{dv}{dy} = \mu_2 \frac{v}{y}$$

Equating the two, we get

$$\mu_1 \frac{v}{(h-y)} = \mu_2 \frac{v}{y}$$

$$\Rightarrow \qquad y = \frac{\mu_2 h}{(\mu_1 + \mu_2)} \qquad \text{**Ans.**}$$

(ii)   Let F is the force required to pull the plate. Suppose A is the area of the plate, then

$$F = f_1 A + f_2 A$$

$$F = A\mu_1 \left(\frac{v}{h-y}\right) + A\mu_2 \left(\frac{v}{y}\right)$$

For F to be minimum,

$$\frac{dF}{dy} = 0$$

or

$$\frac{A\mu_1 v}{(h-y)^2} - \frac{\mu_2 v}{y^2} = 0$$

$$\Rightarrow \qquad y = \frac{h}{1 + \sqrt{\dfrac{\mu_1}{\mu_2}}} \qquad \text{**Ans.**}$$

Ex. 48
A large bottle is filled with a siphon made of capillary glass tubing. Compare the time taken to empty the bottle when it is filled (i) with water (ii) with petrol of density 0.8 cgs unit. The viscosity of water and petrol are 0.01 and 0.02 cgs units respectively.

Sol.
The volume of liquid flowing in time t is through a tube is given by

$$V = Qt = \frac{\pi P r^4}{8\eta \ell} t$$

If t_1 and t_2 be the times taken by water and petrol respectively, then

For water, $\qquad V_1 = \dfrac{\pi (\rho_1 gh) r^4}{8\eta_1 \ell} t_1$

For petrol, $\qquad V_2 = \dfrac{\pi (\rho_2 gh) r^4}{8\eta_2 \ell} t_2$

But $\qquad V_1 = V_2$

or $\qquad \dfrac{\pi (\rho_1 gh) r^4}{8\eta_1 \ell} t_1 = \dfrac{\pi (\rho_2 gh) r^4}{8\eta_2 \ell} t_2$

$$\therefore \qquad \frac{t_1}{t_2} = \frac{\eta_1}{\eta_2} \times \frac{\rho_2}{\rho_1}$$

$$= \frac{0.01}{0.02} \times \frac{0.8}{1.0} = 0.4 \qquad \text{**Ans.**}$$

Ex. 49
The level of liquid in a cylindrical vessel is kept constant at 30 cm. It has three identical horizontal tubes of length 39 cm, each coming out at heights 0, 4 and 8 cm respectively. Calculate the length of a single overflow tube of the same radius as that of identical tubes which can replace the three when placed horizontally at bottom of the cylinder.

Sol.

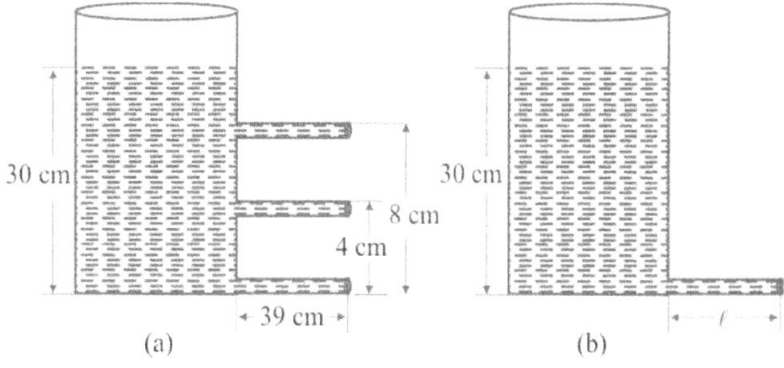

Fig. 2.98

Pressure heads for first tube $= 30 - 0 = 30$ cm

Pressure head for second tube $= 30 - 4 = 26$ cm

Pressure head for third tube $= 30 - 8 = 22$ cm

Length of the each tube $\ell \qquad = 39$ cm

Let radius of the each tube $\qquad = r$ cm

Rate of flow of liquid through the tubes

$$Q_1 = \frac{\pi P_1 r_1^4}{8\eta\ell} = \frac{\pi(\rho g \times 30)}{8\eta\ell} \times r^4$$

Similarly $\qquad Q_2 = \dfrac{\pi(\rho g \times 26) \times r^4}{8\eta\ell}$

and $\qquad Q_3 = \dfrac{\pi(\rho g \times 22) \times r^4}{8\eta\ell}$

The total rate of flow

$$Q = Q_1 + Q_2 + Q_3$$

$$= \frac{\pi\rho g r^4}{8\eta\ell}(30 + 26 + 22)$$

$$= \frac{\pi\rho g r^4}{8\eta \times 39} \times 78 = \frac{\pi\rho g r^4}{4\eta} \quad \ldots \text{(i)}$$

If ℓ' be the length of the equivalent tube, then

$$Q = \frac{\pi(\rho g \times 30)r^4}{8\eta\ell'} \quad \ldots \text{(ii)}$$

From equations (i) and (ii)

$$\frac{\pi(\rho g \times 30)r^4}{8\eta\ell'} = \frac{\pi\rho g r^4}{4\eta}$$

or $\qquad \ell' = 15$ cm $\qquad$ *Ans.*

Ex. 50 In figure *Fig. 2.99* there is a pipe network of uniform cross-sectional area. Pressure at inlet and outlet are $2P_0$ and P_0 respectively. Find ratio of volume of flow in two branches of the pipes. The length of the each pipe is shown in figure. Also find pressure at points *C* and *D*.

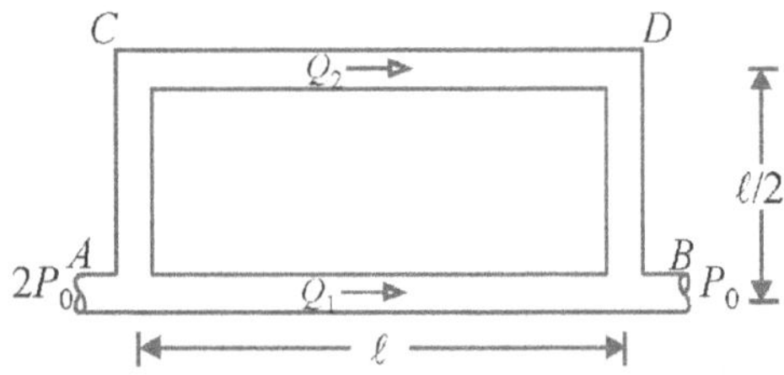

Fig. 2.99

Sol.

Suppose resistance of the pipe *AB* is *r* then resistance of pipes *AC, CD* and *DB* will be $r/2$, r and $r/2$ respectively. The given pipe network can be assumed as an equivalent of electrical circuit shown in *Fig. 2.100*.

The total resistance of the circuit,

$$R = \frac{2r \times r}{2r + r}$$

$$= \frac{2r}{3}$$

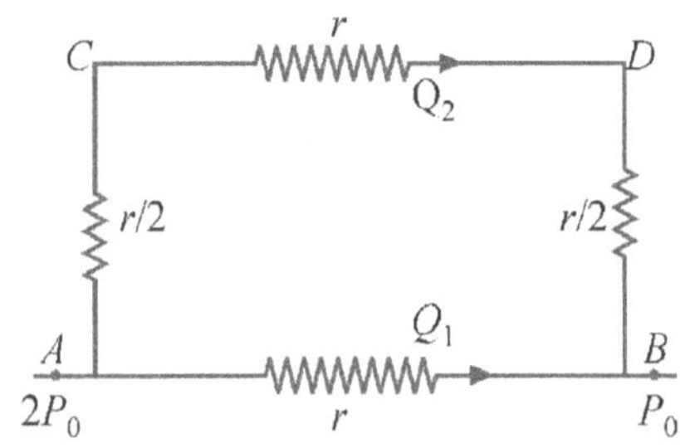

Fig. 2.100

The total input $\qquad Q = \dfrac{\Delta P}{R}$

or $\qquad Q_1 + Q_2 = \dfrac{2P_0 - P_0}{2r/3} = \dfrac{3P_0}{2r} \qquad \ldots \text{(i)}$

As pipe *ACDB* is parallel to *AB*, so

$$Q_1 \times r = Q_2 \times 2r \qquad \ldots \text{(ii)}$$

or $\qquad Q_1 = 2Q_2$

Solving equations (i) and (ii), we get

$$Q_1 = \frac{P_0}{r} \text{ and } Q_2 = \frac{P_0}{2r}$$

$\therefore \qquad \dfrac{Q_1}{Q_2} = 2 \qquad\qquad$ *Ans.*

Pressure difference :

$$P_A - P_C = Q_2 \times \frac{r}{2}$$

$$= \frac{P_0}{2r} \times \frac{r}{2} = \frac{P_0}{4}$$

Given $\qquad P_A = 2P_0 \qquad\qquad$ *Ans.*

$\therefore \qquad P_C = \dfrac{7P_0}{4}$

Similarly $\qquad P_D - P_B = Q_2 \times \dfrac{r}{2}$

$$= \frac{P_0}{2r} \times \frac{r}{2} = \frac{P_0}{4}$$

Given $\qquad P_B = P_0$

$\therefore \qquad P_D = \dfrac{5P_0}{4} \qquad\qquad$ *Ans.*

Review of formulae & Important Points

ELASTICITY

1. **Elastic force is electromagnetic in nature, but it does not obey Coulomb's law.**

2. $$\text{Stress} = \frac{\text{Applied force}}{\text{Area}} = \frac{F}{A}$$

   $$\text{Strain} = \frac{\text{Change in dimension}}{\text{Original dimension}}$$

3. **Hooke's law :** Within elastic limit;
   $$\text{stress} \propto \text{strain}$$
   or $\dfrac{\text{stress}}{\text{strain}} = E\,(\text{modulus of elasticity})$

   Modulus of elasticity is the material property which does not depend on size and shape of the body.

4. **Three types of modulii of elasticity.**
   (i) Young's modulus,
   $$Y = \frac{\text{Longitudinal stress}}{\text{Longitudinal strain}}$$
   $$= \frac{F/A}{\Delta l/l} = \frac{Mgl}{\pi r^2 \Delta l}$$

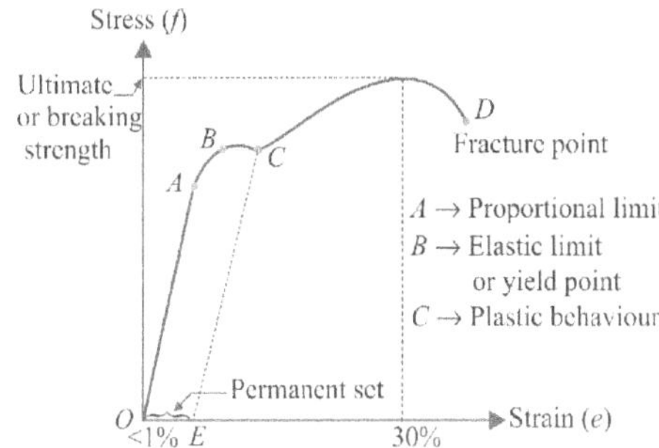

   (ii) Bulk modulus,
   $$B = \frac{\text{Normal stress}}{\text{Volumetric strain}} = \frac{P}{\left(\dfrac{\Delta V}{V}\right)}$$

   In differential form, B can be written as
   $$B = \frac{dP}{\left(\dfrac{-dV}{V}\right)}$$

5. **Shear modulus,**
   $$\eta = \frac{\text{shear stress}}{\text{shear strain}} = \frac{F/A}{\theta}$$
   $$= \frac{F}{A\theta}$$
   Here θ is the shear strain.

6. **Poisson's ratio,**
   $$\sigma = \frac{\text{Lateral strain}}{\text{Longitudinal strain}} = \frac{-\Delta r/r}{\Delta l/l}$$
   Theoretical value of σ lies from -1 to 0.5.

7. $Y = 3B(1-2\sigma)$, $\quad Y = 2\eta(1+\sigma)$
   $$Y = \frac{9\eta B}{\eta + 3B}$$

8. Change in volume,
   $$\frac{\Delta V}{V} = \frac{\Delta l}{l}(1-2\sigma)$$
   Change in density,
   $$\rho' = \frac{\rho}{\left(1 - \dfrac{P}{B}\right)}$$

9. **Thermal stress,** $f_{th} = Y\alpha\Delta T$

10. **Extension due to self weight**
    $$\Delta \ell = \frac{\rho g \ell^2}{2Y} = \frac{W\ell}{2AY}$$

11. **Strain energy,** $U = \dfrac{1}{2} \times \text{stress} \times \text{strain} \times \text{volume}$

    Strain energy per unit volume, $u = \dfrac{f^2}{2Y}$

    Strain energy due to shear of the body $u = \dfrac{f^2}{2\eta}$

12. **Bending of beam :** Deflection of beam,
    $$\delta = \frac{Wl^3}{48YI} \text{ for simply supported beam and } \delta = \frac{Wl^3}{3YI} \text{ for cantilever beam}$$

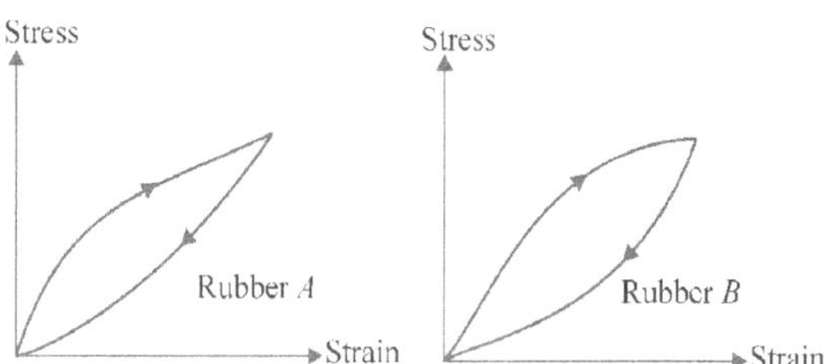

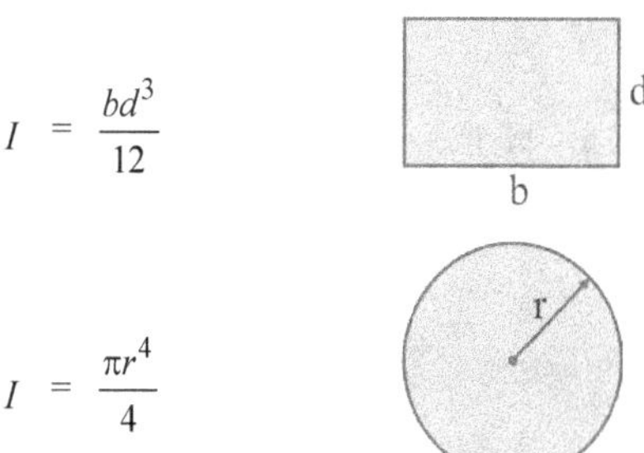

    $$I = \frac{bd^3}{12}$$

    $$I = \frac{\pi r^4}{4}$$

13. **Twisting of a shaft:** Torsional rigidity of material of shaft
    $$\frac{\tau}{\theta} = \frac{\pi \eta r^4}{2l}$$
    Here θ is the angle of twist.

SURFACE TENSION

14. **Surface tension,**
    $$T = \frac{F}{l}$$

or $F = Tl$

(i) Surface tension force on a wire of length l, placed on water

$$F = 2Tl$$

(ii) Surface tension force on circular disc of radius r,

$$F = 2\pi r T$$

(iii) Surface tension force on a ring of radius R.

$$F = 2(2\pi R \times T)$$

15. Surface means a thin layer of approximately 10-15 molecular diameters.

16. **Surface energy :** A molecule in the surface has greater potential energy than a molecule which inside the liquid. The extra energy that a surface film has is called the surface energy.

17. **Work done in increasing the area of the surface film,**

$$W = T\Delta A$$

(i) W.d. in breaking a liquid drop

$$W = T\left[n \times 4\pi r^2 - 4\pi R^2\right]$$

here $r = \dfrac{R}{n^{1/3}}$

(ii) Work done in blowing a soap bubble from zero to radius R.

$$W = T \times 2\left(4\pi R^2\right) = 8\pi T R^2$$

18. **Pressure difference :**

(i) In a liquid drop $P_i - P_0 = \dfrac{2T}{R}$.

(ii) In a soap bubble $P_i - P_0 = \dfrac{4T}{R}$.

(iii) In general, for one free surface

$$P_i \sim P_0 = T\left(\frac{1}{R_1} + \frac{1}{R_2}\right)$$

19. **Angle of contact :**
   (i) Angle of contact is the property of the materials in contact.
   (ii) It decreases with increase in temperature.
   (iii) It decreases with the addition of soap and detergent.
   (iv) It increases with the addition of sugar and salt.
   (v) Angle of contact of water with glass is 8°, and for mercury in glass is 140°.

20. **Capillary rise :** If r is the radius of the capillary tube, then

$$h = \frac{2T\cos\theta}{r\rho g}$$

In terms of radius of curvature $R = \dfrac{r}{\cos\theta}$, $h = \dfrac{2T}{R\rho g}$

21. In case of square tube of side a,

$$h = \frac{4T\cos\theta}{a\rho g}$$

22. **Capillary tube of insufficient length :**
   If h is the free rise of the liquid and l is the length of tube, being
   $l < h$, then $hR = lR'$

   here R' is the radius of curvature of the meniscus of the liquid at the top of the tube.
   The liquid will not spillout.

   As $l < h, so\ R' > R$.

23. **Apparent angle of contact :** If θ and θ' are the true and apparent angle of contact, then $\cos\theta' = \dfrac{l}{h}\cos\theta$

24. Force required to pull the plates apart having some liquid between them :

$$F = \left(P_0 - P_i\right)A = \frac{2TA}{d}$$

Here d is the separation between the plates and A is the area of each plate.

VISCOSITY

25. **Viscosity** is the resistance force between the adjacent layers of fluid.

26. Viscosity of liquids decreases with increase in temperature and viscosity of gases increases with increase in temperature.

27. **Newton's law of viscosity :** For liquid layer of area A with velocity gradient $\dfrac{dv}{dy}$ with the adjacent layer, the viscous force

$$F_v = \eta A\left(\frac{dv}{dy}\right)$$

SI unit of η is $N - s / m^2$.

28. **Stoke's law (experimental law) :**
   Viscous force on a spherical body moving in an infinite liquid is given by $F_v = 6\pi\eta r v$

29. Viscous force on a spherical body by stoke's is little different from that obtained by Newton's law.

30. **Terminal velocity :** A constant velocity in a viscous fluid is given by

$$v_t = \frac{2}{9}r^2\frac{(\sigma - \rho)g}{\eta}$$

31. **Poisulli's equation :**
   Rate of flow of a viscous liquid in a circular pipe is given by

$$Q = \frac{P_1 - P_2}{R}$$

Here R is the resistance of pipe, which is,

$$R = \frac{8\eta l}{\pi r^4}$$

$$\therefore \quad Q = \frac{\pi\left(P_1 - P_2\right)r^4}{8\eta l}$$

32. **Pipes in series :**

Total resistance $R = R_1 + R_2 = \left(\dfrac{8\eta l_1}{\pi r_1^4} + \dfrac{8\eta l_2}{\pi r_2^4}\right)$

and rate of flow, $Q = \left[\dfrac{P_1 - P_2}{R}\right]$

33. **Pipes in parallel :**

Total resistance. $\dfrac{1}{R} = \dfrac{1}{R_1} + \dfrac{1}{R_2}$

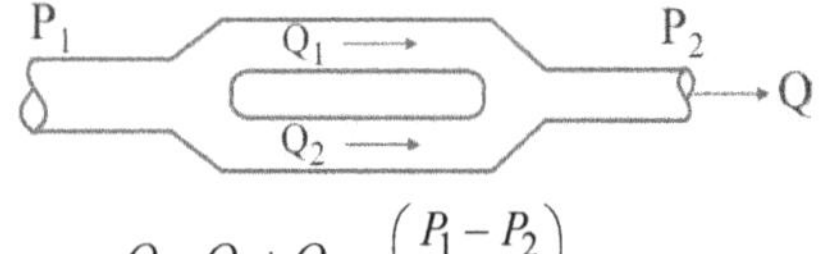

$$Q = Q_1 + Q_2 = \left(\frac{P_1 - P_2}{R}\right)$$

POM MCQ Type 1 *Exercise 2.1*

LEVEL - 1

Only one option correct

1. Two rods of different materials having coefficient of linear expansion α_1, α_2 and Young's modulii Y_1, Y_2 respectively are fixed between two rigid massive walls. The rods are heated such that they undergo the same increase in temperature. There is no bending of the rods. If $\alpha_1 : \alpha_2 = 2 : 3$, the thermal stresses developed in the two rods are equal provided $Y_1 : Y_2$ is equal to :
   (a) $2 : 3$
   (b) $1 : 1$
   (c) $3 : 2$
   (d) $4 : 9$

2. A steel ring of radius r and cross-sectional area A is fitted on to a wooden disc of radius R $(R > r)$. If Young's modulus of steel is Y, then the force with which the steel ring is expanded is :
   (a) $AY\dfrac{R}{r}$
   (b) $AY\dfrac{R-r}{r}$
   (c) $\dfrac{Y}{A}\left(\dfrac{R-r}{r}\right)$
   (d) $\dfrac{Yr}{AR}$

3. Two rods A and B of the same material and length have radii r_1 and r_2 respectively. When they are rigidly fixed at one end and twisted by the same couple supplied at the other end, the ratio
   $$\dfrac{\text{(angle of twist at end of } A)}{\text{(angle of twist at end of } B)}$$
   (a) r_1^2 / r_2^2
   (b) r_2^3 / r_1^3
   (c) r_2^4 / r_1^4
   (d) r_1^4 / r_2^4

4. The ratio (stress/strain) remains constant for a small deformation of a material. When the deformation is made larger, this ratio :
   (a) Increases
   (b) Decreases
   (c) Remains constant
   (d) Becomes zero

5. An elastic string of unstretched length L and force constant k is stretched by a small length x. It is further stretched by another small length y. The work done in the second stretching is :
   (a) $\dfrac{1}{2}ky^2$
   (b) $\dfrac{1}{2}k(x^2 + y^2)$
   (c) $\dfrac{1}{2}k(x+y)^2$
   (d) $\dfrac{1}{2}ky(2x + y)$

6. The end of a uniform wire of length L and of weight W is attached rigidly to a point in the roof and a weight W_1 is suspended from its lower end. If s is the area of cross-section of the wire, the stress in the wire at a height $\dfrac{3L}{4}$ from its lower end is :
   (a) $\dfrac{W_1}{s}$
   (b) $\dfrac{W_1 + \dfrac{W}{4}}{s}$
   (c) $\dfrac{W_1 + \dfrac{3W}{4}}{s}$
   (d) $\dfrac{W_1 + W}{s}$

7. A wire of length L and cross-sectional area 'A' is made of a material of Young's modulus Y. If the wire is stretched by the amount x, the work done is :
   (a) $\dfrac{YAx^2}{2L}$
   (b) $\dfrac{YAx^2}{L}$
   (c) $\dfrac{YAx}{2L}$
   (d) YAx^2L

8. A wire suspended vertically from one of the ends is stretched by attaching a weight of 200 N to the lower end. If the weight stretches the wire by 1 mm, the elastic energy stored in the wire is :
   (a) 20 J
   (b) 10 J
   (c) 0.2 J
   (d) 0.1 J

9. When the pressure on a fluid is changed from 1.01 x 10^5 Pa to 1.165 x 10^5 Pa, the volume changes by 10%, the bulk modulus of fluid is :
   (a) 1.55 x 10^5 Pa
   (b) 0.015 x 10^5 Pa
   (c) 1.015 x 10^5 Pa
   (d) 1.55 x 10^6 Pa

10. If s is stress and Y is Young's modulus of the material of a wire. The energy stored in the wire per unit volume is :
   (a) $\dfrac{s^2}{2Y}$
   (b) $2 s^2 Y$
   (c) $\dfrac{2Y}{s^2}$
   (d) $\dfrac{1}{2}Ys^2$

11. A wire elongates by l mm when a load W is hanged from it. If the wire goes over a pulley and two weights W each are hung at the two ends, the elongation of the wire (in mm) will be :
   (a) l
   (b) $2\,l$
   (c) zero
   (d) $l/2$

Answer Key	1	(c)	3	(c)	5	(d)	7	(a)	9	(a)	11	(a)
Sol. from page 175	2	(b)	4	(b)	6	(c)	8	(d)	10	(a)		

12. The diagram shows a force-extension graph for a rubber band. Consider the following statements
    I. It will be easier to compress this rubber than expand it.
    II. Rubber does not return to its original length after it is stretched.
    III. The rubber band will get heated if it is stretched and released.
    Which of these can be deduced from the graph :

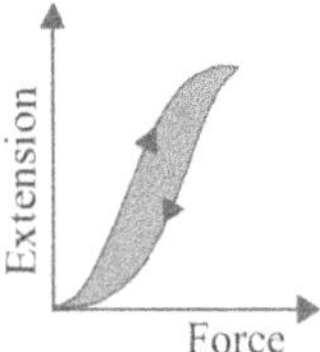

    (a) III only
    (b) II and III
    (c) I and III
    (d) I only

13. The adjacent graph shows the extension (Δl) of a wire of length 1 m suspended from the top of a roof at one end with a load W connected to the other end. If the cross-sectional area of the wire is 10^{-6} m^2, calculate the Young's modulus of the material of the wire :

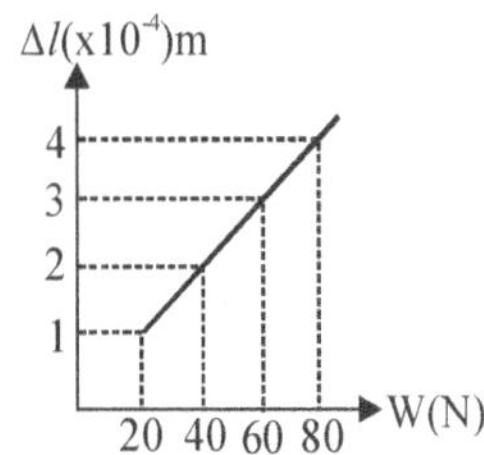

    (a) 2×10^{11} N/m^2
    (b) 2×10^{-11} N/m^2
    (c) 3×10^{-12} N/m^2
    (d) 2×10^{-13} N/m^2

14. The potential energy U between two molecules as a function of the distance x between them has been shown in the figure. The two molecules are :

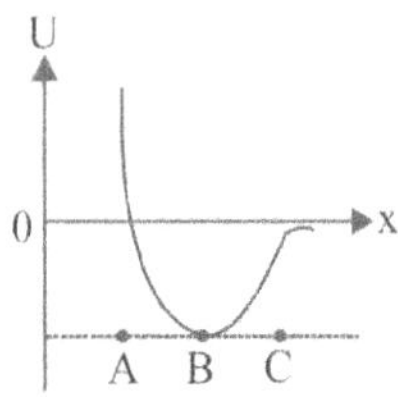

    (a) Attracted when x lies between A and B and are repelled when x lies between B and C
    (b) Attracted when x lies between B and C and are repelled when x lies between A and B
    (c) Attracted when they reach B
    (d) Repelled when they reach B

15. The diagram shows stress v/s strain curve for the materials A and B. From the curves we infer that :

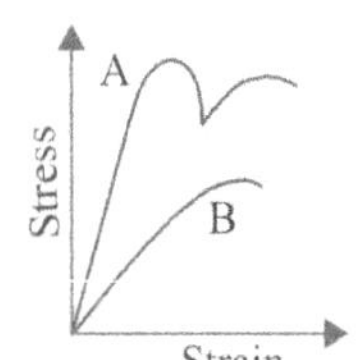

    (a) A is brittle but B is ductile
    (b) A is ductile and B is brittle
    (c) Both A and B are ductile
    (d) Both A and B are brittle

16. An elevator cable is to have a maximum stress of 7×10^7 N/m^2 to allow for appropriate safety factors. Its maximum upward acceleratiom is 1.5 m/s^2. If the cable has to support the total weight of 2000 kg of a loaded elevator, the area of cross–section of the cable should be :
    (a) 3.28 cm^2
    (b) 2.38 cm^2
    (c) 0.328 cm^2
    (d) 8.23 cm^2

17. The temperature of a wire of length l metre and area of cross-section 1 cm^2 is increased from $0°$ C to $100°$ C. If the rod is not allowed to increase in length, the force required will be ($\alpha = 10^{-5}/$ $°$C and $Y = 10^{11}$ N/m^2)
    (a) 10^3 N
    (b) 10^4 N
    (c) 10^5 N
    (d) 10^9 N

18. The breaking stress of a wire depends upon
    (a) Length of the wire
    (b) Radius of the wire
    (c) Material of the wire
    (d) Shape of the cross-section

19. A rod fixed between two points at 20°C. The coefficient of linear expansion of material of rod is $1.1 \times 10^{-5}/°$C and Young's modulus is 1.2×10^{11} N/m^2. Find the stress developed in the rod if temperature of rod becomes 10°C
    (a) 1.32×10^7 N/m^2
    (b) 1.10×10^{15} N/m^2
    (c) 1.32×10^8 N/m^2
    (d) 1.10×10^6 N/m^2

20. When a force is applied on a wire of uniform cross-section area 3×10^{-6} m^2 and length 4m, the increase in length is 1 mm. Energy stored in it will be ($Y = 2 \times 10^{11}$ N/m^2)
    (a) 6250 J
    (b) 0.177 J
    (c) 0.075 J
    (d) 0.150 J

21. The isothermal bulk modulus of a gas at atmosphere pressure is
    (a) 1 mm of Hg
    (b) 13.6 mm of Hg
    (c) 1.013×10^5 N/m^2
    (d) 2.026×10^5 N/m^2

22. The value of Poisson's ratio lies between
    (a) -1 to $\dfrac{1}{2}$
    (b) $-\dfrac{3}{4}$ to $-\dfrac{1}{2}$
    (c) $-\dfrac{1}{2}$ to 1
    (d) 1 to 2

23. To break of wire, a force of 10^6 N/m^2 is required. If the density of the material is 3×10^3 kg/m^3, then the length of the wire which will break by its own weight will be
    (a) 34 m
    (b) 30 m
    (c) 300 m
    (d) 3 m

24. The stress versus strain graphs for wires of two materials A and B are as shown in the figure. If Y_A and Y_B are the Young's moduli of the materials, then
    (a) $Y_B = 2 Y_A$
    (b) $Y_A = Y_B$
    (c) $Y_B = 3 Y_A$
    (d) $Y_A = 3 Y_B$

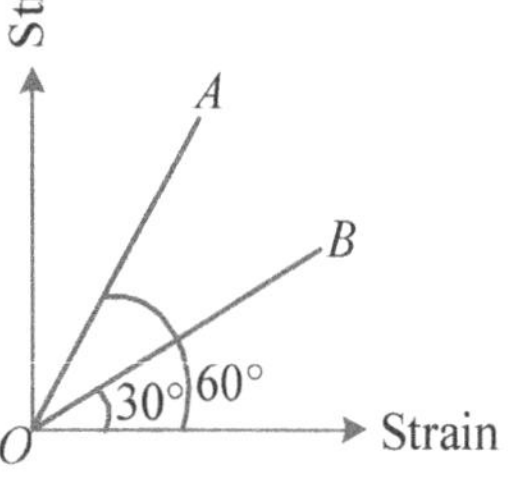

Answer Key	12	(a)	14	(b)	16	(a)	18	(c)	20	(c)	22	(a)	24	(d)
Sol. from page 175	13	(a)	15	(b)	17	(b)	19	(a)	21	(c)	23	(a)		

25. A square frame of side L is dipped in a liquid. On taking out, a membrane is formed. If he surface tension of liquid is T, the force acting on the frame will be

  (a) $2\,T\,L$ (b) $4\,TL$
  (c) $8\,TL$ (d) $10\,TL$

26. Two droplets merge with each other and forms a large droplet. In this process.

  (a) Energy is liberated

  (b) Energy is absorbed

  (c) Neither liberated nor a absorbed

  (d) Some mass is converted into energy.

27. A liquid does not wet the sides of a solid, if the angle of contact is

  (a) Zero   (b) Obtuse (More than 90°)

  (c) Acute (Less than 90°)   (d) 90°

28. The liquid meniscus in capillary tube will be convex, if the angle of contact is

  (a) Greater than 90°   (b) Less than 90°

  (c) Equal to 90°   (d) Equal to 0°

29. Water rises in a vertical capillary tube upto a height of 2.0 cm. If he tube is inclined at an angle of 60° with the vertical, then upto what length the water will rise in the tube

  (a) 2.0 cm   (b) 4.0 cm

  (c) $\dfrac{4}{\sqrt{3}}$ cm   (d) $2\sqrt{2}$ cm

30. In a capillary tube experiment, a vertical 30 cm long capillary tube is dipped in water. The water rises upto a height of 10 cm due to capillary action. If this experiment is conducted in a freely falling elevator. The length of the water column becomes

  (a) 10 cm   (b) 20 cm

  (c) 30 cm   (d) zero

31. Radius of a capillary is 2×10^{-3} m. A liquid of weight 6.28×10^{-4} N may remain in the capillary then the surface tension of liquid will be

  (a) 5×10^{-3} N/ m   (b) 5×10^{-2} N/m

  (c) 5 N/m   (d) 50 N/m

32. A cubical block of side 'a' and density 'ρ' slides over a fixed inclined plane with constant velocity v.

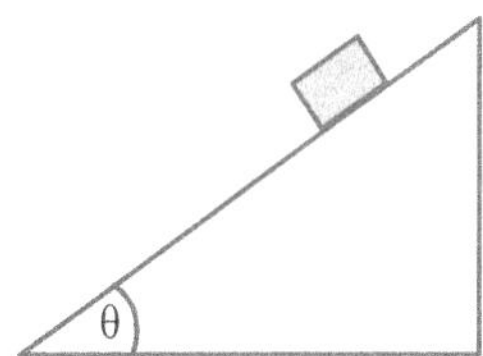

There is a thin film of viscous fluid of thickness 't' between the plane and the block. Then the coefficient of viscosity of the thin film will be

  (a) $\eta = \dfrac{\rho a g t \sin\theta}{v}$ (b) $\dfrac{\rho g t \sin\theta}{a v}$

  (c) $\dfrac{v}{\rho a g t \sin\theta}$ (d) None of these

33. An isolated and charged spherical soap bubble has a radius r and the pressure inside is atmospheric. If T is the surface tension of soap solution, then charge on drop is

  (a) $2\sqrt{\dfrac{2rT}{\varepsilon_0}}$ (b) $8\pi r \sqrt{2rT\varepsilon_0}$

  (c) $8\pi r \sqrt{rT\varepsilon_0}$ (d) $8\pi r \sqrt{\dfrac{2rT}{\varepsilon_0}}$

34. Spherical balls of radius R are falling in a viscous fluid of viscosity η with a velocity v. The retarding viscous force acting on the spherical ball is :

  (a) directly proportional to radius R but inversely proportional to velocity v

  (b) directly proportional to both radius R and velocity v

  (c) inversely proportional to both radius R and velocity v

  (d) inversely proportional to radius R but inversely proportional to velocity v

35. Water flows in a stream line manner through a capillary tube of radius 'a'. The pressure difference is p and rate of flow is Q. If the radius is reduced to 'a'/2 and the pressure is increased to $2p$, then the rate of flow becomes :

  (a) $4\,Q$ (b) Q

  (c) $\dfrac{Q}{2}$ (d) $\dfrac{Q}{8}$

36. The terminal speed of a sphere of gold (density = 19.5 kg/m³) is 0.2 m/s in a viscous liquid (density = 1.5 kg/m³), find the terminal speed of sphere of a silver (density 10.5 kg/m³) of the same size in the same liquid :

  (a) 0.4 m/s   (b) 0.133 m/s

  (c) 0.1 m/s   (d) 0.2 m/s

37. A thin metal disc of radius r floats on water surface and bends the surface downwards along the perimeter making an angle θ with vertical edge of the disc. If the disc displaces a weight of water W and surface tension of water is T, then the weight of metal disc is:

  (a) $2\,\pi rT + W$ (b) $2\,\pi rT \cos\theta - W$

  (c) $2\,\pi rT \cos\theta + W$ (d) $W - 2\,\pi rT \cos\theta$

38. A thread is tied slightly loose to a wire frame as in figure and the frame is dipped into a soap solution and taken out. The frame is completely covered with the film. When the portion A punctured with a pin, the thread :

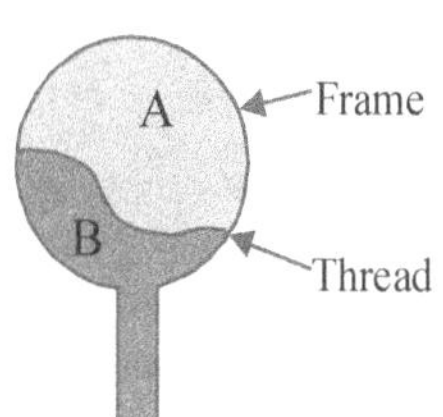

  (a) Becomes concave towards A

  (b) Becomes convex towards A

  (c) Remains in the initial position

  (d) Either (a) or (b) depending on the size of A w.r.t. B

Answer Key	**25**	(c)	**27**	(b)	**29**	(b)	**31**	(b)	**33**	(b)	**35**	(d)	**37**	(c)
Sol. from page 175	**26**	(a)	**28**	(a)	**30**	(c)	**32**	(a)	**34**	(b)	**36**	(c)	**38**	(a)

39. The work done in increasing the size of a soap film from 10 cm × 6 cm to 10 cm × 11 cm is 3×10^{-4} joule. The surface tension of the film is :

(a) 1.5×10^{-2} N/m   (b) 3.0×10^{-2} N/m

(c) 6.0×10^{-2} N/m   (d) 11.0×10^{-2} N/m

40. In a surface tension experiment with a capillary tube water rises upto 0.1 m. If the same experiment is repeated on an artificial satellite, which is revolving around the earth, water will rise in the capillary tube upto a height of :

(a) 1.0 m   (b) 0.2 m

(c) 0.98 m   (d) Full length of capillary tube

41. What will be the height of liquid column in the capillary on the surface of moon if it is h on surface of earth :

(a) h (b) $h/6$

(c) $6h$ (d) information is insufficient

42. A soap bubble is very slowly blown on the end of a glass tube by a mechanical pump which supplies a fixed volume per minute whatever the internal pressure may be. Which graph represents the variation of excess pressure p inside the bubble with time :

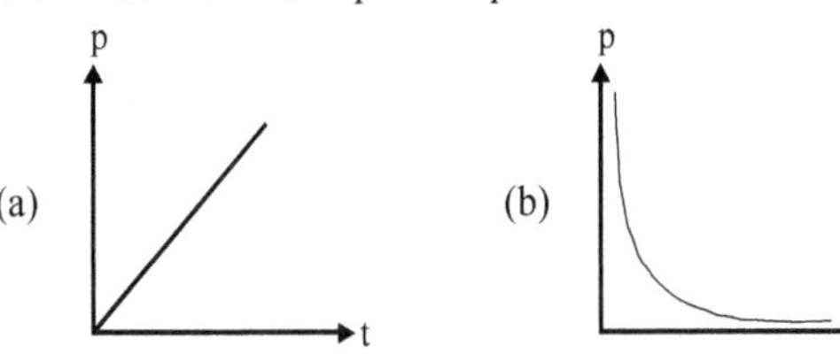

(a)   (b)

(c)   (d)

43. A soap film is slowly blown under isothermal conditions in air at NTP to a radius R. How much work is done? Surface tension of film is T :

(a) $4 \pi R^2 T$ (b) $8 \pi R^2 T$

(c) $18 \pi R^2 T$ (d) Zero

44. The correct curve between the height or depression h of liquid in a capillary tube and its radius is :

(a)   (b)

(c)   (d)

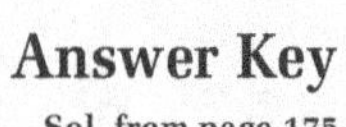

Answer Key
Sol. from page 175

39	(b)	40	(d)	41	(c)	42	(b)	43	(b)	44	(b)

LEVEL - 2

Only one option correct

1. A uniform cylindrical wire (Young's modulus 2×10^{11} N/m²) is subjected to a longitudinal tensile stress of 5×10^7 N-m². If the overall volume change in the wire is 0.02%, the fractional decrease in the radius of the wire, is :

(a) 1.5×10^{-4} (b) 1.0×10^{-4}

(c) 0.5×10^{-4} (d) 0.25×10^{-4}

2. A solid sphere of radius R made of material of bulk modulus K is surrounded by a liquid in a cylindrical container. A massless piston of area A floats on the surface of the liquid when a mass m is placed on the piston to compress the liquid, the fractional change in the radius of the sphere $\delta R / R$ is :

(a) $\dfrac{mg}{AK}$ (b) $\dfrac{mg}{3AK}$

(c) $\dfrac{mg}{A}$ (d) $\dfrac{3mg}{AK}$

3. The table gives the areas of the four surfaces and the magnitude of a force that is applied perpendicular to the surface and uniformly across it. Which surface(s) has greatest stress :

Surface	Area	Force
A	0.25 A	F
B	0.50 A	2F
C	2 A	4F
D	3 A	5F

(a) A (b) A, B

(c) B, C (d) D

4. Four cylindrical rods are stretched by applying forces at their ends. The force magnitudes, the areas of end faces, the changes in length, and the initial lengths are given in the table. The rod which is of greatest Young's modulus is :

Rod	Force	Area	Length change	Initial length
1	F	A	ΔL	L
2	2F	2 A	2 ΔL	L
3	F	2 A	2 ΔL	2L
4	3F	1.5 A	ΔL	2L

(a) 1   (b) 2

(c) 3   (d) 4

5. The velocity of small ball of mass M and density d_1 when dropped in a container filled with glycerine becomes constant after sometime. If the density of glycerine is d_2, the viscous force acting on the ball will be :

(a) $\dfrac{Md_1 g}{d_2}$ (b) $Mg\left(1 - \dfrac{d_2}{d_1}\right)$

(c) $\dfrac{M(d_1 + d_2)}{g}$ (d) $md_1 d_2$

Answer Key
Sol. from page 177

1	(d)	2	(b)	3	(b)	4	(d)	5	(b)		

6. A glass capillary tube of inner diameter 0.28 mm is lowered vertically into water in a vessel. The pressure to be applied on the water in the tube so that water level in the tube is same as that in the vessel in N/m² is (surface tension of water = 0.07 N/m, atmospheric pressure = 10^5 N/m²) :
   (a) 10^3
   (b) 99×10^3
   (c) 100×10^3
   (d) 101×10^3

7. A capillary tube of radius R is immersed in water and water rises in it to a height H. Mass of water in the capillary tube is M. If the radius of the tube is doubled, mass of water that will rise in the capillary tube will now be :
   (a) M
   (b) $2M$
   (c) $M/2$
   (d) $4M$

8. A wire of length L and radius r is rigidly fixed at one end. On stretching the other end of the wire with a force F. the increase in its length is l. If another wire of same material but of length $2L$ and radius $2r$ is stretched with a force of $2F$, the increase in its length will be.
   (a) l
   (b) $2l$
   (c) $\dfrac{l}{2}$
   (d) $\dfrac{1}{4}$

9. The length of an elastic string is a metre when the longitudinal tension is 4 N and b metre when the longitudinal tension is 5 N. The length of the string in metre when the longitudinal tension is 9 N is
   (a) $a - b$
   (b) $5b - 4a$
   (c) $2b - \dfrac{1}{4}a$
   (d) $4a - 3b$

10. A rod of length l and radius r is joined to a rod of length $l/2$ and radius $r/2$ of same material. The free end of small rod is fixed to a rigid base and the free end of larger rod is given a twist of $\theta°$, the twist angle at the joint will be
   (a) $\theta / 4$
   (b) $\theta / 2$
   (c) $5\theta / 6$
   (d) $8\theta / 9$

11. A light rod of length $2m$ suspended from the ceiling horizontally by means of two vertical wires of equal length. A weight W is hung from a light rod as shown in figure. The rod hung by means of a steel wire of cross-sectional area $A_1 = 0.1$ cm² and brass wire of cross-sectional area $A_2 = 0.2$ cm². To have equal stress in both wires, $T_1/T_2 = $

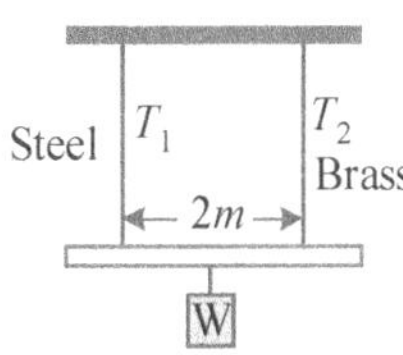

   (a) 1/3
   (b) 1/4
   (c) 4/3
   (d) 1/2

12. A student performs an experiment to determine the Young's modulus of a wire, exactly 2 m long, by Searle's method increase in the length of the wire to be 0.8 mm with an uncertainly of ± 0.05 mm at a load of exactly 1.0 kg. The student also measures of diameter of the wire to be 0.4 mm with an uncertainty of ± 0.01 mm. Take $g = 9.8$ m/s² (exact). The Young's modulus obtained from the reading is
   (a) $(2.0 \pm 0.3) \times 10^{11}$ N/m²
   (b) $(2.0 \pm 0.2) \times 10^{11}$ N/m²
   (c) $(2.0 \pm 0.1) \times 10^{11}$ N/m²
   (d) $(2.0 \pm 0.05) \times 10^{11}$ N/m²

13. If the ratio of lengths, radii and Young's modulus of steel and brass wires shown in the figure are a, b, and c, respectively. The ratio between the increase in length of steel and brass wires would be

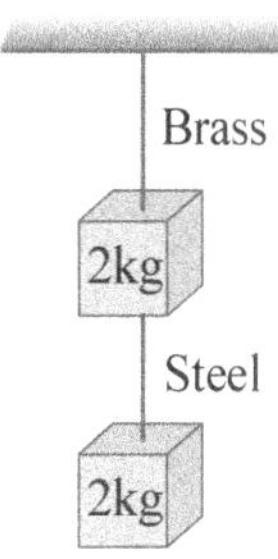

   (a) $\dfrac{b^2 a}{2c}$
   (b) $\dfrac{bc}{2a^2}$
   (c) $\dfrac{ba^2}{2c}$
   (d) $\dfrac{a}{2b^2 c}$

14. A capillary tube (A) is dipped in water. Another identical tube (B) is dipped in a soap-water solution. Which of the following shows the relative nature of the liquid columns in the two tubes.

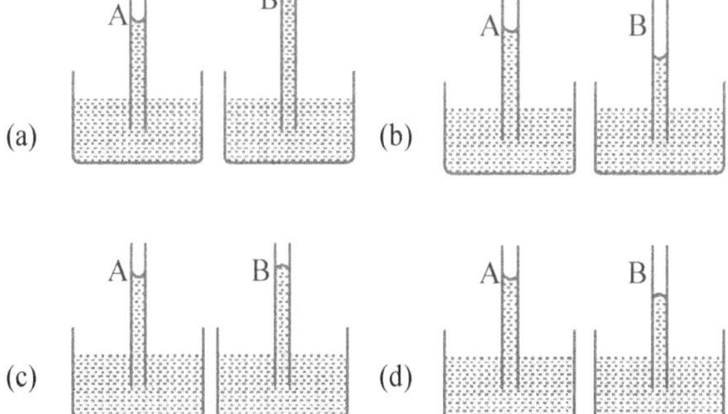

15. By inserting a long capillary tube upto a depth l in water, the water rises to a height h. If the lower end of the capillary is closed inside water and the capillary is taken out and closed end opened, to what height the water will remain in the tube
   (a) Zero
   (b) $l + h$
   (c) $2h$
   (d) h

16. Two soap bubbles A and B are kept in a closed chamber where the air is maintained at pressure 8 N/m^2. The radii of bubbles A and B are 2 cm ad 4 cm, respectively. Surface tension of the soap-water used to make bubbles is 0.04 N/m. Find the ratio n_B / n_A where n_A and n_B are the number of moles of air in bubbles A and B, respectively. [Neglect the effect of gravity].

  (a) 2   (b) 9

  (c) 8   (d) 6

17. A glass tube of uniform internal radius (r) has a valve separating the two identical ends. Initially, the valve is in a tightly closed position End 1 has a hemispherical soap bubble of radius r. End 2 has sub-hemispherical soap bubble as shown in figure. Just after opening the valve.

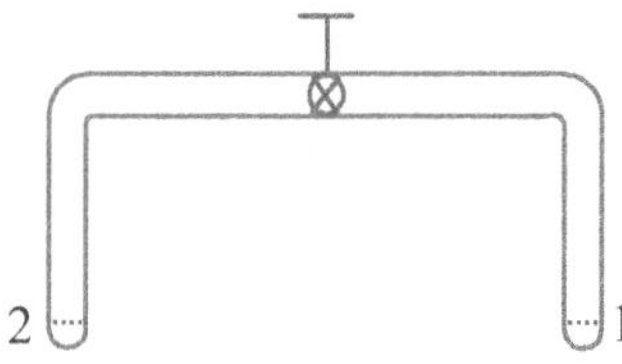

  (a) Air from end 1 flows towards end 2. No change in the volume of the soap bubbles

  (b) Air from end 1 flows towards end 2 . Volume of the soap bubble at end 1 decreases

  (c) No change occurs

  (d) Air from end 2 flows towards end 1. Volume of the soap bubble at end 1 increases.

18. Drops of liquid of density ρ are floating half immersed in a liquid of density σ. If the surface tension of liquid is T, the radius of the drop will be

  (a) $\sqrt{\dfrac{3T}{g(3\rho-\sigma)}}$ (b) $\sqrt{\dfrac{6T}{g(2\rho-\sigma)}}$

  (c) $\sqrt{\dfrac{3T}{g(2\rho-\sigma)}}$ (d) $\sqrt{\dfrac{3T}{g(4\rho-3\sigma)}}$

19. In the figure shown, radius of the limbs of the manometer are r_1 and r_2 ($< r_1$). The surface tension of the liquid is T. The difference of the heights of the liquid column h is equal to (Assume that the angle of contact is zero).

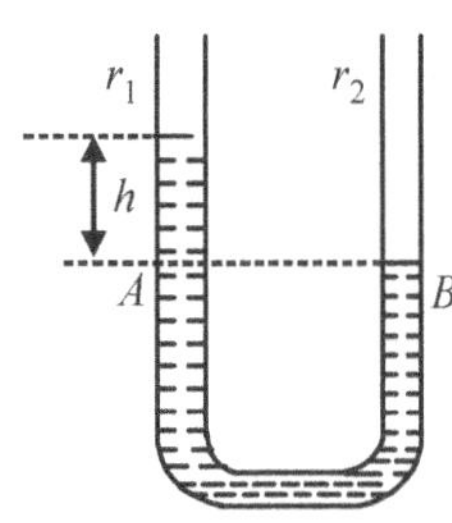

20. A large number of droplets, each of radius a, coalesce to form bigger drop of radius b. Assume that the energy released in process is converted into the kinetic energy of the drop. velocity of the drop is (S = surface tension and ρ = density drop)

  (a) $\left[\dfrac{3S}{\rho}\left(\dfrac{1}{a}-\dfrac{1}{b}\right)\right]^{1/2}$ (b) $\left[\dfrac{6S}{\rho}\left(\dfrac{1}{a}-\dfrac{1}{b}\right)\right]^{1/2}$

  (c) $\left[\dfrac{2S}{\rho}\left(\dfrac{1}{a}-\dfrac{1}{b}\right)\right]^{1/2}$ (d) $\left[\dfrac{S}{\rho}\left(\dfrac{1}{a}-\dfrac{1}{b}\right)\right]^{1/2}$

21. A thin movable plate is separated from two fixed plates P_1 an by two highly viscous liquids of coefficients of viscosity n_1 n_2 as shown, where $n_2 = 9n_1$. Area of contact of movable with each fluid is same. If the distance between two fixed plat h, then the distance h_1 of movable plate form upper plate that movable plate can be moved with a finite velocity by app the minimum possible force on movable plate is (assume linear velocity distribution in each liquid)

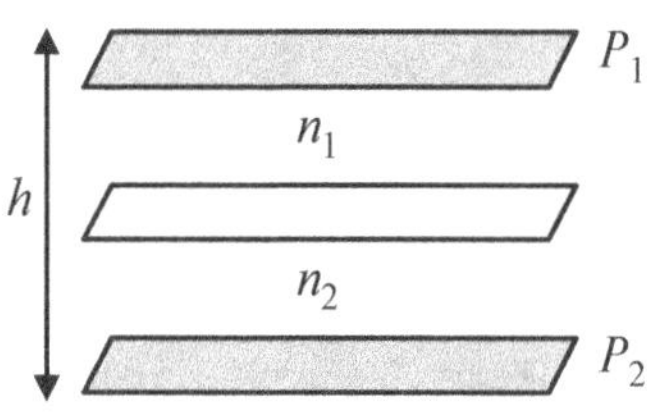

  (a) $\dfrac{h}{4}$ (b) $\dfrac{h}{2}$

  (c) $\dfrac{h}{6}$ (d) $\dfrac{h}{3}$

22. A cylinder with movable piston contains air under pressur and a soap bubble of radius r. The surface tension of soap sol is T and the temperature of the system is kept constant. pressure to which the air should be compressed by slowly pus the pistion into the cylinder for the soap bubble to reduce its by half is

  (a) $8\left[P_0+\dfrac{3T}{r}\right]$ (b) $\left[P_0+\dfrac{T}{r}\right]$

  (c) $8\left[P_0+\dfrac{T}{r}\right]$ (d) $8\left[P_0+\dfrac{7T}{r}\right]$

Answer Key	16	(d)	18	(c)	20	(b)	22	(a)
Sol. from page 177	17	(b)	19	(a)	21	(a)		

POM   MCQ Type 2   *Exercise 2.2*

Multiple correct options

1. Two identical rods each of cross-sectional area A are placed on smooth horizontal surface. These are acted by forces as shown in figure. The breaking strength of material of each rod is F/A, then :

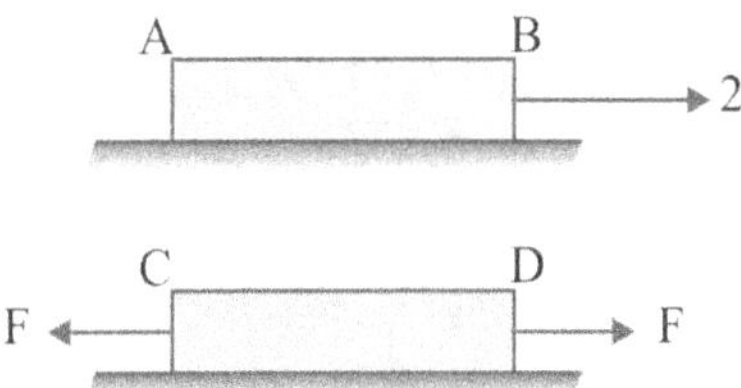

   (a) rod AB will break left of the centre
   (b) rod AB will break right of the centre
   (c) rod CD will break left of the centre
   (d) rod CD will break right of the centre

2. Two wires A and B have equal lengths and are made of the same material, but the diameter of A is twice that of wire B. Then, for a given load
   (a) the extension of B will be four times that of A
   (b) the extensions of A and B will be equal
   (c) the strain in B is four times that in A
   (d) the strains in A and B will be equal

3. Four rods, A, B, C and D of the same length and material but of different radii $r, r\sqrt{2}, r\sqrt{3}$ and $2r$ respectively are held between two rigid walls. The temperature of all rods is increased through the same range. If the rods do not bend, then
   (a) the stress in the rods A, B, C and D are in the ratio $1:2:3:4$
   (b) the forces on them exerted by the wall are in the ratio $1:2:3:4$
   (c) the energy stored in the rods due to elasticity are in the ratio $1:2:3:4$
   (d) the strains produced in the rods are in the ratio $1:2:3:4$

4. A vertical bar of uniform section is fixed at both of its ends and a load $W = 5000$ N is applied axially at an intermediate section as shown in figure. Choose the correct options.

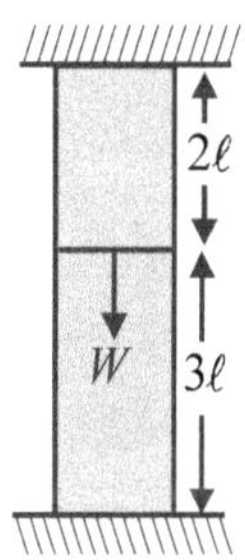

   (a) Reaction at the top support is 3000 N
   (b) Reaction at the bottom support is 2000 N
   (c) Reaction at the top support is 1000 N
   (d) Reaction at the bottom support is 3000 N

5. The wires A and B shown in the Fig., are made of the same material and have radii r_A and r_B respectively. A block of mass m is connected between them. When a force F is mg/3, one of the wires breaks.

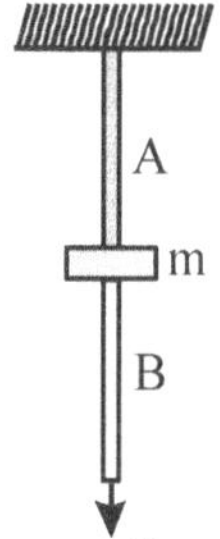

   (a) A will break before B if $r_A < 2\,r_B$
   (b) A will break before B if $r_A = r_B$
   (c) Either A or B will break if $r_A = 2r_B$
   (d) The lengths of A and B must be known to decide which wire will break

6. A metal wire of length L is suspended vertically from a rigid support. When a body of mass M is attached to the lower end of wire, the elongation of the wire is ℓ.
   (a) The loss in gravitational potential energy of mass M is $Mg\ell$
   (b) The elastic potential energy stored in the wire is $Mg\ell$
   (c) The elastic potential energy stored in the wire is $\dfrac{1}{2}Mg\ell$
   (d) Heat produced is $\dfrac{1}{2}Mg\ell$

7. When a wire is stretched to double its length
   (a) strain is unity
   (b) stress is equal to Young's modulus of elasticity
   (c) its radius is halved
   (d) Young's modulus is equal to twice the elastic potential energy per unit volume.

8. A metal wire of length L, area of cross-section A and Young's modulus Y is stretched by a variable force F such that F is always slightly greater than the elastic forces of resistance in the wire. When the elongation of the wire is ℓ
   (a) the work done by F is $\dfrac{YA\ell^2}{L}$
   (b) the work done by F is $\dfrac{YA\ell^2}{2L}$
   (c) the eleastic potential energy stored in the wire is $\dfrac{YA\ell^2}{2L}$
   (d) heat is produced during the elongation.

Answer Key	1	(b, c, d)	3	(b, c)	5	(a, b, c)	7	(a, b, d)
Sol. from page 178	2	(a, c)	4	(a, b)	6	(a, c, d)	8	(b, c)

9. An air bubble in a water tank rises from the bottom to the top. Which of the following statements are true :

    (a) Bubble rises upwards because pressure at the bottom is less than that at the top.

    (b) Bubble rises upwards because pressure at the bottom is greater than that at the top.

    (c) As the bubble rises, its size increases.

    (d) As the bubble rises, its size decreases.

10. The capillary rise of water in a tube depends on

    (a) the outer radius of the tube

    (b) the inner radius of the tube

    (c) the material of the tube

    (d) the length of the tube

11. The contact angle between a solid and a liquid is a property of

    (a) the material of the solid

    (b) the material of the liquid

    (c) the shape of the solid

    (d) the mass of the solid

12. When a capillary tube is dipped into a liquid, the liquid neither rises nor falls in the capillary.

    (a) the surface tension may be zero.

    (b) the surface tension of the liquid must be zero

    (c) the contact angle may be 90°

    (d) none of these

13. A solid sphere moves at a terminal velocity of 10 m/s in air at a place where $g = 10$ m/s². The sphere is taken in a gravity free hall having air at the same pressure and pushed down at a speed of 10 m/s.

    (a) Its initial acceleration will be 10 m/s² downward.

    (b) Its initial acceleration will be 10 m/s² upward

    (c) The magnitude of acceleration will decrease as time passes

    (d) It will eventually stop.

14. The rise of liquid in a capillary tube depends on

    (a) the material of tube and nature of liquid

    (b) the length of tube

    (c) the outer radius

    (d) the inner radius of the tube

15. When a drop splits up into a number of drops

    (a) area increases   (b) volume increases

    (c) energy is absorbed   (d) energy is liberated

16. When a capillary tube is dipped in a liquid, the liquid rises up to a height h in the tube. The free liquid surface inside the tube is hemispherical in shape. The tube is now pushed down so that the height of the tube outside the liquid is less than h.

    (a) The liquid will ooze out of the tube slowly

    (b) The liquid will come out of the tube like in a small fountain

    (c) The free liquid surface inside the tube will not be hemispherical

    (d) The liquid will fill the tube but not come out of its upper end.

17. Choose the correct option (s)

    (a) with the rise in temperature viscosity decreases.

    (b) viscosity of liquid increases with increase in pressure but in case of water, viscosity decreases with rise in pressure

    (c) viscosity of liquid is about 100 times greater than that of gases

    (d) viscosity of gases is independent of pressure

18. The viscous force acting on a solid ball of surface area A moving with terminal velocity v is proportional to

    (a) A (b) $A^{\frac{1}{2}}$

    (c) v (d) $v^{1/2}$

19. An oil drop falls through air with a terminal velocity of 5×10^{-4} m/s. Viscosity of oil is 1.8×10^{-5} N–s/m² and density of oil is 900 kg/m³. Neglecting density of air as compared to that of the oil

    (a) radius of the drop is 6.20×10^{-2} m

    (b) radius of the drop is 2.14×10^{-6} m

    (c) terminal velocity of the drop at half of this radius is 1.25×10^{-4} m/s

    (d) terminal velocity of the drop at half of this radius is 2.5×10^{-4} m/s

Answer Key	**9**	(b, c)	**11**	(a, b)	**13**	(b, c, d)	**15**	(a, c)	**17**	(a, b, c, d)	**19**	(b, c)
Sol. from page 178	**10**	(b, d)	**12**	(a, c)	**14**	(a, b, d)	**16**	(c, d)	**18**	(b, c)		

POM — Statement Questions — *Exercise 2.3*

Read the two statements carefully to mark the correct option out of the options given below:
(a) If both the statements are true and the *statement - 2* is the correct explanation of *statement - 1*.
(b) If both the statements are true but *statement - 2* is not the correct explanation of the *statement - 1*.
(c) If *statement - 1* true but *statement - 2* is false.
(d) If *statement - 1* is false but *statement - 2* is true.

1. **Statement - 1**

   It is better to wash the clothes in hot soap solution.

   Statement - 2

   The surface tension of hot solution is less than the surface tension of cold solution.

2. **Statement - 1**

   When height of a tube is less than liquid rise in the capillary tube, the liquid does not overflow.

   Statement - 2

   Product of radius of meniscus and height of liquid in capillary tube always remains constant.

3. **Statement - 1**

   The impurities always decrease the surface tension of the liquid.

   Statement - 2

   The change in surface tension of the liquid depends upon the degree of contamination of the impurity.

4. **Statement - 1**

   At critical temperature, surface tension of a liquid becomes zero.

   Statement - 2

   At this temperature, intermolecular forces for liquids and gases become equal.

5. **Statement - 1**

   Small drops of liquid resist deforming forces better than bigger drops.

   Statement - 2

   Excess pressure inside a drop is directly proportional to surface tension.

6. **Statement - 1**

   Steel is more elastic than rubber.

   Statement - 2

   Under given deforming force, steel is deformed less than rubber.

7. **Statement - 1**

   A hollow shaft is found to be stronger than a solid shaft made of same amount of material.

   Statement - 2

   The torque required to produce a given twist in hollow shaft is greater than that required to twist a solid shaft made of the same amount of material.

8. **Statement - 1**

   The bridges declared unsafe after a long use.

   Statement - 2

   Elastic strength of bridges decreases with time.

9. **Statement - 1**

   Wet clay does not regain its shape.

   Statement - 2

   Young's modulus for a perfectly plastic body is zero.

10. **Statement - 1**

    Viscosity of gas increases with increase in temperature.

    Statement - 2

    With increase in temperature collisions between the molecules of gas increases.

11. **Statement - 1**

    A bigger rain drop falls faster than a smaller one.

    Statement - 2

    Terminal velocity of the drop is proportional to square of the radius of the drop.

12.. **Statement - 1**

    When two boats sail parallel in the same direction and close to each other, they are pulled towards each other.

    Statement - 2

    The viscous drag on a spherical body is proportional to its speed.

13. **Statement - 1**

    Water flows faster than honey.

    Statement - 2

    The cofficient of viscosity of water is less than honey.

14. **Statement - 1**

    A steel blade placed gently on the surface of water floats on it.

    Statement - 2

    Buoyant force of water is equal to the weight of the blade.

15. **Statement - 1**

    Water in one flask and castor oil in other are violently shaken, castor oil comes to rest earlier.

    Statement - 2

    Surface tension of castor oil is greater than that of water.

Answer Key

Sol. from page 179

1	(a)	3	(d)	5	(a)	7	(a)	9	(a)	11	(a)	13	(a)	15	(b)
2	(a)	4	(a)	6	(b)	8	(a)	10	(a)	12	(b)	14	(c)		

POM   Passage & Matrix   *Exercise 2.4*

PASSAGES

Passage for (Q. 1 - 3) :
The axle of a pulley of mass 1 kg is attached to the end of an elastic string of length 1 m, cross-sectional area $10^{-3}\,m^2$ and Young's modulus $2 \times 10^5\,N/m^2$ whose other end is fixed to the ceiling. A rope of negligible mass is placed on the pulley such that its left end is fixed to the ground and its right end is hanging freely from the pulley which is at rest in equilibrium. The free end of the rope A start pulling with constant force $F = 10$ N. Friction can be neglected between the rope and the pulley.

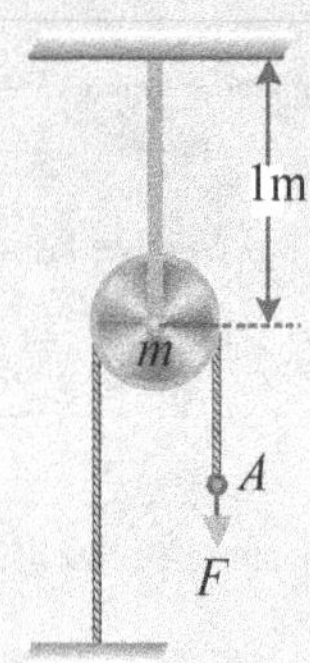

1.   The elongation of the string before applying force is
      (a)   0.05 cm   (b)   0.5 cm
      (c)   5 cm   (d)   50 cm
2.   The greatest elongation of the string is
      (a)   20 cm   (b)   25 cm
      (c)   30 cm   (d)   35 cm
3.   The maximum displacement of point A after applying F
      (a)   30 cm   (b)   40 cm
      (c)   60 cm   (d)   70 cm

Passage for (Q. 4 - 6) :
When viscous liquid flows, adjacent layers oppose their relative motion by applying a viscous force given by

$$F = -\eta A \frac{dv}{dy}$$

When η = coefficient of viscosity, A = surface area of adjacent layers in contact.

$$\frac{dv}{dy} = \text{velocity gradient}$$

Now, a viscous liquid having coefficient of viscosity η is flowing through a fixed tube of length ℓ and radius R under a pressure difference P between the two ends of the tube.
Consider a cylindrical volume of liquid of radius r. Due to steady flow, net force on the liquid in cylindrical volume should be zero.

$$-\eta 2\pi r \ell \frac{dv}{dr} = P\pi r^2$$

$$-\int_v^0 dv = \frac{P}{2\eta\ell}\int_r^R r\,dr$$

(layer in contact with the tube is stationary)

$$v = v_0\left(1 - \frac{r^2}{R^2}\right), \text{ where } v_0 = \frac{PR^2}{4\eta\ell}$$

The volume of the liquid per second through the tube,

$$Q = \int_0^R v.2\pi r\,dr = \int_0^R v_0\left(1 - \frac{r^2}{R^2}\right)2\pi r\,dr$$

$$= v_0 2\pi \left[\frac{r^2}{2} - \frac{r^4}{4R^2}\right]_0^R$$

$$= v_0 2\pi \left[\frac{R^2}{2} - \frac{R^2}{4}\right] = \frac{v_0 \pi R^2}{2} = \frac{\pi PR^4}{8\eta\ell}$$

This is called Poiseuille's equation

4.   Force acting on the tube due to the liquid is .
      (a) $\pi\,\eta\,\ell\,v_0$ (b) $2\pi\,\eta\,\ell\,v_0$
      (c) $4\pi\,\eta\,\ell\,v_0$ (d) $6\pi\,\eta\,\ell\,v_0$
5.   The viscous force on the cylindrical volume of the liquid varies as
      (a) $F \propto r^2$ (b) $F \propto r$
      (c) $F \propto 1/r$ (d) $F \propto 1/r^2$
6.   The momentum of the liquid confined in the tube is
      (a) $\rho\pi R^2\ell v_0$ (b) $\rho\pi R^2\ell v_0/2$
      (c) $2\rho\pi R^2\ell v_0$ (d) $\rho\pi R^2\ell v_0/4$

Passage for (Q. 7 - 9) :
A steel wire has the following properties :
Length = 5 cm
Cross section = $0.5\,cm^2$
Young's modulus = $1.8 \times 10^{11}\,N/m^2$
Shear modulus = $0.6 \times 10^{11}\,N/m^2$
Proportional limit = $3.6 \times 10^8\,N/m^2$
Breaking stress = $7.2 \times 10^8\,N/m^2$
The wire is fastened at its upper end and hangs vertically.

Answer Key	1	(c)	3	(c)	5	(a)
Sol. from page 180	2	(c)	4	(c)	6	(b)

7. The maximum load W that can be supported without exceeding the proportional limit is :
   (a) 600 N   (b) 1200 N
   (c) 1800 N   (d) 2100 N
8. The extension of the wire under this load W is :
   (a) 0.01 m   (b) 0.02 m
   (c) 0.04 m   (d) 0.05 m
9. The maximum load the wire can carry without breaking is :
   (a) 1800 N   (b) 2400 N
   (c) 3000 N   (d) 3600 N

Passage for (Q. 10 - 12) :

A copper rod of length 2 m and cross-sectional area 2.0 cm^2 is fastened end to end to a steel rod of length L and cross-sectional area 1.0 cm^2. The compound rod is subjected to equal and opposite pulls ot magnitude 3×10^4 N at its ends.

$$Y_{steel} = 2.0 \times 10^{11} \text{ N/m}^2$$
$$Y_{copper} = 1.1 \times 10^{11} \text{ N/m}^2$$

10. The length L of the steel rod if the clongation of the two rods are equal is
    (a) 1.82 m   (b) 2.20 m
    (c) 3.04 m   (d) 3.84 m
11. The stress in copper rod is
    (a) 1.20×10^8 N/m^2 (b) 1.50×10^8 N/m^2
    (c) 2.00×10^8 N/m^2 (d) 3.20×10^8 N/m^2
12. The strain in steel rod is
    (a) 1.5×10^{-3} (b) 2.25×10^{-3}
    (c) 3.0×10^{-3} N/m^2 (d) 4.5×10^{-3}

Passage for (Q. 13 - 14) :

The two wires shown in figure are made of the same material which has a breaking stress of 8×10^8 N/m^2. The area of the cross–section of the upper wire is 0.006 cm^2 and that of the lower wire is 0.003 cm^2. The mass m_1= 10 kg, m_2 = 20 kg and the hanger is light.

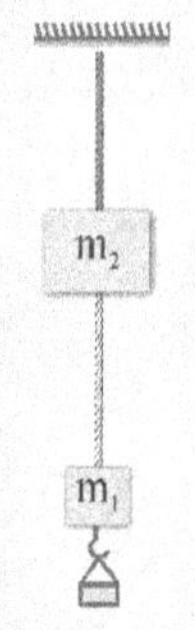

13. Find the maximum load that can be put on the hanger without breaking lower wire
    (a) 7 kg   (b) 10 kg
    (c) 14 kg   (d) 20 kg
14. For m_1 = 10 kg, m_2 = 36 kg; find the maximum load that can be put on the hanger without breaking upper wire is
    (a) 2 kg   (b) 5 kg
    (c) 7 kg   (d) 14 kg

Passage for (Q. 15 - 17) :

When liquid medicine of density ρ is to put in the eye, it is done with the help of a dropper. As the bulb on the top of the dropper is pressed, a drop forms at the opening of the dropper. We wish to estimate the size of the drop. We first assume that the drop formed at the opening is spherical because that requires a minimum increase in its surface energy. To determine the size, we calculate the net vertical force due to the surface tension T when the radius of the drop is R. When this force becomes smaller than the weight of the drop, the drop gets detached from the dropper.

15. If the radius of the opening of the dropper is r, the vertical force due to the surface tension on the drop of radius R (assuming $r <<$ R) is
    (a) $2\pi rT$ (b) $2\pi RT$
    (c) $\dfrac{2\pi r^2 T}{R}$ (d) $\dfrac{2\pi R^2 T}{r}$
16. If $r = 5 \times 10^{-4}$ m, $\rho = 10^3$ kgm^{-3}, $g = 10$ ms^{-2}, $T = 0.11$ Nm^{-1}, the radius of the drop when it detaches from the dropper is approximately
    (a) 1.4×10^{-3} m   (b) 3.3×10^{-3} m
    (c) 2.0×10^{-3} m   (d) 4.1×10^{-3} m
17. After the drop detaches, its surface energy is
    (a) 1.4×10^{-6} J   (b) 2.7×10^{-6} J
    (c) 5.4×10^{-6} J   (d) 8.1×10^{-6} J

MATRIX MATCHING

18. Match the columns correctly.

Column I		Column II	
A.	Bernoulli's theorem	(p)	Elasticity
B.	Stoke's law	(q)	Speed of efflux
C.	Torricelli's theorem	(r)	Venturimeter
D.	Hooke's law	(s)	Viscosity
		(t)	Conservation of energy

Answer Key

Sol. from page 180

7	(c)	9	(d)	11	(b)	13	(c)	15	(c)	17	(a)
8	(a)	10	(a)	12	(a)	14	(a)	16	(c)	18	A→ (q, r, t); B→ (s); C→ (q, t); D→ (p)

19. Column II depends on physical quantity/law given in column I. Match the column correctly.

	Column I		**Column II**
A.	Stoke's law	(p)	radius
B.	Terminal velocity	(q)	density of the material of body
C.	Excess pressure inside mercury drop	(r)	coefficient of viscosity
D.	Viscous force	(s)	surface tension
		(t)	velocity gradient

20. Match the columns correctly.

	Column I		**Column II**
A.	With rise in temperature forces that decreases	(p)	Elastic force
B.	Forces involved in capillary action	(q)	Force due to surface tension
C.	Water flows in a continuous stream down a vertical pipe whereas it breaks into drops when falling freely because of	(r)	Frictional force
D.	Terminal velocity of rain drop	(s)	Viscous force
		(t)	Gravitational force

21. A copper wire ($Y = 10^{11}$ N/m^2) of length 8 m and steel wire ($Y = 2 \times 10^{11}$ N/m^2) of length 4 m each of 0.5 cm^2 cross-section are fastened end to end and stretched with a tension of 500 N.

	Column-I		**Column-II**
A.	Elongation in copper wire in mm	(p)	0.25
B.	Elongation in steel wire in mm	(q)	1.0
C.	Total elongation in mm	(r)	0.8
D.	Elastic potential energy of the system in joules	(s)	$\dfrac{1}{4}$ th the elongation in copper wire

22.

	Column I		**Column II**
A.	Larger Reyonlds number	(p)	Drops in mist
B.	Time to acquire terminal speed	(q)	$v = \dfrac{2r^2 g(\rho - \sigma)}{9\eta}$
C.	Radius of drops of water < 0.01 mm	(r)	Less viscous force
D.	Greater velocity of flow of a liquid	(s)	Independent of the density of liquid

Answer Key	**19.**	A→ (p, r); B→ (p, q, r); C→ (p, s) ; D→ (r, t)	**20.**	A→ (p, q, r, s); B→ (q, t); C→ (q); D→ (s, t)
Sol. from page 180	**21.**	A→ (r) ; B→ (s); C→ (q); D→ (p)	**22.**	A→ (r) ; B→ (s); C→ (p, q) ; D→ (r)

POM Subjective Integer Type *Exercise 2.5*

Solutions from page 181

1. A body of mass 3.14 kg is suspended from one end of a wire of length 10.0 m. The radius of the wire is changing uniformly from 9.8×10^{-4} m at one end to 5.0×10^{-4} m at the other end. Find the change in the length of the wire. What will be the change in length if the ends are interchanged ? Young's modulus of the material of the wire is 2×10^{11} N/m^2.
   Ans. 1 mm, No.

2. A capillary tube of radius 0.50 mm is dipped vertically in a pot of water. Find the difference between the pressure of the water in the tube 5.0 cm below the surface and the atmospheric pressure. Surface tension of water = 0.075 N/m.
   Ans. 190 N/m^2 .

3. Two capillary tubes AB and BC are joined end to end at B, AB is 16 cm long and of diameter 4 mm whereas BC is 4 cm long and of diameter 2 mm. The composite tube is held horizontally with A connected to a vessel of water giving a constant head of 3 cm and C is open to the air. Calculate the pressure difference between B and C.
   Ans. h = 2.4 cm.

4. Eight rain drops of radius 1 mm each falling down with terminal velocity of 5 cm/s coalesce to form a bigger drop. Find the terminal velocity of the bigger drop.
   Ans. 20 cm/s.

5. Two large glass plates are placed vertically and parallel to each other inside a tank of water with separation between the plates equal to 1 mm. Find the rise of water in the space between the plates. Surface tension of water = 0.075 N/m.
   Ans. 1.5 cm.

6. In the bottom of a vessel with mercury there is a round hole of diameter $d = 70$ µm. At what maximum thickness of the mercury layer will the liquid still not flow out through this hole ?
   Ans. $\dfrac{4T}{\rho g d} = 21$ cm .

7. A glass rod of diameter $d_1 = 1.5$ mm is inserted symmetrically into a glass capillary with inside diameter $d_2 = 2$ mm. Then the whole arrangement is vertically oriented and brought in contact with the surface of water. To what height will the water rise in the capillary ?
   Ans. $h = \dfrac{4T}{\rho g (d_2 - d_1)} = 6\,cm$.

8. Find the attraction force between two parallel glass plates separated by a distance $h = 0.10$ mm, after a water drop of mass $m = 70$ mg was introduced between them. The wetting is assumed to be complete.
   Ans. $F = \dfrac{2Tm}{\rho h^2} = 1.0\,N.$

POM Subjective *Exercise 2.6*

Solutions from page 182

1. A structural steel rod has a radius of 10 mm and a length of 1 m. A 100 kN force F stretches it along its length. Calculate (a) the stress, (b) elongation, and (c) strain on the rod. Given that the Young's modulus, Y, of the structural steel is 2.0×10^{11} N/m^2.
   Ans. (a) 3.18×10^8 N/m^2 (b) 1.59 mm (c) 0.159 %.

2. The breaking stress for a metal is 7.8×10^9 N/m^2. Calculate the maximum length of the wire made of this metal which may be suspended without breaking. The density of the metal = 7.8×10^3 kg/m^3. Take g = 10 N/ kg.
   Ans. 10^5 m.

3. A composite wire of uniform diameter 3.0 mm consisting of a copper wire of length 2.2 m and a steel wire of length 1.6 m stretches under a load by 0.7 mm. Calculate the load, given that the Young's modulus for copper is 1.1×10^{11} Pa and for steel is 2.0×10^{11} Pa.
   Ans. 176.8 N.

4. The maximum stress that can be applied to the material of a wire used to suspend an elevator is 1.3×10^8 Nm^{-2}. If the mass of the elevator is 900 kg and it moves up with an acceleration of 2.2 ms^{-2}. What is the minimum diameter of the wire ?
   Ans. 1.0284×10^{-2} m.

5. Figure shows the stress – strain curve for a given material. What are (a) Young's modulus and (b) approximate yield strength for this material ?

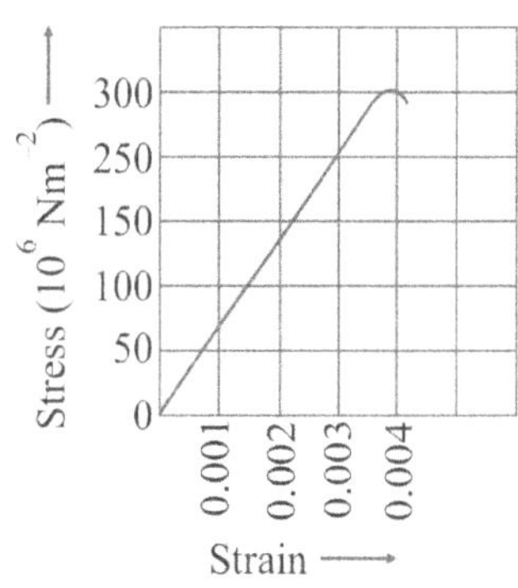

   Ans. 7.5×10^{10} N/m^2, (b) 3×10^8 N/m^2.

6. The average depth of Indian ocean is about 3000 m. Calculate the fractional compression $\Delta V / V$, of water of the bottom of the ocean, given that the bulk modulus of water is 2.2×10^9 Nm^{-2}.
   Ans. 1.36 %.

7. What is the density of ocean water at a depth, where the pressure is 80.0 atm, given that its density at the surface is 1.03×10^3 kgm^{-3} ? Compressibility of water = 45.8×10^{-11} Pa^{-1}. Given 1 atm = 1.013×10^5 Pa.

Ans. 1.034×10^3 kg/m^3.

8. A solid cube is subjected to a pressure of 5×10^5 Nm^{-2}. Each side of the cube is shortened by 1 %. Find volumetric strain and bulk modulus of elasticity of the cube.

Ans. 0.03, 1.67×10^7 N/m^2.

9. A solid sphere of radius R made of a material of bulk modulus K is surrounded by a liquid in a cylindrical container. A massless piston of area A floats on the surface of the liquid. When a mass M is placed on the piston to compress the liquid. Find fractional change in the radius of the sphere.

Ans. $\dfrac{\Delta R}{R} = \dfrac{Mg}{3AK}$

10. A wire of cross–sectional area 4×10^{-4} m^2, modulus of elasticity 2×10^{11} N/m^2 and length 1 m is stretched between two vertical rigid poles. A mass of 1 kg is suspended at its middle. Calculate the angle it makes with the horizontal.

Ans. 17.2'.

11. A sphere of radius 0.1 m and mass $8\,\pi$ kg is attached to the lower end of a steel wire of length 5.0 m and diameter 10^{-3} m. The wire is suspended from 5.22 m high ceiling of a room. When the sphere is made to swing as a simple pendulum, it just grazes the floor at its lowest point. Calculate the velocity of the sphere at the lowest position. Young's modulus of steel is 1.994×10^{11} N/m^2.

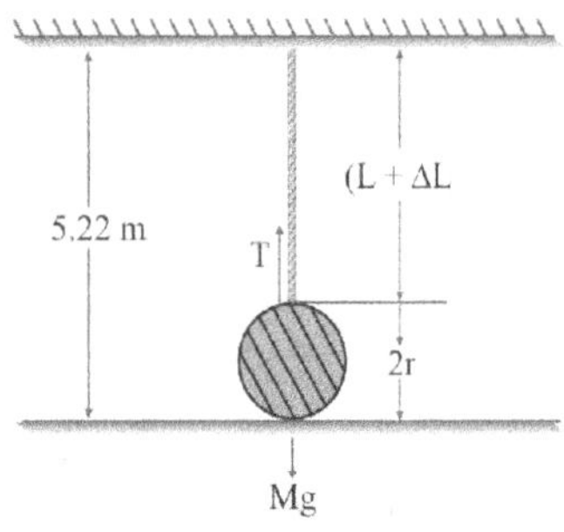

Ans. 8.8 m/s.

12. A stone of 0.5 kg mass is attached to one end of a 0.8 m long aluminium wire 0.7 mm in diameter and suspended vertically. The stone is now rotated in a horizontal plane at a rate such that the wire makes an angle of 85° with the vertical. Find increase in length of the wire. (The Young's modulus of aluminium $= 7 \times 10^{10}$ N/m^2) (sin 85° = 0.9962, cos 85° = 0.0872).

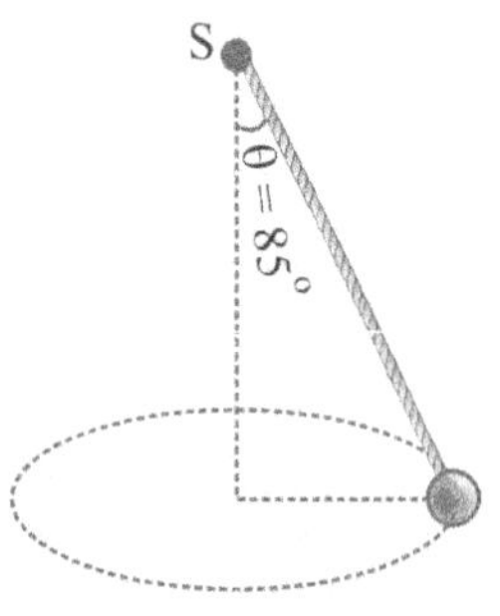

Ans. 1.668 mm.

13. Two rods of different metals but of equal cross–section and length (1.0 m each) are joined to make a rod of length 2.0 m. The metal of one rod has a coefficient of linear thermal expansion 10^{-5}/°C and Young's modulus 3×10^{10} N/m^2. The other metal has the values 2×10^{-5} / °C and 10^{10} N/m^2 respectively. How much pressure must be applied to the ends of the composite rod to prevent its expansion when the temperature is raised to 100°C ?

Ans. 2.25×10^7 N/m^2.

14. Find the change in volume which 1cm^3 water will undergo when taken from the surface to the bottom of an ocean 10 km deep. Volume elasticity of water 22000 atmospheres.

Ans. 0.044 cc.

15. (i) Two wires *AB* and *BC*, one of aluminium and the other of steel, each 1 m long are joined end to end to form a composite wire of length 2 m. The radius of each wire is 1 mm. Calculate the total length of the composite wire if a mass of 10 kg is attached at end *C*. $Y_{Al} = 7 \times 10^{10}$ N/m^2, $Y_{steel} = 2.1 \times 10^{11}$ N/m^2.

(ii) What is the elastic energy per unit volume produced in each wire ?

(iii) What load at end *C* would produce an expension 0.32 mm in both wires combined ?

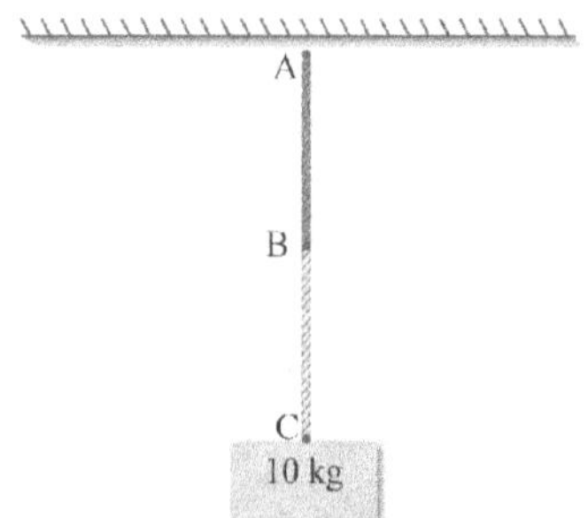

Ans. (i) 2.000606 m (ii) 7.22×10^3 J, 2.41×10^3 J, (iii) 5.28 kg.

16. A composite rod is made by joining a copper rod end to end with a second rod of different material, but of same cross -section. At 25°C, the composite rod is 1 m in length, of which the length of the copper rod is 30 cm. At 125°C the length of the composite rod increases by 1.91 mm. When the composite rod is not allowed to expand by holding it between two rigid walls, it is found that the length of constituents do not change with rise in temperature. Find the Young's modulus and the coefficient of linear expansion of the second rod. Given $\alpha_{cu} = 1.5 \times 10^{-5}$ /°C, $Y_{cu} = 1.3 \times 10^{11}$ N m^2. *Ans.* 1.1×10^{11} N/m^2. 2×10^{-5}/°C

17. A flat steel plate is of trapezoidal form of uniform thickness of t and tapers uniformly from a width b_1 to b_2 in a length of l. Determine the elongation of the plate under an axial force of F at each end. Young's modulus of steel plate is Y.

Ans. $\dfrac{F\,\ell\,\ell n(b_2/b_1)}{(b_2 - b_1)tY}$.

18. One end of a metal wire is fixed to a ceiling and a load of 2 kg hangs from the other end. A similar wire is attached to the bottom of the load and another load of 1 kg hangs from this lower wire. Find the longitudinal strain in both the wires. Area of cross–section of each wire is 0.005 cm^2 and Young's modulus of the metal is 2.0×10^{11} N/m^2. Take g = 10 m/s^2. *Ans.* $3 \times 10^{-4}, 10^{-4}$.

19. Each of the three blocks P, Q and R shown in figure has a mass of 3 kg. Each of the wires A and B has cross– sectional area 0.005 cm^2 and Young's modulus 2×10^{11} N/m^2. Neglect friction. Find the longitudinal strain developed in each of the wires. Take g = 10 m/s^2.

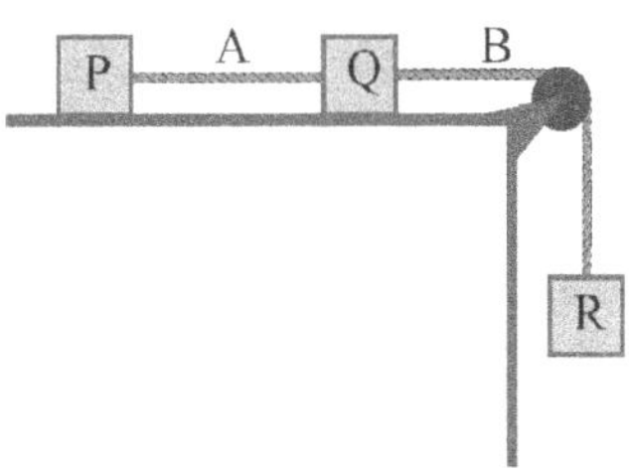

Ans. 2×10^{-4}, 1×10^{-4}.

20. The velocity of water in a river is 18 km/h near the surface. If the river is 5 m deep, find the shearing stress between the horizontal layer of water. The coefficient of viscosity of water = 10^{-2} poise.

Ans. 10^{-3} N/m^2 .

21. Consider the situation shown in figure. The force F is equal to the $m_2 g / 2$. If the area of the cross–section of the string is A and its Young's modulus Y, find the strain developed in it. The string is light and there is no friction anywhere.

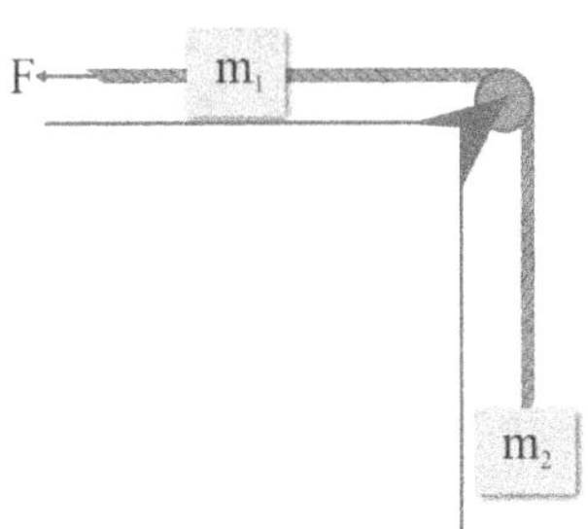

Ans. $\dfrac{m_2 g \,(2m_1 + m_2)}{2\,AY\,(m_1 + m_2)}$.

22. A steel rod of length l_1 = 30 cm and two identical brass rods of length l_2 = 20 cm each, support a light horizontal plateform as shown in figure. Cross–sectional area of each of the three rods is A = 1 cm^2. Calculate stress in each rod when a vertically downward force F = 5000 N is applied on the plateform. Given, Young's modulus of elasticity for steel Y_s = 2×10^{11} Nm^{-2} and brass Y_b = 1×10^{11} Nm^{-2}.

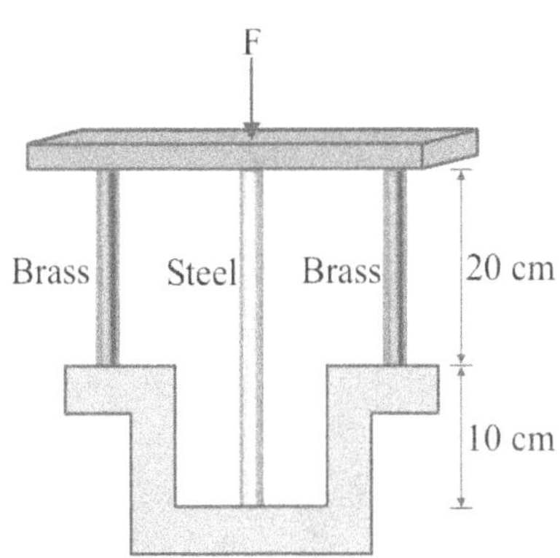

Ans. stress in steel = 2×10^7 N/m^2, stress in brass = 1.5×10^7 N/m^2.

EXERCISE (VISCOSITY)

23. Glycerine flows steadly through a horizontal tube of length 1.5 m and radius 1.0 cm. If the amount of glycerine collected per second at one end is 4.0×10^{-3} kg/s, what is the pressure difference between the two ends of the tube? Density of glycerine = 1.3×10^3 kg/m^3 and viscosity of glycerine = 0.83 Ns/m^2 .

Ans. 9.8×10^2 Pa.

24. Three capillary tubes of the same radius r but of lengths l_1, l_2 and l_3 are fitted horizontally to the bottom of a tall vessel containing a liquid at constant head and flowing through these tubes. Calculate the length of a single out flow tube of the same radius r which can replace the three capillaries.

Ans. $l = l_1 l_2 l_3 / (l_2 l_3 + l_1 l_3 + l_1 l_2)$.

25. A cylindrical tank of height 0.4 m is open at the top and has a diameter 0.16 m. Water is filled in it upto a height of 0.16 m. Calculate how long will it take to empty the tank through a hole of radius 5×10^{-3} m in the bottom.

Ans. 46.2 s.

26. Two tubes A and B of lengths 1 m and 0.5 m have radii 0.1 mm and 0.2 mm respectively. If a liquid is passing through the two tubes, entering A at a pressure of 0.8 m of mercury and leaving B at a pressure of 0.76 m. Find the pressure at the junction of A and B.

Ans. 0.7612 m of Hg.

27. In Millikan's oil drop experiment, what is the terminal speed of a drop of radius 2.0×10^{-5} m and density 1.2×10^3 kg/m^3? Take the viscosity of air at the temperature of the experiment to be 1.8×10^{-5} Ns/m^2. How much is the viscous force on the drop at that speed? Neglect buoyancy of the drop due to air.

Ans. 5.8 cm/s, 3.9×10^{-10} N.

28. A sphere is dropped under gravity through a fluid of viscosity η. Taking the average acceleration as half of the initial acceleration, show that the time taken to attain the terminal velocity is independent of the fluid density.

Ans. $\dfrac{4}{9}\dfrac{r^2 \rho}{\eta}$.

29. The tank at the left in figure has a very large cross–section and is open to the atmosphere. The depth y = 40 cm. The cross–sections of the horizontal tubes leading out of the tank are respectively 1 cm^2, 0.5 cm^2 and 0.2 cm^2. The liquid is ideal, having zero viscosity.
(a) What is the volume rate of flow out of the tank ?
(b) What is the velocity in each portion of the horizontal tube ?
(c) What are the heights of the liquid in the vertical side tubes ?

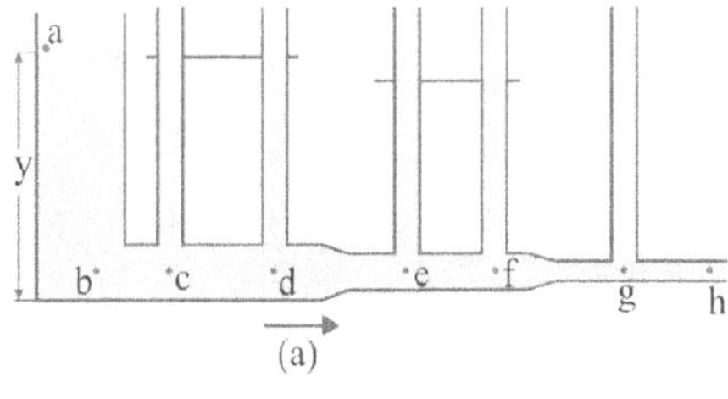

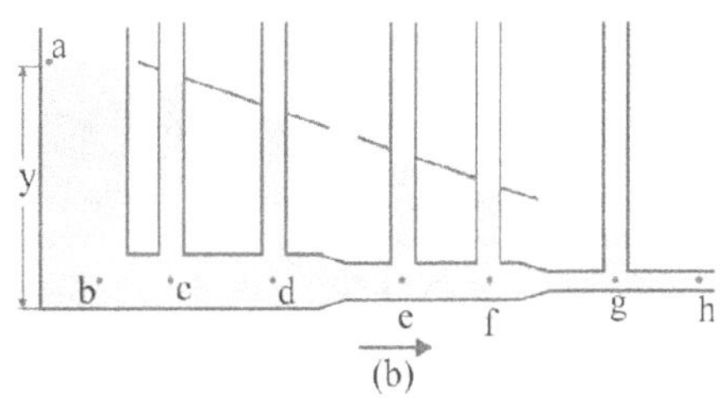

Pressure along a horizontal tube in which in flowing (a) an ideal fluid, (b) a viscous flu.d

Suppose that the liquid is figure has a viscosity of 0.5 poise, a density of 0.8 g/ cm^3, and that the depth of liquid in the large tank is such that the volume rate of flow is the same as in part (a) above. The distance between the side tubes at c and d, and between those at e and f, is 20 cm. The cross-sections of the horizontal tubes are the same in both diagrams.

(d) What is the difference in level between the tops of the liquid column in tubes c and d ?

(e) In tubes e and f ?

(f) What is the flow velocity on the axis of each part of the horizontal tube ?

Ans. (a) 56.0 cm^3/s (b) 56, 112, 280 cm/s

(c) 38.4, 38..4, 33.6, 33.6, 0.0 cm

(d) 18.0 cm (e) 71.8 cm and (f) 112, 224, 560 cm/s.

EXERCISE (SURFACE TENSION)

30. A glass capillary sealed at the upper end is of length 0.11 m and internal diameter 2×10^{-5} m. The tube is immersed vertically into a liquid of surface tension 5.06×10^{-2} N/m. To what length the capillary has to be immersed so that the liquid level inside and outside the capillary becomes the same. What will happen to water level inside the capillary if the seal is now broken ?

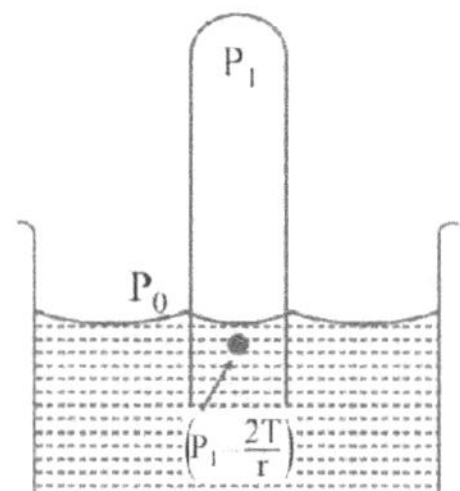

Ans. 0.01 m.

31. A conical glass capillary tube A of length 0.1 m has diameters 10^{-3} m and 5×10^{-4} m at the ends. When it is just immersed in a liquid at 0°C with larger diameter in contact with it, the liquid rises to 8×10^{-2} m in the tube. In another cylindrical glass capillary tube B, when immersed in the same liquid at 0°C, the liquid rises to 6×10^{-2} m height. The rise of liquid in tube B is only 5.5×10^{-2} m when the liquid is at 50°C. Find the rate at which the surface tension changes with temperature considering the change to be linear. The density of liquid is $[\dfrac{1}{14} \times 10^4]$ kg/m^3 and the

angle of contact is zero. Effect of temperature on the density of liquid and glass is negligible.

Ans. – (1 / 600) per 0°C ; Surface tension of liquid decreases linearly by 1 / 600 per °C rise of temperature per unit surface tension.

32. What is the excess pressure inside a bubble of soap solution of radius 5.00 mm? Given that the surface tension of soap solution at the temperature 20°C is 2.50×10^{-2} N/m. If an air bubble of the same dimension were formed at a depth of 40.0 cm inside a container containing the soap solution (of relative density 1.20), what would be the pressure inside the bubble ? (1 atm = 1.01×10^5 Pa)

Ans. 20 Pa, 105714 Pa.

33. The lower end of a capillary tube of diameter 2.00 mm is dipped 8.00 cm below the surface of water in a beaker. What is the pressure required in the tube in order to blow a hemispherical bubble at its end in water ? The surface tension in water at the temperature of the experiment is 7.30×10^{-2} N/m. 1 atmospheric pressure $= 1.01 \times 10^5$ Pa, density of water $= 1000$ kg/m^3, g = 9.80 m/s^2. Also calculate the excess pressure.

Ans. 146 Pa, 1.02×10^5 Pa.

34. A vertical capillary is brought in contact with the water surface. What amount of heat is liberated while the water rises along the capillary ? The wetting is assumed to be complete. The surface tension equals T.

Ans. $\dfrac{2\pi T^2}{\rho g}$.

35. Find the free energy of the surface layer of (a) a mercury droplet of diameter $d = 1.4$ mm; (b) a soap bubble of diameter $d = 6.0$ mm if the surface tension of the soap water solution is equal to $T = 45$ mN/m.

Ans. (a) 3 µ J (b) 10 µ J.

36. An air bubble in a liquid of surface tension 1.0×10^{-3} N/m gradually grows from a radius of 1.0×10^{-5} m to 1.0×10^{-4} m in 6 µs. Calculate the average rate of change of pressure inside.

Ans. 3×10^7 N/m^2–s.

37. A capillary tube is submerged in a broad vessel filled with water such that the upper end of the tube is above the level of water in the vessel by 2 cm. The internal radius of the capillary is 0.5 mm. Find the radius of curvature R of a meniscus in the capillary tube. Consider the wetting to be complete.

Ans. 0.75 mm.

Hints & Solutions

1. (c)
$$f_1 = f_2$$
or $\quad Y_1\alpha_1\Delta T = Y_2\alpha_2\Delta T$
$$\therefore \quad \frac{Y_1}{Y_2} = \frac{\alpha_2}{\alpha_1} = \frac{3}{2}$$

2. (b) Strain, $\quad e = \dfrac{\Delta r}{r} = \dfrac{R-r}{r}$

Stress $\quad f = eY = \left(\dfrac{R-r}{r}\right)Y$

Force needed $\quad F = fA = \left(\dfrac{R-r}{r}\right)YA$.

3. (c) As, $\dfrac{\tau}{\theta} = \dfrac{\pi\eta r^4}{2\ell}$

$$\therefore \quad \frac{\theta_A}{\theta_B} = \frac{r_2^4}{r_1^4}$$

4. (b) The ratio $\left(\dfrac{\text{stress}}{\text{strain}}\right)$ decreases . (see figure)

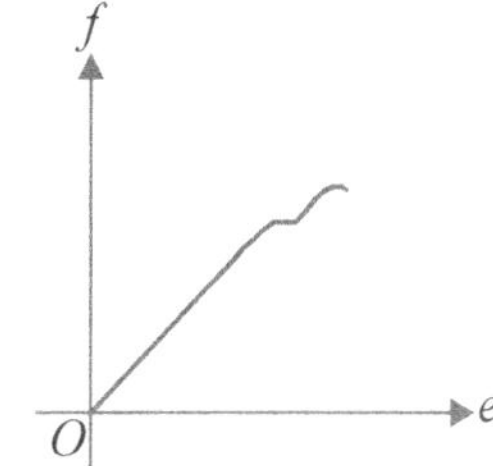

5. (d)
$$W_1 = \frac{1}{2}kx^2$$
and $\quad W_2 = \dfrac{1}{2}k(x+y)^2$

$$\therefore \quad W = W_2 - W_1 = \frac{1}{2}k(x+y)^2 - \frac{1}{2}kx^2$$
$$= \frac{1}{2}ky(2x+y)$$

6. (c)
$$f = \frac{F}{A} = \frac{W_1 + 3W/4}{s}$$

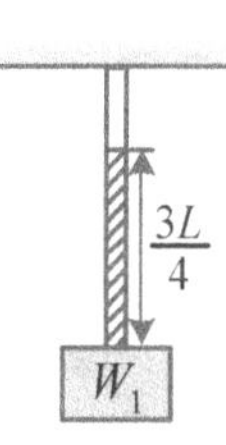

7 (a)
$$W = \frac{1}{2}kx^2 = \frac{1}{2}\left(\frac{YA}{L}\right)x^2$$

8. (d)
$$U = \frac{Fx}{2} = \frac{200 \times 10^{-3}}{2} = 0.1 \text{ J}$$

9. (a) Bulk modulus, $\quad B = \dfrac{\Delta P}{\left(\dfrac{\Delta V}{V}\right)} = \dfrac{0.155 \times 10^5}{0.1}$
$$= 1.55 \times 10^5 \text{ N/m}^2$$

10. (a)
$$U = \frac{1}{2}\frac{f^2}{Y} = \frac{s^2}{2Y}$$

11. (a) In the second case, the deforming force is also W. So, the elongation of the wire is ℓ.

12. (a) The difference in work done in expanding and compressing rubber will appear as heat.

13. (a) $Y = \dfrac{f}{e} = \dfrac{80/10^{-6}}{4 \times 10^{-4}} = 2 \times 10^{11} \text{ N/m}^2$

14. (b) For $x < r_0 \rightarrow$ repulsion and $x > r_0 \rightarrow$ attraction

15. (b) For brittle material, there is no yield point.

16. (a) Given, the breaking strength of cable $f_u = 7 \times 10^7 \text{ N/m}^2$
The force carried by the cable,
$$F = m(g+a)$$
$$= 2000(9.8+1.5) = 22600 \text{ N}$$

The area of cross-section, $A = \dfrac{F}{f_u} = \dfrac{22600}{7 \times 10^7}$
$$= 3.28 \times 10^{-4} \text{ m}^2.$$

17. (b)
$$F = y\alpha\Delta TA$$
$$= 10^{11} \times 10^{-5} \times 100 \times 10^{-4}$$
$$= 10^4 \text{ N}.$$

18. (c) It is the material property, so does not depend on size and shape of the specimen.

19. (a)
$$f = Y\alpha\Delta T$$
$$= 1.2 \times 10^{11} \times 1.1 \times 10^{-5} \times (20-10)$$
$$= 1.32 \times 10^7 \text{ N/m}^2.$$

20. (c)
$$e = \frac{\Delta Y}{\ell} = \frac{1 \times 10^{-3}}{4}$$
$$u = \frac{e^2 Y}{2} = \left(\frac{10^{-3}}{4}\right)^2 \times \frac{2 \times 10^{11}}{2}$$
$$= 0.075 \text{ J}.$$

21. (c) The isothermal bulk modulus of a gas is equal to pressure of the gas.

22. (a) The theoritical value of Poisson's ratio lies between -1 to $\dfrac{1}{2}$.

23. (a)
$$W = mg = (A\ell)\rho g$$
Thus $\quad f A = W$
or $\quad 10^6 A = A\ell\rho g$
or $\quad 10^6 = \ell \times 3 \times 10^3 \times 10$
or $\quad \ell \simeq 34 \text{ m}.$

24. (d) $$Y_A = \tan 60° = \sqrt{3}$$

and $$Y_B = \tan 30° = \frac{1}{\sqrt{3}}$$

$$\therefore \quad Y_A = 3Y_B.$$

25. (c) $$F = 2T \times \text{perimeter}$$
$$= 2T \times 4\,\ell = 8\,T\ell$$

26. (a) In this process, surface area of drop decreases and so energy will liberate.

27. (b) For the liquid does not wet the solid, the angle of contact should be greater than 90°.

28. (a) For the convex meniscus, the angle of contact should be greater than 90°.

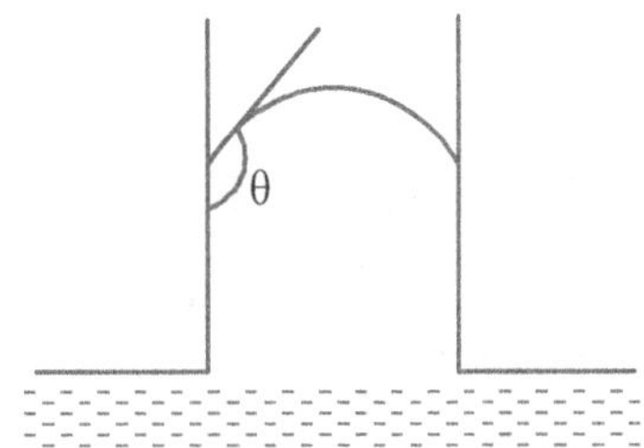

29. (b) $$\ell = \frac{h}{\cos\theta} = \frac{2}{\cos 60°} = 4\,\text{cm}.$$

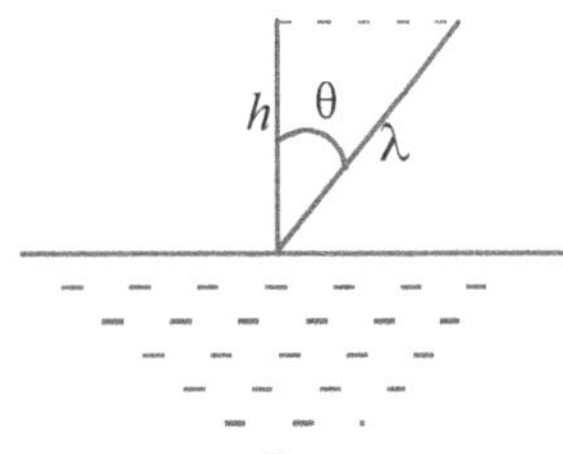

30. (c) In freely falling elevator, the effective value of gravity becomes zero. So liquid will rise upto full length of the tube.

31. (b) $$W = mg = \rho(\pi r^2 h)g$$

or $$W \simeq \rho(\pi r^2) \times \left(\frac{2T}{\rho rg}\right)g$$

or $$W = 2\pi r T$$

$$\therefore \quad T = \frac{W}{2\pi r} = \frac{6.28 \times 10^4}{2\pi \times 2 \times 10^{-3}}$$
$$= 5 \times 10^{-2}\ \text{N/m}.$$

32. (a) $$mg \sin\theta = \eta A\left(\frac{v}{t}\right)$$

or $$\rho a^3 g \sin\theta = \eta a^2\left(\frac{v}{t}\right)$$

$$\therefore \quad \eta = \frac{\rho a g t \sin\theta}{v}$$

33. (b) Inside pressure must be $\dfrac{4T}{r}$ greater than outside pressure in bubble. This excess pressure is provided by charge on bubble.

$$\frac{4T}{r} = \frac{\sigma^2}{2\varepsilon_0}$$

$$\frac{4T}{r} = \frac{Q^2}{16\pi^2 r^2 \times 2\varepsilon_0} \quad \left[\sigma = \frac{Q}{4\pi r^2}\right]$$

$$Q = 8\pi r\sqrt{2rT\varepsilon_0}$$

34. (b) $$F_v = 6\pi\eta R v$$

35. (d) $$Q = \frac{\pi P a^4}{8\eta\ell}$$

and $$Q' = \frac{\pi(2P)(a/2)^4}{8\eta\ell} = \frac{Q}{8}.$$

36. (c) $$\frac{v_1}{v_2} = \frac{(\rho_g - \rho_\ell)}{(\rho_s - \rho_\ell)} = \frac{19.5 - 1.5}{10.5 - 1.5}$$

$$\therefore \quad v_2 = \frac{v_1}{2} = \frac{0.2}{2} = 0.1\,\text{m/s}.$$

37. (c)

For floating disc, $F_{\text{net}} = 0$

or $F_b + 2\pi r T\cos\theta = W'$

or $W + 2\pi r T\cos\theta = W'.$

38. (a) The thread spread out due to surface tension.

39. (b) $$W = T\Delta A$$

$$\therefore \quad T = \frac{W}{\Delta A}$$

$$= \frac{3 \times 10^{-4}}{2(10 \times 11 - 10 \times 6) \times 10^{-4}}$$

$$= 3 \times 10^{-2}\ \text{N/m}^2$$

40. (d) In satellite there is weightlessness, so water will rise to full length of the tube.

41. (c) As $$h = \frac{2T}{R\rho g}$$

$$\therefore \quad h' = \frac{2T}{R\rho g/6} = 6h$$

42. (b) We know that, $P = \dfrac{4T}{r}$. With increase in time r increases and so pressure decreases.

43. (b) $$W = T\Delta A$$
$$= T \times 2[4\pi R^2 - 0]$$
$$= 8\pi R^2 T.$$

44. (b) $h = \dfrac{2T\cos\theta}{r\rho g}$, or $hr = \text{constant}$ (rectangular hyperbola).

Solutions **EXERCISE 2.1 LEVEL -2**

1. (d) Longitudinal strain,

$$e = \frac{f}{Y} = \frac{5 \times 10^7}{2 \times 10^{11}} = 2.5 \times 10^{-4}$$

For cylindrical wire, $V = \pi r^2 \ell$

$$\therefore \quad \frac{\Delta V}{V} = \frac{2\Delta r}{r} + \frac{\Delta \ell}{\ell}$$

or

$$\frac{0.02}{100} = 2\frac{\Delta r}{r} + 2.5 \times 10^{-4}$$

$$\therefore \quad \frac{\Delta r}{r} = -0.25 \times 10^{-4}.$$

2. (b)

$$f = \frac{mg}{A}$$

Volumetric strain,

$$\frac{\Delta V}{V} = \frac{\Delta P}{K}$$

or

$$3\frac{\Delta R}{R} = \frac{mg/A}{K}$$

$$\therefore \quad \frac{\Delta R}{R} = \left(\frac{mg}{3KA}\right).$$

3. (b) $f_A = \dfrac{F}{0.25A} = \dfrac{4F}{A}$; $\quad f_B = \dfrac{2F}{0.50A} = \dfrac{4F}{A}$

$f_C = \dfrac{4F}{2A} = \dfrac{2F}{A}$; $\quad f_D = \dfrac{5F}{3A}$

4. (d) We know that

$$\Delta L = \frac{FL}{AY}$$

$$\therefore \quad Y = \frac{FL}{A\Delta L}.$$

Clearly it is greatest for case 4.

5. (b)

$$F_b + F_v = Mg$$

or

$$F_v = Mg - F_b = Mg\left(1 - \frac{F_b}{Mg}\right)$$

$$= Mg\left(1 - \frac{d_2}{d_1}\right).$$

6. (b)

$$\frac{2T}{r} = \frac{2 \times 0.07}{0.14 \times 10^{-3}} = 10^3 \text{ N/m}^2$$

Pressure applied, $= P_a - \dfrac{2T}{r}$

$$= 10^5 - 10^3 = 99 \times 10^3 \text{ N/m}^2$$

7. (b)

$$M = (\pi r^2 h)\rho = \pi r^2 \left(\frac{2T\cos\theta}{\rho r g}\right)\rho$$

and

$$M' = \pi(2r)^2 \left(\frac{2T\cos\theta}{\rho \times 2r \times g}\right)\rho$$

$$= 2M.$$

8. (a) Increase in length of the wire

$$\ell = \frac{F.L}{\pi r^2 Y}$$

and

$$\ell' = \frac{2F \times (2L)}{\pi(2r)^2 Y} = \ell$$

9. (b) Using Hooke's law, $F = kx$ we can write

$$4 = k(a - \ell_0) \qquad \text{... (i)}$$

and

$$5 = k(b - \ell_0) \qquad \text{... (ii)}$$

If ℓ be the length under tension 9N, then

$$9 = k(\ell - \ell_0) \qquad \text{... (iii)}$$

After solving above equations, we get

$$\ell = (5b - 4a).$$

10. (d)

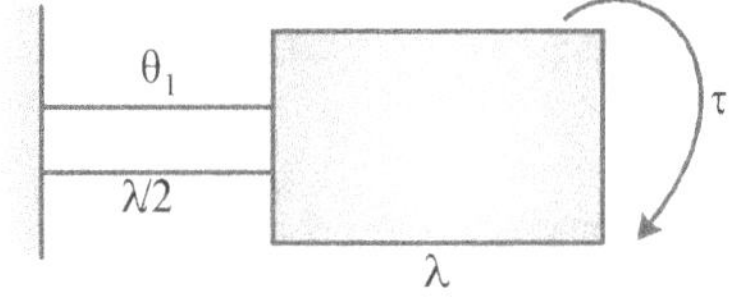

$$\theta_1 + \theta_2 = \theta_0 \qquad \text{... (i)}$$

We know that

$$\frac{\tau}{\theta} = \frac{\pi \eta r^4}{2\ell}$$

$$\therefore \quad \frac{\theta_1}{\theta_2} = \frac{\ell_1}{\ell_2} \times \frac{r_2^4}{r_1^4} = \frac{\ell/2 \times r^4}{\ell \times (r/2)^4} = 8 \quad \text{... (ii)}$$

After solving above equations, we get

$$\theta_1 = \frac{8\theta}{9}.$$

11. (d) For stress to be equal,

$$\frac{T_1}{A_1} = \frac{T_2}{A_2}$$

$$\therefore \quad \frac{T_1}{T_2} = \frac{A_1}{A_2} = \frac{1}{2}.$$

12. (b)

$$Y = \frac{MgL}{\pi r^2 \ell}$$

$$= \frac{1 \times 9.8 \times 2}{\pi(0.2 \times 10^{-3})^2 \times 0.8 \times 10^{-3}}$$

$$= 2 \times 10^{11} \text{ N/m}^2$$

Also

$$\frac{\Delta Y}{Y} = 2\frac{\Delta r}{r} + \frac{\Delta \ell}{\ell}$$

$$= 2\frac{0.01}{4} + \frac{0.05}{0.8} = 0.2$$

Use 1 → steel, 2 → brass,

13. (d)

$$\frac{\Delta\ell_{steel}}{\Delta\ell_{brass}} = \frac{F_1\ell_1/\pi r_1^2 Y_1}{F_2\ell_2/\pi r_2^2 Y_2}$$

$$= \frac{2}{4} \times a \times \left(\frac{1}{b}\right)^2 \times \frac{1}{c}$$

$$= \frac{a}{2b^2 c}.$$

14. (b) The surface tension of soap water is smaller, so it rises upto small height.

15. (c) One free surface rises the water by h, then two free surfaces rise the water by $2h$.

16. (d) From $\quad PV = nRT$, we have

$$\frac{P_A V_A}{P_B V_B} = \frac{n_A}{n_B}$$

$$\Rightarrow \frac{\left(8 + \dfrac{4T}{r_A}\right) \times \dfrac{4}{3}\pi r_A^3}{\left(8 + \dfrac{4T}{r_B}\right) \times \dfrac{4}{3}\pi r_B^3} = \frac{n_A}{n_B}$$

After substituting values, we get

$$\frac{n_B}{n_A} = 6.$$

17. (b) The radius at end 1 is smaller than at end 2, so pressure at end 1 is greater. Air blows from this end.

18. (c) $\quad T \times 2\pi r + mg = F_b$

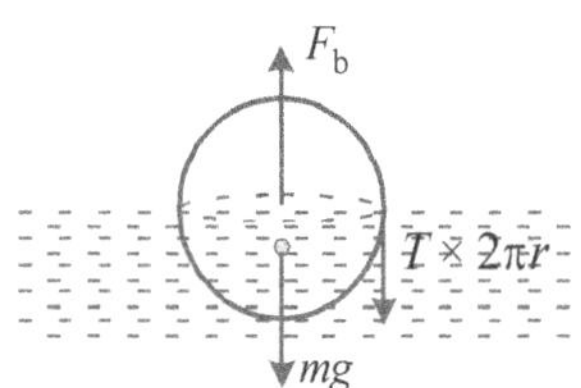

$$\text{or } T \times 2\pi r + \rho\frac{4}{3}\pi r^3 g = \left[\frac{\frac{4}{3}\pi r^3}{2}\right]\sigma g$$

$$\therefore \quad r = \sqrt{\frac{3T}{g(2\rho - \sigma)}}$$

19. (a) $\quad h_1 = \dfrac{2T}{r_1 \rho g}$ and $h_2 = \dfrac{2T}{r_2 \rho g}$

$$\therefore h = h_2 - h_1 = \frac{2T}{\rho g}\left(\frac{1}{r_2} - \frac{1}{r_1}\right).$$

20. (b)

$$n\frac{4}{3}\pi a^3 = \frac{4}{3}\pi b^3$$

$$\therefore \quad n = \frac{b^3}{a^3}$$

$$W = T\Delta A = S[n \times 4\pi a^2 - 4\pi b^2]$$

$$\text{or} \quad \frac{1}{2}mv^2 = S\left[\frac{b^3}{a^3} \times 4\pi a^2 - 4\pi b^2\right]$$

$$\text{or } \frac{1}{2}\rho \times \left(\frac{4}{3}\pi b\right)^3 v^2 = S\left[\frac{b^3}{a^3} \times 4\pi a^2 - 4\pi b^2\right]$$

$$\therefore \quad v = \sqrt{\frac{6S}{\rho}\left(\frac{1}{a} - \frac{1}{b}\right)}.$$

21. (a) $\quad F = \left[n_1\dfrac{v}{h_1} + n_2\dfrac{v}{(h - h_1)}\right]A$

$$\frac{dF}{dh_1} = 0$$

$$h_1 = \frac{h}{4}.$$

22. (a) $\quad \left(P_0 + \dfrac{4T}{r}\right)V = \left(P + \dfrac{4T}{r/2}\right)\dfrac{V}{8}$

$$\Rightarrow P = 8\left(P_0 + \frac{3T}{r}\right)$$

---

1. (b, c, d) The force at the middle of rod AB will be F. So stress right of middle will be greater than F/A. The force at each section of rod CD is F. So stress at each section is F/A.

2. (a, c)

$$\Delta\ell = \frac{F\ell}{\pi r^2 Y}$$

Clearly, $\quad \dfrac{\Delta\ell_A}{\Delta\ell_B} = \dfrac{r_B^2}{r_A^2} = (2)^2 = 4.$

3. (b, c)

$$F = (Y\alpha\Delta T)A = (Y\alpha\Delta T)\pi r^2$$

$$\therefore F_1 : F_2 : F_3 : F_4 = 1 : 2 : 3 : 4$$

$$\text{Energy stored} = \frac{1}{2}Fx = \frac{1}{2}F \times \frac{F\ell}{AY} = \frac{F^2\ell}{2AY} = \frac{F^2\ell}{2\pi r^2 Y}$$

$$\text{or} \quad U \propto \frac{F^2}{r^2}$$

4. (a, b)

$$F_1 + F_2 = 5000$$

$$\text{Also} \quad \Delta\ell_1 = \Delta\ell_2$$

$$\text{or} \quad \frac{F_1(2\ell)}{AY} = \frac{F_2(3\ell)}{AY}$$

$$\text{or} \quad 2F_1 = 3F_2$$

After solving, we get

$$F_1 = 3000N \text{ and } F_2 = 2000N$$

5. (a, b, c)

$$F_A = mg + \frac{mg}{3} = \frac{4mg}{3}$$

$$\text{and} \quad F_B = \frac{mg}{3}$$

$$f_A = \frac{F_A}{\pi r_A^2} = \frac{4mg/3}{\pi r_A^2}$$

and $$f_B = \frac{F_B}{\pi r_B^2} = \frac{mg/3}{\pi r_B^2}$$

For $r_A = 2r_B \Rightarrow f_A = f_B = f$; so either of them break.

For $r_A < 2r_B$; $f_A > f$, A will break before B.

For $r_A = r_B$; $f_A > f$, so A will break before B.

6. (a, c, d)

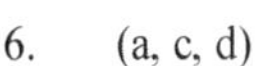

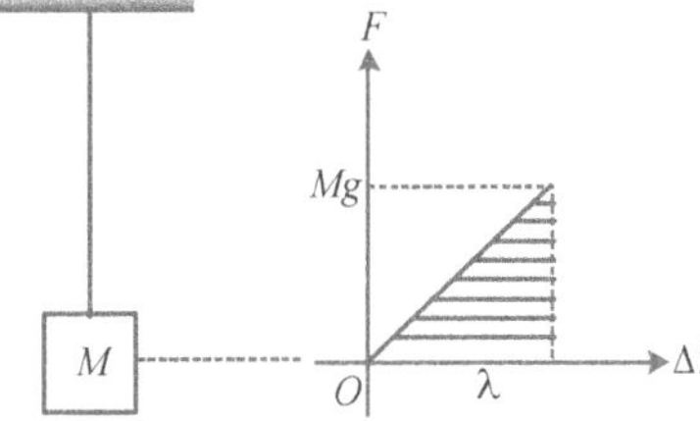

The decrease in PE $= Mg\ell$

Elastic potential energy stored $= Mg\dfrac{\ell}{2}$

Heat produced , $H = Mg\ell - Mg\dfrac{\ell}{2}$

$$= Mg\frac{\ell}{2}$$

7. (a, b, d) Strain, $e = \dfrac{\Delta\ell}{\ell} = \dfrac{\ell}{\ell} = 1$

Stress, $f = eY = 1 \times Y = Y$

Potential energy, U $= \dfrac{e^2 Y}{2} = \dfrac{(1)^2 Y}{2} = Y$.

8. (b, c) $W = U = \dfrac{e^2 Y}{2} \times \text{Vol.}$

$$= \frac{1}{2}\left(\frac{\ell}{L}\right)^2 Y \times AL = \frac{YA\ell^2}{2L}$$

9. (b, c) $$P_{top}V = P_{bottom}V'$$

$$P_{bottom} = (P_{top} + \rho gh)$$

As $P_{bottom} > P_{top}$; $\therefore$ $V > V'$.

10. (b, d) $$h = \frac{2T\cos\theta}{r\rho g}$$

Clearly $h \propto \dfrac{1}{r}$. Also in case of tube of insufficient length,

$h = \ell$.

11. (a, b) Angle of contact is the property of materials in contact.

12. (a, c) $h = \dfrac{2T\cos\theta}{r\rho g}$. For h to be zero, either $T = 0$ or $\theta = 90°$

13. (b, c, d) Initially $mg = 6\pi\eta r \times 10$.
In gravity free space, $mg = 0$, so unbalanced force acts in upward direction. Therefore

$$a = \frac{mg}{m} = g \text{ m/s}^2 .$$

Because of upward acceleration, the downward speed decreases and sphere will stop momentarily.

14. (a, b, d) $$h = \frac{2T\cos\theta}{r\rho g}$$

Clearly, h depends on T, r and length of the tube.

15. (a, c) When a drop splits, surface area increases and energy is to be given in the process.

16. (c, d) The liquid will rise to the full height of the tube and will get meniscus of larger radius.

17. (a, b, c, d) Solution in theory

18. (b, c) Viscous force, $F_v = 6\pi\eta rv$

Clearly, $F_v \propto v$ and $F_v \propto r$

As $A = \pi r^2$; $r = \sqrt{\dfrac{A}{\pi}}$, so $F_v \propto \sqrt{A}$.

19. (b, c) As $v_t \propto r^2$

$$\therefore \frac{v_1}{v_2} = \frac{(r)^2}{(r/2)^2} \Rightarrow v_2 = \frac{v_1}{4} .$$

Solutions EXERCISE-2.3

1. (a) Soap decreases the surface tension, which gives better cleaning.

2. (a) $$h = \frac{2T}{R\rho g} \text{ or } hR = \text{constant}$$

If $\ell < h$, then $hR = \ell R' \Rightarrow R' = R$.

3. (d) Some impurities can decrease the surface tension of the liquid.

4. (a) Critical temperature is the temperature at which vapour can liquify.

5. (b) Pressure difference, $P = \dfrac{2T}{r}$.

6. (a) $Y = \dfrac{f}{e}$, for the given force the strain produced in rubber is greater than steel and so $Y_{steel} > Y_{rubber}$.

7. (a) Size of hollow shaft will be greater than solid shaft made of same amount of material. As

$\dfrac{\tau}{\theta} = \dfrac{\pi\eta r^4}{2\ell}$, so $\tau \propto r^4$.

8. (a) Elasticity of the material decreases with long time.

9. (a) Clay is almost plastic material.

10. (a) Viscosity of the gases is proportional to the number of collisions.

11. (a) $v_t = \dfrac{2}{9}\dfrac{r^2(\rho - \sigma)g}{\eta}$; clearly $v_t \propto r^2$.

12. (b) $P + \dfrac{1}{2}\rho v^2 = \text{constant}$. In between the boats, v increases and so P decreases in comparision outside pressure.

Also, $F_v = 6\pi\eta rv$

13. (a) The coefficient of viscosity of water is smaller than honey.

14. (c) The weight of steel blade is balanced by surface tension force.

15. (b) The viscosity of castor oil is greater than water.

Solutions **EXERCISE-2.4**

Passage (Q1 - 3)

1. (c) $\Delta\ell = \dfrac{F\ell}{AY} = \dfrac{10 \times 1}{10^{-3} \times 2 \times 10^5} = 5$ cm

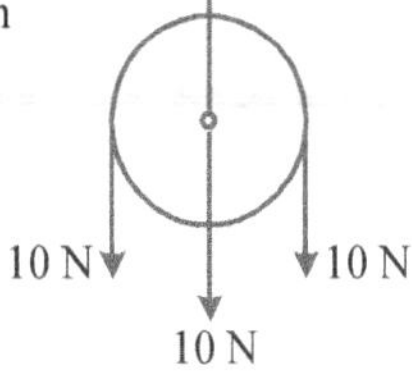

2. (c) $Fx = \dfrac{1}{2}kx^2 \quad \therefore \quad x = \dfrac{2F}{k} = \dfrac{2 \times 30}{(YA/\ell)}$

$= \dfrac{2 \times 30}{2 \times 10^5 \times 10^{-3}} = 30$ cm

3. (c) When pulley moves down by 30 cm, the string will loose from its both sides, so the point A moves down by 60 cm.

Passage (Q4 - 6)

4. (c) $f = 2\eta\pi R\ell\left(\dfrac{dv}{dr}\right) = -2\eta\pi R\ell\left[\dfrac{-2Rv_0}{R^2}\right]$; $F = 4\pi\eta\ell v_0$

5. (a) $F = -\eta 2\pi r\ell\left[\dfrac{-2rv_0}{R^2}\right] \Rightarrow F \propto r^2$

6. (b)

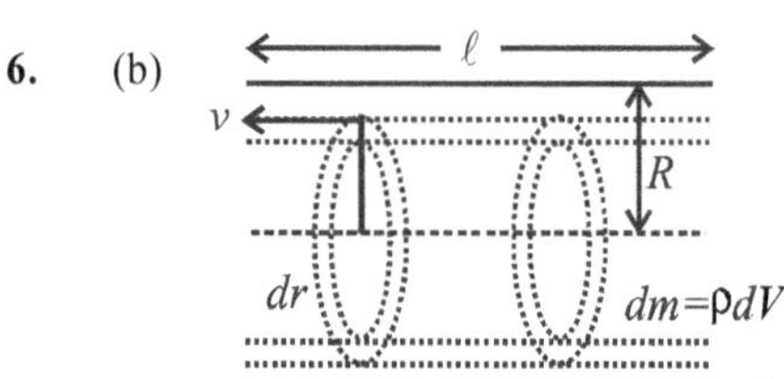

$dm = \rho \, dV = \rho \, dA.\ell$; $dm = \rho \, \ell \, 2\pi r \, dr$
so momentum of mass dm

$dp = v \, dm$; $\displaystyle\int_0^p dp = \int_0^R v \, dm$

$p = 2\pi\rho\ell v_0 \displaystyle\int_0^R r\left(1 - \dfrac{r^2}{R^2}\right) dr$; $p = 2\pi\rho\ell v_0 \left[\dfrac{r^2}{2} - \dfrac{r^4}{4R^2}\right]_0^R$

$= 2\pi\rho\ell v_0 \left[\dfrac{R^2}{2} - \dfrac{R^2}{4}\right] = \dfrac{2\pi\rho\ell v_0 R^2}{4}$; $p = \dfrac{\rho\pi R^2 \ell v_0}{2}$

Passage (Q7 - 9)

7. (c) $W = fA = 3.6 \times 10^8 \times 0.5 \times 10^{-4} = 1800$ N

8. (a) $\Delta\ell = \dfrac{W\ell}{AY} = \dfrac{1800 \times 0.05}{0.5 \times 10^{-4} \times 1.8 \times 10^{11}} = 0.01$ m

9. (d) $W_{max} = f_u A = 7.2 \times 10^8 \times 0.5 \times 10^{-4} = 3600$ N.

Passage (Q10 - 12)

10. (a) $\Delta\ell_{copper} = \Delta\ell_{steel}$

or $\dfrac{F \times 2}{(1.1 \times 10^{11}) \times 2 \times 10^{-4}} = \dfrac{F \times L}{2.0 \times 10^{11} \times 1 \times 10^{-4}}$

or $L = 1.8$ m

11. (b) $f_{copper} = \dfrac{F}{A} = \dfrac{3 \times 10^4}{2 \times 10^{-4}} = 1.50 \times 10^8$ N/m^2

12. (a) $e_{steel} = f_{steel}/Y_{steel} = \left(\dfrac{3 \times 10^4}{1 \times 10^{-4}}\right)\Big/ 2 \times 10^{11}$

$= 1.5 \times 10^{-3}$.

Passage (Q13 - 14)

Suppose m is the load put on the hanger.

13. (c) The stress in upper wire $8 \times 10^8 = \dfrac{(20 + 10 + m)g}{0.006 \times 10^{-4}}$

$\therefore \qquad m = 18$ kg

The stress in lower wire $f = \dfrac{(10 + 18)g}{0.003 \times 10^{-4}}$

$= 9.3 \times 10^9$ N/m^2

Thus lower wire will break by 18 kg load, and so to prevent its breaking let, m' is the required mass

$\therefore \qquad 8 \times 10^8 = \dfrac{(10 + m)g}{0.003 \times 10^{-4}}$

or $\qquad m' = 14$ kg

14. (a) The stress in upper wire $8 \times 10^4 = \dfrac{(10 + 36 + m)}{0.006 \times 10^{-4}}$

$\therefore \qquad m' = 2$ kg.

The stress in lower wire corresponding to this load

$f = \dfrac{(10 + 2)}{0.003 \times 10^{-4}} = 4 \times 10^8$ N/m^2, (safe)

Passage (Q15 - 17)

15. (c) The vertical component of face

$F_v = F \sin\theta$

$\simeq F \tan\theta$

$= (T \times 2\pi r) \times \dfrac{r}{R}$

$= \dfrac{2\pi r^2 T}{R}$.

16. (a) $F_v = mg$

or $\dfrac{2\pi r^2 T}{R} = \dfrac{4}{3}\pi R^3 \rho$

$\therefore \quad R = \left(\dfrac{3r^2 T}{2\rho g}\right)^{r/4}$

17. (b) Surface energy $= T(4\pi R^2) = 2.7 \times 10^{-6}$ J.

18. **A → (q, r, t) ; B→ (s) ; C→(q, t) ; D→(p)**

(A) Bernoulli's equation is based on conservation of energy. From Bernoulli's equation, we can get speed of efflux and rate of flow (venturimeter)

(B) $F_v = 6\pi\eta r v$

(C) Toricelli's theorem, $v_e = \sqrt{2gh}$, which can be obtained by conservation of energy.

(D) Hooke's law : stress $\propto$ strain.

19. **A → (p, r) ; B→ (p, q, r) ; C→(p, s) ; D→(r, t)**

(A) Stoke's law, $F_v = 6\pi\eta r v$

(B) Terminal velocity, $v_t = \dfrac{2}{9}\dfrac{r^2(\rho - \sigma)g}{\eta}$.

(C) Excess pressure, $p = \dfrac{2T}{r}$.

(D) Viscous force, $F = \eta A(-dv/dy)$.

20. **A→ (p, q, r, s); B→ (q, t); C→ (q); D→ (s, t)**

21. A→ (r) ; B→ (s); C→ (q); D→ (p)

(A) $\Delta\ell_{copper} = \dfrac{F\ell}{AY} = \dfrac{500\times 8}{0.5\times 10^{-4}\times 10^{11}} = 0.8$ mm

(B) $\Delta\ell_{steel} = \dfrac{F\ell}{AY} = \dfrac{500\times 4}{0.5\times 10^{-4}\times 2\times 10^{11}} = 0.2$ mm

(C) $\Delta\ell = \Delta\ell_{copper} + \Delta\ell_{steel} = 1.0$ mm

(D) $U = \left[\dfrac{e^2 Y_{copper}}{2} + \dfrac{e^2 Y_{steel}}{2}\right]\times \text{Vol} = 0.25$ J

22. A→ (r) ; B→ (s); C→ (p, q) ; D→ (r)

(A) $R_N = \dfrac{\rho v D}{\eta}$; Clearly less value of η indicates large value of R_N.

(B) Time aquired for terminal velocity does not depend on density of body or liquid.

(C) Radius is related to $v = \dfrac{2}{9} r^2 \dfrac{(\rho - \sigma) g}{\eta}$

(D) Velocity of flow, $v = \dfrac{p r^2}{8\eta\ell}$.

Solutions EXERCISE-2.5

1. The change in length of the wire is given by

$$\Delta L = \frac{FL}{\pi r_1 r_2 Y}$$

$$= \frac{(3.14\times 9.8)\times 10}{\pi (9.8\times 10^{-4})\times (5\times 10^{-4})\times (2\times 10^{11})}$$

$$= 10^{-3} \qquad \textbf{Ans.}$$

2. The pressure just below the free surface of water

$$P_A = \left(P_a - \frac{2T}{R}\right)$$

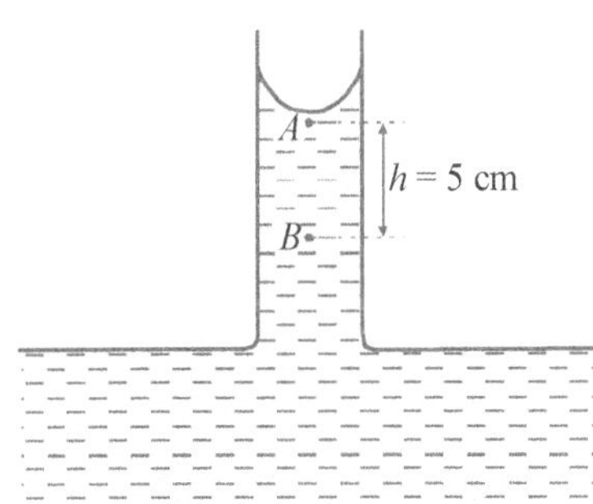

The pressure difference

$$P_B - P_A = \rho g h$$

or $P_B - \left(P_a - \dfrac{2T}{R}\right) = \rho g h$

$\therefore \quad P_B - P_a = \rho g h - \dfrac{2T}{R}$

$$= 1000\times 9.8\times 0.05 - \frac{2\times 0.075}{0.5\times 10^{-3}}$$

$$= 190 \text{ N/m}^2 \qquad \textbf{Ans.}$$

3.

$P_A = 3$ cm, P_B, $P_C = 0$

16 cm — 4 cm

The resistance of two tubes are $R_1 = \dfrac{8\eta l_1}{\pi r_1^4}$

and $R_2 = \dfrac{8\eta l_2}{\pi r_2^4}$

As tubes are connected in series, and so,

$$Q_1 = Q_2$$

or $\dfrac{P_A - P_B}{R_1} = \dfrac{P_B - 0}{R_2}$

or $\dfrac{(3 - P_B)}{\left(\dfrac{8\eta l_1}{\pi r_1^4}\right)} = \dfrac{P_B}{\left(\dfrac{8\eta l_2}{\pi r_2^4}\right)}$

or $(3 - P_B)\dfrac{r_1^4}{l_1} = \dfrac{P_B r_2^4}{l_2}$

After substituting the value and simplifying, we get

$$P_B = 2.4 \text{ cm}.$$

4. If R is the radius of bigger drop, then

$$8\times \frac{4}{3}\pi r^3 = \frac{4}{3}\pi R^3$$

$\therefore \quad R = 2r = 2\times 1 = 2$ mm.

We know that, $v_t \propto r^2$

$\therefore \quad \dfrac{v_2}{v_1} = \dfrac{R^2}{r^2}$

or $v_2 = \dfrac{R^2}{r^2} v_1 = \dfrac{2^2}{1^2}\times 5 = 20$ cm/s **Ans.**

5. If h is the rise in the tube, then

surface tension force= weight of liquid rise

$$2T\ell = \rho\,(\ell b h) g$$

$\therefore \quad h = \dfrac{2T}{\rho b g} = \dfrac{2\times 0.075}{1000\times 10^{-3}\times 9.8}$

$$= 1.5\times 10^{-2} \text{ m} \qquad \textbf{Ans.}$$

6. The height above the hole is given by

$$h = \frac{2T}{r\rho g} = \frac{2T}{\dfrac{d}{2}\rho g} = \frac{4T}{d\rho g} = 21 \text{ cm}.$$

7. If h is the height of water rise, then

weight of water in the tube = surface tension force

$$\frac{\pi}{4}(d_2^2 - d_1^2) h\rho g = \pi\,(d_2 + d_1)\,T$$

$\therefore \quad h = \dfrac{4T}{\rho g (d_2 - d_1)} = 6\,cm$ \qquad **Ans.**

8. Force needed to pull the plate, each of area A

$$F = \frac{2TA}{d}$$

Here $d = h,$

$Ah\rho = m$

$\therefore \quad A = \dfrac{m}{h\rho}$

$\therefore \quad F = \dfrac{2T\left(\dfrac{m}{h\rho}\right)}{h} = \dfrac{2Tm}{\rho h^2}$ \qquad **Ans.**

1. (a) Stress $f = \dfrac{F}{A} = \dfrac{100 \times 10^3}{\pi (0.01)^2}$

$$= 3.18 \times 10^8 \text{ N/m}^2$$

(b) Elonglation $\Delta L = \dfrac{F\ell}{Ay} = \dfrac{F\ell}{\pi r^2 Y}$

$$= \dfrac{(100 \times 10^3) \times 1}{\pi (0.01)^2 \times 2 \times 10^{11}}$$

$$= 1.59 \times 10^{-3} \text{ m}$$

(c) Strain $e = \dfrac{\Delta L}{L} = \dfrac{1.59 \times 10^{-3}}{1}$

$$= 0.159 \,\% \qquad \textbf{\textit{Ans.}}$$

2. If ℓ is the length of wire and A is the area of the cross – section, then mass of the wire

$$m = \rho \ell A$$

Stress $f = \dfrac{mg}{A} = \dfrac{\rho \ell A g}{A} = \rho \ell g$

Thus $7.8 \times 10^9 = 7.8 \times 10^3 \times \ell \times 10$

$\therefore \qquad \ell = 10^5 \text{ m}$

3. The extension $\Delta L_{copper} = \dfrac{F\ell_1}{AY_c} = \dfrac{F \times 2.2}{\pi (0.003)^2 \times 1.1 \times 10^{11}}$

and $\Delta L_{steel} = \dfrac{F\ell_2}{AY_s}$

$$= \dfrac{F \times 1.6}{\pi (0.003)^2 \times 2 \times 10^{11}}$$

Given $\Delta L_{copper} + \Delta L_{steel} = 0.7 \times 10^{-3}$
After simplifying above equations, we get

$$F = 176.8 \text{ N} \qquad \textbf{\textit{Ans.}}$$

4. The load to be carried

$$W = m(g+a)$$
$$= 900(9.8 + 2.2) = 10800 \text{ N}$$

If r is the required radius of the wire, then

$$\dfrac{W}{\pi r^2} = f$$

or $\dfrac{10800}{\pi r^2} = 1.3 \times 10^8$

$\therefore \qquad r = 1.0284 \times 10^{-2} \text{ m} \qquad \textbf{\textit{Ans.}}$

5. (a) Young's modulus, $Y = $ slope of stress-strain curve

$$= \dfrac{150 \times 10^6}{0.002} = 7.5 \times 10^{10} \text{ N/m}^2$$

(b) Appropriate yield strength of the material

$$= 3 \times 10^8 \text{ N/m}^2 \qquad \textbf{\textit{Ans.}}$$

6. The increase in pressure $\Delta P = \rho g h$

$$= 10^3 \times 9.8 \times 3000$$
$$= 29.4 \times 10^6 \text{ N/m}^2$$

The volumetric strain, $\dfrac{\Delta V}{V} = \dfrac{\Delta P}{B} = \dfrac{29.4 \times 10^6}{2.2 \times 10^9}$

$$= 1.36 \,\% \qquad \textbf{\textit{Ans.}}$$

7. Bulk modulus $B = \dfrac{1}{k} = \dfrac{1}{45.8 \times 10^{-11}} Pa$

$$= 2.18 \times 10^9 \text{ Pa}$$

Density is given by $\rho' = \dfrac{\rho}{\left(1 - \dfrac{P}{B}\right)}$

$$= \dfrac{1.03 \times 10^3}{\left[1 - \dfrac{80 \times 1.013 \times 10^5}{2.18 \times 10^9}\right]}$$

$$\simeq 1.034 \times 10^3 \text{ kg/m}^3 \qquad \textbf{\textit{Ans.}}$$

8. Volumetric strain, $\dfrac{\Delta V}{V} = 3 \times \dfrac{\Delta \ell}{\ell} = 3 \times 0.01 = 0.03$

Bulk modulus, $B = \dfrac{\Delta P}{(\Delta V / V)} = \dfrac{5 \times 10^5}{0.03}$

$$= 1.67 \times 10^7 \text{ N/m}^2$$

9. Increase in pressure , $\Delta P = \dfrac{Mg}{A}$

Bulk modulus, $K = \dfrac{\Delta P}{(\Delta V / V)}$

$\therefore \qquad \dfrac{\Delta V}{V} = \dfrac{\Delta P}{K} = \dfrac{Mg}{AK}$

The volume of the sphere, $V = \dfrac{4}{3} \pi R^3$

$\therefore \qquad \dfrac{\Delta V}{V} = 3 \dfrac{\Delta R}{R}$

or $\dfrac{\Delta R}{R} = \dfrac{\Delta V}{3V}$

$$= \dfrac{Mg}{3AK} \qquad \textbf{\textit{Ans.}}$$

10. Suppose θ is the required angle. Then

$$2T\sin\theta = mg$$

$\therefore \qquad T = \dfrac{mg}{2\sin\theta}$

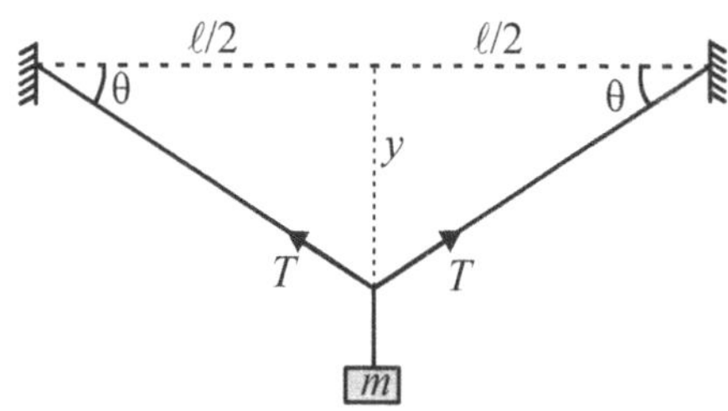

Stress $f = \dfrac{T}{A} = \dfrac{mg}{2A\sin\theta}$

Strain $e = \dfrac{\Delta \ell}{\ell} = \dfrac{\left(\dfrac{\ell}{\cos\theta} - \ell\right)}{\ell}$

$$= \left(\dfrac{1 - \cos\theta}{\cos\theta}\right)$$

We have $Y = \dfrac{f}{e}$

or $\quad 2 \times 10^{11} = \dfrac{mg/2A\sin\theta}{(1-\cos\theta)/\cos\theta}$

$\quad\quad 2 \times 10^{11} = \dfrac{mg}{2A}\cdot\dfrac{\cos\theta}{\sin\theta(1-\cos\theta)}$

After substituting the known values and solving, we get
$$\theta = 17.2'$$

11. The increase in length of the wine
$$\Delta L = 5.22 - 5 - 0.2 = 0.02 \text{ m}$$

Strain, $\quad e = \dfrac{\Delta L}{L} = \dfrac{0.02}{5}$

If v is the velocity of the sphere at the lowest position, then
$$T = mg + \dfrac{mv^2}{r}$$
$$[r = 5.22 - 0.1 = 5.12 \text{ m}]$$

Stress, $\quad f = \dfrac{T}{A} = \dfrac{\left[mg + \dfrac{mv^2}{r}\right]}{A}$

$$Y = \dfrac{f}{A}$$

or $\quad 1.994 \times 10^{11} = \dfrac{\left[mg + \dfrac{mv^2}{r}\right]\Big/A}{(0.20/5)}$

After simplifying, we get $v = 8.8$ m/s $\quad\quad$ ***Ans.***

12. If T is the tension in the wire, then
$$T\cos\theta = mg$$

$\therefore \quad\quad T = \dfrac{mg}{\cos\theta}$

Stress, $\quad f = \dfrac{T}{A}$

$\quad\quad = \dfrac{mg}{A\cos\theta}$

Strain, $\quad e = \dfrac{\Delta L}{L}$

We have $\quad Y = \dfrac{f}{e}$

or $\quad 7 \times 10^{10} = \dfrac{mg/A\cos\theta}{\Delta L/L}$

After simplifying, we get $\Delta L = 1.668$ m.

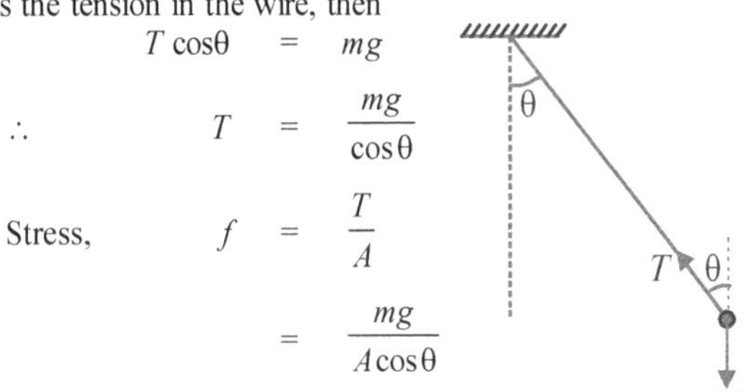

13. The strain produced in rods $e_1 = \dfrac{\Delta L_1}{L_1} = \dfrac{L_1\alpha\,\Delta t}{L_1} = \alpha_1\Delta t$

Total strain $\quad e = e_1 + e_2$

$\quad\quad = (\alpha_1 + \alpha_2)\Delta t$

$\quad\quad = (10^{-5} + 2 \times 10^{-5}) \times 100$

$\quad\quad = 3 \times 10^{-3}$

If f is the stress induced by preventing this strain, then

$$e = \dfrac{f}{Y_1} + \dfrac{f}{Y_2} = f\left(\dfrac{1}{Y_1} + \dfrac{1}{Y_2}\right)$$

$\therefore \quad\quad f = \dfrac{e}{\left(\dfrac{1}{Y_1} + \dfrac{1}{Y_2}\right)}$

$\quad\quad = \dfrac{3 \times 10^{-3}}{\left(\dfrac{1}{3 \times 10^{10}} + \dfrac{1}{10^{10}}\right)}$

$\quad\quad = 2.25 \times 10^7 \quad$ N/m². ***Ans.***

14. The increase in pressure,
$$\Delta P = \rho\, gh$$
$$= 10^3 \times 9.8 \times 10 \times 10^3$$
$$= 9.8 \times 10^7 \quad \text{N/m}^2.$$

The volumetric strain, $\dfrac{\Delta V}{V} = \dfrac{\Delta P}{B}$

$\quad\quad = \left(\dfrac{9.8 \times 10^7}{22000 \times 1.013 \times 10^5}\right)$

$\quad\quad = 4.4 \times 10^{-2}$

$\therefore \quad\quad \Delta V = 0.044 \text{ cm}^3.$ $\quad\quad$ ***Ans.***

15. (i) The change in length of the wire
$$\Delta L_1 = \dfrac{FL}{AY_1} \quad\quad [L = 1\text{m}]$$

and $\Delta L_2 = \dfrac{FL}{AY_2}$

$\therefore \quad \Delta L = \Delta L_1 + \Delta L_2$

$\quad\quad = \dfrac{FL}{A}\left[\dfrac{1}{Y_1} + \dfrac{1}{Y_2}\right]$

$\quad\quad = \dfrac{(10 \times 10) \times 1}{\pi(10^{-3})^2}\left[\dfrac{1}{7 \times 10^{10}} + \dfrac{1}{2.1 \times 10^{11}}\right]$

$\quad\quad = 0.000606 \text{ m}$

Thus total length of the wire
$$= 2 + 0.000606 = 2.000606 \text{ m}.$$

(ii) Stress in each wire $\quad f = \dfrac{mg}{\pi r^2} = \dfrac{10 \times 10}{\pi(10^{-3})^2}$

$\quad\quad = 3.18 \times 10^7 \text{ N/m}^2$

Elastic energy per unit volume is given by

$$u_1 = \dfrac{f^2}{2Y_1} = \dfrac{(3.18 \times 10^7)^2}{2 \times 7 \times 10^{10}}$$
$$= 7.22 \times 10^3 \text{ J}$$

and $\quad u_2 = \dfrac{f^2}{2Y_2} = \dfrac{(3.18 \times 10^7)^2}{2 \times 2.1 \times 10^{11}}$

$\quad\quad = 2.41 \times 10^3 \text{ J}.$ $\quad\quad$ ***Ans.***

16. See example 14 page 133.

17. Choose an element of thickness dx. The area of cross section there,

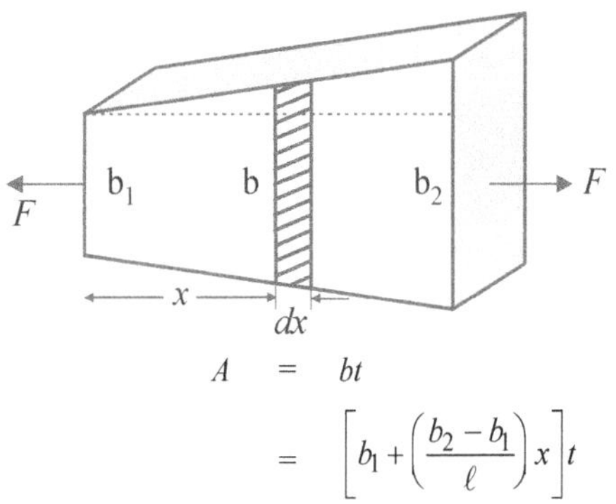

$$A = bt$$
$$= \left[b_1 + \left(\dfrac{b_2 - b_1}{\ell}\right)x\right]t$$

The extension ΔL =

$$\int_0^\ell \frac{F\,dx}{\left[b_1 + \left(\dfrac{b_2 - b_1}{\ell}\right)x\right]t\,Y}$$

$$= \frac{F\ell \ln\left(\dfrac{b_2}{b_1}\right)}{(b_2 - b_1)t\,Y} \qquad \textbf{Ans.}$$

18. Stress in lower wire,

$$f_1 = \frac{mg}{A}$$

$$= \frac{1 \times 10}{0.005 \times 10^{-4}} N/m^2$$

Stress in upper wire, $f_2 = \dfrac{3 \times 10}{0.005 \times 10^{-4}} N/m^2$

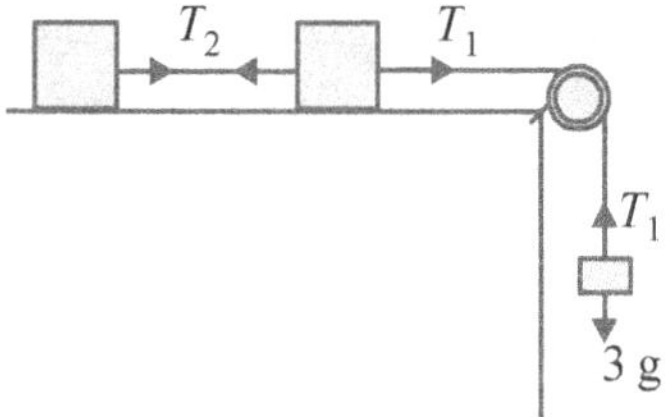

Strain produced in lower wire, $e_1 = \dfrac{f_1}{Y} = 10^{-4}$

and $$e_2 = \frac{f_2}{Y}$$

$$= \frac{3 \times 10}{0.005 \times 10^{-4} \times 2 \times 10^{11}}$$

$$= 3 \times 10^{-4} \qquad \textbf{Ans.}$$

19. If a is the acceleration of the blocks, then

$$3g - T_1 = 3a,$$

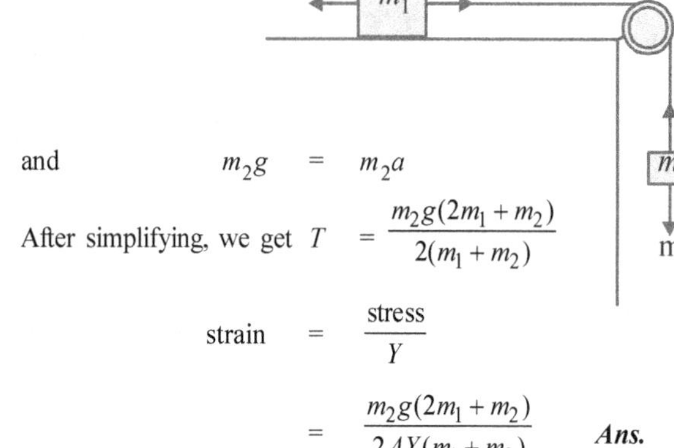

$$T_1 - T_2 = 3a$$
and $$T_2 = 3a$$
After simplifying, we get

$$a = \frac{g}{3}\,m/s^2 = \frac{10}{3}\,m/s^2$$

$$T_1 = 2g$$
$$= 20\,N$$
and $$T_2 = 10\,N$$

Strain developed, $e_1 = \dfrac{T_1/A}{Y}$

$$= \frac{20}{0.005 \times 10^{-4} \times 2 \times 10^{11}}$$

$$= 2 \times 10^{-4}$$

$$e_2 = \frac{T_2/A}{Y}$$

$$= \frac{10}{0.005 \times 10^{-4} \times 2 \times 10^{11}}$$

$$= 1 \times 10^{-4} \qquad \textbf{Ans.}$$

20. The velocity of water, $v = \dfrac{18 \times 5}{18} = 5\,m/s.$

The velocity gradient, $\dfrac{dv}{dy} = \dfrac{5}{5} = 1s^{-1}$

We know that $$F = \eta A\left(\frac{dv}{dy}\right)$$

$$\therefore \quad \frac{F}{A} = \eta\left(\frac{dv}{dy}\right) = \frac{10^{-2}}{10} \times 1$$

or $$f = 10^{-3}\,N/m^2 \qquad \textbf{Ans.}$$

21. If a is the acceleration of the blocks, then

$$T - F = m_1 a$$

and $$m_2 g = m_2 a$$

After simplifying, we get $\quad T = \dfrac{m_2 g(2m_1 + m_2)}{2(m_1 + m_2)}$

$$\text{strain} = \frac{\text{stress}}{Y}$$

$$= \frac{m_2 g(2m_1 + m_2)}{2AY(m_1 + m_2)} \qquad \textbf{Ans.}$$

22. If stresses in brass and steel are f_b and f_s respecting, then

$$2f_b A + f_s A = 5000 \qquad ....(i)$$

The change of length of rods are equal and so

$$\Delta L_b = \Delta L_s$$

or $$\frac{f_b L_b}{Y_b} = \frac{f_s L_s}{Y_s} \qquad ......(ii)$$

After simplifying and substituting the given values, we have

$$f_b = 1.5 \times 10^7\,N/m^2$$
$$f_s = 2 \times 10^7\,N/m^2$$

23. Given $$Q = \frac{4 \times 10^{-3}}{1.3 \times 10^3}$$

$$= 3.08 \times 10^{-6}\,m^3/s$$

We know that $$Q = \frac{\pi P r^4}{8\eta l}$$

or $$3.08 \times 10^{-6} = \frac{\pi P(1 \times 10^{-2})^4}{8 \times 0.83 \times 1.5}$$

$$\therefore \quad P = 9.8 \times 10^2\,N/m^2 \qquad \textbf{Ans.}$$

24. In this case the tubes are in parallel, so

$$\frac{1}{R} = \frac{1}{R_1} + \frac{1}{R_2} + \frac{1}{R_3}$$

As resistance is proportional to the length of the tube (constant) and so

$$\frac{1}{l} = \frac{1}{l_1} + \frac{1}{l_2} + \frac{1}{l_3}$$

$$\frac{1}{l} = \left[\frac{l_1 l_2 + l_1 l_3 + l_2 l_3}{l_1 l_2 l_3}\right]$$

$$\therefore \quad l = \left[\frac{l_1 l_2 l_3}{l_1 l_2 + l_1 l_3 + l_2 l_3}\right] \qquad \textbf{Ans.}$$

25. The time of emptying a tank is given by

$$t = \frac{A\sqrt{2}}{a\sqrt{g}}(\sqrt{h_1} - \sqrt{h_2})$$

Here; $h_1 = 0.16$ m,
$h_2 = 0$

After simplifying, we get $t = 46.2\ s$.

26. $$\frac{\pi(P_A - P)r_A^4}{8\eta\ell_A} = \frac{\pi(P - P_B)r_B^4}{8\eta\ell_8}$$

$\therefore \qquad P = 0.7612$ m of Hg

27. Terminal speed is given by

$$v = \frac{2}{9}r^2\frac{(\sigma - \rho)}{\eta}g$$

$$= 5.8 \text{ cm/s}$$

Viscous force, $F_b = 6\pi\eta\, r\, v$
$$= 3.9 \times 10^{-10} \text{ N.} \qquad \textbf{\textit{Ans.}}$$

28. The initial acceleration of the drop

$$= \frac{mg - F_b}{m}$$

$$= \left[\frac{V\rho g - V\sigma g}{V\rho}\right]$$

$$= \frac{(\rho - \sigma)g}{\rho}$$

The average acceleration, $a = \dfrac{(\rho - \sigma)g}{2\rho}$

The terminal velocity, $v = \dfrac{2}{9}r^2\dfrac{(\rho - \sigma)g}{\eta}$

Now using $v = u + at$, we have,

$$t = \frac{v}{a} = \frac{4}{9}\frac{r^2\rho}{\eta} \qquad \textbf{\textit{Ans.}}$$

29. (a) Volume rate of flow $= a\,v$

$$= a\sqrt{2gy}$$

$$= (0.2) \times \sqrt{2 \times 981 \times 40}$$

$$= 56 \text{ cm}^3/\text{s.}$$

(b) $v_1 \times 1 = v_2 \times 0.5$
$$= v_3 \times 0.2 = 56$$
$v_1 = 56$ cm/s
$v_2 = 112$ cm/s
$v_3 = 280$ cm/s

(c) By using Bernoulli's equation, we have

$$\frac{P_1}{\rho g} + \frac{v_1^2}{2g} = \frac{P_2}{\rho g} + \frac{v_2^2}{2g}$$

$$= \frac{P_3}{\rho g} + \frac{v_3^2}{2g}$$

or $$y_1 + \frac{v_1^2}{2g} = y_2 + \frac{v_2^2}{2g}$$

$$= y_3 + \frac{v_3^2}{2g}$$

Here $y_3 = 0$
After substituting and simplifying, we get
$y_1 = 38.4$ cm.
and $y_2 = 33.6$ cm $\qquad \textbf{\textit{Ans.}}$

(d) For the part cd,

$$Q = \frac{\pi\Delta P r^4}{8\eta l} = \frac{\pi P a^2}{8\pi\eta l}$$

$\therefore \qquad \Delta P = \dfrac{8\pi\eta l\theta}{a^2}$

$$= \frac{8\pi \times 0.5 \times 20 \times 56}{1^2}$$

$$= 14067.2$$

$$\Delta y = \frac{\Delta P}{\rho g}$$

$$= \frac{14067.2}{0.8 \times 981}$$

$$\simeq 18 \text{ cm.}$$

Similar treatment can be made for other parts.

30. When capillary tube is immersed in the liquid, pressure inside it becomes $\left(P_a + \dfrac{2T}{r}\right)$. If ℓ is the length of the tube inside liquid, then

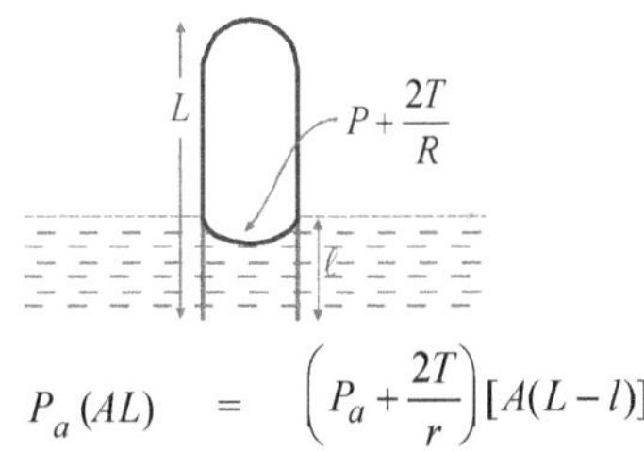

$$P_a(AL) = \left(P_a + \frac{2T}{r}\right)[A(L - l)]$$

After substituting the known values and simplifying, we get
$l = 0.01$ m $\qquad \textbf{\textit{Ans.}}$

31. The radius of the tube at the poistion of meniscus

$$r = r_1 + \frac{(r_2 - r_1)}{\ell}(\ell - h)$$

$$= 2.5 \times 10^{-4} + \left(\frac{1 \times 10^{-3} - 5 \times 10^{-4}}{0.1}\right)(0.1 - 0.08)$$

$$= 3.0 \times 10^{-4} \text{ m.}$$

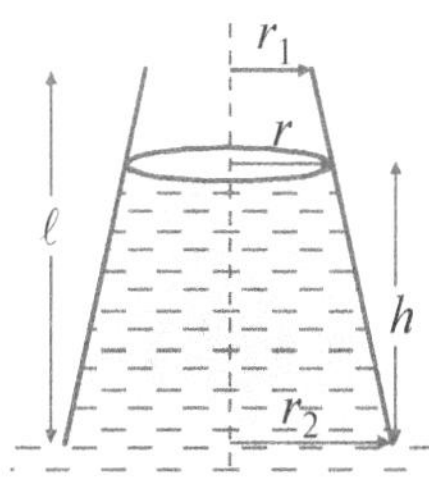

If T_0 is the surface tension at $0°$C, then

$$h = \frac{2T_0}{r\rho g}$$

$\therefore \qquad T_0 = \dfrac{hr\rho g}{2}$

$$= \frac{(8 \times 10^{-2})(3 \times 10^{-4})\left(\frac{1}{4} \times 10^4\right)(9.8)}{2}$$

$$= 0.084 \text{ N/m}$$

As $h \propto T$

$$\therefore \quad \frac{T_{50}}{T_0} = \frac{h_{50}}{h_0}$$

$$\therefore \quad T_{50} = \frac{h_{50}}{h_0} \times T_0$$

$$= \frac{5.5 \times 10^{-2}}{6 \times 10^{-2}} \times 0.084$$

$$= 0.077 \, \text{N/m}$$

If α is the rate with which surface tension changes, then

$$T_{50} = T_0(1 + \alpha \Delta t) \quad [\Delta t = 50^\circ C]$$

$$\therefore \quad \alpha = \frac{(T_{50} - T_0)}{T_0 \, \Delta t}$$

$$= \frac{1}{600} \, perK.$$

32. Excess pressure $\quad P = \dfrac{4T}{R}$

$$= \frac{4 \times 2.50 \times 10^{-2}}{5 \times 10^{-3}}$$

$$= 20 \, \text{N/m}^2$$

At a depth h $\quad P_i - P_o = \dfrac{4T}{R}$

$$\therefore \quad P_i = P_o + \frac{4T}{R}$$

$$= (P_a + \rho \, gh) + \frac{4T}{R}$$

$$= 1.01 \times 10^5 + 12000 \times 9.8 \times 0.4 + \frac{4 \times 2.50 \times 10^{-2}}{5 \times 10^{-3}}$$

$$= 105724 \, \text{N/m}^2 \qquad \textbf{\textit{Ans.}}$$

33. The pressure difference in air bubble

$$P_i - P_o = \frac{2T}{R}$$

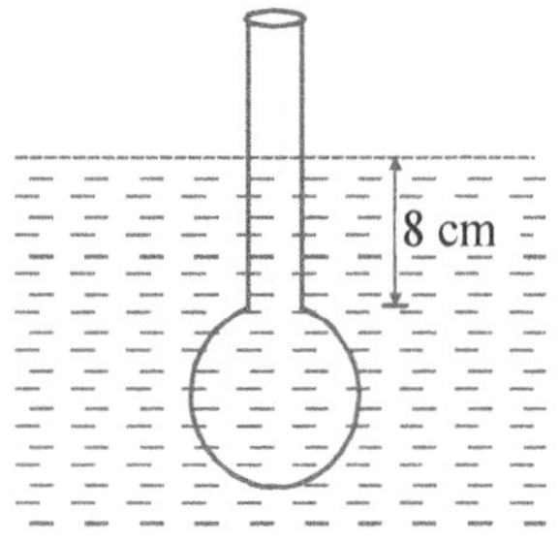

8 cm

$$= \frac{2 \times 7.30 \times 10^{-2}}{1 \times 10^{-3}} = 146 \, \text{Pa}$$

Pressure inside bubble

$$P_i = P_o + \frac{2T}{R}$$

$$= (P_a + h\rho g) + \frac{2T}{r}$$

$$= 1.02 \times 10^3 \, P_a \qquad \textbf{\textit{Ans.}}$$

34. If h is the capillay rise, then

$$h = \frac{2T}{r\rho g}$$

Pressure, $\quad P = \rho \, gh$

$$= \frac{2T}{r}$$

Average pressure $\quad P_{av} = \dfrac{0+P}{2} = \dfrac{T}{r}$

The volume of water rise $= \pi r^2 h$

Heat liberated $=$ work done by surface tension force

$$= P_{av} \times \Delta V$$

$$= \frac{T}{r} \times \pi r^2 h = \pi T r h$$

$$= \pi T r \times \left(\frac{2T}{r\rho g}\right)$$

$$= \frac{2\pi T^2}{\rho g} \qquad \textbf{\textit{Ans.}}$$

35. Surface energy is given by

$$U = T(\Delta A)$$

(a) For mercury droplet, $\Delta A = 4\pi \, r^2$

$$= \pi \, (\, 0.7 \times 10^{-3})^2$$

(b) For soap bubble, $\Delta A = 2(4\pi r^2)$

$$\therefore \quad U = T \times \Delta A$$

$$= 45 \times 10^{-3} \times 8 \, \pi \, (\, 3 \times 10^{-3})^2$$

$$= 10 \, \mu J \qquad \textbf{\textit{Ans.}}$$

36. The pressure difference in air bubble in liquid

$$P_1 = \frac{2T}{r_1}$$

and $\quad P_2 = \dfrac{2T}{r_2}$

$$\therefore \quad P_1 - P_2 = 2T\left(\frac{1}{r_1} - \frac{1}{r_2}\right)$$

$$= 2 \times 1 \times 10^{-3}\left(\frac{1}{10^{-5}} - \frac{1}{10^{-4}}\right)$$

$$= 180 \, \text{N/m}^2$$

Thus $\quad \dfrac{P_1 - P_2}{t} = \dfrac{180}{6 \times 10^{-6}}$

$$= 3 \times 10^7 \, \frac{N}{m^2 - s} \qquad \textbf{\textit{Ans.}}$$

37. The rise of the water in capillary tube that can be

$$h = \frac{2T}{R\rho g}$$

$$\therefore \quad R = \frac{2T}{h\rho g}$$

Fluid Mechanics

(187- 278)

3.1 DEFINITION OF FLUID

Fluid may be defined as a substance which is capable of flowing. It has no definite shape of its own, but can acquire the shape of the containing vessel. Both liquids and gases are fluids.

A liquid possesses a definite volume. It forms a free surface or an interface separating it from the atmosphere. Under ordinary conditions liquids are difficult to compress. So they may be assume incompressible for all practical purposes.

A gas possesses no definite volume but it always expands until its volume is equal to that of the container. All gases are compressible in nature.

Ideal fluids are those which have no viscosity and surface tension and also incompressible. Real fluids are those which are actually possess the properties like; viscosity, surface tension and compressibility.

3.2 FLUID STATICS AND FLUID DYNAMICS

Fluid statics is the branch of physics that deals with the study of fluids at rest. Study of water at rest is called hydrostatics. It includes fluid pressure, Pascal's law, Archimedes principle etc.

Fluid dynamics is the branch of physics that deals with the study of fluids in motion. Its study includes equation of continuity, Bernoulli's theorem, Toricelli's theorem etc.

3.3 MASS DENSITY AND SPECIFIC WEIGHT

Density of any material is defined as the mass per unit volume of the material. Thus

$$\text{density} = \frac{\text{Mass}}{\text{Volume}}$$

or

$$\rho = \frac{M}{V}$$

SI unit of density is kg/m^3. CGS unit of density is g/cm^3.

Specific weight

Specific weight of any material is the weight per unit volume of the material.

$$\text{specific weight} = \frac{\text{Weight}}{\text{Volume}}$$

or

$$\gamma = \frac{W}{V}$$

SI unit of specific weight is N/m^3.

Relative density

Relative density of a substance is defined as the ratio of the density of the substance to the density of water at 4°C.

Thus

$$\text{R.D.} = \frac{\text{Density of substance}}{\text{Density of water at 4°C}}$$

Relative density is a dimensionless quantity. Clearly density of a substance = R.D. × density of water at 4°C.

Specific gravity

Specific gravity of a substance is defined as the specific weight of substance to the specific weight of water. Thus

$$\text{S.G} = \frac{\text{Specific weight of substance}}{\text{Specific weight of water}}$$

Note:

1. Numerically relative density and specific weight are equal.
2. Relative density can be calculated as:

$$\text{R.D.} = \frac{\text{Weight of substance in air}}{\text{Loss in weight in water}}$$

or

$$\text{R.D.} = \frac{W_{air}}{W_{air} - W_{water}}$$

3. If ρ_o is the density of substance at $0°C$, then its density at $t°C$ is given by:

$$\rho_t = \frac{\rho_0}{(1+\gamma t)} \approx \rho_o (1 - \gamma t)$$

Densities of some common fluids at STP

Fluid	Density (kg/m^3)
Water	1.00×10^3
Sea water	1.03×10^3
Ice	0.92×10^3
Mercury	13.6×10^3
Blood	1.06×10^3
Air	1.29

3.4 DENSITY OF MIXTURE

If $m_1, m_2, \ldots\ldots, m_n$ are the masses and $V_1, V_2, \ldots\ldots V_n$ are the volumes of the different substances, then density of their mixture is defined as:

$$\rho = \frac{M}{V} = \frac{m_1 + m_2 + \ldots\ldots + m_n}{V_1 + V_2 + \ldots\ldots\ldots + V_n}$$

(i) If two substances are mixed in equal volumes, then

$$\rho = \frac{m_1 + m_2}{V_1 + V_2}$$

$$= \frac{\rho_1 V + \rho_2 V}{V + V} = \frac{\rho_1 + \rho_2}{2}$$

(ii) If two substances are mixed in equal amount, i.e., $m_1 = m_2$

or

$$\rho_1 V_1 = \rho_2 V_2 \Rightarrow \frac{V_2}{V_1} = \frac{\rho_1}{\rho_2}$$

$$\therefore \qquad \rho = \frac{m_1 + m_2}{V_1 + V_2}$$

$$= \frac{\rho_1 V_1 + \rho_2 V_2}{V_1 + V_2} = \frac{2\rho_1 V_1}{V_1 \left(1 + \frac{V_2}{V_1}\right)}$$

$$= \frac{2\rho_1}{1 + \frac{\rho_1}{\rho_2}} = \frac{2\rho_1 \rho_2}{\rho_1 + \rho_2}$$

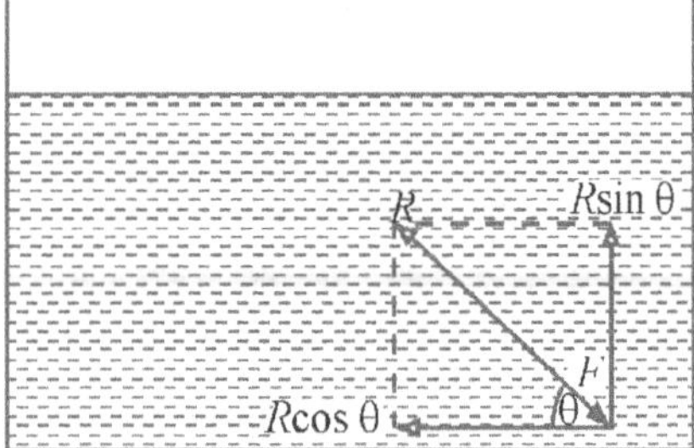

Fig. 3.1

3.5 THRUST OR FORCE OF A LIQUID

When a certain liquid is held in static equilibrium against boundary surfaces, the forces exert by liquid always be perpendicular to the surface in contact. This is so because a liquid at rest can not resist any tangential force. To understand this, consider a liquid contained in a vessel in the equilibrium, as shown in *Fig. 3.1*. Suppose the liquid exerts a force F at the bottom of the vessel, whose direction makes angle θ with the horizontal. The bottom surface of the vessel exerts an equal reaction force R on water.

The reaction force has two components:

(i)   Tangential component $= R\cos\theta$

(ii)   Normal component $= R\sin\theta$

Since liquid can not sustain any tangential force, so liquid begins to flow along tangentially. But the liquid is at rest, so tangential component of R must be zero, i.e.,

$$R\cos\theta = 0$$

As $R \neq 0$, $\therefore \cos\theta = 0$ or $\theta = 90°$

Hence a liquid always exerts force perpendicular to the surface of the container at every point.

3.6 PRESSURE

The pressure or intensity of pressure at any point may be defined as the normal force exerted on a unit area around that point. If force ΔF acts normally over a flat area ΔA, then pressure

$$P = \frac{\Delta F}{\Delta A}$$

Pressure at any point can be defined as:

$$P = \underset{\Delta A \to 0}{Lim} \frac{\Delta F}{\Delta A}$$

or

$$P = \frac{dF}{dA}$$

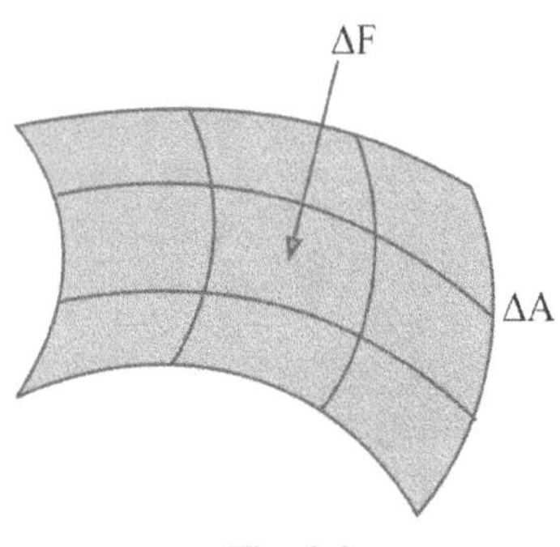

Fig. 3.2

Units of pressure

(i)   SI unit of pressure $= N/m^2$ or pascal (Pa) i.e., $1\,Pa = 1\,N/m^2$

(ii)   In metrology the pressure is measured in bar and millibar.

$$1\,bar = 10^5\,N/m^2$$

Also, $1\,torr = 1\,mm\ of\ Hg\ height$

(iii) **Atmospheric (atm) :** It is the pressure exerted by 76 cm of mercury column or 10.3 m of water column.

$1\,atm = 1.013 \times 10^5\,N/m^2$

Some pressures (in Pa)

Atmosphere at sea level	1.01×10^5
Systolic blood pressure (gauge)	1.60×10^4 (120 torr)
Highest laboratory pressure	10^{12}
Exceptional laboratory vacuum	10^{-12}

Blood pressure

When heart is contracted to its smallest size, the pumping of blood is the hardest and the pressure of blood flowing in major arteries is nearly 120 mm of Hg (120 torr). This is known as **systolic pressure**. When the heart is expanded to its largest size the blood pressure is nearly 80 mm of Hg (80 torr). This is known as **diastolic** pressure. The sphygmomanometer is a device, which measures these extreme pressures.

Ex. 1 The two thigh bones, each of cross - sectional area 10 cm^2 support the upper part of a human body of mass 40 kg. Estimate the average pressure sustained by the bones. Take $g = 10$ m/s^2

Sol.

Total cross-sectional area of the thigh bones

$$A = 2\,(10 \times 10^{-4}) = 2 \times 10^{-3} \text{ m}^2$$

Force acting on the bones $= mg = 40 \times 10$

$$= 400 \text{ N}$$

$$\therefore \quad P_{av} = \frac{F}{A} = \frac{400}{2 \times 10^{-3}} = 2 \times 10^5 \text{ N/m}^2 \text{ } \textit{Ans.}$$

Ex. 2 A cylindrical vessel containing liquid is closed by a smooth piston of mass m. The area of cross-section of the piston is A. If the atmospheric pressure is P_o, find the pressure of the liquid just below the piston.

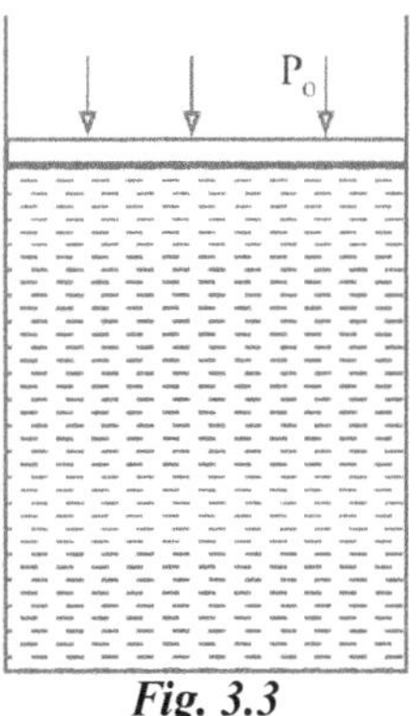

Fig. 3.3

Sol.

The pressure due to weight of the piston, $P = \dfrac{mg}{A}$

Atmospheric pressure $= P_0$

$\therefore$ Total pressure just below the piston $= \dfrac{mg}{A} + P_0$ $\qquad$ *Ans.*

3.7 VARIATION OF LIQUID PRESSURE WITH DEPTH

Consider a liquid of density ρ in static equilibrium. Take a liquid sample contained in an imaginary cylindrical element of area A and thickness dy, at a height y from the bottom of the container. Various forces acting of the element are:

(i) Upward force PA on the bottom of the element.

(ii) Downward force $(P + \Delta P)\,A$ on the top of the element.

(iii) Weight of the liquid in the cylindrical element.

It is $dW = mg = (A\,dy)\rho g$

As the liquid element is in equilibrium, so

$$PA - (P + dP)\,A = dW$$

or $\qquad (-dP)\,A = A(dy)\rho g$

or $\qquad -dP = \rho g\,(dy)$

$\Rightarrow \qquad \dfrac{dP}{dy} = -\rho g$

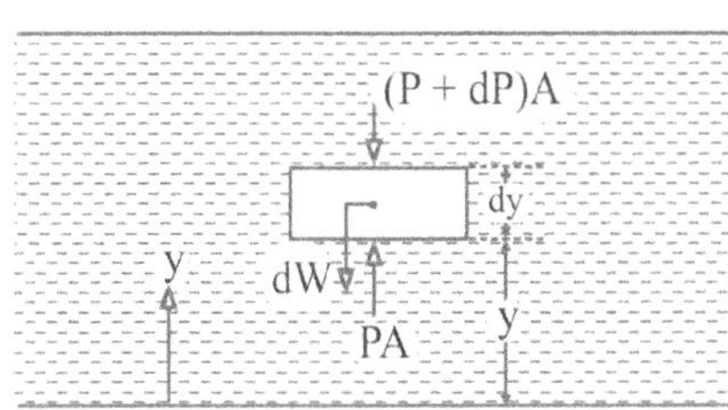

Fig. 3.4

If P_1 and P_2 be the pressures at elevation y_1 and y_2 respectively and assuming ρ and g constant, then on integrating above equation, we get

$$\int_{P_1}^{P_2} dP = \int_{y_1}^{y_2} -\rho g \, dy$$

$$\left[P\right]_{P_1}^{P_2} = -\rho g\left[y\right]_{y_1}^{y_2}$$

$$P_2 - P_1 = -\rho g\,(y_2 - y_1)$$

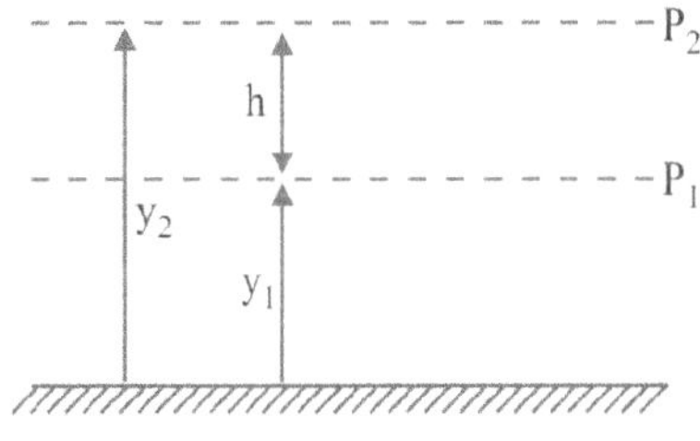

Fig. 3.5

Pressure at a depth h below the free surface can be obtained as:

$$y_2 - y_1 = h$$

If $P_2 = P_0$ (Pressure at free surface of liquid), then pressure P at a depth h,

$$P = P_0 + h\rho g \qquad (P_1 = P)$$

1. If $P_0 = 0$, then $P = h\rho g$.

2. Pressure at any point inside the liquid depends on depth h.

3. Pressure does not depend on the area of cross-section or the shape of the vessel .

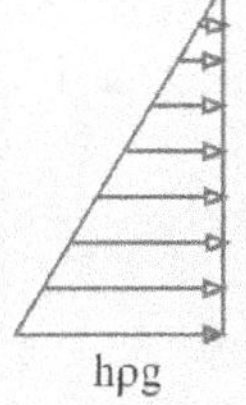

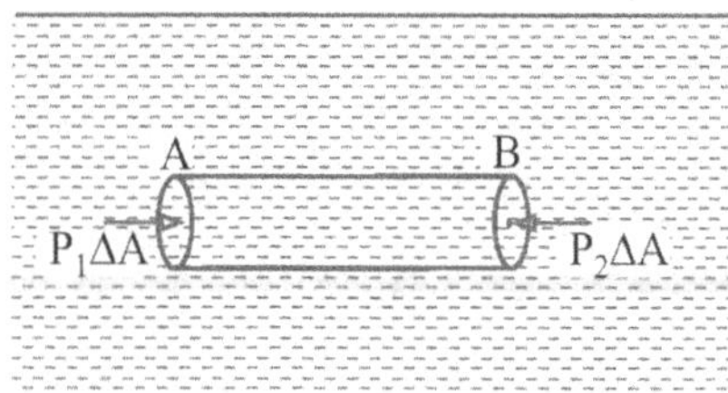

Fig. 3.6

Now consider two points A and B in the same horizontal line inside the liquid. Imagine a small vertical area ΔA containing the point A and a similar vertical area ΔA containing the point B. If the pressure at A and B are P_1 and P_2 respectively, then the forces on element AB are:

(i) $P_1 \Delta A$ towards right and

(ii) $P_2 \Delta A$ towards left.

As the liquid is in static equilibrium, so

$$P_1 \Delta A = P_2 \Delta A \Rightarrow P_1 = P_2$$

Thus, the pressure is same at different points on the same horizontal level.

3.8 PASCAL'S LAW

This law tells about the transmission of pressure in a liquid. It can be stated in the following equivalent ways:

(i)   The pressure exerted at any point on an enclosed liquid is transmitted equally in all directions.

(ii)   A change in pressure applied to an enclosed incompressible liquid is transmitted undiminished to every point of the liquid and the walls of the container.

(iii)   The pressure in a liquid at rest is same at all points if we ignore gravity.

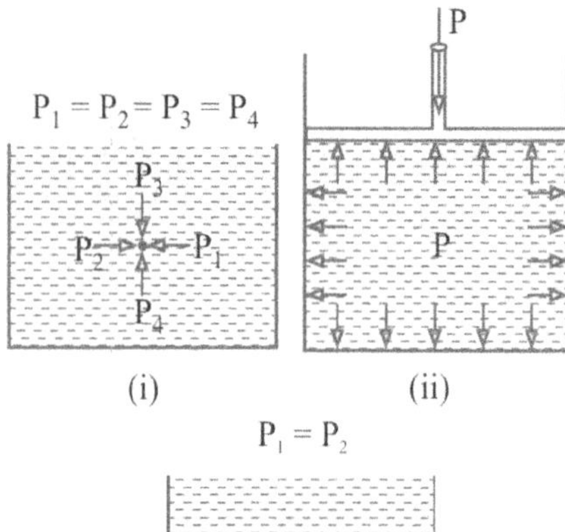

Fig. 3.7

Proof of Pascal's law:

Consider a small element ABC-DEF in the form of a right angled prism inside a liquid at rest.

Suppose the liquid exerts pressure P_a, P_b and P_c on the faces $BEFC$, $ADFC$ and $ADEB$ respectively of the element. If F_a, F_b and F_c are the corresponding forces on these faces, then

$$F_a = P_a (BC)\ell; \quad F_b = P_b(AC)\ell \; ; \quad F_c = P_c (AB)\ell \qquad [AD = BE = CE = \ell]$$

As the element is at rest, so net force on it must be zero. We can write:

For the equilibrium in horizontal direction

$$F_b \sin \theta = F_c$$

or $\qquad P_b (AC)\,\ell \sin \theta = P_c (AB)\,\ell$

or $\qquad P_b \sin \theta = P_c \left(\dfrac{AB}{AC} \right)$

or $\qquad P_b \sin \theta = P_c \sin \theta$

$\therefore \qquad P_b = P_c$

For the equilibrium in vertical direction

$$F_b \cos \theta = F_a$$

$$P_b (AC)\,\ell \cos \theta = P_a (BC)\ell$$

or $\qquad P_b \cos \theta = P_a \left(\dfrac{BC}{AC} \right)$

or $\qquad P_b \cos \theta = P_a \cos \theta$

$\therefore \qquad P_b = P_a$

Hence $\qquad P_a = P_b = P_c$

This proves Pascal's law.

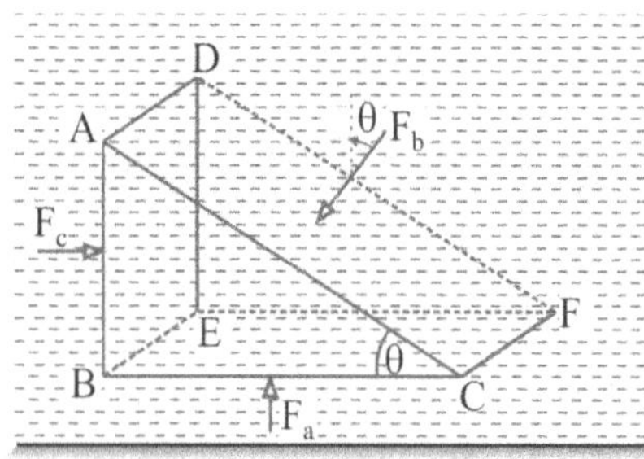

Fig. 3.8

3.9 APPLICATIONS OF PASCAL'S LAW

(i) Hydraulic lift or jack

It is used to lift heavy load (cars, trucks) for small height. A piston of small cross-sectional area 'a' is used to exert a small effort f on a liquid such as oil. The pressure $P = \dfrac{f}{a}$ is transmitted to a larger cylinder equipped with a larger piston of area A through a pipe (see *Fig. 3.9*). According to Pascal's law

Pressure at smaller piston = Pressure at larger piston

or
$$\frac{f}{a} = \frac{W}{A}$$

$$\Rightarrow \qquad W = f\left(\frac{A}{a}\right)$$

As $A > a$, $\quad \therefore \qquad W > f.$

Hence by making $\left(\dfrac{A}{a}\right)$ larger, heavy loads can be lifted by applying small effort.

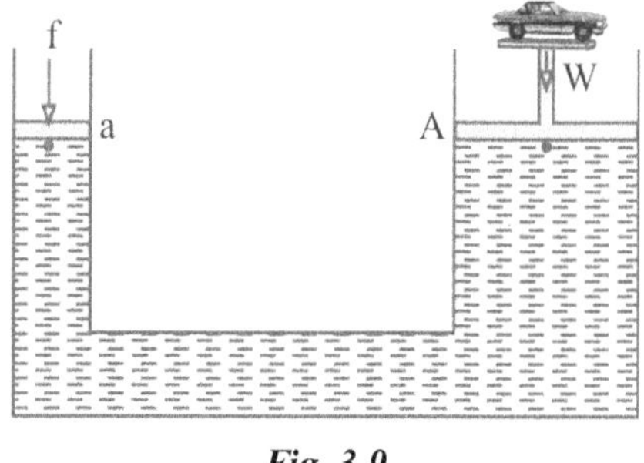

Fig. 3.9

(ii) Hydraulic brakes

Construction : Hydraulic brakes consists of a tube T containing brake oil. One end of this tube is connected to a master cylinder fitted with piston P. The piston P is attached to the brake pedal through a lever system (see *Fig. 3.10*). The other end of the tube is connected to the wheel cylinder having two pistons P_1 and P_2. These pistons are attached to the brake shoes S_1 and S_2. The area of cross-section of the wheel cylinder is larger than that of master cylinder.

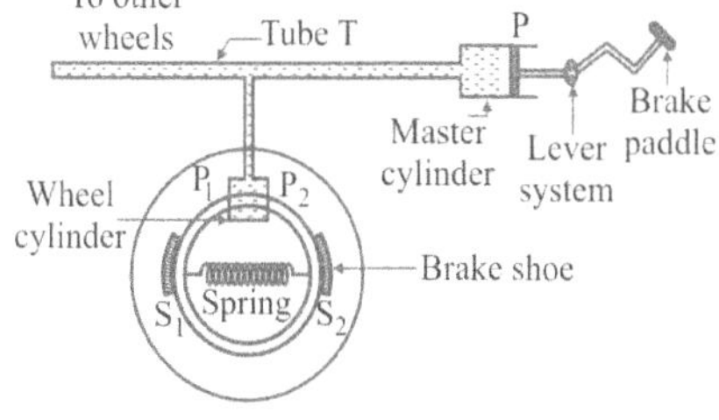

Fig. 3.10 Hydraulic brake.

Working : When the brake pedal is pressed, its lever system pushes the piston P into the master cylinder. By doing this the pressure is transmitted through the oil to the pistons P_1 and P_2. These piston are pushed outwards. The brake shoes get pressed against the inner rim of the wheel, retarding its motion. As the cross-sectional area of wheel cylinder is larger than that of master cylinder, a small force applied to the pedal produces a large retarding force.

Ex. 3 In a car lift compressed air exerts a force F_1 on a small piston having a radius of 5 cm. This pressure is transmitted to a second piston of radius 15 cm. If the mass of the car to be lifted is 1350 kg, what is F_1? What is the pressure necessary to accomplish this task? Take g= 9.81 m/s².

Sol.

As the pressure through air is transmitted equally on both the pistons, so

$$\frac{F_1}{A_1} = \frac{F_2}{A_2}$$

Here
$$F_2 = mg = 1350 \times 9.81 \text{ N}$$

$$\therefore \qquad F_1 = \frac{A_1}{A_2} F_2$$

$$= \frac{\pi r_1^2}{\pi r_2^2} F_2 = \frac{r_1^2}{r_2^2} F_2$$

$$= \frac{5^2}{15^2} \times 1350 \times 9.81$$

$$= 1.47 \times 10^3 \text{ N} \qquad\qquad \textit{Ans.}$$

Required air pressure,

$$P = \frac{F_1}{A_1} = \frac{1.47 \times 10^3}{\pi (0.05)^2}$$

$$= 1.87 \times 10^5 \text{ N/m}^2 \qquad \textit{Ans.}$$

Ex. 4 Two pistons of hydraulic press have diameters of 30.0 cm and 2.5 cm. What is the force exerted by larger piston, when 50.0 kg-wt is placed on the smaller piston? If the stroke of the smaller piston is 4.0 cm, through what distance will be larger piston move after 10 strokes?

Sol.

Radius of the pistons: $r = 1.25$ cm and $R = 15$ cm

As
$$\frac{f}{a} = \frac{F}{A}$$

$$\therefore \qquad F = f\frac{A}{a} = f\frac{\pi R^2}{\pi r^2}$$

$$= f\left(\frac{R}{r}\right)^2 = 50.0\left(\frac{15}{1.25}\right)^2$$

$$= 7200 \text{ kg-wt} \qquad\qquad \textit{Ans.}$$

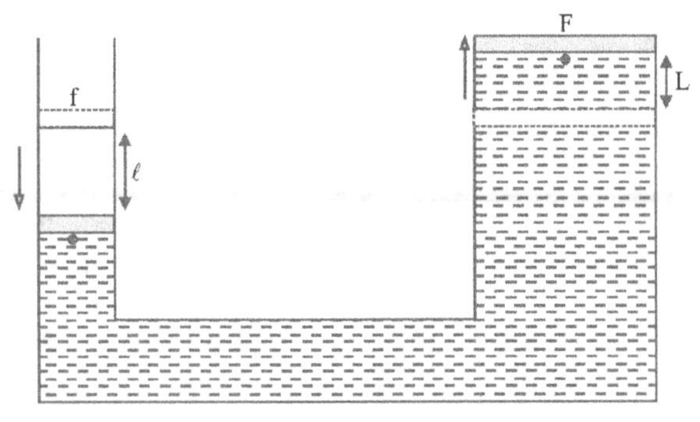

Fig. 3.11

If ℓ and L are the distances moved by the small and large piston in one stroke, then

$$f\ell = FL$$

$$\therefore \quad L = \frac{f\ell}{F}$$

$$= \frac{50 \times 4.0}{7200} = 0.028 \text{cm}$$

The distance moved by larger piston is 10 strokes

$$= 0.028 \times 10 = 0.28 \text{ cm} \qquad \textit{Ans.}$$

Pressure head

The vertical height of the free surface above any point in a liquid at rest is known as pressure head. It is expressed as $h = \dfrac{P}{\rho g}$.

Since the pressure at any point in a liquid depends on the height of the free surface above the point, so it is convenient to express a liquid pressure in terms of pressure head.

Hydrostatic paradox

It was experimentally demonstrated by Pascal that the pressure exerted by a liquid depends only on the height of the liquid and not on the shape of the containing vessel. *Fig. 3.12* shows three vessels of different shapes. When the vessels are filled with the same liquid upto the same height, the pressure meters record the same pressure in all the three vessels, even the amount of liquids is different in the vessels. This apparent result is known as hydrostatic paradox.

Explanation : In vessel A, the pressure exerted by liquid is normal to the wall. The pressure acts horizontally on the walls. The reaction R of the walls is also horizontal.

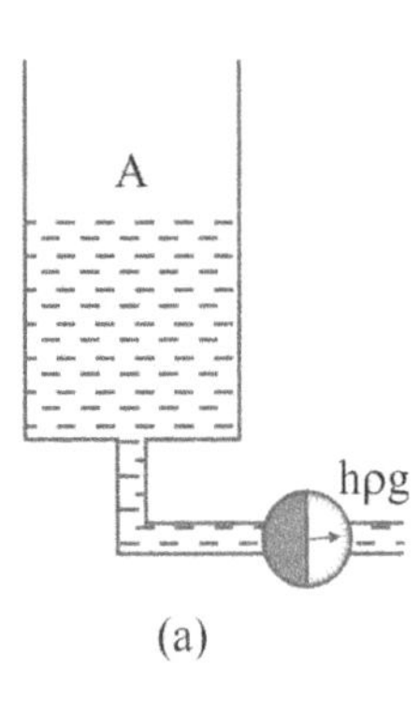

(a)

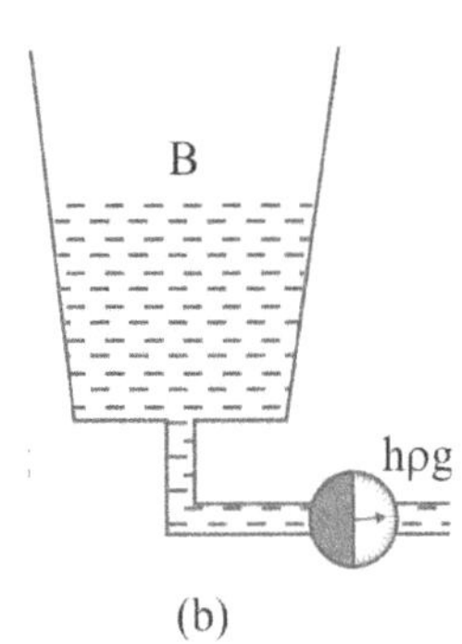

(b)

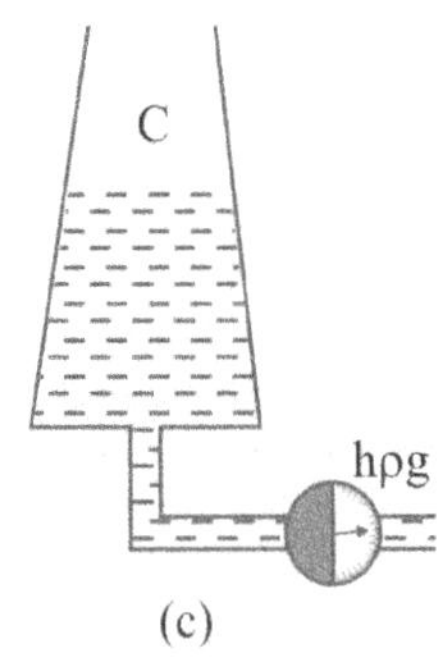

(c)

Fig. 3.12

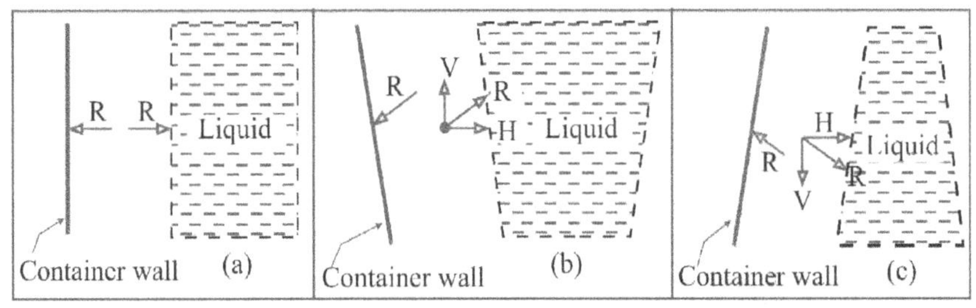

Fig. 3.13

In vessel B, the reaction R of the wall is inclined upwards. The vertical component V of which decreases the downwards thrust due to extra liquid.

In vessel C, the reaction R is involved in the downward direction. The vertical component V of which increases the downwards thrust of the liquid.

If W is the weight of liquid in vessel A and if base area of all the vessels are equal then thrust at the bottom of vessel $P_A = \dfrac{W}{A}$.

Note:

If W_B and W_C are weight of liquids in vessels B and C respectively, then thrust at bottom of vessel B,

$$P_B = \frac{W_B - V}{A} \quad \text{and} \quad P_C = \frac{W_C + V}{A}$$

As
$$P_A = P_B = P_C$$

$$\therefore \quad W_B - V = W \Rightarrow W_B = W + V$$

Also,
$$W_C + V = W \Rightarrow W_C = W - V$$

Atmospheric pressure

Earth is surrounded by different gases. The pressure exerted by atmospheric gases is called atmospheric pressure. The atmospheric pressure at sea level is 1.013×10^5 N/m^2.

3.10 MEASURING PRESSURE

The mercury barometer

Fig. 3.14 shows a mercury barometer which was first deviced by Torricelli. A long glass tube (may be 1m long) is filled with mercury and inverted with its open end in a dish of mercury. The mercury level in the tube falls and comes to rest at a vertical height of 76 cm above the mercury level in the dish.

The space above mercury in the tube is almost a vacuum, so $P_A = 0$. At point C there is only atmospheric pressure, so $P_c = P_a$ which is equal to the pressure at B, because points B and C are at the same level. Thus

$$P_C = P_B$$
$$= P_A + \rho gh$$

As $P_A = 0$, $\qquad \therefore P_C = \rho gh$

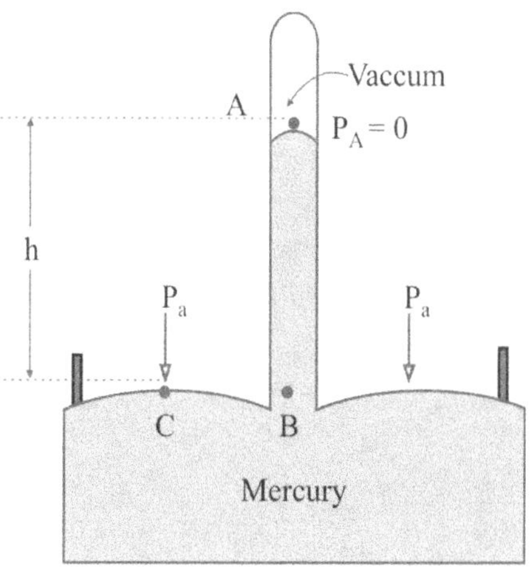

Fig. 3.14 Barometer

For mercury barometer, $h = 76$ cm $= 0.76$ m, $\rho = 13.6 \times 10^3$ kg/m^3

$$\therefore \quad P_c = P_a = 0.76 \times 13.6 \times 10^3 \times 9.81$$
$$= 1.013 \times 10^5 \text{ N/m}^2$$

The open tube manometer

It is used to measure the gauge pressure of the gas. It consists of a U-tube containing a liquid (mercury), with one end of the tube connected to the vessel whose pressure is to be measured.

The total pressure P of the gas is equal to the pressure at A.

By Pascal's law, $P_A = P_B$

or $\qquad\qquad P = P_a + \rho gh$

or $\qquad\qquad P - P_a = \rho gh$

or $\qquad\qquad P - P_a = \rho gh$

Here $P - P_a$ is the gauge pressure of the gas.

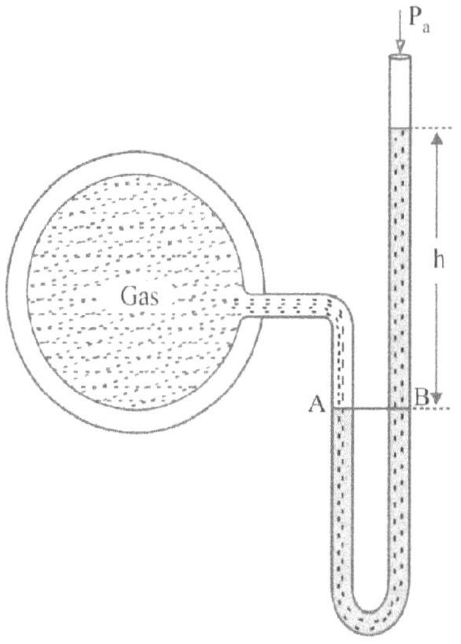

Fig. 3.15. Manometer.

Absolute pressure and gauge pressure

Fluid pressure may be measured with respect to any arbitrary reference level (datum). The two most commonly used datum are (i) absolute zero pressure and (ii) local atmospheric pressure. When pressure is measured above absolute zero, it is called an absolute pressure. When it is measured either above or below atmospheric pressure as a datum, it is called gauge pressure. Thus

Gauge pressure = Absolute pressure – Atmospheric pressure

or $\qquad\qquad P_{gauge} = P_{absolute} - P_a$

or $\qquad$ we can write $P_{absolute} = P_{gauge} + P_a$

Height of atmosphere

In actual practice the value of g and density of air decrease with height, so the atmosphere extends with decreasing pressure even beyond hundreds of kilometer. Making the following assumptions:

(i)   The density of air, assuming constant $\rho = 1.3$ kg/m^3.

(ii)   Temperature remains constant throughout the atmosphere.

(iii)   The value of g does not change with height.

       Atmospheric pressure $P_a = \rho gh$

$$\therefore \qquad h = \frac{P_a}{\rho g} = \frac{1.013 \times 10^3}{1.3 \times 9.81} = 7950 \text{ m} \approx 8 \text{ km}$$

Isothermal atmosphere

If it is assumed that pressure P and density ρ vary according to isothermal condition, then according to gas law, we have

$$PV = \frac{m}{M}RT$$

and

$$P\Delta V = \frac{\Delta m}{M}RT$$

or

$$P = \left(\frac{\Delta m/\Delta V}{M}\right)RT$$

or

$$P = \rho\left(\frac{RT}{M}\right)$$

Also

$$P_0 = \rho_0\left(\frac{RT}{M}\right)$$

$$\therefore \quad \frac{P}{P_0} = \frac{\rho}{\rho_0} \Rightarrow \rho = \left(\frac{P}{P_0}\right)\rho_0$$

where P_0 and ρ_0 are the values of the pressure and density of the air at reference level (At ground level).

We know that

$$dP = -\rho g\, dy$$

$$= -\left(\frac{P\rho_0}{P_0}\right)g\, dy$$

$$\therefore \quad \frac{dP}{P} = \frac{\rho_0 g}{P_0}(-dy)$$

Integrating above equation, we have

$$\int_{P_0}^{P}\frac{dP}{P} = -\frac{\rho_0 g}{P_0}\int_{0}^{h} dy$$

$$\left|lnP\right|_{P_0}^{P} = \frac{-\rho_0 g}{P_0}\left|y\right|_{0}^{h}$$

$$ln\frac{P}{P_0} = \frac{-\rho_0 g h}{P_0}$$

or

$$P = P_0 e^{-\rho_0 gh/P_0}$$

Differential Manometer

It is used to measure pressure difference between two points. Pressure difference between the points A and B can be obtained as:

By Pascal's law

$$P_M = P_N$$

or

$$P_A + \rho_3 g(x+y+z) = P_B + \rho_2 gx + \rho_1 gy$$

$$\therefore \quad P_A - P_B = (\rho_2 - \rho_3)gx + (\rho_1 - \rho_3)gy - \rho_3 gz$$

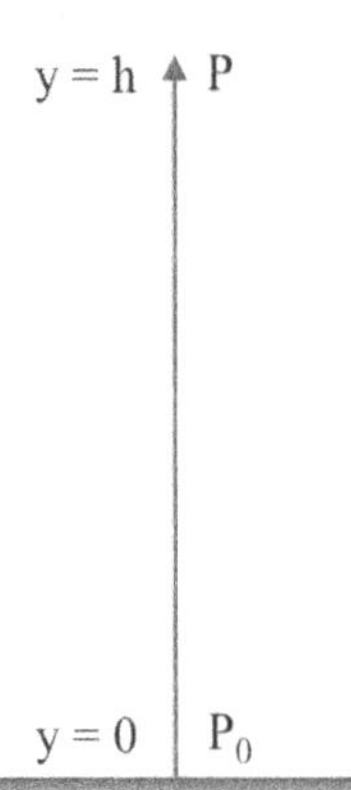

Fig. 3.16. Manometer.

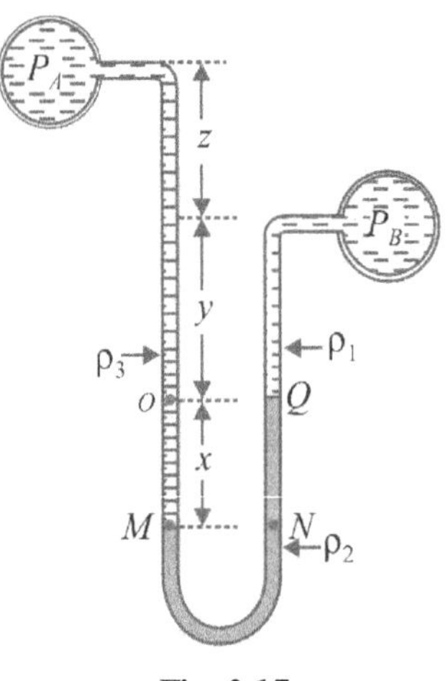

Fig. 3.17

Ex. 5 What is the pressure on a swimmer 10 m below the surface of a lake? Take atmospheric pressure = 1×10^5 N/m^2.

Sol.

Pressure at any depth h from the free surface of the water is given by

$$P = \rho g h + P_a$$
$$= (1000) \times 9.8 \times 10 + 1.0 \times 10^5$$
$$= 1.98 \text{ N/m}^2 \qquad Ans.$$

Ex. 6 What will be the length of mercury column in a barometer tube, when the atmospheric pressure is 75 cm of mercury and the tube is inclined at an angle of 60° with the horizontal direction?

Sol.

The barometric height $h = 75$ cm

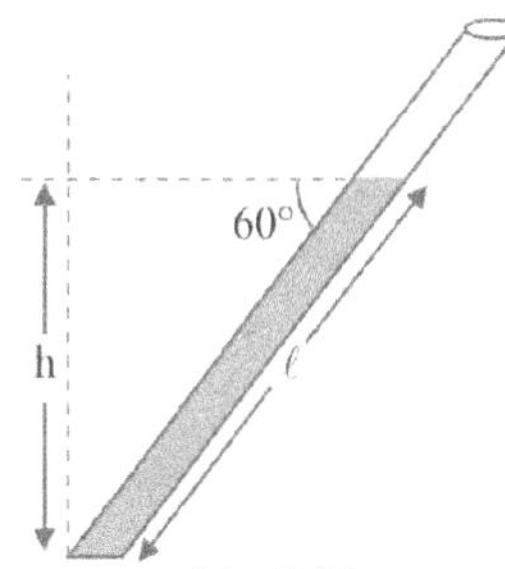

Fig. 3.18

If ℓ is the length of the mercury column in the tube,

then $\qquad \dfrac{h}{\ell} = \sin 60°$

or $\qquad \ell = \dfrac{h}{\sin 60°} = \dfrac{75}{\left(\sqrt{3}/2\right)}$

$$= 86.6 \text{ cm}. \qquad Ans.$$

Ex. 7 A U-tube contains water and methylated spirit separated by mercury. The mercury columns in the two arms are in level with 10.0 cm of water in one arm and 12.5 cm of spirit in the other. What is the specific gravity of spirit?

Sol.

As the mercury column in the two arms of the U-tube are the same, so
$$P_A = P_B$$

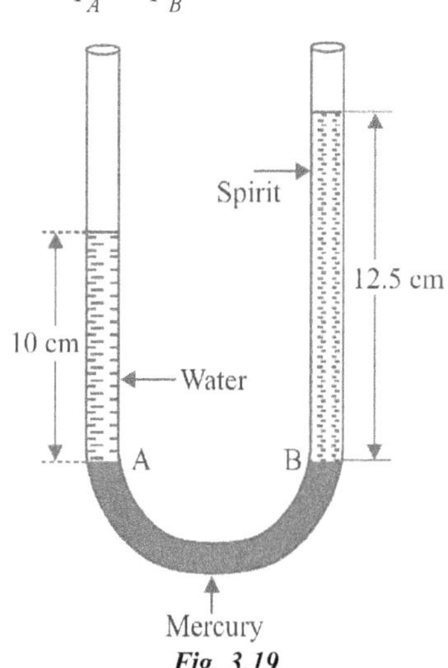

Fig. 3.19

or $\qquad \rho_w g h_w = \rho_s g h_s$

or $\qquad \dfrac{\rho_s}{\rho_w} = \dfrac{h_w}{h_s}$

$$= \dfrac{10}{12.5} = 0.8 \qquad Ans.$$

Thus specific gravity of spirit is 0.8.

Ex. 8 What is the absolute and gauge pressure of the gas above the liquid surface in the tank shown in *Fig. 3.20*. Density of oil = 820 kg/m^3, density of mercury = 13.6×10^3 kg/m^3. Given 1 atmospheric pressure = 1.01×10^5 N/m^2.

Sol.

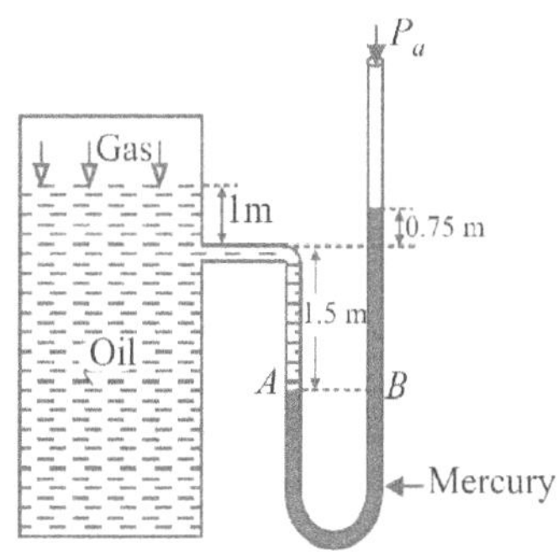

Fig. 3.20

Suppose P_{gas} is the pressure of the gas on the oil. As the points A and B are at the same level in the mercury columns, so
$$P_A = P_B$$

or $\qquad P_{gas} + \rho_{oil} \, gh_{oil} = P_a + \rho_{Hg} \, g \, h_{Hg}$

or $P_{gas} + 820 \times 9.8 \times (1 + 1.50) =$

$$P_a + 13.6 \times 10^3 \times 9.8 \times (1.5 + 0.75)$$

or $P_{gas} + 20.09 \times 10^3 = P_a + 299.88 \times 10^3$

$\therefore \qquad P_{gas} - Pa = 299.88 \times 10^3 - 20.09 \times 10^3$

or $\qquad [P_{gas}]_{gauge} = 279.8 \times 10^3 \text{ N/m}^2$

$$= 2.8 \times 10^5 \text{ N/m}^2 \qquad Ans.$$

Absolute pressure of gas

$$[P_{gas}]_{absolute} = [P_{gas}]_{gauge} + P_a$$
$$= 2.8 \times 10^5 + 1.01 \times 10^5$$
$$= 3.81 \times 10^5 \text{ N/m}^2 \qquad Ans.$$

Ex. 9 A U-tube in which the cross-sectional area of the limb on the left is one third of the limb on the right contains mercury (density 13.6 g/cm^3). The level of mercury in the narrow limb extends to a distance of 30 cm from the upper end of the tube. What will be the rise in the level of mercury in the right limb. If the left limb is filled to the top with water (neglect surface tension effects).

Sol.

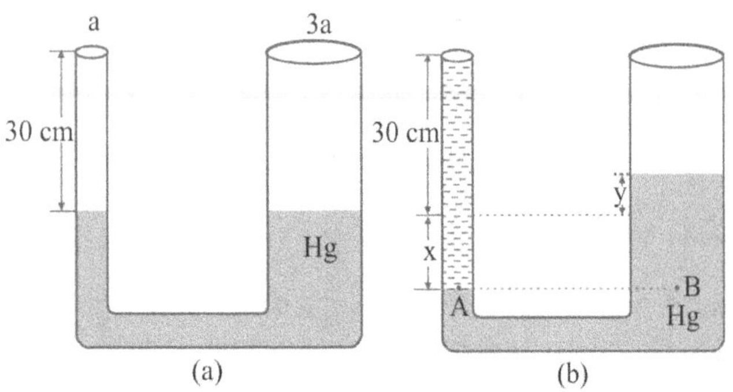

Fig. 3.21

Suppose area of cross-section of narrow limb is a, then area of cross-section of right limb will be $3a$. Let level of mercury in left limb falls by x and the rise of level in right limb is y, then

$$ax = (3a)y$$

or $$x = 3y$$

According to Pascal's law, $P_A = P_B$

or $$(30 + x)\rho_w g = (x + y)\rho_{Hg}\, g$$

$$(30 + 3y) \times 1 \times g = (3y + y) \times 13.6 \times g$$

$$\Rightarrow \qquad y = 0.58\ \text{cm} \qquad \textbf{\textit{Ans.}}$$

Ex. 10 A thin tube, sealed at both ends is 1.0 m long. It lies horizontally, the middle 0.1m containing mercury and the two equal ends containing air at standard atmospheric pressure. If the tube now turned to vertical position, by what amount will the column of mercury be displaced? (Standard atmospheric pressure = 0.76 m of Hg)

Sol.

Let a be the cross-sectional area of the tube. When the tube is in horizontal position, the length of air column on either side of mercury is 0.45m.

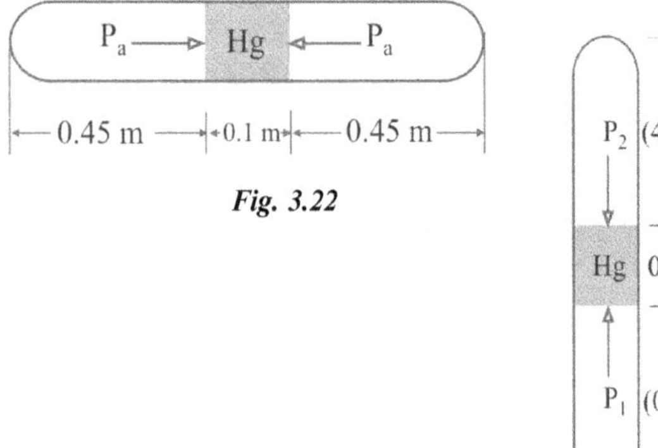

Fig. 3.22

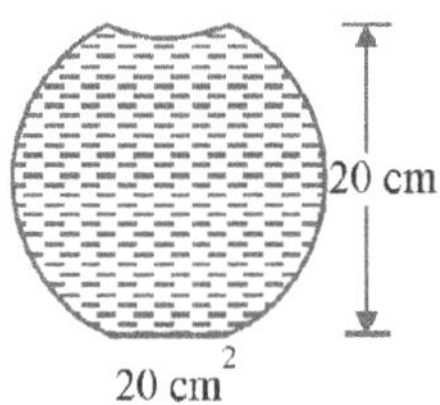

Fig. 3.23

When tube is placed in vertical position, let the mercury level is displaced down by x. Therefore the length of air column in lower portion of tube becomes $(0.45 - x)$ and in upper portion it becomes $(0.45 + x)$ (assuming mercury as incompressible).

Using Boyle's law, i.e PV = Constant, we have

$$P_a\,(0.45a) = P_1\,(0.45 - x)a \qquad \ldots\text{(i)}$$

Also $$P_a\,(0.45a) = P_2\,(0.45 + x)a \qquad \ldots\text{(ii)}$$

and $$P_1 = P_2 + 0.1 \text{ of Hg} \qquad \ldots\text{(iii)}$$

Given, $$P_a = 0.76 \text{ m of Hg}$$

From equations (i) and (ii), we have

$$P_1 = \frac{0.45 P_a}{0.45 - x}$$

and $$P_2 = \frac{0.45 P_a}{0.45 + x}$$

Substituting these values in equation (iii), we get

$$x = 0.0295\ \text{m} \qquad \textbf{\textit{Ans.}}$$

Ex. 11 A glass full of water has a bottom of area 20 cm², top of area 20 cm², height 20 cm and volume half a litre.

(a)   Find the force exerted by the water on the bottom.

(b)   Considering the equilibrium of the water, find the resultant force exerted by the sides of the glass on the water. Atmospheric pressure = 1.0×10^5 N/m² . Density of water = 1000 kg/m³ and g = 10 m/s².

Sol.

(a)   The pressure intensity at the bottom of the container is

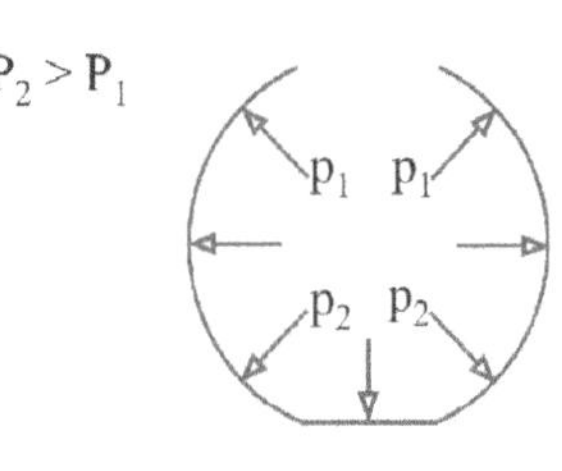

Fig. 3.24

$$P = h\rho g = 0.20 \times 1000 \times 10 = 2 \times 10^3 \text{ N/m}^2$$

Force at the bottom of container

$$= P \times \text{base area}$$
$$= 2 \times 10^3 \times (20 \times 10^{-4})$$
$$= 4\ \text{N}$$

(Force exerted by water only) **_Ans._**

(b)   Weight of the water in the container

$$= \text{Volume} \times \text{density of water} \times g$$
$$= 0.5 \times 10^3 \times 1000 \times 10 = 5\ \text{N}$$

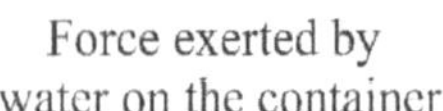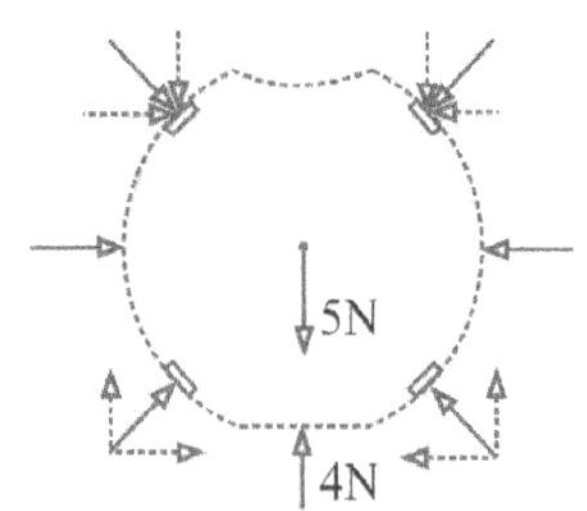

Force exerted by   Force exerted by
water on the container   container on water

Fig. 3.25

From the diagram, the force exerted by the container is in upward direction (because $(P_2 > P_1)$). Let force exerted by sides of container is F, then

$$\therefore \qquad 4 + F = 5\ N$$

$$\Rightarrow \qquad F = 1\ N \qquad \textbf{\textit{Ans.}}$$

Ex. 12 A tube 1 cm² in cross- section is attached to the top of a vessel 1 cm high and of cross- section 100 cm². Water is powered into the system, filling it to a depth of 100 cm above the bottom of the vessel.

(a) What is the force exerted by the water against the bottom of the vessel?

(b) What is the weight of the water in the vessel?

(c) Explain why (a) and (b) are not equal.

Sol.

(a) Intensity of pressure at the bottom of the container is

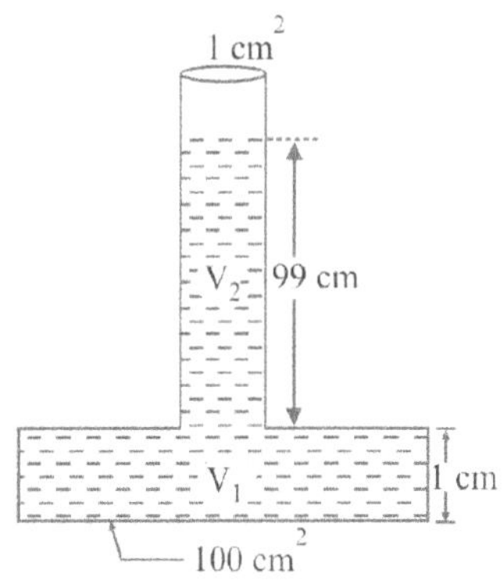

Fig. 3.26

$$P = h\rho g$$
$$= 1 \times 1000 \times 10$$
$$= 1 \times 10^4 \text{ N/m}^2$$

Force exerted by water at the bottom

$$F = P \times A$$
$$= (1 \times 10^4) \times (100 \times 10^{-4})$$
$$= 100 \text{ N}$$

(b) Weight of the water in the container

$$W = (V_1 + V_2)\,\rho\, g$$
$$= [100 \times 10^{-4} \times 1 \times 10^{-2} + 1$$
$$\times 10^{-4} \times 99 \times 10^{-2}] \times 1000 \times 10$$
$$= 1.99 \text{ N}$$

(c) As we have seen in (a) and (b) the thrust of water at the bottom of the vessel is greater than the weight of the water. It is because of the force exerted by the top face of the vessel on the water. Water transfer this force to the bottom of the vessel.

3.11 HYDROSTATIC FORCE ON SURFACES

Total pressure and centre of pressure

When a static fluid comes in contact with a surface, either plane or curved, a normal force is exerted by the fluid on the surface. This force is known as total pressure. The point of application of total pressure on the surface is known as centre of pressure.

(i) **Total pressure on a plane horizontal surface**

Consider a plane surface inside a liquid of density ρ, such that it is held in a horizontal position at a depth h below the free surface of the liquid as shown in *Fig. 3.27*. Since every point on the surface is at the same depth h, so the intensity of pressure is constant over the entire surface, being equal to ρgh. Thus if A is the area of the surface, then the total pressure on the horizontal surface is

$$F = PA = \rho gh A.$$

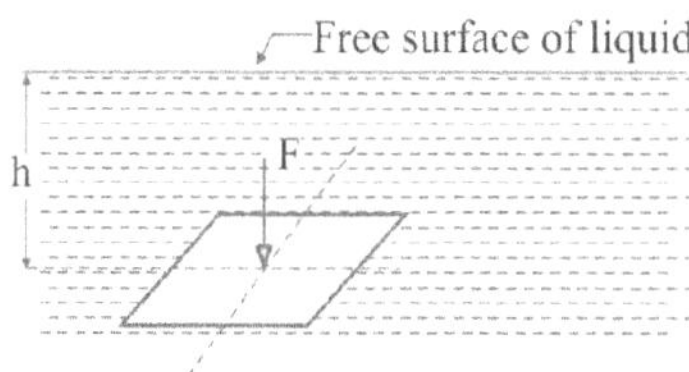

Fig. 3.27

(ii) **Total pressure on inclined/vertical plane surface**

Consider a plane surface of length 'a' and width 'b' which is inside a liquid of density ρ as shown in the *Fig. 3.28*.

Choose an element of length (dy) at a distance y from O.

The depth of the element $\quad h = y \cos\theta$

The intensity of pressure at the position of element

$$P = \rho gh = \rho g\,(y\cos\theta)$$

The force on the element, $\quad dF = P\,(bdy)$
$$= \rho\, g\,(y\cos\theta)\, bdy$$
$$= \rho\, gb\cos\theta\; y(dy)$$

The force on the entire surface, $F = \displaystyle\int_{\ell}^{(\ell+a)} dF$

$$= \rho\, g\, b\cos\theta \int_{\ell}^{(\ell+a)} y\, dy$$

$$= \rho g\,\frac{b\cos\theta}{2}\Big|y^2\Big|_{\ell}^{(\ell+a)}$$

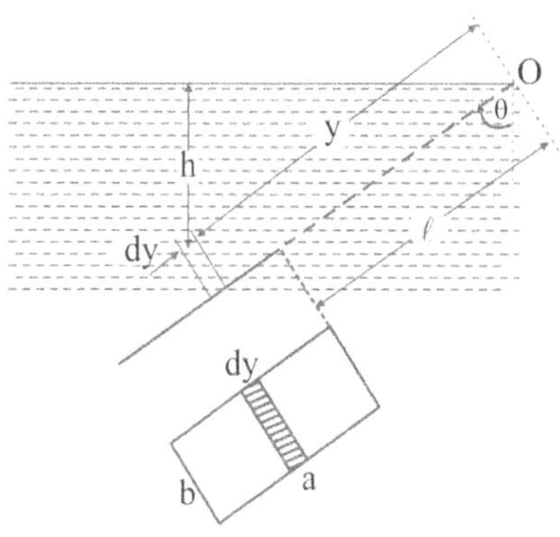

Fig. 3.28

or
$$F = \rho g b \frac{\cos\theta}{2}\left[(\ell+a)^2 - \ell^2\right]$$

$$F = \frac{\rho g b \cos\theta}{2}\left[a^2 + 2a\ell\right]$$

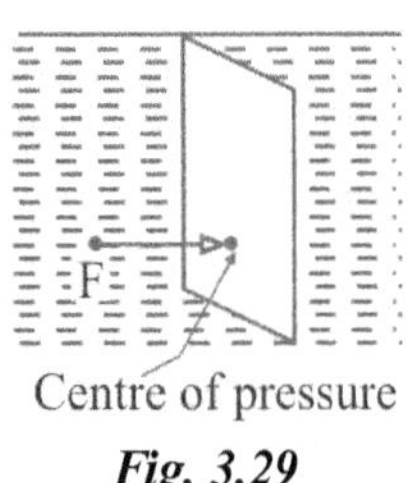

Centre of pressure

Fig. 3.29

Special cases

(i) For $\ell = 0$,
$$F = \frac{\rho g b \cos\theta}{2}\left[a^2 + 0\right]$$

$$= \frac{1}{2}\rho g b a^2 \cos\theta$$

(ii) For $\ell = 0$, and $\theta = 0°$,
$$F = \frac{1}{2}\rho g b \cos 0° \, a^2$$

$$= \frac{\rho g b a^2}{2}$$

Pressure diagram

Net force (total pressure) as well as point of application of force (centre of pressure) for a plane surface wholly submerged in a static liquid, either vertically or inclined, may also be determined by drawing a pressure diagram. A pressure diagram is a graphical representation of the variation of the pressure intensity over a surface. Such a diagram may be prepared by plotting to some convenient scale the pressure intensities at various points on the surface.

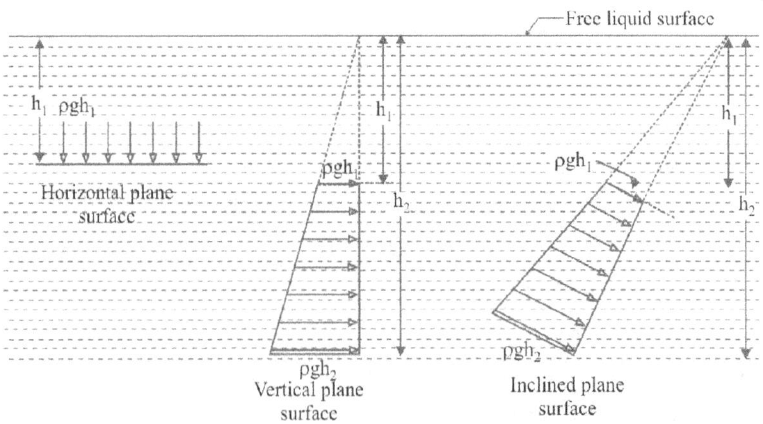

Fig. 3.30

Since force at any point acts in the direction normal to the surface, the pressure intensities at various points on the surface are plotted normal to the surface. Figure shows typical pressure diagrams for horizontal, vertical and inclined plane surfaces. Consider a rectangular plane surface of depth a and width b, held vertically in a static liquid of density ρ as shown in *Fig. 3.32*. Let top and bottom edges of the plane surface be at vertical depth of h_1 and h_2 respectively below the free surface of the liquid. The pressure intensity at the top edge, $P_1 = \rho g h_1$

The pressure intensity at the bottom edge, $P_2 = \rho g h_2$. As the pressure intensity increases

linearly from $\rho g h_1$ to $\rho g h_2$, so the average pressure intensity over the entire surface,

$$P_{av} \;=\; \frac{P_1 + P_2}{2}$$

$$=\; \rho g \left(\frac{h_1 + h_2}{2} \right)$$

Thus the net force on the vertical surface

$$F \;=\; P_{av} \times \text{Area of the surface}$$

or

$$F \;=\; \rho g \left(\frac{h_1 + h_2}{2} \right) \times ab$$

Force on curved surface

Consider a curved surface inside a static liquid of density ρ. *Fig. 3.34* shows the trace of the curved surface which extends in the direction normal to the plane of the paper. At any point on the curved surface the force acts normal to the surface. Choose a small element of area dA of the curved surface lying at a vertical depth of h below the free surface of the liquid. The force on the element

$$dF \;=\; P(dA) = \rho g h(dA) \qquad \text{...(i)}$$

The force dF acting on the element can be resolved into horizontal and vertical components

$$dF_H \;=\; dF \sin\theta = \rho g h(dA) \sin\theta \qquad \text{...(ii)}$$

and

$$dF_V \;=\; dF \cos\theta = \rho g h(dA) \cos\theta \qquad \text{...(iii)}$$

Here θ is the inclination of the elementary area with the horizontal. The total horizontal and vertical components of the force can be obtained by integrating equations (ii) and (iii), so

$$F_H \;=\; \int dF_H = \rho g \int h(dA) \sin\theta \qquad \text{...(iv)}$$

and

$$F_V \;=\; \int dF_V = \rho g \int h(dA) \cos\theta \qquad \text{...(v)}$$

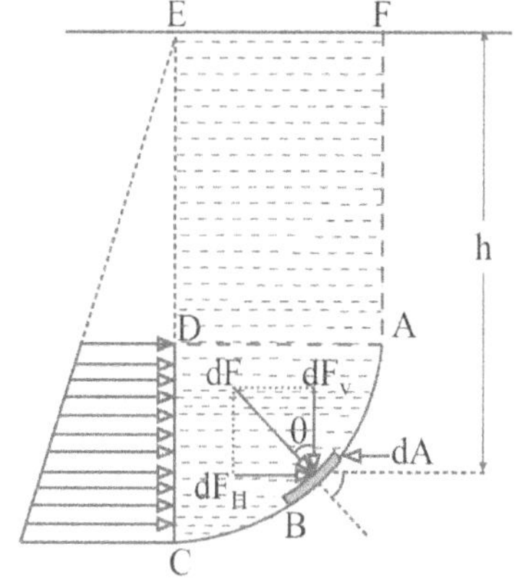

Fig. 3.31

In equation (iv) $(dA \sin\theta)$ is the vertical projection of the area dA and in equation (v), $(dA \cos\theta)$ is the horizontal projection of the elementary area dA. Thus $\rho g \int h(dA) \sin\theta$ represents the total force on the vertical projection of the curved surface. i.e.,

$$F_H \;=\; \begin{bmatrix} \text{Total force on the projected area of the} \\ \text{curved surface on the vertical plane, the} \\ \text{trace of which is represented by CD} \end{bmatrix}$$

Further $\rho g \int h(dA) \cos\theta$ represents the total force on the horizontal projection of the curved surface, and it is equal to the weight of the liquid contained in the portion extending above the curved surface in the portion $ABCDEFA$. i.e.,

$$F_v \;=\; \begin{bmatrix} \text{The weight of the liquid contained in the portion} \\ \text{extending vertically above the curved surface upto} \\ \text{the free surface of the liquid.} \end{bmatrix}$$

The resultant force on the curved surface $F = \sqrt{F_H^2 + F_V^2}$.

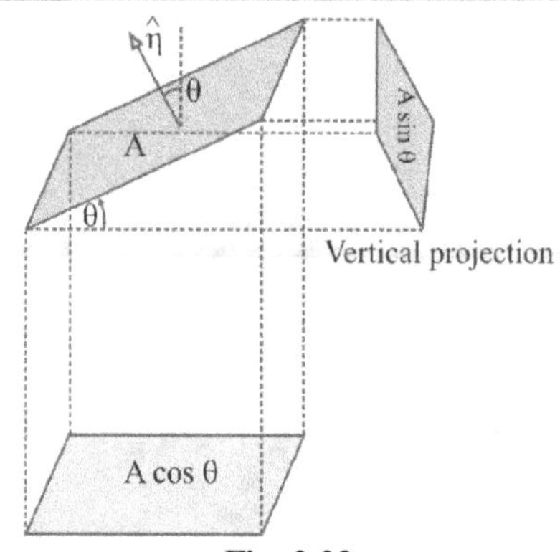

Fig. 3.32

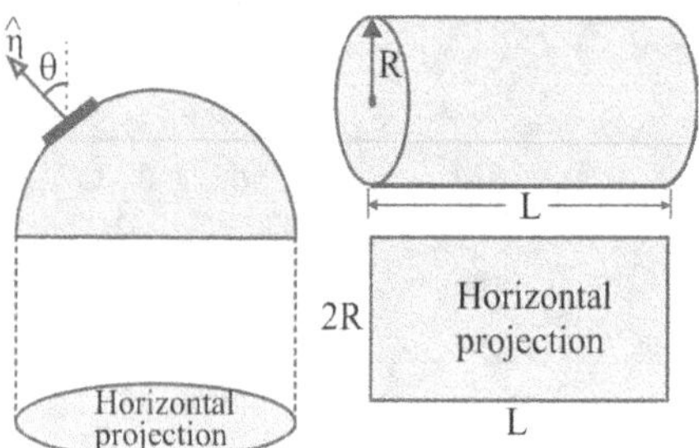

Fig. 3.33

About projected area

1. Horizontal and vertical projection of area $\vec{A}$: (*Fig.* 3.32)

   Horizontal projection of $\vec{A}$ $\qquad = A\cos\theta$

   Vertical projection of $\vec{A}$ $\qquad = A\sin\theta$

2. Horizontal projection of hemisphere of radius R:

   Consider a small element of area ΔA, its horizontal projection

   $$= \Delta A\cos\theta$$

   The horizontal projection of whole hemisphere

   $$A_H \;=\; \sum \Delta A\cos\theta$$

   $$=\; \pi R^2 \quad (\textit{Fig. } 3.33)$$

3. Horizontal projection of the cylinder of radius R and length $L = 2RL$.

Ex. 13 Suppose water stands at a depth of H behind the vertical face of a dam of width L. Find force exerted by the water on the wall and centre of pressure.

Sol.

Choose an element of thickness (dy) at a depth y. The pressure at the position of the element

$$P \;=\; \rho g y$$

The force on the element $\quad dF \;=\; P\,(Ldy)$

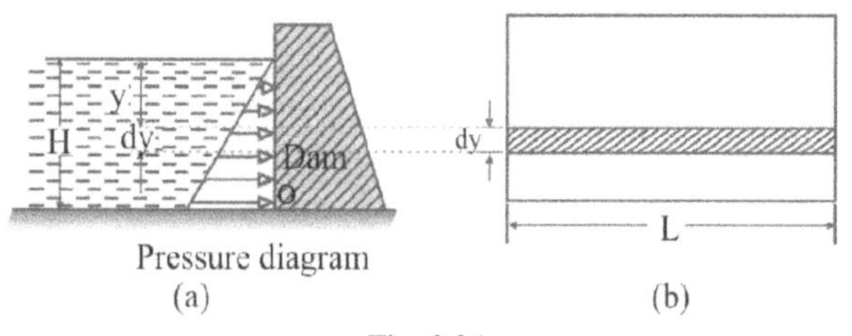

Pressure diagram
(a) $\hspace{6cm}$ (b)

Fig. 3.34

or $\hspace{3cm} dF \;=\; \rho\, gy\,(Ldy) = \rho\, gL\,(ydy)$

The total force on the dam

$$F \;=\; \int_0^H dF = \rho g L \int_0^H y\,dy$$

$$=\; \frac{\rho g L}{2}\Big|y^2\Big|_0^H$$

or $\hspace{3cm} F \;=\; \frac{\rho g L H^2}{2}$

Centre of pressure

The moment of the force dF about an axis through O

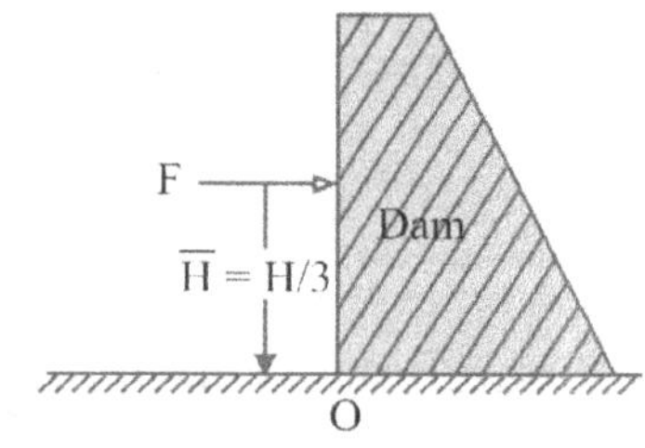

Fig. 3.35

or torque $\hspace{2cm} d\tau \;=\; dF\,(H-y)$

$$=\; \rho g L\,(ydy)(H-y)$$

$$=\; \rho g L (Hy - y^2)dy$$

Net torque $\hspace{1.5cm} \tau \;=\; \rho g L \int_0^H (Hy - y^2)dy$

$$=\; \rho g L \left|\frac{Hy^2}{2} - \frac{y^3}{3}\right|_0^H$$

$$=\; \rho g L \left(\frac{H^3}{2} - \frac{H^3}{3}\right)$$

$$\tau \;=\; \frac{1}{6}\rho g L H^3$$

If $\bar{H}$ is the height above O at which the total force F would have to act to produce this torque, then

$$F\,\bar{H} = \tau$$

or

$$\bar{H} = \frac{\tau}{F} = \frac{\dfrac{1}{6}\rho g L H^3}{\dfrac{\rho g L H^2}{2}} = \frac{H}{3}$$

Ex. 14
To what height should a cylindrical vessel of radius R be filled with a homogeneous liquid to make the force with which the liquid presses on the sides of the vessel equal to the force exerted by the liquid on the bottom of the vessel?

Sol.

Let h be the height of the liquid in the vessel.
The average pressure at the side of the vessel

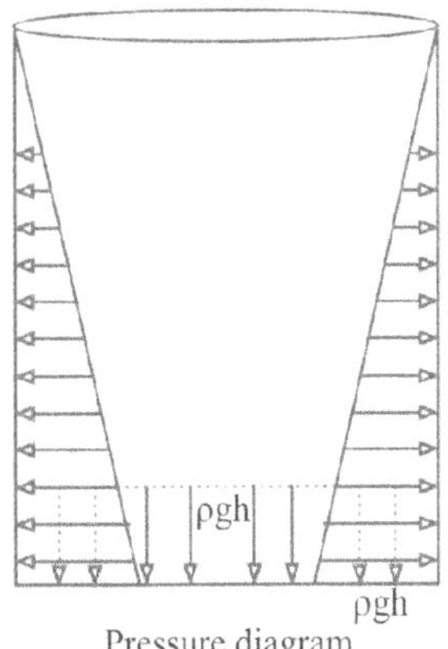

Pressure diagram

Fig. 3.36

$$P_{av} = \frac{0+\rho gh}{2} = \frac{\rho gh}{2}$$

Force at the side of vessel, $F_{side} = P_{av}\,(2\pi Rh)$

$$= \left(\frac{\rho gh}{2}\right)(2\pi Rh)$$

The pressure at the bottom of the vessel remain uniform,

$$P = \rho gh$$

Force at the bottom of the vessel,

$$F_{bottom} = P\left(\pi R^2\right)$$

$$= \rho gh\left(\pi R^2\right)$$

Given, $\qquad F_{side} = F_{bottom}$

or $\qquad \dfrac{\rho gh}{2}(2\pi Rh) = \rho gh(\pi R^2)$

$\Rightarrow \qquad h = R \qquad$ *Ans.*

Ex. 15
Compute the resultant force on the gate AB as a result of hydrostatic pressure *Fig. 3.37*. The gate is 1.5 m wide. Determine the line of action of this force.

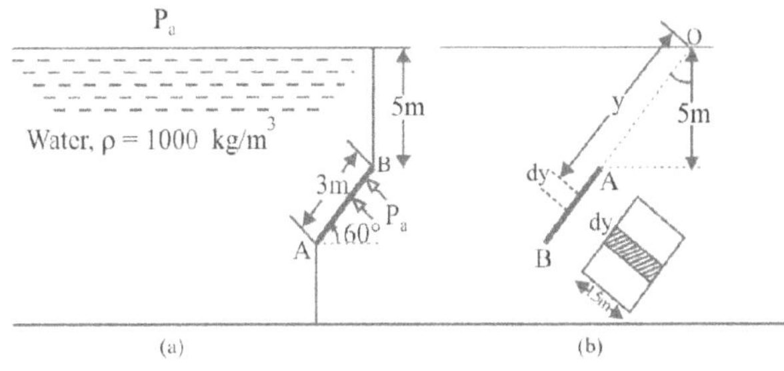

Fig. 3.37

Sol.

From the figure (b) distance $OA = \dfrac{5}{\sin 60°} = 5.77\,\text{m}$

The distance $OB = 3+5.77 = 8.77$ m

Choose a small strip of the gate of length (dy) at a distance y from O. The pressure intensity at the position of the strip,

$$P = \rho g(y\sin 60°) = 0.87\rho gy$$

The force of this strip, $\qquad dF = P\,(1.5dy)$

$$= 0.87\,\rho gy \times 1.5(dy)$$

$$= 1.305\,\rho gy\;(dy)$$

The resultant force on the gate

$$F = 1.305\,\rho\,g\int_{OA}^{OB} ydy = 1.305\,\rho g\left.\frac{y^2}{2}\right|_{5.77}^{8.77}$$

$$= 1.305\times 1000\times 9.8\times\left(\frac{8.77^2-5.77^2}{2}\right)$$

$$= 2.78\times 10^5\,N \qquad\qquad\qquad \textit{Ans.}$$

The effect of air pressure get cancelled out from both sides of the gate. To find the line of action of this force, assume that resultant force acts at a distance $\bar{y}$ from O, now equal the moment of this resultant about O with the moment of the distribution about the same axis. Thus

$$F\,\bar{y} = \int_{5.77}^{8.77} (dF)\,y$$

$$= \int_{5.77}^{8.77} 1.305\rho gy(dy)\,y$$

$$= 1.305\rho g\int_{5.77}^{8.77} y^2 dy$$

$$= 1.305\,\rho g\left.\frac{y^3}{3}\right|_{5.77}^{8.77}$$

$$\therefore\quad \bar{y} = \frac{1.305\rho g}{F}\left(\frac{8.77^3-5.77^3}{3}\right)$$

$$= \frac{1.305\times 1000\times 9.8}{2.78\times 10^5}\left(\frac{8.77^3-5.77^3}{3}\right) = 7.4\,\text{m}$$

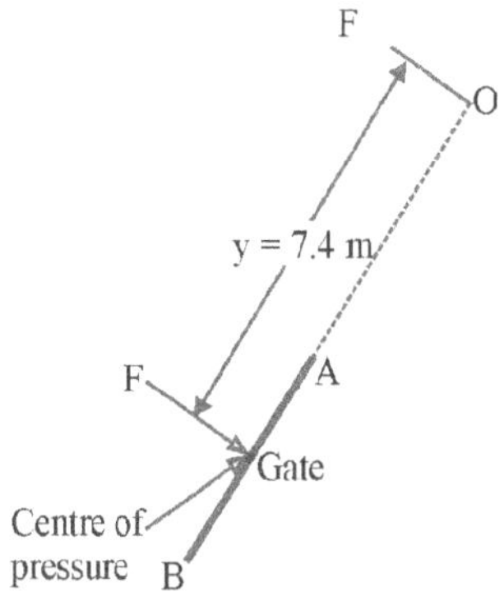

Fig. 3.38

Ex. 16 A conical cup of height b, semivertical angle α rests open end down on a flat surface as shown in *Fig. 3.39*. The cup is filled to height h with liquid of density ρ. What is the upward lifting force on the cup?

Sol.

Let W is the weight of the liquid and F is the thrust of the liquid at the bottom of the container, then for equilibrium of the liquid

$$F = W + F_v$$

where F_v is the vertical force.

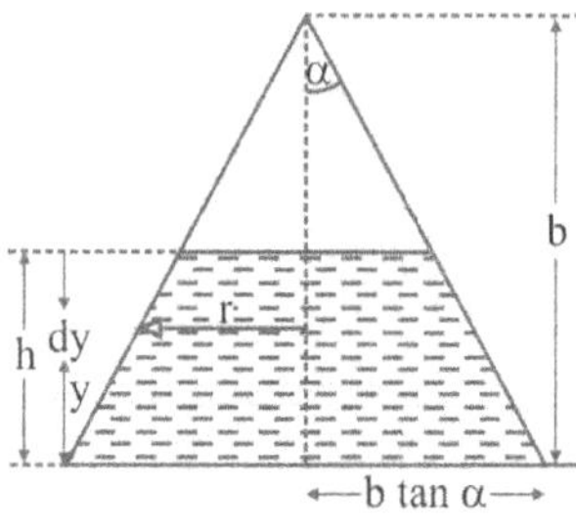

Fig. 3.39

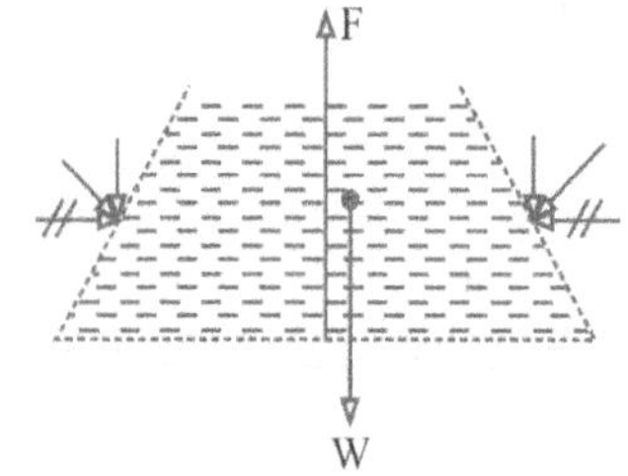

Fig. 3.40

$\therefore$

$$F_v = F - W \qquad \ldots(i)$$

$$F = P \times \text{base area}$$

$$= (\rho g h) \times \pi (b \tan \alpha)^2$$

$$= \pi \rho g h b^2 \times \tan^2 \alpha$$

$$W = (\rho \times \text{volume}) g$$

$$= g\rho \int_0^h \pi r^2 dy$$

$$= \pi g \rho \int_0^h \left[(b - y)\tan \alpha\right]^2 dy$$

$$= \pi g \rho \tan^2 \alpha \int_0^h (b - y)^2 dy$$

$$= \pi \rho g \tan^2 \alpha \left(b^2 h - bh^2 + \frac{h^3}{3}\right)$$

Substituting these values in equation (i),

we get

$$F_v = F - W$$

$$= \pi \rho g \tan^2 \alpha \left(bh^2 - \frac{h^3}{3}\right) \quad \textbf{Ans.}$$

Ex. 17 Compute the horizontal and vertical components of the resultant of the hydrostatic pressure distribution on the gate *AB*, which is a quarter of a cylinder *Fig. 3.41*. Assume the gate is 3 m wide.

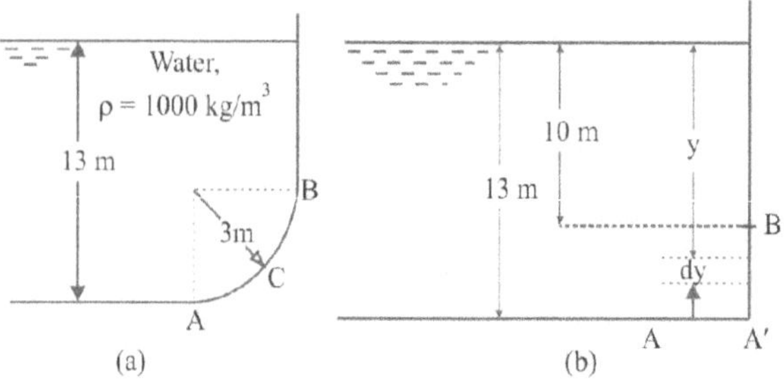

Fig. 3.41

Sol.

(a) **Horizontal component :** The horizontal component of the resultant force on the gate is equal to the force on the vertical projection BA' of the gate. The pressure at a depth y from free surface of the water, $P = \rho g y$. The force on the strip of area $(3dy)$ of the gate,

$$dF_H = P(3dy) = \rho g y (3dy)$$

$$= 3\rho g y\, dy$$

Total horizontal force,

$$F_H = 3\rho g \int_{10}^{13} y\, dy = 3\,\rho g \left.\frac{y^2}{2}\right|_{10}^{13}$$

$$= 3 \times 1000 \times 9.8 \times \left(\frac{13^2 - 10^2}{2}\right)$$

$$= 1.014 \times 10^6 \, N \qquad \textbf{Ans.}$$

(b) **Vertical component:** It is equal to the weight of the water above the curved surface. Dividing the volume above the curved surface into a rectangular parallelopiped and a quarter cylinder, we thus have:

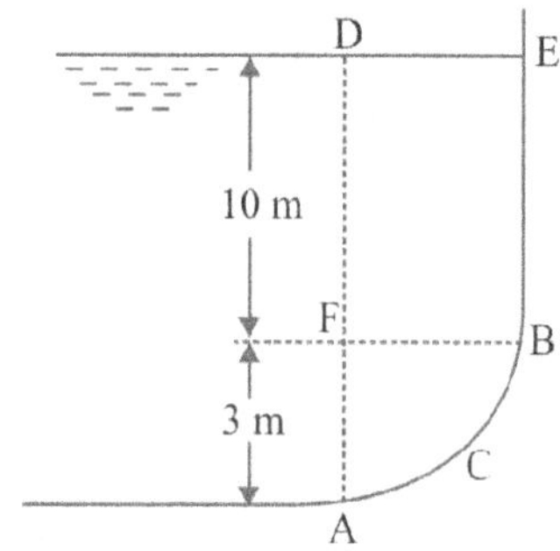

Fig. 3.42

$$F_v = \text{Weight of water in } DEFB + \text{weight of water in } ACBF$$

$$= \rho [V_1 + V_2] g$$

$$= 1000 \left[10 \times 3 \times 3 + \frac{\pi(3)^2 \times 3}{4}\right] \times 9.8$$

$$= 1.09 \times 10^6 \, N \qquad \textbf{Ans.}$$

The resultant force on the gate

$$F = \sqrt{F_H{}^2 + F_V{}^2}$$

$$= 1.49 \times 10^6 \; N \qquad \textbf{Ans.}$$

3.12 BUOYANT FORCE AND BUOYANCY

Body inside a fluid experiences pressure on its all faces. As the fluid pressure increases with depth, so the upward thrust at the bottom is more than the downward thrust on the top. Hence a net force acts in upward direction. This upward force acting on a body in a fluid is called **upthrust or buoyant force** and the phenomenon is called buoyancy. The point of application of buoyant force is called centre of buoyancy. It is the centre of gravity of the displaced fluid.

Archimedes' Principle

The principle was discovered by the Greek scientist, Archimedes around 225 B.C. It states that when a body is immersed in a fluid, partially or wholly, it experiences an upward force equal to the weight of the volume of the fluid displaced by the body.

Proof: To understand easily, take a body of height h and area A, lying inside a liquid of density ρ. The top face of the body is at a distance y from the free surface of the liquid. Pressure at the top face of the body,

$$P_1 = \rho g y$$

Pressure at the bottom face of the body,

$$P_2 = \rho g(y+h)$$

Thrust on the top face of the body,

$$F_1 = P_1 A = \rho g h A \text{ acting vertically downwards.}$$

Thrust acting on the bottom face of the body

$$F_2 = P_2 A = \rho g (y+h) A \text{ acting vertically upwards.}$$

The resultant force $(F_2 - F_1)$ acts on the body in the upward direction and is called buoyant force (F_b). Thus

$$F_b = F_2 - F_1 = \rho g (y+h) A - \rho g y A$$
$$= (Ah)\rho g$$

But $Ah = V$, the volume of the body, which is equal to the volume of the liquid displaced.

$$\therefore \quad F_b = V \rho g$$

Thus buoyant force is equal to the weight of the fluid displaced.

Apparent weight of immersed body

$$\text{Apparent weight} = \text{Actual weight} - \text{buoyant force}$$
$$W_{app} = W - F_b$$

For a body completely inside liquid, $F_b = V \rho g$

$$\therefore \quad W_{app} = V \sigma g - V \rho g$$

$$= V \sigma g \left(1 - \frac{\rho}{\sigma}\right)$$

or

$$W_{app} = W \left(1 - \frac{\rho}{\sigma}\right)$$

Here σ is the density of the material of the body.

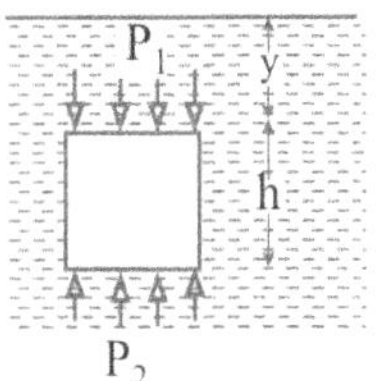

Fig. 3.43

Note:

1. For a wholly immersed body of homogeneous composition the centre of buoyancy will coincide with the centre of gravity.

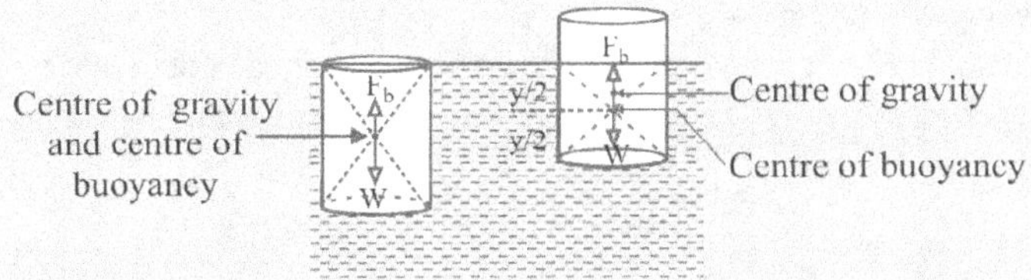

Fig. 3.44

2. When a body lies inside two or more immiscible liquids, the buoyant force on the body is given by

$$F_b = F_{b1} + F_{b2} + \text{------------}$$

For two liquids

$$F_b = V_1\rho_1 g + V_2\rho_2 g$$

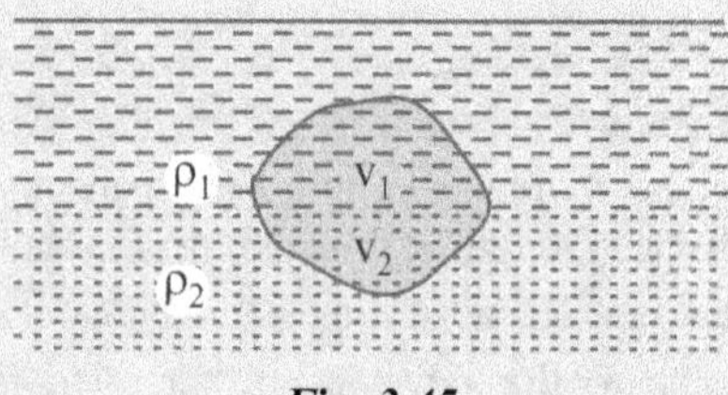

Fig. 3.45

3.13 RELATIVE DENSITY

We know that,

$$\text{Loss in weight} = \text{Buoyant force on the immersed body}$$
$$= \text{Weight of the body in air} - \text{weight of the body in water}$$

or $$F_b = W_{air} - W_{water}$$
or $$W_{air} = F_b + W_{water} \qquad \text{...(1)}$$

or $$W_{air} = F_b\left(1 + \frac{W_{water}}{F_b}\right) \qquad \text{...(2)}$$

If σ is the density of material of body and ρ_w is the density of the water, then equation (2) can be written as;

$$V\sigma g = V\rho_w g\left(\frac{F_b + W_{water}}{F_b}\right)$$

In view of equations (1) and (2), we have

or $$\frac{\sigma}{\rho_w} = \frac{W_{air}}{W_{air} - W_{water}}$$

or $$\text{R.D.} = \frac{W_{air}}{W_{air} - W_{water}}$$

3.14 PRINCIPLE OF FLOATATION

The principle of floatation states that:

(i) Weight of a body floating in a fluid is equal to the buoyant force which in turn is equal to the weight of the fluid displaced by the body.

(ii) The lines of action of weight of the body (C.G.) and the buoyant force (centre of buoyancy) must lie on the same vertical line, so that their moment about any axis is zero.

Three possible cases:

(i) When $W > F_b$: In case, when weight of the body is greater than the buoyant force, the net force $(W - F_b)$ acts in the downward direction and hence the body will sink.

$$W > F_b \Rightarrow V\sigma g > V\rho g \ \text{or}\ \sigma > \rho.$$

Thus the body will sink in a liquid if its density is greater than the density of the liquid.

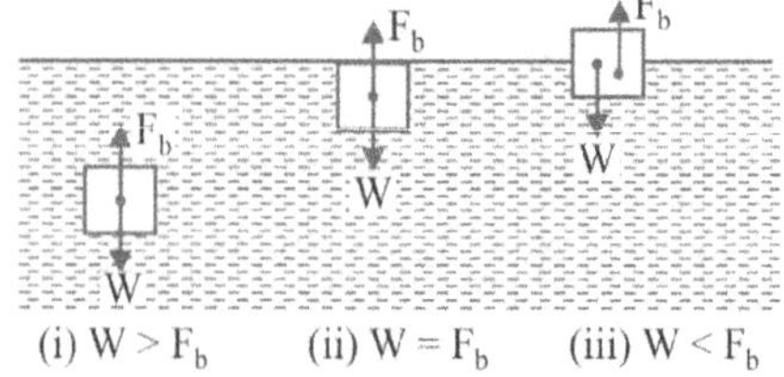

Fig. 3.46

(ii)   When $W = F_b$: The weight of the body is just equal to the buoyant force. No net force acts on the body. The body floats fully immersed.

$$W = F_b \Rightarrow V\sigma g = V\rho g \quad or \quad \sigma = \rho$$

(iii)   When $W < F_b$: In case when weight of the body is less than buoyant force on a fully immersed body, the body will again float with less volume inside liquid. Here $\sigma < \rho$.

Fractional submerged volume of a floating body

When density of the body (σ) is less than the density of the liquid (ρ), the body floats partially submerged. If V is the volume of the body and V′ is the submerged volume, then for a floating body

$$W = F_b$$
$$V\sigma g = V'\rho g$$

or
$$\frac{V'}{V} = \frac{\sigma}{\rho}$$

Volume of cavity inside metal

Consider a metal piece of mass M and density σ. The volume of metal, $V = \dfrac{M}{\sigma}$.

When metal weighs in water, let its weight is W'. Thus

Loss in weight in water   =   Weight in air – weight in water

or
$$F_b = W - W'$$

If V' is the total volume of the metal body, then

$$V'\rho_w g = W - W'$$

$$\therefore \quad V' = \frac{W - W'}{\rho_w g}$$

The volume of cavity   = $V' - V$

$$= \left(\frac{W - W'}{\rho_w g}\right) - \frac{M}{\sigma}$$

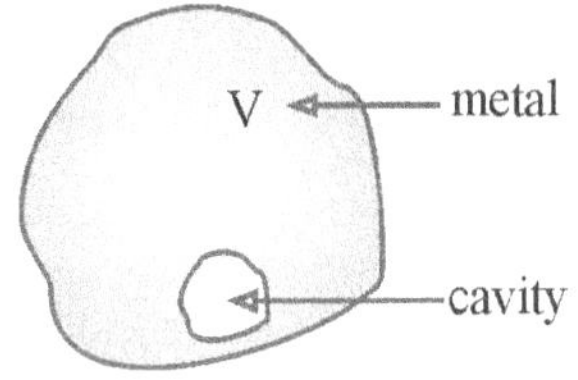

Fig. 3.47

Ex. 18 The density of ice is 917 kg/m³. What fraction of ice lies below water? The density of sea water is 1024 kg/m³. What fraction of the ice berg do we see assuming that it has the same density as ordinary ice (917 kg/m³)?

Sol.

According to law of floatation:

Weight of the ice   =   Weight of the water displaced

$$V\rho_{ice}g = V'\rho_w g$$

$$\therefore \quad V' = \frac{\rho_{ice}}{\rho_w}V = \frac{917}{1000}V = 0.917V$$

so,   91.7% of the ice is inside water.

If V_1 is the volume of ice inside sea water, then

$$V\rho_{ice}g = V_1\rho_w g$$

$$\therefore \quad V_1 = \frac{\rho_{ice}}{\rho_w}V = \frac{917}{1024}V = 0.895V$$

The fraction of ice visible to us is;

$$= V - V_1 = V - 0.895V$$
$$= 0.105V \qquad \textit{Ans.}$$

So 10.5% of the ice is visible to us.

Ex. 19 A solid floats in water with 3/4 of its volume below the surface of water. Calculate the density of the solid.

Sol.   If V is the volume and σ is the density of the solid, then

$$V\sigma g = \left(\frac{3}{4}V\right)\rho_w g$$

or
$$\sigma = \frac{3}{4}\rho_w$$

$$= \frac{3}{4} \times 1000 = 750\,kg/m^3 \; \textit{Ans.}$$

Ex. 20 A solid weighs 10 N in air. Its weight decreases by 2N when weighted in water. What is the density of the solid?

Sol.   R.D. of solid $= \dfrac{\text{Weight in air}}{\text{Loss in weight in water}}$

$$= \frac{10}{2} = 5$$

or
$$\frac{\sigma}{\rho_w} = 5$$

$$\therefore \quad \sigma = 5\rho_w$$
$$= 5 \times 1000 = 5000 \; kg/m^3 \; \textit{Ans.}$$

Ex. 21 A body of density ρ floats with a volume V_1 of its total volume V immersed in one liquid of density ρ_1 and with the remainder of volume V_2 immersed in another liquid of density ρ_2, where $\rho_1 > \rho_2$. Find the relative volume immersed in two liquids.

Sol.

For a floating body in two liquids

Weight of the body = Buoyant force of I liquid + buoyant force of II liquid

$$V\rho g = V_1\rho_1 g + V_2\rho_2 g$$

or $\quad\quad V\rho = V_1\rho_1 + V_2\rho_2 \quad\quad \text{... (i)}$

Also $\quad\quad V = V_1 + V_2 \quad\quad \text{... (ii)}$

After solving equations (i) and (ii), we get

$$V_1 = V\left(\frac{\rho - \rho_2}{\rho_1 - \rho_2}\right)$$

and $\quad\quad V_2 = V\left(\frac{\rho_1 - \rho}{\rho_1 - \rho_2}\right) \quad\quad$ ***Ans.***

Ex. 22 A large block of ice 5m thick has a vertical hole drilled through it and is floating in the middle of a lake. What is the minimum length of the rope required to scoop up a bucket full of water through the hole? (Relative density of ice = 0.9).

Sol.

The length of the rope required is equal to the height of the block above the water level. Let it is y. If A is the area of base of the block, then

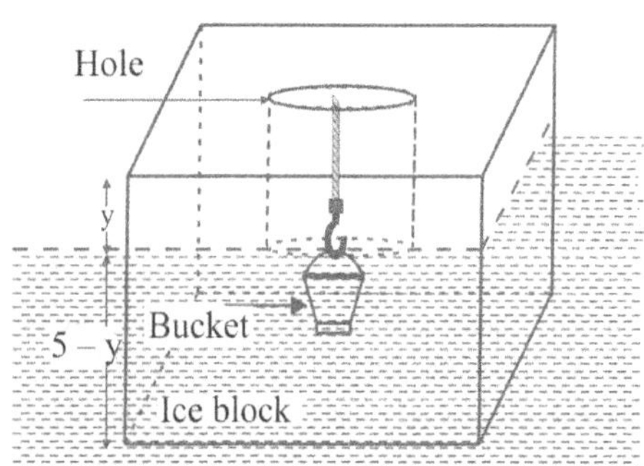

Fig. 3.48

Weight of ice block = Weight of the water displaced

$$(A \times 5)\rho_{ice}g = A \times (5 - y)\rho_w g$$

or $\quad\quad 5\rho_{ice} = (5 - y)\rho_w$

or $\quad\quad 5 \times 900 = (5 - y) \times 1000$

which after solving gives, $\quad y = 0.5\text{m} \quad\quad$ ***Ans.***

Ex. 23 A block of wood is floating on water at 0°C with a certain volume V above the water level. The temperature of water is slowly raised from 0°C to 20°C. How will the volume V change with the rise in temperature?

Sol.

Suppose V' be the volume of the block of wood and W be the weight of the block.

For the floating block :

$\quad\quad$ Weight of the block = weight of the water displaced.

$$W = (V' - V)\rho_t g$$

where ρ_t is the density of water at t°C which is

$$\rho_t = \frac{\rho_o}{1 + \gamma t}$$

$\therefore \quad\quad W = (V' - V)\frac{\rho_o}{(1 + \gamma t)}g$

or $\quad\quad V = V' - \frac{W(1 + \gamma t)}{\rho_o g}$

Clearly V decreases with increase in temperature. $\quad$ ***Ans.***

Ex. 24 A ball floats on the surface of water in a container exposed to the atmosphere. Will the ball remain immersed at its initial depth or will it sink or rise some what if the container is shifted to the moon?

Sol.

The gravity on moon is about one sixth of that on the earth. i.e.,

$$g_m = g/6$$

On the earth, water and air both exert buoyant force on the ball, but on the moon as there is no air so weight of the ball is balanced only by buoyant force of the water. Thus

On the earth $\quad\quad mg = V_w\,\rho_w g + V_a\rho_a g$

or $\quad\quad m = V_w\rho_w + V_a\rho_a \quad\quad \text{...(i)}$

On the moon $\quad\quad m\left(\dfrac{g}{6}\right) = V'_w\,\rho_w\left(\dfrac{g}{6}\right) \quad\quad \text{... (ii)}$

or $\quad\quad m = V'_w\rho_w$

From equations (i) and (ii), we have

$$V'_w = V_w + \frac{V_a\rho_a}{\rho_w}$$

Clearly $V'_w > V_w$. That is, the volume of the ball immersed in water on the moon will be greater than that on the earth. Hence ball will sink slightly more in water on the moon.

Ex. 25 A balloon filled with air weighted so that it barely floats in water, as shown in *Fig. 3.49*. Explain why it sinks to the bottom when it is submerged more by a small distance.

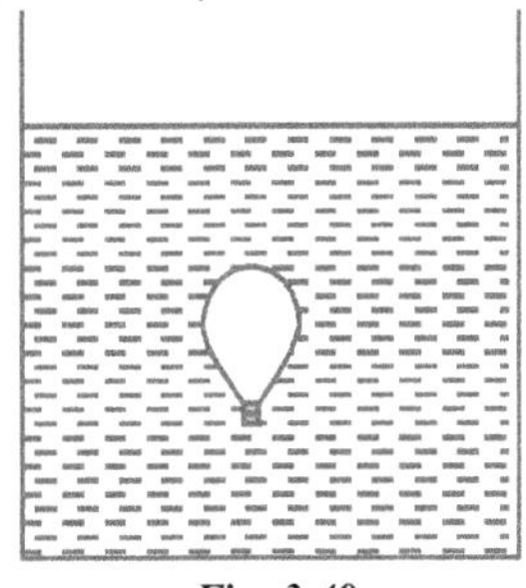

Fig. 3.49

Sol.

When the balloon is submerged slightly into water, the pressure exerted by water increases and hence the air inside the balloon is slightly compressed (PV = constant). The buoyant force on the balloon therefore decreases ($F_b \propto V$), and so it sinks to the bottom.

Ex. 26 A beaker containing water of weight W is placed on a spring balance. A stone weight W' is hung and lowered into the water without touching the sides and bottom of the beaker. Explain how the reading of the balance and tension in the string will change.

Sol.

When stone is submerged into water, water exerts buoyant force F_b on the stone in upward direction. The stone also exerts an equal downward force on water. So tension in the string becomes,

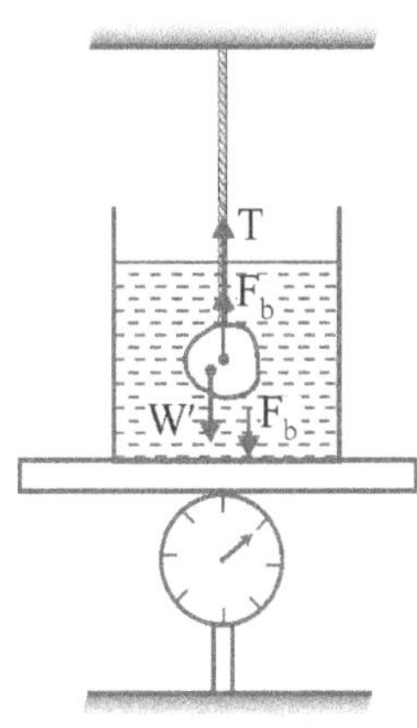

Fig. 3.50

$T = W' - F_b$ and reading of spring balance becomes $= W + F_b$

Note :

1. When bottom of the body is quite plane, and no water enters below it, the buoyant force on the body will be zero (*Fig. 3.51.* a).

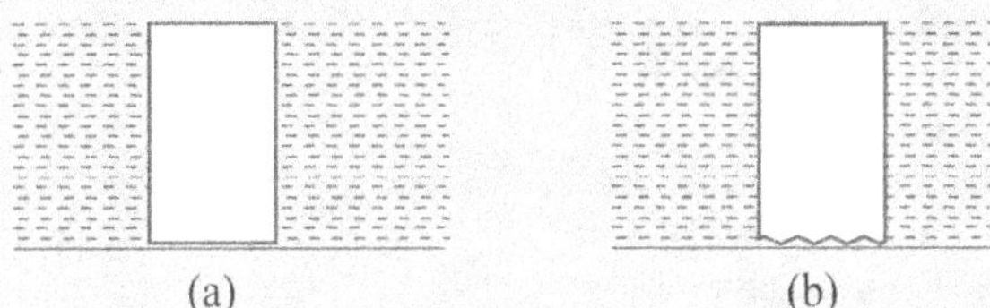

(a)   (b)

Fig. 3.51

When bottom face of the body is rough, the water enters below it and exerts buoyant force (*Fig. 3.51.* b).

2. Weight of empty balloon and inflated balloon are equal : Suppose weight of empty balloon is Mg. Let m amount of air is in inflated balloon. On the inflated balloon buoyant force is also there, so net weight of the balloon

$$= (M+m)g - F_b$$
$$= (M+m)g - V_{air}\, \rho_{air}\, g$$
$$= (M+m)g - \frac{m}{\rho_{air}}\rho_{air}g$$
$$= Mg$$

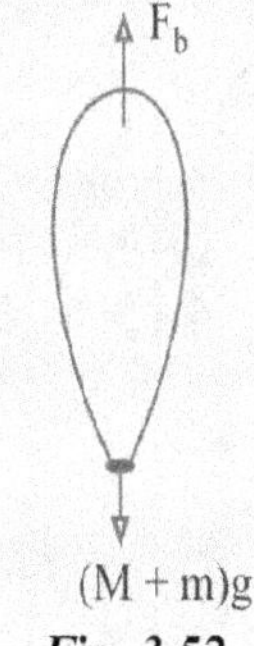

Fig. 3.52

Ex. 27 Compute the depth that a 500 N force will submerge the buoy shown in *Fig. 3.53*. It is a right circular cone whose weight we shall neglect.

Sol.

Let x be the depth of immersion. By similar triangles the radius of the cone cross-section at the free surface is:

$$\frac{r}{y} = \frac{0.3}{3}$$

$$\therefore \quad r = \frac{y}{10}$$

Fig. 3.53

Using the principle of buoyancy, we have

Downward force exerted on the cone

= Buoyant force on the submerge portion of the cone

or

$$500 = \left(\frac{1}{3}\pi r^2 y\right)\rho_w g$$

$$= \frac{1}{3}\pi\left(\frac{y}{10}\right)^2 y \times 100 \times 9.8$$

$$y = 1.69\,\text{m} \qquad \textit{Ans.}$$

Ex. 28 A piece of wax weighs 18.03 g in air. A piece of metal weighs 17.03 g in water. It is tied to the wax and both together weigh 15.23 g in water. What is the specific gravity of wax?

Sol.

Weight of the wax in air, $W_1 = 18.03$ g-wt

Let F_{b1} and F_{b2} are the buoyant forces on wax and metal respectively.

Weight of the metal in air, $W_2 = 17.03g + F_{b2}$

Combined weight of wax + metal in water $= 15.23$ g-wt

or $(W_1 + W_2) - (F_{b1} + F_{b2}) = 15.23g$

or $(18.03g + 17.03g + F_{b2}) - (V_{wax}\,\rho_w g + F_{b2}) = 15.23g$

or $35.06g - V_{wax}\,\rho_w g = 15.23g$

or $\dfrac{m_{wax}}{\rho_{wax}}\rho_w g = 19.83g$

or $\dfrac{18.03}{\rho_{wax}}\rho_w = 19.83$

or $\dfrac{\rho_{wax}}{\rho_w} = 0.909$

Thus specific gravity of wax = 0.909   ***Ans.***

Ex. 29 (i)   A piece of ice floats in water in a beaker. What happens to the level of liquid in beaker when the ice melts completely?

(ii)   A small metal piece is inside an ice block which is floating in water in a beaker. What happens to the level in beaker when ice melts completely?

(iii)   Stones are unloaded from the boat into the lake. What happens to the level of water in the lake?

(iv)   A cork piece is inside an ice block which is floating in water in a beaker. What happens to the level of water in the beaker when ice melts completely?

Sol.

(i)   Suppose M is the mass of the ice block and ρ_w the density of water. For a floating ice block, let V_1 is the volume of water displaced, then

$$Mg = V_1 \rho_w g$$

$$\Rightarrow \qquad V_1 = \frac{M}{\rho_w}$$

After melting of ice, the volume of water forms

$$V_2 = \frac{M}{\rho_w}$$

As, $V_1 = V_2$, so the level of water in the beaker will not change.

(ii)   Suppose m and ρ_{metal} are the mass and density of metal, then for a floating ice block,

$$(M+m)g = V_1 \rho_w g$$

$$\Rightarrow \qquad V_1 = \frac{M}{\rho_w} + \frac{m}{\rho_w}$$

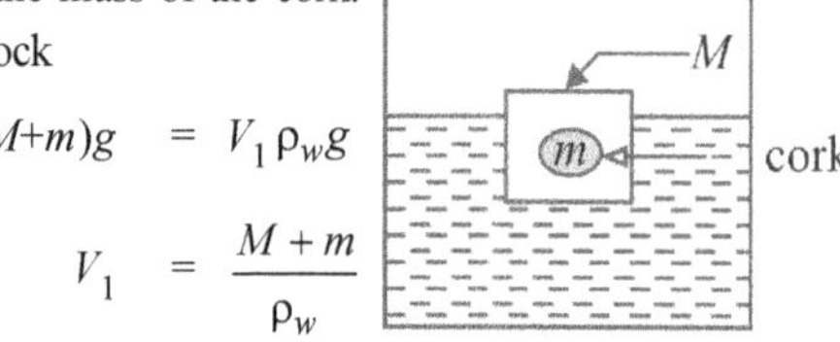

Fig. 3.54

When ice melts, the metal piece sink into the water.

So total volume of water forms + displaced by metal piece

$$V_2 = \frac{M}{\rho_w} + \frac{m}{\rho_{metal}}$$

As $\rho_{metal} > \rho_w$ $\therefore$ $V_2 < V_1$

So the level of water in the beaker will decrease.

(iii)   As explained in (ii).

(iv)   Suppose M is the mass of the cork.

For the floating in block

$$(M+m)g = V_1 \rho_w g$$

$$\Rightarrow \qquad V_1 = \frac{M+m}{\rho_w}$$

Fig. 3.55

After melting of ice, cork piece will float such that,

$$mg = V'\rho_w g \Rightarrow V' = \frac{m}{\rho_w}$$

The volume of water forms $= \dfrac{M}{\rho_w}$

Total volume of water forms + displaced by cork, $V_2 = \dfrac{M}{\rho_w} + \dfrac{m}{\rho_w}$

As $V_2 = V_1$, so the level of water in the beaker will not change.

3.15 EQUILIBRIUM OF A SUBMERGED BODY

Consider a body floating completely in a liquid. It is acted upon by two forces viz., the weight of the body W acting at the centre of gravity G of the body and the buoyant force F_b acting at the centre of buoyancy B. The forces W and F_b are equal and opposite and the points G and B must lie on a same vertical line.

(i)   **Stable equilibrium:** Consider a body as shown in figure (a) the centre of gravity of which lies below the centre of buoyancy. If such a body is tilted slightly in clockwise direction, the buoyant force and weight produce a couple in the anticlockwise direction which restores the body to its original position. This corresponds to stable equilibrium.

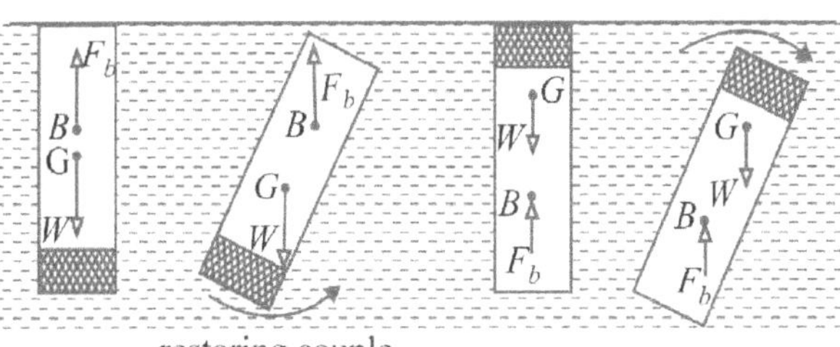

Fig. 3.56

(ii) **Unstable equilibrium:** Consider a body as shown in figure (b). The centre of gravity of which lies above centre of buoyancy. If such a body is tilted slightly from its initial position, the couple produced by weight (W) and buoyant force (B) rotate the body away from its original position. This corresponds to unstable equilibrium.

(iii) **Neutral equilibrium:** If centre of gravity and centre of buoyancy coincide with each other, then body tilted from initial position, remain in that position. It renders in a state of neutral equilibrium *Fig. 3.57* (c).

Metacentre: Let a body in *Fig. 3.58* tilted slightly from its equilibrium position. In the tilted position of the body the buoyant force acts in a vertical upward direction at B_1. Now if a vertical line is drawn through the new centre of buoyancy B_1. It intersects the axis of the body BG at point M, which is known as metacentre. Metacentre is used to understand the stability of the partially submerged floating body.

Thus metacentre may be defined as the point of intersection between the axis of the floating body passing through the points B and G and a vertical line passing through the new centre of buoyancy B_1.

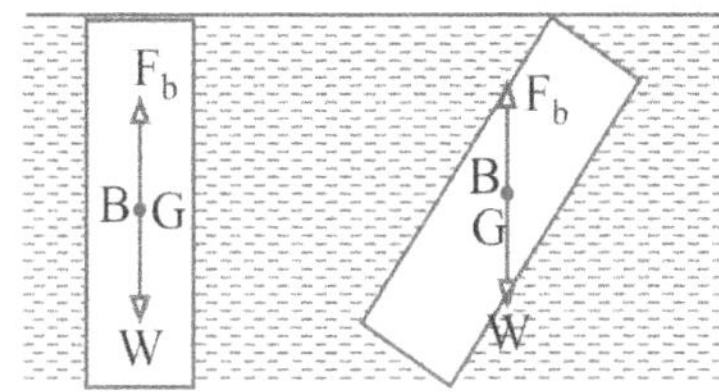

(c) Neutral equilibrium

Fig. 3.57

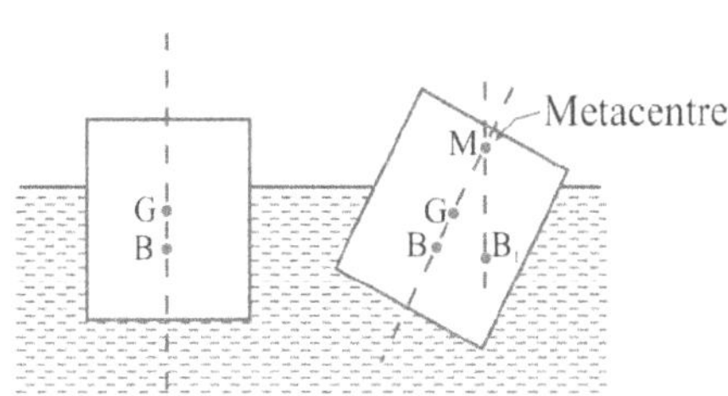

Fig. 3.58

Stability of partially submerged floating body

(i) For stable equilibrium, the centre of gravity lies below metacentre.

(ii) If the metacentre lies below its centre of gravity, then the body is said to be in an unstable equilibrium.

(iii) If metacentre coincides with the centre of gravity of the body, then the body will be in a neutral equilibrium.

Accelerating liquid

(i) **Pressure difference when liquid is accelerating in vertical direction:**

Consider a cylindrical element of height h and area A. The force on the top face of the element is $P_1 A$ and force on the bottom face is $P_2 A$. If a is the acceleration of the liquid, then

$$P_2 A - (mg + P_1 A) = ma$$

here m is the mass of the element of liquid which is equal $hA\rho$.

Thus we have

$$P_2 A - (hA\rho g + P_1 A) = (hA\rho) a$$

After simplification, we get

$$P_2 - P_1 = \rho(g + a)h$$

(ii) **Buoyant force:**

Suppose the body is submerged into a liquid of density ρ, which is accelerating upwards. If a is the acceleration of the liquid, then

$$F_b - mg = ma$$

or

$$F_b = m(g + a)$$

here m is the mass of the displaced liquid, which is equal to $V\rho$.

$$\therefore \quad F_b = \rho V(g + a)$$

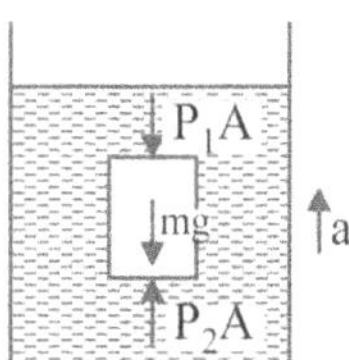

Fig. 3.59

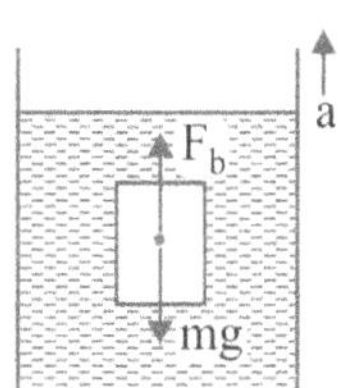

Fig. 3.60

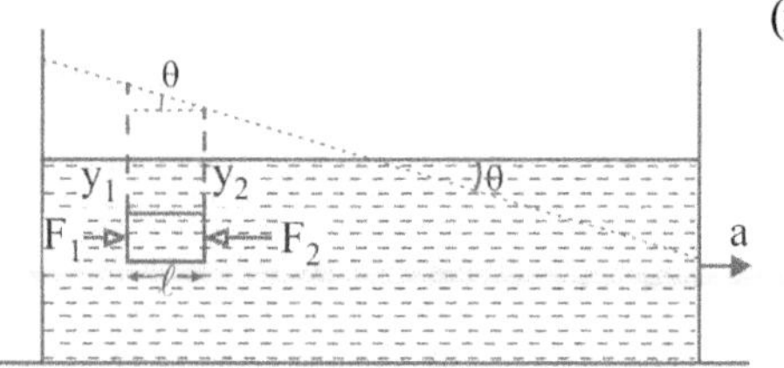

Fig. 3.61

(iii) Liquid subjected to horizontal acceleration:

Consider a liquid in a tank which is moving on a horizontal surface with constant acceleration a. The free surface of the liquid takes the shape as shown in *Fig. 3.61*. Suppose a cylinder of liquid of length ℓ and area of cross-section A. The force on the left face of the cylinder, $F_1 = P_1 A$ and force on the right face of the cylinder, $F_2 = P_2 A$. Here $P_1 = \rho g y_1$ and $P_2 = \rho g y_2$.

Mass of the liquid cylinder, $m = (A \ell \rho)$

Using Newton's second law for the liquid cylinder.

$$F_1 - F_2 \;=\; ma$$

or $$P_1 A - P_2 A \;=\; ma$$

or $$(\rho g y_1 - \rho g y_2)A \;=\; (A\ell\rho)a$$

or $$\frac{y_1 - y_2}{\ell} \;=\; \frac{a}{g}$$

From the figure, $$\frac{y_1 - y_2}{\ell} \;=\; \tan\theta$$

$$\therefore \qquad \tan\theta \;=\; \frac{a}{g}.$$

The above equation can be written as: $\tan\theta = \dfrac{a_x}{a_y}$.

(iv) Liquid subjected to combined horizontal and vertical accelerations:

Resolve the acceleration a into two components, a_x and a_y.

In view of the previous analysis, we can write

$$\tan\theta \;=\; \frac{a_x}{g + a_y}.$$

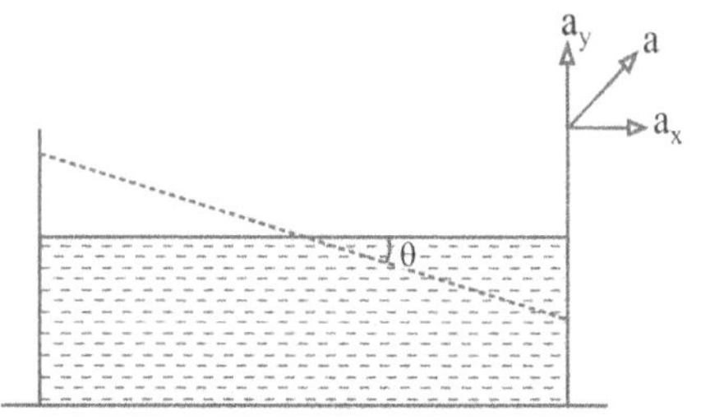

Fig. 3.62

Ex. 30   A barometer kept in an elevator accelerating upwards reads 76 cm of Hg. What will be the possible air pressure inside the elevator?

Sol.

Let a be the acceleration of the elevator, then pressure inside the elevator
$$P \;=\; \rho(g + a)h = \rho \times (g + a)0.76 \ \text{N/m}^2$$
Atmospheric pressure $P_a \;=\; \rho g \times 0.76 \ \text{N/m}^2$

Clearly, the air pressure inside elevator will be greater than P_a, i.e., 76 cm of Hg.

Ex. 31   A barometer kept in elevator reads 76cm, when it is at rest. What will be the barometric reading when elevator accelerates upwards?

Sol.

Let a be the acceleration of the elevator and h be the barometric height, then
$$P_a \;=\; \rho(g + a)h \qquad \dots (i)$$

For the static elevator with barometric height h_0
$$P_a \;=\; \rho g h_0 \qquad \dots(ii)$$
From equations (i) and (ii), we get

$$h \;=\; \frac{g h_0}{(g + a)}$$

Clearly $h < h_0$, so barometric reading in an accelerating elevator will be less than 76 cm.

Ex. 32   A barometer accelerating downwards reads 76 cm of Hg. What will be the possible air pressure inside the jar?

Sol.

If a is the acceleration, then pressure $P = \rho(g - a)h = \rho(g - a) \times 0.76$

Clearly, the pressure is less than $\rho g \times 0.76$, i.e., 76 cm of Hg.

(v) **Liquid in a container subjected to rotation:**

Consider a liquid in a container which is rotating with constant angular velocity ω. Take an element of liquid of mass (dm) at a radial distance x from the axis of rotation.

If liquid element makes angle θ with the horizontal, then

$$N \sin\theta = (dm)\omega^2 x \qquad \text{...(i)}$$

and

$$N \cos\theta = (dm)g \qquad \text{...(ii)}$$

Dividing equation (i) by (ii), we get

$$\tan\theta = \frac{\omega^2 x}{g}$$

As

$$\tan\theta = \frac{dy}{dx}$$

$\therefore$

$$\frac{dy}{dx} = \frac{\omega^2 x}{g}$$

or

$$dy = \frac{\omega^2 x}{g} dx$$

On integrating, we get

$$y = \frac{\omega^2 x^2}{2g}$$

The difference in level of free surface between axis and at a distance x is: $y = \dfrac{\omega^2 x^2}{2g}$

At the boundary of the container, $x = R$

$\therefore$

$$y = \frac{\omega^2 R^2}{2g}.$$

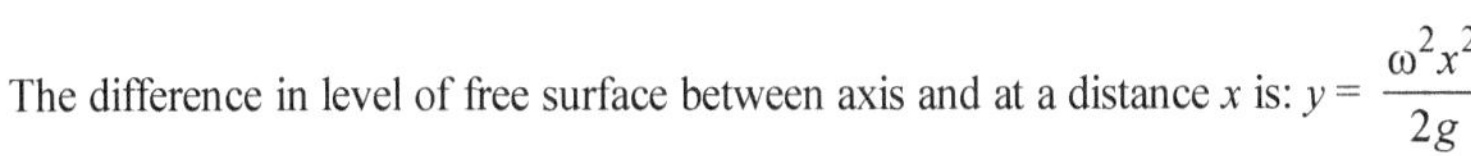
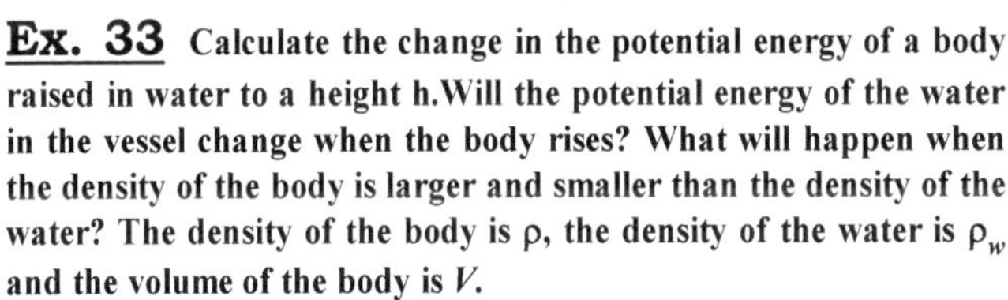

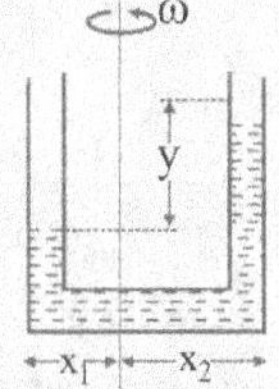

Fig. 3.63

Ex. 33 **Calculate the change in the potential energy of a body raised in water to a height h. Will the potential energy of the water in the vessel change when the body rises? What will happen when the density of the body is larger and smaller than the density of the water? The density of the body is ρ, the density of the water is ρ_w and the volume of the body is V.**

Sol.

The body in water is simultaneously subjected to the force of gravity and the buoyant force. We know that the change in potential energy of the body is equal to the work done by conservative forces. i.e.,

$$\Delta U = -W_C$$
$$= -[-F_g + F_b] \times h$$
$$= (F_g - F_b)h$$

For the body completely inside water

$$F_b = V\rho_w g \text{ and } F_g = mg = V\rho g$$

$\therefore$

$$\Delta U = Vgh(\rho - \rho_w) \qquad \textit{Ans.}$$

If $\rho > \rho_w$, then $\Delta U > 0$ and the energy of the body increases. If $\rho < \rho_w$, then $\Delta U < 0$ and the energy of the body diminishes.

When the body moves up to the height h a volume of water V is displaced downwards by the same distance. In this case the potential energy of this volume in the fluid of the force of gravity will diminish by $V\rho_w gh$ and the energy due to the buoyant force will increase by $V\rho_w gh$. Therefore, the total potential energy of the water will remain constant.

$$\Delta U_{water} = 0 \qquad \textit{Ans.}$$

Note:

If a U-tube is rotated about an axis as shown, then $y = \dfrac{\omega^2}{2g}(x_2^2 - x_1^2)$

Fig. 3.64

Ex. 34 A hydrometer has a uniform stem graduated downward from 0,1,2, - - - - - - - -upto 10. When floating in pure water it reads 0 and in a liquid of relative density 1.5 it reads 10. Calculate the relative density of a liquid in which it reads 5.

Sol.

The floating of hydrometer in different liquids is shown in figure. If m is the mass of the hydrometer, then by principle of floatation :

In water, $\qquad mg = (V + V')\rho_w g \qquad$ ... (i)

In know liquid $\qquad mg = V' \times 1.5 \times g \qquad$ ... (ii)

Suppose density of liquid is ρ_ℓ, then $mg = \left(V' + \dfrac{V}{2}\right)\rho_\ell g$

After solving above equations, we get $\rho_\ell = 1.20$ *Ans.*

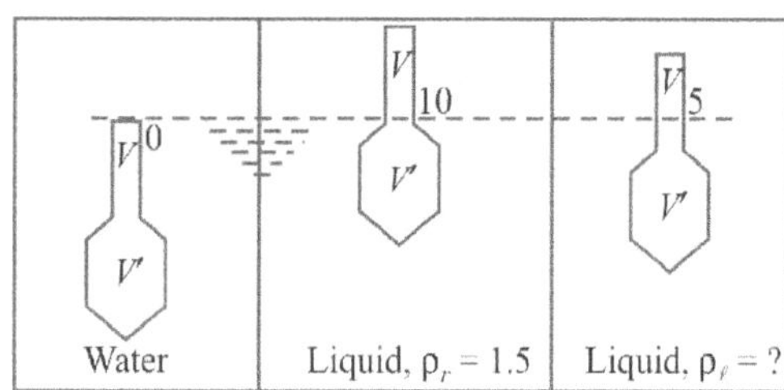

Fig. 3.65

Ex. 35 A tube of length h, which is wide enough to make surface tension effects negligible, is closed at one end. It is then lowered into a tank of mercury to a depth h as shown in *Fig. 3.67*, so that mercury rises a distance x into the tube. If mercury barometer stands at h, then find relationship between h and x.

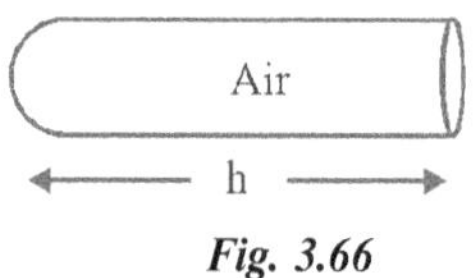

Fig. 3.66

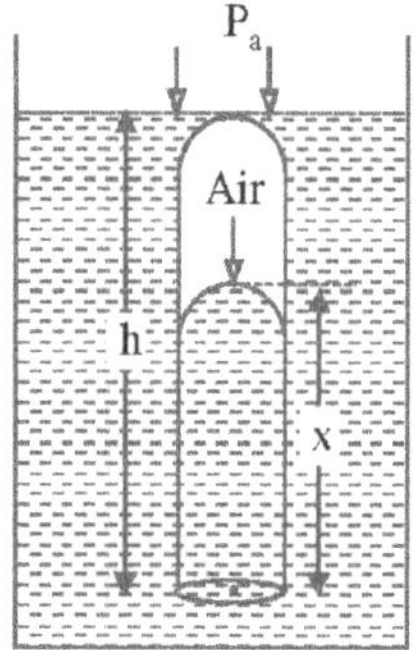

Fig. 3.67

Sol.

Let area of cross-section of tube is A. When it is in air the volume of air in it, $V_1 = Ah$, and pressure $P_1 = h$ of mercury.

When the tube lowered into mercury, then volume of air

$$V_2 = A(h - x);$$
$$P_2 + x = 2h$$
$$\Rightarrow \qquad P_2 = (2h - x) \text{ of mercury}$$

Now by Boyle's law

$$P_1 V_1 = P_2 V_2$$
$$\text{or} \qquad h(Ah) = (2h - x)[A(h - x)]$$
$$\Rightarrow \qquad h^2 = (2h - x)(h - x) \qquad \textit{Ans.}$$

Ex. 36 An ornament weighing 36 g in air, weighs only 34 g in water. Assuming that some copper is mixed with gold to prepare the ornament, find the amount of copper in it. Specific gravity of gold is 19.3 and that of copper is 8.9.

Sol.

Let m_g and m_c are the masses of gold and copper in the ornament, then

$$m_g + m_c = 36 \qquad \text{... (i)}$$

Loss in weight in water $= (36 - 34)g = 2g$

$$\therefore \qquad 2g = V_{total}\, \rho_w\, g$$

$$\text{or} \qquad V_{total} = \frac{2}{\rho_w}$$

$$\text{or} \qquad \frac{m_g}{19.3} + \frac{m_c}{8.9} = \frac{2}{1} \qquad \text{... (ii)}$$

After solving equations (i) & (ii), we get

$$m_c = 2.2\,g \qquad \textit{Ans.}$$

Ex. 37 A cubical block of wood of edge 3 cm floats in water. The lower surface of the cube just touches the free end of a vertical spring fixed at the bottom of the pot. Find the maximum weight that can be put on the block without wetting it. Density of wood = 800 kg/m³ and spring constant of spring = 50 N/m. Take g = 10 m/s².

Sol.

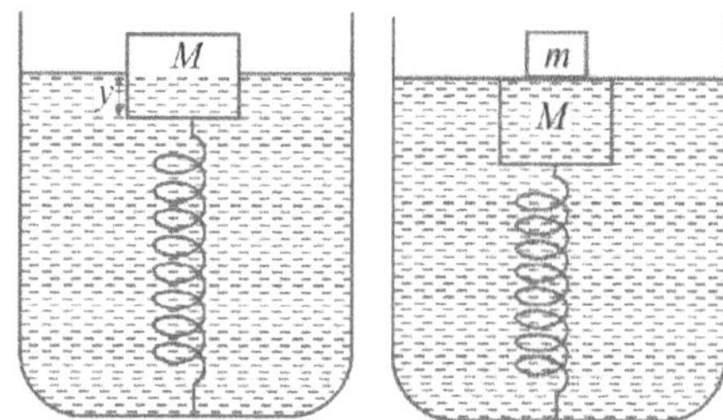

Fig. 3.68

When block just touches the spring, it floats freely on water. Let y is the portion of block inside water, then

$$\text{Weight of block} = \text{buoyant force}$$
$$V\rho_{wood}\, g = \forall \rho_w\, g$$
$$\text{or} \quad (3 \times 3 \times 3 \times 10^{-6}) \times 800g = (y \times 3 \times 3 \times 10^{-6}) \times 1000 \times g$$
$$y = 2.4 \text{ cm.}$$

$\therefore$ Height of block out of water $= 3 - 2.4 = 0.6$ cm

Let m is the mass, that can be placed on the block without wetting it.

The additional weight is balanced by the buoyant force on additional dipped portion + spring force

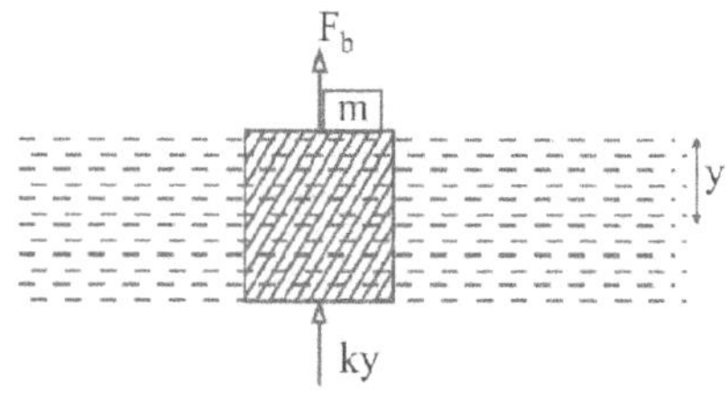

Fig. 3.69

i.e. $\qquad mg = \forall \rho_w g + ky$

$$= (0.6 \times 3 \times 3 \times 10^{-6}) \times 1000 \times 10 + 50 \times (0.6 \times 10^{-2})$$
$$= 0.354 \text{ N} \qquad \textit{Ans.}$$

Ex. 38 A cube of ice of edge 4 cm is placed in an empty cylindrical glass of inner diameter 6 cm. Assume that the ice melts uniformly from each side so that it always retains its cubical shape. Remembering that ice is lighter than water, find the length of the edge of the ice cube at the instant it just leaves the contact with the bottom of the glass.

Sol.

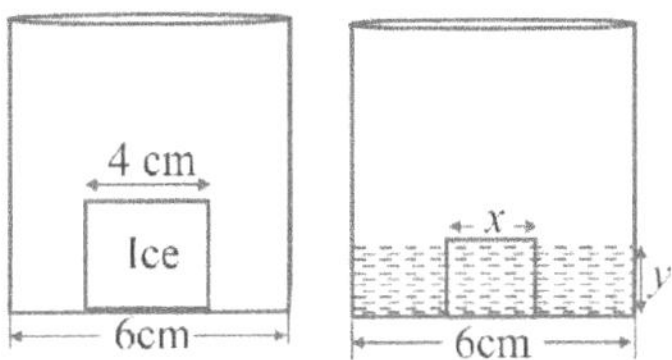

Fig. 3.70　　　*Fig. 3.71*

Let size of ice block remaining is x^3 when it just about to float, then

$$\therefore \qquad x^3 \times \rho_{ice}\, g = (x^2 y)\rho_w g \qquad ...(i)$$

$$\Rightarrow \qquad x^3 \rho_{ice} = x^2 y\, \rho_w$$

Also mass of ice melt = mass of water forms

$$(4^3 - x^3) \times \rho_{ice} = \left(\pi \times 3^2 \times y - x^2 y\right)\rho_w \qquad ...(ii)$$

$$\text{or} \quad 4^3\rho_{ice} - x^3\,\rho_{ice} = \pi \times 3^2\, y\rho_w - x^2 y\rho_w$$

$$\text{or} \qquad 4^3\rho_{ice} = \pi \times 3^2\, y\rho_w$$

$$\text{or} \qquad y = \left(\frac{7.11\rho_{ice}}{\pi\rho_w}\right)$$

Substituting the value of y in equation (i), we get

$$x^3 \times \rho_{ice}\, g = x^2 \times \left(\frac{7.11\rho_{ice}}{\pi\rho_w}\right)\rho_w g$$

$$\text{or} \qquad x = 2.26 \text{ cm} \qquad \textit{Ans.}$$

Ex. 39 A wooden plank of length 1m and uniform cross-section is hinged at one end to the bottom of a tank as shown in *Fig. 3.72*. The tank is filled with water up to a height of 0.5m. The specific gravity of the plank is 0.5. Find the angle θ that the plank makes with the vertical in the equilibrium position (Exclude the case $\theta = 0$).

Sol.

Let y is the length of the plank inside water

$$\therefore \qquad y = \frac{0.5}{\cos\theta}$$

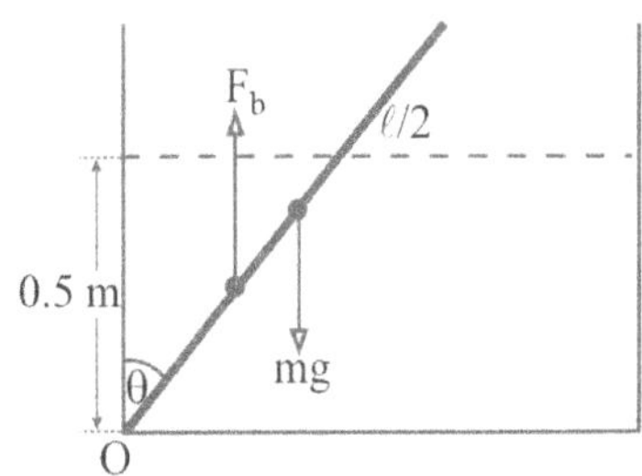

Fig. 3.72

Let A be the cross-sectional area of the plank, then buoyant force on it

$$F_b = V\rho_w g$$

$$= (Ay)\rho_w g$$

Since plank is in rotational equilibrium, so

$$\sum \vec{\tau}_o = 0$$

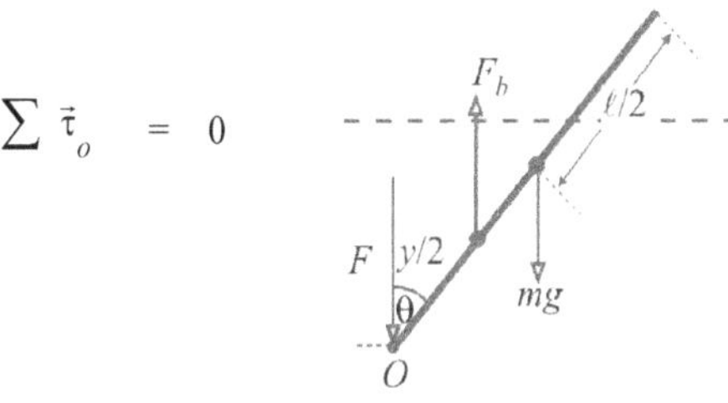

Fig. 3.73

$$\text{or} \quad mg \times \frac{\ell}{2}\sin\theta - F_b \times \frac{y}{2}\sin\theta = 0$$

$$\text{or} \qquad mg\,\ell - F_b \times y = 0$$

$$(A\,\ell \times 0.5)\text{g}\,\ell - (Ay)\,d_w y = 0$$

$$\text{or} \qquad 0.5\,\ell^2 = y^2$$

$$\text{or} \qquad 0.5 \times (1)^2 = \left(\frac{0.5}{\cos\theta}\right)^2$$

$$\Rightarrow \qquad \cos^2\theta = \frac{1}{2}$$

$$\text{or} \qquad \cos\theta = \frac{1}{\sqrt{2}}$$

$$\text{or} \qquad \theta = 45° \qquad \textit{Ans.}$$

Ex. 40 A trolley containing a liquid slides down a smooth inclined plane of angle α with the horizontal. Find the angle of inclination θ of the free surface with the horizontal.

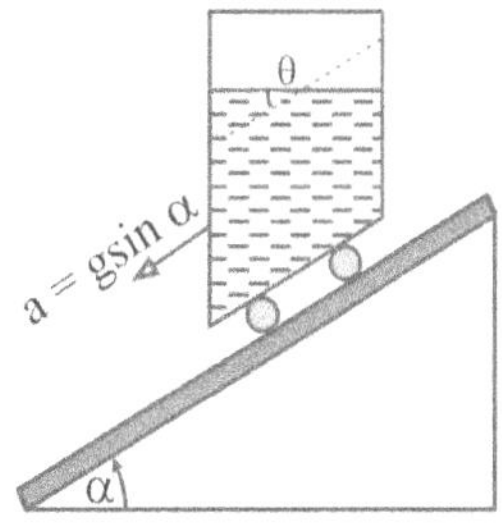

Fig. 3.74

Sol.

The acceleration of the trolley is $a = g\sin\theta$ down the inclined plane

$$\therefore \quad a_x = a\cos\alpha = (g\sin\alpha)\cos\alpha$$

$$a_y = a\sin\alpha = (g\sin\alpha)\sin\alpha = g\sin^2\alpha$$

Let θ is the angle made by free surface of liquid then

$$\tan\theta = \frac{a_x}{g - a_y}$$

$$= \frac{g\sin\alpha\cos\alpha}{g - g\sin^2\alpha} = \tan\alpha$$

$$\Rightarrow \qquad \theta = \alpha \qquad \textit{Ans.}$$

Ex. 41 The *Fig. 3.75* shows a semi-cylindrical massless gate pivoted at the point *O* holding a stationary liquid of density ρ. The length of the cylinder is ℓ. Calculate horizontal force exerted by the liquid on the gate.

Sol.

The force exerted by liquid on the gate

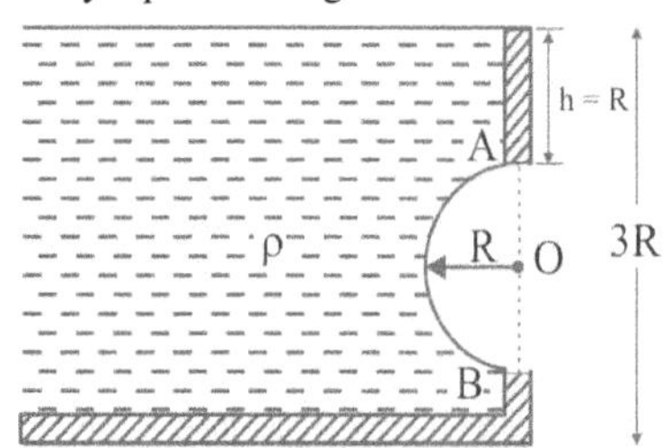

Fig. 3.75

$$F_H = P_{av} \times \text{vertical projected area of the gate}$$

$$= \left(\frac{P_A + P_B}{2}\right) \times (2R\ell)$$

$$= \left(\frac{R\rho g + 3R\rho g}{2}\right) \times 2R\ell$$

$$= 4\rho g R^2 \ell \qquad \textit{Ans.}$$

Ex. 42 A closed rectangular tank 1.2 m high, 2.4 m 10 m long and 1.5 m wide is two-third full of gasoline of relative density 0.8. Calculate the acceleration which may be imparted to the tank so that the bottom front end of the tank is just exposed. Also calculate the total forces on each end of the tank.

Sol.

The height of gasoline $= \dfrac{2}{3} \times 1.2 = 0.8\,\text{m}$

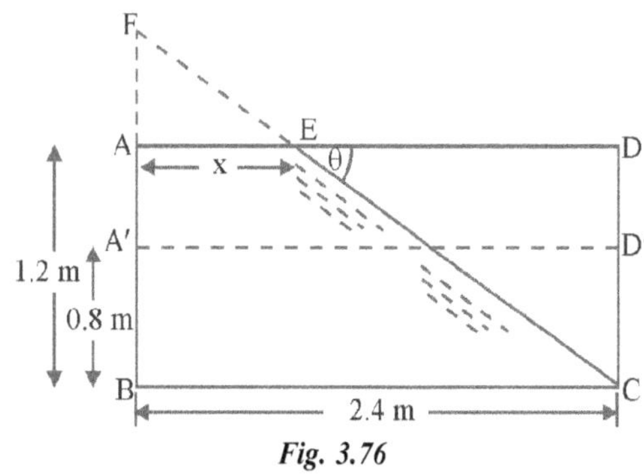

Fig. 3.76

Since tank is closed, therefore volume of liquid inside it remain as such. Suppose free surface makes θ with the horizontal and x is the distance of free surface from *A*, then

Volume of $AECBA$ = Volume of $A'D'CB$

$$\therefore \quad \frac{1}{2}(2.4 + x) \times 1.2 \times 1.5 = 2.4 \times 1.5 \times 0.8$$

$$\Rightarrow \qquad x = 0.8\,\text{m}$$

From geometry $\tan\theta = \dfrac{CD}{DE}$

$$= \left(\frac{1.2}{2.4 - 0.8}\right) = 0.75$$

Also $\qquad \tan\theta = \dfrac{a_x}{g}$

$$= 0.75$$

or $\qquad a_x = 0.75 \times g$

$$= 7.35\,\text{m/s}^2$$

At *A* the pressure head is equal to an imaginary column of gasoline of height equal to *AE*.

$$\frac{AF}{AE} = \tan\theta = 0.75$$

or $\qquad AF = 0.75\,AE$

$$= 0.75 \times 0.8 = 0.6\,\text{m}$$

Therefore effective height of liquid at end *B*

$$= 1.2 + 0.6 = 1.8\,\text{m}$$

$$P_A = 0.6\rho g$$

$$P_B = 1.8\rho g$$

$$\therefore \qquad P_{av} = \frac{P_A + P_B}{2} = \frac{(0.6 + 1.8)}{2}\rho g$$

$$= 1.2\rho g$$

Force acting on the back face

$$F_1 = P_{av} \times \text{area of face}$$

$$= (1.2\rho g) \times (1.2 \times 1.5)$$

$$= (1.2 \times 800 \times 9.8) \times (1.2 \times 1.5)$$

$$= 16934.4\,\text{N} \qquad \textit{Ans.}$$

Force on the front face

$$F_2 = 0 \qquad \textit{Ans.}$$

3.16 FLUID DYNAMICS

Flow characteristics

Steady and un-steady flow : Steady flow may be defined as the flow in which at any point in the flowing fluid various characteristics which describe the behaviour of flow are independent of time. How ever these characteristics may be different at different points in the direction of flow. Mathematically steady flow can be expressed as:

$$\left(\frac{\partial v}{\partial t}\right) = 0 \; ; \; \left(\frac{\partial P}{\partial t}\right) = 0 \; ; \; \left(\frac{\partial \rho}{\partial t}\right) = 0$$

Fluid flow is said to be unsteady if at any point in the flowing fluid any one or all the characteristics which describe the behaviour of the flow change with time. Thus for unsteady flow,

$$\left(\frac{\partial v}{\partial t}\right) \neq 0 \text{ and } \left(\frac{\partial P}{\partial t}\right) \neq 0$$

Uniform and non-uniform flow:
If velocity of flow does not change from point to point in a flowing fluid for any given instant of time, the flow is said to be uniform otherwise non-uniform. Thus,

for uniform flow, $$\left(\frac{\partial v}{\partial s}\right) = 0$$

for non-uniform flow, $$\left(\frac{\partial v}{\partial s}\right) \neq 0$$

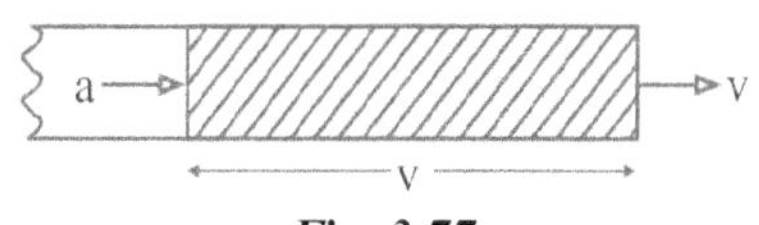
Fig. 3.77

Rate of flow: Consider a pipe of cross-sectional area a carrying liquid with a velocity v, the volume of liquid flows in one second, i.e.,

$$Q = \frac{dV}{dt} = \frac{\text{volume of shaded portion}}{1\,\text{second}} = av$$

Ex. 43 Discuss the flow characteristics in the pipes shown in figure, for (i) constant flow (ii) variable flow.

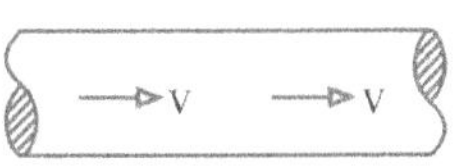
Fig. 3.78

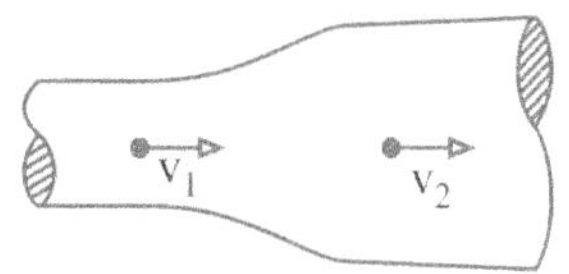
Fig. 3.79

Sol.

(i) For constant rate of flow, velocity at different points in the direction of flow do not change with time, so flow in both the pipes is steady. But in pipe of varying cross-section, the velocity of flow changes with distance, so the flow will be non-uniform. Thus in first pipe flow is steady-uniform and in second pipe it is steady-non-uniform.

(ii) When flow rate changes, the velocity at any point will change with time. So in first pipe flow is unsteady-uniform but in second pipe it is unsteady-nonuniform.

Laminar flow

A flow is said to be laminar when different liquid particles move in layers with one layer of fluid over an adjacent layer. In the laminar flow, the viscosity of fluid plays an important role. The flow of viscous liquid may be in general be treated as laminar.

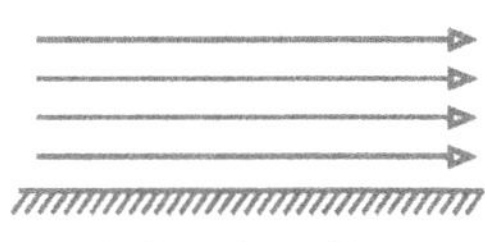
(a) Laminar flow
Fig. 3.80

Turbulent flow

When liquid particles move on zig-zag path or disorderly manner, the flow of liquid leads to turbulent flow. The occurrence of turbulent flow is more frequent than that of laminar flow. Flow in streams, channels, water supply pipes, sewers etc. are few examples of turbulent flow.

(b) Turbulent flow
Fig. 3.81

Velocity profile

The surface obtained by joining the heads of velocity vectors for the particles in a section normal to the direction of flow is called velocity profile.

(a) **Velocity profile of a non-viscous liquid:** In this case, the velocity of all the particles at any section of pipe is same, so the velocity profile is plane as shown in figure (a).

(b) **Velocity profile of viscous liquid :** The velocity of fluid particles in the contact of pipe is zero and maximum at the centre of the pipe. In this case velocity profile will be parabolic.

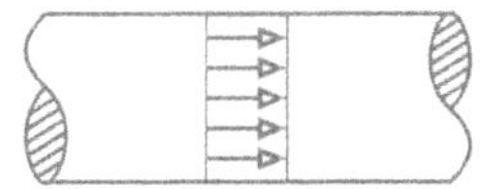
(a) Non- viscous liquid
Fig. 3.82

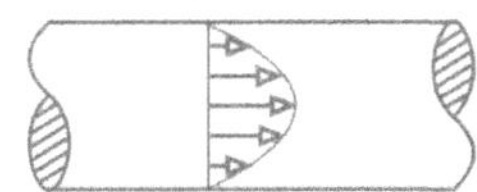
(b) Viscous liquid
Fig. 3.83

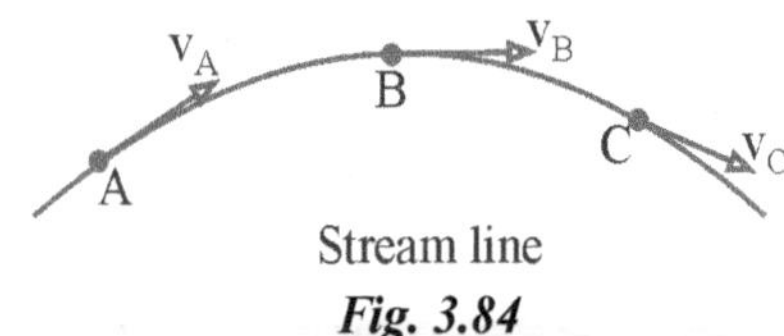

Stream line

Fig. 3.84

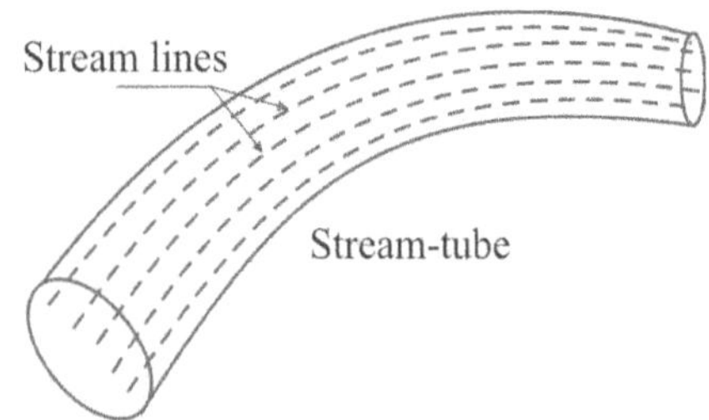

Stream lines

Stream-tube

Fig. 3.85

Streamline flow

Consider the flow of a liquid along the path ABC as shown in *Fig. 3.84*. If every successive particle passes through A, B and C with velocities $\vec{v}_A$, $\vec{v}_B$ and $\vec{v}_C$ respectively, the flow is said to be steady or streamlined flow. The path ABC along which the particles move one after other is called **streamline**. A group of streamlines passing through a small closed curve, which may or may not be circular, is called stream tube.

Critical velocity

At low velocity, the flow of liquid is laminar. As the velocity of flow increases, the flow becomes turbulent after a certain velocity of flow. Thus the velocity at which flow changes from laminar to turbulent, is called **critical velocity**. The critical velocity v_c of a liquid flowing through a pipe depends on

(i) density of liquid (ρ)   (ii) diameter of pipe (D)   (iii) coefficient of viscosity (η)

and is equal to

$$v_c = \frac{k\eta}{\rho D}$$

Here k is a constant.

3.17 REYNOLDS NUMBER

It is a dimensionless parameter which describes the nature of flow of fluid. It is defined as:

$$R_e = \frac{\text{Inertia per force unit area of fluid}(F_i)}{\text{viscous force per unit area}(F_v)}$$

$$F_i = F/A = \frac{\Delta P / \Delta t}{A} = \frac{\Delta m}{\Delta t}\frac{v}{A}$$

$$= \rho\frac{\Delta V}{\Delta t}\frac{v}{A} = \rho\frac{Qv}{A} = \rho v^2$$

$$F_v = \eta \times \text{velocity gradient}$$

$$= \eta\frac{v}{D}$$

$$\therefore \qquad R_e = \frac{\rho v^2}{\eta v/D}$$

$$\text{or} \qquad R_e = \frac{\rho v D}{\eta}$$

For flow of liquid in a pipe

If R_e is less than equal to 2000, the flow will be laminar. If $R_e > 3000$, the flow is turbulent. If R_e lies between 2000 and 3000, the flow is unstable.

Ex. 44 (a) What is the largest average velocity of blood flow in an artery of radius 2×10^{-3} m if the flow must remain laminar? (b) What is the corresponding flow rate? Take viscosity of blood to be 2.084×10^{-3} Pa-s and density of blood = 1.06×10^3 kg/m³.

Sol.

(a) The maximum value of Reynolds number for blow to be laminar is 2000. If v_c is the average velocity of flow, then

$$R_e = \frac{\rho v_c D}{\eta}$$

$$\therefore \qquad v_c = \frac{\eta R_e}{\rho D} = \frac{\eta R_e}{2r}$$

$$= \frac{2.084 \times 10^{-3} \times 2000}{1.06 \times 10^3 \times 2 \times 2 \times 10^{-3}}$$

$$= 0.98 \text{ m/s} \qquad \textit{Ans.}$$

(b)   The flow rate of blood

$$Q = v_c \times \text{area of cross-section of the artery}$$

$$= 0.98 \times \pi r^2$$

$$= 0.98 \times \pi (2 \times 10^{-3})^2$$

$$= 1.23 \times 10^{-5} \text{ m}^3/\text{s} \qquad \textit{Ans.}$$

Ex. 45 The flow rate from a tap of diameter 1.25 cm is 3 litre/min the coefficient of viscosity of water is 10^{-3} Pa-s. Characteristics the flow.

Sol.

Given, $\quad D = 1.25 \times 10^2\,\text{m}$

$$Q = 3\ \text{litre/min} = \frac{3 \times 10^{-3}}{60} = 5 \times 10^{-5}\,\text{m}^3/\text{s}$$

As $\quad Q = v_c A = v_c \times \dfrac{\pi D^2}{4}$

$$v_c = \frac{Q}{\frac{\pi}{4}D^2} = \frac{5 \times 10^{-5}}{\frac{\pi}{4}\left(1.25 \times 10^{-2}\right)^2} = 4.08\,\text{m}^3/\text{s}$$

$$\text{Reynolds number, } R_e = \frac{\rho v_c D}{\eta} = \frac{1000 \times 4.08 \times 1.25 \times 10^{-2}}{10^{-3}}$$

$$= 5095$$

As $R_e > 3000$, so the flow will be turbulent.

3.18 IDEAL FLUID

An ideal fluid has the following characteristics:

(i) **Incompressible :** The density of fluid does not change with change in fluid pressure.

(ii) **Non-viscous :** The fluid layers offer no internal resistance and hence total mechanical energy of non-viscous fluid remain constant. In practice water can be taken as ideal fluid.

3.19 EQUATION OF CONTINUITY

The equation of continuity is the mathematical statement of the principle of conservation of mass.

Consider a fluid is flowing in a pipe of varying area of cross-section as shown in *Fig. 3.86*. Let v_1 and v_2 are the velocities of flow at cross-sections A_1 and A_2 respectively.

The mass of the fluid enters into section 1 in time Δt,

$$m_1 = \rho_1 V_1$$

$$= \rho_1(A_1 v_1 \Delta t)$$

The mass of the fluid leaving the section 2 in the same interval of time,

$$m_2 = \rho_2 V_2$$

$$= \rho_2(A_2 v_2 \Delta t)$$

By conservation of mass

$$m_1 = m_2$$

or $\quad \rho_1(A_1 v_1 \Delta t) = \rho_2\left(A_2 v_2 \Delta t\right)$

or $\quad \rho_1 A_1 v_1 = \rho_2 A_2 v_2$

For incompressible fluid $\quad \rho_1 = \rho_2$

$\therefore \quad A_1 v_1 = A_2 v_2$

or $\quad Av = \text{Constant (Q)}$

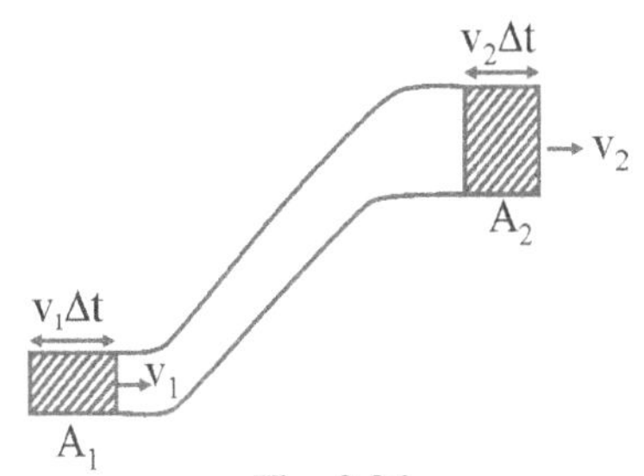

Fig. 3.86

The above equation is the equation of continuity. It states that for an incompressible fluid product of flow velocity and corresponding area of cross-section of a pipe remain constant.

3.20 ENERGY OF A FLOWING FLUID

A flowing fluid may have three kinds of energy.

(i) **Kinetic energy:** The energy possessed by a fluid by virtue of motion is called its kinetic energy. Kinetic energy of m mass of the fluid flowing with velocity v is given by

$$\text{K.E.} = \frac{1}{2}mv^2$$

$$\text{K.E. per unit volume} = \frac{1}{2}\frac{mv^2}{V} = \frac{1}{2}\rho v^2$$

The kinetic energy per unit weight of the fluid is given by $\frac{1}{2}\frac{mv^2}{mg} = \frac{v^2}{2g}$. It is measured in metre and called the **velocity head**.

(ii) **Potential energy:** The energy possessed by a fluid by virtue of its position is called its potential energy. Potential energy of fluid at a height h above earth's surface is given by

$$\text{P.E.} = mgh$$

$$\text{P. E. per unit volume} = \frac{mgh}{V} = \rho gh.$$

P. E. per unit weight of the fluid is given by $\frac{mgh}{mg} = h$ and is called **potential or gravitational head**.

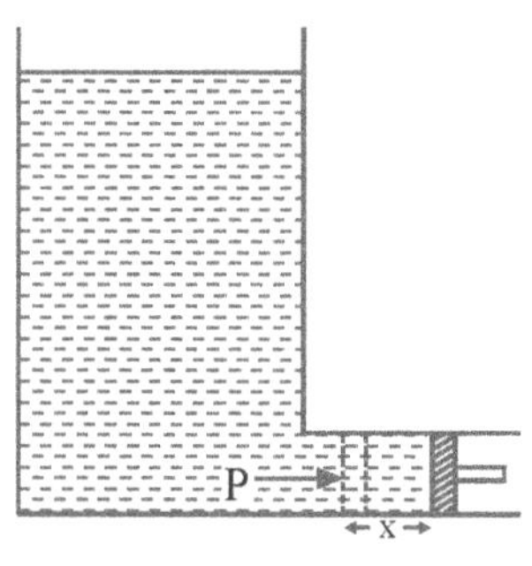

Fig. 3.87

(iii) **Pressure energy :** The energy possessed by a fluid by virtue of its pressure is called its pressure energy. To understand this, consider a liquid in a cylinder fitted with a piston. Let P be the pressure at the piston. Suppose the piston moves through a distance x.

The work done against this pressure,

$$\begin{aligned} W &= \text{Force} \times \text{displacement} \\ &= (PA)x \\ &= P(Ax) = PV \end{aligned}$$

where V is the volume swept by the piston. This work done is stored as the pressure energy of the fluid of the volume V.

Thus pressure energy of fluid of volume $V = PV$

$$\text{Pressure energy per unit volume} = \frac{PV}{V} = P \text{ (Excess pressure)}$$

Pressure energy per unit weight is given by $\frac{PV}{mg} = \frac{P}{\rho g}$ and is called **pressure head**.

3.21 BERNOULLI'S PRINCIPLE

The Swiss scientist Daniel Bernoulli in 1738 first derived the principle which is based on the law of conservation of energy and applies to ideal fluid. According to this principle the sum of pressure energy, kinetic energy and potential energy of an ideal fluid flowing along a streamline is a constant. Bernoulli's principle mathematically can be expressed in terms of an equation, is called Bernoulli's equation :

$$P + \frac{1}{2}\rho v^2 + \rho gh = \text{Constant}$$

3.22 DERIVATION OF BERNOULLI'S EQUATION

To derive Bernoulli's equation, we can apply the work-energy theorem to the fluid in a section of a flow tube. Consider the fluid initially lies between the two sections respectively. In a time interval Δt, the fluid was initially at a moves to a', a distance $v_1 \Delta t$. It the same time the fluid initially at b moves to b', a distance $v_2 \Delta t$.

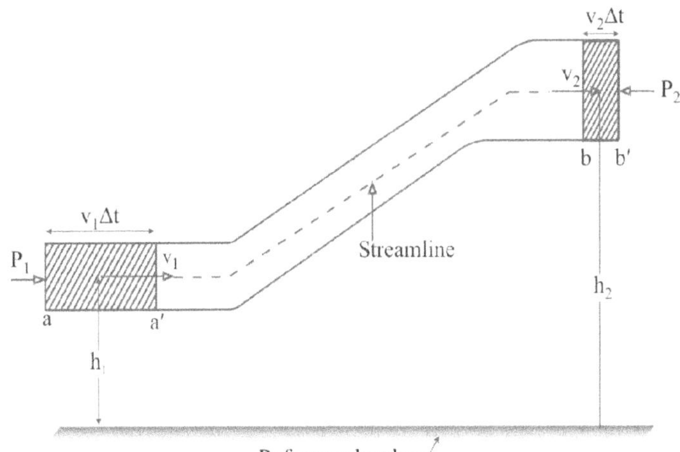

Fig. 3.88

If A_1 and A_2 are the cross-sectional areas at the two ends, then by equation of continuity, the volume of fluid ΔV passing any cross-section in time Δt is

$$\Delta V = A_1(v_1\Delta t) = A_2(v_2\Delta t)$$

or

$$\Delta V = A_1\Delta s_1 = A_2\Delta s_2$$

If P_1 and P_2 are the pressures at the two ends, then force at the cross-section a is P_1A_1, and that at b is P_2A_2. The network done on the element during this displacement

$$W = F_1\Delta s_1 - F_2\Delta s_2$$

$$= P_1A_1\Delta s_1 - P_2A_2\Delta s_2$$

$$= P_1\Delta V - P_2\Delta V = (P_1 - P_2)\Delta V \qquad ...(i)$$

Change in K. E. from a to b:

The mass of the fluid between a and a'

$$\Delta m = \text{Density} \times \text{volume}$$

$$= \rho\Delta V$$

The kinetic energy of the fluid between a and a'

$$K_1 = \frac{1}{2}\Delta mv_1^2$$

$$= \frac{1}{2}\rho\Delta Vv_1^2$$

Similarly, at the end of Δt, the kinetic energy of the fluid between b and b',

$$K_2 = \frac{1}{2}\rho\Delta Vv_2^2$$

Thus the change in kinetic energy of the fluid between a and b,

$$\Delta K = K_2 - K_1$$

$$= \frac{1}{2}\rho\Delta V(v_2^2 - v_1^2) \qquad ...(ii)$$

Change in potential energy:

The potential energy of the mass entering at a in time Δt is,

$$U_1 = \Delta mgh_1 = \rho\Delta Vgh_1$$

The potential energy of the mass leaving at b is,

$$U_2 = \Delta mgh_2 = \rho\Delta Vgh_2$$

The change in potential energy between a and b is,

$$\Delta U = U_2 - U_1 = \rho\Delta Vg(h_2 - h_1) \qquad ...(iii)$$

Now using work-energy theorem

$$W = \Delta K + \Delta U$$

or

$$(P_1 - P_2)\Delta V = \frac{1}{2}\rho\Delta V\left(v_2^2 - v_1^2\right) + \rho\Delta V g(h_2 - h_1)$$

After rearranging above expression, we get

$$P_1 + \frac{1}{2}\rho v_1^2 + \rho g h_1 = P_2 + \frac{1}{2}\rho v_2^2 + \rho g h_2$$

We can write

$$P + \frac{1}{2}\rho v^2 + \rho g h = \text{Constant} \qquad \text{...(1)}$$

Bernoulli's equation can also be written as:

$$\frac{P}{\rho g} + \frac{v^2}{2g} + h = \text{Constant} \qquad \text{...(2)}$$

Note:

1. In Bernoulli's equation P is the absolute pressure, not gauge pressure.
2. In equation (1) each term has unit N/m^2 and in equation (2) each term has unit metre.
3. For horizontal streamline, $h_1 = h_2$, so $\quad P + \frac{1}{2}\rho v^2 = \text{Constant}$
4. In Bernoulli's equation, the term $(P + \rho g h)$ is called static pressure, because it is the pressure of the fluid even if it is at rest, and the term $\frac{1}{2}\rho v^2$ is called dynamic pressure of the fluid. Bernoulli's equation thus can be written as:
   Static pressure + kinetic pressure = Constant.

Ex. 46 Water enters a house through a pipe 2.0 cm inside diameter, at an absolute pressure of 4×10^5 pa. The pipe leading to the second - floor bathroom 5 m above is 1.0 cm in diameter. When the flow velocity at the inlet pipe is 4 m/s, find the flow velocity and pressure in the bathroom.

Sol.

By continuity equation the flow velocity

$$v_2 = \frac{A_1 v_1}{A_2} = \frac{\pi(0.01)^2}{\pi(0.005)^2} \times 4 = 16\,\text{m/s} \quad Ans$$

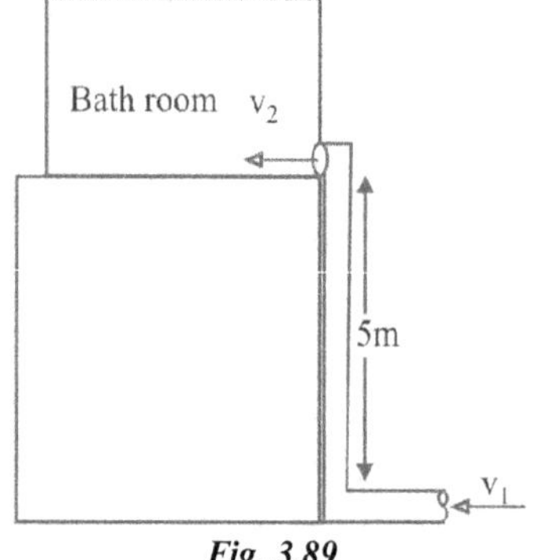

Fig. 3.89

Using Bernoulli's equation between 1 & 2, we have

$$P_1 + \frac{1}{2}\rho v_1^2 + \rho g h_1 = P_2 + \frac{1}{2}\rho v_2^2 + \rho g h_2$$

or

$$P_2 = P_1 - \frac{1}{2}\rho\left(v_2^2 - v_1^2\right) - \rho g\left(h_2 - h_1\right)$$

$$= 4\times10^5 - \frac{1}{2}\times1000\left(16^2 - 4^2\right) - 1000\times9.8\times5$$

$$= 2.3 \times 10^5 \text{ Pa} \qquad Ans.$$

Ex. 47 The reading of pressure-meter attached with a closed pipe is 3.5×10^5 N/m^2. On opening the valve of the pipe, the reading of the pressure-meter is reduced to 3.0×10^5 N/m^2. Calculate the speed of the water flowing in the pipe.

Sol.

Before opening the valve

$$P_1 = 3.5\times10^5\,N/m^2,\; v_1 = 0$$

After opening the valve

$$P_2 = 3.0\times10^5\,N/m^2$$

Let v_2 is the speed of the water after opening of the valve, then for the horizontal pipe

$$P_1 + \frac{1}{2}\rho v_1^2 = P_2 + \frac{1}{2}\rho v_2^2$$

$$\therefore \qquad v_2 = \left[v_1^2 + \frac{2(P_1 - P_2)}{\rho} \right]^{1/2}$$

As $\qquad v_1 = 0$

$$\therefore \qquad v_2 = \left[\frac{2(P_1 - P_2)}{\rho} \right]^{1/2}$$

$$= \left[\frac{2\left(3.5 \times 10^5 - 3.0 \times 10^5\right)}{1000} \right]^{1/2}$$

$$= \quad 10 \text{ m/s} \qquad\qquad \textit{Ans.}$$

3.23 APPLICATIONS OF BERNOULLI'S EQUATION

1. **Pressure difference:** When v_1 and v_2 are zero, the Bernoulli's equation reduces to

$$P_1 - P_2 = \rho g \left(h_2 - h_1\right).$$

This is the same equation as we have derived in hydrostatics. Thus the equation of hydrostatics are special cases of Bernoulli's equation.

2. **Venturimeter:** It is an ideal device of measuring rate of flow of a liquid in a pipe. It is also known as venturi tube or flow meter. The basic principle of venturimeter is that by reducing the cross-sectional area of the flow passage, a pressure difference is created and the measurement of the pressure difference enables the determination of the rate of flow through the pipe.

Construction: As shown in figure a venturimeter consists of (1) an inlet section followed by a convergent cone, (2) a cylindrical throat, and (3) a gradually divergent cone. The inlet section of the venturimeter is of the same diameter as that of the pipe which is followed by a convergent cone.

Let area of cross-sections of inlet and throat are A_1 and A_2 respectively. By continuity equation

$$A_1 v_1 = A_2 v_2 = Q \qquad \text{(Rate of flow)}$$

$$\therefore \qquad v_1 = \frac{Q}{A_1} \text{ and } v_2 = \frac{Q}{A_2} \qquad \text{...(i)}$$

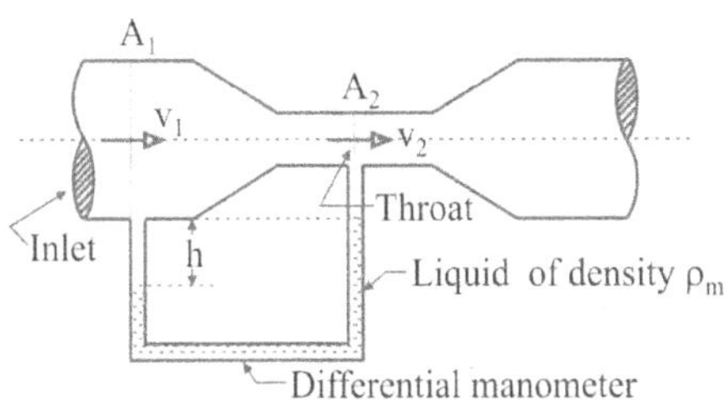

Fig. 3.90. Venturimeter placed horizontally

If ρ is the density of the flowing fluid and P_1 and P_2 are the pressures of fluid at inlet and throat, then by Bernoulli's equation

$$P_1 + \frac{1}{2}\rho v_1^2 = P_2 + \frac{1}{2}\rho v_2^2$$

or $\qquad v_2^2 - v_1^2 = \dfrac{2(P_1 - P_2)}{\rho} \qquad \text{...(ii)}$

Substituting values of v_1 and v_2 from equation (i) into (ii), we have

$$\frac{Q^2}{A_2^2} - \frac{Q^2}{A_1^2} = \frac{2(P_1 - P_2)}{\rho}$$

or $\qquad Q^2 \left[\dfrac{A_1^2 - A_2^2}{A_1^2 A_2^2} \right] = \dfrac{2(P_1 - P_2)}{\rho}$

$$\therefore \qquad Q = A_1 A_2 \sqrt{\frac{2(P_1 - P_2)}{\rho\left(A_1^2 - A_2^2\right)}} \qquad \text{...(1)}$$

From the manometer $\qquad P_1 - P_2 = \rho_m g h$

$$\therefore \qquad Q = A_1 A_2 \sqrt{\frac{2\rho_m g h}{\rho\left(A_1^2 - A_2^2\right)}} \qquad \text{...(2)}$$

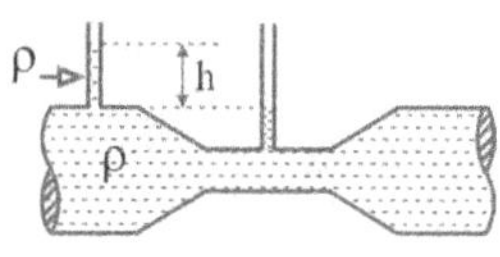

Fig. 3.91

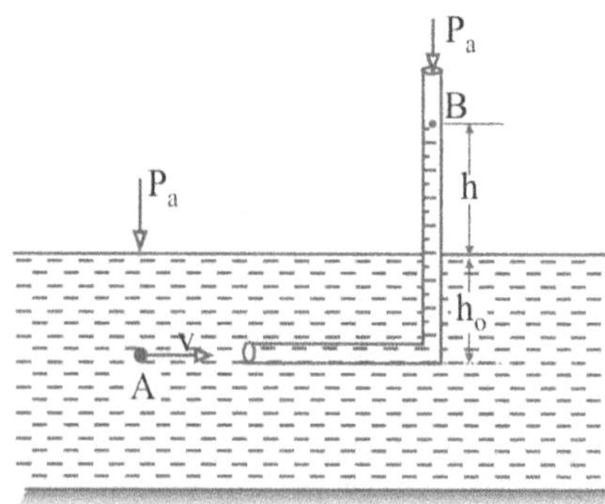

Fig. 3.92

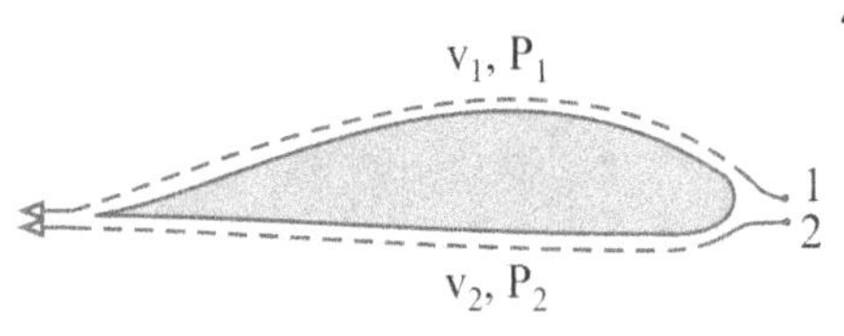

Fig. 3.93

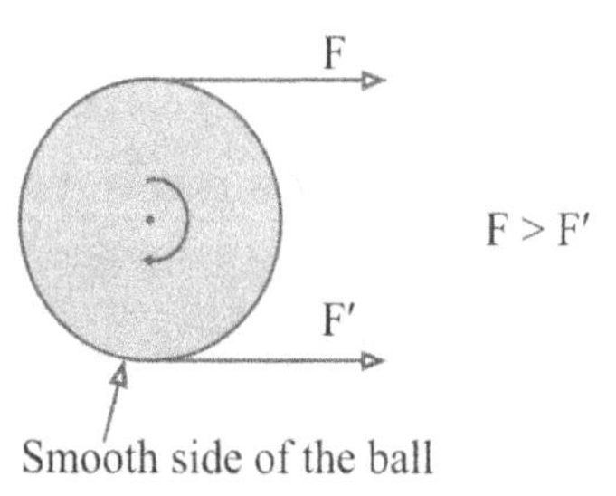

$F > F'$

Smooth side of the ball

Fig. 3.94

If simple manometers are inserted in inlet and throat, then $\rho_m = \rho$

$$\therefore \qquad Q = A_1 A_2 \sqrt{\frac{2gh}{A_1^2 - A_2^2}}.$$

3.   **The Pitot tube :** A Pitot tube is a simple device which is used to measure the velocity of flow in the river. It is named in honour of its invertor Henry de Pitot. The basic principle used in the device is that if the velocity of flow at a particular point is reduced to zero, which is known a stagnation point, the pressure there is increased due to conversion of kinetic energy into pressure energy. By measuring pressure head, we can calculate velocity of flow.

Consider two points A and B as shown in the *Fig. 3.92*. Using Bernoulli's equation between these points.

$$(P_a + \rho g h_0) + \frac{1}{2}\rho v^2 + 0 = (P_a) + 0 + \rho g(h_o + h)$$

After simplifying above expression, we get

$$v = \sqrt{2gh}.$$

4.   **Dynamic lift on aeroplane wings :** The design of aeroplane wing is made in such a way that the curvature length of the upper part of the wing is greater than the lower part. The orientation of the wing relative to the flow direction causes flow lines to crowd together above the wing, corresponding increased flow velocity and decreased pressure in this region, while below the wing the pressure remains nearly atmosphere. Because of this pressure difference, there is a net upward force or lift on the wing.

Suppose v_1 and v_2 are the velocities and P_1 and P_2 are the pressures at 1 and 2 respectively. Clearly $v_1 > v_2$ and $P_1 < P_2$.

Lift force on the wing F = Pressure difference × projected area of wing

or $\qquad\qquad F = (P_2 - P_1) \times$ projected area of wing

5.   **Swing of the ball : Magnus effect**

When one side of the ball is made smoother by rubbing, it experiences greater drag force by air on the rough side, and the ball starts spinning due to a net torque.

When such a ball is thrown horizontally with large speed, it deviated from its usual parabolic path.

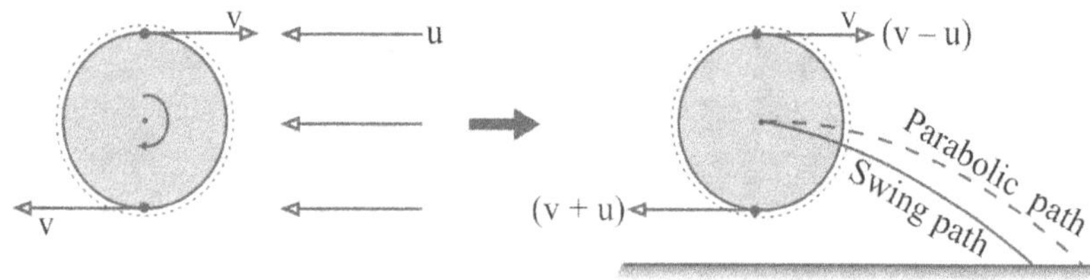

Fig. 3.95   **Fig. 3.96**

Suppose v is the speed of the air molecules in contact with the ball due to its turning figure (a).

When the ball moves forward, the air ahead of the ball rushes towards the ball with speed u. The layer above the ball moves in a direction opposite to that of the spinning, so the net speed becomes $(v - u)$. The layer below the ball moves in the direction of spin, so the net speed there becomes $(v + u)$. Because of this difference in speed, the net difference of pressure is created and the ball gets deviate from its usual parabolic path.

6. **Atomizer :** *Fig. 3.97* shows an atomizer. When the rubber or sprayer balloon is pressed, the air rushed out on the horizontal tube. By Bernoulli's principle, pressure there P_2 becomes less than the pressure P_1 in the container $(P + \frac{1}{2}\rho v^2 = \text{constant})$.

   As a result, the liquid rises up in the vertical tube. The liquid mixed together with high speed air in the tube produces fine spray.

7. **Blowing off the roof during storm:** During wind storm, high speed wind over the roof creates low pressure. While pressure below the roof is equal to the atmospheric pressure. This difference in pressure causes an upward thrust and the roof is lifted up. Once the roof is lifted up, it will blown off with the wind.

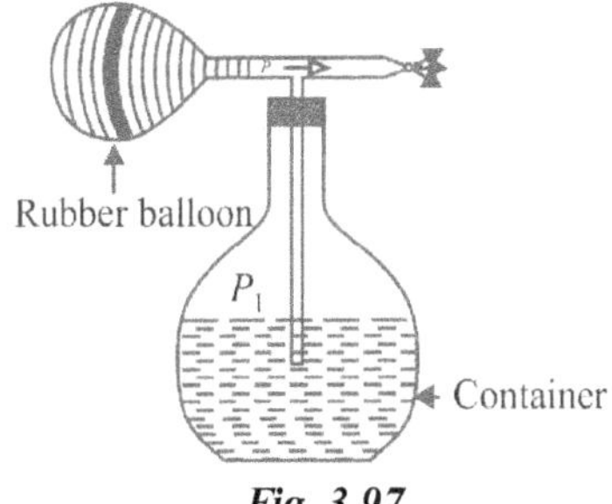

Fig. 3.97

3.24 SPEED OF EFFLUX : TORRICELLI'S THEOREM

Consider a tank containing liquid of density ρ with a small hole on its side at a depth h from the free surface of the liquid. Let P be the air pressure above the liquid surface. If A_1 and A_2 are the cross-sectional areas of the hole and the tank respectively, and v_1 and v_2 are the liquid velocities at points 1 and 2, then by equation of continuity

$$A_1 v_1 = A_2 v_2$$

or

$$v_2 = \frac{A_1}{A_2} v_1$$

For small hole in a large container, $\dfrac{A_1}{A_2} \to 0,$ $\qquad \therefore v_2 = 0$

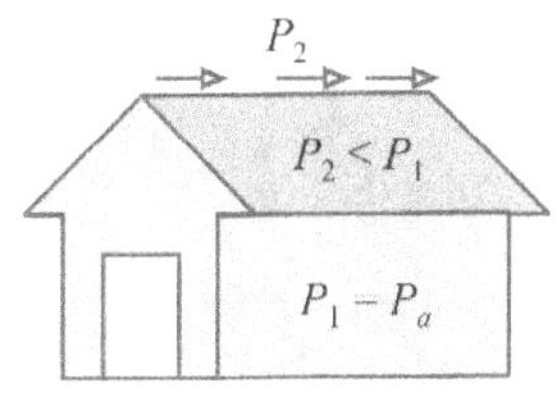

Fig. 3.98 : Blowing off the roof during wind storm

Now applying Bernoulli's equation between points 1 and 2, we have

$$P_1 + \frac{1}{2}\rho v_1^2 + 0 = P_2 + \frac{1}{2}\rho v_2^2 + \rho g h$$

Substituting $v_1 = v_e$, $v_2 = 0$ and $P_1 = P_a$, $P_2 = P$ in the above expression, we have

$$P_a + \frac{1}{2}\rho v_e^2 = P + \rho g h$$

After solving, we get

$$v_e = \sqrt{2gh + \frac{2(P - P_a)}{\rho}}.$$

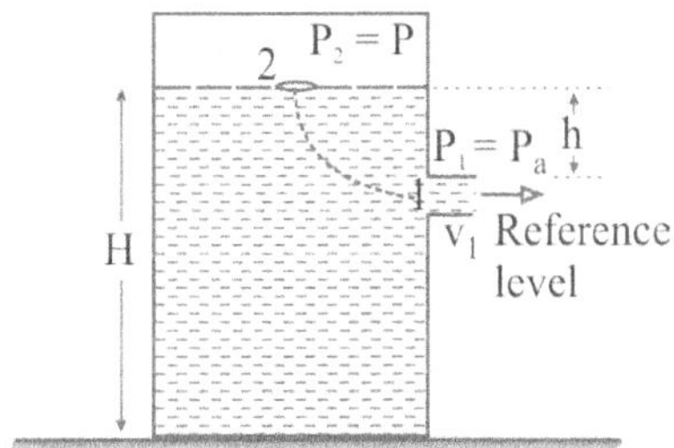

Fig. 3.99

Special cases

1. For large tank with large P, the term $2gh$ can be neglected

$$\therefore \qquad v_e = \sqrt{\frac{2(P - P_a)}{\rho}}.$$

2. When the tank is open to atmosphere

$$P = P_a \qquad \therefore v_e = \sqrt{2gh}$$

   Thus the speed of efflux of a liquid through a small hole in an open tank is equal to the velocity which a body acquires in falling freely from the free liquid surface to the orifice. This is called **Torricelli's theorem.**

3. The reaction force on the container due to emerging of the liquid

$$F = \rho A_1 v_e^2 = \rho A_1 \times 2gh$$
$$= 2\rho g h A_1$$

4. For water in a closed tank without any pressure over its free surface
$$P = 0 \text{ and } v_e \geq 0$$

$$\Rightarrow \qquad h \ge \frac{P_a}{\rho g} \;=\; \frac{1.03 \times 10^5}{1000 \times 9.8} \simeq 10.3 \text{ m}$$

i.e., water will come out from a closed tank when height of water above hole is greater than equal to 10.3 m.

5. The distance at which liquid strikes:

Let H is the height of liquid in the open container.

The time taken by liquid to hit the ground

$$(H - h) \;=\; 0 + \frac{1}{2} g t^2$$

$$\therefore \qquad t \;=\; \sqrt{\frac{2(H-h)}{g}}$$

The distance $\qquad x \;=\; v_e t$

$$=\; \sqrt{2gh} \times \sqrt{\frac{2(H-h)}{g}}$$

or $\qquad x \;=\; 2\sqrt{h(H-h)}$

For maximum x, $\qquad \dfrac{dx}{dh} \;=\; 0$

or $\qquad \dfrac{d}{dh}\left[2\sqrt{h(H-h)} \right] \;=\; 0$

$$\Rightarrow \qquad h \;=\; \frac{H}{2}$$

and $\qquad x_{\max} \;=\; 2\sqrt{\dfrac{H}{2}\left(H - \dfrac{H}{2} \right)}$

or $\qquad x_{\max} \;=\; H$

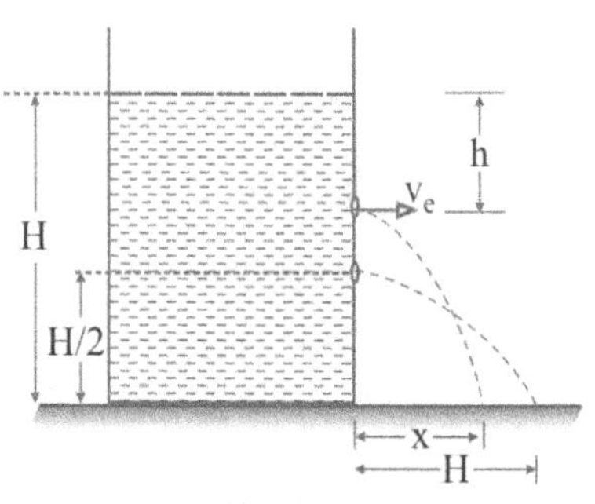

Fig. 3.100

Ex. 48 In a test experiment on a model aeroplane in a wind tunnel, the flow speeds on the upper and lower surfaces of the wing are 70 m/s and 63 m/s respectively. What is the lift on the wing if its area is 2.5 m²? Density of air =1.3 kg/m³.

Sol.

Let P_1 and P_2 be the presences on the upper and lower surfaces of the wing. Using Bernoulli's equation

$$P_1 + \frac{1}{2}\rho v_1^2 \;=\; P_2 + \frac{1}{2}\rho v_2^2$$

Fig. 3.101

(Neglecting gravitation head between lower and upper surfaces)

or $\qquad (P_2 - P_1) \;=\; \dfrac{\rho}{2}\left(v_2^2 - v_1^2\right)$

$$=\; \frac{1.3}{2}\left(70^2 - 63^2\right)$$

$$=\; 605.15 \text{ N/m}^2$$

Lift force on the wing $\;=\; (P_2 - P_1) \times$ Projected area of wing

$$=\; 605.15 \times 2.5$$

$$=\; 1.51 \times 10^3 \text{ N} \qquad\qquad \textit{Ans.}$$

Ex. 49 A Pitot tube is mounted on an aeroplane wing to measure the speed of the plane. The tube contains alcohol and shows a level difference of 40 cm. What is the speed of the plane relative air ? (sp.gr of alcohol = 0.8 and density of air = 1kg/m³)

Sol.

Let v be the velocity of the plane w.r.t. air which is equal to the velocity of the air in main pipe (see figure)

Using Bernoulli's equation between A and B

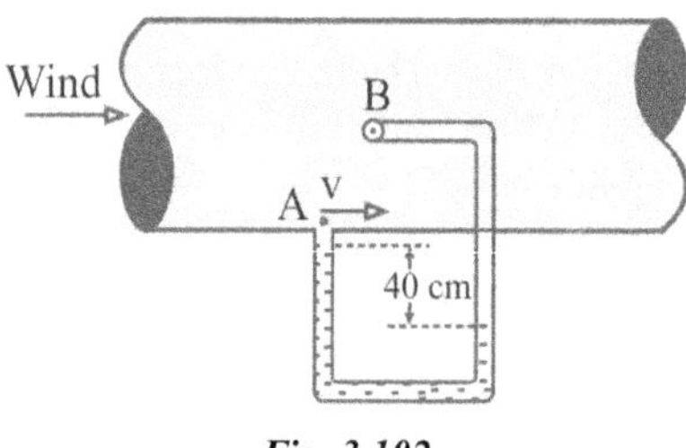

Fig. 3.102

$$P_A + \frac{1}{2}\rho v_A^2 \;=\; P_B + \frac{1}{2}\rho v_B^2$$

But
$$v_A = v \text{ and } v_B = 0$$

$$\therefore \quad \frac{1}{2}\rho v^2 = P_B - P_A$$

If ρ' is the density of alcohol in the tube, then
$$P_B - P_A = \rho' g h$$

$$\therefore \quad v = \sqrt{\frac{2\rho' g h}{\rho}}$$

$$= \sqrt{\frac{2 \times 800 \times 9.8 \times 0.40}{1}}$$

$$= 79.18 \text{ m/s} \qquad \textit{Ans.}$$

Ex. 50 A fully loaded Boeing aircraft 747 has a mass of 3.3×10^5 kg. Its total wing area is 500 m². It is in level flight with a speed of 960 km/h. (a) Estimate the pressure difference between the lower and upper surfaces of the wings. (b) Estimate the fractional increase in the speed of the air on the upper surface of the wing relative to the lower surface. The density of air is $\rho = 1.2$ kg/m³ and $g = 9.81$ m/s².

Sol.

(a) If P_1 and P_2 are the pressures at upper and lower surfaces of the aircraft, the pressure difference

$$\Delta P = P_2 - P_1 = \frac{mg}{A}$$

$$= \frac{3.3 \times 10^5 \times 9.81}{500} = 6.5 \times 10^3 \text{ N/m}^2$$

$$\textit{Ans.}$$

(b) If v_1 and v_2 are speeds of air on the upper and lower surfaces of the aircraft, then by Bernoulli's equation

$$P_1 + \frac{1}{2}\rho v_1^2 = P_2 + \frac{1}{2}\rho v_2^2$$

or $$\frac{v_1^2 - v_2^2}{2} = \frac{P_2 - P_1}{\rho}$$

or $$(v_1 - v_2)\left(\frac{v_1 + v_2}{2}\right) = \frac{\Delta P}{\rho}$$

or $$(v_1 - v_2)v_{av} = \frac{\Delta P}{\rho}$$

$$v_1 - v_2 = \frac{(\Delta P/\rho)}{v_{av}}$$

and $$\frac{(v_1 - v_2)}{v_{av}} = \frac{(\Delta P/\rho)}{v_{av}^2}$$

Here $$v_{av} = 960 \text{ km/h} = 267 \text{ m/s}$$

$$\therefore \quad \frac{v_1 - v_2}{v_{av}} = \frac{6.5 \times 10^3}{1.2 \times 267^2} \approx 0.08 = 8\% \quad \textit{Ans.}$$

Ex. 51 *Fig. 3.103* shows how the stream of water emerging from a faucet "necks down" as it falls. The indicated cross-sectional areas are $A_0 = 1.2$ cm² and $A = 0.35$ cm². The two levels are separated by a vertical distance $h = 45$ mm. What is the volume flow rate from the tap?

Sol.

If v_0 and v are the speeds at the respective sections, then by continuity equation

$$A_0 v_0 = Av \qquad \ldots\text{(i)}$$

Using Bernoulli's equation , we have

$$P_a + \frac{1}{2}\rho v_0^2 + \rho g h = P_a + \frac{1}{2}\rho v^2 + 0$$

or $$v^2 = v_0^2 + 2gh \qquad \ldots \text{(ii)}$$

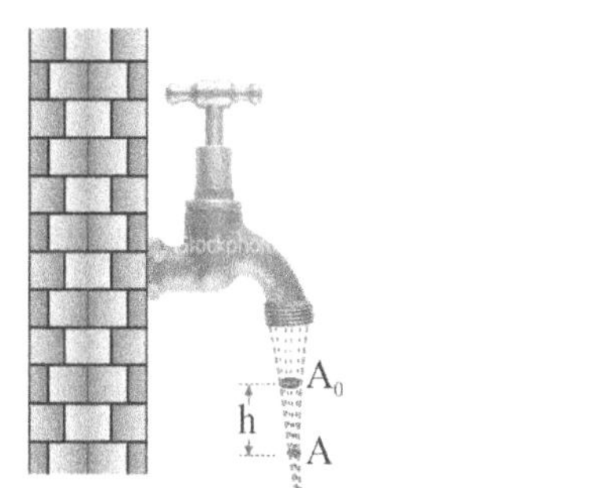

Fig. 3.103

Solving equations (i) and (ii) , we get

$$v_0 = \sqrt{\frac{2ghA^2}{A_0^2 - A^2}}$$

$$= \sqrt{\frac{2 \times 9.8 \times 0.045 \times 0.35}{(1.2^2 - 0.35^2)}}$$

$$= 0.286 \text{ m/s}$$

The volume rate of flow

$$Q = A_0 v_0$$
$$= (1.2 \times 10^{-4}) \times 0.286$$
$$= 34 \times 10^{-6} \text{ m}^3/\text{s} \qquad \textit{Ans.}$$

Ex. 52 A cylindrical tank has a hole of 1 cm² at its bottom. If the water is allowed to flow into the tank from a tube above it at the rate of 70 cm³/s, then find the maximum height upto which water can rise in the tank.

Sol.

As well as height of water in the tank increases, the efflux velocity and hence rate of flow of emerging water also increases. At a certain height h the output become equal to input and the level of water becomes constant.

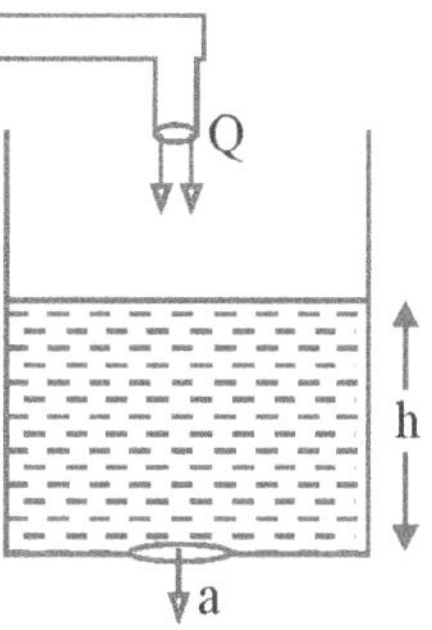

Fig. 3.104

$$\therefore \quad Q_{in} = Q_{out}$$

$$Q = a\sqrt{2gh}$$

$$h = \frac{Q^2}{2ga^2}$$

$$= \frac{(70 \times 10^{-6})^2}{2 \times 9.8 \times (1 \times 10^{-4})^2}$$

$$= 2.5 \times 10^{-2} \text{ m} \qquad \textit{Ans.}$$

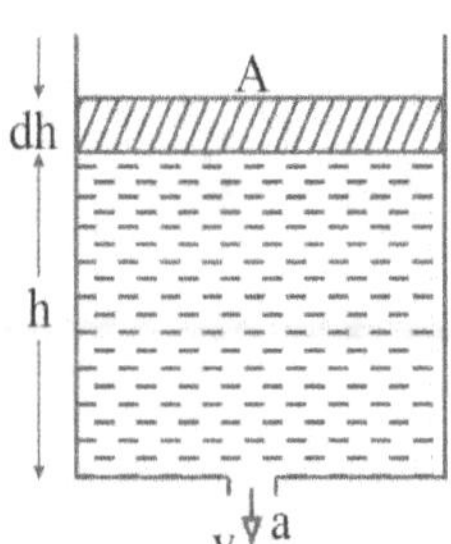

Fig. 3.105

3.25 TIME OF EMPTYING OF TANK

Consider a large tank of cross–sectional area A, with a small hole of area a at the bottom of the tank .

At any instant when height of liquid is h, the speed of the efflux through the hole $v = \sqrt{2gh}$ and rate of out flow

$$q = a\sqrt{2gh}.$$

Let in time dt, the level of liquid in the tank is decreased by dh. Thus

Volume of liquid emerging out from the hole

= volume of the shaded portion of the liquid

or $$g\,(dt) = A\,(dh)$$

or $$a\sqrt{2gh}\,dt = A\,(dh)$$

$$\therefore \qquad dt = \frac{A}{a\sqrt{2g}}\,\frac{dh}{\sqrt{h}}$$

With increases in time, h decreases, so

$$dt = \frac{A}{a\sqrt{2g}}\,\frac{-dh}{\sqrt{h}}$$

Time of emptying the tank from h_1 to h_2

$$\int_0^t dt = \frac{A}{a\sqrt{2g}}\int_{h_1}^{h_2}\frac{-dh}{\sqrt{h}} \qquad \int_0^t dt = \frac{A}{a\sqrt{2g}}\int_{h_1}^{h_2}\frac{-dh}{\sqrt{h}}$$

or $$t = \frac{A\sqrt{2}}{a\sqrt{g}}\left(\sqrt{h_1}-\sqrt{h_2}\right)$$

3.26 TIME OF EMPTYING (OR FILLING) A TANK WITH INFLOW

Consider a large tank of cross-sectional area A, with a small hole of area a at its bottom (or at side wall). Let there be a constant inflow of liquid $Q\,\mathrm{m^3/s}$ and at the same time the liquid is discharging through the hole.

Let at any instant liquid surface be at a height h above the centre of the hole and in time dt the level is increased by dh. Then volume of liquid added to the tank is Adh. Further in time dt the volume of the inflow of the liquid into tank is Qdt, and during the same time the volume of the liquid discharged through the hole is qdt, where

$$q = a\sqrt{2gh}.$$

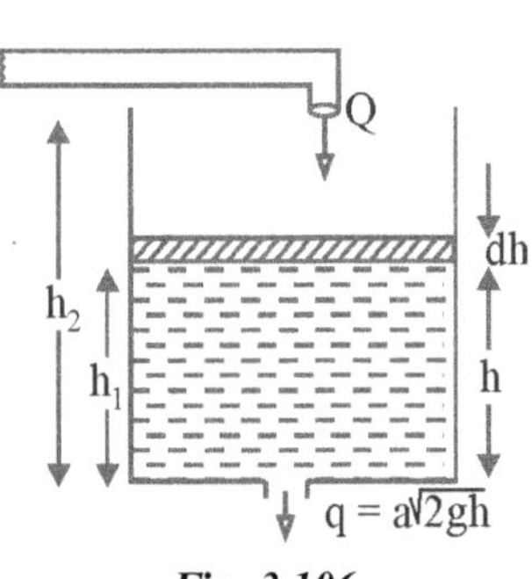

Fig. 3.106

Thus net volume of the liquid added in time dt

$$= Qdt - qdt = (Q-q)\,dt$$

$$= (Q - a\sqrt{2gh})dt$$

Thus $$Adh = (Q - a\sqrt{2gh})dt$$

or $$dt = \frac{Adh}{\left(Q - a\sqrt{2gh}\right)}$$

If liquid level rises from h_1 to h_2 in time t, then

$$\int_0^t dt = \int_{h_1}^{h_2}\frac{Adh}{\left(Q - a\sqrt{2gh}\right)} \qquad \ldots(1)$$

Substituting

$$Q - a\sqrt{2gh} = z$$

or

$$h = \frac{(Q-z)^2}{2ga^2}$$

Also

$$dh = -\frac{(Q-z)}{ga^2}\,dz$$

Substituting these values in equation (1), we get

$$t = \int \frac{A\left[-\dfrac{(Q-z)dz}{ga^2}\right]}{z}$$

$$= -\frac{A}{ga^2}\int\left(\frac{Q}{z}-1\right)dz$$

$$= -\frac{A}{ga^2}\left[Q\ln z - z\right]_{h_1}^{h_2}$$

$$= -\frac{A}{ga^2}\left[Q\ln\left(Q-a\sqrt{2gh}\right)-\left(Q-a\sqrt{2gh}\right)\right]_{h_1}^{h_2}$$

$$= -\frac{A}{ga^2}\left[Q\ln\left\{\frac{Q-a\sqrt{2gh_2}}{Q-a\sqrt{2gh_1}}\right\}+a\sqrt{2g}\left(\sqrt{h_2}-\sqrt{h_1}\right)\right] \quad \ldots (2)$$

Ex. 53 A liquid is poured into a vessel at rest with the hole in a wall closed by a valve . It is filled by liquid upto height h above the valve. What horizontal acceleration 'a' should the vessel moved, so that liquid does not come out when valve is opened?

Sol.

Method 1: Let A is the area of hole. The liquid which comes out from the hole, exerts force on the rest part of liquid . Let Δm amount of liquid leaves the hole in Δt time with velocity v. By Newton's second law

$$F = \frac{\Delta P}{\Delta t} = \frac{\Delta mv}{\Delta t}$$

$$= v\rho\frac{\Delta V}{\Delta t}$$

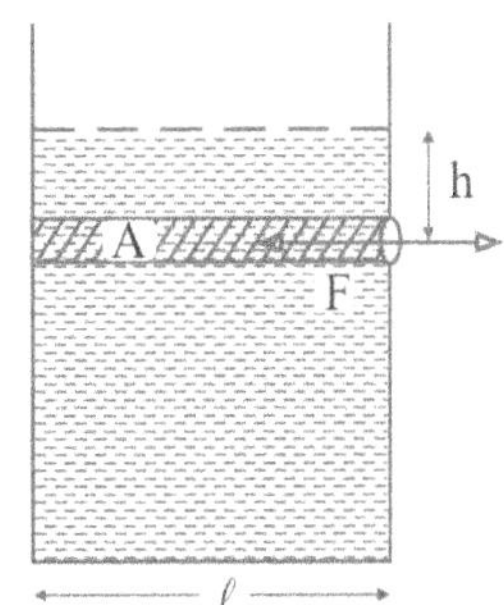

Fig. 3.107

where $\dfrac{\Delta V}{\Delta t} = Q$, rate of liquid coming out of the hole.

This force acts in backward directions of liquid confined in shaded portion.

The acceleration

$$a = \frac{F}{m} = \frac{\rho vQ}{\rho A\ell} = \frac{\rho Av^2}{\rho A\ell} \quad (Q = Av)$$

As

$$v = \sqrt{2gh} \quad \therefore \ a = \frac{v^2}{\ell} = \frac{2gh}{\ell} \quad \textit{Ans.}$$

Method II: The vessel is given an acceleration of such a value so that level of liquid at valve become zero. Let a be the acceleration of the vessel towards right, then

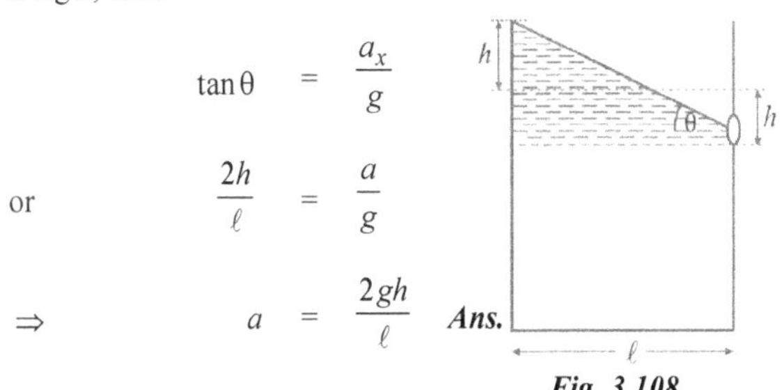

$$\tan\theta = \frac{a_x}{g}$$

or

$$\frac{2h}{\ell} = \frac{a}{g}$$

$$\Rightarrow \quad a = \frac{2gh}{\ell} \quad \textit{Ans.}$$

Fig. 3.108

Ex. 54 A tank filled with water (density ρ_ω =1000 kg/m³) and oil of (density ρ_{oil} = 900 kg/m³). The height of water is 1.00m and of the oil is 4.00m . Find the velocity of efflux through a hole at the bottom of the tank.

Sol.

Method I Applying Bernoulli's equation between (1) and (2) , we get

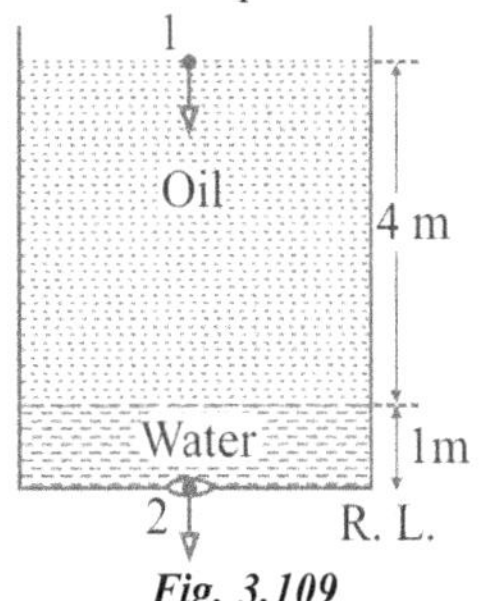

Fig. 3.109

$$P_a + \frac{1}{2}\rho v_1^2 + (\rho_w g \times 1 + \rho_{oil} \times g \times 4) = P_a + \frac{1}{2}\rho_w v_2^2 + 0$$

Since $v_1 \ll v_2$, so $\frac{1}{2}\rho v_1^2$ can be neglected.

$$\therefore \qquad v_2 = \sqrt{\frac{2(\rho_w g \times 1 + \rho_{oil} \times g \times 4)}{\rho_w}}$$

$$= \sqrt{\frac{2(1000 \times 9.8 \times 1 + 900 \times 9.8 \times 4)}{1000}}$$

$$= 9.5 \text{ m/s} \qquad \textbf{\textit{Ans.}}$$

Method II : Height of water which exerts the same pressure on interface, whatever oil exerts, let it is h.

$$\therefore \qquad h\,\rho_w g = 4 \times \rho_{oil} \times g$$

$$\text{or} \qquad h = \frac{4 \times 900}{1000} = 3.6\text{m}$$

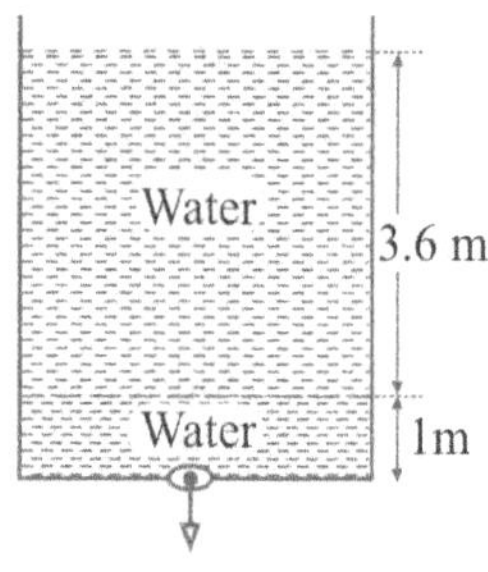

Fig. 3.110

Effective height of water over the hole
$$H = 1 + 3.6 = 4.6 \text{ m}$$
$$\therefore \qquad v_e = \sqrt{2gh} = \sqrt{2 \times 9.8 \times 4.6}$$
$$= 9.5 \text{ m/s} \qquad \textbf{\textit{Ans.}}$$

Ex. 55 A bent tube is lowered into a water stream as shown in *Fig. 3.112*. The velocity of stream relative to be tube is equal to v = 2.5 m/s. The closed upper end of the tube located at the height h_0 = 12 cm as a small orifice. To what height h will the water jet spurt?

Sol.

Consider two points 1 and 2. Point (1) is y_0 below the free surface of the liquid. Applying Bernoulli's equation between (1) and (2), we have

$$(P_a + y_0\rho g) + \frac{1}{2}\rho v^2 + 0 = P_a + 0 + \rho(y_0 + h_0 + h)g$$

$$\text{or} \qquad \frac{1}{2}\rho v^2 = \rho(h_0 + h)g$$

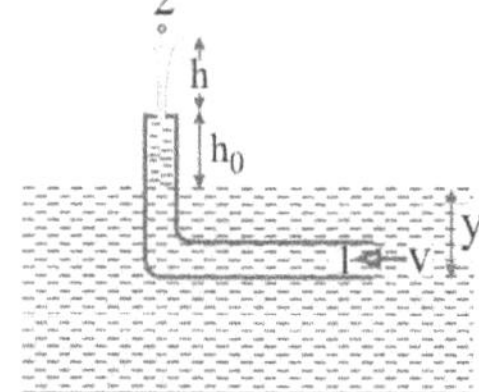

Fig. 3.111

$$\text{or} \qquad \frac{1}{2} \times 2.5^2 = (0.12 + h) \times 9.8$$

$$\therefore \qquad h = 0.2 \text{ m} \qquad \textbf{\textit{Ans.}}$$

Ex. 56 In the arrangement shown in *Fig. 3.113* a viscous liquid whose density is ρ = 1.0 g/cm³ flows along a tube out of a wide tank A. Find the velocity of the liquid flow, if h_1 = 10 cm, h_2 = 20 cm, and h_3 = 35 cm. All distances ℓ are equal.

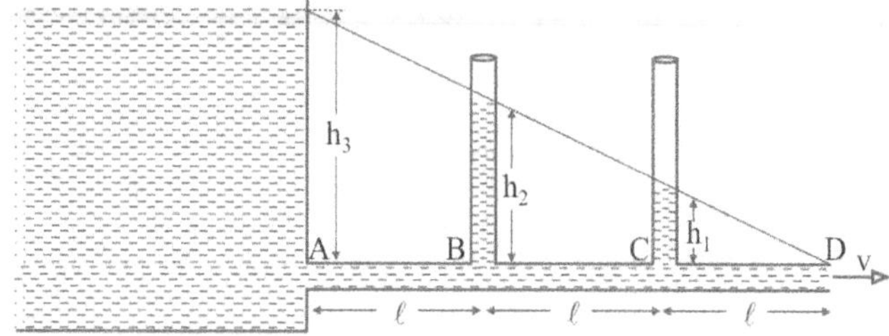

Fig. 3.112

Sol.

Loss of head from A to $B = h_3 - h_2 = 35 - 20 = 15$ cm
from B to $C = h_2 - h_1 = 20 - 10 = 10$ cm.
On the similar way from C to $D = 5$ cm
$$\therefore \qquad \text{Kinetic head available at } D, h = 35 - (15 + 10 + 5) = 5 \text{ cm}$$

$$\therefore \qquad \frac{1}{2}\rho v^2 = (0.05)\rho g$$

$$\text{or} \qquad v = \sqrt{2 \times 0.05 \times 10}$$

$$= 1 \text{ m/s} \qquad \textbf{\textit{Ans.}}$$

Ex. 57 A large open top container of negligible mass and uniform cross-sectional area A has a small hole of cross-sectional area $A/100$ in its side wall near the bottom. The container is kept on a smooth horizontal floor and contains a liquid of density ρ and mass m_0. Assuming that the liquid starts flowing out horizontally through the hole at $t = 0$, calculate

(i)   the acceleration of the container and

(ii)   its velocity when 75% of the liquid has drained out.

Sol.

(i)   The height of liquid in the container $h = \dfrac{m_0}{\rho A}$

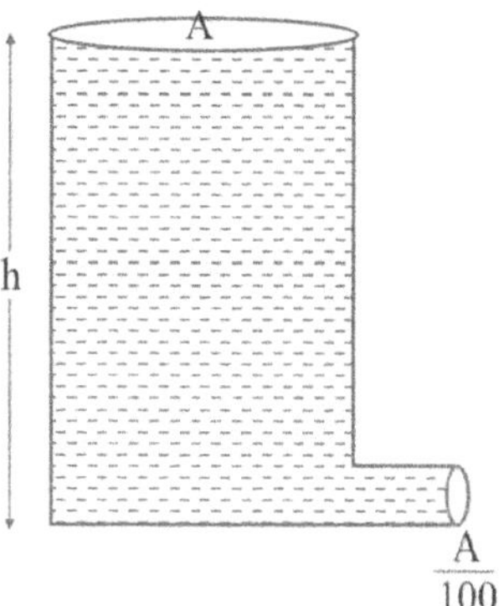

Fig. 3.113

Initially the velocity of efflux $v = \sqrt{2gh}$

Force acts on the container

$$F = \rho v Q = \rho a v^2$$

$$= \rho \times \frac{A}{100} \times 2gh$$

$$\therefore \quad \text{acceleration } a_x = \frac{F}{m_0} = \frac{\rho\left(\dfrac{A}{100}\right)\times 2gh}{m_0}$$

$$= \frac{\rho\left(\dfrac{A}{100}\right)\times 2g \times \dfrac{m_0}{\rho A}}{m_0}$$

$$= \frac{2g}{100} = \frac{1}{5}\,\text{m/s}^2 \quad \text{(Constant value) } \textbf{\textit{Ans.}}$$

(ii) Let in time t the level of liquid falls from h to $\dfrac{h}{4}$ (75% of the liquid drained out). The time of emptying a tank from h_1 to h_2 is given by

$$t = \frac{A\sqrt{2}}{a\sqrt{g}}\left(\sqrt{h_1} - \sqrt{h_2}\right)$$

$$= \frac{A\sqrt{2}}{\dfrac{A}{100}\sqrt{g}}\left(\sqrt{h} - \sqrt{\dfrac{h}{4}}\right)$$

$$= \frac{100\sqrt{2}}{\sqrt{g}}\left(1 - \frac{1}{2}\right)\sqrt{h}$$

$$= \frac{100}{\sqrt{2g}}\sqrt{h}$$

$$= \frac{100}{\sqrt{2g}}\sqrt{\frac{m_0}{\rho A}}$$

Velocity of the container in time t

$$v = at$$

$$= \frac{1}{5}\times\frac{100}{\sqrt{2g}}\sqrt{\frac{m_0}{\rho A}} \quad \textbf{\textit{Ans.}}$$

Ex. 58 A liquid of density 900 kg/m³ is filled in a cylindrical tank of upper radius 0.9 m and lower radius 0.3m. A capillary tube of length ℓ is attached at the bottom of the tank as shown in the Fig. 3.115. The capillary has outer radius 0.002m and inner radius a. When pressure P is applied at the top of the tank volume flow rate of the liquid is 8×10^{-6} m³/s and if capillary tube is detached, the liquid comes out from the tank with a velocity of 10 m/s . Determine the coefficient of viscosity of the liquid.

[Given $\pi a^2 = 10^{-6} m^2$ and $\dfrac{a^2}{\ell} = 2\times 10^{-6}$ m]

Sol.

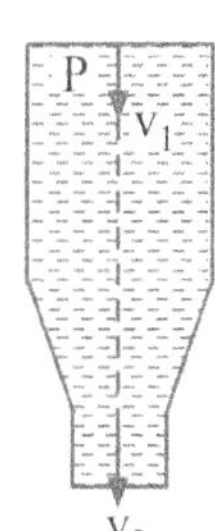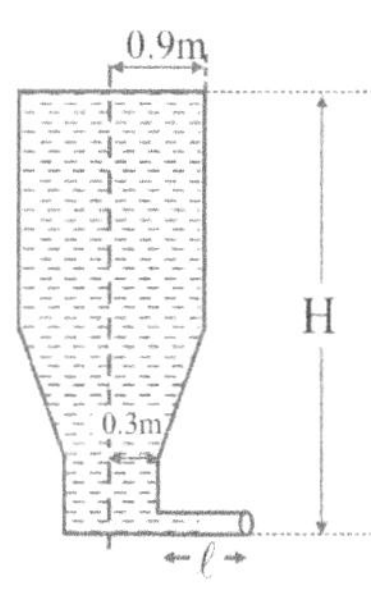

Fig. 3.114

Without the capillary tube, the liquid comes out from the narrower part of the cylinder

$$\therefore \quad a_1 v_1 = a_2 v_2 \Rightarrow v_1 = \frac{a_2 v_2}{a_1}$$

Applying Bernoulli's equation between (1) and (2), we have

$$(P + P_a) + \frac{1}{2}\rho v_1^2 + \rho g H = P_a + \frac{1}{2}\rho v_2^2 + 0$$

$$\text{or} \quad (P + \rho g H) = \frac{1}{2}\rho\left(v_2^2 - v_1^2\right)$$

$$= \frac{1}{2}\rho\left[v_2^2 - \left(\frac{a_2 v_2}{a_1}\right)^2\right]$$

$$= \frac{1}{2}\rho v_2^2\left[1 - \frac{a_2^2}{a_1^2}\right]$$

$$\text{where} \quad v_2 = 10 \text{ m/s}$$

$$\therefore \quad P + \rho g H = \frac{1}{2}\times 900\times(10)^2\left[1 - \left[\frac{\pi(0.3)^2}{\pi(0.9)^2}\right]^2\right]$$

$$= \frac{1}{2}\times 900\times 100\left(1 - \frac{1}{81}\right)$$

$$= \frac{1}{2}\times 900\times 100\times\frac{80}{81}$$

$$= \frac{4}{9}\times 10^5\,\text{N/m}^2$$

With the capillary tube the rate of flow = 8×10^{-6} m³/s. Pressure difference across the tube

$$\Delta P = (P_a + P + H\rho g - P_a)$$

Fig. 3.115

$$= P + H\rho g$$

$$= \frac{4}{9}\times 10^5\,\text{N/m}^2$$

Now using Poisulli's equation, we have

$$Q = \frac{\pi(\Delta P)r^4}{8\eta\ell}$$

$$\text{or} \quad 8\times 10^{-6} = \frac{\left(\dfrac{4}{9}\times 10^5\right)(\pi a^2)}{8\eta}\left(\frac{a^2}{\ell}\right)$$

$$\text{or} \quad 8\times 10^{-6} = \frac{\left(\dfrac{4}{9}\times 10^5\right)(10^{-6})(2\times 10^{-6})}{8\eta}$$

After solving, $\quad \eta = \dfrac{1}{720}\dfrac{N-s}{m^2} \quad \textbf{\textit{Ans.}}$

Ex. 59 The gate OA shown is hinged at O and is in the form of a quadrant of a circle of radius 1m. It supports water on one side as shown. If the width of the gate is 3m, calculate the force required to hold the gate in position

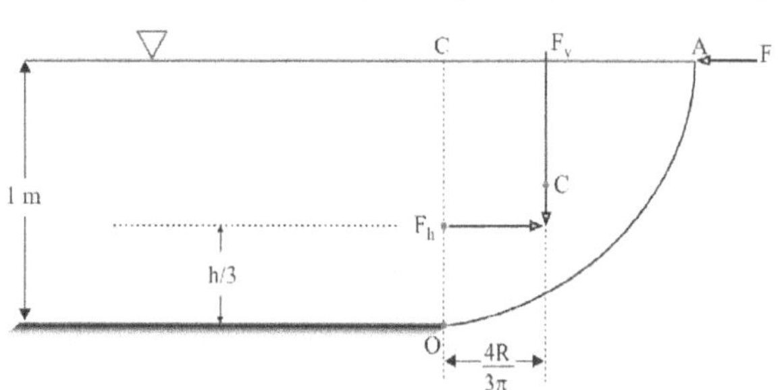

Fig. 3.116

Sol..

Given radius,

$$R = 1\ m$$

Width of the gate,

$$b = 3\ m$$

$$F_n = \text{force on vertical projection of } AOC$$

$$= p_{av} \times (OC \times b)$$

$$= \frac{\rho g h}{2} \times (1 \times 3)$$

$$= \frac{1000 \times 9.81 \times 1}{2}(1 \times 3)$$

$$= 14715\ n$$

$$F_v = \text{weight of the water contained in } OAC.$$

$$= \left(\frac{1}{4}\pi R^2 \times b\right)\rho g$$

$$= \frac{1}{4}\pi(1)^2 \times 3 \times 1000 \times 9.81$$

$$= 23102.5\ N$$

The horizontal force F_n acts at a height $\dfrac{h}{3} = \dfrac{1}{3}m$ above the hinge whereas the force F_v acts through the centroid of OAC which is located at a distance $\dfrac{4R}{3\pi} = \dfrac{4 \times 1}{3\pi}$ from OC.

Taking moment of forces about the hinge O

$$F \times 1 = 14715 \times \frac{1}{3} + 23102.5 \times \left(\frac{4 \times 1}{3\pi}\right)$$

$$\therefore \qquad F = 14715\ N \qquad \textbf{Ans.}$$

Ex. 60 A tube ABC bent at a right angle open at A and closed at C, filled with water, is accelerated to the right as shown. Determine the acceleration at which the pressure at C becomes atmospheric.

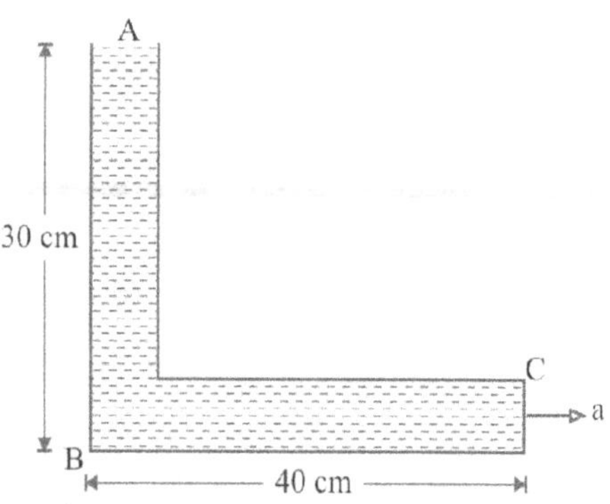

Fig. 3.117

Sol.

The pressure at C to be atmospheric, the force exerted by the water column of height 30 cm and 40 cm long column is to be balanced by the pseudo force. If A is the area of cross-section of the tube, then

$$P_B A = m_{BC} a$$

$$\rho g h A = (\rho \ell A) a$$

$$\therefore \qquad a = \frac{h}{\ell} g$$

$$= \frac{0.30}{0.40} \times 9.8$$

$$= 7.36\ m/s^2 \qquad \textbf{Ans.}$$

Ex. 61 A tank and a through are placed on a trolley as shown. Water issues from the tank through a 5 cm diameter nozzle at 5 m/s and strikes the through which turns it by 45°. Determine the compression of the spring of stiffness 2000 N/m.

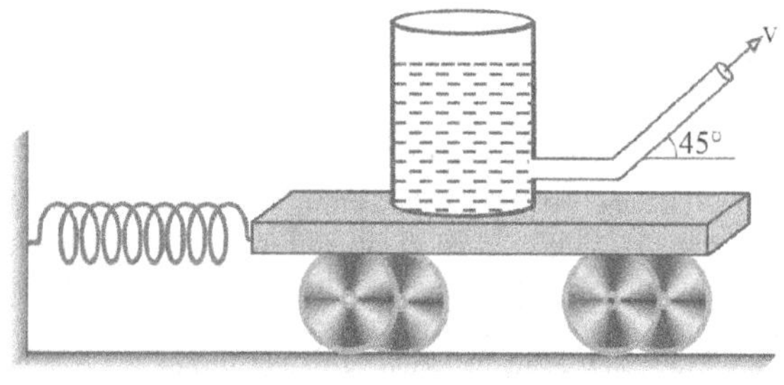

Fig. 3.118

Sol.

The rate of flow through the nozzle

$$Q = Av = \frac{\pi}{4}(0.05)^2 \times 5$$

$$= 9.81 \times 10^{-3}\ kg/m^3$$

The reaction force at the mouth of nozzle

$$F = \rho v Q$$

$$= 1000 \times 5 \times 9.81 \times 10^{-3}$$

$$= 49.05\ N$$

The direction of F is along the direction of nozzle.
The horizontal component of this force

$$F_x = F\cos 45° = \frac{49.05}{\sqrt{2}} \, N$$

If x is the compression of spring, then

$$F_x = kx$$

$$\therefore \quad x = F_x/k = \frac{49.05}{\sqrt{2} \times 2000}$$

$$= 0.0173 \, m \qquad \textit{Ans.}$$

Ex. 62 A bellmouth entry in front of an air-compressor is to be calibrated for discharge through it in terms of height h of water in a single tube manometer as shown. If $h = 0.2$ m and the density of air is 1.2 kg/m³, estimate the discharge of air through the compressor.

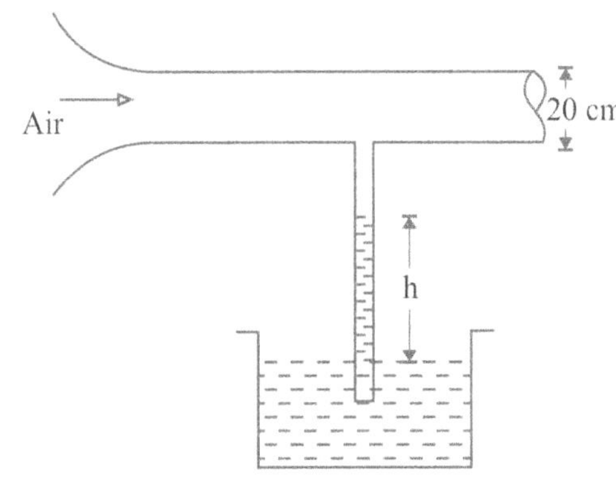

Fig. 3.119

Sol.

If v is the velocity of flow of the air then

$$\frac{1}{2}\rho_{air}v^2 = \rho_\omega gh$$

$$\therefore \quad v = \sqrt{\frac{2\rho_\omega gh}{\rho_{air}}}$$

$$= \sqrt{\frac{2 \times 1000 \times 9.81 \times 0.2}{1.2}} = 57.14 \, m/s$$

The rate of flow of air or discharge through the compressor

$$Q = Av$$

$$= \frac{\pi}{4}d^2 \times v$$

$$= \frac{\pi}{4}(0.20)^2 \times 57.14$$

$$= 1.8 \, m^3/s \qquad \textit{Ans.}$$

Ex. 63 A lawn sprinkler with two nozzles 0.1 cm diameter each at 20 cm and 10 cm radii is connected across at tap capable of 6 litre /minute discharged. The nozzle discharge water upwards and outwards from the plane of rotation. What torque will the sprinkler exert on the hand?

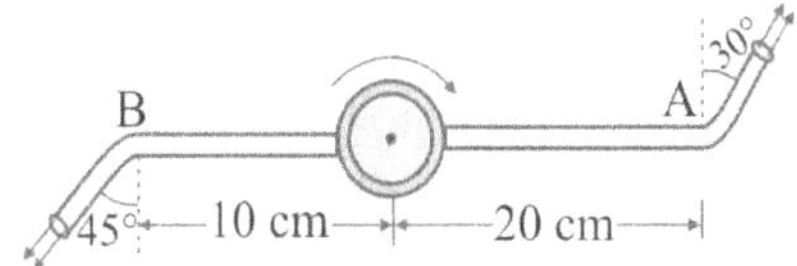

Fig. 3.120

Sol.

Assuming the discharge to be divided equally between the two nozzles, so

$$Q_A = Q_B = 3 \text{ litre/minute}$$

$$= \frac{3 \times 10^{-3}}{60} = 50 \times 10^{-6} \, m^3/s$$

The force exerted by the discharging water on the nozzle is given by

$$F = \rho v Q = \rho \frac{Q^2}{A}$$

Thus

$$F_A = F_B = \frac{1000 \times (50 \times 10^{-6})^2}{\frac{\pi}{4}(0.01)^2}$$

$$= 31.85 \times 10^{-3} \, N$$

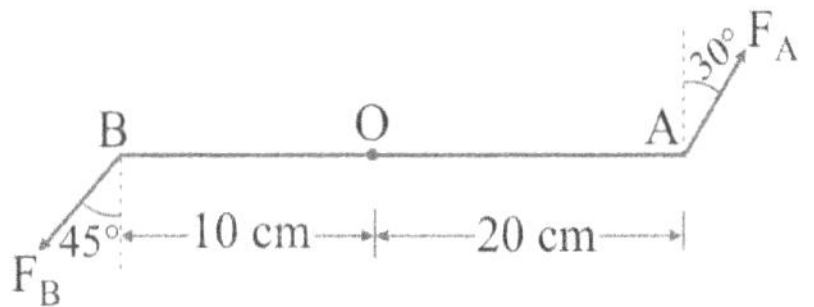

Fig. 3.121

The net torque at the hand (about)

$$\tau =$$

$$F_A \cos 30° \times 0.20 + F_B \cos 45° \times 0.10$$

$$= 31.85 \times 10^{-3} \times \frac{\sqrt{3}}{2} \times 0.20 + 31.85 \times 10^{-3} \times \frac{1}{\sqrt{2}} \times 0.10$$

$$= 0.078 \, N\text{-}m \qquad \textit{Ans.}$$

Ex. 64 Determine the torque required to turn a 10 cm long 5 cm diameter shaft at 500 revolutions per minute in a 5.1 cm diameter concentric bearing flooded with a lubricating oil of viscosity 100 centipoise.

Sol.

Angular speed of the shaft $\omega = 2\pi n$
Peripheral speed of the shaft $v = \omega r = 2\pi nr$

$$= 2\pi \times \frac{500}{60} \times 0.025 = 1.31 \, m/s$$

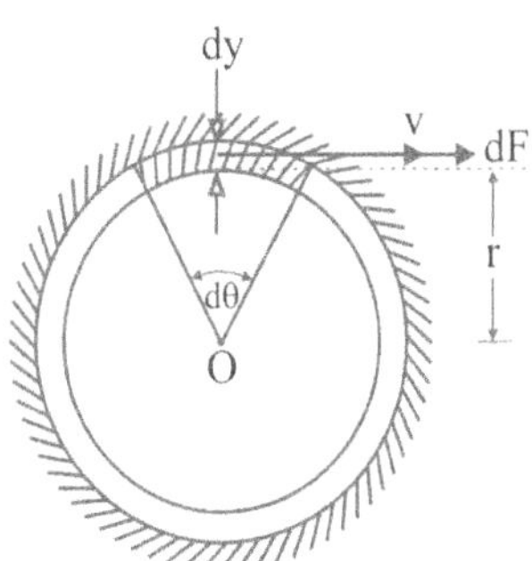

Fig. 3.122

Since bearing is at rest, so velocity gradient

$$\frac{dv}{dy} = \frac{1.31}{(5.1-5)\times10^{-2}}$$

$$= 2620 \text{ /s}$$

Now choose an element of angular width $d\theta$, the area over which viscous force of the element acts,

$$dA = (rd\theta)\ell \,.$$

The viscous force on the element

$$dF = \eta(dA)\frac{dv}{dy}$$

Torque of this force, $\quad d\tau = (dF)r$

The torque required to turn the shaft

$$\tau = \int_0^{2\pi}(dF)r = \int_0^{2\pi}\eta(dA)\frac{dv}{dy}r$$

$$= \int_0^{2\pi}\eta(rd\theta\ell)\frac{dv}{dy}r$$

$$= \eta r^2\ell\left(\frac{dv}{dy}\right)\times2\pi$$

$$= 0.1\times(0.025)^2\times0.10\times2620\times2\pi$$

$$= 0.1028 \text{ N-m} \qquad \textbf{\textit{Ans.}}$$

Review of formulae & Important Points

1. Density : $\quad \rho = \dfrac{M}{V}$

Relative density :

$$\text{R.D.} = \frac{\text{Density of substance}}{\text{Density of water at } 4^\circ C}$$

R.D. can be obtained by the formula $R.D.=\left(\dfrac{W_{air}}{W_{air}-W_{water}}\right)$

Density of mixture is given by

$$\rho = \left(\frac{M_1+M_2+........+M_n}{V_1+V_2+.........+V_n}\right)$$

2. Pressure :

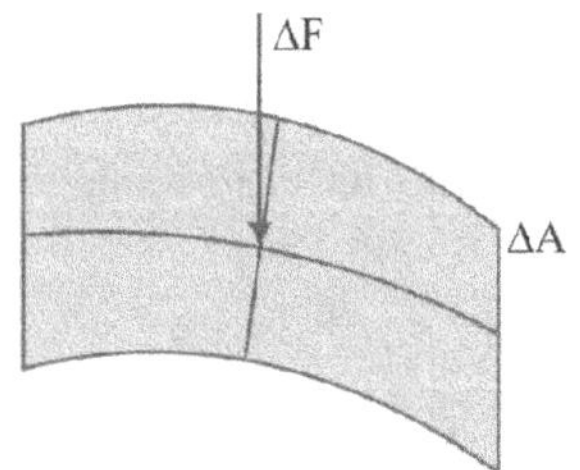

Average pressure, $P = \dfrac{\Delta F}{\Delta A}$

Pressure at any point is defined as :

$$P = \lim_{\Delta A\to0}\frac{\Delta F}{\Delta A}$$

or $\qquad P = \dfrac{dF}{dA}$

SI unit of pressure is $\dfrac{N}{m^2}$. $\dfrac{1N}{m^2}=1Pa.$ 1 bar $= 10^5 N/m^2$.

3. Variation of pressure with depth.

$$P = \rho g h$$

here h is the depth of the point from free surface of the liquid.

4. Pascal's law : It can be stated in the following equivalent ways.

(i) The pressure exerted at any point on an enclosed liquid is transmitted equally in all directions.

(ii) A change in pressure applied to an enclosed incompressible liquid is transmitted undiminished to every point of the liquid and the walls of the container

(iii) The pressure in a liquid at rest is same at all points of liquid at some levels of we ignore gravity.

In hydraulic lift, the load lifted W by effort ρ is given by:

$$W = P\frac{A}{a}$$

5. Atmospheric pressure :

1 atmospheric pressure = 76 cm of mercury height

$$= 10.3 \text{ m of water height}$$

$$= 1.013\times10^5 \, N/m^2$$

Gauge pressure = Absolute pressure–Atmospheric pressure

or $\qquad P_{gauge} = P_{absolute} - P_a$

Assuming isothermal atmosphere, pressure at any height h is given by

$$P = P_0 e^{-\rho_0 g h/P_0}$$

here P_0 is the pressure at ground level.

6. Manometer : It is used to measure the gauge pressure of a gas. If h is the difference of levels of liquid in the arms of manometer tube, then

$$P_{gauge} = \rho g h$$

7. Force exerted by liquid on the vertical face of the wall :

$F = P_{av} \times$ Area of the wall in contact with the liquid

$$= \frac{\rho g h}{2}\times Lh = \frac{\rho g L h^2}{2}$$

This force acts at a height $\dfrac{h}{3}$ from the base of the wall.

8. Archimedes' principle :

Buoyant force on the immersed body

$$F_b = V \rho g$$

Apparent weight of the body

$$= W - F_b = W\left(1 - \frac{\rho}{\sigma}\right)$$

9. For floating body :

weight of the body = buoyant force on the body

10. If V' and V are the submerged and total volume of the body, then

$$\frac{V'}{V} = \frac{\sigma}{\rho}$$

here $\sigma \leq \rho$.

11. Equilibrium of a submerged body : For completely submerged floating body;

(i) If C.G. his below centre of buoyancy, then there will be stable equilibrium.

(ii) If C.G. lies above centre of buoyancy, then there will be unstable equilibrium.

(iii) If C.G. concides with the centre of buoyancy, then there will be neutral equilibrium

12. Accelerating liquid :

(i) Pressure difference between two points at a vertical height h in a liquid accelerating upwards is given by

$$P_2 - P_1 = \rho(g + a)h$$

Buoyant force,

$$F_b = V\rho(g + a)$$

(iii) When liquid is subjected to horizontal acceleration :

$$\tan\theta = \frac{a}{g}$$

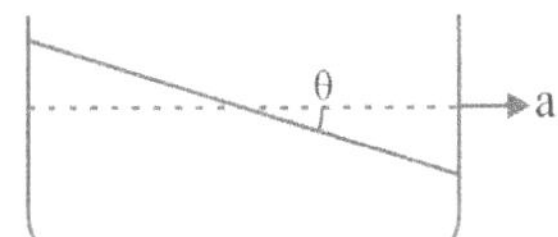

(iv) When liquid is subjected to rotation :

The difference in elevation between the axis and at a distance x,

$$y = \frac{\omega^2 x^2}{2g}$$

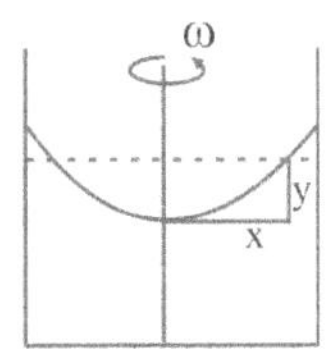

FLUID DYNAMICS

13. Rate of flow or discharge

$$Q = Av$$

14. Reynolds number

$$R_e = \frac{\rho v D}{\eta}.$$

If $R_e \leq 2000$, the flow will be laminar. If $R_e > 3000$, the flow is turbulent. If R_e lies between 2000 and 3000, the flow is unstable.

15. Equation of continuity :

$$Q = Av = \text{constant}$$

16. Bernoulli's equation :

(i)

$$P + \frac{1}{2}\rho v^2 + \rho g h = \text{constant}$$

(ii)

$$\frac{P}{\rho g} + \frac{v^2}{2g} + h = \text{constant}$$

17. Venturimeter or flow meter :

$$Q = A_1 A_2 \frac{\sqrt{2gh}}{\sqrt{A_1^2 - A_2^2}}$$

here h is the difference of readings of simple manometers.

18. Speed of efflux : The speed of the liquid emerging from a small hole under head h is given by

$$v_e = \sqrt{2gh}$$

$$x = 2\sqrt{h(H - h)}$$

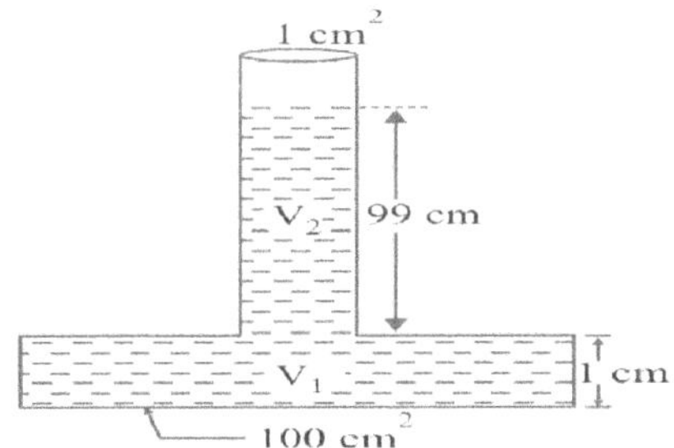

For maximum x, $h = \dfrac{H}{2}$, and $x_{\max} = H$.

19. Time of emplying a tank :

$$t = \frac{A\sqrt{2}}{a\sqrt{g}}\left(\sqrt{h_1} - \sqrt{h_2}\right)$$

FM   **MCQ Type 1**   *Exercise 3.1*

LEVEL - 1

Only one option is correct

1. We fully submerge an irregular 5 kg lump of material in a certain fluid. The fluid that would have been in the space now occupied by the lump has a mass of 3.5 kg. When we release the lump, it will move
   - (a) upward
   - (b) downward
   - (c) remain in place
   - (d) none of these

2. A block floats in water in a stationary elevator. When elevator moves upward with an acceleration, the block floats now with volume inside water :
   - (a) same
   - (b) less
   - (c) greater
   - (d) any of the above depending on the density of the block

3. A siphon in use is demonstrated in the following figure. The density of the liquid flowing in siphon is 1.5 gm/cc. The pressure difference between the point P and S will be

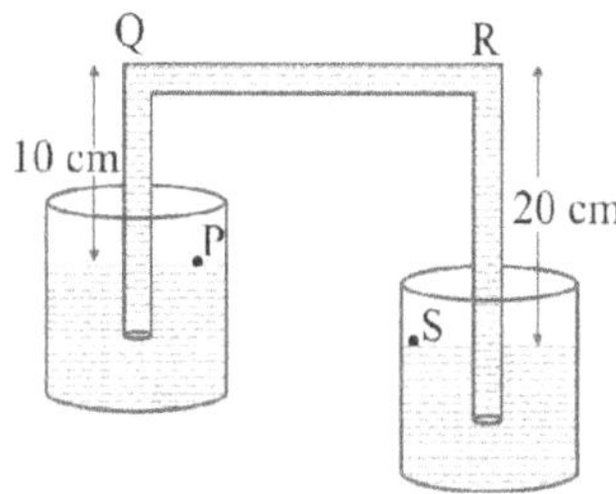

   - (a) 10^5 N/m
   - (b) 2×10^5 N/m
   - (c) Zero
   - (d) Infinity

4. Density of ice is ρ and that of water is σ. What will be decrease in volume when a mass M of ice melts
   - (a) $\dfrac{M}{\sigma - \rho}$
   - (b) $\dfrac{\sigma - \rho}{M}$
   - (c) $M\left[\dfrac{1}{\rho} - \dfrac{1}{\sigma}\right]$
   - (d) $\dfrac{1}{M}\left[\dfrac{1}{\rho} + \dfrac{1}{\sigma}\right]$

5. A closed rectangular tank is completely filled with water and is accelerated horizontally with an acceleration a towards right. Pressure is (i) maximum at, and (ii) minimum at

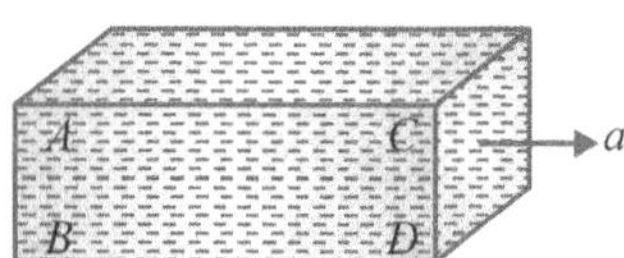

   - (a) (i) B (ii) D
   - (b) (i) C (ii) D
   - (c) (i) B (ii) C
   - (d) (i) B (ii) A

6. A vertical U-tube of uniform inner cross- section contains mercury in both sides of its arms. A glycerin (density = 1.3 g/cm^3) column of length 10 cm is introduced into one of its arms. Oil of density 0.8 gm/cm^3 is poured into the other arm until the upper surfaces of the oil and glycerin are in the same horizontal level. Find the length of the oil column. Density of mercury = 13.6 g/cm^3

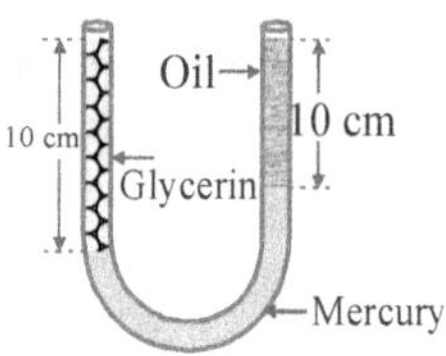

   - (a) 10.4 cm
   - (b) 8.2 cm
   - (c) 7.2 cm
   - (d) 9.6 cm

7. Three liquids of densities d, $2d$ and $3d$ are mixed in equal proportions of weights. The relative density of the mixture is
   - (a) $\dfrac{11d}{7}$
   - (b) $\dfrac{18d}{11}$
   - (c) $\dfrac{13d}{9}$
   - (d) $\dfrac{23d}{18}$

8. From the adjacent figure, the correct observation is

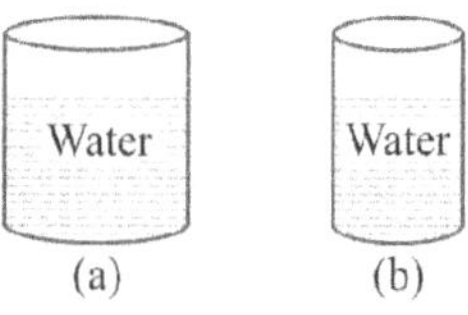

   - (a) The pressure on the bottom of tank (a) is greater than at the bottom of (b)
   - (b) The pressure on the bottom of the tank (a) is smaller than at the bottom of (b)
   - (c) The pressure depend on the shape of the container
   - (d) The pressure on the bottom of (a) and (b) is the same

Answer Key	1	(a)	3	(c)	5	(a)	7	(b)
Sol. from page 259	2	(a)	4	(c)	6	(d)	8	(d)

9. A given shaped glass tube having uniform cross section is filled with water and is mounted on a rotatable shaft as shown in figure. If the tube is rotated with a constant angular velocity ω, then

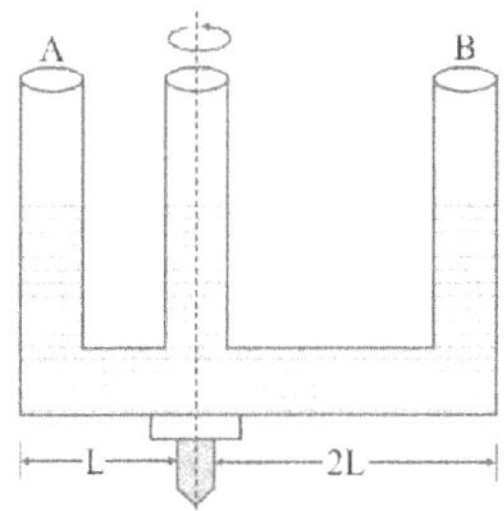

(a) Water levels in both sections A and B go up
(b) Water level in section A goes up and that in B comes down
(c) Water level in section A comes down and that in B it goes up
(d) Water levels remains same in both sections

10. A cubical block is floating in a liquid with half of its volume immersed in the liquid. When the whole system accelerates upwards with acceleration of g/3, the fraction of volume immersed in the liquid will be

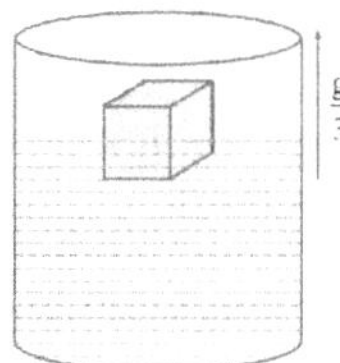

(a) $\dfrac{1}{2}$

(b) $\dfrac{3}{8}$

(c) $\dfrac{2}{3}$

(d) $\dfrac{3}{4}$

11. An incompressible liquid flows through a horizontal tube shown in the following fig. Then the velocity v of the fluid is

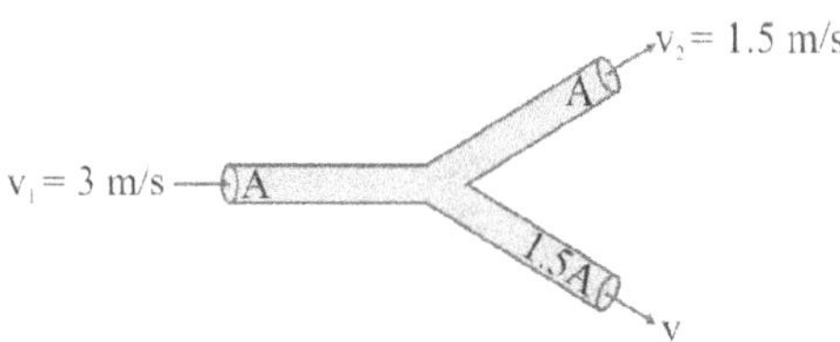

(a) 3.0 m/s
(b) 1.5 m/s
(c) 1.0 m/s
(d) 2.25 m/s

12. Water is moving with a speed of 5.18 ms^{-1} through a pipe with a cross-sectional area of 4.20 cm^2. The water gradually descends 9.66 m as the pipe increase in area to 7.60 cm^2. The speed of flow at the lower level is

(a) 3.0 ms^{-1}
(b) 5.7 ms^{-1}
(c) 3.82 ms^{-1}
(d) 2.86 ms^{-1}

13. A manometer connected to a closed tap reads 3.5×10^5 N/m^2. When the valve is opened, the reading of manometer falls to 3.0×10^5 N/m^2, then velocity of flow of water is

(a) 100 m/s
(b) 10 m/s
(c) 1 m/s
(d) $10\sqrt{10} \ m/s$

14. A ball of radius r and density ρ falls freely under gravity through a distance h before entering water. Velocity of ball does not change even on entering water. If viscosity of water is η, the value of h is given by

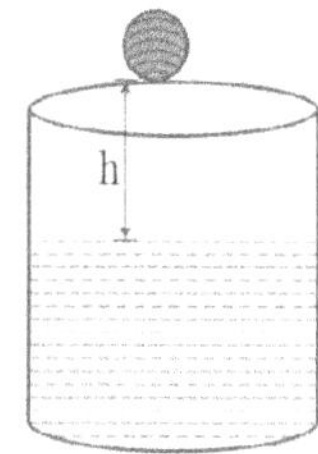

(a) $\dfrac{2}{9}r^2\left(\dfrac{1-\rho}{\eta}\right)g$

(b) $\dfrac{2}{81}r^2\left(\dfrac{\rho-1}{\eta}\right)^2 g$

(c) $\dfrac{2}{81}r^4\left(\dfrac{\rho-1}{\eta}\right)^2 g$

(d) $\dfrac{2}{9}r^4\left(\dfrac{\rho-1}{\eta}\right)^2 g$

15. An application of Bernoulli's equation for fluid flow is found in
(a) dynamic lift of an aeroplane
(b) viscosity meter
(c) capillary rise
(d) hydraulic press

16. A cylindrical vessel of 90 cm height is kept filled upto the brim. It has four holes 1, 2, 3, 4 which are respectively at heights of 20 cm, 30 cm, 45 cm and 50 cm from the horizontal floor PQ. The water falling at the maximum horizontal distance from the vessel comes from

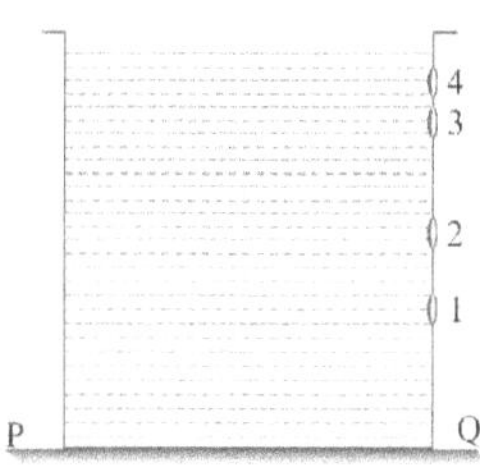

(a) Hole number 4
(b) Hole number 3
(c) Hole number 2
(d) Hole number 1

Answer Key	9	(a)	11	(c)	13	(b)	15	(a)
Sol. from page 259	10	(a)	12	(d)	14	(c)	16	(b)

17. A *U*-tube in which the cross-sectional area of the limb on the left is one quarter, the limb on the right contains mercury (density 13.6 g/cm^3). The level of mercury in the narrow limb is at a distance of 36 cm from the upper end of the tube. What will be the rise in the level of mercury in the right limb if the left limb is filled to the top with water

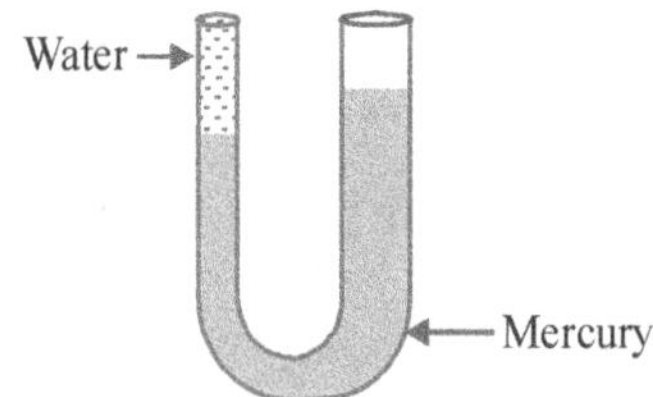

   (a) 1.2 cm   (b) 2.35 cm
   (c) 0.56 cm   (d) 0.8 cm

18. A vessel contains oil (density $= 0.8$ gm/cm^3) over mercury (density $= 13.6$ gm/cm^3). A homogeneous sphere floats with half of its volume immersed in mercury and the other half in oil. The density of the material of the sphere in gm/cm^3 is
   (a) 3.3   (b) 6.4
   (c) 7.2   (d) 12.8

19. A body floats in a liquid contained in a beaker. The whole system as shown falls freely under gravity. The upthrust on the body due to the liquid is

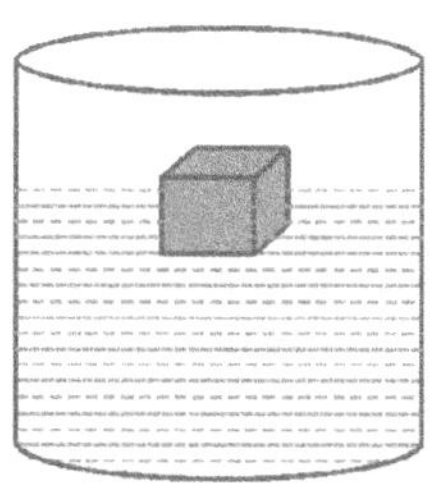

   (a) zero
   (b) equal to the weight of the liquid displaced
   (c) equal to the weight of the body in air
   (d) equal to the weight of the immersed position of the body

20. A block of ice floats on a liquid of density 1.2 in a beaker, then level of liquid when ice completely melt
   (a) Remains same   (b) Rises
   (c) Lowers   (d) (a), (b) or (c)

21. A lead shot of 1 mm diameter falls through a long column of glycerine. The variation of its velocity v with distance covered is represented by

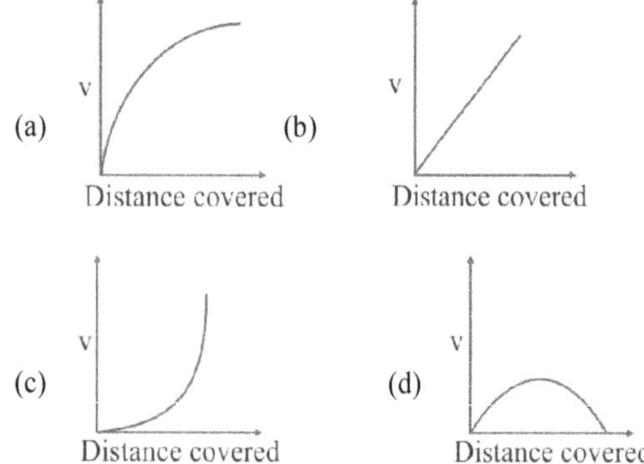

22. Consider the following statements : In a streamline flow of a liquid,
  1. the kinetic energies of all particles arriving at a given point are same.
  2. the momenta of all particles arriving at a given point are same.
  3. the speed of particles are below the critical velocity.
  Which of the statements given above are correct:
   (a) 1 and 2 only   (b) 2 and 3 only
   (c) 1 and 3 only   (d) 1, 2 and 3

23. For cylindrical pipes, the Reynolds number corresponding to the critical speed is 2000. Water (viscosity coefficient 10^{-3} N s/m^2) flows through a pipe of diameter 2 cm. What is the critical speed
   (a) 4 cm/s   (b) 10 cm/s
   (c) 12 cm/s   (d) 100 cm/s

24. Consider the following statements :
  1. Magnus effect is a consequence of Bernoulli's principle.
  2. A cricketer, while spinning a ball makes it to experience magnus effect.
  Which of the statements given above is/are correct
   (a) 1 only   (b) 2 only
   (c) Both 1 and 2   (d) Neither 1 nor 2

25. Consider the following statements :
  There is a small hole near the bottom of an open tank filled with water. The speed of water ejected depends on
  1. area of the hole
  2. density of liquid
  3. height of liquid from the hole
  4. acceleration due to gravity
  Which of the statements given above are correct
   (a) 1 and 2 only   (b) 1, 3 and 4 only
   (c) 3 and 4 only   (d) 2, 3 and 4 only

26. In the figure shown, water drains out through a small hole of a large tank.

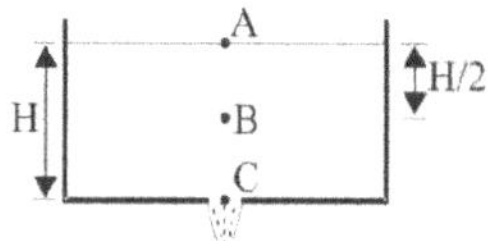

   (a) pressure at the point C is greater than atmospheric
   (b) pressure at the point B is $\rho g \dfrac{H}{2}$
   (c) pressure at the point B is less than $\rho g \dfrac{H}{2}$
   (d) velocity head at the point B is negligible

27. A jar is filled with two non-mixing liquids 1 and 2 having densities ρ_1 and ρ_2 respectively. A solid ball made of a material of density ρ_3 is dropped in the jar. It comes to equilibrium in the position shown in the figure. Which of the following is true for ρ_1, ρ_2 and ρ_3

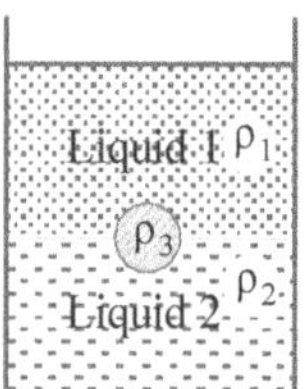

   (a) $\rho_1 > \rho_3 > \rho_2$ (b) $\rho_1 > \rho_2 > \rho_3$
   (c) $\rho_1 < \rho_3 < \rho_2$ (d) $\rho_3 < \rho_1 < \rho_2$

Answer Key	17	(c)	19	(a)	21	(a)	23	(b)	25	(c)	27	(c)
Sol. from page 259	18	(c)	20	(b)	22	(d)	24	(c)	26	(c)		

28. A triangular lamina of area A and height h is immersed in a liquid of density ρ in a vertical plane with its base on the surface of the liquid. The thrust on the lamina is

(a) $\dfrac{1}{2} A\rho gh$

(b) $\dfrac{1}{3} A\rho gh$

(c) $\dfrac{1}{6} A\rho gh$

(d) $\dfrac{2}{3} A\rho gh$

29. By sucking through a straw, a student can reduce the pressure in his lungs to 750 mm of Hg (density = 13.6 gm/cm³). Using the straw, he can drink water from a glass up to a maximum depth of
(a) 10 cm
(b) 75 cm
(c) 13.6 cm
(d) 1.36 cm

30. The area of cross-section of wider tube shown in figure is 800 cm². If a mass of 12 kg is placed on the massless piston, the difference in heights h in the level of water in the two tubes is :

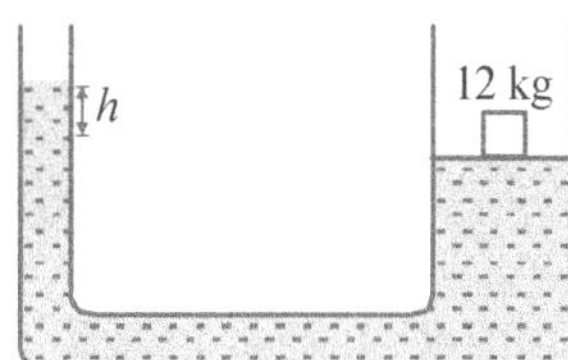

(a) 10 cm
(b) 6 cm
(c) 15 cm
(d) 2 cm

31. Some liquid is filled in a cylindrical vessel of radius R. Let F_1 be the force applied by the liquid on the bottom of the cylinder. Now the same liquid is poured into a vessel of uniform square cross-section of side R. Let F_2 be the force applied by the liquid on the bottom of this new vessel. (Neglect atmosphere pressure) Then

(a) $F_1 = \pi F_2$

(b) $F_1 = \dfrac{F_2}{\pi}$

(c) $F_1 = \sqrt{\pi} F_2$

(d) $F_1 = F_2$

32. The pressure at the bottom of a tank of water is $3P$ where P is the atmospheric pressure. If the water is drawn out till the level of water is lowered by one fifth, the pressure at the bottom of the tank will now be
(a) $2P$
(b) $(13/5)P$
(c) $(8/5)P$
(d) $(4/5)P$

33. A cylindrical block of area of cross-section A and of material of density ρ is placed in a liquid of density one-third of density of block. The block compresses a spring and compression in the spring is one-third of the length of the block. If acceleration due to gravity is g, the spring constant of the spring is

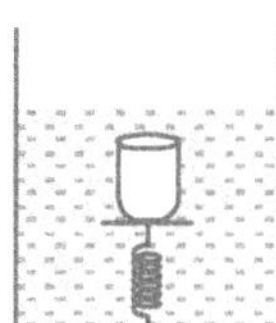

(a) $\rho A g$
(b) $2\rho A g$
(c) $2\rho A g/3$
(d) $\rho A g/3$

34. An open water tanker moving on a horizontal straight road has a cubical block of cork floating over its surface. If the tanker has an acceleration a, then the acceleration of the cork w.r.t. container is

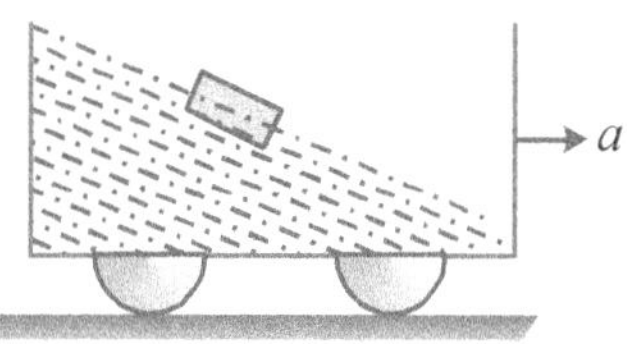

(a) a
(b) a^2/g
(c) $\sqrt{a^2 + g^2}$
(d) zero

35. A cup of water is placed in a car under contant acceleration to the left as shown. Inside the water there is a small air bubble. The following figures show the shape of the water surface and the direction of motion of the bubble as indicated by the arrow on the bubble. Choose the correct one

(a) 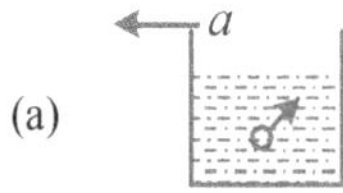

(b) 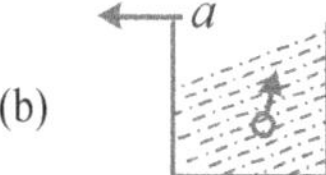

(c) 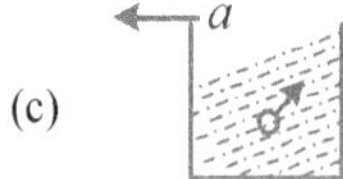

(d) 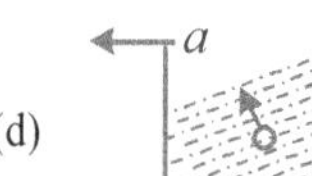

36. A multitube manometer is employed to determine the pressure in a pipe. For the levels in the manometers as shown, compute the pressure in the pipe. What would be the length of a single mercury filled U-tube to record this pressure?

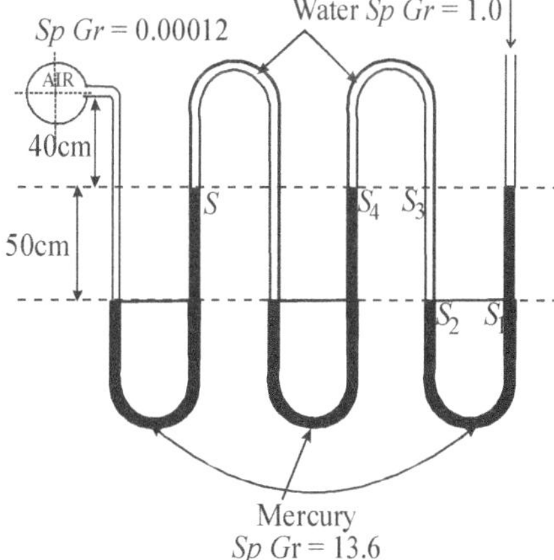

(a) 193cm
(b) 165cm
(c) 121cm
(d) 153cm

Only one option correct

1. Two evacuated brass hemisphere of thin walls, each of radius 1 m are pulled apart by exerting force F on each of them. Taking inside pressure 0.5 atm and the outside pressure as 1.0 atm, the value of F is

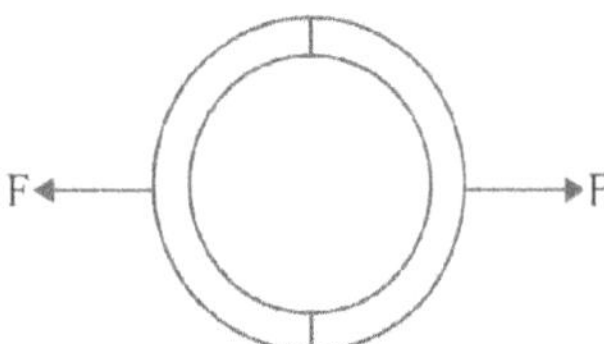

  (a) 1×10^5 N   (b) 1.57×10^5 N
  (c) 3.14×10^5 N   (d) 6.28×10^5 N

2. A body of density d_1 is counterpoised by Mg of weights of density d_2 in air of density d. Then the true mass of the body is

  (a) M (b) $M\left(1 - \dfrac{d}{d_2}\right)$

  (c) $M\left(1 - \dfrac{d}{d_1}\right)$ (d) $\dfrac{M\left(1 - d/d_2\right)}{\left(1 - d/d_1\right)}$

3. The volume of an air bubble becomes three times as it rises from the bottom of a lake to its surface. Assuming atmospheric pressure to be 75 cm of Hg and the density of water to be 1/10 of the density of mercury, the depth of the lake is
  (a) 5 m   (b) 10 m
  (c) 15 m   (d) 20 m

4. A concrete sphere of radius R has a cavity of radius r which is packed with sawdust. The specific gravities of concrete and sawdust are respectively 2.4 and 0.3 for this sphere to float with its entire volume submerged under water. Ratio of mass of concrete to mass of sawdust will be
  (a) 8   (b) 4
  (c) 3   (d) zero

5. A solid sphere of density $\eta\,(>1)$ times lighter than water is suspended in a water tank by a string tied to its base as shown in fig. If the mass of the sphere is m, then the tension in the string is given by

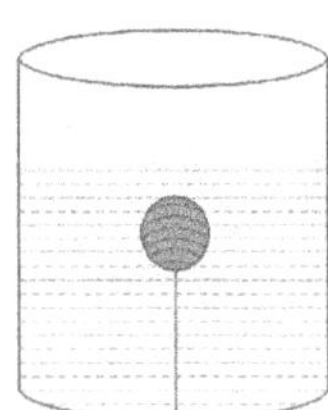

  (a) $\left(\dfrac{\eta - 1}{\eta}\right) mg$ (b) ηmg

  (c) $\dfrac{mg}{\eta - 1}$ (d) $(\eta - 1) mg$

6. A candle of diameter d is floating on a liquid in a cylindrical container of diameter D ($D >> d$) as shown in figure. If it is burning at the rate of 2 cm/hour, then the top of the candle will

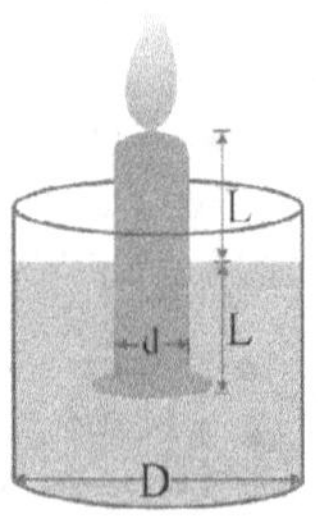

  (a) remain at the same height
  (b) fall at the rate of 1 cm/hour
  (c) fall at the rate of 2 cm/hour
  (d) go up the rate of 1 cm/hour

7. A large tank filled with water to a height 'h' is to be emptied through a small hole at the bottom. The ratio of time taken for the level of water to fall from h to $\dfrac{h}{2}$ and $\dfrac{h}{2}$ to zero is

  (a) $\sqrt{2}$ (b) $\dfrac{1}{\sqrt{2}}$

  (c) $\sqrt{2} - 1$ (d) $\dfrac{1}{\sqrt{2} - 1}$

8. Two spheres of volume 250cc each but of relative densities 0.8 and 1.2 are connected by a string and the combination is immersed in a liquid in vertical position as shown in figure. The tension in the string is ($g = 10$ m/s^2)

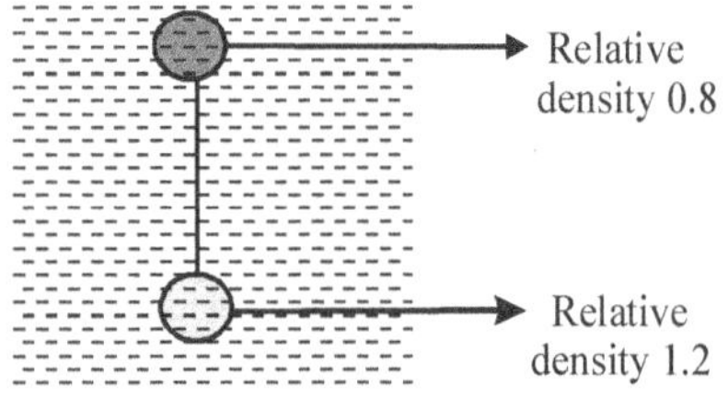

  (a) 5.0N   (b) 0.5N
  (c) 1.0N   (d) 2.0N

9. Two capillary tubes of the same length but different radii r_1 and r_2 are fitted in parallel to the bottom of a vessel. The pressure head is P. What should be the radius of a single tube that can replace the two tubes so that the rate of flow is same as before

  (a) $r_1 + r_2$ (b) $r_1^2 + r_2^2$

  (c) $r_1^4 + r_2^4$ (d) None of these

Answer Key	1	(b)	3	(c)	5	(d)	7	(c)	9	(c)
Sol. from page 260	2	(d)	4	(b)	6	(b)	8	(b)		

10. A homogeneous solid cylinder of length L ($L < H/2$). Cross-sectional area $A/5$ is immersed such that it floats with its axis vertical at the liquid-liquid interface with length $L/4$ in the denser liquid as shown in the fig. The lower density liquid is open to atmosphere having pressure P_0. The density D of solid is given by

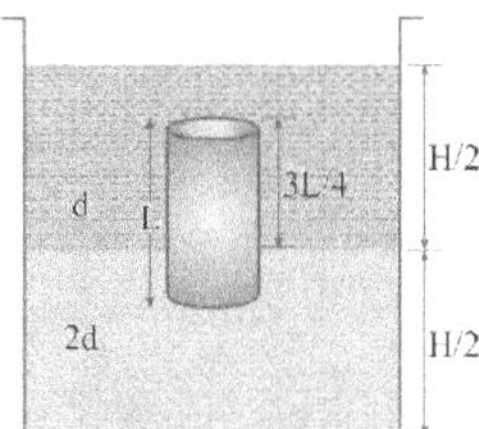

(a) $\dfrac{5}{4}d$

(b) $\dfrac{4}{5}d$

(c) d

(d) $\dfrac{d}{5}$

11. A wooden block, with a coin placed on its top floats in water as shown in fig. The distance l and h are shown there. After some time the coin falls into the water. Then

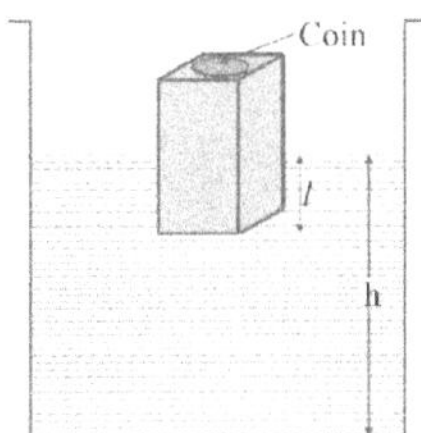

(a) l decreases and h increases
(b) l increases and h decreases
(c) Both l and h increase
(d) Both l and h decrease

12. Water is filled in a cylindrical container to a height of 3m. The ratio of the cross-sectional area of the orifice and the beaker is 0.1. The square of the speed of the liquid coming out from the orifice is ($g = 10$ m/s^2)

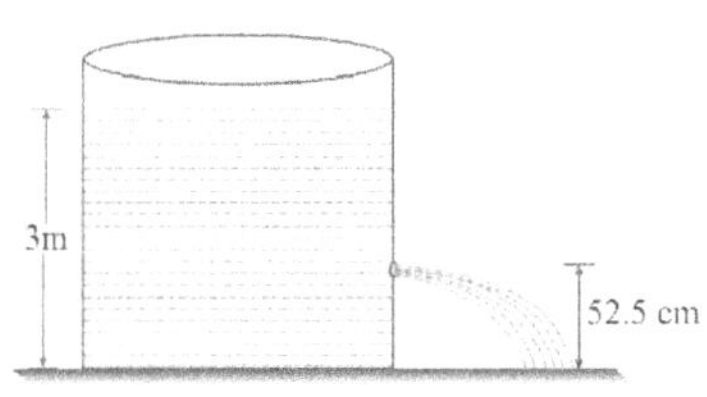

(a) $50\ \text{m}^2/\text{s}^2$

(b) $50.5\ \text{m}^2/\text{s}^2$

(c) $51\ \text{m}^2/\text{s}^2$

(d) $52\ \text{m}^2/\text{s}^2$

13. A large open tank has two holes in the wall. One is a square hole of side L at a depth y from the top and the other is a circular hole of radius R at a depth $4y$ from the top. When the tank is completely filled with water the quantities of water flowing out per second from both the holes are the same. Then R is equal to

(a) $2\pi L$

(b) $\dfrac{L}{\sqrt{2\pi}}$

(c) L

(d) $\dfrac{L}{2\pi}$

14. There are two identical small holes of area of cross-section a on the opposite sides of a tank containing a liquid of density ρ. The difference in height between the holes is h. Tank is resting on a smooth horizontal surface. Horizontal force which will has to be applied on the tank to keep it in equilibrium is

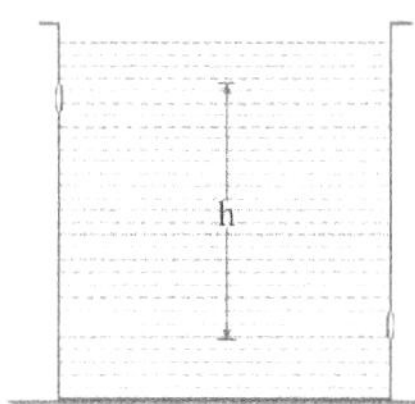

(a) $gh\rho a$

(b) $\dfrac{2gh}{\rho a}$

(c) $2\rho agh$

(d) $\dfrac{\rho gh}{a}$

15. Two communicating vessels contain mercury. The diameter of one vessel is n times larger than the diameter of the other. A column of water of height h is poured into the left vessel. The mercury level will rise in the right-hand vessel (s = relative density of mercury and ρ = density of water) by

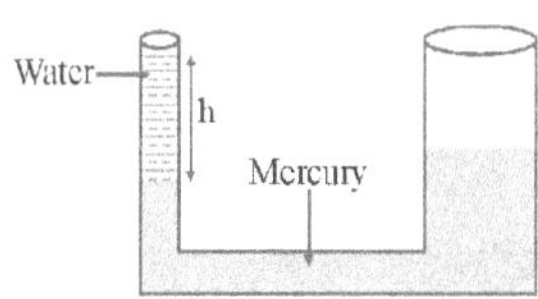

(a) $\dfrac{n^2 h}{(n+1)^2 s}$

(b) $\dfrac{h}{(n^2+1)s}$

(c) $\dfrac{h}{(n+1)^2 s}$

(d) $\dfrac{h}{n^2 s}$

16. A log of wood of mass 120 kg floats in water. The weight that can be put on the log to make it just sink, should be (density of wood = 600 kg/m^3)
(a) 80 kg
(b) 50 kg
(c) 60 kg
(d) 30 kg

17. A hemispherical bowl just floats without sinking in a liquid of density 1.2×10^3 kg/m^3. If outer diameter and the density of the bowl are 1 m and 2×10^4 kg/m^3 respectively, then the inner diameter of the bowl will be
(a) 0.94 m
(b) 0.97 m
(c) 0.98 m
(d) 0.99 m

Answer Key	10	(a)	12	(a)	14	(c)	16	(a)
Sol. from page 260	11	(d)	13	(b)	15	(b)	17	(c)

18. An L-shaped glass tube is just immersed in flowing water such that its opening is pointing against flowing water. If the speed of water current is v, then

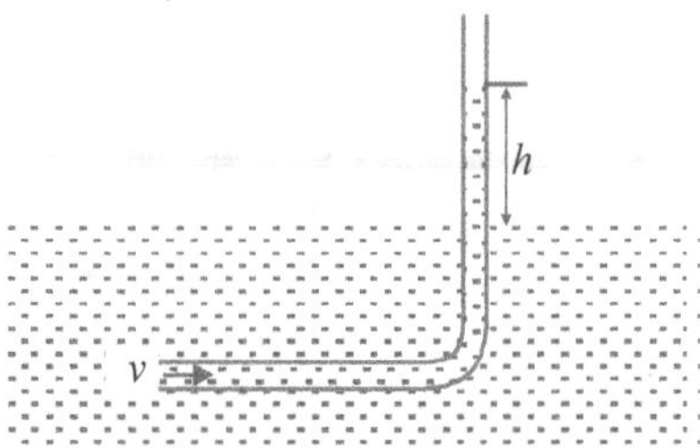

  (a) The water in the tube rises to height $\dfrac{v^2}{2g}$

  (b) The water in the tube rises to height $\dfrac{g}{2v^2}$

  (c) The water in the tube does not rise at all

  (d) None of these

19. Water is filled upto a height h in a beaker of radius R as shown in the figure. The density of water is ρ, the surface tension of water is T and the atmospheric pressure is P_0. Consider a vertical section $ABCD$ of the water column through a diameter of the beaker. The force on water on one side of this section by water on the other side of this section has magnitude

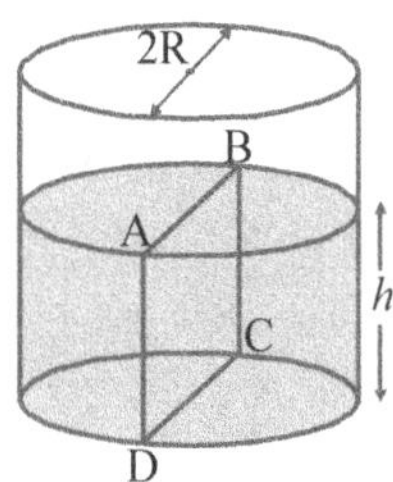

  (a) $|2P_0Rh + \pi R^2 \rho g h - 2RT|$ (b) $|2P_0Rh + R\rho g h^2 - 2RT|$

  (c) $|P_0\pi R^2 + R\rho g h^2 - 2RT|$ (d) $|P_0\pi R^2 + R\rho g h^2 + 2RT|$

20. A cylindrical vessel of height 500 mm has an orifice (small hole) at its bottom. The orifice is initially closed and water is filled in it up to height H. Now the top is completely sealed with a cap and the orifice at the bottom is opened. Some water comes out from the orifice and the water level in the vessel becomes steady with height of water column being 200 mm. Find the fall in height (in mm) of water level due to opening of the orifice. [Take atmospheric pressure = 1.0×10^5 N/m², density of water = 1000 kg/m³ and g = 10 m/s². Neglect any effect of surface tension]

  (a) 5 mm   (b) 6 mm

  (c) 2 mm   (d) 1 mm

21. A small spherical solid ball is dropped from a great height in a viscous liquid. Its journey in the liquid is best described in the diagram given below by the

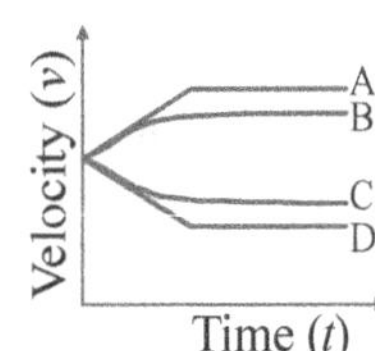

(a) Curve A (b) Curve B

(c) Curve C (d) Curve D

22. A cone of radius R and height H, is hanging inside a liquid of density ρ by means of a string as shown in the figure. The force, due to the liquid acting on the slant surface of the cone is (Neglect atmosphere pressure)

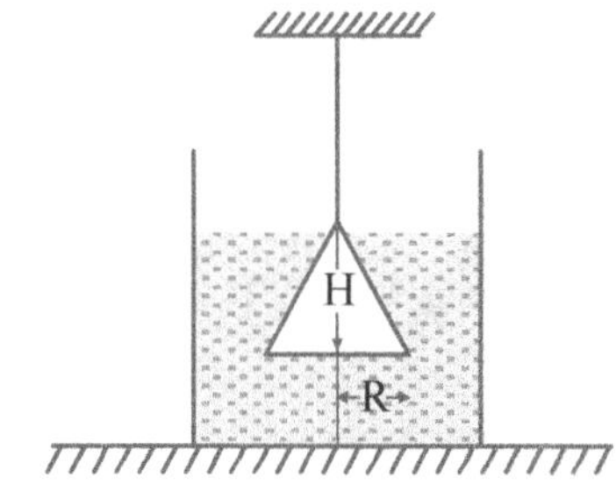

  (a) $\rho\pi gHR^2$ (b) $\pi\rho HR^2$

  (c) $\dfrac{4}{3}\pi\rho gHR^2$ (d) $\dfrac{2}{3}\pi\rho gHR^2$

23. A slender homogeneous rod of length 2 L floats partly immersed in water, being supported by a string fastened to one of its ends, as shown. The specific gravity of the rod is 0.75. The length of rod that extends out of water is

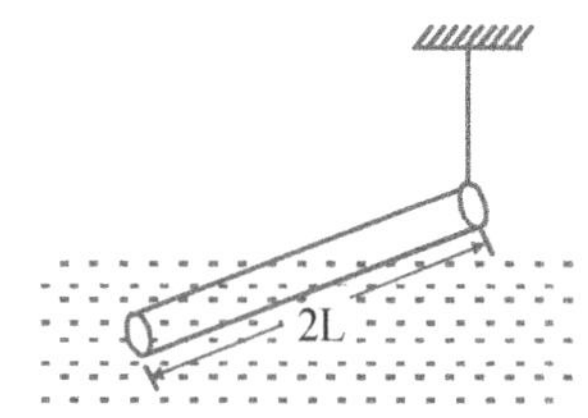

  (a) L (b) $\dfrac{1}{2}L$

  (c) $\dfrac{1}{4}L$ (d) $3L$

24. A hollow sphere of mass M and radius R is immersed in a tank of water (density ρ_w). The sphere would float if it were set free. The sphere is tied to the bottom of the tank by two wires which makes angle 45° with the horizontal as shown in the figure. The tension T_1 in the wire is

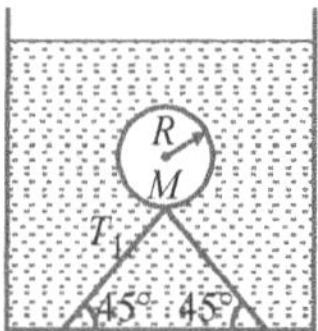

  (a) $\dfrac{\dfrac{4}{3}\pi R^3\rho_w g - Mg}{\sqrt{2}}$ (b) $\dfrac{2}{3}\pi R^3\rho_w g - Mg$

  (c) $\dfrac{4}{3}\pi R^3\rho_w g - Mg$ (d) $\dfrac{4}{3}\pi R^3\rho_w g + Mg$

Answer Key	18	(a)	20	(b)	22	(d)	24	(a)
Sol. from page 260	19	(b)	21	(c)	23	(a)		

25. A body having volume V and density ρ is attached to the bottom of a container as shown. Density of the liquid is $d\ (>\rho)$. Container has a constant upward acceleration a. Tension in the string is

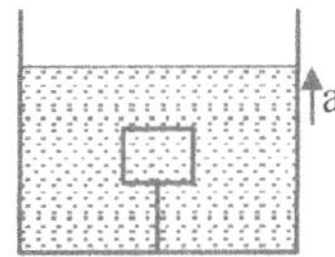

   (a) $V[dg - \rho(g+a)]$ (b) $V[(g+a)(d-\rho)]$

   (c) $V(d-\rho)g$ (d) none

26. A cubical box of wine has a small spout located in one of the bottom corners. When the box is full and placed on a level surface, opening the spout results in a flow of wine with a initial speed of v_0 (see figure). When the box is half empty, someone tilts it at 45° so that the spout is at the lowest point (see figure). When the spout is opened the wine will flow out with a speed of

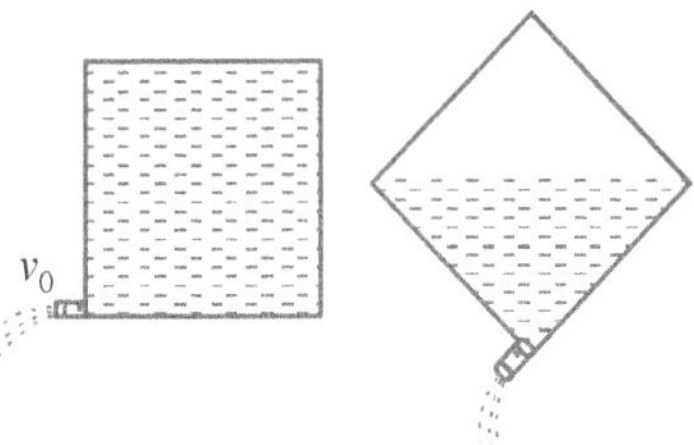

   (a) v_0 (b) $v_0/2$

   (c) $v_0/\sqrt{2}$ (d) $v_0/\sqrt[4]{2}$

27. A fire hydrant delivers water of density ρ at a volume rate Q. The water travels vertically upward through the hydrant and then does 90° turn to emerge horizontally at speed v. The pipe and nozzle have uniform cross-section throughout. The force exerted by the water on the corner of the hydrant is

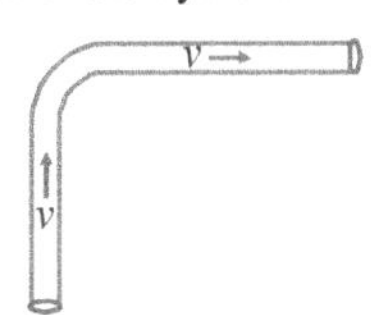

   (a) $\rho v Q$ (b) zero

   (c) $2\rho v Q$ (d) $\sqrt{2}\rho v Q$

28. A large tank is filled with water (density = 10^3 kg/m³). A small hole is made at a depth 10 m below water surface. The range of water issuing out of the hole is R on ground. What extra pressure must be applied on the water surface so that the range becomes $2R$ (take 1 atm = 10^5 Pa and g = 10 m/s²)

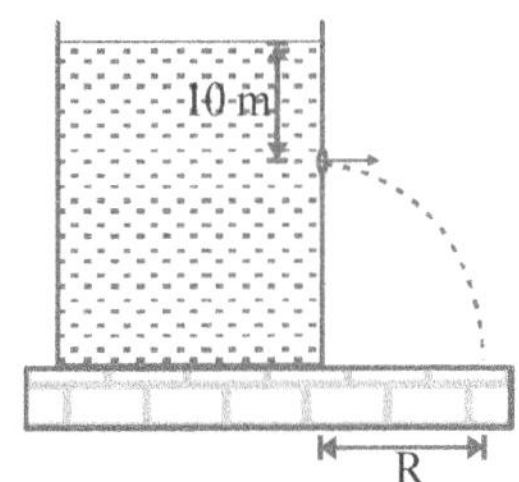

   (a) 9 atm   (b) 4 atm

   (c) 5 atm   (d) 3 atm

29. Equal volumes of two immiscible liquids of densities ρ and 2ρ are filled in a vessel as shown in figure. Two small holes are punched at depth $h/2$ and $3h/2$ from the surface of lighter liquid. If v_1 and v_2 are the velocities of a flux at these two holes, then v_1/v_2 is

   (a) $\dfrac{1}{2\sqrt{2}}$

   (b) $\dfrac{1}{2}$

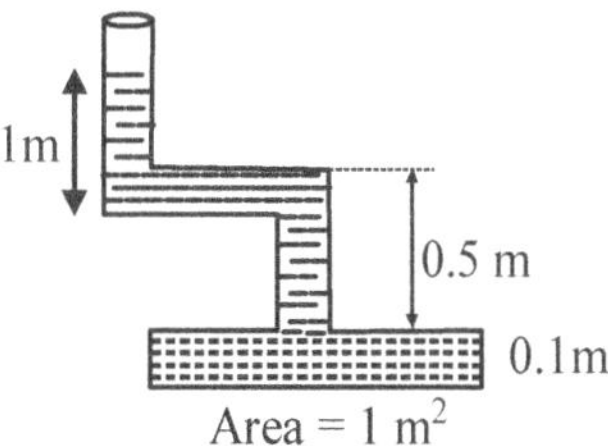

   (c) $\dfrac{1}{4}$

   (d) $\dfrac{1}{\sqrt{2}}$

30. A vessel has the shape shown in the figure. Water, which has density of 10^3 kg/m³, is filled in the vessel. The pressure due to liquid column at the bottom will be (take g = 10 m/s²) (area of bottom = 1 m²)

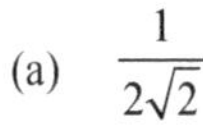

   (a) 1.6×10^3 N/m²   (b) 1.5×10^4 N/m²

   (c) 1×10^4 N/m²   (d) 1.6×10^4 N/m²

31. A cubical block is floating in a liquid with $\dfrac{3}{4}$ of its volume immersed in the liquid. When the whole system accelerates downwards with a net acceleration of g/4, the fraction of volume immersed in the liquid will be

   (a) $\dfrac{1}{2}$ (b) $\dfrac{1}{4}$

   (c) $\dfrac{3}{4}$ (d) $\dfrac{3}{8}$

32. A uniform rod of density ρ is placed in a wide tank containing a liquid of density $\sigma(\sigma > \rho)$. The depth of liquid in the tank is half the length of the rod. The rod is in equilibrium, with its lower end resting on the bottom of the tank. In this position, the rod makes an angle θ with the horizontal. Then $\sin\theta$ is equal to

   (a) $\dfrac{1}{2}\sqrt{\dfrac{\sigma}{\rho}}$ (b) $\dfrac{1}{2}\dfrac{\sigma}{\rho}$

   (c) $\sqrt{\dfrac{\rho}{\sigma}}$ (d) $\sqrt{\dfrac{\sigma}{\rho}}$

33. A cubical block of wood 20.0 cm on a side and density of 500 kg/m³ floating on water. From its equilibrium floating position, it is pushed further by 4.0 cm into the water. What is the force needed to keep the block in this new position? g = 10 m/s².

   (a) 16 N   (b) 32 N

   (c) 40 N   (d) 56 N

Answer Key	25	(b)	27	(d)	29	(d)	31	(c)	33	(a)
Sol. from page 260	26	(d)	28	(d)	30	(d)	32	(a)		

34. A bird of mass 1.23 kg is able to hover by imparting a downward velocity 10 m/s uniformly to air of density ρ kg/m³ over an effective area 0.1 m². If the acceleration due to gravity is 10 m/s², then the magnitude of ρ in kg/m³ is

(a)   0.0123   (b)   0.123

(c)   1.23   (d)   1.32

35. The presseure of air in the tank as shown in figure is : (oil has density ρ_1, mercury has density ρ_{Hg}, density of air negligible small in comparison to that of liquid and mercury. Atmospheric pressure is P_0.

(a) $\rho g \ell_1 + \rho_{Hg} g \ell_3 + P_0$

(b) $\rho g \ell_2 + \rho_{Hg} g \ell_3$

(c) $\rho_1 g (\ell_2 - \ell_1) + \rho_{Hg} g \ell_3 + P_0$

(d)   none of these

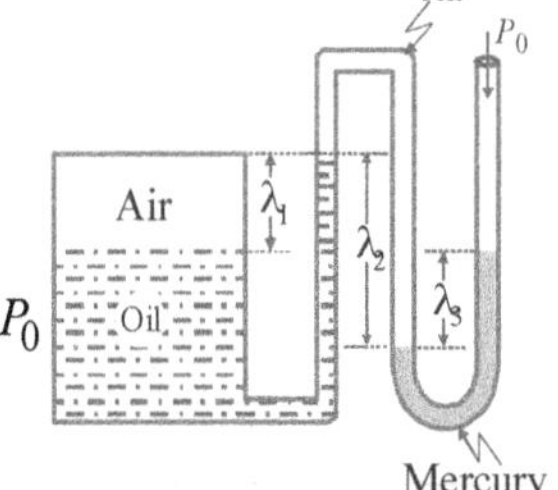

36. The limbs of a glass U-tube are lowered into vessels A and B as shown in figure. Some air is pumped out thorugh a valve, placed at the top of tube and then the valve is closed. The liquid is the left hand limb then rises to $h_1 = 20$ cm and in the right hand it rises to a height $h_2 = 10$ cm. Vessel A has water, then the density of liquid in vessel B is :

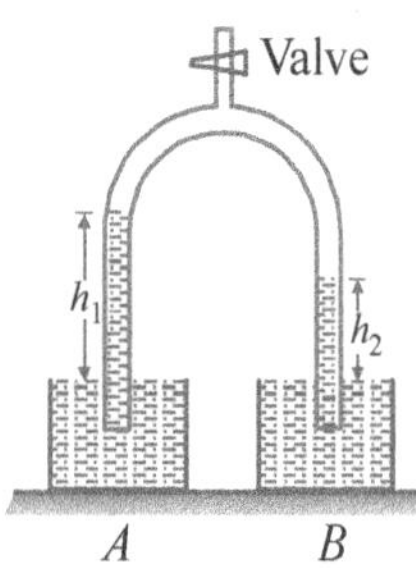

(a) $2 \times 10^3 \, \text{kg/m}^3$ (b) $3 \times 10^3 \, \text{kg/m}^3$

(c) $4 \times 10^3 \, \text{kg/m}^3$ (d) $4.5 \times 10^3 \, \text{kg/m}^3$

37. A hemispherical portion of radius R is removed from the bottom of a cylinder of radius R. The volume of the remaining cylinder is V and its mass M. It is suspended by a string in a liquid of density ρ where it stays vertical. The upper surface of the cylinder is at a depth h below the liquid surface. The force on the bottom of the cylinder by the liquid is

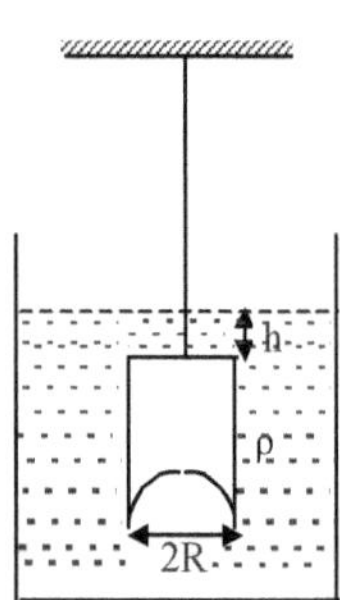

(a) Mg (b) $Mg - V\rho g$

(c) $Mg + \pi R^2 h \rho g$ (d) $\rho g (V + \pi R^2 h)$

38. A uniform wooden stick of length L, cross-section area A and density d is immersed in a liquid of density $4d$. A small body of mass m and negligible volume is attached at the lower end of the rod so that the stick floats vertically in stable equilibrium then

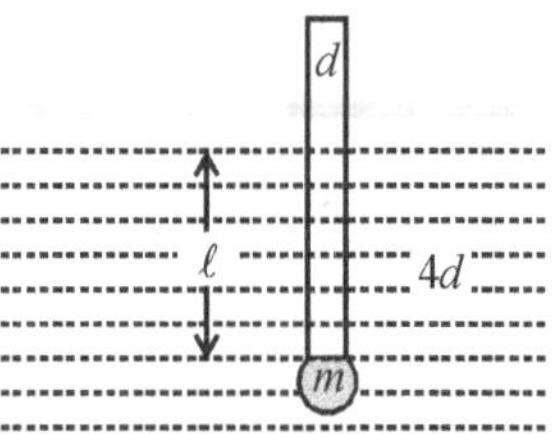

(a) $m > dAL$ (b) $m < dAL$

(c) $m < dAL/2$ (d) $m < dAL/4$

39. A right circular cone of density ρ, floats just immersed with its vertex downwards in a vessel containing two liquids of densities σ_1 and σ_2 respectively, the planes of separation of the two liquids cuts off from the axis of the cone a fraction z of its length. Find z.

(a) $\left(\dfrac{\rho + \sigma_2}{\sigma_1 + \sigma_2} \right)^{1/3}$ (b) $\left(\dfrac{\rho - \sigma_2}{\sigma_1 - \sigma_2} \right)^{1/3}$

(c) $\left(\dfrac{\rho - \sigma_2}{\sigma_1 + \sigma_2} \right)^{1/2}$ (d) $\left(\dfrac{\rho - \sigma_2}{\sigma_1 - \sigma_2} \right)$

40. A bent tube of uniform cross-section is mounted on a cart, which is accelerating towards right with constant acceleration a. The total length of the liquid in the tube is $2\sqrt{2}\ell$. The level difference between two limbs is :

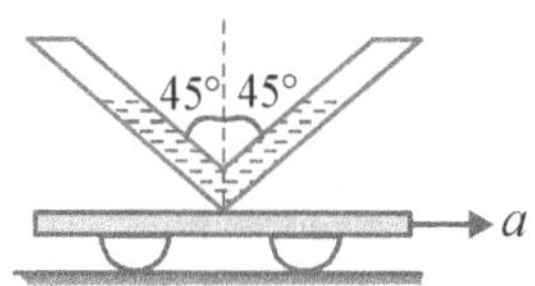

(a) $\dfrac{a\ell}{g}$ (b) $\dfrac{2a\ell}{g}$

(c) $\dfrac{a\ell}{2g}$ (d)   none of these

41. A bent tube is of uniform cross-section has a liquid of density ρ (see figure). The height of liquid in each limb of the tube is h. The acceleration of the tube so that pressure due to liquid at A becomes zero is :

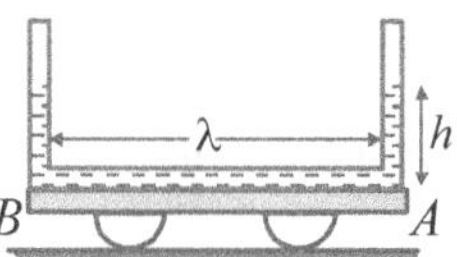

(a) gh/ℓ towards right

(b) $2gh/\ell$ towards right

(c) $gh/2\ell$ towards left

(d)   none of these

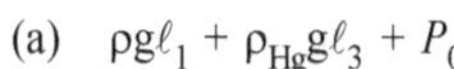

Answer Key	34	(c)	36	(a)	38	(a)	40	(b)
Sol. from page 260	35	(a)	37	(d)	39	(b)	41	(b)

FM MCQ Type 2 *Exercise 3.2*

Multiple options are correct

1. In this figure, an ideal liquid flows through the tube, which is of uniform cross-section. The liquid has velocities v_A and v_B and pressure P_A and P_B at points A and B respectively

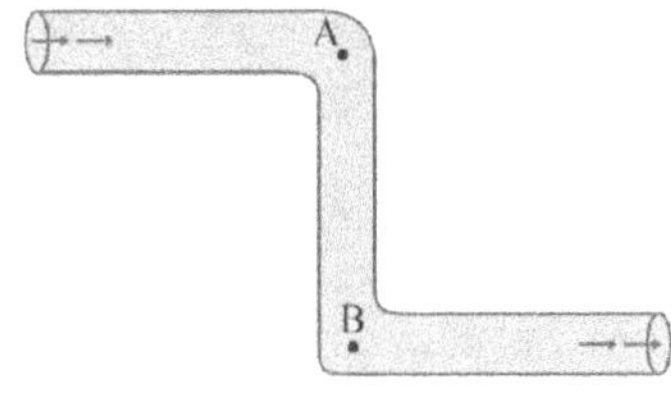

(a) $v_A = v_B$ (b) $v_B > v_A$

(c) $P_A = P_B$ (d) $P_B > P_A$

2. In a streamline flow
   (a) the speed of a particle always remains same
   (b) the velocity of a particle always remains same
   (c) the kinetic energies of all the particles arriving at a given point are the same
   (d) the momenta of all the particles arriving at a given point are the same

3. An upright U-tube manometer with its limbs 0.6m high and spaced 0.3m apart contains a liquid to a height of 0.4m in each limb. If the U-tube is rotated at 10 radians/second about a vertical axis at 0.1m from one limb. Choose the correct options

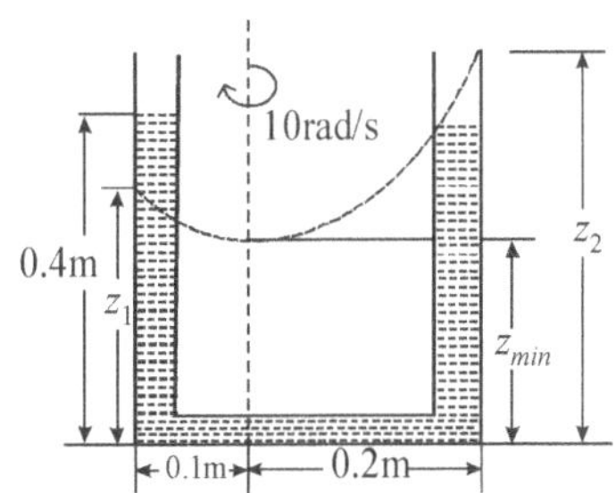

(a) $z_1 = 0.324$ (b) $z_2 = 0.477$

(c) $z_{min} = 0.273$ (b) $z_1 + z_2 = 0.8$

4. A body of weight W volume V is floating in liquid with V' of its volume inside liquid. When the container of liquid is accelerated, then
   (a) buoyant force on the body is equal to W
   (b) buoyant force on the body is greater than W
   (c) body floats with volume V' inside liquid
   (d) body floats with volume greater than V' inside liquid

5. A cylindrical container has water and closed at the top. If v_1, v_2, v_3 represent the efflux velocities, then

(a) $v_1 = \sqrt{2g \times 6}$

(b) $v_1 = 0$

(c) $v_2 = \sqrt{2g \times 9}$

(d) $v_3 \neq \sqrt{2g \times 12}$

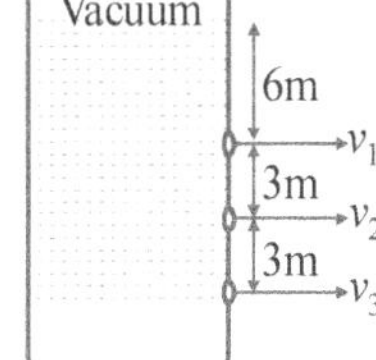

6. A completely filled closed aquarium is kept on a weighing machine. It can be assumed that the density of the fish is greater than the density of the water. The total mass of the aquarium and its contents put together is M. If now all the fish start accelerating upwards with an acceleration a, then the incorrect option (s) is/are
   (a) the weight recorded will be equal to Mg.
   (b) the weight reading will be less than Mg.
   (c) the weight reading will be more than Mg.
   (d) no conclusion can be drawn from the given information.

7. The spring balance A reads 2 kg with a block m suspended from it. A balance B reads 5 kg when a beaker with liquid is put on the pan of the balance. The two balances are now so arranged that the hanging mass is inside the liquid in the beaker as shown in the figure. In this situation:

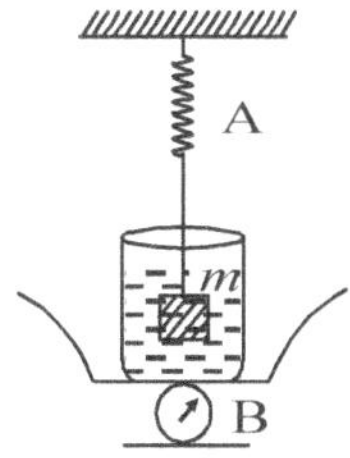

(a) the balance A will read more than 2 kg
(b) the balance B will read more than 5 kg
(c) the balance A will read less than 2 kg and B will read more than 5 kg
(d) the balance A and B will read 2 kg and 5 kg respectively

Answer Key	1	(a,c)	3	(c, d)	5	(b, d)	7	(b, c)
Sol. from page 264	2	(c, d)	4	(b, c)	6	(a, b, d)		

8. A liquid flows through a horizontal tube. The velocities of the liquid in the two sections, which have areas of cross-section A_1 and A_2, are v_1 and v_2 respectively. The difference in the levels of the liquid in the two vertical tubes is h

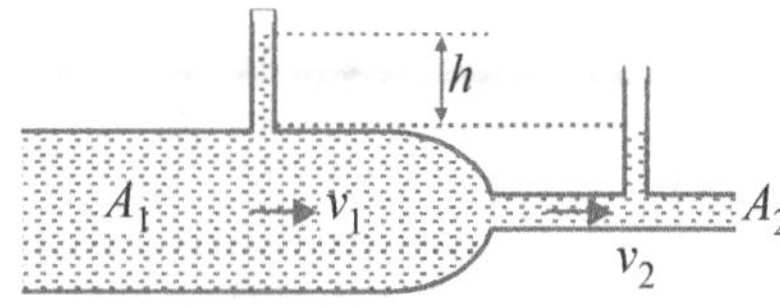

(a) The volume of the liquid flowing through the tube in unit time is $A_1 v_1$

(b) $v_2 - v_1 = \sqrt{2gh}$

(c) $v_2^2 - v_1^2 = 2gh$

(d) The energy per unit mass of the liquid is the same in both sections of the tube

9. A beaker is filled with water is accelerated a m/s^2 in $+x$ direction. The surface of water shall make an angle

(a) $\tan^{-1}(a/g)$ backwards   (b) $\tan^{-1}(a/g)$ forwards

(c) $\cot^{-1}(g/a)$ backwards   (d) $\cot^{-1}(g/a)$ forwards

10. Figure shows a siphon. Choose the correct statement :

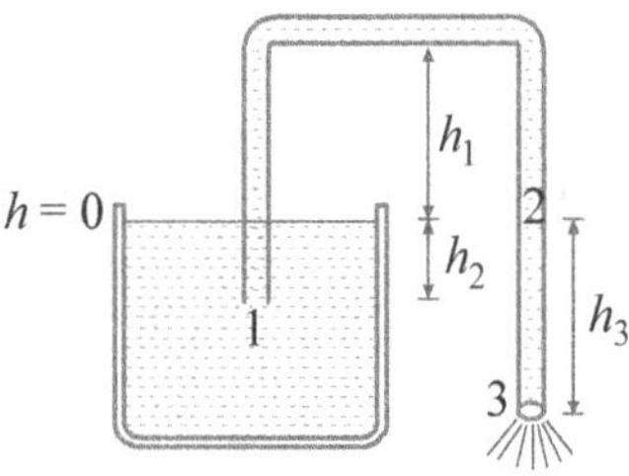

(a) Siphon works when $h_3 > 0$
(b) Pressure at point 2 is $P_2 = P_0 - \rho g h_3$
(c) Pressure at point 3 is P_0
(d) None of the above
    (P_0 = atmospheric pressure)

11. A tank is filled upto a height h with a liquid and is placed on a platform of height h from the ground. To get maximum range x_m a small hole is punched at a distance of y from the free surface of the liquid. Then

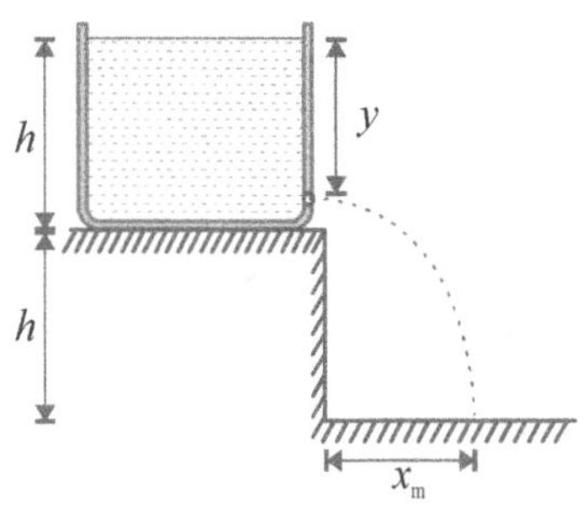

(a) $x_m = 2h$ (b) $x_m = 1.5\,h$
(c) $y = h$ (d) $y = 0.75\,h$

12. Water coming out of a horizontal tube at a speed v strikes normally a vetical wall close to the mouth of the tube and falls down vertically after impact. When the speed of water is increased to 2v.
(a) the thrust exerted by the water on the wall will be doubled
(b) the thrust exerted by the water on the wall will be four times
(c) the energy lost per second by water strike up the wall will also be four times
(d) the energy lost per second by water striking the wall be increased eight times

13. A piston is pressed with a force F on a hydroulic cylinder containing water ($\rho = 10^3$ kg/m^3). The cross-sectional area of the cylinder is $A = 100$ cm^2. The water is forced into pipe with a cross-sectional area of 1 cm^2 that reses a height $h = 50$ cm (Atmospheric pressure $P_0 = 10^5$ N/m^2)

(a) Force F required to make water eject with a speed of 10 m/s is 550 N.
(b) Force F required to make water eject with a speed of 10 m/s at the top is 5500 N.
(c) The pressure inside the cylinder at the bottom when water ejects at 10 m/s is 1.55×10^5 Pa.
(d) none of the above

14. Ideal fluid flows along a tube of uniform cross-section, located in a horizontal plane and bent as shown in figure. The flow is steady; 1 and 2 are two points and v_1 and v_2 are the velocity of flow at these points, then

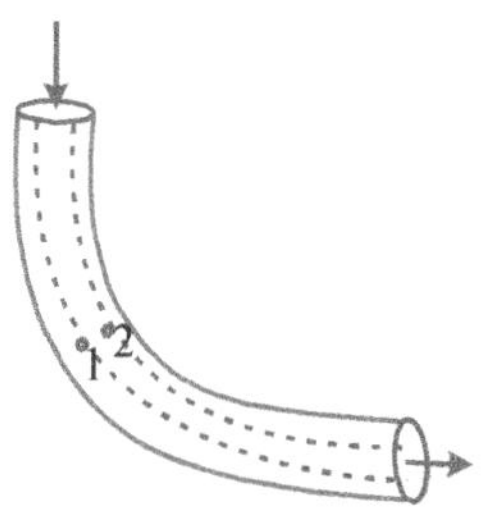

(a) $P_1 < P_2$ (b) $P_1 > P_2$
(c) $v_1 < v_2$ (d) $v_1 > v_2$

Answer Key	8	(a, c, d)	10	(a, b, c)	12	(b, d)	14	(b, c)
Sol. from page 264	9	(a, c)	11	(a, c)	13	(a, c)		

 **FM** Statement Questions *Exercise 3.3*

Read the two statements carefully to mark the correct option out of the options given below:
(a) If both the statements are true and the *statement - 2* is the correct explanation of *statement - 1*.
(b) If both the statements are true but *statement - 2* is not the correct explanation of the *statement - 1*.
(c) If *statement - 1* true but *statement - 2* is false.
(d) If *statement - 1* is false but *statement - 2* is true.

1. *Statement 1*

Paper pins are made to have pointed end.

Statement 2

Because pointed pins have very small area due to which even for small applied force it exert large pressure on the surface.

2. *Statement 1*

It is difficult to stop bleeding from a cut in the body at high altitude.

Statement 2

The atmospheric pressure at high altitude is lesser than the blood pressure.

3. *Statement 1*

The blood pressure in humans is greater at the feet than at the brain.

Statement 2

Pressure of liquid at any point is proportional to height of liquid at that point.

4. *Statement 1*

Pressure is a vector quantity.

Statement 2

Pressure is force divided by area and force is a vector quantity.

5. *Statement 1*

A man in a boat which is floating on a pond. If the man drinks some water from the pond the level of water in the pond decreases.

Statement 2

According to Archimede's principle, the weight of water displaced by body is equal to the weight of the body.

6. *Statement 1*

The shape of automobiles is made streamlined.

Statement 2

The resistance offered by streamline shape of the body is minimum.

7. *Statement 1*

Bernoulli's theorem holds for incompressible, non-viscous fluids.

Statement 2

For incompressible fluid, $\dfrac{p}{\rho g}+\dfrac{v^2}{2g}$ = constant.

8. *Statement 1*

A fluid flowing out of a small hole in a vessel apply a backward thrust on the vessel.

Statement 2

According to equation of continuity, the product of area and velocity of flow is constant.

9. *Statement 1*

For a floating body to be in stable equilibrium, its centre of buoyancy must be located above the centre of gravity.

Statement 2

The torque produced by the weight of the body and the upthrust will restore body back to its normal position, after body is disturbed.

10. *Statement 1*

Sudden fall of pressure at a place indicates storm.

Statement 2

Air flows from higher pressure to lower pressure.

11. *Statement 1*

Aeroplane are made to run on the runway before take off, so that they acquire the necessary lift.

Statement 2

According to Bernoulli's theorem, as velocity increases, pressure decreases.

12. *Statement 1*

A block of wood in floating in a tank containing water. The apparent weight of the floating block is equal to zero.

Statement 2

Because the entire weight of the block is supported by the buoyant force due to water.

Answer Key	1	(a)	3	(a)	5	(d)	7	(c)	9	(a)	11	(a)
Sol. from page 265	2	(a)	4	(d)	6	(a)	8	(b)	10	(a)	12	(a)

FM — Passage & Matrix — *Exercise 3.4*

PASSAGES

Passage for (Q. 1 - 3) :

A common method for testing gold for purity is to measure its density by weighing it in air and then in water. In an era of rising gold prices, a swindler proposed to make a fake gold ingot by using a hollow slab of iridium (density 22.5 g/cm^3) and plating it with a thin layer of gold (density 19.3 g/cm^3)

1. To make fake ingot of total mass 0.5 kg. What should be the total volume ?
    - (a) 12.4 cm^3
    - (b) 25.9 cm^3
    - (c) 18.6 cm^3
    - (d) 27.3 cm^3
2. The volume of interior air space (cavity) in the ingot is
    - (a) 3.68 cm^3
    - (b) 4.24 cm^3
    - (c) 8.24 cm^3
    - (d) 12.20 cm^3
3. Select the correct one
    - (a) iridium is cheaper than gold
    - (b) gold is cheaper than iridium
    - (c) cost can not be decided by these observations
    - (d) none of the above

Passage for (Q. 4 - 6) :

Water stands at a depth of 1 m in an enclosed tank whose side walls are vertical. The space above the water surface contains air at a gauge pressure of 8×10^5 Pa. The tank rests on a platform 2 m above the floor. A hole of cross-sectional area 1cm^2 is made in one of the side walls just above the bottom of the tank.

4. The horizontal distance at which stream of water strike the floor is
    - (a) 12.3 m
    - (b) 25.2 m
    - (c) 30.80 m
    - (d) 35.5 m
5. The vertical force exerted by the stream on the floor is
    - (a) 25.2 N
    - (b) 50.4 N
    - (c) 75.6 N
    - (d) none of these
6. The horizontal force exerted on the tank is (Assume the water level and pressure in the tank to remain constant.)
    - (a) 80 N
    - (b) 123 N
    - (c) 160 N
    - (d) 182 N

Passage for (Q. 7 - 9) :

The section of pipe shown in figure has a cross-section of 40 cm^2 at the wider portion and 10 cm^2 at the contriction. The discharge of water from the pipe is 3000 cm^3/s.

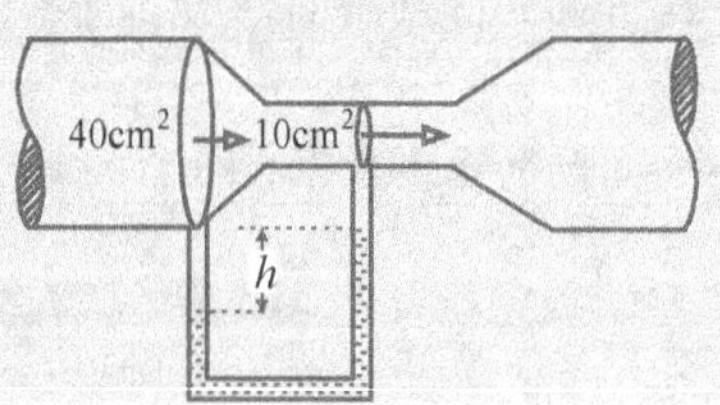

7. The velocity at the wide portion is
    - (a) 0.75 m/s
    - (b) 3.0 m/s
    - (c) 3.75 m/s
    - (d) 4.50 m/s
8. The pressure difference between wider and narrow section is
    - (a) 4000 N/ m^2
    - (b) 4219 N/m^2
    - (c) 4872 N/m^2
    - (d) 5200 N/m^2
9. The difference in height of mercurry column in the U-tube is
    - (a) 1.68 cm
    - (b) 3.16 cm
    - (c) 4.20 cm
    - (d) 5.20 cm

Passage for (Q. 10 - 12) :

A uniform solid cylinder of density 0.8 g/cm^3 floats in equilibrium in a combination of two non-mixing liquids A and B with its axis vertical. The densities of liquids A and B are 0.7 g/cm^3 and 1.2 g/cm^3 respectively. The height of liquid A is h_A=1.2 cm. The length of the part of the cylinder in liquid B is h_B = 0.8 cm.

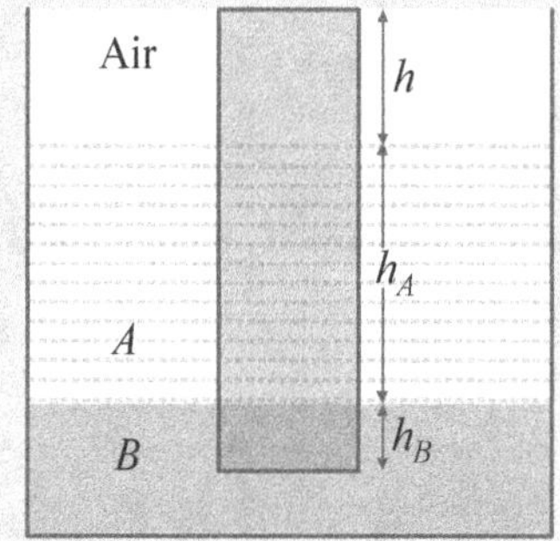

10. The total force exerted by liquid A on the cylinder is
    - (a) 200 N
    - (b) 350 N
    - (c) 450 N
    - (d) zero
11. The length h of the cylinder in air is
    - (a) 0.25 cm
    - (b) 0.50 cm
    - (c) 0.75 cm
    - (d) 1.20 cm
12. The cylinder is depressed in such a way that its top surface is just below the upper surface of liquid A and then released. The acceleration of the cylinder just after release is
    - (a) g m/s^2
    - (b) $\dfrac{g}{2}$ m/s^2
    - (c) $\dfrac{g}{6}$ m/s^2
    - (d) $\dfrac{g}{8}$ m/s^2

Answer Key	1	(b)	3	(a)	5	(a)	7	(a)	9	(b)	11	(a)
Sol. from page 265	2	(a)	4	(b)	6	(c)	8	(b)	10	(d)	12	(c)

Passage for (Q. 13 - 15) :
When an object moves in a viscous fluid, it experiences a viscous force, which is proportional to the speed of the object. According to stoke, the viscous force on a spherical body of radius r_1, moving with a speed is, $6\pi\eta rv$. According to poisualli the rate of flow given by

$$Q = \frac{\pi r^4 \Delta P}{8\eta L}$$

Here η is the coefficient of viscosity and ΔP is the pressure drop in a length L of the pipe. r is the radius of the pipe. For the laminar flow in a pipe, the Reynolds number is given by

$$R = \frac{\rho v D}{\eta}$$

Here ρ is the density of the liquid, D is the diameter of the pipe and v is the average velocity of flow. For laminar flow in a pipe, the Reynolds number should be less than equal to 2000.

13. The viscous force on a glass sphere of radius r = 1 mm falling through water ($\eta = 10^{-3}$Pa -s) with a speed of 3 m/s is
    (a) 2.5×10^{-5} N
    (b) 2.7×10^{-2}N
    (c) 3.7×10^{-3} N
    (d) 5.6×10^{-5} N

14. Blood vessel is 0.10 m in length and has a radius of 1.5×10^{-3} m. Blood flows at rate of 10^{-7} m^3/s through this vessel. The pressure difference that must be maintained in this flow, between the two ends of the vessel is 20 Pa. What is the coefficient of viscosity of the blood?
    (a) 1×10^{-3} Pa-s
    (b) 2×10^{-3} Pa-s
    (c) 4×10^{-3} Pa-s
    (d) 5×10^{-4} Pa-s

15. Calculate the highest average speed that blood (ρ = 1000 kg/m^3) could have and still remain in laminar flow when it flows through the aorta (r = 8×10^{-3}m.) Take $\eta = 4 \times 10^{-3}$ Pa-s
    (a) 0.5 m/s
    (b) 1.0 m/s
    (c) 1.5 m/s
    (d) 2.0 m/s

Passage for (Q. 16 - 18) :
A cylinder of radius R is kept embedded along the wall of a dam as shown. Take density of water as ρ. Take length as L.

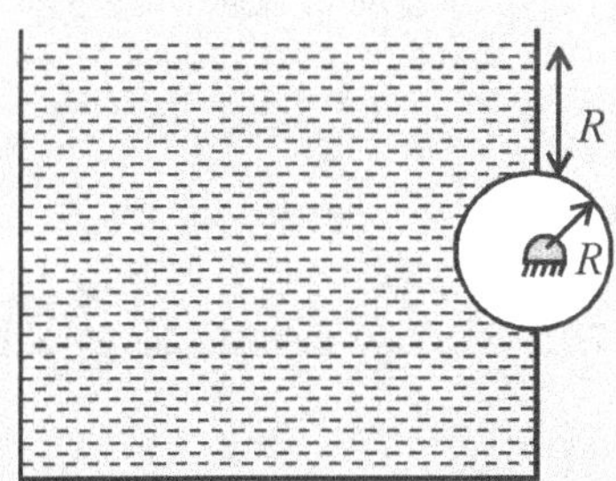

16. The vertical force exerted by water on the cylinder is
    (a) $\rho\pi R^2 Lg$
    (b) $\rho\pi R^2 Lg/2$
    (c) zero
    (d) None of these

17. The net torque exerted by liquid on the cylinder is
    (a) $\dfrac{2\rho R^3 Lg}{3}$
    (b) $\dfrac{\rho R^3 Lg}{3}$
    (c) $\dfrac{\rho R^3 Lg}{2}$
    (d) 0

18. The force exerted by liquid on the cylinder in horizontal direction is [Neglecting atmospheric pressure]
    (a) $2R^2\rho gL$
    (b) $R^2\rho gL$
    (c) $4R^2\rho gL$
    (d) $1.61\,R^2\rho gL$

Passage for (Q. 19 - 21) :
One way of measuring a person's body fat content is by "weighing" them under water. This works because fat tends to float on water as it is less dense than water. On the other hand muscle and bond tend to sink as they are more dense. Knowing your "weight" under water as well as your real weight out of water, the percentage of your body's volume that is made up of fat can easily be estimated. This is only an estimate since it assumes that your body is made up of only two substances, fat (low density) and everything else (high density). The "weight" is measured by spring balance both inside the outside the water. Quotes are placed around weight to indicate that the measurement read on the scale is not your true weight, i.e. the force applied to you body by gravity, but a measurement of the net downward force on the scale.

19. Ram and Shyam are having the same weight when measured outside the water. When measured under water, it is found that weight of Ram is more than that of Shyam, then we can say that
    (a) Ram is having more fat content than Shyam
    (b) Shyam is having more fat content than Ram
    (c) Ram and Shyam both are having the same fat content
    (d) None of these

20. A person of mass 165kg having one fourth of his volume consisting of fat (relative density 0.4) and rest of the volume consisting of everything else (average relative density 4/3) is weighed under water by the spring balance. The reading shown by the spring balance is
    (a) 15 kg
    (b) 65 kg
    (c) 150 kg
    (d) None of these

21. Suppose that Ram is floating in water with two-third of his volume immersed. Now the system is taken in a lift which is accelerating upward with acceleration g/3. The new fraction immersed is
    (a) one-third
    (b) half
    (c) two-third
    (d) three-fourth

Passage for (Q. 22 - 24) :
A container of large uniform cross-sectional area A resting on a horizontal surface holds two immiscible, non-viscous and incompressible liquids of densities d and $2\,d$, each of height $H/2$ as shown. The lower density liquid is open to the atmosphere having pressure P_0. A tiny hole of area $s(s << A)$ is punched on the vertical side of the container at a height h ($h < H/2$). Determine :

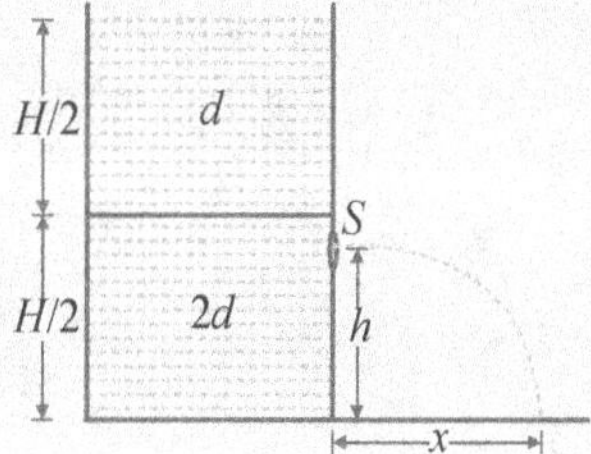

22. The initial speed of efflux of the liquid at the hole is

    (a) $\sqrt{2gH}$

    (b) $\sqrt{2g(3H-4h)}$

    (c) $\sqrt{\dfrac{g}{2}(3H-4h)}$

    (d) $\sqrt{g(H-3h)}$

23. The horizontal distance x travelled by the liquid initially is

    (a) $\sqrt{(3H-4h)h}$

    (b) $\sqrt{(4H-3h)h}$

    (c) 150 kg

    (d) None of these

24. The height h at which the hole should be punched so that the liquid travels the maximum distance x_m is

    (a) $3H/4$

    (b) $H/2$

    (c) $3H/8$

    (d) None of these

Passage for (Q. 25 - 27) :

A cylindrical tank 1 m in radius rests on a platform 5 m high. Initially the tank is filled with water to a height of 5 m. A plug whose area is 10^{-4} m^2, is removed from an orifice on the side of the tank at the bottom. Calculate the following:

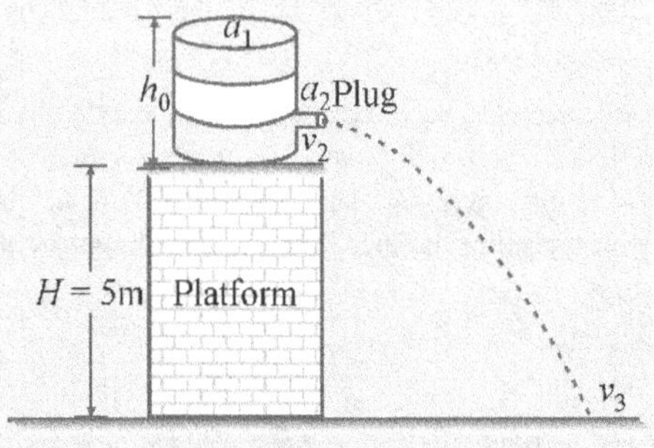

25. Initial speed with which the water flows from the orifice is

    (a) 5 m/s

    (b) 10 m/s

    (c) 12 m/s

    (d) 15 m/s

26. Initial speed with which the water strikes the ground is

    (a) 10 m/s

    (b) 14.1 m/s

    (c) 16.4 m/s

    (d) 18.2 m/s

27. Time taken to empty the tank to half its original value is

    (a) 444 s

    (b) 512 s

    (c) 628 s

    (d) 942 s

Passage for (Q. 28 - 30) :

A cubical beaker contains two immiscible liquids of density ρ and 2ρ each, filled upto height h as shown in figure

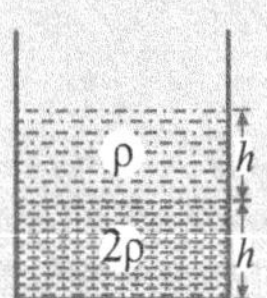

28. The distance of point of application of the force due to the liquids on the vertical wall of the beaker from the bottom is

    (a) h

    (b) $h/3$

    (c) $3h/2$

    (d) $3h/5$

29. The beaker is given a horizontal acceleration a. The liquid of density ρ finally makes an angle θ_1 with the horizontal while the liquid of density 2ρ makes an angle θ_2 with the horizontal, then

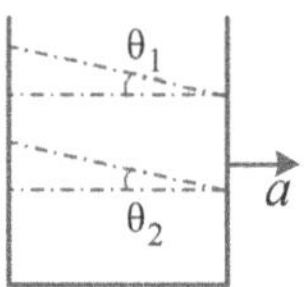

    (a) $\theta_1 < \theta_2$

    (b) $\theta_1 > \theta_2$

    (c) $\theta_1 = \theta_2$

    (d) none of these

30. Two holes are made in the beaker as shown. Find the initial acceleration of the beaker. The area of cross-section of beaker is A_0 and that of each hole is A. Neglect the mass of the beaker.

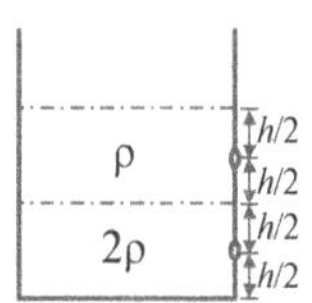

    (a) $\dfrac{3A}{A_0}g$

    (b) $\dfrac{Ag}{A_0}$

    (c) $\dfrac{5A}{3A_0}g$

    (d) none of these

Passage for (Q. 31 - 33) :

A U tube containing two different liquid of density ρ and 2ρ is fixed vertically on a rotating table about a vertical axis passing through the centre of the table. The interface of two liquids of densities ρ and 2ρ respectively lies at the point A in a U tube at rest height of liquid column above A is $\dfrac{8}{3}a$, where $AB = 2a$. The cross-sectional area of the tube is S.

Now the table is whirled with angular velocity ω about a vertical axis as shown in figure such that the interface of the liquids shifts towards B by $\dfrac{2}{3}a$, then at this instant

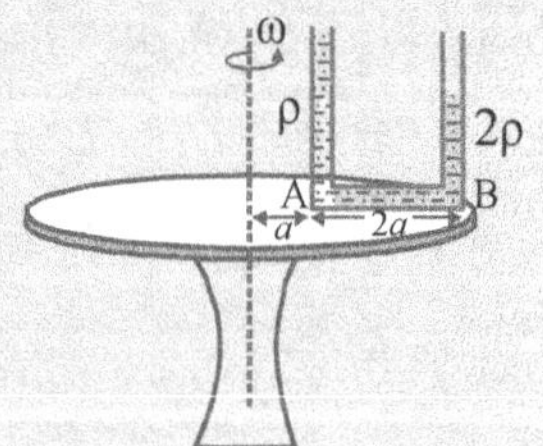

Answer Key	22	(c)	24	(c)	26	(b)	28	(d)	30	(c)
Sol. from page 265	23	(a)	25	(b)	27	(d)	29	(c)		

31. The value of $P_B - P_A$ is
    (a) ρga (b) $2\rho ga$
    (c) $3\rho ga$`   (d) $4\rho ga$

32. The force exerted by liquid ρ on liquid 2ρ at the interface is

    (a) $\rho Sag\left(\dfrac{9}{4}\right)$ (b) $\rho Sag\left(\dfrac{29}{3}\right)$

    (c) $\rho Sag\left(\dfrac{9}{10}\right)$ (d) $\rho Sag\left(\dfrac{29}{10}\right)$

33. The value of ω is

    (a) $\sqrt{\dfrac{9g}{4a}}$ (b) $\sqrt{\dfrac{9g}{32a}}$

    (c) $\sqrt{\dfrac{9g}{8a}}$ (d) $\sqrt{\dfrac{9g}{16a}}$

Passage for (Q. 34 - 36) :

A cylindrical tank has a hole of diameter $2r$ in its bottom. The hole is covered with a wooden cylindrical block of diameter $4r$, height h and density $\rho/3$.

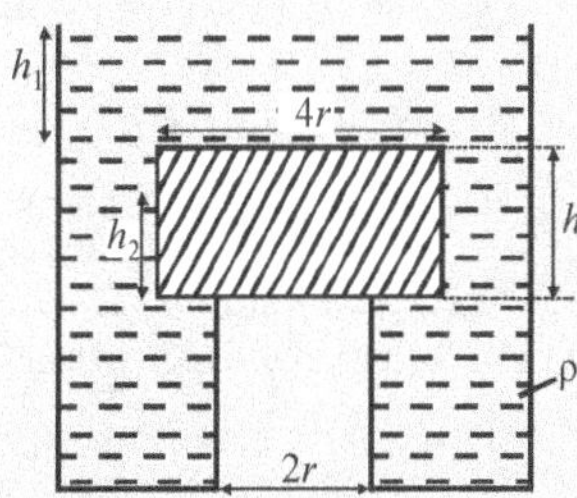

Process 1 : Initially, the tank is filled with water of density ρ to a height such that the height of water above the top of the block is h_1 (measured from the top of the block).

Process 2 : The water is removed from the tank to a height h_2 (measured from the bottom of the block), as shown in the figure. The height h_2 is smaller than h (height of the block) and thus the block is exposed to the atmosphere.

34. Find the minimum value of height h_1 (in process1), for which the block just starts to move up?

    (a) $\dfrac{2h}{3}$ (b) $\dfrac{5h}{4}$

    (c) $\dfrac{5h}{3}$ (d) $\dfrac{5h}{2}$

35. Find the height of the water level h_2 (in process 2), for which the block remains in its original position without the application of any external force

    (a) $\dfrac{h}{3}$ (b) $\dfrac{4h}{9}$

    (c) $\dfrac{2h}{3}$ (d) h

36. In process 2, if h_2 is further decreased, then
    (a) cylinder will not move up and remains at its original position

    (b) for $h_2 = \dfrac{h}{3}$, cylinder again starts moving up

    (c) for $h_2 = \dfrac{h}{4}$, cylinder again starts moving up

    (d) for $h_2 = \dfrac{h}{5}$, cylinder again starts moving up

MATRIX MATCHING

37. Match **Column I** (Property at fluid) with **Column II** (Law of fluid motion) and select the correct answer :

    Column-I
    A. Volume rate of flow
    B. Viscous drag
    C. Speed of efflux (exit)
    D. Pressure difference between two points

    Column-II
    p. Bernoulli's theorem
    q. Torricelli's theorem
    r. Stoke's law
    s. Poisuilli's law points in a flow tube

38. The vessel has two sections of areas of cross-section A_1 and A_2. A liquid of density fills both the sections, up to a height in each. Neglect atmospheric pressure.

    Column-I
    A. The pressure at the base of the vessel
    B. The force exerted by the liquid on the base of vessel
    C. The weight of the liquid is less than
    D. Downward force on the liquid by the walls of the vessel at the level X

    Column-II
    p. $2h\rho gA_2$
    q. $2h\rho g$
    r. $h\rho g\,(A_2 - A_1)$
    s. $2h\rho gA_1$

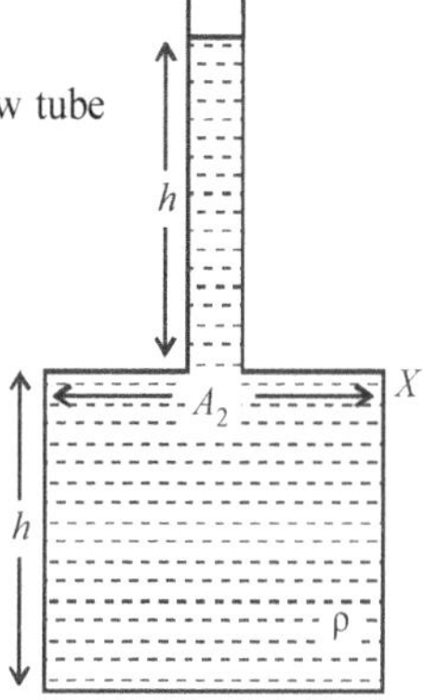

Answer Key	31	(b)	33	(b)	35	(b)	37	A → (s) ; B→ (r) ; C → (q); D → (p)
Sol. from page 265	32	(a)	34	(c)	36	(a)	38	A→ (q) ; B→ (p) ; C→ (p); D → (r)

39. Figure shows a siphon. It is a long pipe which is used to drain water from the reservoir at higher level to a reservoir at lower level. Regarding with the siphon match the following columns :

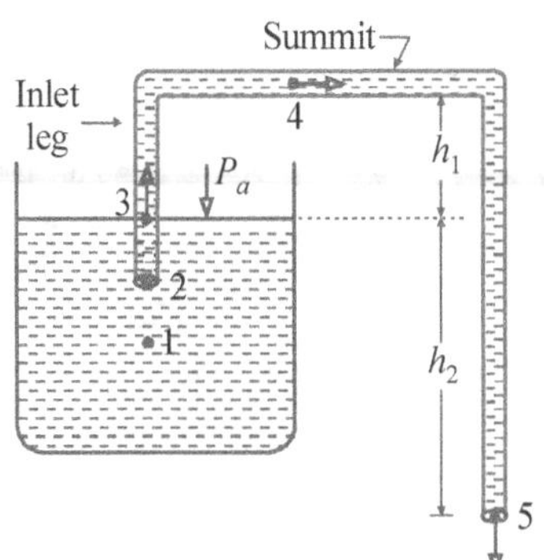

Column-I		Column-II	
A.	Pressure is more than atmospheric pressure at	(p)	1
B.	Pressure is less than atmospheric pressure at	(q)	2
C.	Pressure is highest of all the five points at	(r)	3
D.	Pressure is least of all the five points	(s)	4
		(t)	5

40. **Column II** shows five system in which two objects are labelled as X and Y. Also in each case a point P is shows

Column I gives some statements about X and/ or Y. Match these statements to the appropriate system (s) from **Column II**.

Column-I

A. The force exerted by X and Y has a magnitude Mg. (p)

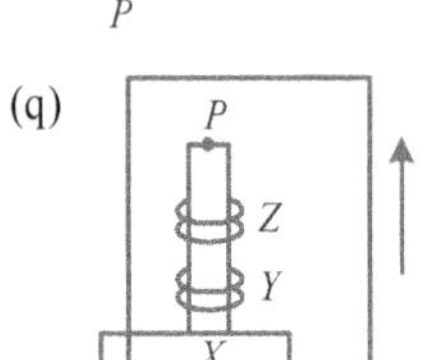

Column-II

Block Y of mass M left on a fixed inclined plane X, slides on it with a constants velocity

B. The gravitational potential energy of X is continuously increasing (q)

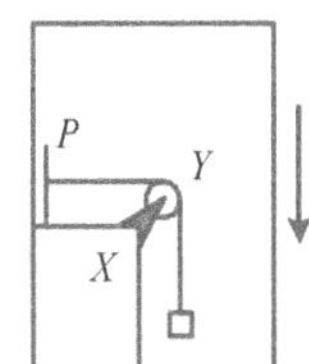

Two ring magnets Y and Z, each of mass M, are kept in frictionless vertical plastic stand so that they repel each other. Y rests on the base X and Z hangs in air in equilibrium. P is the top most point of the stand on the common axis of the two rings The whole system is in a lift that is going up with a constant velocity

C. Mechanical energy of the system $X + Y$ is continuously decreasing (r)

A pulley Y of mass m_0 is fixed to a table through a clamp X. A block of mass M hang from a string that goes over the pulley and is fixed at point P of the table. The whole system is kept in a lift that is going down with a constant velocity

D. The torque of the weight of Y about point P is zero (s)

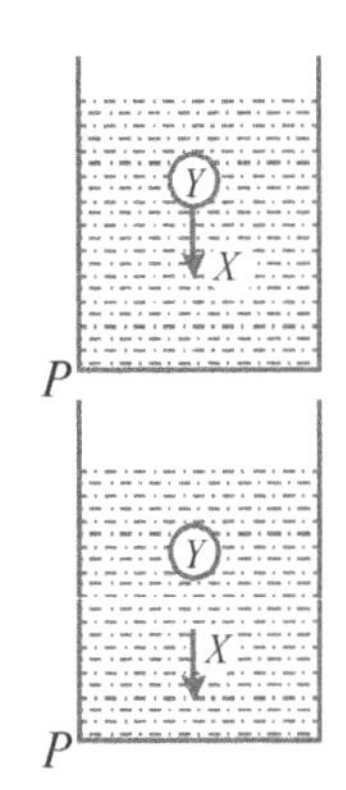

A sphere Y of mass M is put in a non viscous liquid X kept in a container at rest. The sphere is released and it moves down in the liquid.

(t)

A sphere Y of mass M is falling with its terminal velocity in a viscous liquid X kept in a container.

Solution from page 270

1. In a hydraulic press used for compressing cotton, the area of the piston is $0.1\ m^2$ and the force exerted along the piston rod is 200 N. If the area of the larger cylinder is $0.8\ m^2$, find the pressure produced in the cylinder and the total crushing force exerted on the bale of cotton.

    Ans. 1600 N, 1280 N/m^2 .

2. A metal piece of mass 1600 g lies in equilibrium inside a glass of water. The piece touches the bottom of the glass at a small number of points. If the density of the metal is $8000\ kg/m^3$, find the normal force exerted by the bottom of the glass on the metal piece.

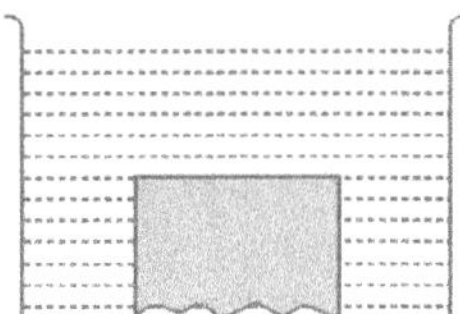

    Ans. 14 N.

3. A U-tube contains water and liquid separated by mercury. The mercury columns in the two arms are in level with 10 cm of water in one arm and 5 cm of liquid in the other. What is the specific gravity of liquid ?

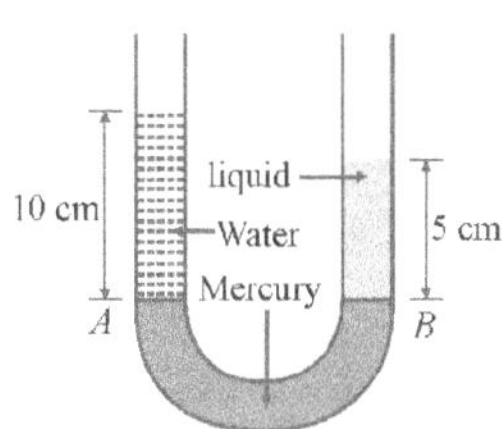

    Ans. 2

4. The pressure in tank A measures 700 kg/m^2 gauge. What is the pressure in tank B if $\rho_{oil} = 800\ kg/m^3$.

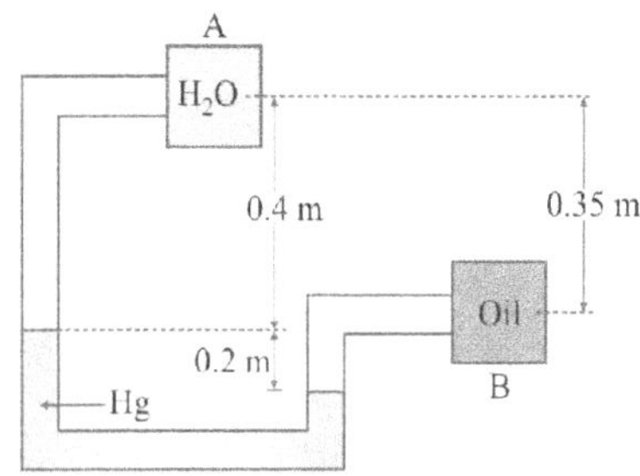

    Ans. 3620 kg/m^2 .

5. Water flows through a horizontal tube as shown in figure. If the difference of heights of water column in the vertical tube is 2 cm, and the areas of cross-section at A and B are 4 cm^2 and 2 cm^2 respectively, find the rate of flow of water across any section.

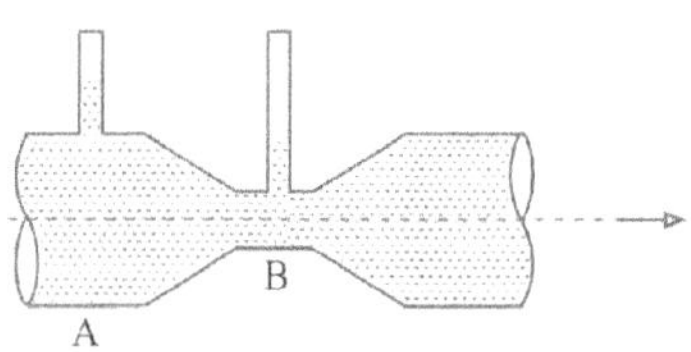

    Ans. 146 cc/s.

6. Water flows into a horizontal pipe whose one end is closed with a valve and the reading of a pressure gauge attached to the pipe is $3 \times 10^5\ N/m^2$. This reading of the pressure gauge falls to $1 \times 10^5\ N/m^2$ when the valve is opened. Calculate the speed of water flowing into the pipe. ***Ans.*** 20 m/s.

7. The side wall of a wide vertical vessel of height h = 75 cm has a narrow vertical slit running all the way down to the bottom of the vessel. The length of the slit is l = 50 cm and the width b = 1.0 mm. With the slit closed, the vessel is filled with water. Find the resultant force of reaction of water flowing out the vessel immediatly after the slit is opened.

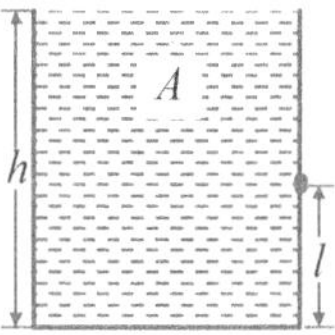

    Ans. 5 N.

8. A side wall of a wide open tank is provided with a narrowing tube through which water flows out. The cross–sectional area of the tube decreases from S = 3.0 cm^2 to s = 1.0 cm^2 . The water level in the tank is h = 4.6 m higher than in the tube. Neglecting the viscosity of water, find the horizontal component of the force tending to pull the tube out of the tank.

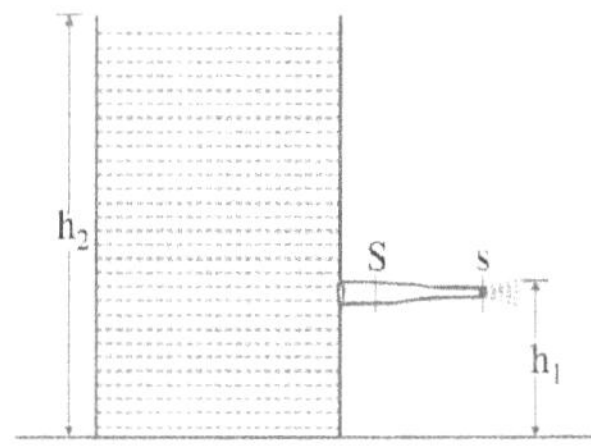

    Ans. $\rho g h\dfrac{(S-s)^2}{S} = 6N$

FM Subjective *Exercise 3.6*

Solution from page 271

1. An automobile back is lifted by a hydraulic jack that consists of two pistons. The large piston is 1 m in diameter and the small piston is 10 cm in diameter. If W be the weight of the car, how much smaller a force is needed on the small piston to lift the car ?
   Ans. 1% of the weight of the car.

2. A tank with a square base of area 1.0 m^2 is divided by a vertical partition in the middle. The bottom of the partition has a small hinged door of area 20 cm^2. The tank is filled with water in one compartment, and an acid (of relative density 1.7) in the other, both to a height of 4.0 m. Compute the force necessary to keep the door closed. *Ans.* 54.88 N.

3. A manometer reads the pressure of a gas in an enclosure as shown in figure. (a) When some of the gas is removed by a pump, the manometer reads as in figure (b). The liquid used in the manometer is mercury and the atmospheric pressure is 76 cm of mercury.
   (i) Give the absolute and gauge pressure of the gas in the enclosure for cases (a) and (b) in units of cm of mercury.
   (ii) How would the levels change in case (b) if 13.6 cm of water (immiscible with mercury) are poured into the right limb of the manometer ? (Ignore the small change in volume of the gas)

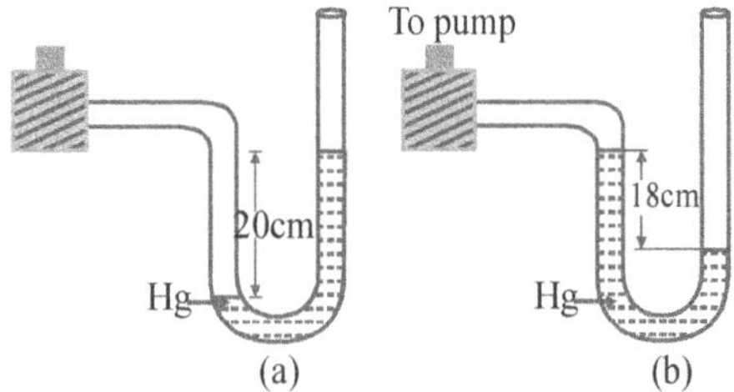

   Ans. (i) 20 cm of Hg, – 18 cm of Hg (ii) 19 cm.

4. A liquid stands at the same level in the U–tube when at rest. If A is the area of cross–section and g the acceleration due to gravity, what will be the difference in height h of the liquid in the two limbs of U–tube, when the system is given an acceleration a towards right, as shown in figure.

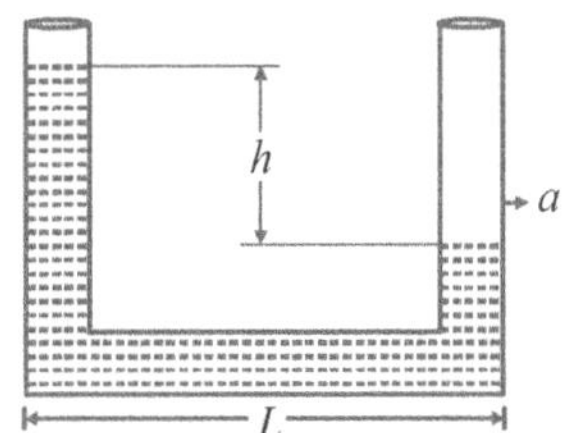

   Ans. $h = \dfrac{La}{g}$.

5. A piece of pure gold (ρ = 19.3 g /cm^3) is suspected to be hollow from inside. It weighs 38.250 g in air and 33.865 g in water. Calculate the volume of the hollow portion in gold, if any.
   Ans. 2.403 cm^3 .

6. A spring balance reads 10 kg when a bucket of water is suspended from it. What is the reading on the spring balance when (i) an ice cube of mass 1.5 kg is put into the bucket (ii) an iron piece of mass 7.8 kg suspended by another spring is immersed with half its volume inside the water in the bucket ? Relative density of iron = 7.8. *Ans.* (i)11.5 kg f (ii) 10.5 kg f.

7. A hemispherical tank of radius R has an orifice of cross–sectional area a at its base. Determine the time required to empty the tank, if height of liquid in the tank is H.

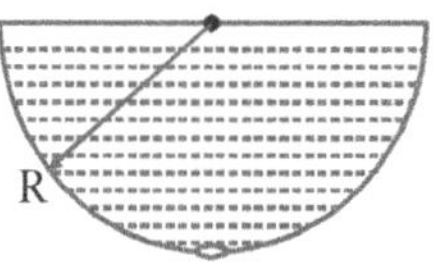

   Ans. $T = \dfrac{\pi}{a\sqrt{2g}}\left[\dfrac{4}{3}RH^{3/2} - \dfrac{2}{5}H^{5/2}\right].$

8. A barometer is a device for measuring atmospheric pressure. If we use a liquid having a specific gravity of 13,600 kg/m^3 and invert a tube full of this material as shown in figure. What is the value of h if the vapour pressure of the liquid is 21 kg/m^2 ?

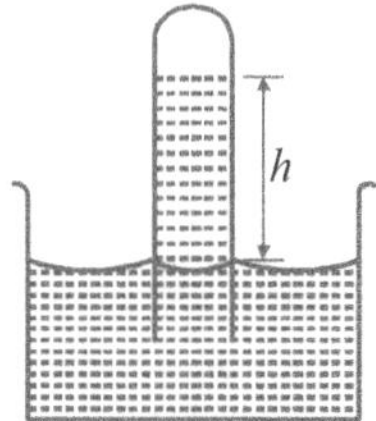

   Ans. 75.85 cm.

9. The vessel has two immiscible fluids, water and oil is evacuated to a pressure of 0.5 atm. What is the resultant force on the door from fluids inside the container (the specific gravity of oil is 0.8)?

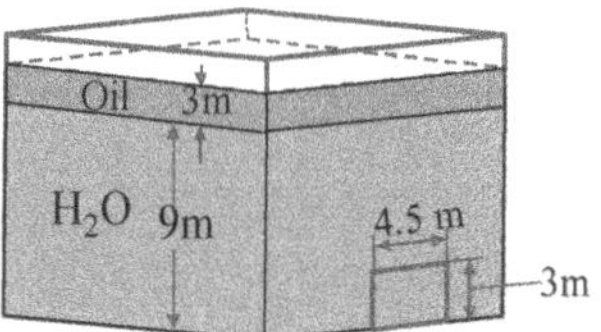

   Ans. 8.21×10^5 N.

10. Find the resultant force vector acting on the unit width of the wall from the water.

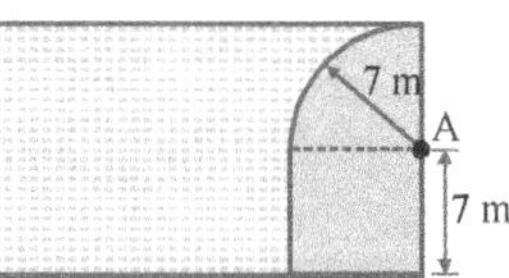

   Ans. (961.38 **i** – 103.16 **j**) kN.

11. The area of cross–section of a large tank is 0.5 m^2. It has an opening near the bottom having area of cross–section 1 cm^2. A load of 20 kg is applied on the water at the top. Find the velocity of the water coming out of the opening at the time when the height of water level is 50 cm above the bottom. Take g = 10 m/s^2.
   Ans. 3.3 m/s.

12. A large slab rests on soft ground at the bottom of a lake. The slab has sunk into the ground a slight distance so that water cannot reach the under surface. If the slab of mass 1000 kg, has a cross-sectional area parallel to the free surface of 1 m², what initial force is required to start moving it up? When it has moved a slight distance up so that water reaches the lower surface, what is the force required to hold the slab ?

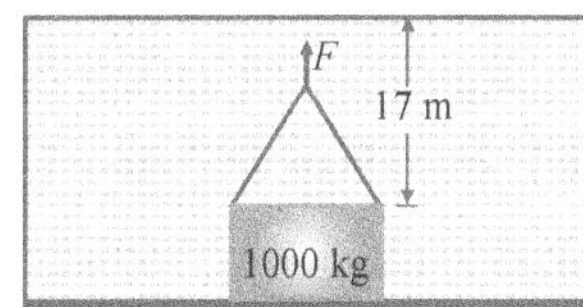

Ans. 176.58 kN, 9810 N.

13. A wooden stick of length L, radius R and density ρ has a small metal piece of mass m (of negligible volume) attached to its one end. Find the minimum value for the mass (in terms of given parameters) that would make the stick float vertically in equilibrium in a liquid of density σ (> ρ).   ***Ans.*** $\pi R^2 L\rho\left\{\sqrt{\dfrac{\sigma}{\rho}}-1\right\}$.

14. A solid ball of density half that of water falls freely under gravity from a height of 19.6 m and then enters water. Upto what depth will the ball go ? How much time will it take to come again to the water surface ? Neglect air resistance and viscosity effects in water.
Ans. 19.6 m, 4 s.

15. A balloon filled with hydrogen has a volume of 1000 litres and its mass 1 kg. What would be the volume of the block of a very light material which it can just lift ? One litre of the material has mass of 91.3 g. (Density of air = 1.3 g/ litre)   ***Ans.*** 3.33 litre.

16. A container of a large uniform cross-sectional area A resting on a horizontal surface holds two immiscible, non viscous and incompressible liquids of densities d and 2 d, each of height $\dfrac{H}{2}$ as shown in figure. The lower density liquid is open to atmosphere.

A homogeneous solid cylinder of length L $\left(L<\dfrac{H}{2}\right)$, cross –sectional area $\dfrac{A}{5}$ is immersed such that it floats with its axis vertical at the liquid – liquid interface with length $\dfrac{L}{4}$ in denser liquid. Determine (i)   density of the solid and (ii) the total pressure at the bottom of the container. (Atmospheric pressure = P_0)

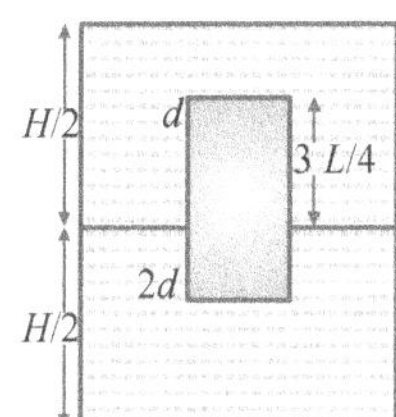

Ans. (i) $\dfrac{5d}{4}$ (ii) $\left(\dfrac{6H+L}{4}\right)dg+P_0$.

17. An open and wide glass tube is immersed vertically in mercury in such a way that a length 0.05 m extends above the   mercury level. The open end of the tube is then closed and the tube is raised further by 0.43 m. Calculate the length of the air column above the mercury level in the tube.
Ans. 0.10 m.

18. A closed tank filled with water is mounted on a cart. The cart moves with an acceleration, 'a' on a plane road. Find the value of the pressure at any point which is at a depth h and a distance l from the front wall.

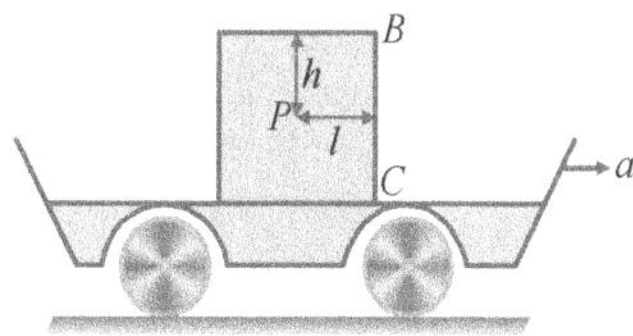

Ans. (hg + la)d.

19. A body of density ρ is released gently on the surface of a layer of a liquid of depth d and density σ (ρ > σ). Show it will reach the bottom of the liquid after a time $\left[\dfrac{2d\rho}{g(\rho-\sigma)}\right]^{\frac{1}{2}}$.

20. A cubical tank of side 2 m is filled with 1.5 m of glycerine of specific gravity 1.6. Find the force acting on the side of the tank when
(a)   it is accelerated vertically upward at 5 m/s², and
(b)   it is accelerated vertically downward at 5 m/s².
Ans. (a) 53.316 kN (b) 17.316 kN.

21. A tank contains water and mercury as shown in figure. An iron cube of edge 6 cm is in equilibrium as shown. What is the fraction of cube inside the mercury ? Given density of iron = 7.7 × 10³ kg m³ and density of mercury = 13.6 × 10³ kg/m³.

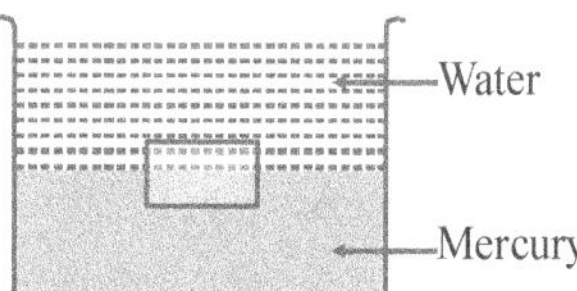

Ans. 0.533.

22. Water flows through the tube shown in figure. The areas of cross–section of the wide and the narrow portions of the tube are 5 cm² and 2 cm² respectively. The rate of flow of water through the tube is 500 cm³/s. Find the difference of mercury levels in the U–tube.

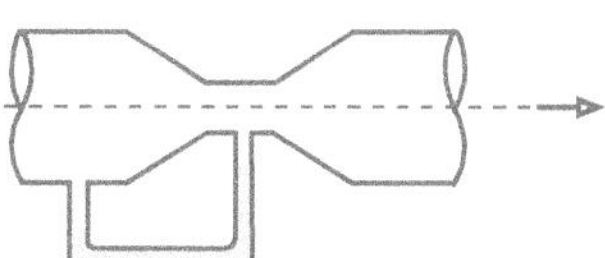

Ans. 1.97 cm

23. Figure shows a siphon in action. The liquid flowing through the siphon has a density of 1.5 g/cc. Calculate the pressure difference between points

(a)   (i) A and D   (ii) B and C, neglecting density of air.

(b)   (i) A and D (ii) B and C, taking into account the density of air = 1.3 kg/m^3.

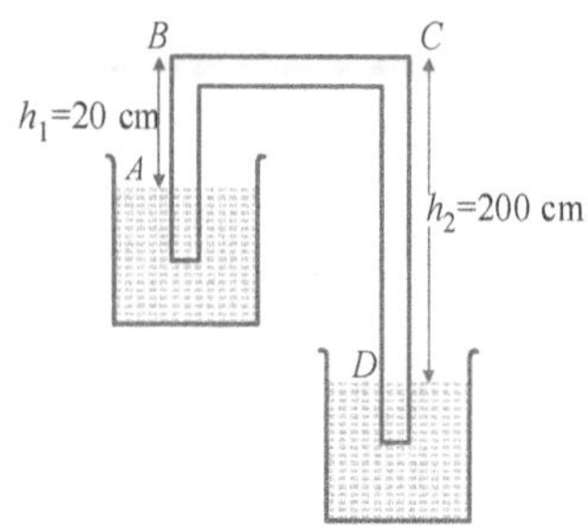

Ans. (a)   (i) $P_D - P_A = 0$ (ii) $P_B - P_C = 2.646 \times 10^4 \, N/m^2$

(b) $P_D - P_A = 22.93 \, N/m^2$, $P_B - P_C = 2.644 \times 10^4 \, N/m^2$.

24. Water-flows steadily from a reservoir as in figure. The elevation of point 1 is 10 m; of points 2 and 3 it is 1 m. The cross section at point 2 is 0.04 m^2 and at point 3 it is 0.02 m^2. The area of the reservoir is very large compared with the cross-sections of the pipe.

(a)   Compute the gauge pressure at point 2.

(b)   Compute the discharge rate in cubic metre per second.

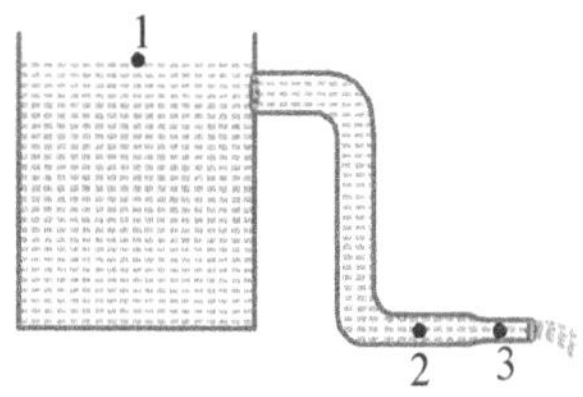

Ans. (a) 6.62×10^4 Pa (b) 0.266 m^3/s.

25. Two very large open tanks, A and F both contain the same liquid. A horizontal pipe BCD, having a constriction at C, leads out of the bottom of tank A, and a vertical pipe E opens into the constriction at C and dips in tothe liquid in tank F. Assume streamline flow and no viscosity. If the cross section at C is one half that at D, and if D is at distance h_1 below the level of the liquid in A, to what height h_2 will liquid rise in pipe E ? Express your answer in terms of h_1. Neglect changes in atmospheric pressure with elevation.

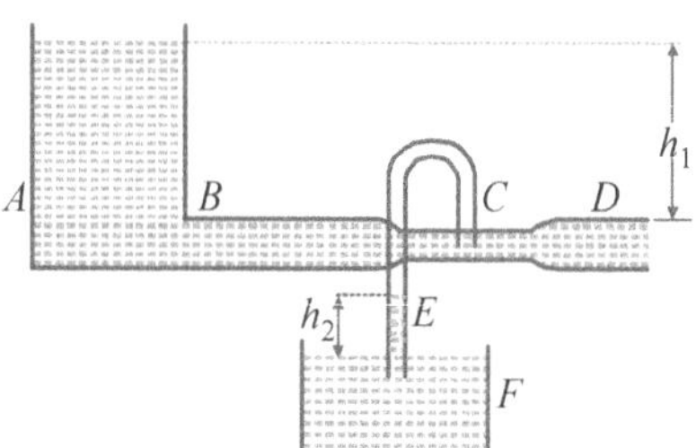

Ans. $h_2 = 3\, h_1$.

26. A plane is in level flight at constant speed and each of its two wings has an area of 25 m^2. If the speed of the air is 180 km/h over the lower wing and 234 km/h over the upper wing surface, determine the plane's mass. Take air density to be 1 kg/m^3 and g = 9.81 m/s^2.

Ans. 4396 kg.

27. Water is flowing through two horizontal pipes of different diameters which are connected together. In the first pipe the speed of water is 4 m/s and the pressure is 2.0×10^4 N/m^2. Calculate the speed and pressure of water in the second pipe. The diameters of the pipes are 3 cm and 6 cm respectively.

Ans. 1 m/s, 2.75×10^4 N/m^2.

28. The flow of blood in a large artery of an anesthetized dog is diverted through a venturi metre. The wider part of the   metre has a cross–sectional area equal to that of the artery, A = 8 mm^2. The narrower part has an area a = 4 mm^2. The pressure drop in the artery is 24 Pa. What is the speed of the blood in the artery?

Ans. 0.125 m/s.

29. What work should be done in order to squeeze all water from a horizontally located cylinder during the time t by means of a constant force acting on the piston ? The volume of water in the cylinder is equal to V, the cross–sectional area of the orifice is s, with s being considerably less than the piston area. The friction and viscosity are negligibly small.

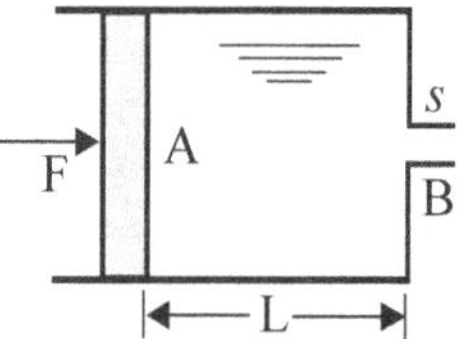

Ans. $W = \dfrac{1}{2}\rho\left(\dfrac{V^3}{s^2 t^2}\right)$.

30. On the opposite sides of a wide vertical vessel filled with water two identical holes are opened, each having cross-sectional area S. The height difference between them is equal to Δh. Find the resultant force of reaction of the water flowing out of the vessel.

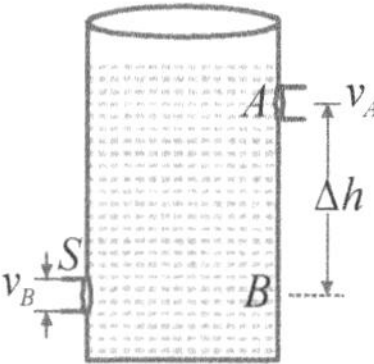

Ans. $F = (2\,\Delta h\, \rho\, g\, S)$.

31. Two manometric tubes are mounted on a horizontal pipe of varying cross–section at the sections S_1 and S_2 as shown in figure. Find the volume of water flowing across the pipe's section per unit time if the difference in water columns is equal to Δh.

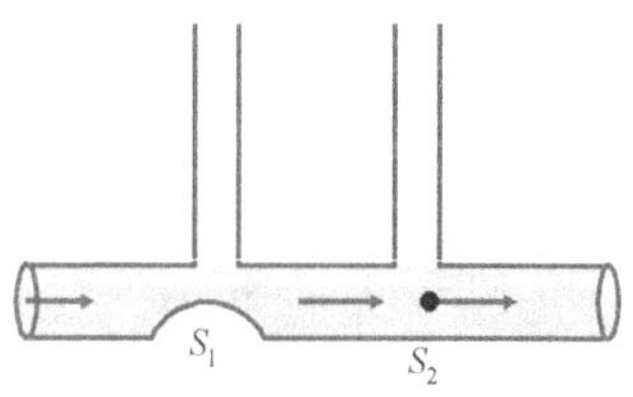

Ans. $S_1 S_2 \sqrt{\dfrac{2\,\Delta h g}{S_2^2 - S_1^2}}$.

32. The horizontal bottom of a wide vessel with an ideal fluid has a round orifice of radius R_1 over which a round closed cylinder is mounted, whose radius $R_2 > R_1$. The clearance between the cylinder and the bottom of the vessel is very small, the fluid density is ρ. Find the static pressure of the fluid in the clearance as a function of the distance r from the axis of the orifice (and the cylinder), if the height of the fluid is equal to h.

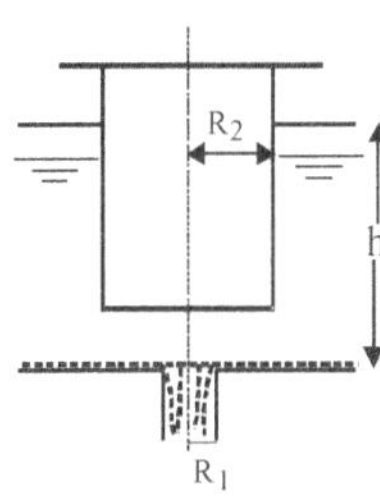

$$\textbf{Ans. } P_a + \rho g h\left[1 - \frac{R_1^2}{r^2}\right].$$

33. A horizontally oriented tube AB of length l rotates with a constant angular velocity ω about a stationary vertical axis OO' passing through the end A. The tube is filled with an ideal fluid. The end A of the tube is open, the closed end B has a very small orifice. Find the velocity of the fluid relative to the tube as a function of the column height h.

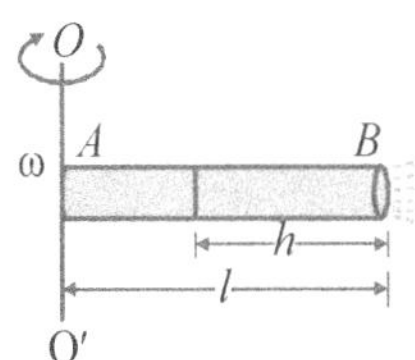

$$\textbf{Ans. } \omega h\sqrt{\left(\frac{2\ell}{h} - 1\right)}.$$

34. Water flows out of a big tank along a tube bent at right angles : the inside radius of the tube is equal to r. The length of the horizontal section of the tube is equal to l. The water flow rate is Q litres/s. Find the moment of reaction forces of flow in water, acting on the tube's walls, relative to the point O.

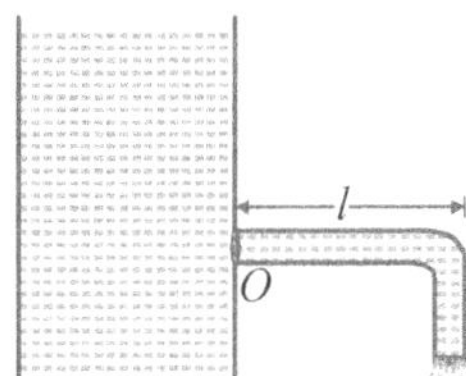

$$\textbf{Ans. } \left(\frac{Q^2\rho}{\pi r^2}\right)\ell.$$

35. In the figure shown a vessel kept on a trolley. The diameter of the exit pipe is 5 cm, the water issues out at 5 m/s and is turned through 45° by the bent pipe. What is the compression produced in the spring ? Spring constant is $k = 20$ N/cm.

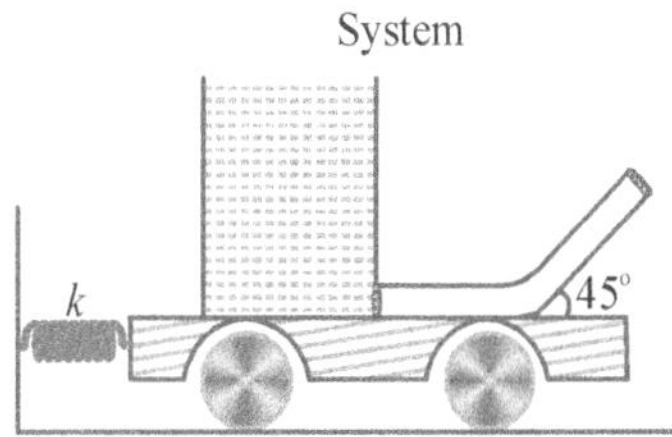

$$\textbf{Ans. } 1.74 \text{ cm.}$$

36. A vessel with a hole in its bottom is fastened on a cart. The mass of the vessel and the cart is M and cross–section area A. What force F is required to pull the cart so that a maximum amount of water remains in the vessel ? The dimensions of the vessel are shown in the figure.

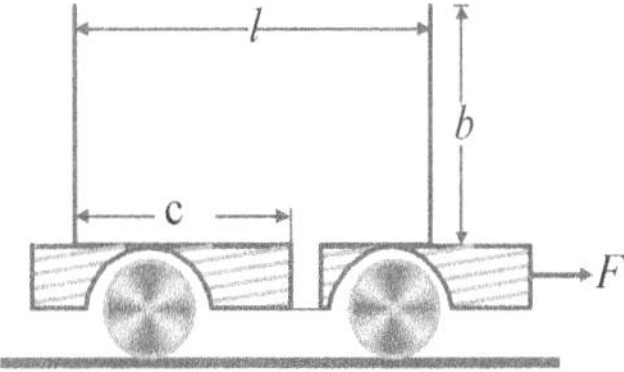

$$\textbf{Ans. } F = \left(M + \frac{bcA}{2\ell}\rho\right)g\frac{b}{c}.$$

37. A non viscous liquid of constant density 1000 kg/m³ flows in a streamline motion along a tube of variable cross-section. The tube is kept inclined in the vertical plane as shown in figure. The area of the cross–section of the tube at two points P and Q at heights of 2 m and 5 m are respectively 4×10^{-3} m² and 8×10^{-3} m². The velocity of the liquid at point P is 1 m/s. Find the work done per unit volume by the pressure and the gravity forces as the liquid flows from point P to Q.

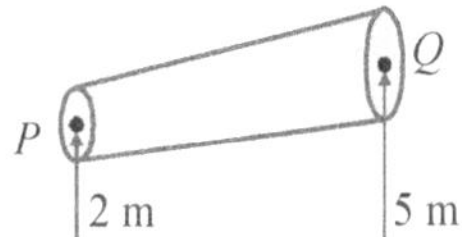

$$\textbf{Ans. } 29025 \text{ J/m}^3, -2.94 \times 10^4 \text{ J/m}^3$$

38. A metal rod of length 80 cm and mass 1.6 kg has a uniform cross–sectional area of 6.0 cm². Due to a nonuniform density, the centre of mass of the rod is 20 cm from one end of the rod. The rod is suspended in a horizontal position in water by ropes attached to both ends.

(a) What is the tension in the rope closer to the centre of mass?

(b) What is the tension in the rope further from the centre of mass?

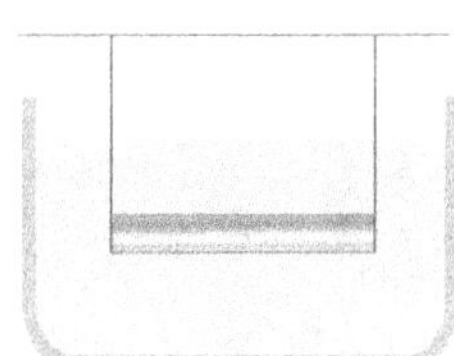

(**Hint:** The buoyancy force on the rod effectively acts at the rod's centre)

$$\textbf{Ans. } \text{(a) } 9.4 \text{ N, (b) } 1.6 \text{ N.}$$

39. A Pitot tube is used to determine the air speed of an airplane. It consists of an outer tube with a number of small holes B (four are shown) that allow air in to the tube; that tube is connected to one arm of a U–tube. The other arm of the U–tube is connected to hole A at the front end of the device, which points in the direction the plane is headed. At A the air becomes stagnant so that $v_A = 0$. At B, however the speed of the air presumely equals the air speed, v of the aircraft.

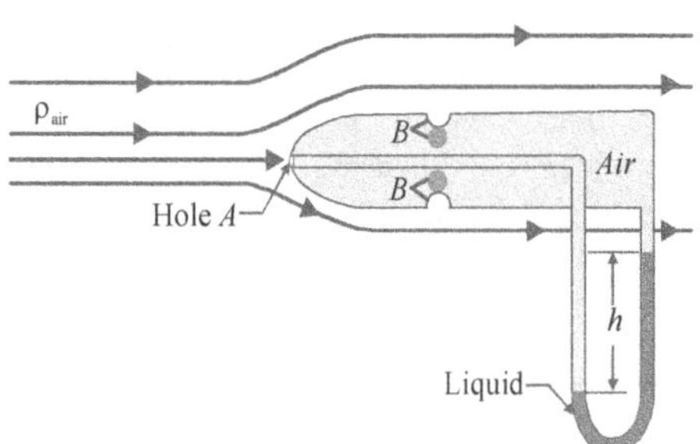

(a) Use Bernoulli's equation to show that $v = \sqrt{\dfrac{2\rho gh}{\rho_{air}}}$ where

ρ is the density of the liquid in the U–tube and h is the difference in the fluid levels in that tube.

(b) Suppose that the tube contains alcohol and indicates a level difference h of 26.0 cm. What is the plane's speed relative to the air? The density of the air is 1.03 kg/m^3 and that of alcohol is 810 kg/m^3.

Ans. (b) 63.3 m/s.

40. Water in a clean aquarium forms a meniscus, as illustrated in figure. Calculate the difference in height h between the centre and the edge of the meniscus. The surface tension of water is $T = 0.073$ N/m.

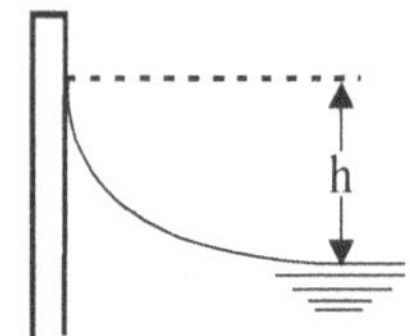

Ans. Water rises by approximately 4 mm up the wall of the aquarium.

41. A 1×1 m cover AB on a container under pressure as shown in figure is held in position by a force F. Calculate the force and the reaction at the hinge B.

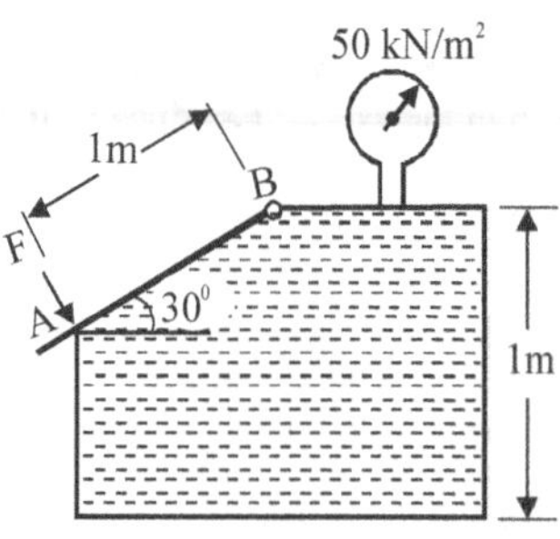

Ans. 26.24 kN.

42. A small tank practically filled with liquid is mounted at the end of a long rotating arm of radius R which rotates steadily in the horizontal plane at an angular velocity ω. The remaining space in the tank is at uniform pressure. The free surface of liquid, which may be taken as a plane, from an angle θ with the horizontal. Show that θ is given by tan $\theta = - (\omega^2 R / g)$.

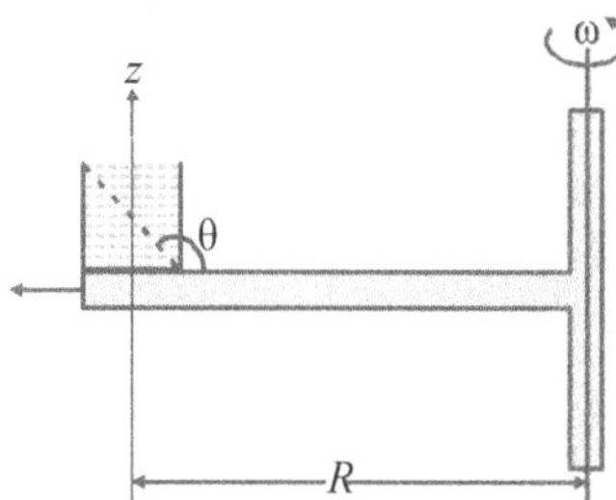

43. W–tube system as shown is rotated about an axis AA at 10 rpm. Determine the levels in columns C_1, C_2 and C_3 in the new position of equilibrium. Determine also the levels in the tubes if the axis of rotation was BB instead of AA. Assume the tubes to be long enough not to allow spillage.

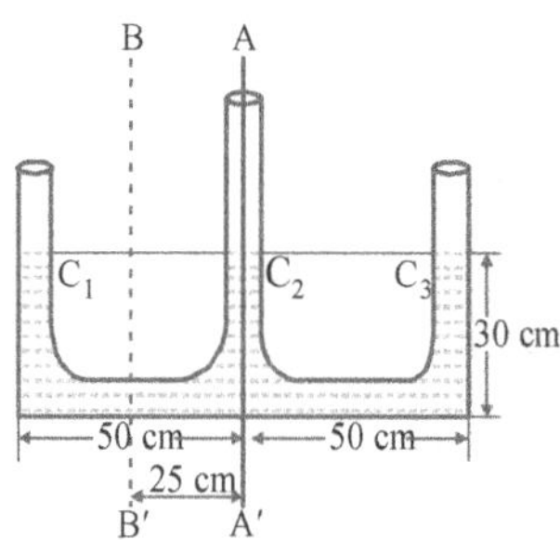

Ans. 30.47, 29.06, 30.47; 29.07, 31.86 cm

Hints & Solutions

1. (a) Previously buoyant force, $F_b = 5g$. When 3.5 kg is put in that place, it has an unbalanced force in upward direction.

2. (a) For floating
$$mg = V\rho g$$
$$\therefore \quad V = \frac{m}{\rho}$$
Thus submerge volume is free from acceleration due to gravity.

3. (c) Both the points are exposed to atmosphere, so they have atmospheric pressure.

4. (c) The volume of ice $V = \dfrac{M}{\rho}$ and that of water $\dfrac{M}{\sigma}$. Therefore decrease in volume
$$= \frac{M}{\rho} - \frac{M}{\sigma} = M\left[\frac{1}{\rho} - \frac{1}{\sigma}\right]$$

5. (a) Because of rightward acceleration, the water level at backward side tend to increase and so pressure at B will increase and at C will decrease.

6. (d)

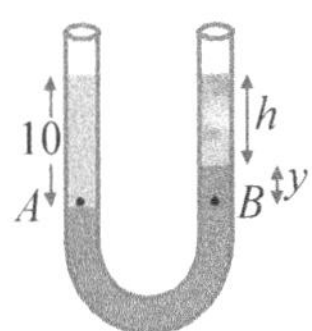

$$h + y = 10 \text{ cm} \qquad \ldots(i)$$
$$P_A = P_B$$
or $\quad 1.3g \times 10 = 13.6 \times g \times y + 0.8 \times g \times h$
or $\quad 13 = 13.6\, y + 0.8\, h \qquad \ldots (ii)$
After solving above equations, we get
$$h = 9.6 \text{ cm.}$$

7. (b)
$$\rho_{mit} = \frac{3m}{\left(\dfrac{m}{d} + \dfrac{m}{2d} + \dfrac{m}{3d}\right)} = \frac{18d}{11}$$

8. (d) As, $P = \rho g h$, so pressure in both the tank at the bottom is same.

9. (a) The water levels in A and B goes up. But level in B rises greater than A.

10. (a) The volume of liquid displaced $V = \dfrac{m}{\rho}$, does not depend on g so it remains as such.

11. (c)
$$A\, v = A_1 v_1 + A_2 v_2$$
or $\quad A \times 3 = A \times 1.5 + 1.5 A \times v$
$\therefore \quad v = 1 \text{ m/s}$

12. (d)
$$A_1 v_1 = A_2 v_2$$
$$\therefore \quad v_2 = \frac{A_1 v_1}{A_2} = \frac{4.20 \times 5.18}{7.60} = 2.86 \text{ m/s}$$

13. (b) Decrease in pressure energy is equal to increase in kinetic energy of water, so
$$\frac{1}{2}\rho v^2 = (P_1 - P_2)$$
or $\quad \dfrac{1}{2} \times 1000 \times v^2 = (3.5 - 3) \times 10^5$
$\therefore \quad v = 10 \text{ m/s}$

14. (c) The velocity of ball just penetration the water $v = \sqrt{2gh}$. This to be constant.
$$\left(\frac{4}{3}\pi r^3\right)\rho g = 6\pi \eta r(\sqrt{2gh}) + \left(\frac{4}{3}\pi r^3\right)\rho_w g$$
$$h = \frac{2}{81}r^4\left(\frac{\rho-1}{\eta}\right)^2 g$$

15. (a) For dynamic lift on aeroplane,
$$P + \frac{1}{2}\rho v^2 = \text{constant}$$

16. (b) For maximum range,
$$h = \frac{H}{2} = \frac{90}{2} = 45 \text{ cm}$$

17. (c)
$$Ax = (4A)y$$
or $\quad x = 4\, y$
From Pascal's law
$$P_A = P_B$$
or $\quad \rho_w g(36 + x) = \rho_{Hg} g(x + y)$
or $\quad 1 \times g(36 + 4y) = 13.6 \times g\,(4y + y)$
$\therefore \quad y = 0.56 \text{ cm}$

18. (c)

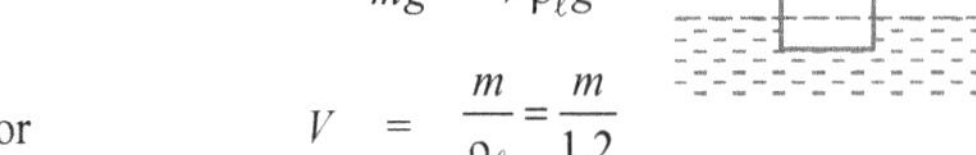

$$mg = \frac{V}{2}\rho_{oil}g + \frac{V}{2}\rho_{Hg}g$$
or $\quad V\rho g = V \times \dfrac{0.8 \times g}{2} + \dfrac{V}{2} \times 13.6 \times g$
$\therefore \quad \rho = 7.2 \text{ g/cm}^3$

19. (a) If V is the volume of liquid displaced then,
$$F_b = V\rho(g - a) = V\rho(g - g) = 0$$

20. (b)
$$mg = V\rho_\ell g$$
or $\quad V = \dfrac{m}{\rho_\ell} = \dfrac{m}{1.2}$

When ice melt, the volume of water formed
$$V' = \frac{m}{\rho_w} = \frac{m}{1} = m$$

Clearly $V' > V$, so level of liquid will rise.

21. (a) The velocity of the body becomes constant after travelling for some distance.

22. (d) For streamline flow, all are correct.

23. (b)
$$R_N = \frac{\rho v d}{\eta}$$

or
$$2000 = \left[\frac{1000 \times v \times (2 \times 10^{-2})}{10^{-3}}\right]$$

$\therefore \qquad v = 0.1 \text{ m/s}$

24. (c) Go to theory.

25. (c) Velocity of efflux, $v_e = \sqrt{2gh}$, clearly v_e depends on g and h.

26. (c) For the static liquid, pressure at B will be, $P = \rho g H / 2$. Due to velocity of liquid at B, the pressure at the point will decrease, so that $P + \dfrac{1}{2}\rho v^2 = \text{constant}$.

27. (c)
$$V\rho_3 g = \frac{V}{2}\rho_1 g + \frac{V}{2}\rho_2 g$$

or
$$\rho_3 = \frac{\rho_1 + \rho_2}{2},$$

Clearly $\rho_1 < \rho_3 < \rho_2$.

28. (a) The thrust, $\quad F = P_{av} \times A = \dfrac{\rho g h}{2} A$.

29. (c) The pressure difference between lungs and atmosphere,
$$= 760 - 750 = 10 \text{ mm of Hg}$$

$\therefore \qquad h\rho_\omega g = 1 \times \rho_{Hg} \times g$

or
$$h = \frac{\rho_{Hg}}{\rho_w} = 13.6 \text{ cm.}$$

30. (c) From Pascal's law
$$\rho_w g \times h = \frac{mg}{A}$$

or
$$h = \left(\frac{12}{800 \times 10^{-4} \times 10^3}\right) = 0.15 \text{ m}$$

31. (d)
$$\pi R^2 h_1 = R^2 h_2$$

$\therefore \qquad \pi h_1 = h_2$

$$\frac{F_1}{F_2} = \frac{\rho g h_1 \times \pi R^2}{\rho g h_2 \times R^2}$$

$$= \frac{\pi h_1}{h_2} = 1$$

32. (b) The pressure of liquid $= 3P - P = 2P$

Thus, in the next case pressure, $P' = \dfrac{4}{5} \times 2P + P = \dfrac{13P}{5}$.

33. (b) For the equilibrium of the block
$$mg = kx + V\rho g$$

$$\rho(Ah)g = k(h/3) + (Ah)\frac{\rho}{3}g$$

$\therefore \qquad k = 2\rho A g$

34. (d) The acceleration of the cork is also a w.r.t ground observer, so acceleration w.r.t. water becomes zero.

35. (d) The pressure on right side of the bubble is greater than left, and so bubble will have the shape as in case (d).

36. (d) $p_{s_1} = 50$ cm. mercury $= \dfrac{50}{100} \times 13.6 = 6.8$ m WG

($WG \rightarrow$ water gauge)

$p_{s_2} = p_{s_1} = 6.8$ m WG

$p_{s_3} = 6.8 - 0.5 = 6.3$ m WG

Equating p_{s_4} to p_{s_3} etc.

$p_s = 6.3 \times 2 = 12.6$ m WG

$$p_{pipe} = 12.6 + \frac{50}{100} \times 13.6 - 0.0012 \times \frac{90}{100} = 19.4 \text{ m WG}$$
$$= 19.4 \times 1000 \times 9.81 = 190 \times 10^3 \text{ N/m}^2$$
$$= 190 \text{ kN/m}^2 \text{ (gauge)}$$

The pressure, 19.4m WG equals 1.43m mercury gauge. Allowing, say, 10 cm. to stay in the bottom U-space, the single U-tube mercury manometer would be 153cm. long.

Solutions **EXERCISE 3.1 LEVEL -2**

1. (b) $\quad F = P \times \pi R^2 = (1 - 0.5) \times 10^5 \times \pi(1)^2$
$\qquad\qquad = 1.57 \times 10^5 \text{ N}$

2. (d) $\quad mg - Vdg = Mg - V'dg$

or
$$mg - \frac{m}{d_1}dg = Mg - \frac{M}{d_2}dg$$

$\therefore \qquad m = \dfrac{M\left(1 - \dfrac{d}{d_2}\right)}{\left(1 - \dfrac{d}{d_1}\right)}$

3. (c)

$$3V \times 75 = V(75 + h)$$
$\therefore \qquad h = 150 \text{ cm of Hg}$
or $\qquad h = 1.50 \times 10 = 15 \text{ m of water}$

4. (b)

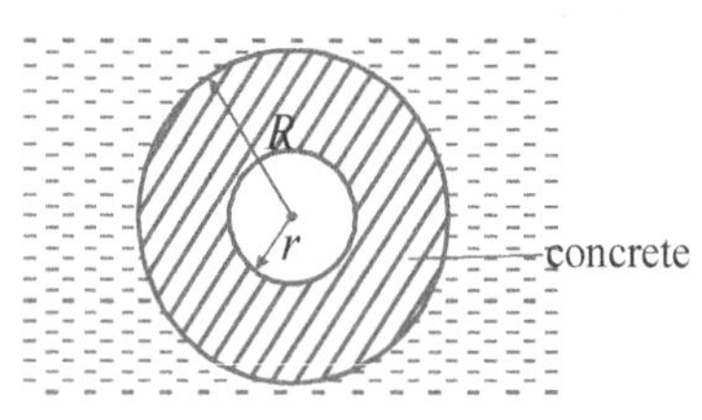

$$\left(m_{concrete} + m_{sawdust}\right)g = V\rho_w g$$

$$2.4 \times \frac{4}{3}\pi(R^3 - r^3) + 0.3 \times \frac{4}{3}\pi r^3 = \frac{4}{3}\pi R^3 \times 1$$

or $\qquad R^3 \;=\; \dfrac{3}{2}r^3$

$\therefore \qquad \dfrac{m_{concrete}}{m_{sawdust}} \;=\; \dfrac{\rho_{concrete}\,\dfrac{4}{3}\pi(R^3 - r^3)}{\rho_{sawdust}\,\dfrac{4}{3}\pi r^3}$

$\qquad\qquad\qquad =\; \dfrac{2.4}{0.3}\dfrac{\left(\dfrac{3}{2}r^3 - r^3\right)}{r^3} = 4$

5. (d) $\qquad T + mg \;=\; F_b$

$\qquad \therefore \qquad T \;=\; F_b - mg$

$\qquad\qquad\qquad =\; V\rho_w g - mg$

$\qquad\qquad\qquad =\; \dfrac{m}{(\rho_w/\eta)}\rho_w g - mg$

$\qquad\qquad\qquad =\; (\eta - 1)mg\,.$

6. (b) Initially, $\qquad mg \;=\; (AL)P_\omega g$

$\qquad$ or $\qquad \rho(A \times 2L)g \;=\; (AL)\rho_w g \qquad \ldots\text{(i)}$

$\qquad$ After one hour,

$\qquad \rho[A \times (2L - 2)]g \;=\; (A\ell)\rho_w g \qquad \ldots\text{(ii)}$

$\qquad$ Dividing (ii) by (i), we get

$\qquad\qquad \ell \;=\; (L - 1)$

7. (c) $\qquad t \;=\; k(\sqrt{h_1} - \sqrt{h_2})$

$\qquad \therefore \qquad t_1 \;=\; k(\sqrt{h} - \sqrt{h/2})$

$\qquad$ and $\qquad t_2 \;=\; k\left(\sqrt{h/2} - 0\right)$

$\qquad \therefore \qquad \dfrac{t_1}{t_2} \;=\; \sqrt{2} - 1$

8. (b) $\quad T + 0.8 \times 250 \times 10^{-3}g = 250\, d_\ell g$

$\qquad T + 250\, d_\ell g = 1.2 \times 250 \times 10^{-3}g$

$\qquad$ Solving, $T = 0.5$ N

9. (c) $\qquad Q_1 + Q_2 \;=\; Q$

$\qquad \dfrac{\pi p r_1^4}{8\eta\ell} + \dfrac{\pi p r_2^4}{8\eta\ell} \;=\; \dfrac{\pi p r^4}{8\eta\ell}$

$\qquad$ or $\qquad r^4 \;=\; r_1^4 + r_2^4$

10. (a) $\qquad mg \;=\; F_1 + F_2$

$\qquad$ or $\quad (AL)Dg \;=\; A \times \dfrac{L}{4} \times 2dg + A \times \dfrac{3L}{4} \times dg$

$\qquad \therefore \qquad D \;=\; \dfrac{5d}{4}$

11. (d) Suppose m and M are the masses of coin and block respectively, then

$\qquad (M + m)g \;=\; V\rho_w g$

$\qquad \therefore \qquad V \;=\; \dfrac{M + m}{\rho_w}$

When coin falls into water, volume of water displaced

$\qquad V' \;=\; \dfrac{M}{\rho_w} + \dfrac{m}{\rho_{coin}}$

As $\rho_{coin} > \rho_w,\; \therefore\; V' < V$.

12. (a) If v_2 is the required speed then

$\qquad A_1 v_1 \;=\; A_2 v_2$

$\qquad$ or $\qquad v_1 \;=\; \dfrac{A_2}{A_1}v_2 = 0.1v_2 \qquad \ldots\text{(i)}$

From Bernoulli's equation, we have

$\qquad P_a + \dfrac{1}{2}\rho v_1^2 + \rho g(3 - 0.525) = P_a + \dfrac{1}{2}\rho v_2^2 + 0 \qquad \ldots\text{(ii)}$

After solving above equations, we get

$\qquad v_2^2 \;=\; 50 \;\; \text{m}^2/\text{s}^2$

13. (b) Rate of flow, $\quad Q \;=\; av$

$\qquad\qquad\qquad =\; L^2 \times \sqrt{2gy} = \pi R^2 \times \sqrt{2g(4y)}$

$\qquad \therefore \qquad R \;=\; \dfrac{L}{\sqrt{2\pi}}$

14. (c)

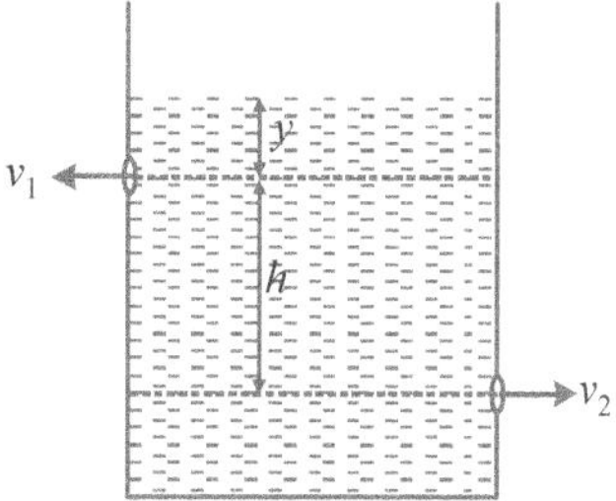

Force $\qquad F \;=\; \rho Q v = \rho a v^2$

$\qquad\qquad\qquad =\; \rho a \times 2gh$

Thus net force $\;=\; F_2 - F_1$

$\qquad\qquad\qquad =\; \rho a v_2^2 - \rho a v_1^2$

$\qquad\qquad\qquad =\; \rho a(v_2^2 - v_1^2) = \rho a[2g(y + h) - 2gy]$

$\qquad\qquad\qquad =\; \rho a \times 2gh$

15. (b)

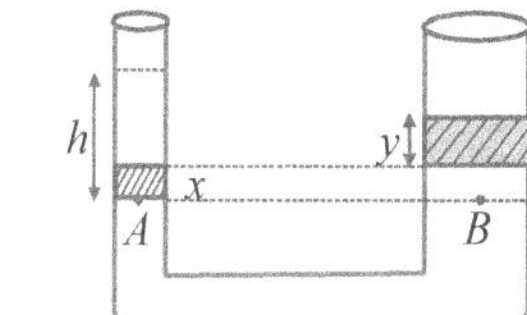

$\qquad x \times \dfrac{\pi d^2}{4} \;=\; y\dfrac{\pi(nd)^2}{4}$

$\qquad \therefore \qquad x \;=\; n^2 y$

From Pascal's law

$\qquad \rho_w g h \;=\; \rho_{Hg}g(x + y)$

$\qquad$ or $\qquad 1 \times gh \;=\; sg(n^2 y + y)$

$\qquad \therefore \qquad y \;=\; \dfrac{h}{s(1 + n^2)}$

16.   **(a)**   If m be the mass put on the log, then

$$mg + 120g = V\rho_w g$$

or $\quad m + 120 = \dfrac{120}{600} \times 1000$

$\therefore \quad m = 80\,\text{kg}.$

17.   **(c)**

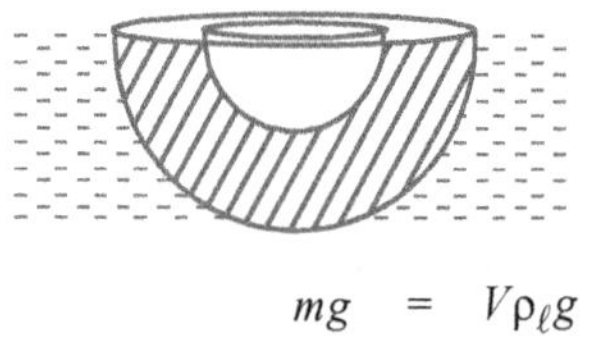

$$mg = V\rho_\ell g$$

or $\dfrac{4}{3}\pi(R^3 - r^3)\rho g = \dfrac{4}{3}\pi R^3 \times \rho_\ell g$

or $(R^3 - r^3) \times 2 \times 10^4 = 1.2 \times 10^3 \, R^3$

or $(0.5^3 - r^3) \times 20 = 1.2 \times (0.5)^3$

or $\quad r = 0.98\,\text{m}.$

18.   **(a)**   Using Bernoulli's equation, we have

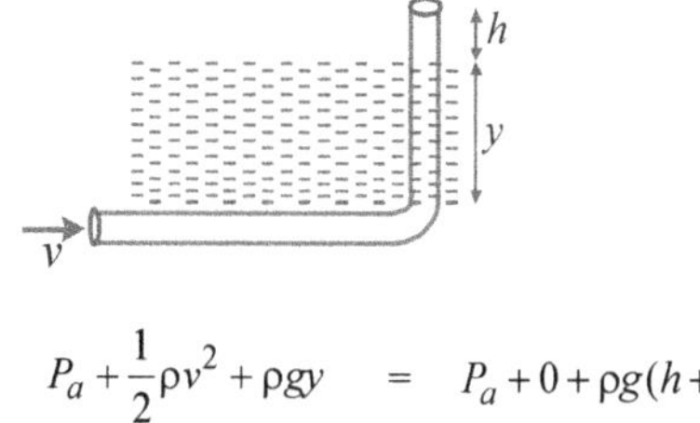

$$P_a + \dfrac{1}{2}\rho v^2 + \rho g y = P_a + 0 + \rho g(h + y)$$

$\therefore \quad h = \dfrac{v^2}{2g}.$

19.   **(b)**

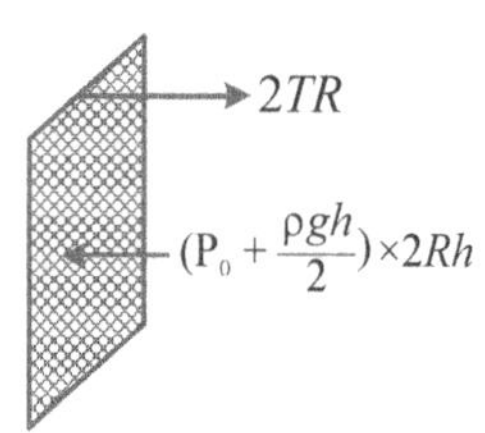

The net force

$$F = \left(P_0 + \dfrac{\rho g h}{2}\right) \times 2Rh - 2TR$$

$$= [2P_0 Rh + R\rho g h^2 - 2TR].$$

20.   **(b)** $P_1 = P_a$, $V_1 = (500 - H)A$

and $\quad P_2 + 200 = P_a \Rightarrow P_2 = (P_a - 200)$,

$\quad V_2 = (500 - 200)A = 300A$

From Boyle's law, we have

$P_a \times (500 - H)A = (P_a - 200) \times 300A$

After substituting values and simplifying, we get

$\quad H = 206\,\text{mm}.$

21.   **(c)**   When ball fall from great height, its initial velocity before entering into liquid is quite enough. So viscous force together with buoyant force becomes greater than weight of the cone. So first ball retarted and thereafter will move with constant velocity.

22.   **(d)**   The buoyant force

$$F_b = F_{\text{bottom}} + F_{\text{vertical force on slint force}}$$

or $\left(\dfrac{\pi R^2 H}{3}\right)\rho g = \pi R^2 \times \rho g H + F_{\text{vertical force on slint face}}$

$\Rightarrow F_{\text{vertical force on slint face}} = -\dfrac{2}{3}\pi \rho g H R^2$. (downward)

23.   **(a)**

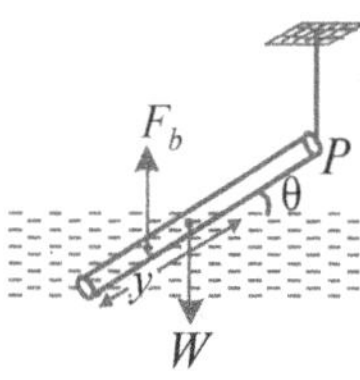

$W = (2LA) \times 0.75g$, $\quad F_b = (Ay) \times 1 \times g$

As rod is in equilibrium, so $\Sigma \tau_P = 0$

or $W \times L\cos\theta - F_b \times (2L - y/2)\cos\theta = 0$

After substituting and simplifying, we get

$\quad y = L$

So the length of rod out of water is L.

24.   **(a)**   For the equilibrium of the sphere,

$Mg + 2T_1\cos 45° = F_b$

$$= \left(\dfrac{4}{3}\pi R^3\right)\rho_w g$$

$\therefore \quad T_1 = \left[\dfrac{\dfrac{4}{3}\pi R^3 \rho_w g - Mg}{\sqrt{3}}\right]$

25.   **(b)**

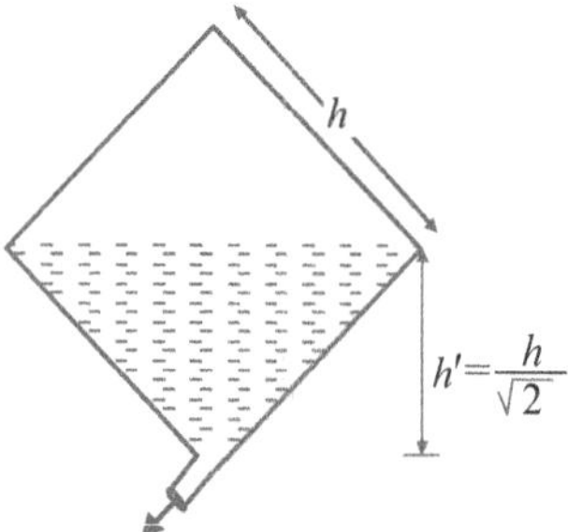

$$F_b = Vd(g + a)$$

$$F_b - (T + mg) = ma$$

or $\quad T = Vd(g + a) - V\rho(g + a)$

$$= V(d - \rho)(g + a).$$

26.   **(d)** $v_0 = \sqrt{2gh}$

Now, $\quad v = \sqrt{2gh'} = \sqrt{2g\dfrac{h}{\sqrt{2}}} = \dfrac{\sqrt{2gh}}{\sqrt[4]{2}}$

$$= \dfrac{v_0}{\sqrt[4]{2}}.$$

27. (d)

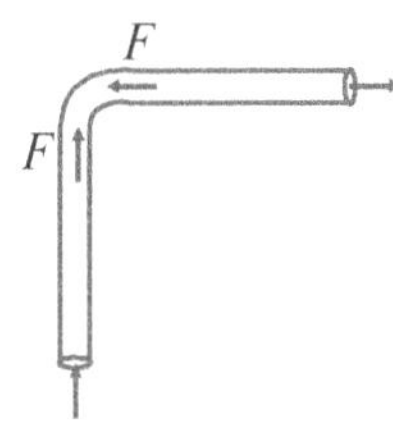

The resultant force at the corner of the hydrant

$$F' = \sqrt{F^2 + F^2} = \sqrt{2}F$$
$$= \sqrt{2}\rho v Q.$$

28. (d) Range, $\quad R = vt = \sqrt{2gh} \times t \qquad \dots (i)$

Also $\qquad 2R = \sqrt{2gh'} \times t \qquad \dots (ii)$

From above equations, we get $h' = 4h = 40m$

$\therefore$ Extra height of water = 30 m = 3 atm.

29. (d)

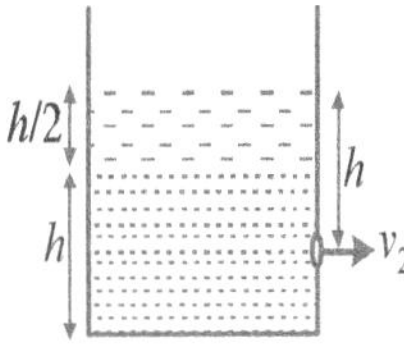

$v_1 = \sqrt{2g(h/2)}.$

For v_2 we can replace the liquid of density ρ and height h to

a liquid of density 2ρ and height $h/2$. Thus $v_2 = \sqrt{2gh} = \sqrt{2}v$

30. (d)
$$\begin{aligned} P &= \rho g h \\ &= 1000 \times 10 \times (1 + 0.5 + 0.1) \\ &= 1.6 \times 10^4 \text{ N/m}^2. \end{aligned}$$

31. (c) The volume of liquid displaced, $V = \dfrac{m}{\rho}$, does not depend

on acceleration due to gravity, so it remains as such.

32. (a)

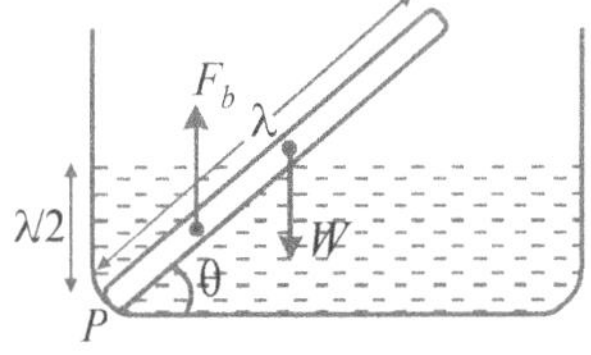

$W = A\ell\rho, \quad F_b = (Ay)\sigma g$
$$= \left(A\frac{\ell}{2\sin\theta}\right)\sigma g.$$

Taking moment of all the forces acting on the rod about P, and put equal to zero, we get

$$W \times \frac{\ell}{2}\cos\theta - F_b \times \frac{y}{2}\cos\theta = 0$$

After substituting and simplifying, we get

$$\sin\theta = \frac{1}{2}\sqrt{\frac{\sigma}{\rho}}.$$

33. (a) The extra buoyant force,
$$\begin{aligned} F_b &= V\rho g \\ &= (0.20 \times 0.20 \times 0.04) \times 1000 \times 10 = 16 \text{ N}. \end{aligned}$$

34. (c) For floating, we have
$$mg = \rho A v^2$$
$$\therefore \quad \rho = \frac{mg}{Av^2} = \frac{1.23 \times 10}{0.1 \times 10^2}$$
$$= 1.23 \text{ kg/m}^3$$

35. (a) $\qquad P_{air} - \rho g\ell_1 = \rho_{Hg}g\ell_3 + P_0$

or $\qquad P_{air} = \rho g\ell_1 + \rho_{Hg}g\ell_3 + P_0$

36. (a) $\qquad P + \rho_1 g h_1 = P + \rho_2 g h_2$

$$\therefore \quad \rho_2 = \frac{\rho_1 h_1}{h_2} = \frac{1000 \times 20}{10} = 2000 \text{ kg/m}^3$$

37. (d) The buoyant force,
$$F_b = P_{\text{bottom}}A - P_{\text{top}}A$$
$$\Rightarrow \quad P_{\text{bottom}}A = F_b + P_{top}A$$
$$= V\rho g + \rho g h \times \pi R^2.$$

38. (a) For equilibrium
$$4dA\ell g = (dAL + m)\, g$$

and $\dfrac{\ell}{2} > Y_{cm}$ (for rotational equilibrium)

$$Y_{cm} = \frac{m \times 0 + dAL(L/2)}{m + dAL} = \frac{dAL^2}{2(m + dAL)}$$

$$\ell > \frac{AL^2 d}{(ALd + m)} \Rightarrow \frac{m + dAL}{4dA} > \frac{AL^2 d}{(ALd + m)}$$

$m > ALd$

39. (b) VAB is the given cone. Let its height be h and semi-vertical angle α. Let the base AB of the cone be in the surface. CD is the surface of separation of two liquids, O and O' are the centres of the base AB and surface of separation CD.

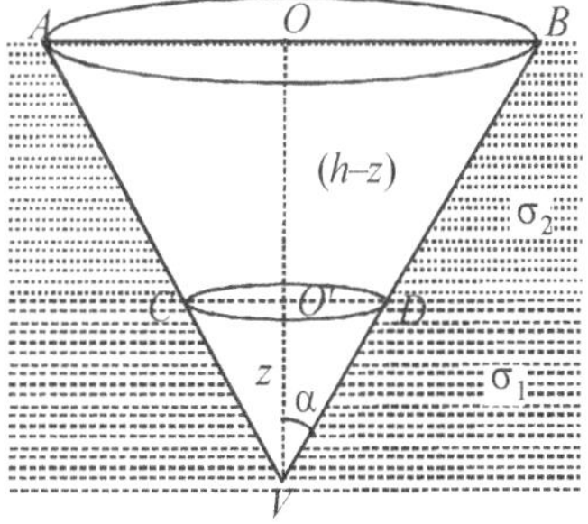

Let $VO' = z$ then $OO' = h - z$

$\therefore$ The weight of the cone = (vol. of the cone) ρg

$$= \frac{1}{3}\pi h^3 \tan^2\alpha\, \rho\, g$$

Volume of liquid (of density σ_1) displaced

$$= \text{volume of cone } (VCD) = \frac{1}{3}\pi z^3 \tan^2\alpha$$

and volume of liquid of density σ_2 displaced = volume of the

frustum $ABDC = \left(\frac{1}{3}\pi h^3 \tan^2 \alpha\right) - \left(\frac{1}{3}\pi z^3 \tan^2 \alpha\right)$

$\therefore$ For equilibrium,

weight of the cone = (weight of liquid of density σ_1 displaced) + (weight of liquid of density σ_2 displaced)

or $\dfrac{1}{3}\pi h^3 \tan^2\alpha.\rho g = \dfrac{1}{3}\pi z^3 \tan^2\alpha.\sigma_1 g$

$$+\dfrac{1}{3}\pi\,(h^3 - z^3)\tan^2\alpha.\sigma_2 g$$

or $h^3\rho = z^3\sigma_1 + (h^3 - z^3)\,\sigma_2$

or $h^3(\rho - \sigma_2) = z^3(\sigma_1 - \sigma_2)$

or $z = h\left(\dfrac{\rho - \sigma_2}{\sigma_1 - \sigma_2}\right)^{1/3}$.

Solutions EXERCISE 3.2

1. **(a, c)** For uniform cross-section
$$av_A = av_B \Rightarrow v_A = v_B,$$
From Bernoulli's equation, we have
$$P_A + \frac{1}{2}\rho v_A^2 = P_B + \frac{1}{2}\rho v_B^2$$
As $v_A = v_B$, $\therefore$ $P_A = P_B$,

2. **(c, d)** In a streamline flow, particles arriving at a given point must have same velocity and so K.E. and momenta.

3. **(a, b, c, d)** Let z_{min} be the minimum reference level of the dotted parabola and z_1 and z_2 the liquid levels above the base.
$$z_1 = \frac{r_1^2\omega^2}{2g} + z_{min} = \frac{0.1^2 \times 10^2}{2\times 9.81} + z_{min},$$
$$z_2 = \frac{r_2^2\omega^2}{2g} + z_{min} = \frac{0.2^2 \times 10^2}{2\times 9.81} + z_{min}$$
But $z_1 + z_2 = 2 \times 0.4 = 0.8\text{m}$

Hence, $0.8 = \dfrac{0.2^2 \times 10^2 + 0.1 \times 10^2}{2\times 9.81} + 2z_{min}$

whence, $z_{min} = 0.273\text{m}$
Consequently,
$$z_1 = 0.273 + \frac{0.1^2 \times 10^2}{2\times 9.81} = 0.324\text{m}$$
$$z_2 = 0.273 + \frac{0.2^2 \times 10^2}{2\times 9.81} = 0.477\text{m}$$

4. **(b, c)** Buoyant force on the body, $F_b = V\rho(g + a) > W$

The volume of liquid displaced, $V' = \dfrac{m}{\rho}$, which is constant.

5. **(b, d)** $0 + \dfrac{1}{2}\rho v^2 + \rho gh = P_a + \dfrac{1}{2}\rho v_e^2 + 0$

For large container $v << v_e$, and so can be neglected.
$$\therefore \quad v_e = \sqrt{2(\rho gh - P_a)}$$
For $v_e >> 0$,
$$\text{or}\,(\rho gh - P_a) \geq 0$$
or $\quad h \geq \dfrac{P_a}{\rho g} \simeq \dfrac{1\times 10^5}{1000 \times 10} = 10\text{ m}$

Thus $v_1 = 0$ and $v_2 = 0$

6. **(a, b, d)** When all the fish start accelerating up, the weight
$$W' = M(g + a).$$

7. **(b, c)** If F_b is the buoyant force on the block, then
Reading of balance $A = 2g - F_b$,
and reading of balance $B = 5g + F_b$

8. **(a, c, d)** The rate of flow, $Q = A_1 v_1 = A_2 v_2$
From Bernoulli's equation,
$$P_1 + \frac{1}{2}\rho v_1^2 = P_2 + \frac{1}{2}\rho v_2^2$$
or $\quad v_2^2 - v_1^2 = \dfrac{2}{\rho}(P_1 - P_2) = 2gh$

9. **(a, c)** The free surface of water makes an angle
$$\tan\theta = \frac{a}{g}\ \text{backward}$$
or $\quad \cot\theta = g/a$.

10. **(a, b, c)** Using Bernoulli's equation between points 2 and 3, we have
$$P_2 + \frac{1}{2}\rho v^2 + \rho gh_3 = P_0 + \frac{1}{2}\rho v^2 + 0$$
$$\therefore \quad P_2 = (P_0 - \rho gh_3)$$
Now between free surface on container and point 2, we have
$$P_0 + 0 + 0 = P_2 + \frac{1}{2}\rho v^2 + 0$$
or $\quad P_0 = P_0 - \rho gh_3 + \dfrac{1}{2}\rho v^2$
$$\Rightarrow \quad v = \sqrt{2gh_3},$$
Clearly, $h_3 > 0$

11. **(a, c)** $H = 2h$; $\quad x = \sqrt{y(H - y)}$

For maximum, $\dfrac{dx}{dy} = 0$, which give $y = \dfrac{H}{2} = h$.

Also $x_m = H = 2h$.

12. **(b, d)** $F = \rho vQ = \rho Av^2$,
Clearly when velocity becomes two times, the thrust becomes four times.

Energy lost per second, $P = Fv = \rho Av^3$, so it becomes eight times.

13. (a, c)
$$P = \frac{500}{100 \times 10^{-4}} = 5 \times 10^4 \text{ N/m}^2$$

Using Bernoulli's equations, we have

$$P + 0 + 0 = P_a + \frac{1}{2}\rho v^2 + \rho g h$$

$$= 1 \times 10^5 + \frac{1}{2} \times 10^3 \times 10^2 + 10^3 \times 10 \times 0.50$$

$$= 1.55 \times 10^5 \text{ N/m}^2$$

If F is the force applied then

$$P_a + \frac{F}{A} = 1.55 \times 10^5$$

$$\text{or } 1 \times 10^5 + \frac{F}{A} = 1.55 \times 10^5$$

$$\therefore \quad F = 0.55 \times 10^5 \times 100 \times 10^{-4} = 550 \text{ N}$$

14. (b, c) At point 1, the space available for fluid is large and so speed becomes smaller.

Thus $v_1 < v_2$ and $P_1 > P_2$.

Solutions EXERCISE-3.3

1. (a) $P = \dfrac{F}{A}$, so small area will cause greater pressure.

2. (a) With height the depth of air column decreases and so pressure decreases.

3. (a) $P = \rho g h$.

4. (d) Pressure is a scalar quantity, $P = \dfrac{F}{A}$.

5. (d) If man drink m kg of water, then level of water in the pond decreases by $\dfrac{m}{\rho_w}$. Due to increased weight of man the water displaced, $V = \dfrac{m}{\rho_w}$. So no change in level of water in the pond.

6. (a) In a streamlined body, there are least obstruction for air blow.

7. (c) Bernoulli's equation can be used for non-viscous and incompressible fluid.

8. (b) $F = \rho v Q$ and $Q = Av = $ constant.

9. (a) When centre of buoyancy is above centre of buoyancy, after disturbance, they constitute restoring torque.

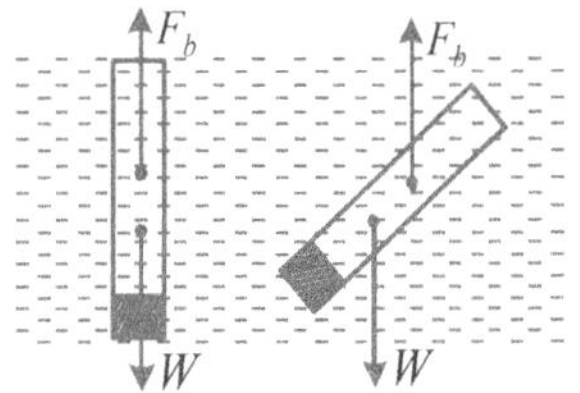

10. (a) With sudden decrease in pressure, there become a pressure difference, which will cause storm.

11. (a) $P + \dfrac{1}{2}\rho v^2 = 0$, with increase in v, pressure there will decrease and pressure difference will provide lift force.

12. (a) For a floating body, $W = F_b$.

The apparent weight $W' = W - F_b = W - W = 0$

Solutions EXERCISE-3.4

Passage (Q. 1 – 3) :

1. (b) The volume of 0.5 kg of gold

$$V = \frac{500}{19.3} = 25.91 \text{ cm}^3$$

2. (a) The volume of 0.5 kg of iridium

$$V' = \frac{500}{22.5} = 22.22 \text{ cm}^3$$

To appear this size like gold, the cavity left inside

$$\Delta V = V - V' = 25.91 - 22.22$$
$$= 3.68 \text{ cm}^3.$$

3 (a) Iridium should be cheaper.

Passage (Q. 4 – 6) :

4 (b)

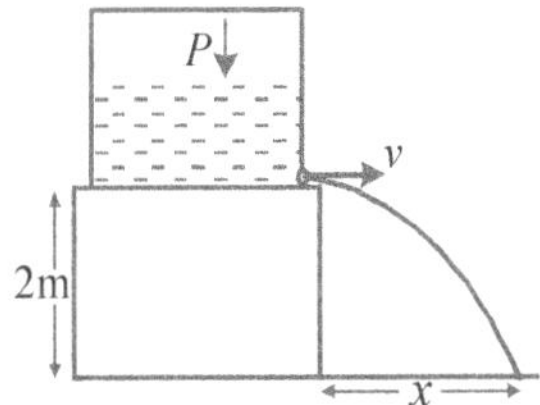

The velocity of efflux,

$$v = \sqrt{\frac{2(P - P_a)}{\rho}}$$

$$= \sqrt{\frac{2 \times 8 \times 10^5}{1000}}$$

$$= 40 \text{ m/s}$$

The time to fall the height 2m,

$$t = \sqrt{\frac{2h}{g}} = \sqrt{\frac{2 \times 2}{9.8}} = 0.63 \text{ s}$$

The distance, $x = vt = 40 \times 0.63 = 25.2 \text{ m}$

5. (a) The vertical component of velocity,

$$v_y^2 = 0 + 2g \times 2$$

$$\therefore \quad v_y = 6.32 \text{ m/s}$$

The vertical component of force

$$F_y = \rho A v_y^2 + \rho g h A$$

$$= 25.2 \text{ N}$$

6. (c) The horizontal component of force on the tank

$$F_x = \rho A v_x^2 = 1000 \times 10^{-4} \times (40)^2$$

$$= 160 \text{ N}.$$

Passage (Q. 7 – 9) :

7. (a) $\quad v_1 = \dfrac{Q}{A_1} = \dfrac{3000 \times 10^{-6}}{40 \times 10^{-4}} = 0.75 \text{ m/s}$

8. (b) $\quad v_2 = \dfrac{Q}{A_2} = \dfrac{3000 \times 10^{-6}}{10 \times 10^{-4}} = 3 \text{ m/s}$

Using Bernoulli's equation, we have

$$P_1 + \frac{1}{2}\rho v_1^2 = P_2 + \frac{1}{2}\rho v_2^2$$

$$\therefore \quad P_1 - P_2 = \frac{1}{2}\rho(v_2^2 - v_1^2)$$

$$= \frac{1}{2} \times 1000(3^2 - 0.75)^2$$

$$= 4219 \text{ N/m}^2$$

9. (b) $\quad h = \dfrac{4219}{13.6 \times 10^3 \times 9.8}$

$$= 0.0316 = 3.16 \text{cm}$$

Passage (Q. 10 – 12) :

10. (d) Liquid A exerts all round horizontal force on the cylinder and so net on it is zero.

11. (a) If A is the area of cross – section of the cylinder, then for the floating cylinder
weight of the cylinder= buoyant force by the liquids
$(h_A + h_B + h)A \times 0.8\, g =$ $(h_A A)\rho_A\, g + (h_B A)\rho_B\, g$
$(1.2 + 0.8 + h)\, A \times 0.8\, g = (1.2\, A) \times 0.7\, g + (0.8\, A) \times 1.2\, g$
$\therefore \quad h = 0.25$ cm.

12. (c) The extra buoyant force
$$F_b = (A\, h)\,\rho_B\, g$$

Acceleration $\quad a = \dfrac{F_b}{m}$

$$= \dfrac{Ah\rho_B g}{m}$$

Here $\quad m = (h_A + h_B + h)A \times 0.8$
$$= (1.2 + 0.8 + 0.25)\, A \times 0.8$$
$$= 1.8\, A$$

$$\therefore \quad a = \dfrac{A \times 0.25 \times 1.2\, g}{1.8\, A}$$

$$= \dfrac{g}{6}\, m/s^2.$$

Passage (Q. 13 – 15) :

13. (d) $\quad f = 6\pi\eta r v = 6\pi \times 10^{-3} \times 10^{-3} \times 3$
$$= 5.65 \times 10^{-5} \text{ N}$$

14. (c) From $Q = \dfrac{\pi R^4 (P_2 - P_1)}{8\eta L}$

We have, $\quad \eta = \dfrac{\pi R^4 (P_2 - P_1)}{8LQ}$

Substituting the value, we get $\eta \approx 4 \times 10^{-3}$ Pa.s

15. (a) From $R_e = \dfrac{2\bar{v}\,\rho R}{\eta}$

$$\bar{v} = \dfrac{\eta\, R_e}{2\rho R}$$

Flow remains laminar till $R_e = 2000$

$$\therefore \quad \bar{v} = \dfrac{4 \times 10^{-3} \times 2000}{2 \times 1000 \times 8 \times 10^{-3}} = 0.5\, m/s$$

Passage (Q. 16 – 18) :
16. (b), 17. (d), 18. (c).

$$F_v = \int_0^{\pi} [\rho g\,(2R - R\cos\theta)] \times [Rd\theta \times L]\cos\theta$$

$$F_v = \rho g R^2 L \int_0^{\pi} \cos\theta\,(2 - \cos\theta)\, d\theta$$

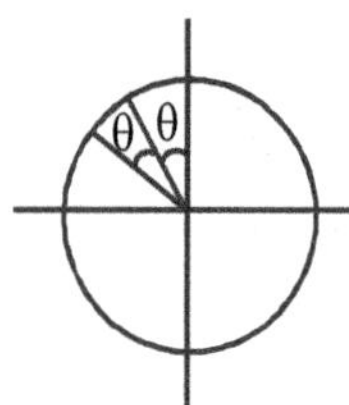

$$= \rho g R^2 L \int_0^{\pi} (2\cos\theta - \cos^2\theta)\, d\theta = -\rho g R^2 L \frac{\pi}{2}$$

$\therefore$ Force $= \rho g R^2 L \dfrac{\pi}{2}$ upwards

As all forces are radial and all pass through axis and hence torque is zero.

$$F_x = \int_0^{\pi} \rho g\,(2R - R\cos\theta)\,(Rd\theta \times L)\sin\theta = 4R^2\rho g L$$

Passage (Q. 19 – 21) :

19. (b) Weight of Ram is more than that of Shyam in water means upthrust on Ram is less hence less volume and less fat content.

20. (a) Let Fat mass $= m_1$, Other mass $= m_2$.
Total volume $= V$

Given : $\dfrac{m_1}{0.4 d_w} = \dfrac{V}{4}, \dfrac{m_2}{(4/3)d_w} = \dfrac{3V}{4}$ and

$$m_1 + m_2 = 165$$

Solving, $V = \dfrac{1650}{11 d_w}$

Spring balance reading $= 165 - \dfrac{1650}{11 d_w} d_w = 15$ kg

21. (c) Upthrust and effective weight changes by same factor hence fraction immersed remains same.

Passage (Q. 22 - 24) :

The liquid of density d and height $H/2$ can be replaced by liquid of density $2d$ and of height h_0, where h_0 is

$$(2d)\, g\, h_0 = dg\, H/2$$

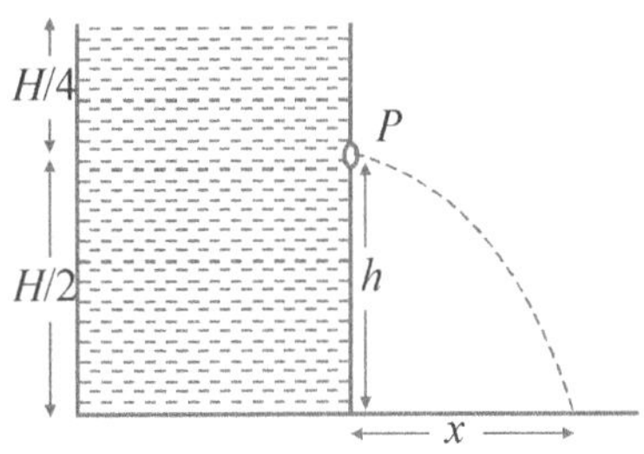

$$\therefore \qquad h_0 = \frac{H}{4}.$$

Thus the equivalent system is as shown in figure. The head of liquid over the hole

$$y = \frac{H}{2} + \frac{H}{4} - h$$

$$= \frac{(3H - 4h)}{4}.$$

22. (c) The velocity of efflux $v = \sqrt{2gy}$

$$= \sqrt{2g \frac{(3H - 4h)}{4}}$$

$$= \sqrt{\frac{g}{2}(3H - 4h)}$$

23. (a) The horizontal distance $x = v\,t$

$$= \sqrt{2gy} \times \sqrt{\frac{2h}{g}}$$

$$= \sqrt{(3H - 4h)h}.$$

24. (c) For maximum x,

$$\frac{dx}{dh} = 0$$

or $\quad \frac{1}{2}(3Hh - 4h^2)^{1/2} \times (3h - 8h) = 0$

or $\dfrac{-5h}{2}(3Hh - 4h^2)^{1/2} = 0$

Thus $\quad 3Hh - 4h^2 = 0$

or $\qquad h = \dfrac{3H}{4}$

Passage (Q. 25 - 27) :

25. (b) Speed of efflux

$$v_2 = \sqrt{2gh}$$

$$= \sqrt{2 \times 10 \times 5}$$

$$= 10 \text{ m/s}$$

26. (b) By using conservation of mechanical energy, we have

$$\frac{1}{2}\rho v_2^2 + \rho gH = \frac{1}{2}\rho v_3^2 + 0$$

$$\therefore \qquad v_3 = \sqrt{v_2^2 + 2gH}$$

$$= \sqrt{10^2 + 2 \times 10 \times 5}$$

$$= 14.14 \text{ m/s}.$$

27. (d) Time to empty the tank is given by

$$t = \frac{A\sqrt{2}}{a\sqrt{g}}(\sqrt{h_1} - \sqrt{h_2})$$

where $\quad A = \pi\,(1)^2$

$$= 3.14 \text{ m}^2$$

$$a = 10^{-4} \text{ m}^2,$$

$$h_1 = 5\text{m}$$

$$h_2 = 2.5 \text{ m}.$$

After substituting the values and simplifying, we get

$$t = 942 \text{ s}.$$

Passage (Q. 28 - 30) :

28. (d)

29. (c) $\tan\theta = \dfrac{a}{g}$; which does not depend on density. so, $\theta_1 = \theta_2$

30. (c)

The velocity of efflux at hole1, $v_1 = \sqrt{2g\dfrac{h}{2}} = \sqrt{gh}$.

$$\therefore \ F_1 = \rho A v_1^2 = \rho Agh.$$

Using Bernoulli's equation between a point on free surface and 2, we have

$$P_a + 0 + \left(\rho gh + 2\rho g \times \frac{h}{2}\right) = P_a + \frac{1}{2}(2\rho)v_2^2$$

$$\therefore \qquad v_2 = \sqrt{2gh}.$$

Force $F_2 = (2\rho)A v_2^2 = 2\rho A \times 2gh = 4\rho Agh$.

The mass of liquid,

$$m = \rho A_0 h + 2\rho A_0 h = 3\rho A_0 h.$$

The initial acceleration of tank

$$a = \frac{F_1 + F_2}{m} = \frac{5\rho Agh}{3\rho A_0 h}$$

$$= \frac{5Ag}{3A_0}$$

Passage (Q. 31 - 33) :

31. (b) The level in tube A becomes,

$$h_A = \frac{8a}{3} - \frac{2a}{3} = 2a.$$

The level in tube B becomes,

$$h_B = \frac{4a}{3} + \frac{2a}{3} = 2a.$$

Thus $\quad P_B - P_A = (2\rho)gh_B - \rho gh_A$

$$= 2\rho g \times 2a - \rho g \times 2a = 2a\rho g$$

32. (a)

33. (b) $\qquad S(P_x - P_A) = \displaystyle\int_{a}^{(a + 2a/3)} (dm)\omega^2 x$

$$= \int_{a}^{(5a/3)} (\rho s dx)\omega^2 x$$

$$= \frac{8}{9}\rho s\omega^2 a^2 \qquad \ldots (i)$$

Similarly $S(P_B - P_x) = \frac{56}{9}\rho s\omega^2 a^2 \qquad \ldots (ii)$

From above equations

$$F_x = P_x s = \frac{9}{4}\rho sag$$

and

$$\omega = \sqrt{\frac{9g}{32a}}.$$

Passage (Q. 34 - 36) :

34.   (c)   Consider the equilibrium of wooden block. Forces acting in the downward direction are

$$P_1 \times \pi(4r)^2$$

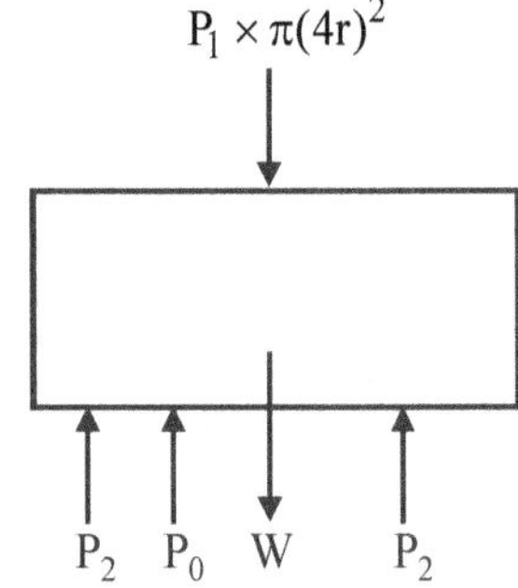

(i)   Weight of wooden cylinder (W)

$$= \pi(4r)^2 \times h \times \frac{\rho}{3} \times g = \pi \times 16r^2 \frac{h\rho}{3}g$$

(ii)   Force due to pressure (P_1) created by liquid of height h_1 above the wooden block is

$= P_1 \times \pi(4r)^2 = [P_0 + h_1\rho g] \times \pi (4r)^2$

$= [P_0 + h_1\rho g] \pi \times 16r^2$

Force acting in the upward direction due to pressure P_2 exerted from below the wooden block and atmospheric pressure is

$= P_2 \times \pi [(4r)^2 - (2r)^2] + P_0 \times (2r)^2$

$= [P_0 + (h_1 + h) \rho g] \times \pi \times 12r^2 + 4r^2 P_0$

At the verge of rising

$[P_0 + (h_1 + h) \rho g] \pi \times 12r^2 + 4r^2 P_0$

$$= \pi \times 16r^2 h \times \frac{\rho}{3}g + [P_0 + h_1\rho g] \times \pi \times 16r^2$$

$$\Rightarrow \quad 12h_1 + 12h = \frac{16h}{3} + 16h_1$$

$$\Rightarrow \quad 12h - \frac{16h}{3} = 4h_1 \Rightarrow \frac{5h}{3} = h_1$$

35.   (b)   Again considering equilibrium of wooden block.

Total downward force = Total upward force

Wt. of block + force due to atmospheric pressure = Force due to pressure of liquid + Force due to atmospheric pressure

$$\therefore \quad \pi(16r^2)\frac{\rho}{3}hg + P_0\pi \times 16r^2$$

$$= [h_2\rho g + P_0] \pi [16r^2 - 4r^2] + P_0 \pi 4r^2$$

$$\Rightarrow \quad \pi (16r^2) h \frac{\rho}{3}g = h_2\rho g \times \pi \times 12r^2$$

$$\Rightarrow \quad 16\frac{h}{3} = 12h_2 \Rightarrow h_2 = \frac{4}{9}h$$

36   (a)   When the height h_2 of water level is further decreased, then the upward force acting on the wooden block decreases. The total force downward remains the same. This difference will be compensated by the normal reaction by the tank wall on the wooden block. Thus the block does not move up and remains at its original position.

37.   **A→s ; B→r ; C→q ; D→p**

(A)   Poisulli's law gives,

$$Q = \frac{\pi P r^4}{8\eta \ell}$$

(B)   Viscous change on a spherical body is given by Stoke's law,

$$F_b = 6\pi\eta rv.$$

(C)   Speed of efflux is related to Toricelli's theorem $v = \sqrt{2gh}$.

(D)   Pressure difference between two points can be obtained by Bernoulli's equation.

38.   **A→q ; B→p ; C→p ; D→r**

39.   **A→p ; B→q, r, s ; C→p ; D→r**

For pipe of uniform cross-section $v_3 = v_4 = v_5 = v$

Applying Bernoulli's equation between (1) and (5) , we have

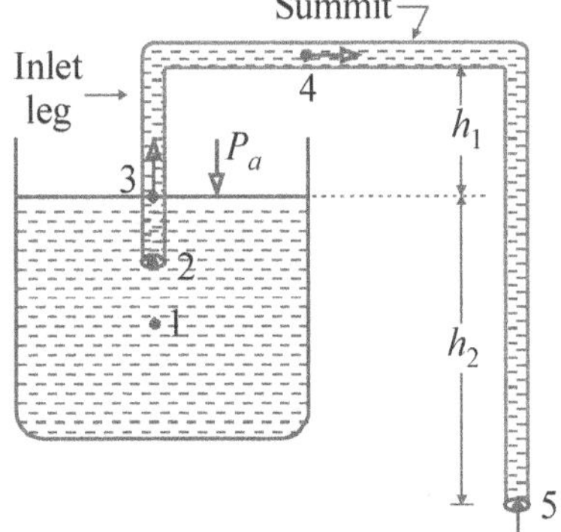

$$P_a = P_a + \frac{1}{2}\rho v_2^2 - \rho g h_2$$

$$\Rightarrow \quad v_2 = \sqrt{2gh_2}$$

Thus for $v_2 > 0$, $h_2 > 0$

Also

$$P_a = P_3 + \frac{1}{2}\rho v^2 = P_4 + \frac{1}{2}\rho v^2 + \rho g h_1$$

$$= P_a + \frac{1}{2}\rho v^2 - \rho g h_2$$

From the above equation following conclusion can be made

(i) $P_4 < P_3 < P_a$

(ii) $\rho g(h_1 + h_2) = P_a - P_4$

$$\Rightarrow (h_1 + h_2) = \frac{P_a - P_4}{\rho g}$$

or $h_1 + h_2 < \dfrac{P_a}{\rho g}$

40.   A→p, t ; B→q, s, t ; C→ p, r, t ; D→q

(p)

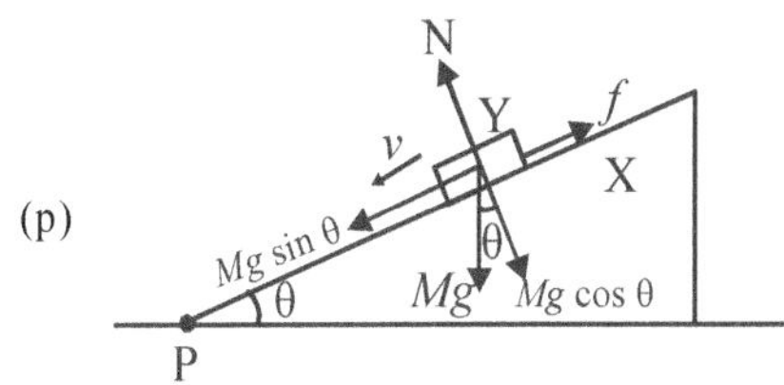

As the velocity is constant,

$$f = Mg \sin\theta \qquad ..... (i)$$

But $f = \mu N = \mu Mg \cos\theta \qquad ..... (ii)$

From (i) and (ii),

$$\mu Mg \cos\theta = Mg \sin\theta \;\Rightarrow\; \mu = \tan\theta$$

The force by X on Y is the resultant of f and N and is equal to

$$\sqrt{f^2 + N^2} = \sqrt{\mu^2 N^2 + N^2} = (\sqrt{\mu^2 + 1})N$$

$$= (\sqrt{\tan^2\theta + 1})\,Mg\cos\theta = \sec\theta Mg\cos\theta = Mg$$

= weight of Y.

Therefore, option (A) is correct.

Now, due to the presence of frictional force between Y and X, the mechanical energy of the system $(X + Y)$ decreases continuously as Y slides down.

Therefore, option (C) is correct.

(q)

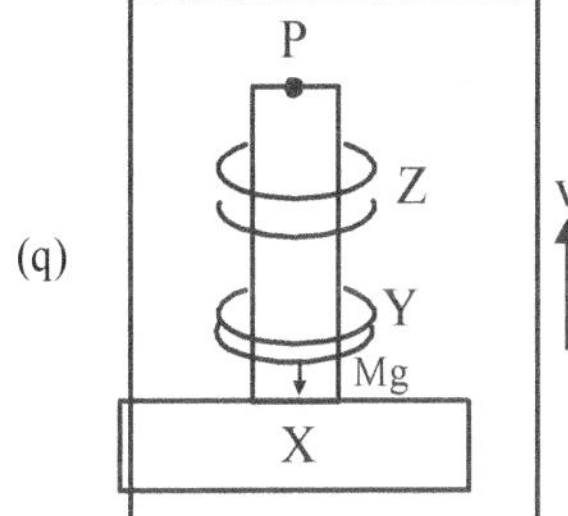

As the lift moves up, X also moves up and therefore the gravitational energy of X is continuously increasing.

∴ Option (B) is correct.

The torque of the weight of Y about P is zero as the perpendicular distance of the line of action of force from the point P is zero.

∴ Option (D) is correct.

The force exerted by X on Y will be equal to $Mg + Mg = 2Mg$ where Mg is wt. of Y and Mg is the force on Y due to Z.

Option (A) is incorrect.

(r)

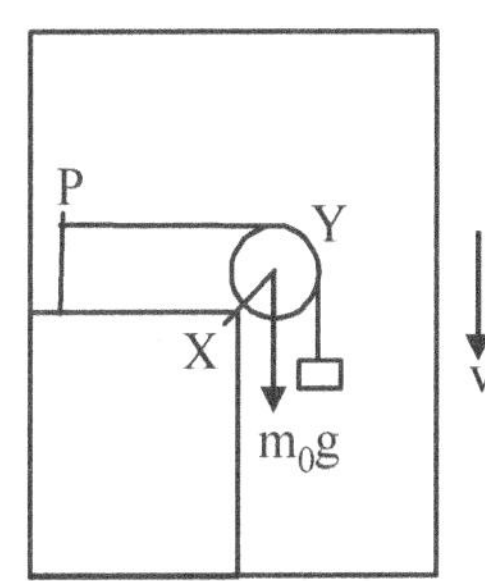

In this case the force exerted by X on Y is same as the force exerted by Y on X. The force on X due to Y is

$$R = \sqrt{(Mg)^2 + [(m_0 + M)g]^2} \neq Mg$$

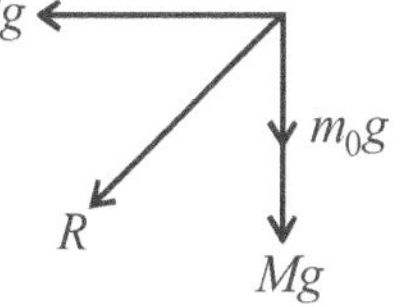

Therefore, option (A) is incorrect.

The mechanical energy of the system $(X + Y)$ is continuously decreasing as the system is coming down and its potential energy is decreasing, the kinetic energy remaining the same. Therefore, option (C) is correct and (B) is incorrect.

The torque of the weight of Y about P is not zero.

(s)

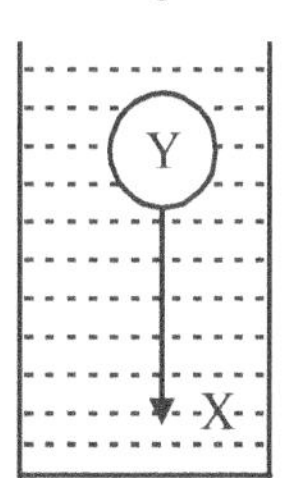

The force on Y by X is equal to the wt. of liquid displaced which cannot be equal to Mg as the density of Y is greater than density of X (as Y is sinking)

Therefore, option (A) is incorrect.

The gravitational potential energy of X increases continuously because as Y moves down, the centre of mass of X moves up.

Therefore, option (B) is correct.

(t)

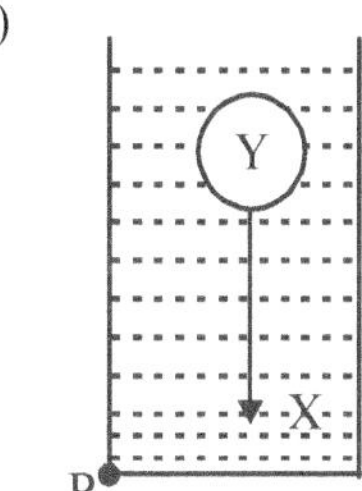

Sphere Y is moving with terminal velocity. Therefore, the net force on Y is zero, i.e.,

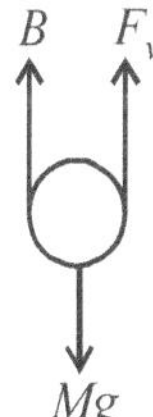

$$Mg = B + F_v$$

where B = buoyant force and F_v = viscous force.

$B + F_v$ are exerted by X on Y.

Therefore, option (A) is correct.

The gravitational potential energy of X is continuously increasing because as Y moves down, the centre of mass of X moves up.

Option (B) is correct.

The mechanical energy of the system $(X + Y)$ is continuously decreasing to overcome the viscous forces.

Option (C) is correct.

1. For hydraulic press

$$\frac{f}{a} = \frac{F}{A}$$

$$\therefore \quad F = \frac{A}{a}\cdot f$$

$$= \frac{0.8}{0.1}\times 200$$

$$= 1600 \text{ N.}$$

2. For the equilibrium of the block

$$mg = F_b + N$$
$$\therefore \quad N = mg - F_b$$
$$= 1.4\,N \qquad \textbf{\textit{Ans.}}$$

3. By Pascal's law

$$P_A = P_B$$
or $$\rho_w g \times 10 = \rho_{sp}\, g \times 5$$

$$\therefore \quad \rho_{sp} = \frac{10}{5}$$

$$= 2 \qquad \textbf{\textit{Ans.}}$$

4. By Pascal's law, we have

$$P_A + \rho_{\text{Hg}}\, g\times 0.2 + \rho_w g \times 0.4 = P_B + \rho_{oil}\, g \times 0.25$$
Given $P_A = 700\,kg/m^2$.
After simplifying, we get $P_B = 3620\,kg/m^2$. **\textit{Ans.}**

5. The rate of flow in the horizontal venturimeter is given by

$$Q = \frac{A_1 A_2 \sqrt{2gh}}{\sqrt{A_1^2 - A_2^2}}$$

Here, $$h = 2\text{cm,}$$
$$A_1 = 4\text{cm}^2,$$
$$A_2 = 2\text{cm}^2$$
$$\therefore \quad Q = 146 \text{ cm}^3/\text{s} \qquad \textbf{\textit{Ans.}}$$

6. If v is the speed, then,

$$\frac{1}{2}\rho v^2 = (P_1 - P_2)$$

or $$v = \sqrt{\frac{2(P_1 - P_2)}{\rho}}$$

$$= \sqrt{\frac{2(3\times 10^5 - 1\times 10^5)}{1000}}$$

$$= 20 \text{ m/s} \qquad \textbf{\textit{Ans.}}$$

7. The force on small element of the slit

$$dF = \rho\,(dA)\,v^2$$
$$= \rho\,(\,bdx\,) \times 2\,g\,(h-x)$$

$$\therefore \quad F = 2\rho bg \int_0^l (h-x)dx$$

$$= 2\rho bg\left(hl - \frac{l^2}{2}\right)$$

$$= 2\times 1000 \times 10^{-3} \times 10\left(0.75\times 0.5 - \frac{0.5^2}{2}\right)$$

$$= 5\text{ N} \qquad \textbf{\textit{Ans.}}$$

8. Suppose P_1 and P_2 be the pressures at sections 1 and 2 respectively. If v_1 and v_2 are the velocities at the sections, then

$$Sv_1 = sv_2$$

$$\therefore \quad \frac{v_1}{v_2} = \frac{s}{S} \qquad ....(i)$$

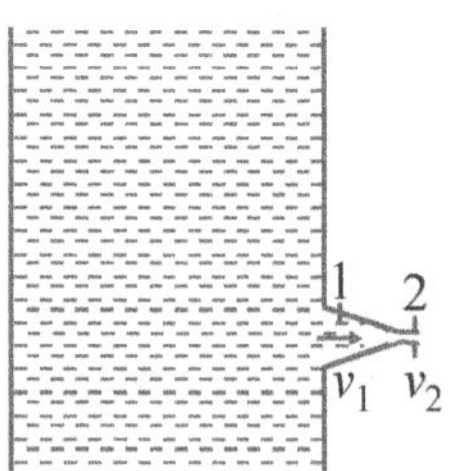

The rate of change of momentum between 1 and 2

$$F = \frac{m}{t}(v_2 - v_1)$$

$$= \rho\, sv_2\,(v_2 - v_1) \qquad ....(ii)$$

The force exerted due to pressure difference on water

$$= (P_1 - P_2)\,s \qquad ....(iii)$$

From equations (ii) and (iii), we get

$$P_1 - P_2 = \rho\, v_2\,(v_2 - v_1) \qquad ....(iv)$$

Uisng Bernoulli's equations between 1 and 2, we have

$$P_1 + \frac{1}{2}\rho v_1^2 + \rho g h_1 = P_2 + \frac{1}{2}\rho v_2^2 + \rho g h_2 + U$$

where U is the loss of potential energy per unit volume due to water flow

$$\therefore \quad P_1 - P_2 = \frac{1}{2}\rho(v_2^2 - v_1^2) + U \qquad ......(iv)$$

From (i), (iv) and (v), we have

$$U = \frac{\rho}{2}v_2^2\left(1 - \frac{s}{S}\right)^2$$

As $$v_2 = \sqrt{2gh},$$

$$\therefore \quad U = \frac{\rho}{2}\times 2gh\frac{(S-s)^2}{S^2}$$

$$= \rho g h\frac{(S-s)^2}{S^2}$$

The force exerted $$F = \left|\frac{dU}{dx}\right|$$

$$= \frac{d(uSx)}{dx}$$

$$= uS$$

$$= \rho g h\frac{(S-s)^2}{S^2}\times S$$

$$= \rho g h\frac{(S-s)^2}{S}$$

$$= 6 \text{ N.} \qquad \textbf{\textit{Ans.}}$$

Solutions EXERCISE-3.6

1. For hydraulic jack

$$\frac{W}{A} = \frac{f}{a}$$

$$\therefore \quad f = \left(\frac{a}{A}\right)W = \left(\frac{\pi r^2}{\pi R^2}\right)W$$

$$= \frac{r^2}{R^2}W$$

$$= \left(\frac{10}{100}\right)^2 W = 0.01\ W.\ \textit{Ans.}$$

2. The force necessary to keep the door closed

$$F = (\rho_1 gh - \rho_2 gh) \times A$$
$$= (1700 - 1000) \times 9.8 \times 4 \times 20 \times 10^{-4}$$
$$= 54.88\ \text{N}. \qquad \textit{Ans.}$$

3. The reading of manometer are:
   (i) (a) 20 cm gauge (b) -18 cm gauge.
   (ii) The pressure exerted by 13.6 cm of water column.

$$= \frac{13.6}{13.6}$$

$$= 1\ \text{cm of mercury column.}$$

So level of mercury in right limb of manometer will decrease by 1 cm. Thus reading will be 19 cm.

4. If h *is* the difference in height, then

$$\tan\theta = \frac{h}{L} = \frac{a}{g}$$

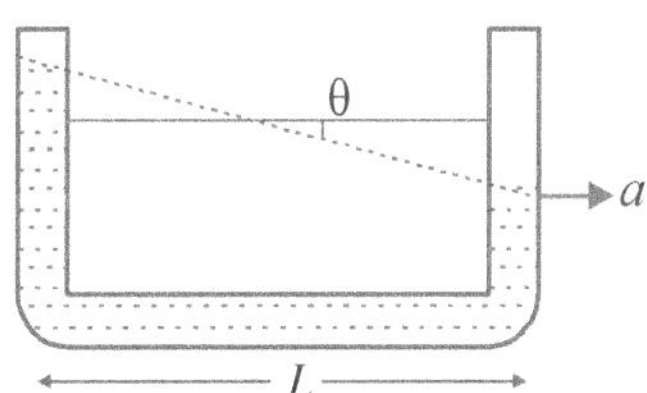

$$\therefore \quad h = \frac{La}{g}. \qquad \textit{Ans.}$$

5. The volume of metal $V = \dfrac{38.25}{19.3}.$

$$= 1.98\ \text{cm}^3.$$

The loss in weight in water $= 38.250 - 33.865$
$$= 4.385\ \text{g}.$$

If V' is the total volume of the piece of gold then

$$4.385\ \text{g} = V'\rho_\omega g$$

$$\therefore \quad V' = 4.385\ \text{cm}^3$$

Thus volume of cavity inside piece
$$= 2.405\ \text{cm}^3. \qquad \textit{Ans.}$$

6. (i) The ice block becomes the part of the system, so reading of

spring balance
$$= 10 + 1.5$$
$$= 11.5\ \text{kg-}f$$

(ii) The buoyant force on the iron piece

$$= \frac{V}{2}\rho_\omega g$$

$$= \left[\frac{7.8/7.8}{2}\right] \times 1 \times g$$

$$= 0.5\ \text{kg-}f$$

Thus reading of the spring balance becomes
$$= 10 + 0.5$$
$$= 10.5\ \text{kg-}f \qquad \textit{Ans.}$$

7. Suppose in time dt the level of liquid decreases by dy. Then volume of liquid empty

$$= \text{volume of liquid emerges out from the hole}$$

$$\pi r^2\,(-dy) = Q\,dt$$

or $\quad \pi r^2\,(-dy) = a\sqrt{2gy}\ dt \quad ....(i)$

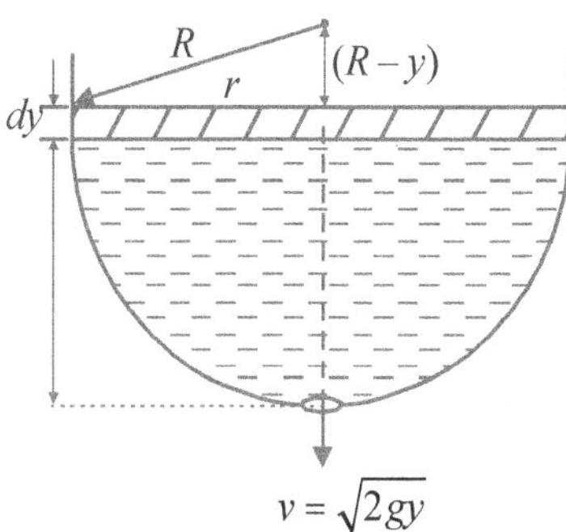

From the geometry, we have
$$(R-y)^2 + r^2 = R^2$$

$$\therefore \quad r^2 = R^2 - (R-y)^2$$

$$= 2Ry - y^2$$

$$\therefore \quad \pi\,(2Ry - y^2)\,(-dy) = a\sqrt{2gy}\ dt$$

or $\quad \displaystyle\int_0^t dt = \frac{-\pi}{a\sqrt{2g}}\int_H^0 (2Ry^{1/2} - y^{3/2})\,dy$

$$\therefore \quad t = \frac{-\pi}{a\sqrt{2g}}\left[\frac{4}{3}RH^{3/4} - \frac{2}{5}H^{5/2}\right].\ \textit{Ans.}$$

8. The vapour pressure $= 21\ \text{kg/m}^2$

$$= \frac{21}{136000}m$$

$$= 0.15\ cm.$$

The barometric height $\quad = 76 - 0.15$
$$= 75.85\ \text{cm}. \qquad \textit{Ans.}$$

9. Pressure intensity at a depth y from surface of water

$$P = \left[0.5\,Pa + \rho_{oil}\,g \times 3 + \rho_w g y\right] \quad (i)$$

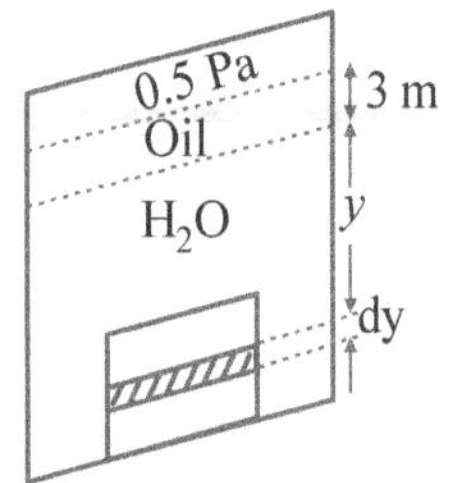

The force on the dy height of gate

$$dF = P\,(4.5\,dy)$$

Total force

$$F = \int_6^9 P(4.5\,dy) \quad ....(ii)$$

After solving equations (i) and (ii), we get

$$F = 8.21 \times 10^5 \text{ N.} \qquad \textbf{\textit{Ans.}}$$

10. Force on the curved portion of the wall:

$$h = R - R\sin\theta$$

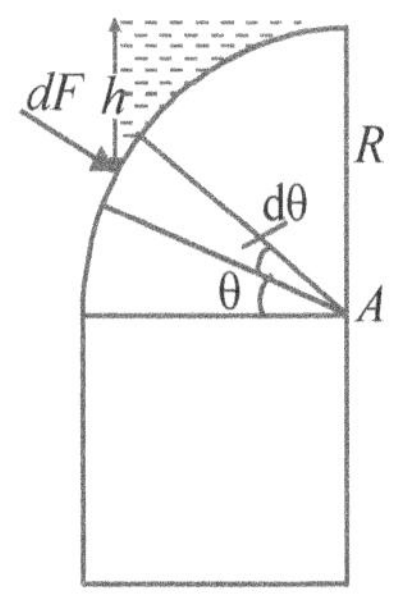

$$= R\,(1 - \sin\theta)$$

The force on the element

$$dF = (\rho\,gh)(R\,d\theta \times 1)$$
$$dFx_1 = dF\cos\theta$$
$$= (\rho\,ghR\,d\theta)\cos\theta$$
$$= \rho\,gR^2(1 - \sin\theta)\cos\theta\,d\theta$$

$$\therefore \qquad Fx_1 = \rho gR^2 \int_0^{\pi/2}\left(\cos\theta - \frac{\sin 2\theta}{2}\right)d\theta$$

$$= \rho gR^2\left[\sin\theta + \frac{\cos 2\theta}{4}\right]_0^{\pi/2}$$

$$=$$

$$\rho gR^2\left[\left(\sin\frac{\pi}{2} + \frac{\cos\pi}{4}\right) - (\sin 0 + \cos 0)\right]$$

$$= \rho gR^2\left[\left(1 + \frac{1}{4}\right) - 1\right]$$

$$= \frac{\rho gR^2}{4}$$

$$F_y = \rho gR^2 \int_0^{\pi/2}(1 - \sin\theta)\sin\theta\,d\theta$$

$$= \rho gR^2 \int_0^{\pi/2}(\sin\theta - \sin^2\theta)\,d\theta$$

$$= \rho gR^2\left[-\cos\theta + \frac{\sin 2\theta}{4} - \frac{\theta}{2}\right]_0^{\pi/2}$$

$$= \rho gR^2\left[\left(-\cos\frac{\pi}{2} + \sin\frac{\pi}{4} - \frac{\pi}{4}\right) - (-\cos 0 + \sin 0 - 0)\right]$$

$$= \rho gR^2\left(1 - \frac{\pi}{4}\right)$$

$$= \rho gR^2\frac{(4 - \pi)}{4}$$

Force on the flat vertical position of the gate

$$F_{x2} = P_{av} \times A$$

$$= \left(\frac{\rho gR + \rho g(2R)}{2}\right) \times (R \times 1)$$

$$= \frac{3}{2}\rho gR^2$$

Thus

$$F_x = F_{x1} + F_{x2}$$

$$= \frac{\rho gR^2}{4} + \frac{3}{2}\rho gR^2$$

$$= \frac{7}{4}\rho gR^2$$

Thus resultant force

$$\vec{F} = F_x\hat{i} + F_y(-\hat{j})$$

$$= \frac{7}{4}\rho gR^2\hat{i} - \rho gR^2\frac{(4-\pi)}{4}\hat{j}\,.$$

After substituting the valus and simplifying, we get

$$\vec{F} = (961.38\hat{i} - 103.16\hat{j}) \text{ kN.} \quad \textbf{\textit{Ans.}}$$

11. The pressure exerted by 50 kg weight is corresponding to h height of water, then

$$\rho\,gh = 50g$$

$$\therefore \qquad h = \frac{50}{\rho}$$

$$= \frac{50}{1000}$$

$$= 0.05 \text{ m}$$

Thus total height of water above opening

$$H = 0.50 + 0.05$$

$$= 0.55 \text{ m.}$$

The efflux velocity $= \sqrt{2gH}$

$$= \sqrt{2g \times 0.55}$$

$$= 3.3 \text{ m/s.} \qquad \textbf{\textit{Ans.}}$$

12. In first case, there is no thrust of water below the slab, so

$$F = mg + (\rho g h) \times A$$
$$= 1000 \times 9.8 + (1000 \times 9.8 \times 17) \times 1$$
$$= 17658 \text{ N} \qquad Ans.$$

In second case

$$F = mg - F_b$$

If F_b is small enough, them

$$F \simeq mg$$
$$= 9800 \text{ N} \qquad \textbf{Ans.}$$

13. For the equilibrium weight of stick $+ mg = F_b$

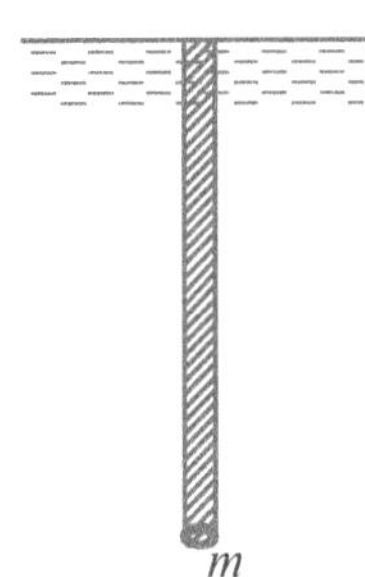

or $\qquad \pi R^2 L \rho g + mg = (\pi R^2 L)\sigma g$

$$\therefore \qquad m = \pi R^2 L \rho \left[\frac{\sigma}{\rho} - 1\right]. \qquad \textbf{Ans.}$$

14. The velocity of the ball after falling height 19.6 m

$$v = \sqrt{2g \times 19.6}$$
$$= 19.6 \ m/s.$$

The retardation of the ball in water

$$a = \frac{F_b - mg}{m}$$
$$= \frac{V\rho g - V\dfrac{\rho}{2}g}{V\rho/2}$$
$$= g \ m/s^2$$

If h is the depth upto which ball goes, then

$$o = v^2 - 2ah$$

$$\therefore \qquad h = \frac{v^2}{2a} = \frac{19.6}{2 \times g} = 19.6 \ m. \textbf{Ans.}$$

Time taken $\qquad t = \dfrac{v}{g} = \dfrac{19.6}{9.8} = 2s.$

Total time taken to return to the surface $= 4s$.

15. To just lift off the block

$$(m + M)g = F_{b1} + F_{b2}$$
$$(1000 + V \times 91.3)g = 1000 \times 1.3 g + V \times 1.3 \times g$$

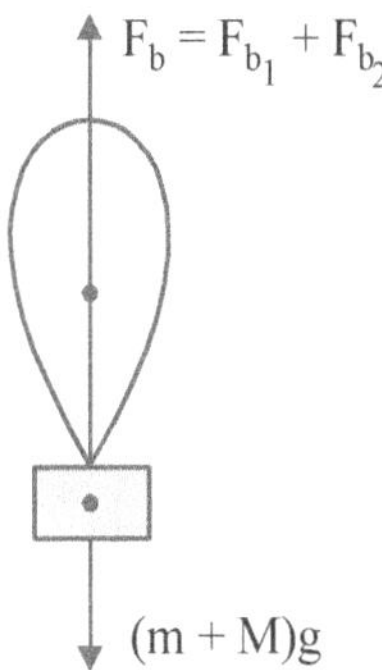

$$\therefore \qquad V = 3.333 \text{ litre} \qquad \textbf{Ans.}$$

16. (i) For the floating of the cylinder, we have

$$Mg = F_b$$

$$\therefore \qquad \rho (AL) g = \left(A\frac{L}{4}\right) \times 2dg + \left(\frac{3AL}{4}\right) \times dg$$

$$\therefore \qquad \rho = \frac{5d}{4}. \qquad \textbf{Ans.}$$

(ii) The total Pressure

$$P = dg (H/2) + 2dg (H/2) + \frac{\rho(A/5L)g}{A} + P_0$$

$$= dg \, H/2 + dgH + \left(\frac{5d}{4}\right) L/5 \ g + P_0$$

$$= \left(\frac{6H + L}{4}\right) dg + P_0. \qquad \textbf{Ans.}$$

17.

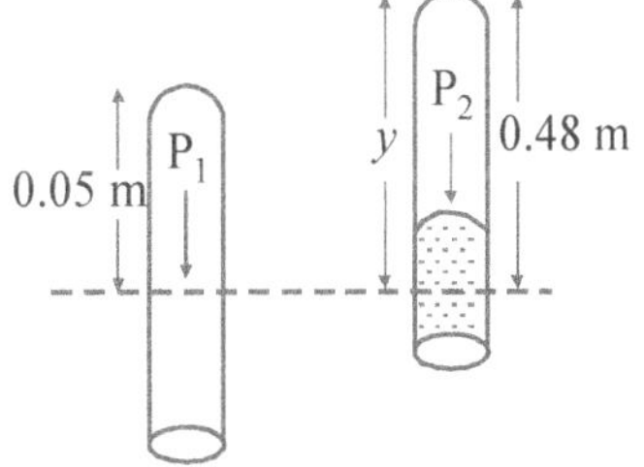

Initially $\qquad P_1 = P_a$
$\qquad\qquad\qquad = 0.76$ m of Hg
and $\qquad\quad V_1 = A \times 0.05$
Finally $\qquad P_2 = P_a - (0.48 - y)$
$\qquad\qquad\qquad = P_a + y - 0.48$
$\qquad\qquad\qquad = 0.76 - 0.48 + y$
$\qquad\qquad\qquad = 0.28 + y$
$\qquad\qquad V_2 = Ay.$

Thus $\qquad P_1 V_1 = P_2 V_2$
$\qquad 0.76 \times (A \times 0.05) = (0.28 + y) \times (Ay)$

$$\therefore \qquad y = 0.10 \text{ m} \qquad \textbf{Ans.}$$

18. Because of the acceleration of the tank, the pressure increases towards backward side of the tank. The equivalent profile is shown in figure. We know that

$$\tan\theta = \frac{a}{g}$$

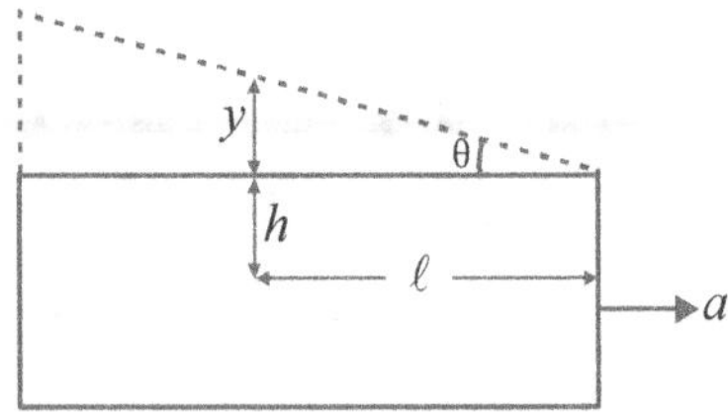

$$= \frac{y}{R}$$

$$\therefore \qquad y = \frac{al}{g}$$

The pressure at the point

$$= (h+y)\,dg$$

$$= \left(h+\frac{al}{g}\right)dg$$

$$= (hg+al)\,d \qquad \textbf{\textit{Ans.}}$$

19. The acceleration of the body

$$a = \frac{mg-F_b}{m}$$

$$= \left(\frac{\rho-\sigma}{\rho}\right)g$$

The distance $\qquad d = 0+\frac{1}{2}at^2$

$$\therefore \qquad t = \sqrt{\frac{2d}{a}}$$

$$= \sqrt{\frac{2d\rho}{g(\rho-\sigma)}}. \qquad \textbf{\textit{Ans.}}$$

20. The pressure intensity at the bottom of the tank

$$P = \rho(g+a)h$$

The average pressure intensity $P_{av} = \dfrac{0+P}{2}$

$$= \frac{\rho(g+a)h}{2}$$

(a) The force on the side of the tank,

$$F = P_{av} \times \text{wetted area of wall}$$

$$= \frac{\rho(g+a)h}{2} \times (bh)$$

$$= \frac{\rho(g+a)bh^2}{2}$$

$$= \frac{1600(9.8+5)\times 2\times 1.5^2}{2}$$

$$\simeq 53.316 \text{ kN.}$$

(b) In case of acceleration downward

$$F = \frac{\rho(g-a)bh^2}{2}$$

$$= \frac{1600(9.8-5)\times 2\times 1.5^2}{2}$$

$$= 17.316 \text{ kN.} \qquad \textbf{\textit{Ans.}}$$

21. Suppose y depth of the cube is inside the mercury, then for floating block.

$$\text{weight of the block} = \text{buoyant force}$$

$$7.7\times 10^3 \times [0.06^3]\,g$$

$$=[\,y\times(0.06)^2\,]\times 13.6\times 10^3\,g + [\,(0.06-y)\times(0.06)^2\times 10^3]g$$

After simplifying $\quad y = 3.2$ cm

Fraction $\qquad f = \dfrac{y}{6}$

$$= \frac{3.2}{6}$$

$$= 0.533. \qquad \textbf{\textit{Ans.}}$$

22. In this case, the rate of flow is given by

$$Q = A_1 A_2 \sqrt{\frac{2\rho_m gh}{\rho(A_1^2-A_2^2)}}$$

or $\qquad 500 = 5\times 2\sqrt{\dfrac{2\times 13.6\times 981\times h}{1(5^2-2^2)}}$

After simplifying, we get $h = 1.97$ cm. $\qquad \textbf{\textit{Ans.}}$

23. (a) (i) As both the points are exposed to atmosphere, so

$$P_A = P_D$$

$$= P_a$$

and hence, $P_A - P_D = 0$

(ii) $\quad P_B - P_C = (P_A - h_1\rho g) - (P_D - h_2\rho g)$

As $\quad P_A = P_D$

$$= P_a$$

$$\therefore \quad P_B - P_C = (h_2-h_1)\rho g$$

$$= (2.0-0.2)\times 1.5\times 10^3 \times 9.8$$

$$= 2.646\times 10^4 \text{ N/m}^2 \qquad \textbf{\textit{Ans.}}$$

(b) (i) $\quad P_D - P_A = (h_2-h_1)\,\rho_{\text{air}}\,g$

$$= (2.0-0.20)\times 1.3\times 9.8$$

$$= 22.93 \text{ N/m}^2$$

(ii) $\quad P_B - P_C = (P_A - P_D)+(h_2-h_1)\,\rho g$

$$= -(h_2-h_1)\,\rho_{\text{air}}\,g+(h_2-h_1)\rho g$$

$$= -22.93+2.646\times 10^4 \text{ N/m}^2.$$

$$= 2.644\times 10^4 \text{ N/m}^2.$$

24. (a) Using Bernoulli's theorem between points 1 and 3, we have

$$P_1+\frac{1}{2}\rho v_1^2+\rho gh_1 = P_3+\frac{1}{2}\rho v_3^2+\rho gh_3$$

Here $\qquad P_1 = P_3$

$$= P_a$$

$$v_1 \ll v_2 \text{ and } h_1 = 10\,m,$$

$$h_3 = 1\,m$$

$$\therefore \qquad \rho\,g \times 9 = \frac{1}{2}\rho \times v_3^2$$

$$\therefore \qquad v_3 = \sqrt{2g \times 9}$$

$$= 13.3 \text{ m/s}$$

Now using equation of continuity between sections 2 and 3, we have

$$A_2 v_2 = A_3 v_3$$

$$\therefore \qquad v_2 = \frac{0.02 \times 19.8}{0.04}$$

$$= 6.64 \text{ m/s}$$

Again using Bernoulli's equation between 2 and 3, we have

$$P_2 + \frac{1}{2}\rho v_2^2 = P_3 + \frac{1}{2}\rho v_3^2$$

As $\qquad P_3 = P_a$

$$\therefore \qquad P_2 - P_a = \frac{1}{2}\rho(v_3^2 - v_2^2)$$

$$= \frac{1}{2} \times 1000(13.30^2 - 6.64^2)$$

$$= 6.62 \times 104 \text{ N/m}^2 \qquad \textbf{\textit{Ans.}}$$

(b) The rate of flow $Q = A_3 v_3$

$$= 0.02 \times 13.3$$

$$= 0.266 \text{ m}^3/\text{s} \qquad \textbf{\textit{Ans.}}$$

25. Using Bernoulli's equation between top of tank A and B, we get

$$v_D = \sqrt{2gh_1}$$

Now by equation of continuity

$$A_C v_C = A_D v_D$$

$$\therefore \qquad v_C = \frac{A_D}{A_C} v_D$$

$$= 2\sqrt{2gh_1}$$

Now using Bernoulli's equations between C and free surface of liquid in A, we have

$$P_a + 0 + \rho\,g h_1 = P_c + \frac{1}{2}\rho v_2^2 + 0 \qquad .....\text{(i)}$$

From tank $F, P_c + \rho\,g h_2 = P_a$

$$\therefore \qquad P_c = P_a - \rho\,g h_2 \qquad ....\text{(ii)}$$

From equations (i) and (ii), we have

$$h_2 = \frac{v_2^2}{2g} - h_1$$

$$= \frac{(2\sqrt{2gh_1})^2}{2g} - h_1$$

$$= 3\,h_1. \qquad \textbf{\textit{Ans.}}$$

26. The lift force on the plane

$$F = (P_2 - P_1)\,A$$

$$= mg \qquad ....\text{(i)}$$

By using Bernoulli's theorem, we have

$$P_1 + \frac{1}{2}\rho v_1^2 = P_2 + \frac{1}{2}\rho v_2^2$$

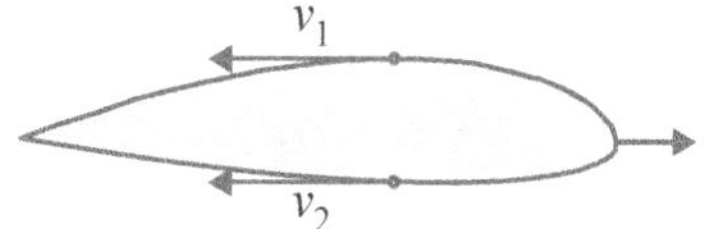

$$\therefore \qquad P_2 - P_1 = \frac{1}{2}\rho(v_1^2 - v_2^2)$$

$$= \frac{1}{2} \times 1(65^2 - 50^2)$$

$$= 1725 \text{ N/m}^2.$$

From equation (i), we have

$$m = \frac{(P_2 - P_1)A}{g}$$

$$= \frac{1725 \times 25}{9.81}$$

$$= 4396 \text{ kg.} \qquad \textbf{\textit{Ans.}}$$

27. We have $\qquad A_1 v_1 = A_2 v_2$

$$\therefore \qquad v_2 = \frac{A_1 v_1}{A_2}$$

$$= \frac{\pi(1.5)^2}{\pi(3)^2} \times 4$$

$$= 1 \text{ m/s.}$$

By using Bernoulli's theorem, we have

$$P_1 + \frac{1}{2}\rho v_1^2 = P_2 + \frac{1}{2}\rho v_2^2$$

$$\therefore \qquad P_2 = P_1 + \frac{1}{2}\rho(v_1^2 - v_2^2)$$

$$= 2 \times 10^4 + \frac{1}{2} \times 10^3(4^2 - 1^2)$$

$$= 2.75 \times 10^4 \text{ N/m}^2 \qquad \textbf{\textit{Ans.}}$$

28. If v_1 is the speed of the blood in artery, then

$$P_1 + \frac{1}{2}\rho v_1^2 = P_2 + \frac{1}{2}\rho v_2^2 \qquad .....\text{(i)}$$

Also $\qquad A_1 v_1 = A_2 v_2$

or $\qquad \rho\, v_1 = 4 \times v_2$

$$\therefore \qquad v_2 = 2\, v_1$$

Now from equation (i),

$$P_1 + \frac{1}{2}\rho v_1^2 = P_2 + \frac{1}{2}\rho(2v_1)^2$$

or $\qquad \dfrac{3}{2}\rho v_1^2 = P_1 - P_2$

$$\therefore \qquad v_1 = \sqrt{\frac{2(P_1 - P_2)}{3\rho}}$$

$$= \sqrt{\frac{2 \times 24}{3 \times 1000}}$$

$$= 0.125 \text{ m/s}$$

29. Using Bernoulli's equation between A and B, we have

$$P = P_a + \frac{1}{2}\rho v^2$$

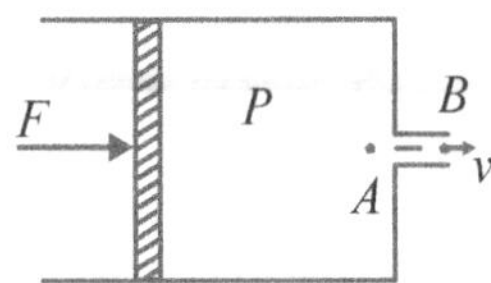

$$\therefore \qquad P - P_a = \frac{1}{2}\rho v^2$$

The net force on the piston, $F = (P - P_a)A$

Thus work done $\quad W = (P - P_0)\Delta V$

$$= \frac{1}{2}\rho v^2 \times (V - 0)$$

$$= \frac{1}{2}\rho v^2 V$$

Given $\qquad V = v\,s\,t$

$$\therefore \qquad W = \frac{1}{2}\rho\left(\frac{V^3}{s^2 t^2}\right).$$

Ans.

30. Force of reactions $\quad F_A = \rho A v_A^2$

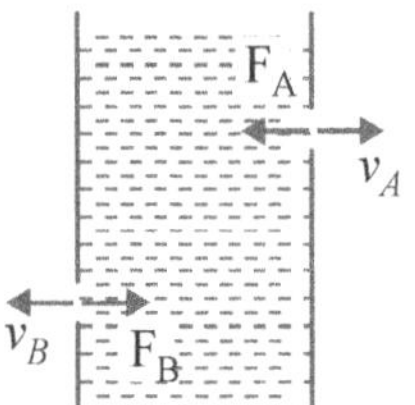

and $\qquad F_B = \rho A v_B^2$

Thus resultant force of reaction $F = F_B - F_A$

$$= \rho A(v_B^2 - v_A^2)$$

$$= \rho S(2gh_2 - 2gh_1)$$

$$= \rho S \times 2g(h_2 - h_1)$$

$$= 2\rho s g \Delta h. \qquad ***Ans.***$$

31. See analysis of venturimeter

32. Using equation of continuity between sections A and B, we have

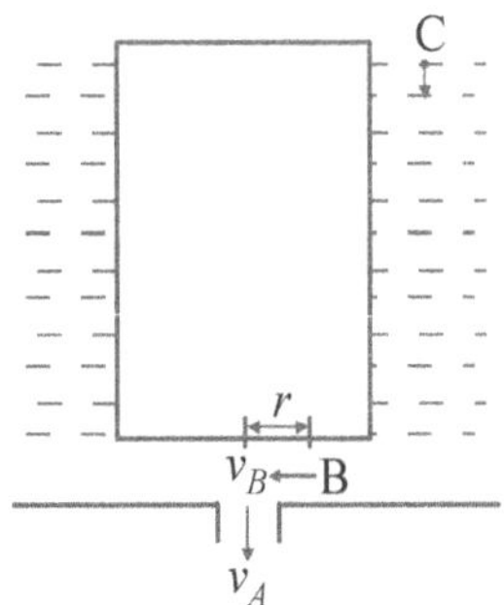

$$(2\pi rd)\,v_B = (2\pi R_1 d)\,v_A$$

or $\qquad r\,v_B = R_1 v_A \qquad .....(i)$

Now using Bernoulli's equation between A and C and between A and B, we have

$$P_a + \frac{1}{2}\rho v_A^2 = P_a + \rho\,gh \qquad ......(ii)$$

and $\qquad P_a + \frac{1}{2}\rho v_A^2 = P + \frac{1}{2}\rho v_B^2 \qquad ....(iii)$

After simplifying, we get

$$P = P_0 + \rho gh\left(1 - \frac{R_1^2}{r^2}\right) \qquad ***Ans.***$$

33. Take an element of fluid of thickness dx. By Newton's second law

$$ma = mw^2 x$$

or $\qquad v\dfrac{dv}{dx} = w^2 x$

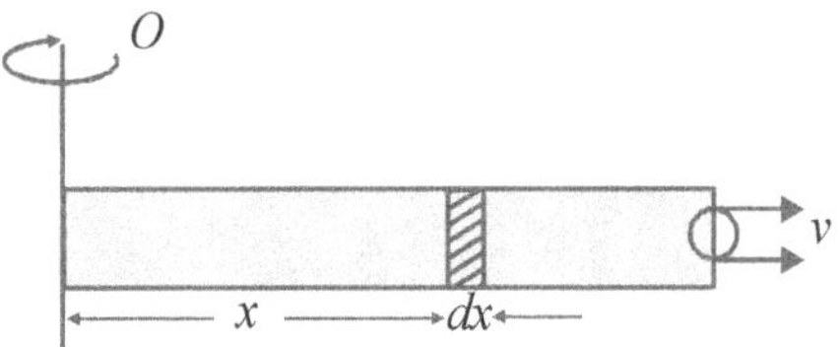

or $\qquad \displaystyle\int_0^v v\,dv = \int_{(l-h)}^h w^2 x\,dx$

$$\therefore \qquad v = wh\sqrt{\frac{2l}{h} - 1} \qquad ***Ans.***$$

34. The force acting on the tube

$$F = \rho\,vQ$$

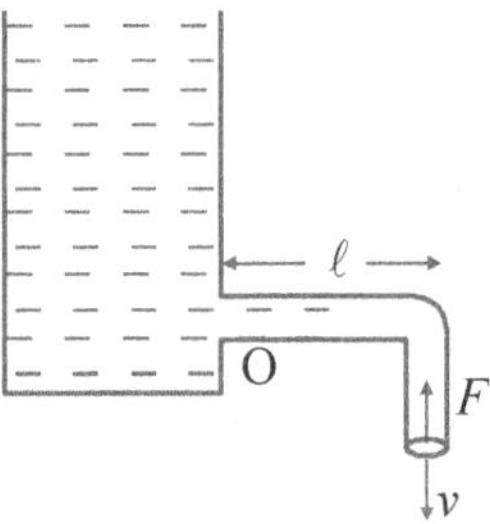

$$= \frac{\rho Q^2}{A}$$

$$= \frac{\rho Q^2}{\pi r^2}$$

The moment of this force about O

$$\tau = F\ell$$

$$= \frac{\rho Q^2 \ell}{\pi r^2}. \qquad ***Ans.***$$

35. The reaction force on the pipe is given by

$$F = \rho\, vQ$$
$$= \rho\, Av^2$$
$$= 1000 \times \frac{\pi}{4}(0.05)^2 \times 5^2$$
$$= 49\ \text{N}$$

If x is the compression the spring, then

$$F \cos 45° = k\, x$$

or

$$49 \times \frac{1}{\sqrt{2}} = 20\, x$$
$$x = 1.74\ \text{cm.}\qquad\textbf{\textit{Ans.}}$$

36. For maximum amount of water in the vessel, the situation is shown in figure.

If θ is the angle made by free surface from the horizontal, then

$$\tan \theta = \frac{a}{g}$$

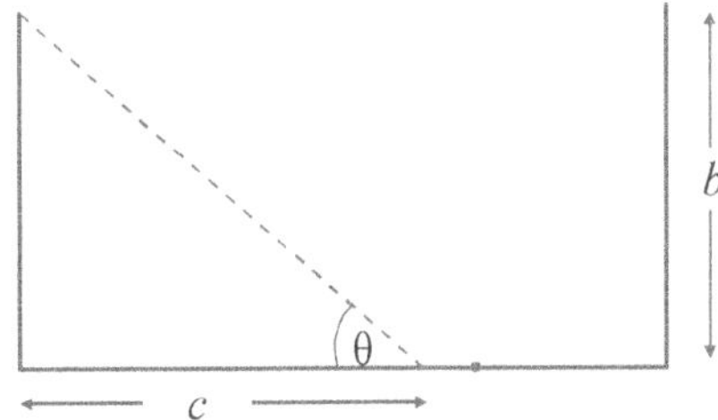

From the geometry, $\tan \theta = \dfrac{b}{c}$

$$\therefore \qquad \frac{a}{g} = \frac{b}{c}$$

$$\Rightarrow \qquad a = \frac{bg}{c}$$

The total mass of the system

$$= \left[M + \frac{1}{2}bc\frac{A}{\ell}\rho \right]$$

Thus force needed $\quad F = \left[M + \frac{1}{2}bc\frac{A\rho}{\ell} \right]a$

$$= \left[M + \frac{bcA\rho}{2\ell} \right]\frac{bg}{c}\qquad\textbf{\textit{Ans.}}$$

37. By equation of continuity, we have

$$A_1 v_1 = A_2 v_2$$

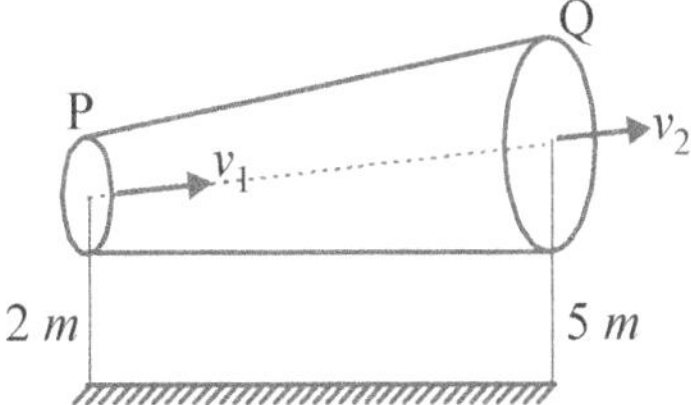

$$v_2 = \frac{A_1 v_1}{A_2}$$

$$= \frac{4 \times 10^{-3}}{8 \times 10^{-3}} \times 1$$
$$= 0.5\ \text{m/s}$$

Now using Bernoulli's equation between 1 and 2, we have

$$P_1 + \frac{1}{2}\rho v_1^2 + \rho g h_1 = P_2 + \frac{1}{2}\rho v_2^2 + \rho g h_2$$

or $\quad (P_1 - P_2) = \frac{1}{2}\rho(v_2^2 - v_1^2) + \rho g(h_2 - h_1)$

or work done by pressure per units volume of water

$$W = \frac{1}{2}\rho(v_2^2 - v_1^2) + \rho g(h_2 - h_1)$$

$$= \frac{1}{2} \times 1000(0.5^2 - 1^2) + 1000 \times 9.8 \times (5-2)$$

$$= 2.9025 \times 10^4\ \text{J/m}^3$$

Work done by gravity per unit volume

$$= \rho g(h_1 - h_2)$$
$$= 1000 \times 9.8 \times (2-5)$$
$$= -2.94 \times 10^4\ \text{J/m}^3\qquad\textbf{\textit{Ans.}}$$

38. Buoyants force on the rod $F_b = V \rho g$

$$= (6 \times 80 \times 10^{-6}) \times 1000 \times 9.8$$
$$= 4.7\ \text{N}$$

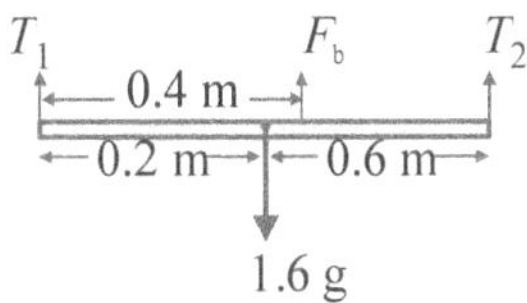

We have

$$T_1 + T_2 + F_b = W$$
$$\therefore \qquad T_1 + T_2 = W - F_b = 1.6\, g - 4.7 = 10.98\ \text{N.}$$

Taking moment of all the forces acting on the rod about left end and put equals to zero,

$$-(1.6 \times 9.8) \times 0.2 + 4.7 \times 0.4 + T_2 \times 0.8 = 0$$
$$\therefore \qquad T_2 = 1.6\ \text{N}$$
and $\qquad T_1 = 9.4\ \text{N.}\qquad\textbf{\textit{Ans.}}$

39. (a) By using Bernoulli's equation between A and B, we have

$$P_A + \frac{1}{2}\rho_{air} v_A^2 = P_B + \frac{1}{2}\rho_{air} v_B^2$$

As $\qquad v_A = 0$

$$\therefore \qquad \frac{1}{2}\rho_{air} v_B^2 = (P_A - P_B) = \rho\, gh$$

$$\therefore \qquad v_B = v = \sqrt{\frac{2\rho gh}{\rho_{air}}}\qquad\textbf{\textit{Ans.}}$$

(b) $\qquad v = \sqrt{\dfrac{2 \times 810 \times 9.8 \times 0.26}{1.03}}$

$$= 63.3\ \text{m/s}$$

40. Water in equilibrium, experiences, two forces

(i) attraction force due to surface tension

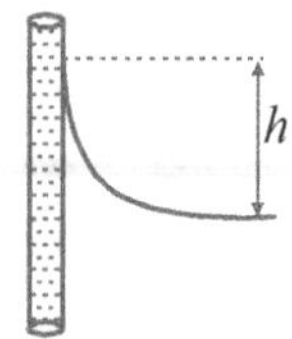

(ii) reaction force of the wall.

Thus $\quad P_{av} \times (\ell\, h) \;=\; T\ell$

or $\quad \left(\dfrac{\rho g h}{2}\right)(\ell h) \;=\; T\ell$

$\therefore \qquad h \;=\; \sqrt{\dfrac{2T}{\rho g}} \simeq 0.004\,\text{m}$ ***Ans.***

41. The force on the gate due to pressure in the container,

$$F_1 \;=\; P \times A$$
$$\;=\; 50 \times (1 \times 1) = 50\,\text{kN}.$$

This force acts at a distance 0.5 m from B. The force on the gate due to water

$$F_2 = P_{av} \times A$$
$$\;=\; \dfrac{\rho g h}{2} \times (1 \times 1)$$
$$\;=\; \dfrac{1000 \times 9.8 \times 1 \sin 30^\circ}{2} \times 1$$
$$\;=\; 2.45\,\text{kN}.$$

This force acts at a distance of 2/3 m from B.

For the equilibrium of the gate, we have

$$F_1 \times 0.5 + F_2 \times \dfrac{2}{3} - F \times 1 \;=\; 0$$

$\therefore \qquad F \;=\; F_1 \times 0.5 + F_2 \times \dfrac{2}{3}$

$$\;=\; 50 \times 0.5 + 2.45 \times \dfrac{2}{3}$$
$$\simeq\; 26.24\,\text{kN}.$$ ***Ans.***

42. If a be the centripetal acceleration, then

$$a_x \;=\; \omega^2 R$$

If α is the inclination, then

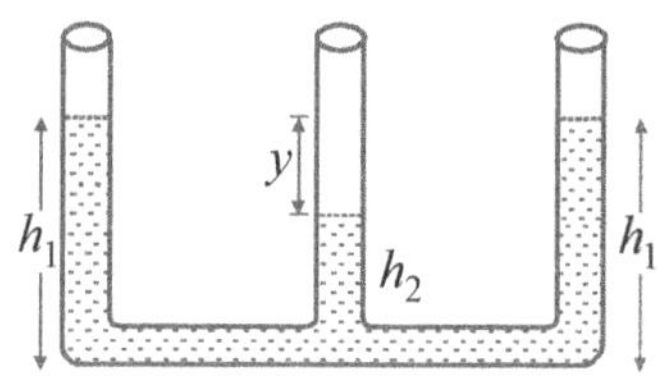

$$\tan \alpha \;=\; \dfrac{a_x}{g}$$

or $\quad \tan(180^\circ - \theta) \;=\; \dfrac{\omega^2 R}{g}$

or $\quad -\tan\theta \;=\; \dfrac{\omega^2 R}{g}$

$\therefore \qquad \tan\theta \;=\; -\dfrac{\omega^2 R}{g}$ ***Ans.***

43. The rise in the tubes c_1 or c_3 rises with respect to c_2, is

$$y \;=\; \dfrac{w^2 x^2}{2g}$$

$$\;=\; \dfrac{\left[2\pi\left(\dfrac{10}{60}\right)\right]^2 \times 0.5^2}{2 \times 9.8}$$

$$\;=\; 1.4 \times 10^{-2}\,\text{m}$$

If h_1 and h_2 be the heights of the liquid in tubes, then

$$h_1 - h_2 \;=\; 1.4 \qquad\qquad \text{.....(i)}$$

and $\quad 2h_1 + h_2 \;=\; 30 + 30 + 30$
$$\;=\; 90 \qquad\qquad \text{.....(ii)}$$

After solving above equations, we get

$$h_1 \;=\; 30.47\,\text{cm}$$

and $\quad h_2 \;=\; 29.06\,\text{cm}$ ***Ans.***

Do the other part similarly.

Simple Harmonic Motion

(279- 364)

4.1 PERIODIC MOTION

Motion which repeats itself in position and phase after equal interval of time is called periodic or harmonic motion. The smallest time after which the motion repeated is called its time period (T). Examples : The motion of the moon around earth, motion of the earth around the sun, motion of clock etc.

4.2 OSCILLATORY MOTION

To and fro or back and forth motion of an object about its mean position is called oscillatory or vibratory motion. Example : Motion of simple pendulum, oscillations of mass block system etc.

Note: Every oscillatory motion is necessarily periodic, but every periodic motion need not be oscillatory motion.

Periodic harmonic functions

Any function which repeats itself after regular intervals of its argument, is called a period function i.e.,

$$f(\theta + T) \quad = \quad f(\theta)$$

For trigonometric function like $\sin\theta$ and $\cos\theta$ are periodic with a period of 2π radians, so

$$\sin(\theta + 2\pi) \quad = \quad \sin\theta$$

and $$\cos(\theta + 2\pi) \quad = \quad \cos\theta$$

If the independent variable θ stands for some dimensionless quantity such as time t, then we can make a periodic function with period T as :

$$f(t) \quad = \quad \sin\frac{2\pi t}{T} \text{ and } g(t) = \cos\frac{2\pi t}{T}.$$

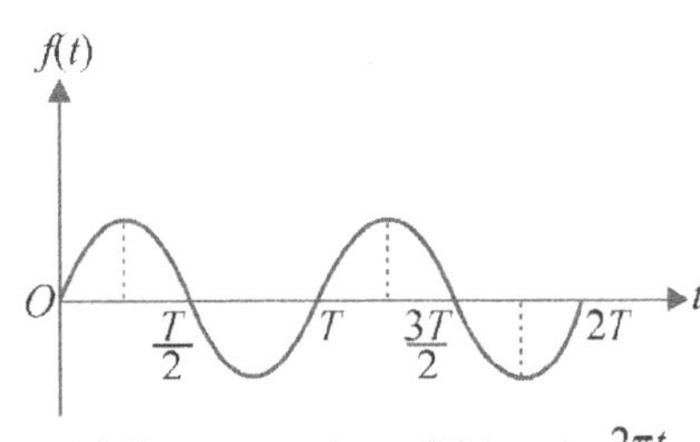

(a) Representation of $f(t) = \sin\dfrac{2\pi t}{T}$

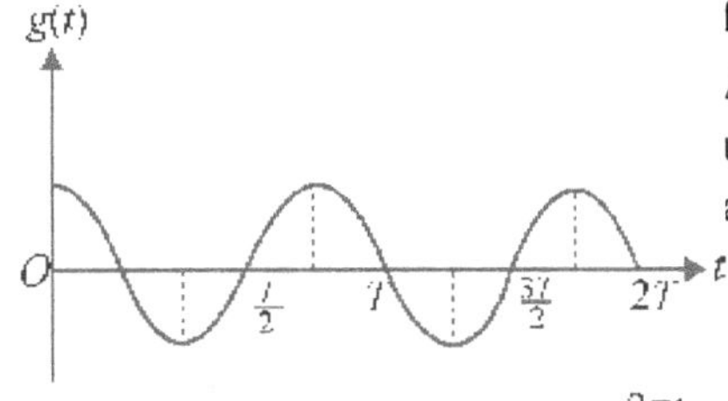

(b) Representation of $g(t) = \cos\dfrac{2\pi t}{T}$

Fig. 4.1

The functions which can be expressed by a sine or cosine curve are called **harmonic function**.

According to Fourier, an arbitrary function $F(t)$ with period T can be represented by a unique combination of the functions $f_n(t)$ and $g_n(t)$. Mathematically it can be expressed as :

$$F(t) = a_0 + a_1 \sin(2\pi t/T) + a_2 \sin(4\pi t/T) + a_3 \sin(6\pi t/T) + \dots$$

$$+ b_1 \cos(2\pi t/T) + b_2 \cos(4\pi t/T) + b_3 \cos(6\pi t/T) + \dots$$

Or it can be written as :

$$F(t) \quad = \quad a_0 + \Sigma a_n \sin n(\omega t) + \Sigma b_n \cos n(\omega t)$$

where $\qquad \omega = \dfrac{2\pi}{T} \cdot a_0, a_1, a_2, \dots ; b_1, b_2, \dots$ are called Fourier coefficients.

Suppose all the Fourier coefficients except a_1 and b_1 are zero, then

$$F_t \quad = \quad a_1 \sin(2\pi t/T) + b_1 \cos(2\pi t/T)$$

Above equation is a special period function which represents **simple harmonic motion**.

Ex. 1 Which of the following examples represent periodic motion?

(i) A swimmer completing one (return) trip from one bank of a river to the other and back.

(ii) A freely suspended bar magnet displaced from its N-S direction and released.

(iii) A hydrogen molecule rotating about its centre of mass

(iv) An arrow released from a bow.

(v) Halley's comet.

Sol. (i) Not periodic   (ii) Periodic

(iii) Periodic   (iv) Not periodic

(v) Periodic

Note:

1. The periodic function which cannot be represented by single sine or cosine function is called non-harmonic functions.

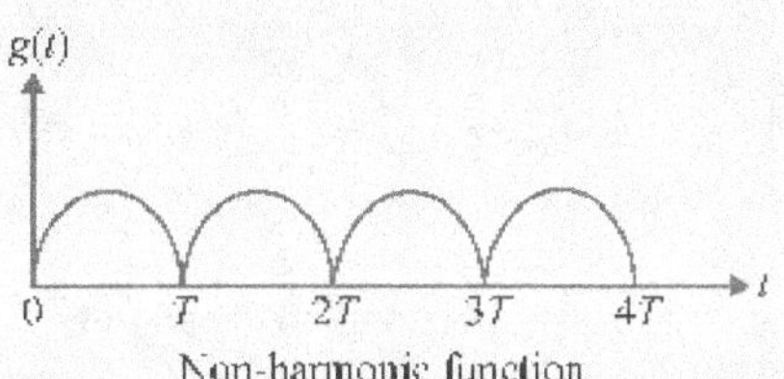

Fig. 4.2

2. Functions $\tan \omega t$ and $\cot \omega t$ are periodic with period π/ω while $\sec \omega t$ and $\csc \omega t$ are periodic with period $2\pi/\omega$. But their values lie between zero to infinity, so these functions can not be used to represent displacement.

Ex. 2 Which of the following functions of time represent

    (a) periodic and   (b) non -periodic motion ?

Give the period for each case of periodic motion. (ω is any positive constant)

(i) $\sin\omega t + \cos\omega t$ (ii) $\sin\omega t + \cos 2\omega t + \sin 4\omega t$

(iii) $e^{-\omega t}$ (iv) $\log(\omega t)$

Sol.

(i)

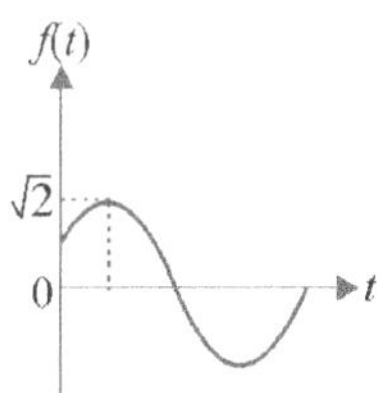

Fig. 4.3

Given, $\qquad f(t) = \sin\omega t + \cos\omega t$

$$= \sqrt{2}\left[\frac{1}{\sqrt{2}}\sin\omega t + \frac{1}{\sqrt{2}}\cos\omega t\right]$$

$$= \sqrt{2}[\cos \pi/4 \cdot \sin\omega t + \sin \pi/4 \cdot \cos\omega t]$$

$$f(t) = \sqrt{2}\sin(\omega t + \pi/4)$$

Hence $\sin\omega t + \cos\omega t$ is a periodic function with time period $2\pi/\omega$.

(ii) Given, $\qquad f(t) = \sin\omega t + \cos 2\omega t + \sin 4\omega t$

Here, $\sin\omega t$ is a periodic function with period $\dfrac{2\pi}{\omega} = T$

$\cos 2\omega t$ is a periodic function with period $\dfrac{2\pi}{2\omega} = \dfrac{\pi}{\omega} = \dfrac{T}{2}$

$\sin 4\omega t$ is a periodic function with period $\dfrac{2\pi}{4\omega} = \dfrac{\pi}{2\omega} = \dfrac{T}{4}$

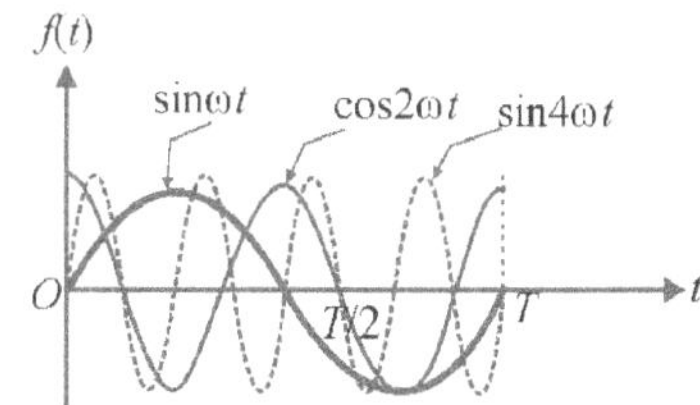

Fig. 4.4

(iii) The function $e^{-\omega t}$ is an exponential function which decreases to zero as $t \to \infty$. It does not repeat its value, so it is not a periodic function.

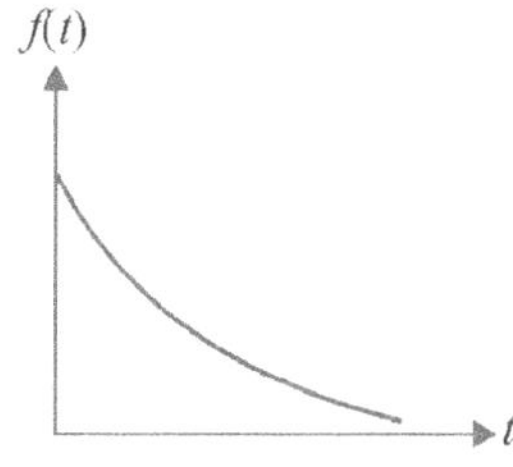

Fig. 4.5

(iv) The function $\log \omega t$ increases with time and becomes ∞ as $t \to \infty$.

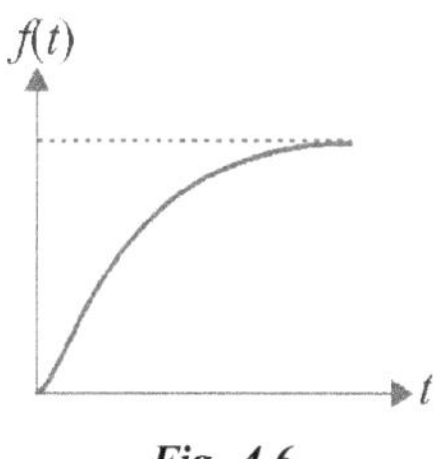

Fig. 4.6

4.3 SIMPLE HARMONIC MOTION

To and fro motion of a particle about its mean position such that the restoring force /torque is proportional to the displacement from mean position is known as simple harmonic motion (SHM).

Two types of SHM

1. Linear SHM: In this case particle moves on a straight line. Ex. oscillations of block-spring system.

2. Angular SHM : In this case particle moves on an arc of a circle. Ex. Oscillations of simple pendulum.

4.4 DIFFERENTIAL EQUATION OF SHM

1. Linear SHM

In linear SHM, the restoring force is proportional to the displacement from mean position. Thus

$$-\vec{F} = k\vec{x}$$

or

$$\vec{F} = -k\vec{x}$$

Here k is called force constant.

By Newton's second law, $F = m\dfrac{d^2\vec{x}}{dt^2}$, so we can write

$$m\dfrac{d^2\vec{x}}{dt^2} = -k\vec{x}$$

or

$$m\dfrac{d^2\vec{x}}{dt^2} + k\vec{x} = 0$$

or

$$\dfrac{d^2\vec{x}}{dt^2} + \dfrac{k\vec{x}}{m} = 0 \qquad \ldots(1)$$

Fig. 4.7

2. Angular SHM

In angular SHM, the restoring torque is proportional to the angular displacement from the mean position. Thus

$$-\vec{\tau} = C\vec{\theta}$$

or

$$\vec{\tau} = -C\vec{\theta}$$

Here C is called torsional rigidity.

By Newton's second law, $\vec{\tau} = I\dfrac{d^2\vec{\theta}}{dt^2}$, so we can write

$$I\dfrac{d^2\vec{\theta}}{dt^2} = -C\vec{\theta}$$

or

$$I\dfrac{d^2\vec{\theta}}{dt^2} + C\vec{\theta} = 0$$

or

$$\dfrac{d^2\vec{\theta}}{dt^2} + \dfrac{C}{I}\vec{\theta} = 0 \qquad \ldots(2)$$

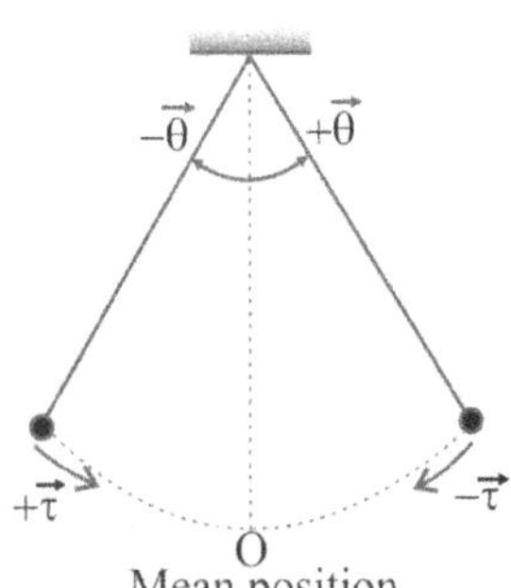

Fig. 4.8

Solution of differential equation of SHM : value of $\vec{x}$ or $\vec{\theta}$

Any of the following expressions can give the Solution of differential equations (1) or (2).

(i) $x = A\sin(\omega t + \phi_0)$ for linear SHM

and $\theta = \theta_0 \sin(\omega t + \phi_0)$ for angular SHM. $\qquad \ldots(i)$

(ii) $x = A\cos(\omega t + \phi_0)$ $\qquad \ldots(ii)$

(iii) $x = A\sin\omega t + B\cos\omega t$ $\qquad \ldots(iii)$

where A is called amplitude of motion, ω is called angular frequency and ϕ is called initial phase or epoch.

Relationship between k and ω

We have, $\qquad\qquad x = A\sin(\omega t + \phi_0)$

On differentiating above equation twice w.r.t. time, we get

$$\dfrac{d^2x}{dt^2} = -\omega^2 A\sin(\omega t + \phi_0)$$

or
$$\frac{d^2x}{dt^2} = -\omega^2 x$$

or
$$\frac{d^2x}{dt^2} + \omega^2 x = 0$$

From equation (1)
$$\frac{d^2x}{dt^2} + \frac{k}{m}x = 0$$

$\therefore$
$$\omega = \sqrt{\frac{k}{m}} \quad \text{or} \quad k = m\omega^2$$

Similarly for angular SHM, we can get

$$\frac{d^2\theta}{dt^2} + \omega^2\theta = 0$$

and
$$\omega = \sqrt{\frac{C}{I}} \quad \text{or} \quad C = I\omega^2$$

4.5 SOME IMPORTANT TERMS CONNECTED WITH SHM

(i) Amplitude

The maximum displacement of the oscillating particle on either side of its mean position is called its amplitude. It can be denoted by A. Thus $x_{max} = \pm A$.

(ii) Time period

The time taken by a oscillating particle to complete one oscillation is called its time period. It is denoted by T.

(iii) Frequency

It is the number of oscillations completed in one second. It can be denoted by f.

We can write
$$f = \frac{1}{T}$$

The SI unit of frequency is $s^{-1} = cps = Hz$.

(iv) Angular frequency

It is the number of oscillations completed in one second and expressed in terms of radian/s. Thus we have angular frequency

$$\omega = 2\pi f = \frac{2\pi}{T}.$$

S.I. unit of angular frequency = rad/s.

(v) Total phase

The total phase of the oscillating particle at any instant gives an idea about the state of the particle with regards to its position and direction of motion. Suppose a SHM is represented by

$x = A\sin(\omega t + \phi_0)$, then total phase $\phi = \omega t + \phi_0$.

Here ϕ_0 is known as initial phase.

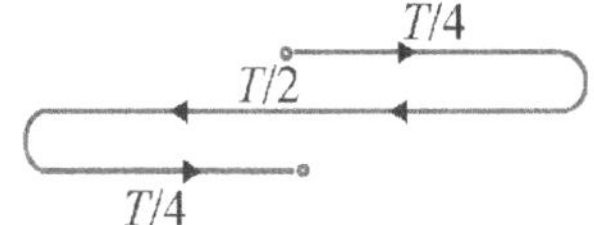

Fig. 4.9
One complete oscillation starting from mean position

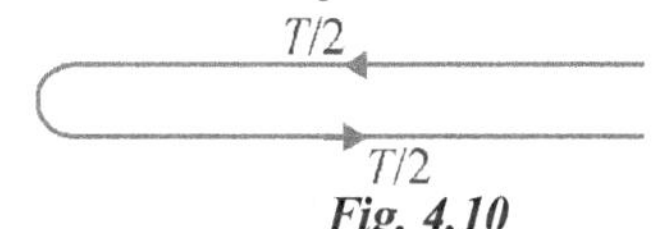

Fig. 4.10
One complete oscillation starting from extreme position

(vi) The initial phase

It gives idea about the position of oscillating particle at $t = 0$. The initial phase corresponds to different positions of the particle are :

(a) If particle is at mean position at $t = 0$, then $x = 0$

$$\therefore 0 = A\sin(\omega \times 0 + \phi_0) \Rightarrow \phi_0 = 0$$

(b) If particle is at right extreme at $t = 0$, then $x = +A$

$$\therefore A = A\sin(\omega \times 0 + \phi_0) \Rightarrow \phi_0 = \frac{\pi}{2}$$

(c) If particle is at left extreme at $t = 0$, then $x = -A$

$$\therefore -A = A\sin(\omega \times 0 + \phi_0) \Rightarrow \phi_0 = -\pi/2,\, 3\pi/2$$

(d) For $x = A/2$, at $t = 0$

$$A/2 = A\sin(\omega \times 0 + \phi_0) \Rightarrow \phi_0 = \pi/6$$

Position at $t = 0$	0	$+A/2$	A	$-A/2$	$-A$
ϕ_0	0	$\pi/6$	$\pi/2$	$-\pi/6$	$-\pi/2$ or $3\pi/2$

Note :

It can be now concluded that, if particle starts from mean position at $t = 0$, then

$$x = A\sin(\omega t + 0) = A\sin \omega t.$$

If particle starts oscillating from extreme position at $t = 0$, then

$$x = A\sin(\omega t + \pi/2) = A\cos \omega t$$

Ex. 3 Calculate the time taken by the particle to reach the half of the amplitude from mean position.

Sol.

Let particle takes t_1 time to cover the displacement $= A/2$.

Fig. 4.11

$$\therefore \quad \frac{A}{2} = A\sin(\omega t_1 + 0)$$

or $\quad \omega t_1 = \pi/6$

or $\quad \dfrac{2\pi t_1}{T} = \pi/6$

or $\quad t_1 = \dfrac{T}{12}$

Time taken to travel from $+A/2$ to $+A$ will be

$$t_2 = \frac{T}{4} - \frac{T}{12} = \frac{T}{6}$$

$$\therefore \quad \frac{t_1}{t_2} = \frac{1}{2} \qquad \qquad Ans.$$

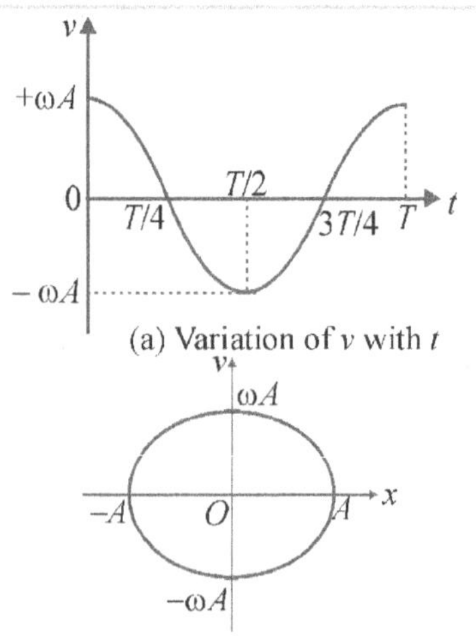

(a) Variation of v with t

(b) Variation of v with x

Fig. 4.12

Velocity in SHM

The displacement of the oscillating particle is given by,

$$x = A\sin(\omega t + \phi_0)$$

$$\therefore \quad \text{Velocity,} \quad v = \frac{dx}{dt} = \frac{d}{dt}[\sin(\omega t + \phi_0)]$$

or $\quad v = \omega A\cos(\omega t + \phi_0)$

or $\quad v = \omega A\sqrt{1 - \sin^2(\omega t + \phi_0)}$

$$= \omega A\sqrt{1 - x^2/A^2}$$

$$v = \omega\sqrt{A^2 - x^2}$$

at $x = 0$, $\qquad v_{max} = \omega A$

After rearranging above equation, we can write

$$\frac{v^2}{\omega^2 A^2} + \frac{x^2}{A^2} = 1$$

Acceleration in SHM

The velocity of the oscillating particle is given by,

$$v = \omega A \cos(\omega t + \phi_0)$$

Differentiating above equation w.r.t. time, we get

$$a = \frac{dv}{dt} = \frac{d}{dt}[\omega A \cos(\omega t + \phi_0)]$$

or

$$a = -\omega^2 A \sin(\omega t + \phi_0)$$

As $x = A\sin(\omega t + \phi_0)$, so

$$a = -\omega^2 x$$

SHM - time	SHM - displacement
$x = A\sin(\omega t + \phi_0)$	x
$v = \omega A\sin(\omega t + \phi_0 + \pi/2)$	$v = \omega\sqrt{A^2 - x^2}$
$a = \omega^2 A\sin(\omega t + \phi_0 + \pi)$	$a = -\omega^2 x$

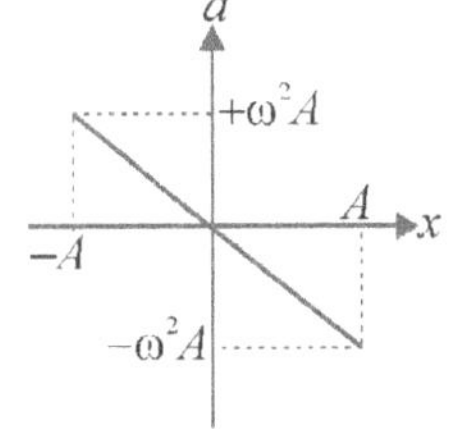

(a) Variation of acceleration with time

(b) Variation of acceleration with x

Fig. 4.13

Kinetic energy in SHM

K.E. as a function of time	K.E. as a function of displacement
$k = \dfrac{1}{2}mv^2$	$k = \dfrac{1}{2}mv^2$
$= \dfrac{1}{2}m[\omega A\cos(\omega t + \phi_0)]^2$	$= \dfrac{1}{2}m[\omega\sqrt{(A^2 - x^2)}]^2$
$= \dfrac{1}{2}m\omega^2 A^2 \cos^2(\omega t + \phi_0)$	$k = \dfrac{1}{2}m\omega^2(A^2 - x^2)$

Potential energy in SHM

$U = \dfrac{1}{2}kx^2$	$U = \dfrac{1}{2}kx^2$
$= \dfrac{1}{2}k[A\sin(\omega t + \phi_0)]^2$	$= \dfrac{1}{2}m\omega^2 x^2$
$= \dfrac{1}{2}m\omega^2 A^2 \sin^2(\omega t + \phi_0)$	

Total mechanical energy :

$$E = K + U$$

$E = \dfrac{1}{2}m\omega^2 A^2[\cos^2(\omega t + \phi) + \sin^2(\omega t + \phi)]$	$E = \dfrac{1}{2}m\omega^2(A^2 - x^2) + \dfrac{1}{2}m\omega^2 x^2$
$= \dfrac{1}{2}m\omega^2 A^2$ (constant)	$= \dfrac{1}{2}m\omega^2 A^2$

As total mechanical energy of the oscillating particle is constant, so $\dfrac{dE}{dt} = 0$ and $\dfrac{dE}{dx} = 0$.

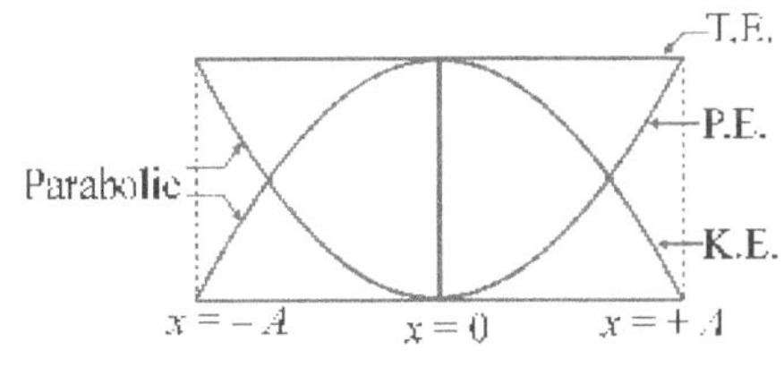

Fig. 4.14

Ex. 4 The position of the oscillating particle where its kinetic energy is equal to its potential energy.

Sol.

For kinetic energy and potential energy to be equal

$$\frac{1}{2}m\omega^2(A^2 - x^2) = \frac{1}{2}m\omega^2 x^2$$

or $A^2 - x^2 = x^2$

or $x = \dfrac{A}{\sqrt{2}}$ *Ans.*

Ex. 5 Show that for a particle in linear SHM, the average kinetic energy over a period of oscillations is equal to the average potential energy over the same period.

Sol.

Let a particle of mass m performs SHM with angular frequency ω. Its displacement at any instant is given by

$$x = A\sin\omega t$$

and velocity $v = A\omega\cos\omega t$

Its kinetic energy $K = \dfrac{1}{2}mv^2 = \dfrac{1}{2}m\omega^2 A^2 \cos^2 \omega t$

Average kinetic energy over the period T

$$K_{av} = \frac{1}{T}\int_0^T \frac{1}{2}m\omega^2 A^2 \cos^2 \omega t\, dt$$

$$= \frac{m\omega^2 A^2}{2T}\int_0^T \frac{(1+\cos 2\omega t)}{2}\, dt$$

$$= \frac{m\omega^2 A^2}{4T}\left[t + \frac{\sin 2\omega t}{2\omega}\right]_0^T$$

$$= \frac{m\omega^2 A^2}{4T}[T] = \frac{1}{4}m\omega^2 A^2$$

Potential energy of the particle

$$U = \frac{1}{2}kx^2 = \frac{1}{2}m\omega^2 A^2 \sin^2 \omega t$$

Average potential energy over the period T

$$U_{av} = \frac{1}{T}\int_0^T \frac{1}{2}m\omega^2 A^2 \sin^2 \omega t\, dt$$

$$= \frac{m\omega^2 A^2}{2T}\int_0^T \frac{(1-\cos 2\omega t)}{2}\, dt$$

$$= \frac{m\omega^2 A^2}{4T}\left[t - \frac{\sin 2\omega t}{2\omega}\right]_0^T$$

$$= \frac{m\omega^2 A^2}{4T}[T] = \frac{1}{4}m\omega^2 A^2$$

Thus $K_{av} = U_{av}.$

Ex. 6 A particle is in linear simple harmonic motion between two points, A and B, 10 cm apart. Take the direction from A to B as the positive direction and give the signs of velocity, acceleration and force on the particle when it is

   (a) at the end A,
   (b) at the end B,
   (c) at the mid-point of AB going towards A,
   (d) at 2 cm away from B going towards A.
   (e) at 3cm away from A going towards B, and
   (f) at 4 cm away from A going towards A.

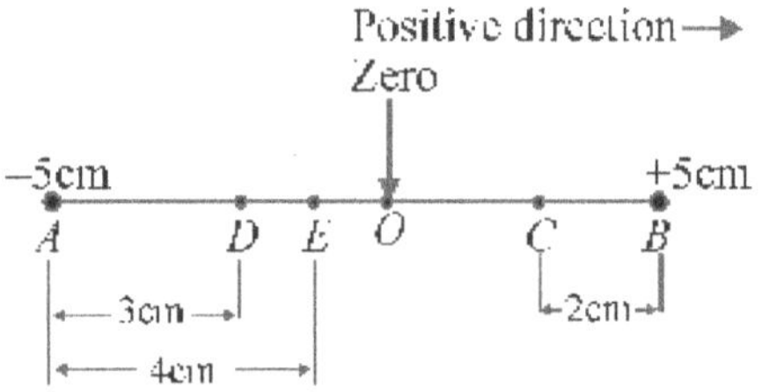

Positive direction→
Zero
−5cm   +5cm
A D E O C B
3cm
2cm
4cm

Fig. 4.15

Sol.

Position	Velocity	Acceleration	Force
(a) At A	0 (at extreme position)	+ve (acts from A to O)	+ve (acts from A to O)
(b) At B	0 (at extreme position)	−ve (acts from B to O)	−ve (acts from B to O)
(c) At mid point O going towards A	−ve and maximum (acts from O to A)	0 (at midpoint)	0 (at midpoint)
(d) At C, going towards A	−ve (acts from C to O)	−ve (acts from C to O)	−ve (acts from C to O)
(e) At D, going towards B	+ve (acts from D to O)	+ve (acts from D to O)	+ve (acts from D to O)
(f) At E, going towards A	−ve (acts from E to A)	+ve (acts from E to O)	+ve (acts from E to O)

Graphical representation of SHM

Motion of a particle moving on a circular path with constant speed is periodic, but not SHM. But the foot of perpendicular drawn over any diameter executes SHM.

Let us consider a particle is moving along a circular path with constant speed. In time t, it rotated angle

$$\theta = \omega t$$

Drop perpendicular from P on diameter CD. Let the length of foot is y

$$\therefore \qquad y = A\sin\omega t \qquad \ldots(1)$$

Also perpendicular drawn over AB gives

$$x = A\cos\omega t \cdot \qquad \ldots(2)$$

Equation (1) and (2) represent SHM.

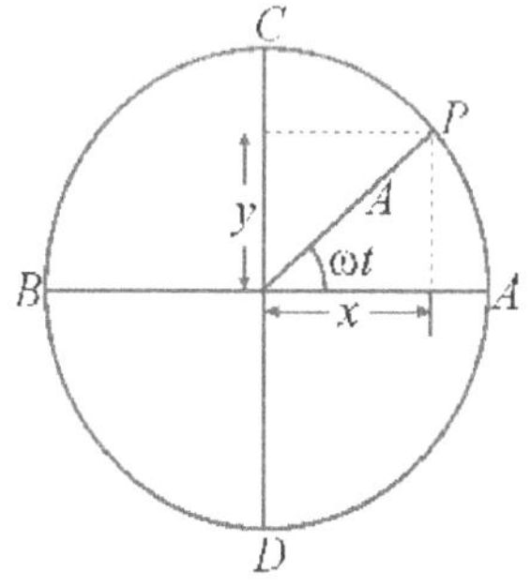

Fig. 4.16

Note:

Kinetic energy,
$$K = \frac{1}{2}m\omega^2 A^2 \cos^2(\omega t + \phi_0)$$

$$= \frac{1}{2}m\omega^2 A^2\left[\frac{1+\cos 2(\omega t + \phi_0)}{2}\right]$$

It is clear from the above expression that the frequency of K.E. is twice that of the frequency of oscillations.

Ex. 7 (i) Is $x = a\sin\omega t + b\cos\omega t$ represents SHM? If yes, find amplitude of motion.

(ii) Is $x = a(\sin 2\omega t + \cos\omega t)$ represents SHM?

Sol.

Any expression which satisfy the differential equation of SHM,

$\dfrac{d^2 x}{dt^2} + \omega^2 x = 0$ will represent SHM.

(i) Given that $\qquad x = a\sin\omega t + b\cos\omega t \qquad \ldots$ (i)

$$\therefore \qquad \frac{dx}{dt} = a\omega\cos\omega t - b\omega\sin\omega t$$

and $\qquad \dfrac{d^2 x}{dt^2} = -a\omega^2\sin\omega t - b\omega^2\cos\omega t$

$$= -\omega^2(a\sin\omega t + b\cos\omega t)$$

$$= -\omega^2 x$$

or $\qquad \dfrac{d^2 x}{dt^2} + \omega^2 x = 0$

Therefore given expression will represent SHM.

We have $\qquad x = A\sin(\omega t + \phi)$

$$= A\sin\omega t\cos\phi + A\cos\omega t\sin\phi \quad \ldots(ii)$$

Comparing equation (ii) with (i), we get

$$A\cos\phi = a \qquad \ldots(iii)$$

and $\qquad A\sin\phi = b \qquad \ldots(iv)$

Squaring and adding (iii) and (iv), we get

$$A = \sqrt{a^2 + b^2} \qquad \textbf{\textit{Ans.}}$$

(ii) Given,

$$x = a[\sin 2\omega t + \cos\omega t]$$

$$\frac{dx}{dt} = a[2\omega\cos 2\omega t - \omega\sin\omega t]$$

and $\qquad \dfrac{d^2 x}{dt^2} = a[-2\omega\times 2\omega\sin 2\omega t - \omega\times\omega\cos\omega t]$

$$= -\omega^2 a\{4\sin 2\omega t + \cos\omega t\}$$

It is clear that the above expression is not like differential equation of SHM, so the given expression will not represent SHM.

Ex. 8 The following figure depict two circular motions. The radius of the circle, the period of revolution, the initial position and the sense of revolution are indicated on the *Fig. 4.18*. Obtain the simple harmonic motions of the x-projection of the radius vector of the rotating particle P in each case.

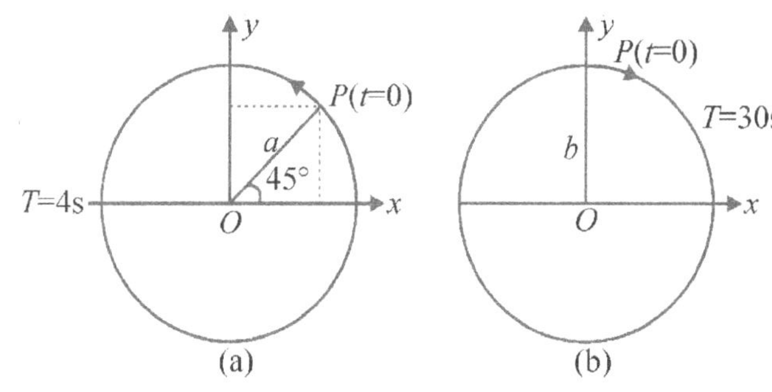

Fig. 4.17

Sol.

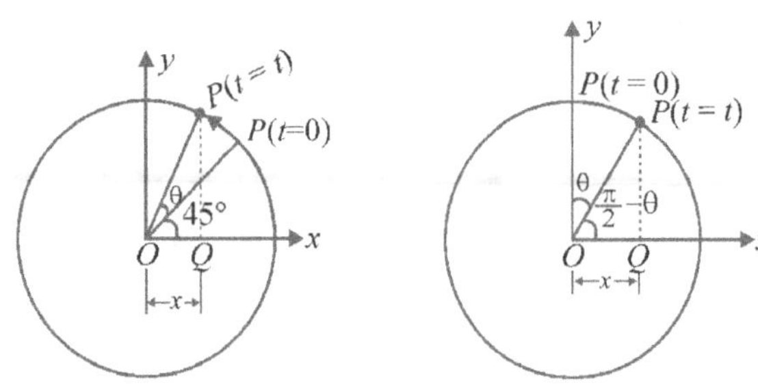

Fig. 4.18

(a)   Given time period $T = 4$ s

∴ Angular frequency $\omega = \dfrac{2\pi}{T} = \dfrac{2\pi}{4} = \dfrac{\pi}{2}\,\text{rad}/s$

Angle traverses by particle in time t, $\theta = \omega t = \dfrac{\pi t}{2}$

The radial position of the particle at time t makes an angle $\left(\dfrac{\pi}{4} + \theta\right)$.

The displacement of the particle = Projection of P on x-axis

or $\qquad x = OQ = a\cos\left(\dfrac{\pi}{4} + \theta\right)$

$\qquad\qquad = a\cos\left(\omega t + \dfrac{\pi}{4}\right)$

or $\qquad x = a\cos\left(\dfrac{\pi t}{2} + \dfrac{\pi}{4}\right)$

(b)   Given time period $T = 30$ s

∴ Angular frequency $\omega = \dfrac{2\pi}{T} = \dfrac{2\pi}{30} = \dfrac{\pi}{15}$ rad / s

Angle traverses by particle in time t, $\theta = \omega t = \dfrac{\pi t}{15}$

The radial position of the particle at any time t makes an angle $(\pi/2 - \theta)$.

The displacement of the particle = Projection of P on x-axis.

or $\qquad x = OQ = b\cos(\pi/2 - \theta)$

$\qquad\qquad = b\cos\left(\pi/2 - \dfrac{\pi t}{15}\right)$

$\qquad\qquad = b\cos\left(\dfrac{\pi t}{15} - \dfrac{\pi}{2}\right)$ *Ans.*

Ex. 9   **A particle in SHM is described by the displacement function** $x(t) = A\cos(\omega t + \varphi)$, $\omega = \dfrac{2\pi}{T}$.

If the initial ($t = 0$) position of the particle is 1 cm and its initial velocity is π cm/s. What are its amplitude and initial phase angle? The angular frequency of the particle is π rad/s

Sol.

Given, displacement at any time t

$$x = A\cos(\omega t + \phi)$$

Since at $t = 0$, $x = 1$, therefore

$$1 = A\cos(\omega \times 0 + \phi)$$

or $\qquad A\cos\phi = 1$ ... (i)

Velocity, $\qquad v = \dfrac{dx}{dt} = \dfrac{d}{dt}A\cos(\omega t + \phi)$

$\qquad\qquad = -\omega A\sin(\omega t + \phi)$

Given at $t = 0$, $v = \pi\,cm/s$, $\omega = \pi\,rad/s$, so we have

$$\pi = -A(\pi)\sin(\omega \times 0 + \phi)$$

or $\qquad A\sin\phi = -1$ ... (ii)

Squaring and adding equations (i) and (ii), we get

$$A^2(\sin^2\phi + \cos^2\phi) = 2$$

or $\qquad A = \sqrt{2}$ cm   *Ans.*

Dividing equation (ii) by (i), we get

$$\tan\phi = -1$$

or $\qquad \phi = \dfrac{3\pi}{4}$ or $\dfrac{7\pi}{4}$ *Ans.*

Ex. 10 **A particle of mass m is located in a unidimensional potential field where the potential energy of the particle depends on the coordinate x as $U(x) = U_0(1 - \cos cx)$; U_0 and c are constants. Find the period of small oscillation that the particle performs about the equilibrium position.**

Sol.

Given, $\qquad U(x) = U_0(1 - \cos cx)$

We know that the field force is given by

$$F = -\dfrac{dU}{dx}$$

or $\qquad F = -\dfrac{d}{dx}[U_0(1 - \cos cx)]$

$\qquad\qquad = -U_0 c\sin cx$

For small value of x, $\sin cx \simeq cx$

∴ $\qquad F = -U_0 c(cx) = -U_0 c^2 x$

Acceleration $\qquad a = \dfrac{F}{m} = \dfrac{U_0 c^2}{m}(-x)$

As $a \propto (-x)$, so above equation represents SHM. Compare this with standard equation of SHM $a = -\omega^2 x$, we get

$$\omega = \sqrt{\dfrac{U_0 c^2}{m}}$$

and $\qquad T = \dfrac{2\pi}{\omega} = 2\pi\sqrt{\dfrac{m}{U_0 c^2}}$ *Ans.*

Ex. 11 The maximum acceleration of a simple harmonic oscillator is a_0 and the maximum velocity is v_0. What is the displacement amplitude.

Sol. Let A be the displacement amplitude and ω be the angular frequency of SHM. Then

$$v_0 = \omega A \qquad \ldots (i)$$

and $$a_0 = \omega^2 A \qquad \ldots (ii)$$

Squaring (i) and dividing by (ii), we get

$$A = \frac{v_0^2}{a_0} \qquad \text{\textit{Ans.}}$$

Ex. 12 What is the ratio between the potential energy and the total energy of a particle, and kinetic energy and total energy of a particle, executing SHM, when its displacement is half of its amplitude?

Sol. The total energy of a particle executing SHM with amplitude A and angular frequency ω,

$$E = \frac{1}{2} m\omega^2 A^2$$

The potential energy at $y = \frac{A}{2}$ is given by

$$U = \frac{1}{2} m\omega^2 y^2 = \frac{1}{2} m\omega^2 \left(\frac{A}{2}\right)^2$$

$$= \frac{E}{4} \qquad \text{\textit{Ans.}}$$

Kinetic energy at $y = \frac{A}{2}$ is given by

$$K = \frac{1}{2} m v^2$$

$$= \frac{1}{2} m\omega^2 (A^2 - y^2) = \frac{1}{2} m\omega^2 \left(A^2 - \frac{A^2}{4}\right)$$

$$= \frac{3E}{4} \qquad \text{\textit{Ans.}}$$

Ex. 13 A body moves along a straight line OAB simple harmonically. It has zero velocity at the points A and B which are at distances a and b respectively from O and has velocity v when half way between them. Find the period of SHM.

Sol.

Fig. 4.19

It is clear from the figure that C is the mean position of SHM. The amplitude of oscillations

$$A = \frac{b - a}{2}$$

The velocity at the mean position C will be

$$v = \omega A = \frac{2\pi}{T}\left(\frac{b - a}{2}\right)$$

$$\therefore \qquad T = \frac{\pi(b - a)}{v} \qquad \text{\textit{Ans.}}$$

Ex. 14 A small block is placed on a wooden plank which is oscillating hormonically in vertical direction with a period of T. At what amplitude of motion will the block separate from the plank?

Sol. The max acceleration of the oscillating plank, $a = \omega^2 A$

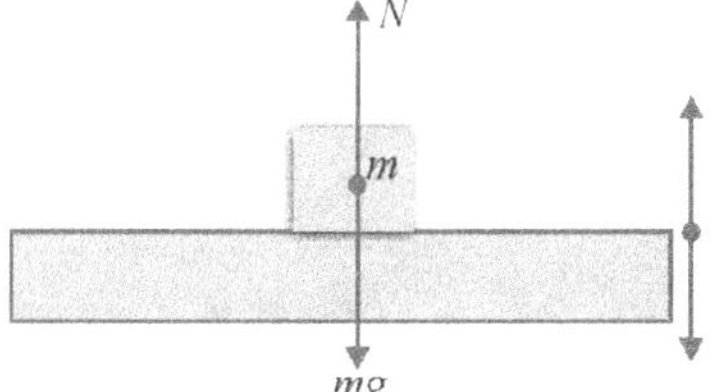

Fig. 4.20

The block can separate from the plank when it goes down. By Newton's second law

$$mg - N = ma$$

$$\text{or} \qquad N = m\,(g - a)$$

$$= m\,(g - \omega^2 A)$$

The block will separate from the plank when

$$N \leq 0$$

$$\text{or} \quad m(g - \omega^2 A) \leq 0$$

$$\text{or} \qquad A \geq \frac{g}{\omega^2}$$

$$\geq \frac{g}{(2\pi/T)^2}$$

$$\geq \frac{gT^2}{4\pi^2} \qquad \text{\textit{Ans.}}$$

Determination of time period of motion

1. **Dynamical method**

Step I : Displace the body from its mean position and then find restoring force or restoring torque acting on the body.

Step II: Find acceleration of the body using Newton's second law

$$a = \frac{F_{rest}}{m} \quad \text{or} \quad \alpha = \frac{\tau_{rest}}{I}$$

Step III: Compare the obtained acceleration with the acceleration in SHM. i.e.,

$$a = -\omega^2 x \quad \text{or} \quad \alpha = -\omega^2 \theta$$

On doing this, we will get ω.

Step IV : By using $T = \dfrac{2\pi}{\omega}$, find time period of oscillations.

2. Energy method

Step I : Find mechanical energy of the oscillating body at any instant, excluding mean and extreme position.

Step II : Since M.E. of the oscillating body is constant at any instant of motion, so

$$\frac{dE}{dt} = 0 \text{ , on doing this we will get acceleration } a.$$

Step III : Compare with standard equation of SHM $a = -\omega^2 x$,to get ω

Step IV : By using $T = \dfrac{2\pi}{\omega}$, find time period of oscillations.

Simple pendulum

A small heavy bob is suspended with an inextensible string constitutes a simple pendulum.

As angular SHM	As linear SHM
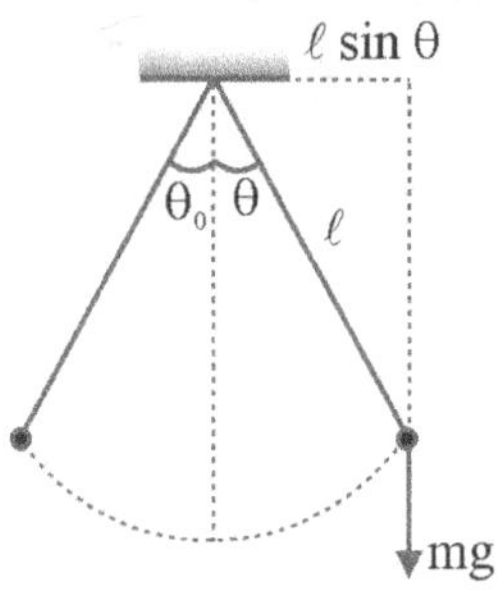	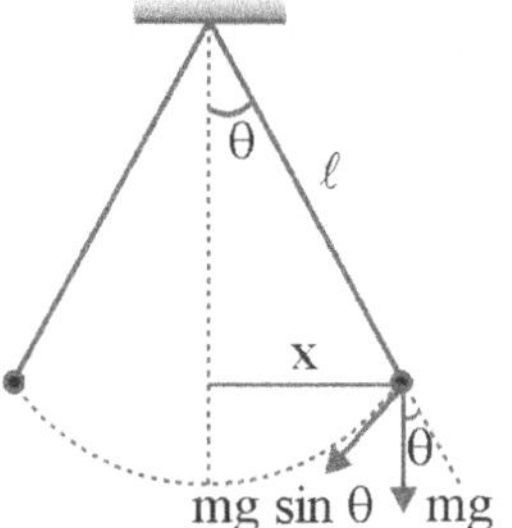
Fig. 4.21	*Fig. 4.22*

$\theta = \theta_0 \sin \omega t$	$x = A \sin \omega t$
The restoring torque on the bob,	The restoring force on the bob,
$\tau_{rest} = -mg \times \ell \sin \theta$	$F_{rest} = -mg \sin \theta$
For small θ, $\sin \theta \simeq \theta$	$= -mg \dfrac{x}{\ell}$
$\therefore \quad \tau = -mg\ell(\theta)$	$a = \dfrac{F_{rest}}{m}$
or $\quad \alpha = \dfrac{\tau}{I} = \dfrac{mg\ell}{I}(-\theta)$	$= \dfrac{g}{\ell}(-x)$
Now compare with $\alpha = -\omega^2 \theta$, we get	Now compare with $a = -\omega^2 x$, we get
$\omega = \sqrt{\dfrac{mg\ell}{I}}$	$\omega = \sqrt{\dfrac{g}{\ell}}$
and $\quad T = \dfrac{2\pi}{\omega} = 2\pi\sqrt{\dfrac{I}{mg\ell}}$	and $\quad T = \dfrac{2\pi}{\omega} = 2\pi\sqrt{\dfrac{\ell}{g}}$
where $I = m\ell^2$	
$\therefore \quad T = 2\pi\sqrt{\dfrac{\ell}{g}}$	

Note:

1. For a spherical bob of radius r

$$I = I = \frac{2}{5}mr^2 + m\ell^2$$

$$\therefore \quad T = 2\pi\sqrt{\frac{\left(\frac{2}{5}mr^2 + m\ell^2\right)}{mg\ell}}$$

2. The time period of a simple pendulum is independent of amplitude, provided it to be small.
   For practical purpose $\theta < 15°$.

3. Second pendulum is one whose time period is 2 s.

So, $$2 = 2\pi\sqrt{\frac{\ell}{g}} \Rightarrow \ell \simeq 1\,m$$

4. If T_0 is the time period of simple pendulum with small amplitude, then time period of the pendulum with large amplitude of oscillation θ will be

$$T = T_0\left(1 + \frac{\theta^2}{16}\right)$$

Here $$T_0 = T_0 = 2\pi\sqrt{\frac{\ell}{g}}$$

$$\therefore \quad T = 2\pi\sqrt{\frac{\ell}{g}}\left(1 + \frac{\theta^2}{16}\right)$$

5. For $\ell = 1m$, $T_0 = 2\,s$. If $\theta = 30° = \frac{\pi}{6}rad,$, then

$$T = 2\left[1 + \frac{(\pi/6)^2}{16}\right]$$

$$= 2.03\,s$$

Time period of simple pendulum when point of suspension is accelerating

Suppose point of suspension is accelerating at an angle β with the vertical. The net force acting on the bob (in accelerating frame)

$$F_{net} = \sqrt{(mg)^2 + (ma)^2 + 2(mg)(ma)\cos\beta}$$

and $$a_{net} = \sqrt{g^2 + a^2 + 2ga\cos\beta}$$

$$\therefore \quad T = 2\pi\sqrt{\frac{\ell}{a_{net}}} = \sqrt{\frac{\ell}{(g^2 + a^2 + 2ga\cos\beta)^{1/2}}}$$

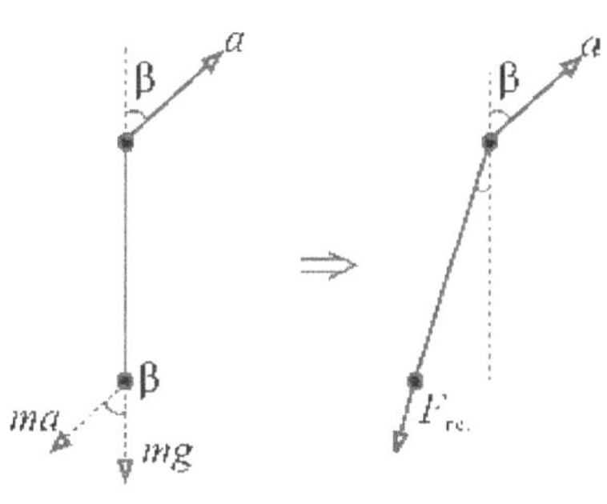

Fig. 4.23

Simple cases :

1.   Acceleration up or retardation down, $\beta = 0$

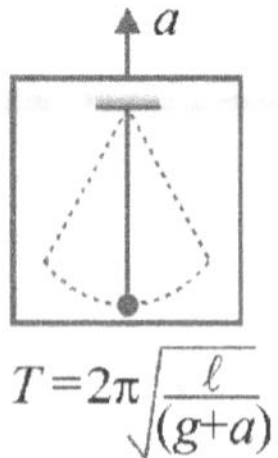

$$T = 2\pi \sqrt{\frac{\ell}{(g+a)}}$$

Fig. 4.24

2.   Acceleration down or retardation up, $\beta = 180°$

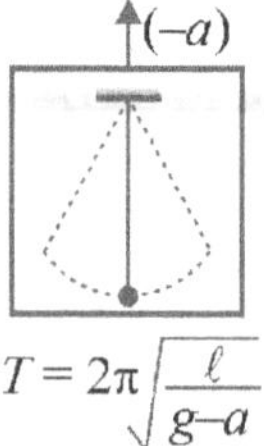

$$T = 2\pi \sqrt{\frac{\ell}{g-a}}$$

Fig. 4.25

3.   Pendulum is accelerating horizontally, $\beta = 90°$

$$\therefore \; a_{net} = \sqrt{g^2 + a^2}$$

$$T = 2\pi \sqrt{\frac{\ell}{g^2 + a^2}}$$

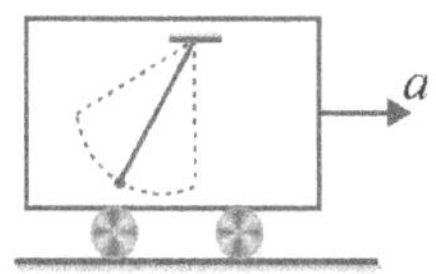

Fig. 4.26

4. $a_{net} = \sqrt{g^2 + (g\sin\theta)^2 + 2g(g\sin\theta)\cos(90° + \theta)}$

$$= g\cos\theta$$

$$T = 2\pi \sqrt{\frac{\ell}{g\cos\theta}}$$

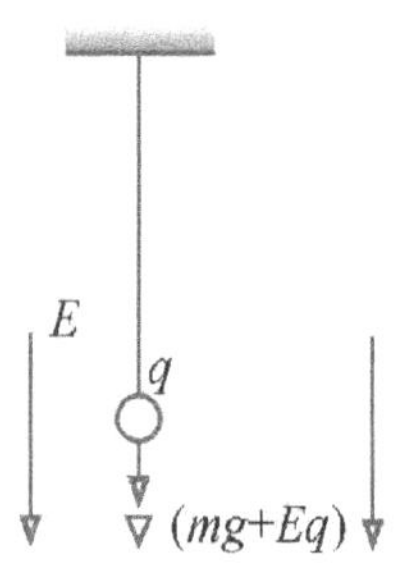

Fig. 4.27

5.   Pendulum is placed in vertical electric field.

The net force on the bob

$$F_{net} = mg + Eq$$

and $a_{net} = \dfrac{F_{net}}{m} = g + \dfrac{Eq}{m}$

$$T = 2\pi \sqrt{\frac{\ell}{\left(g + \dfrac{Eq}{m}\right)}}$$

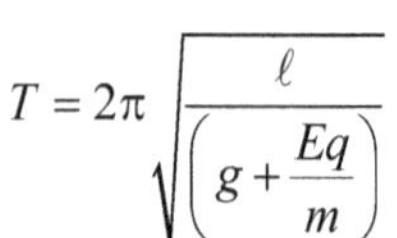

Fig. 4.28

6.   Pendulum is placed in horizontal electric field.

The net force on the bob

$$F_{net} = \sqrt{(mg)^2 + (Eq)^2}$$

and $a_{net} = \dfrac{F_{net}}{m} = \sqrt{g^2 + \left(\dfrac{Eq}{m}\right)^2}$

$$T = 2\pi \sqrt{\frac{\ell}{\sqrt{g^2 + \left(\dfrac{Eq}{m}\right)^2}}}$$

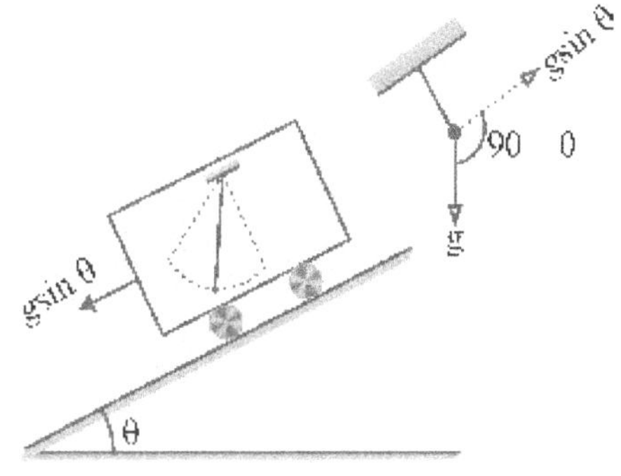

Fig. 4.29

Pendulum of large length but small amplitude

Consider the situation shown in the *Fig. 4.30*, the restoring force acting on the bob

$$F = -mg\sin(\theta + \phi)$$

For small amplitude $\sin(\theta + \phi) \simeq (\theta + \phi)$

$$\therefore \qquad F \simeq -mg\left(\theta+\phi\right)$$

$$\simeq -mg\left(\sin\theta+\sin\phi\right)$$

$$\simeq -mg\left(\frac{x}{\ell}+\frac{x}{R}\right)$$

and

$$\omega = g\left(\frac{1}{\ell}+\frac{1}{R}\right)(-x)$$

Comparing this with standard equation of SHM $a = -\omega^2 x$, we get

$$\omega = \sqrt{g\left(\frac{1}{\ell}+\frac{1}{R}\right)} = \sqrt{\frac{g}{R}\left(1+\frac{R}{\ell}\right)}$$

and

$$T = \frac{2\pi}{\omega} = 2\pi\sqrt{\frac{R}{g\left(1+\dfrac{R}{\ell}\right)}}$$

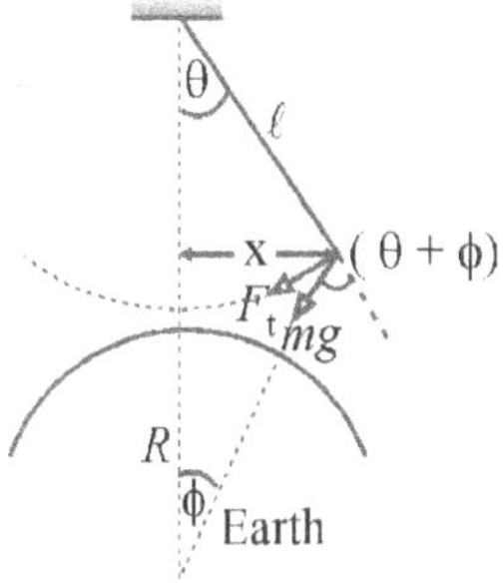

Fig. 4.30

Special cases :

(i) For $\ell = R$,

$$T = 2\pi\sqrt{\frac{R}{2g}}$$

On substituting the value of R and g, we get $T = 59.8$ minute.

(ii) For $\ell \to \infty, \dfrac{R}{\ell} \to 0$,

$$\therefore \qquad T = 2\pi\sqrt{\frac{R}{g}}$$

$$= 84.6 \text{ minute.}$$

Ex. 15 A ball is suspended by a thread of length ℓ at the point O on the wall, forming a small angle α with the vertical. Then the thread with the ball was deviated through a small angle β $(\beta > \alpha)$ and set free. Assuming the collision of the ball against the wall to be perfectly elastic, find the oscillation period of such a pendulum.

Sol. The time period of free oscillations is $T = 2\pi\sqrt{\dfrac{\ell}{g}}$, and $\omega = \sqrt{\dfrac{g}{\ell}}$

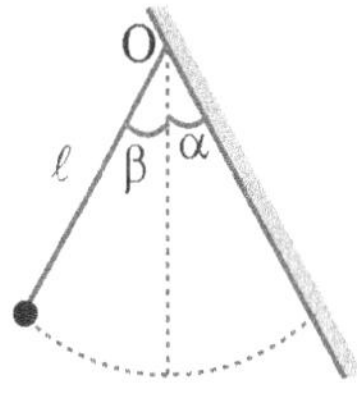

Fig. 4.31

Let t_1 is the time, the ball takes to cover angle β and t_2 is the time to cover angle α.

$$\therefore \qquad T_0 = 2t_1 + 2t_2$$

where

$$t_1 = \frac{T}{4} = \frac{2\pi}{4}\sqrt{\frac{\ell}{g}} = \frac{\pi}{2}\sqrt{\frac{\ell}{g}}$$

We have

$$\theta = \theta_0 \sin\omega t$$

or

$$\alpha = \beta\sin\left(\sqrt{\frac{g}{\ell}}\,t_2\right)$$

or

$$t_2 = \sqrt{\frac{\ell}{g}}\sin^{-1}\left(\frac{\alpha}{\beta}\right)$$

$$\therefore \qquad T_0 = 2\left[\frac{\pi}{2}\sqrt{\frac{\ell}{g}} + \sqrt{\frac{\ell}{g}}\sin^{-1}\left(\frac{\alpha}{\beta}\right)\right]$$

Physical pendulum

Any rigid body suspended from a fixed point constitute a physical pendulum. Consider a body of mass m and its c.m. is at a distance d from the point of suspension.

For small angular displacement θ, restoring torque

$$\tau \;=\; -mg\left(d\,\sin\theta\right)$$

For small amplitude $\sin\theta \simeq \theta$

$$\therefore \qquad \tau \;=\; mg\,d(-\theta)$$

If I is the moment of inertia of the body about point of suspension, then

$$\alpha \;=\; \frac{mgd}{I}\,(-\theta) \to \text{SHM}$$

Comparing this with standard equation of angular SHM, $\alpha = -\omega^2\theta$, we get

$$\omega \;=\; \sqrt{\frac{mgd}{I}}$$

and

$$T \;=\; \frac{2\pi}{\omega} = 2\pi\sqrt{\frac{I}{mgd}}$$

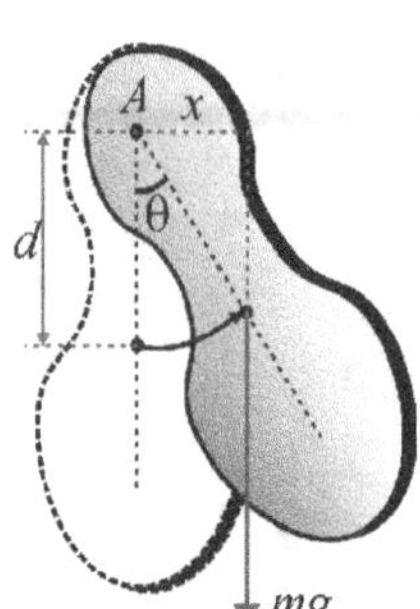

Fig. 4.32

Special cases :

1. For ring, $I = mR^2 + mR^2$
$$= 2mR^2$$

2. For disc, $I = \dfrac{mR^2}{2} + mR^2 = \dfrac{3}{2}mR^2$

3. For rod, $I = \dfrac{m\ell^2}{3}$

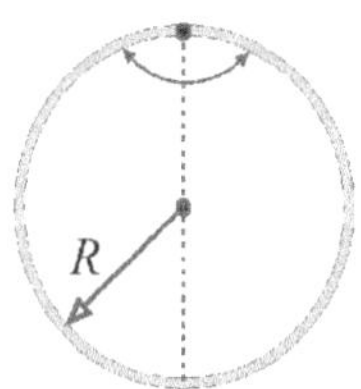

Fig. 4.33

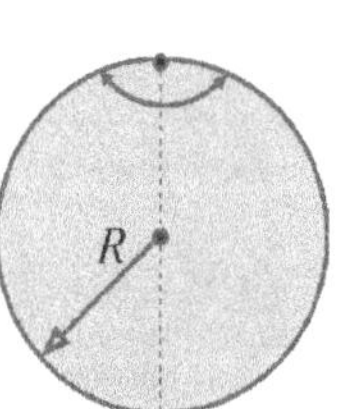

Fig. 4.34

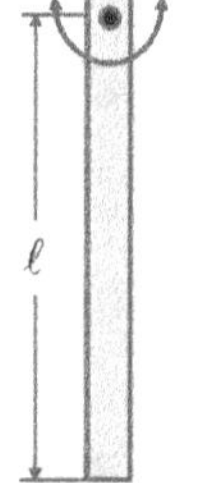

Fig. 4.35

Mass – spring system: Consider a block of mass m is connected to a massless spring of force constant k. The block is displaced slightly from its mean position and left free. It starts oscillating. Find time period of oscillations.

Method I : Dynamical method	**Method II : Energy method**
Displace the block slightly from its mean position, the restoring force on the block	Displace the block slightly from its mean position, the mechanical energy of the system

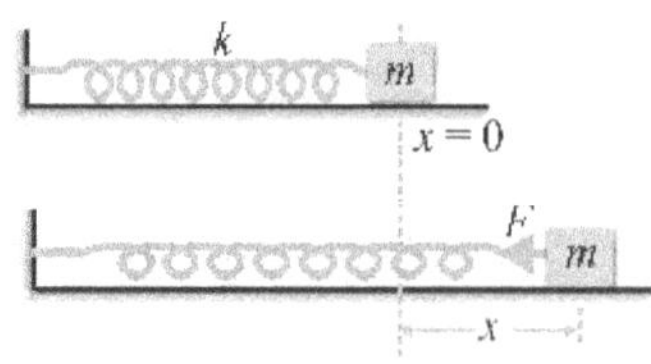

Fig. 4.36

$$F_{\text{rest}} = -k\,x$$

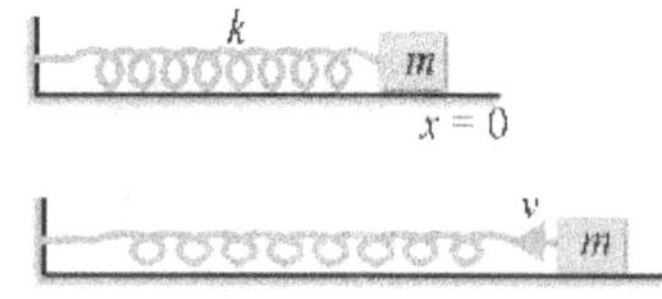

Fig. 4.37

$$E = \frac{1}{2}mv^2 + \frac{1}{2}kx^2$$

$$a = \frac{k}{m}(-x)$$

Compare with $a = -\omega^2 x$

$$\omega = \sqrt{\frac{k}{m}}$$

and $T = \dfrac{2\pi}{\omega} = 2\pi\sqrt{\dfrac{m}{k}}$

For free oscillations, $\dfrac{dE}{dt} = 0$

or $\dfrac{d}{dt}\left(\dfrac{1}{2}mv^2 + \dfrac{1}{2}kx^2\right) = 0$

or $\dfrac{m}{2} \times 2v \times \dfrac{dv}{dt} + \dfrac{k}{2} \times 2x \times \dfrac{dx}{dt} = 0$

or $m\dfrac{dv}{dt} + kx = 0$ or $a = \dfrac{k}{m}(-x)$

Comparing with $a = -\omega^2 x$, we get

$$\omega = \sqrt{\frac{k}{m}} \quad \text{and} \quad T = \frac{2\pi}{\omega} = 2\pi\sqrt{\frac{m}{k}}$$

Oscillation of block in vertical direction

When spring held vertical and block is attached to its lower end. At mean position of the block $ky_0 = mg$, (fig. 4.38)

where y_0 is the extension of the spring from its unstretched position. Now displaces the block slightly from its mean position, the restoring force

$$F = -[k(y + y_0) - mg]$$

As

$$ky_0 = mg$$

$$\therefore \quad F = -ky$$

and acceleration

$$a = \frac{F}{m} = -\frac{k}{m}y$$

Comparing this with standard equation of SHM, we get

$$\omega = \sqrt{\frac{k}{m}} \quad \text{and} \quad T = 2\pi\sqrt{\frac{m}{k}}$$

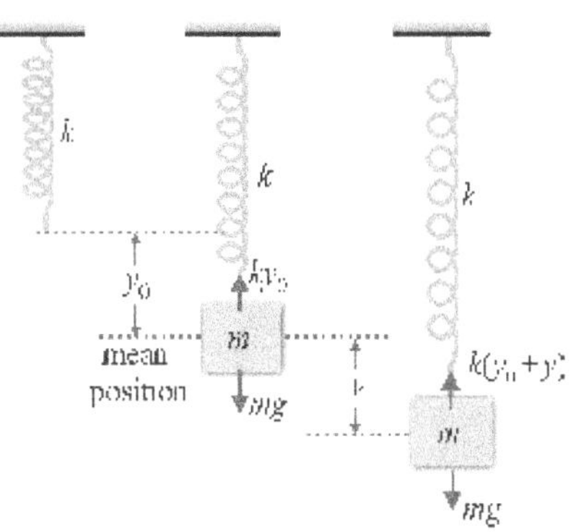

Fig. 4.38

Note:

1. The following devices have same time period of $T = 2\pi\sqrt{\dfrac{m}{k}}$

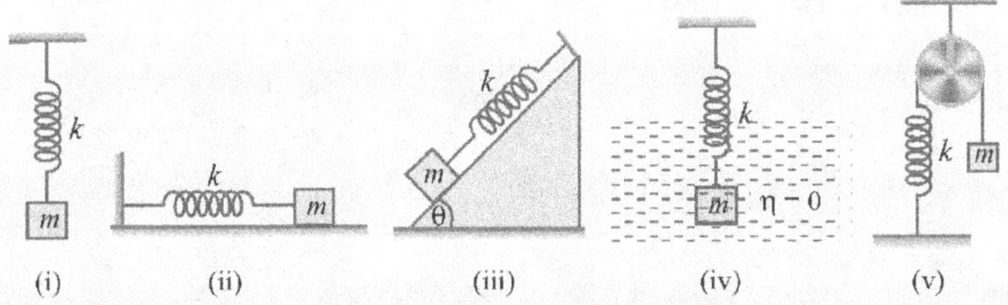

2. The following devices have same time period of $T = 2\pi\sqrt{R/g}$.

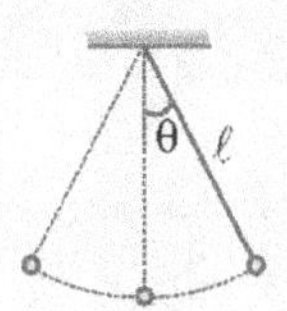
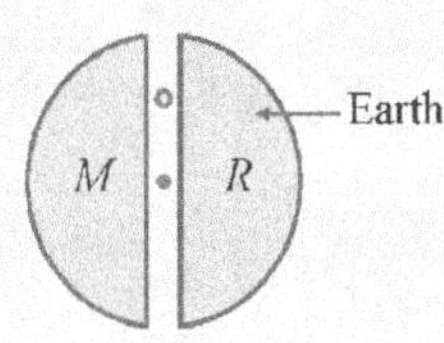

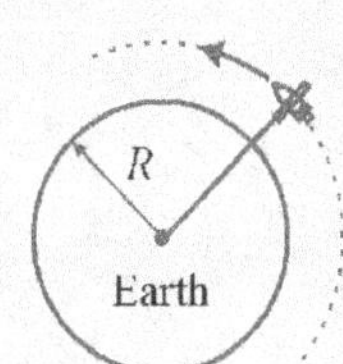

(i) A pendulum of infinite length

(ii) A pendulum of infinite length

(ii) A satellite revolves near the earth surface

Ex. 16 Find the time period of simple pendulum when it oscillates in a non-viscous liquid of density ρ.

Sol.   The bob of the pendulum experiences buoyant force due to liquid $= V\rho g$, in addition to gravitational force.

Thus net force on the bob $= (mg - V\rho g)$

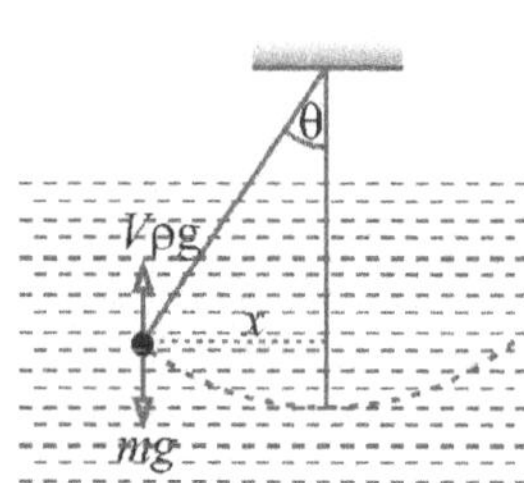

Fig. 4.39

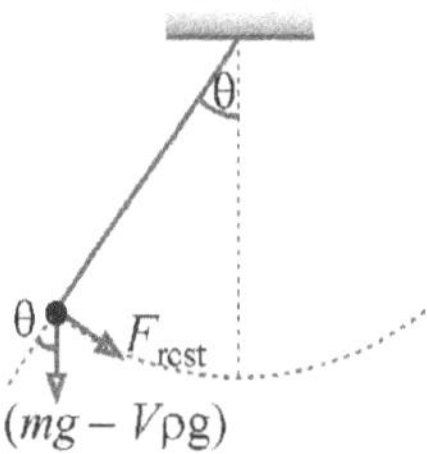

Fig. 4.40

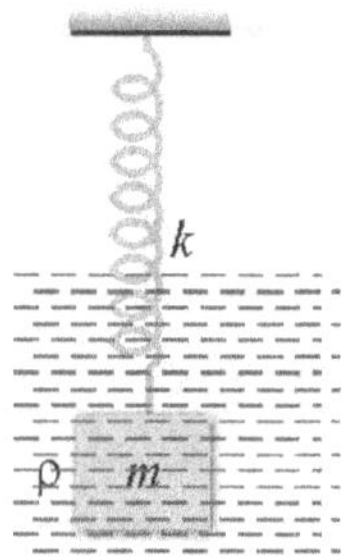

Fig. 4.41

For small displacement x of the bob, restoring force

$$F_{rest} = (mg - V\rho g) \sin\theta$$

$$= -(mg - V\rho g)\frac{x}{\ell}$$

and acceleration $= -\left(g - \dfrac{V\rho g}{m}\right)\dfrac{x}{\ell}$

On comparing with standard equation

of SHM, $a = -\omega^2 x$, we get

$$\omega = \sqrt{\frac{\left(g - \dfrac{V\rho g}{m}\right)}{\ell}}$$

and $T = 2\pi \sqrt{\dfrac{\ell}{\left(g - \dfrac{V\rho g}{m}\right)}}$

When the block oscillates all the time inside liquid, the restoring force on the block for small displacement y, will be

$$F_{rest} = -ky$$

and acceleration $a = \dfrac{k}{m}(-y)$

On comparing with standard equation

of SHM, $a = \omega^2 y$, we get $\omega = \sqrt{\dfrac{k}{m}}$

and $T = \dfrac{2\pi}{\omega} = 2\pi\sqrt{\dfrac{m}{k}}$

Ex. 17 A long rod of mass m and cross-sectional area A is connected to a spring of force constant k. The rod is partially submerged in a non-viscous liquid of density ρ. Find time period of oscillations of the rod.

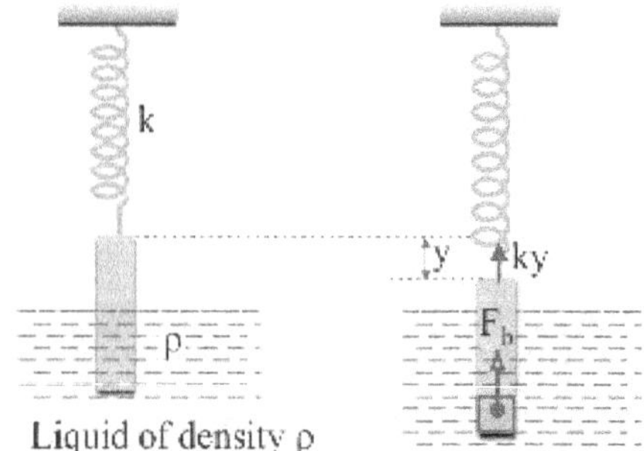

Fig. 4.42   **Fig. 4.43**

Sol.

Let rod is displaced down by y. The restoring force on the rod

$$F_{rest} = -\begin{bmatrix} \text{The force exerted by spring} \\ + \text{buoyant force on the} \\ \text{shaded portion of the rod} \end{bmatrix}$$

$$= -\left[ky + (Ay)\rho g\right]$$

and acceleration of the rod,

$$a = \frac{F_{rest}}{m} = \frac{k + A\rho g}{m}(-y)$$

Now comparing this with standard equation of SHM, we get

$$\omega = \sqrt{\frac{k + A\rho g}{m}} \quad \text{and} \quad T = \frac{2\pi}{\omega} = 2\pi\sqrt{\frac{m}{(k + A\rho g)}} \qquad \textit{Ans.}$$

Combinations of springs

1. **Series combination:** When springs are connected in series and force F is applied at the free end of the last spring, the each spring experiences the same force. Let y_1 and y_2 are the extensions of the springs of force constants k_1 and k_2, then total extension

$$y = y_1 + y_2$$

Here $y_1 = \dfrac{F}{k_1}$ and $y_2 = \dfrac{F}{k_2}$

For the equivalent spring of force constant k, we have $y = \dfrac{F}{k}$

$\therefore$ $\qquad \dfrac{F}{k} = \dfrac{F}{k_1} + \dfrac{F}{k_2}$

or $\qquad \dfrac{1}{k} = \dfrac{1}{k_1} + \dfrac{1}{k_2}$

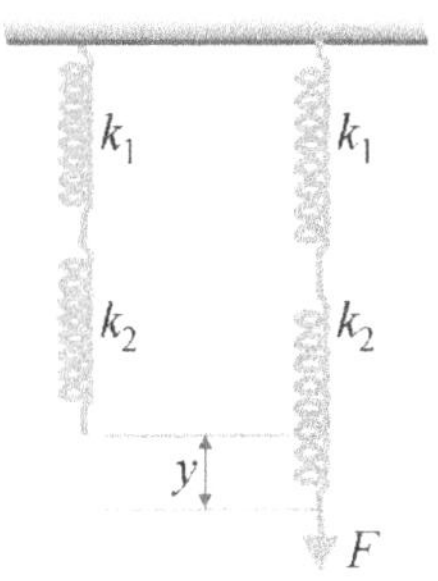

Fig. 4.44

2. **Parallel combination:** When springs are connected in parallel and force F is applied at the free ends of the springs together, the each spring extends by equal amount. If F_1 and F_2 are the forces in springs of force constants k_1 and k_2, then $F = F_1 + F_2$

Here $F_1 = k_1 y$ and $F_2 = k_2 y$

For equivalent spring of force constant k, we have

$$F = ky$$

$\therefore$ $\qquad ky = k_1 y + k_2 y$

or $\qquad k = k_1 + k_2$

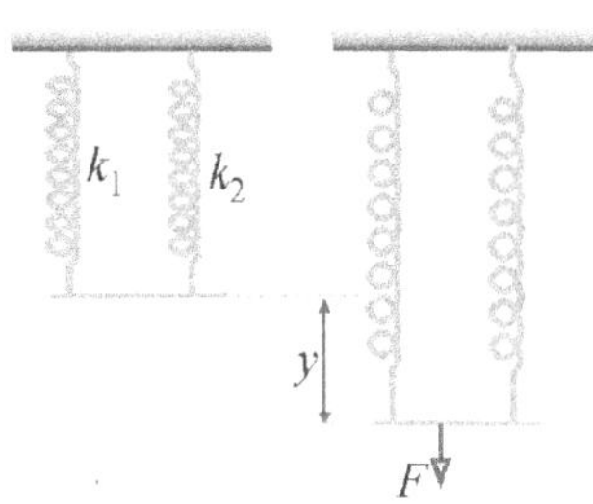

Fig. 4.45

Ex. 18 A spring balance has a scale that reads 0 to 50 kg. The length of the scale is 20cm. A body suspended from this spring, when displaced and released, oscillates with a period of 0.60s. What is the weight of the body?

Sol. Force constant of the spring,

$$k = \frac{Mg}{x} = \frac{50 \times 9.8}{0.20} = 2450 \, N/m$$

The time period of oscillations is given by $T = 2\pi \sqrt{\dfrac{M}{k}}$

$\therefore$ $\qquad M = \dfrac{T^2 k}{4\pi^2} = \dfrac{(0.60)^2 \times 2450}{4\pi^2}$

$\qquad\qquad = 22.36 \, kg$

Weight of the body $= Mg = 22.36 \times 9.8$

$\qquad\qquad = 219.13 \, N$ $\qquad\qquad$ *Ans.*

Ex. 19 A tray of mass 12 kg is supported by two identical springs as shown in the *Fig. 4.46*. When the tray is pressed down slightly and released, it executes SHM with a time period of 1.5s. What is the force constant of each spring? When a block of mass M is placed on the tray, the period of SHM changes to 3.0 s. What is the mass of the block?

Fig. 4.46

Sol. Let k be the force constant of each spring. The equivalent force constant $k' = 2k$

The time period $\qquad T = 2\pi \sqrt{\dfrac{m}{k'}}$ $\qquad$ ......(i)

or $\qquad k' = \dfrac{4\pi^2 m}{T^2}$

$\qquad\qquad = \dfrac{4\pi^2 \times 12}{(1.5)^2} = 210.34 \, N/m$

$\therefore$ $\qquad k = \dfrac{k'}{2} = 105.17 \, \dfrac{N}{m}$ $\qquad$ *Ans.*

When the block of mass M is placed in the tray, the period of oscillation becomes.

$$T' = 2\pi\sqrt{\frac{(M+m)}{k'}} \qquad ...(ii)$$

Dividing equation (ii) by (i), we have

$$\frac{T'}{T} = \sqrt{\frac{M+m}{m}}$$

or $$\left(\frac{3.0}{1.5}\right)^2 = \frac{M+m}{m}$$

or $$4 = \frac{M+12}{12}$$

$$\therefore \qquad M = 36\,\text{kg} \qquad \qquad \textit{Ans.}$$

Ex. 20 A simple pendulum of length ℓ and having a bob of mass M is suspended in a car. The car is moving on a circular track of radius R with a uniform speed v. If the pendulum makes small oscillations in a radial direction about its equilibrium position, what will be its time period?

Sol. The net acceleration of the bob

$$a_{net} = \sqrt{g^2 + a_c^2}$$

where $$a_c = \frac{v^2}{R}$$

$$\therefore \qquad a_{net} = \sqrt{g^2 + \left(\frac{v^2}{R}\right)^2} = \sqrt{g^2 + \frac{v^4}{R^2}}$$

The period of simple pendulum

$$T = 2\pi\sqrt{\frac{\ell}{a_{net}}}$$

$$= 2\pi\sqrt{\frac{\ell}{\left(g^2 + \frac{v^4}{R^2}\right)^{\frac{1}{2}}}} \qquad \textit{Ans.}$$

Ex. 21 A pendulum clock shows accurate time. If the length increases by 0.1%, deduce the error in time per day.

Sol. If ℓ is the length of the pendulum, then

$$\frac{\Delta\ell}{\ell}\times 100 = 0.1.$$

Time period of simple pendulum

$$T = 2\pi\sqrt{\frac{\ell}{g}} = 2\pi\frac{\ell^{1/2}}{g^{1/2}}$$

If ΔT is the small change in time period due to small change in length $\Delta\ell$ of the pendulum, then

$$\frac{\Delta T}{T}\times 100 = \frac{1}{2}\left(\frac{\Delta\ell}{\ell}\times 100\right)$$

Given $T = 1 \times 24 \times 60 \times 60 = 86400$ s

$$\therefore \qquad \frac{\Delta T}{86400}\times 100 = \frac{1}{2}\times 0.1$$

$$\therefore \qquad \Delta T = 43.2\text{s}$$

As time period of the clock increases, so it will loss time by 43.2 s per day.

Ex. 22 A spring of force constant k is cut into n equal parts. If force constant of each part is k', then find k'.

Sol. With decrease in length of the spring force constant increases,

$$k \propto \frac{1}{\ell}.$$

If ℓ' is the length of each part, then

$$\ell' = \frac{\ell}{n}$$

$$\therefore \qquad \frac{k'}{k} = \frac{\ell}{\ell'} = n$$

or $$k' = nk. \qquad \qquad \textit{Ans.}$$

Ex. 23 If a spring of force constant k is cut into two parts, such that one part is twice in length of the other part. Find force constant of each part.

Sol. Suppose the length of the parts are ℓ_1 and ℓ_2 then

$$\ell_1 = 2\ell_2 \qquad ...(i)$$

Also $$\ell_1 + \ell_2 = \ell \qquad ...(ii)$$

Solving (i) and (ii), we get $\ell_1 = 2\dfrac{\ell}{3}$ and $\ell_2 = \dfrac{\ell}{3}$

$$\therefore \quad k_1 = \frac{k}{2/3} = \frac{3k}{2} \text{ and } k_2 = \frac{k}{1/3} = 3k \qquad \textit{Ans.}$$

Ex. 24 Find the time period of the block-springs system shown in the figure 4.49.

Sol.

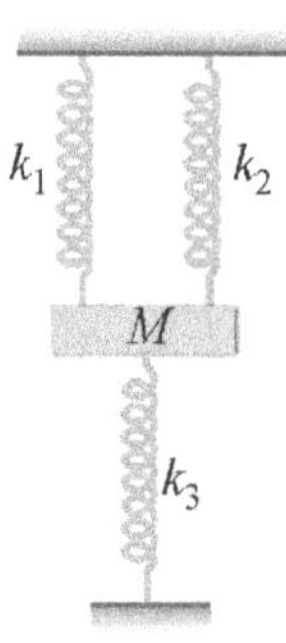

Fig. 4.47

The effective value of force constant

$$k = k_1 + k_2 + k_3$$

Time period $$T = 2\pi\sqrt{\frac{M}{k}}$$

or $$T = 2\pi\sqrt{\frac{M}{(k_1 + k_2 + k_3)}} \qquad \textit{Ans.}$$

Ex. 25 A block of mass m is connected to three springs as shown in the *Fig. 4.48, 4.49* . The block is displaced down slightly and left free, it starts oscillating. Find time period of oscillations.

Sol. Let block is displaced down slightly (y) from its mean position. The extension of the side springs $y' = y\cos\theta$ each. Thus

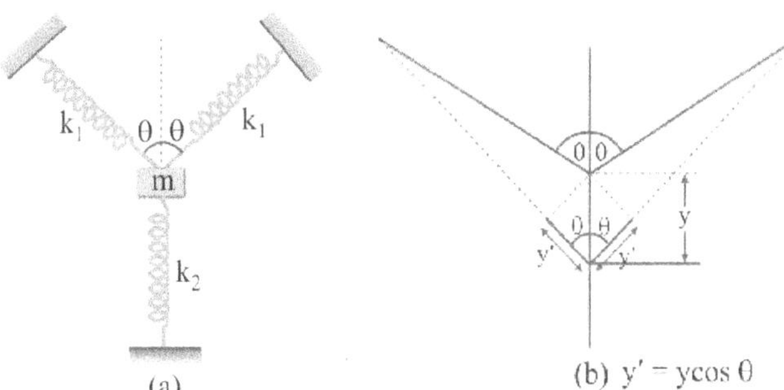

(a)

(b) $y' = y\cos\theta$

Fig. 4.48   *Fig. 4.49*

restoring force on the block

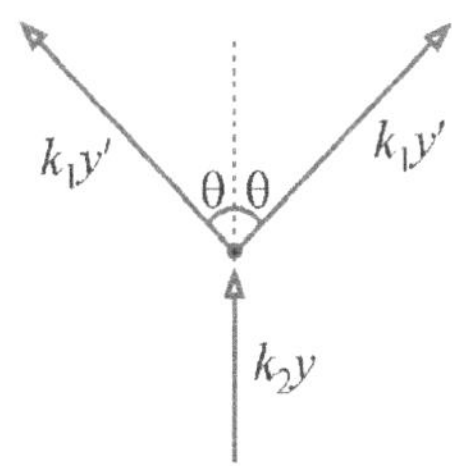

Fig. 4.50

$$F_{rest} = -(2k_1 y'\cos\theta + k_2 y)$$

$$= -\left[2k_1(y\cos\theta)\cos\theta + k_2 y\right]$$

$$= \left(2k_1\cos^2\theta + k_2\right)(-y)$$

and

$$a = \frac{\left(2k_1\cos^2\theta + k_2\right)}{m}(-y)$$

Comparing with standard equation of SHM, we get

$$\omega = \sqrt{\frac{2k_1\cos^2\theta + k_2}{m}}$$

and

$$T = 2\pi\sqrt{\frac{m}{\left(2k_1\cos^2\theta + k_2\right)}} \qquad Ans.$$

Ex. 26 A small block is connected to a massless rod, which in terns attached to a spring of force constant k as shown in *Fig. 4.53*. The block is displaced down slightly, and left free. Find time period of oscillations.

Sol.

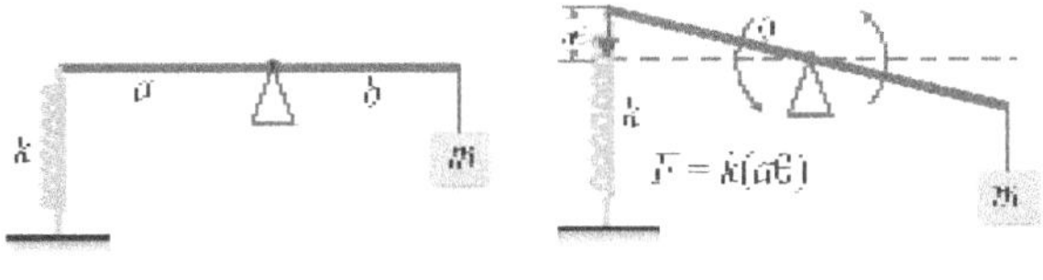

Fig. 4.51   *Fig. 4.52*

Let angular displacement of the block is θ , then extension of the spring will be a θ . If F is the force in the spring, then restoring torque,

$$\tau_{rest} = -Fa$$

$$= -k(a\theta)\times a \qquad [F = kx = ka\theta]$$

and

$$\alpha = \frac{\tau_{rest}}{I} = \frac{ka^2}{I}(-\theta)$$

Now comparing with $\alpha = -\omega^2\theta$, we get

$$\omega = \sqrt{\frac{ka^2}{I}} \text{ and } T = 2\pi\sqrt{\frac{I}{ka^2}}$$

Here

$$I = mb^2$$

$$\therefore \qquad T = 2\pi\sqrt{\frac{mb^2}{ka^2}}$$

$$= 2\pi\frac{b}{a}\sqrt{\frac{m}{k}} \qquad Ans.$$

Ex. 27 In *Fig. 4.53*, the spring has a force constant k. The pulley is light and smooth, the spring and string are light. The suspended block has a mass m kg. If the block is slightly displaced vertically down from its equilibrium position and released, find the period of its vertical oscillations.

Sol. Let the block is displaced down a small displacement y. The corresponding extension of the spring will be $\dfrac{y}{2}$. The extra force developed in the spring is $\dfrac{ky}{2}$. If T be the tension in the string, then

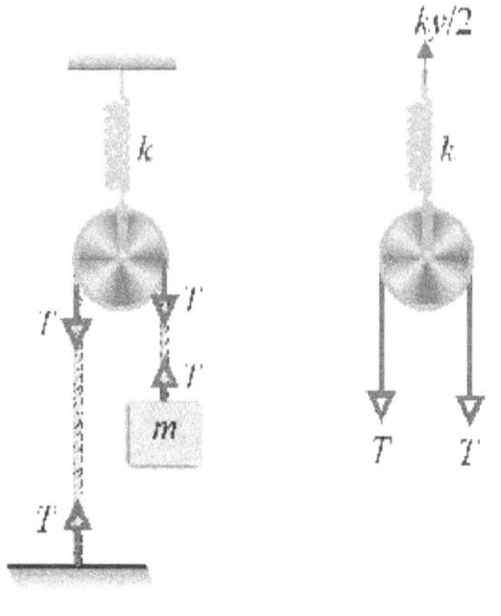

Fig. 4.53   *Fig. 4.54*

$$2T = \frac{ky}{2}$$

or

$$T = \frac{ky}{4}$$

The restoring force on the block $F_{rest} = -T$

$$= \frac{-ky}{4}$$

and

$$a = \frac{F_{rest}}{m} = \frac{k}{4m}(-y)$$

As force is proportional to the displacement from mean position, so it represents SHM. Compare this with standard equation of SHM, $a = -\omega^2 y$, we get

$$\omega = \sqrt{\frac{k}{4m}}$$

and time period $T = \dfrac{2\pi}{\omega} = 2\pi\sqrt{\dfrac{4m}{k}}$.   **Ans.**

Note:

The expression $T = 2\pi\sqrt{\dfrac{4m}{k}}$ can be written as $T = 2\pi\sqrt{\dfrac{m}{k_e}}$, where $k_e = \dfrac{k}{4}$. The given device is equivalent to a block of mass m connected to a spring of force constant k_e.

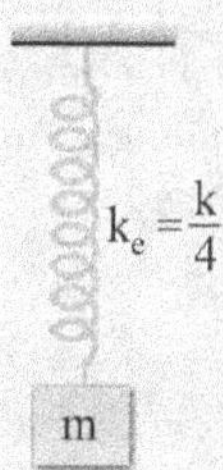

Fig. 4.55

Ex. 28   In the *Fig. 4.56* the spring has a force constant k. The pulley is light and smooth. The spring and string are light. The suspended block has a mass m kg. If the block is displaced down slightly and released, find the time period of oscillations.

Sol. Let block is displaced down by y. The corresponding extension of the spring will be $2y$. The extra force developed in the spring is $2ky$. If T is the tension in the string, then

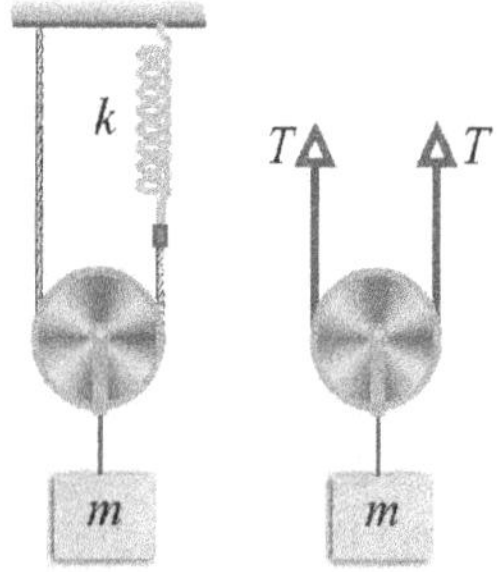

Fig. 4.56   Fig. 4.57

$$T = 2ky$$

The restoring force on the block

$$F_{rest} = 2T$$
$$= -2(2ky) = -4ky$$

and the acceleration of the block

$$a = \frac{F_{rest}}{m} = \frac{4k}{m}(-y)$$

As force acting on the block is proportional to the displacement from mean position, so it will represent SHM. Comparing this with standard equation of SHM, $a = -\omega^2 y$, we get

$$\omega = \sqrt{\frac{4k}{m}}$$

and time period $T = \dfrac{2\pi}{\omega} = 2\pi\sqrt{\dfrac{m}{4k}}$ **Ans.**

Note:

The expression $T = 2\pi\sqrt{\dfrac{m}{4k}}$ **can be written as,** $T = 2\pi\sqrt{\dfrac{m}{k_e}}$, **where** $k_e = 4k$. **Thus the given device is equivalent to a block of mass m connected to a spring of force constant** k_e.

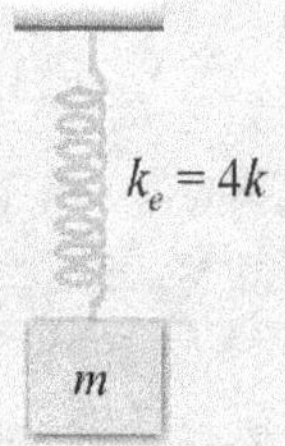

Fig. 4.58

Ex. 29   A block of mass m is attached to one end of a light inextensible string passing over a smooth light pulley A and under another smooth light pulley B as shown in *Fig. 4.59*. The other end of a string is fixed to a ceiling. A and B are held by springs of force constants k_1 and k_2. Find time period of small oscillations of the system.

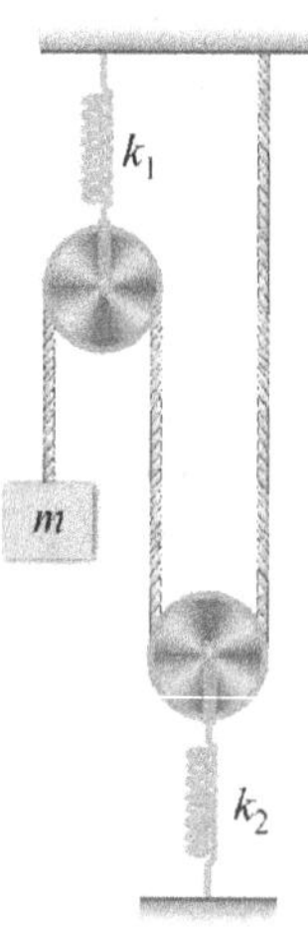

Fig. 4.59

Sol. The given system is equivalent to a system shown in *Fig. 4.60*.

Here $\qquad k'_1 = \dfrac{k_1}{4}$ and $k'_2 = \dfrac{k_2}{4}$

The equivalent force constant

$$k = \frac{k'_1 k'_2}{k'_1 + k'_2} = \frac{\dfrac{k_1}{4} \times \dfrac{k_2}{4}}{\dfrac{k_1}{4} + \dfrac{k_2}{4}}$$

$$= \frac{k_1 k_2}{4(k_1 + k_2)}$$

The time period of equivalent system is given by

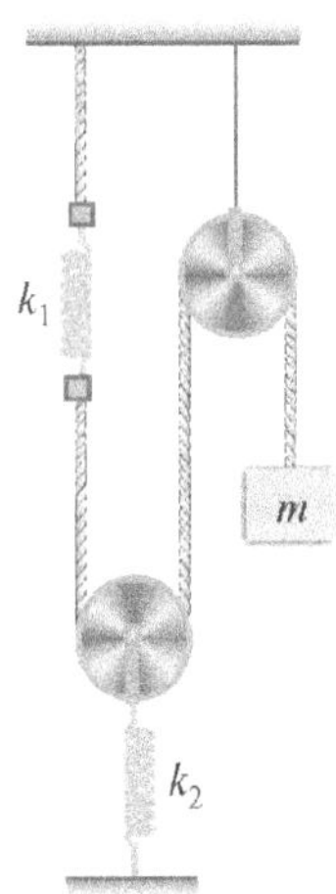

Fig. 4.60

$$T = 2\pi \sqrt{\frac{m}{k}}$$

$$= \frac{2\pi}{\sqrt{\dfrac{m}{\dfrac{k_1 k_2}{4(k_1 + k_2)}}}} = 2\pi \sqrt{\frac{4m(k_1 + k_2)}{k_1 k_2}}$$

$$= 4\pi \sqrt{\frac{m(k_1 + k_2)}{k_1 k_2}} \qquad \textit{Ans.}$$

<u>**Ex. 30**</u> I n the device shown in *Fig. 4.61*, the block m is displaced down slightly and released, it starts oscillating. Pulleys are smooth and massless, string and springs are also massless. Find time period of oscillations.

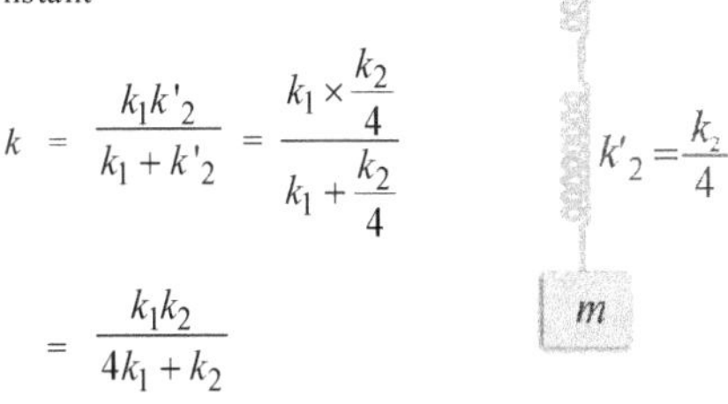

Fig. 4.61

Sol. The given device is equivalent to a device shown in *Fig. 4.62*. In this equivalent device, the spring k_2 is replaced by a spring of force constant k'_2 which is equal to $\dfrac{k_2}{4}$.

The equivalent force constant

$$k = \frac{k_1 k'_2}{k_1 + k'_2} = \frac{k_1 \times \dfrac{k_2}{4}}{k_1 + \dfrac{k_2}{4}}$$

$$= \frac{k_1 k_2}{4k_1 + k_2}$$

Fig. 4.62

The time period of the oscillations of the block is given by

$$T = 2\pi \sqrt{\frac{m}{k}}$$

$$= 2\pi \sqrt{\left(\frac{m}{\dfrac{k_1 k_2}{4k_1 + k_2}} \right)}$$

$$= 2\pi \sqrt{\frac{m(4k_1 + k_2)}{k_1 k_2}} \qquad \textit{Ans.}$$

<u>**Ex. 31**</u> **A block of mass *M* is attached to a spring of mass *m* and force constant *k*. Find time period of oscillation of the block-spring system.**

Sol. Suppose the length of the spring is ℓ. The mass per unit length of the spring is $\dfrac{m}{\ell}$ and the mass of an element of length $d\ell$ will be $\dfrac{m}{\ell} d\ell$. Let at a given instant, the velocity of the end *A* of the spring (and therefore also of the block) be v.

The velocity of the different element of the spring decreases linearly from v to 0 from end *A* to *B*. The velocity of the element $v_x = \dfrac{v}{\ell}(\ell - x)$

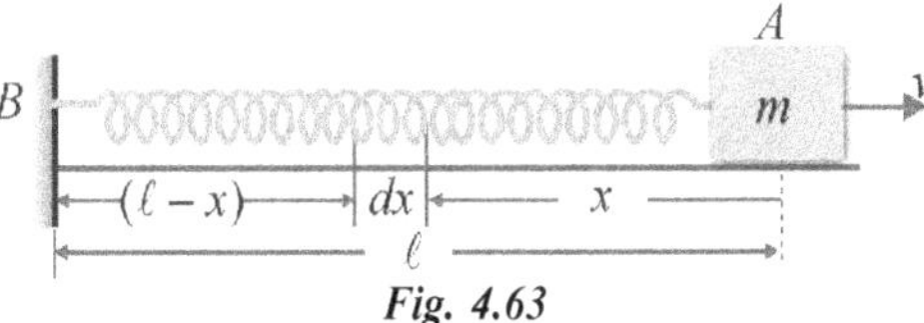

Fig. 4.63

The kinetic energy of the element $dK = \dfrac{1}{2}(dm)v_x^2$

The kinetic energy of the whole spring

$$K = \int_0^\ell \frac{1}{2}(dm)v_x^2 = \frac{1}{2}\int_0^\ell \left(\frac{m}{\ell} dx\right)\left(\frac{v}{\ell}(\ell - x)\right)^2$$

$$= \frac{1}{6}mv^2$$

The mechanical energy of the oscillating system
$\qquad$ E = K.E. of the block + K.E.of the spring + P.E. of the spring.

$$\text{or} \qquad E = \frac{1}{2}Mv^2 + \frac{1}{6}mv^2 + \frac{1}{2}kx^2$$

Energy E of the oscillating body remain constant, so

$$\frac{dE}{dt} = 0$$

$$\text{or} \qquad \frac{d}{dt}\left[\frac{1}{2}Mv^2 + \frac{1}{6}mv^2 + \frac{1}{2}kx^2\right] = 0$$

$$\text{or} \qquad \frac{M}{2} \times 2v \times \frac{dv}{dt} + \frac{m}{6} \times 2v \frac{dv}{dt} + \frac{k}{2} \times 2x \frac{dx}{dt} = 0$$

$$\text{or} \qquad \left(M + \frac{m}{3}\right)\frac{dv}{dt} = -kx$$

$$\text{or} \qquad \frac{dv}{dt} = \frac{k}{\left(M + \dfrac{m}{3}\right)}(-x)$$

Now compare the above expression, with standard equation of SHM,

$a = -\omega^2 x$, we get

$$\omega = \sqrt{\dfrac{k}{\left(M + \dfrac{m}{3}\right)}}$$

and
$$T = 2\pi\sqrt{\dfrac{\left(M + \dfrac{m}{3}\right)}{k}}$$
Ans.

4.6 COUPLED OSCILLATOR

A system of two bodies connected by a spring so that both are free to oscillate simple harmonically along the length of the spring constitutes a coupled oscillator. (*Fig. 4.64*) Let us consider a two-body oscillator consisting of two blocks of masses m_1 and m_2, connected by a horizontal massless spring of force constant k, so as free to oscillate along the length of the spring on a smooth horizontal surface. Suppose the unstretched length of the spring be ℓ_0 and let at any given instant, the coordinates of the two ends of the spring (the position of blocks) are as shown. Then, clearly extension of the spring

$x = (x_2 - x_1) - \ell_0$

As length of the spring ℓ_0 is constant, so

$$\frac{d^2 x}{dt^2} = \frac{d^2 (x_2 - x_1)}{dt^2}.$$

The force F exerted by the spring on the two blocks are equal and opposite. Thus if $\dfrac{d^2 x_1}{dt^2}$ be the acceleration of the block m_1, then

$$m_1 \frac{d^2 x_1}{dt^2} = +kx \qquad \text{...(i)}$$

Similarly for block m_2,

$$m_2 \frac{d^2 x_2}{dt^2} = -kx \qquad \text{...(ii)}$$

Multiplying equation (i) by m_2 and equation (ii) by m_1 and then subtracting equation (i) from equation (ii), we get

$$\left(\frac{m_1 m_2}{m_1 + m_2}\right) \frac{d^2}{dt^2}(x_2 - x_1) = -kx$$

Substituting $\left(\dfrac{m_1 m_2}{m_1 + m_2}\right) = \mu$, the reduced or effective mass of the system, we get

$$\mu \frac{d^2 x}{dt^2} = -kx$$

or
$$\frac{d^2 x}{dt^2} = \frac{k}{\mu}(-x) \qquad \text{...(iii)}$$

Now compare equation (iii) with standard equation of SHM $a = -\omega^2 x$, we get

$$\omega = \sqrt{\frac{k}{\mu}}$$

and
$$T = \frac{2\pi}{\omega} = 2\pi\sqrt{\frac{\mu}{k}}$$

The two-body oscillator is equivalent to a single body oscillator with a reduced mass μ.

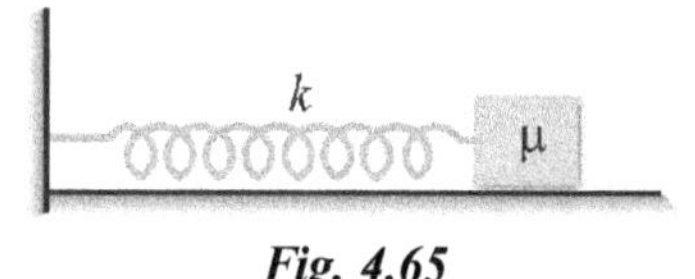

Fig. 4.65

Fig. 4.64

Ex. 32 Find time period of the oscillations of the devices shown in the figure.

Sol.

Reduced mass of the system

$$\mu = \left(\frac{mM}{m+M}\right)$$

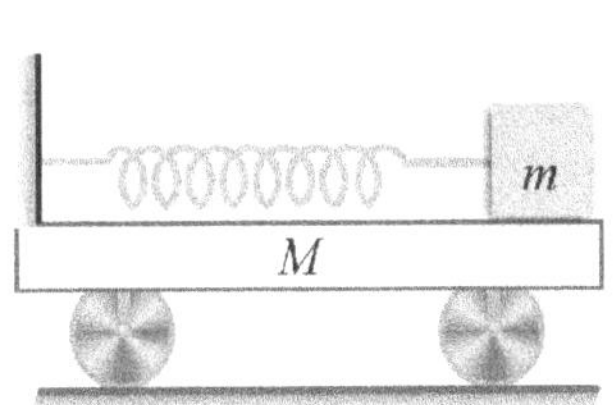

Fig. 4.66

$$\therefore \quad T = 2\pi\sqrt{\frac{\mu}{k}}$$

Reduced mass of the system

$$\mu = \frac{mm}{m+m} = \frac{m}{2}$$

and $\quad k_e = k + k = 2k$

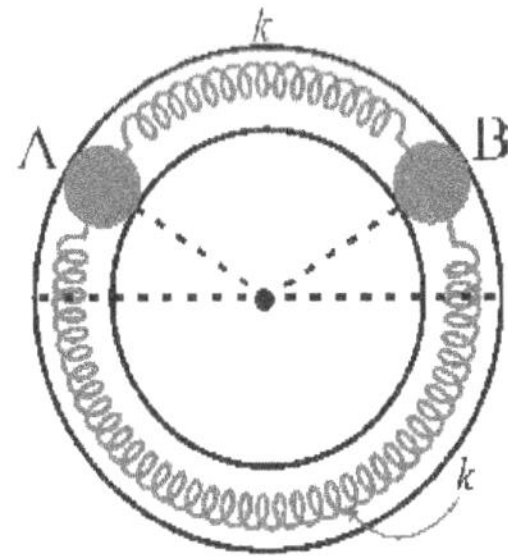

Fig. 4.67

$$\therefore \quad T = 2\pi\sqrt{\frac{\mu}{k_e}}$$

Ex. 33 The pulley shown in *Fig. 4.70* has a moment of inertia I about its axis and mass m. Find time period of vertical oscillations of its centre of mass. The spring has spring constant k and the spring does not slip over the pulley.

Sol.

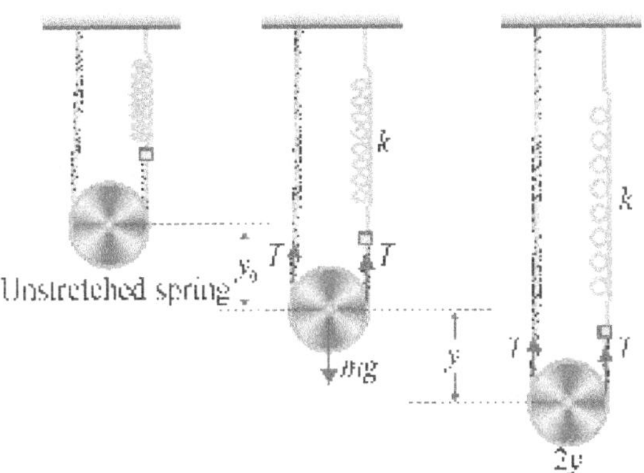

Fig. 4.68

Let at mean position, the extension of the spring is y_0, so force in the spring and string will be $T = ky_0$. For the equilibrium of the pulley, $2T = mg$

or $\qquad 2(ky_0) = mg \Rightarrow y_0 = \dfrac{mg}{2k}$

Let the centre of pulley now displaced down by y from mean position. The extension in the spring will be $2y$. Total extension of the spring becomes $(y_0 + 2y)$.

The total mechanical energy of the system is (with reference to mean position)

$$E = \frac{1}{2}mv^2 + \frac{1}{2}I\omega^2 - mgy + \frac{1}{2}k\left(y_0 + 2y\right)^2$$

or $\qquad E = \dfrac{1}{2}mv^2 + \dfrac{1}{2}I\omega^2 - mgy + \dfrac{1}{2}k\left(\dfrac{mg}{2k} + 2y\right)^2$

Here, $\qquad \omega = \dfrac{v}{r}$

$$\therefore \quad E = \frac{1}{2}mv^2 + \frac{1}{2}I\left(\frac{v}{r}\right)^2 - mgy + \frac{1}{2}k\left(\frac{mg}{2k} + 2y\right)^2$$

$$= \frac{1}{2}\left(m + \frac{I}{r^2}\right)v^2 - mgy + \frac{1}{2}k\left(\frac{mg}{2k} + 2y\right)^2$$

Since mechanical energy of oscillating body remain constant,

$$\therefore \qquad \frac{dE}{dt} = 0$$

or $\quad \dfrac{d}{dt}\left[\dfrac{1}{2}\left(m + \dfrac{I}{r^2}\right)v^2 - mgy + \dfrac{1}{2}k\left(\dfrac{mg}{2k} + 2y\right)^2\right] = 0$

or $\quad \left(m + \dfrac{I}{r^2}\right)v\dfrac{dv}{dt} - mg\left(\dfrac{dy}{dt}\right) + \dfrac{k}{2} \times 2\left(\dfrac{mg}{2k} + 2y\right) \times 2\dfrac{dy}{dt} = 0$

or $\quad \left(m + \dfrac{I}{r^2}\right)v\dfrac{dv}{dt} - mgv + k\left(\dfrac{mg}{2k} + 2y\right) \times 2v = 0$

or $\quad \left(m + \dfrac{I}{r^2}\right)\dfrac{dv}{dt} + 4ky = 0$

or $\qquad \dfrac{dv}{dt} = \dfrac{4k}{\left(m + \dfrac{I}{r^2}\right)}(-y)$

Now comparing the above equation with standard equation of SHM, $a = -\omega^2 y$, we get

$$\omega = \sqrt{\frac{4k}{\left(m + \dfrac{I}{r^2}\right)}}$$

and $\qquad T = \dfrac{2\pi}{\omega} = 2\pi\sqrt{\dfrac{m + \dfrac{I}{r^2}}{4k}}$

Short-cut method: When centre of the pulley is displaced y from mean position, the spring will be stretched by $2y$. So the force in the spring and string will be $2ky$.

$$\therefore \quad (\text{Total inertia}) \times a = -4ky$$

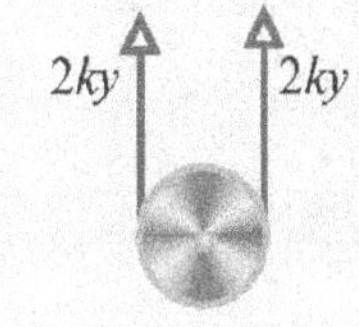

Fig. 4.69

where total inertia = inertia of translation (m) + inertia of rotation $\left(\dfrac{I}{r^2}\right)$

$$\therefore \quad \left(m + \frac{I}{r^2}\right) \times a = -4ky$$

or $\qquad a = \dfrac{4k}{\left(m + \dfrac{I}{r^2}\right)}(-y)$

Ex. 34 Use energy method to find the natural frequency of the homogenous cylinder as shown in *Fig. 4.70*. Assuming cylinder to be in pure rolling.

Sol.

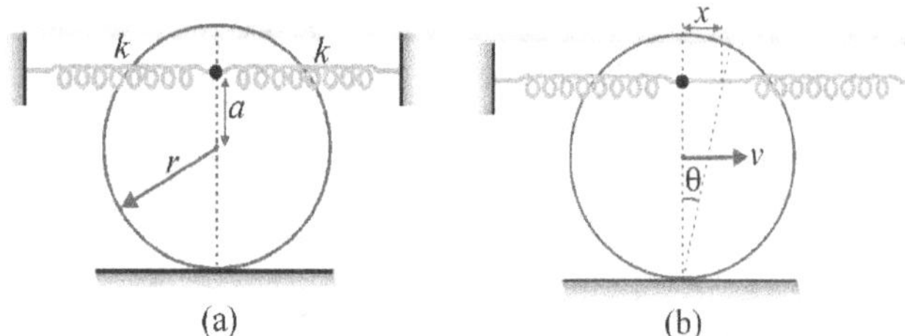

(a)   (b)

Fig. 4.70

Let cylinder is rotated slightly about its axis. The extension/compression in the springs

$$x = (r+a)\theta$$

$\therefore$ Total M.E. of the system

$$E = \frac{1}{2}mv^2 + \frac{1}{2}I\omega^2 + 2\left(\frac{1}{2}kx^2\right)$$

For pure rolling, $v = \omega r$

$\therefore$ $E = \frac{1}{2}m(\omega r)^2 + \frac{1}{2}I\omega^2 + 2\times\frac{1}{2}k\left[(r+a)\theta\right]^2$

For free oscillations, $\dfrac{dE}{dt} = 0$

or $\dfrac{d}{dt}\left[\dfrac{1}{2}m\omega^2 r^2 + \dfrac{1}{2}I\omega^2 + k(r+a)^2\theta^2\right] = 0$

or $\dfrac{1}{2}mr^2\times 2\omega\dfrac{d\omega}{dt} + \dfrac{I}{2}\times 2\omega\dfrac{d\omega}{dt} + k(r+a)^2\times 2\theta\dfrac{d\theta}{dt} = 0$

or $\left(I+mr^2\right)\dfrac{d\omega}{dt} + 2k(r+a)^2\theta = 0$

or $\dfrac{d\omega}{dt} = -\left[\dfrac{2k(r+a)^2}{I+mr^2}\right]\theta$

Comparing with standard equation of angular SHM, $\alpha = -\omega^2\theta$, we have

$$\omega = \sqrt{\frac{2k(r+a)^2}{I+mr^2}}$$

and $f = \dfrac{\omega}{2\pi} = \dfrac{1}{2\pi}\sqrt{\dfrac{2k(r+a)^2}{\left(I+mr^2\right)}}$ *Ans.*

Ex. 35 In figure $k = 100$ N/m, $M = 1$kg and $F = 10$N.

(a) Find the compression of the spring in the equilibrium position.

(b) A sharp below by some external agent imparts a speed of 2 m/s to the block toward left. Find the sum of the potential energy of the spring and the kinetic energy of the block at this instant.

(c) Find the time period of resulting simple harmonic motion.

(d) Find the amplitude.

(e) Write the potential energy of the spring when the block is at the left extreme.

(f) Write the potential energy of the spring when the block is at the right extreme.

Sol.

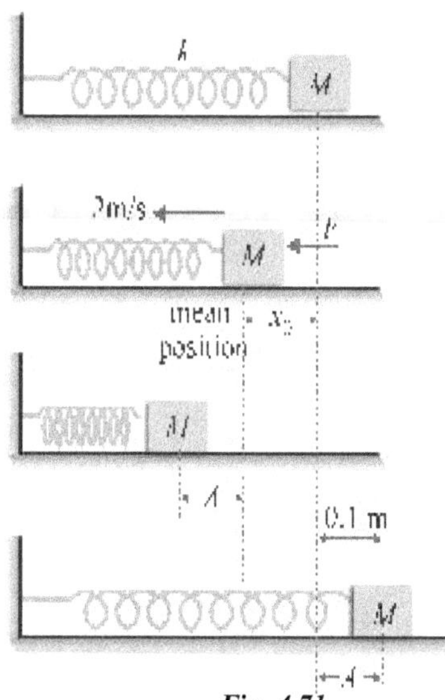

Fig. 4.71

(a) By Hooke's law, we have $F = kx$

$\therefore$ $x = \dfrac{F}{k} = \dfrac{10}{100} = 0.1m$

(b) K.E. imparted to block

$$K.E. = \frac{1}{2}\times 1\times 2^2 = \text{kJ}$$

$\therefore$ $E = P.E. + K.E. = \dfrac{1}{2}\times 100\times(0.1)^2 + 2 = 2.5J$

(c) $T = 2\pi\sqrt{\dfrac{M}{k}} = 2\pi\sqrt{\dfrac{1}{100}} = \dfrac{\pi}{5}s$

(d) $\dfrac{1}{2}mv^2 = \dfrac{1}{2}kA^2$

or $1\times 2^2 = 100\times A^2$

$\therefore$ $A = 0.2$ m

(e) P.E. of spring when block is at left extreme

$$P.E. = \frac{1}{2}\times 100\times(0.1+0.2)^2 = 4.5 \text{ J}$$

(f) The extension of the spring $= 0.1$ m,

$\therefore$ P.E. $= \dfrac{1}{2}\times 100\times(0.1)^2 = 0.5$ J   *Ans.*

Ex. 36 The speed v of a particle moving along x – axis is given by, $v^2 = 8bx - x^2 - 12b^2$, where b is a constant. Find amplitude of oscillations.

Sol. Amplitude of oscillations is the displacement of the particle from mean position to the extreme position. Also the speed of the particle becomes zero at extreme positions. Let x represents these positions, then

    $8bx - x^2 - 12b^2 = 0$

or $x^2 - 8bx + 12b^2 = 0$

or $(x-6b)(x-2b) = 0$

$\therefore$ $x = 2b$ and $6b$

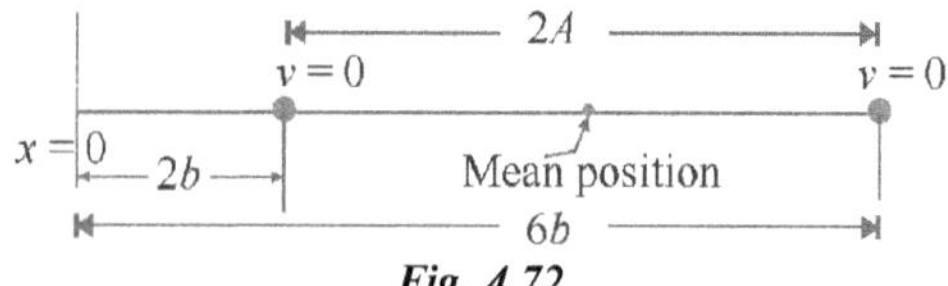

Fig. 4.72

It shows that particle moves along x-axis from $x = 2b$ to $6b$. If A is the amplitude of oscillations, then $2A = 6b - 2b = 4b$

or $A = 2b$ *Ans.*

4.7 OSCILLATIONS OF LIQUID IN U-TUBE

Let us consider a U-tube of area of cross-section A and contains liquid of mass m. The viscosity of liquid is neglected. When liquid is displaced slightly from its mean position, it starts oscillating. (*Fig. 4.73*)

Let liquid is displaced slightly by y downward in left arm. The level of right arm will rise by the same amount (because area of cross-section of tube on both sides is equal). Therefore unbalanced head of liquid becomes $2y$. This head exerts force on the rest of the liquid.

$$\therefore \quad F_{rest} = -\text{Force exerted by } (2y) \text{ height of liquid}$$
$$= -\text{ pressure intensity}$$
$$\times \text{ area of cross-section of tube}$$
$$= -(2y\rho g)\times A$$

Acceleration of the liquid $\quad a = \dfrac{F_{rest}}{m} = \dfrac{2\rho g A}{m}(-y)$

Comparing above equation with the standard equation of SHM, we get

$$\omega = \sqrt{\frac{2\rho g A}{m}}$$

and

$$T = \frac{2\pi}{\omega} = 2\pi\sqrt{\frac{m}{2\rho g A}}$$

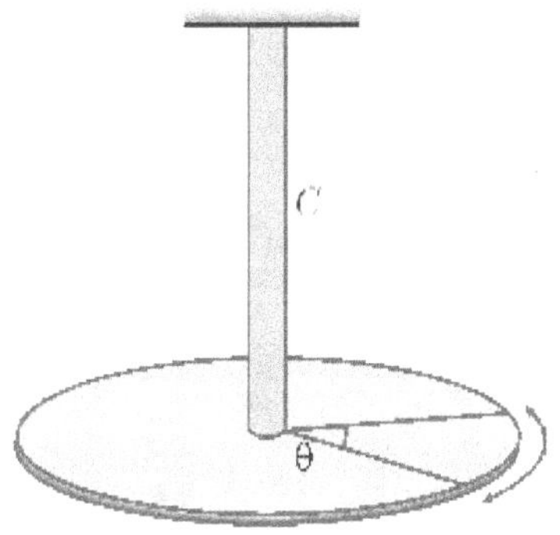

Fig. 4.73

4.8 TORISIONAL PENDULUM

Consider a disc of moment of inertia I which is attached to a rod of torsional rigidity C. This constitutes a torsional pendulum.(*Fig. 4.74*)

Suppose the rod is given a small twist (θ) by rotating the disc. When the pendulum is released from the position shown, the restoring torque acting on the disc

$$\tau_{rest} = -C\theta$$

Angular acceleration of the disc $\quad \alpha = \dfrac{\tau}{I} = \dfrac{C}{I}(-\theta)$

Now compare with $\quad \alpha = -\omega^2\theta$, we get

$$\omega = \sqrt{\frac{C}{I}}$$

and

$$T = \frac{2\pi}{\omega} = 2\pi\sqrt{\frac{I}{C}} .$$

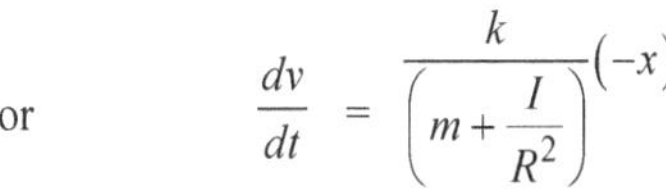

Fig. 4.74

Ex. 37 Find time period of the system shown in *Fig. 4.75*. Assuming pure rolling of the cylinder.

Sol. Short-cut method:

(Total inertia) $\left(\dfrac{dv}{dt}\right) = -kx$

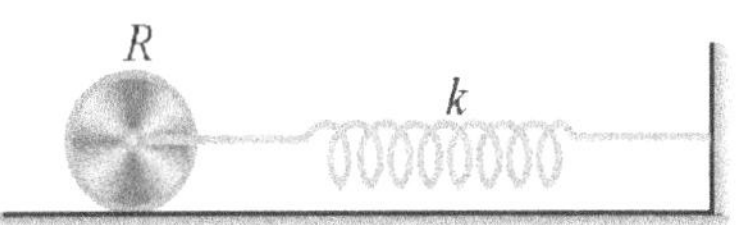

Fig. 4.75

$\left(m+\dfrac{I}{R^2}\right)\dfrac{dv}{dt} = -kx$

or $\quad \dfrac{dv}{dt} = \dfrac{k}{\left(m+\dfrac{I}{R^2}\right)}(-x)$

$\therefore \quad \omega = \sqrt{\dfrac{k}{\left(m+\dfrac{I}{R^2}\right)}} = \sqrt{\dfrac{k}{\left(m+\dfrac{mR^2/2}{R^2}\right)}}$

or $\quad \omega = \sqrt{\dfrac{2k}{3m}}$ and $T = 2\pi\sqrt{\dfrac{3m}{2k}}$ *Ans.*

Ex. 38   **Find the time period of oscillations of a body placed in a tunnel dug into earth;**
(a)   **along the diameter of the earth.**
(b)   **anywhere in the earth.**

Sol.

(a)   Suppose the body is at a distance y from the centre of the earth, the restoring force acting on the body

$$F = -\frac{GM'm}{y^2}$$

where M' is the mass of the dotted sphere,

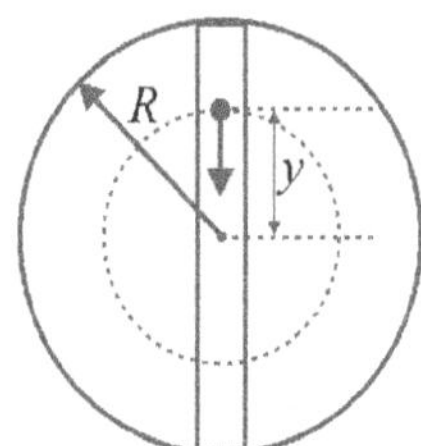

Fig. 4.76

$$\therefore \quad F = -\frac{G\left(\dfrac{M}{\frac{4}{3}\pi R^3}\right)\left(\dfrac{4}{3}\pi y^3\right)m}{y^2}$$

$$= -\frac{GMmy}{R^3}$$

As $\quad \dfrac{GM}{R^2} = g, \therefore F = \dfrac{mg}{R}(-y)$

and $\quad a = \dfrac{F}{m} = \dfrac{g}{R}(-y)$

Comparing above equation with standard equation of SHM, $a = -\omega^2 y$, we get

$$\omega = \sqrt{\frac{g}{R}} \text{ and } T = 2\pi\sqrt{\frac{R}{g}}.$$

(b)   Suppose a tunnel is dug at a radial distance x from the centre of the earth.
If y is the distance of the body from the centre of the tunnel, then
$$y = x\sin\theta.$$
The restoring force acting on the body

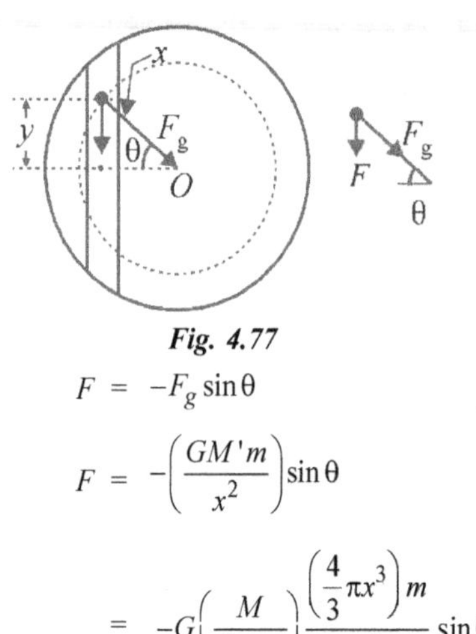

Fig. 4.77

$$F = -F_g \sin\theta$$

$$F = -\left(\frac{GM'm}{x^2}\right)\sin\theta$$

$$= -G\left(\frac{M}{\frac{4}{3}\pi R^3}\right)\frac{\left(\frac{4}{3}\pi x^3\right)m}{x^2}\sin\theta$$

$$= \frac{-GMm}{R^3}x\sin\theta$$

Acceleration of the body, $a = \dfrac{F}{m}$

$$= \frac{-GM}{R^3}(x\sin\theta)$$

Substituting $\dfrac{GM}{R^2} = g$ and $x\sin\theta = y$, we get

$$a = \frac{g}{R}(-y)$$

Comparing above equation with standard equation of SHM, $a = -\omega^2 y$, we get

$$\omega = \sqrt{\frac{g}{R}} \text{ and } T = 2\pi\sqrt{\frac{R}{g}}.$$

4.9 OSCILLATIONS OF A FLOATING BODY

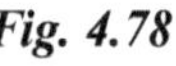

Fig. 4.78

Consider a block of mass M floating in a liquid of density ρ. Area of cross-section of the block is A. Let the block is displaced down slightly (y) from its mean position.
The restoring force = Buoyant force on the extra dipped portion of the cylinder
$$= -(Ay)\rho g$$

Acceleration, $\quad a = \dfrac{F}{m} = \dfrac{A\rho g}{m}(-y)$

Compare with standard equation of SHM, $a = -\omega^2 y$, we get

$$\omega = \sqrt{\frac{A\rho g}{M}}$$

and

$$T = 2\pi\sqrt{\frac{M}{A\rho g}}$$

Ex. 39 A body executes SHM under the action of a force F_1 with frequency n_1. If the force is changed to F_2, it executes SHM with a frequency n_2. If both the forces act simultaneously in the same direction on the body, then find the new frequency of oscillations.

Sol. We have

$$F_1 = -ma_1 \quad \text{and} \quad F_2 = -ma_2$$
$$= -m\omega_1^2 y \qquad\qquad = -m\omega_2^2 y$$

$$\therefore \qquad F = F_1 + F_2 = m\left(\omega_1^2 + \omega_2^2\right)(-y) \qquad \dots (i)$$

If ω is the new frequency, then

$$F = -m\omega^2 y \qquad \dots (ii)$$

On comparing equations (i) and (ii),

$$\omega^2 = \omega_1^2 + \omega_2^2$$
$$\text{or} \qquad n^2 = n_1^2 + n_2^2$$

$$\text{and} \qquad \frac{1}{T^2} = \frac{1}{T_1^2} + \frac{1}{T_2^2} \qquad\qquad \textit{Ans.}$$

Ex. 40 A body of mass m falls from a height h onto the pan of a spring balance. The masses of the pan and spring are negligible. The force constant of the spring is k. The body sticks to the pan and oscillates simple harmonically. Find time period of oscillations and amplitude of motion.

Sol. Let the spring is compressed by y, then by conservation of mechanical energy, we have

$$mg(h+y) = \frac{1}{2}ky^2$$

$$\text{or} \quad \frac{ky^2}{2} - mgy - mgh = 0$$

$$\text{or} \qquad y = \frac{mg \pm \sqrt{(mg)^2 + 4 \times \dfrac{k}{2} \times mgh}}{2\left(\dfrac{k}{2}\right)}$$

$$\text{or} \qquad y = \frac{mg}{k} \pm \frac{\sqrt{(mg)^2 + 2k\,mgh}}{k}$$

where $\dfrac{mg}{k}$ is known as static deflection and $\dfrac{\sqrt{(mg)^2 + 2kmgh}}{k}$ is known as amplitude of motion.

The time period of motion is given by $T = 2\pi\sqrt{\dfrac{m}{k}}$

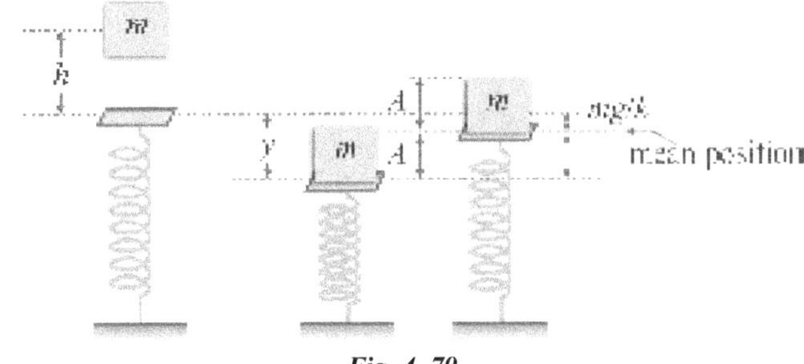

Fig. 4..79

Ex. 41 A cylindrical piston of mass M and cross-sectional area A slides smoothly inside a long cylinder closed at one end, enclosing a certain mass of a gas. The cylinder is kept with its axis horizontal. If the piston is disturbed from its equilibrium position, it oscillates simple harmonically. Find time period of oscillations.

Sol. If P is the pressure and V is the volume of the gas, then by Boyle's law

$$PV = \text{constant}$$

On differentiating, $PdV + VdP = 0$

$$\text{or} \qquad dP = -P\frac{dV}{V}$$

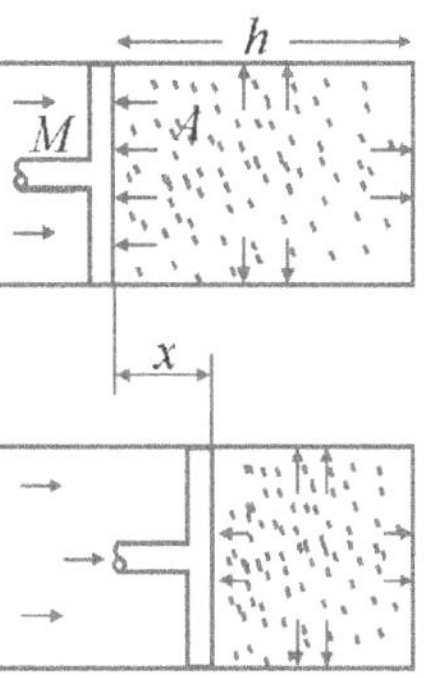

Fig. 4.80

Let piston is displaced slightly by x, then $dV = Ax$, and restoring force

$$F = (dP)A$$
$$= -\left(P\frac{dV}{V}\right)A$$
$$= -P\frac{(Ax)}{(Ah)} = A = \frac{PA}{h}(-x)$$

$$\text{Acceleration of the piston} = \frac{F}{M}$$

$$\text{or} \qquad a = \frac{PA}{Mh}(-x)$$

Now comparing with standard equation of SHM, $a = -\omega^2 x$ we get

$$\omega = \sqrt{\frac{PA}{Mh}}$$

$$\text{and} \qquad T = 2\pi\sqrt{\frac{Mh}{PA}} \qquad\qquad \textit{Ans.}$$

Ex. 42 A spherical ball of mass m and radius r rolls without slipping on a rough concave surface of large radius R. It makes small oscillations about the lowest point. Find the time period.

Sol. Let any instant, the body is at angular position θ with respect to the vertical line drawn from the centre of the mirror. If ϕ is the angular displacement of the ball about its centre, then

$$(R-r)\theta = r\phi$$

$$\therefore \qquad \theta = \left(\frac{r}{R-r}\right)\phi$$

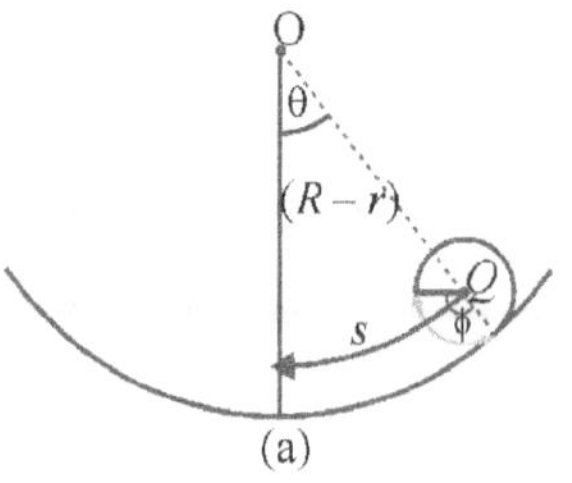

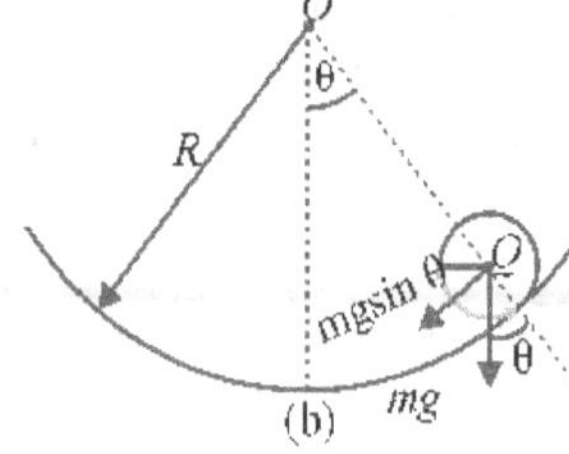

Fig. 4.81

Restoring torque acting on the ball

$$\tau = -mg\sin\theta \times r$$

For small $\theta, \sin\theta \simeq \theta$

$$\therefore \qquad \tau = -mg\,\theta \times r$$

$$\text{or} \qquad \tau = -mg\left[\frac{r}{R-r}\right]\phi\,r$$

$$= mg\left(\frac{r^2}{R-r}\right)(-\phi)$$

Angular acceleration, $\alpha = \dfrac{mg}{I}\left(\dfrac{r^2}{R-r}\right)(-\phi)$

Now comparing above equation with standard equation of SHM, $\alpha = -\omega^2\phi$, we get

$$\omega = \sqrt{\frac{mg}{I}\left(\frac{r^2}{R-r}\right)}$$

Here I is the moment of inertia of the rolling ball about point of contact which is $I = \dfrac{7}{5}mr^2$

$$\therefore \qquad \omega = \sqrt{\frac{mg}{\dfrac{7}{5}mr^2}\left(\frac{r^2}{R-r}\right)}$$

$$= \sqrt{\frac{5}{7}\frac{g}{(R-r)}}$$

$$\text{and} \qquad T = \frac{2\pi}{\omega} = 2\pi\sqrt{\frac{7(R-r)}{5g}} \qquad \qquad \textbf{\textit{Ans.}}$$

Composition of two SHM^s of equal frequency in perpendicular directions

Consider two SHM^s of different amplitudes and having phase difference ϕ

$$x = a\sin\omega t \qquad \qquad \text{...(i)}$$

$$\text{and} \qquad y = b\sin(\omega t + \phi) \qquad \qquad \text{...(ii)}$$

Expanding equation (ii), we have

$$y = b(\sin\omega t\cos\phi + \cos\omega t\sin\phi) \qquad \text{...(iii)}$$

From equation (i), $\sin\omega t = \dfrac{x}{a}$ and $\cos\omega t = \sqrt{1-\dfrac{x^2}{a^2}}$

Fig. 4.82

Substituting these values in equation (iii), we get

$$y = b\left(\frac{x}{a}\cos\phi + \sqrt{\left(1-\frac{x^2}{a^2}\right)}\sin\phi\right)$$

$$\text{or} \qquad \frac{y}{b} - \frac{x}{a}\cos\phi = \sqrt{\left(1-\frac{x^2}{a^2}\right)}\sin\phi$$

$$\text{or} \qquad \left(\frac{y}{b} - \frac{x}{a}\cos\phi\right)^2 = \left(1-\frac{x^2}{a^2}\right)\sin^2\phi$$

$$\text{or} \qquad \frac{y^2}{b^2} + \frac{x^2}{a^2}\cos^2\phi - \frac{2xy}{ab}\cos\phi = \sin^2\phi - \frac{x^2}{a^2}\sin^2\phi$$

$$\text{or} \qquad \frac{x^2}{a^2} + \frac{y^2}{b^2} - \frac{2xy}{ab}\cos\phi = \sin^2\phi$$

The above equation is the general equation of an ellipse.

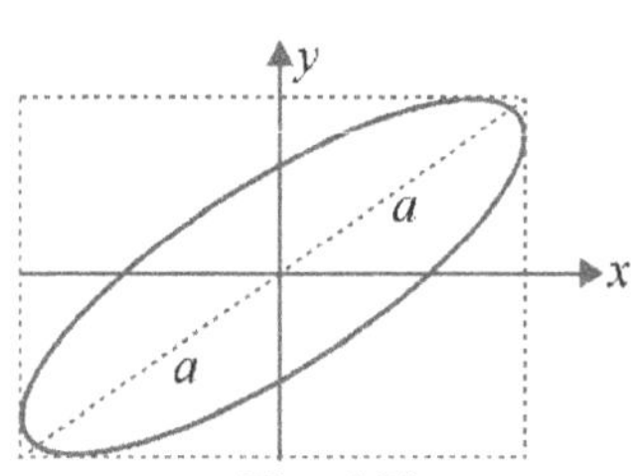

Fig. 4.83

Special cases:

1. $\phi = 0$

$$\frac{x^2}{a^2} + \frac{y^2}{b^2} - \frac{2xy}{ab} = 0$$

or $\left(\dfrac{y}{b} - \dfrac{x}{a}\right)^2 = 0$

or $\boxed{y = \dfrac{b}{a}x}$

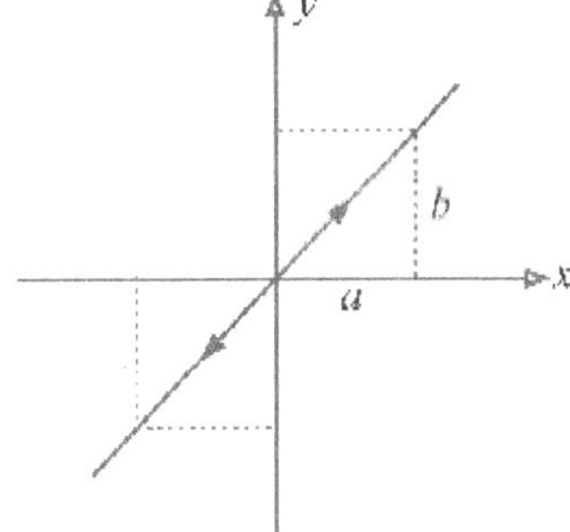

2. $\phi = \pi$

$$\frac{x^2}{a^2} + \frac{y^2}{b^2} - \frac{2xy}{ab} = 0$$

or $\left(\dfrac{y}{b} + \dfrac{x}{a}\right)^2 = 0$

or $\boxed{y = -\dfrac{b}{a}x}$

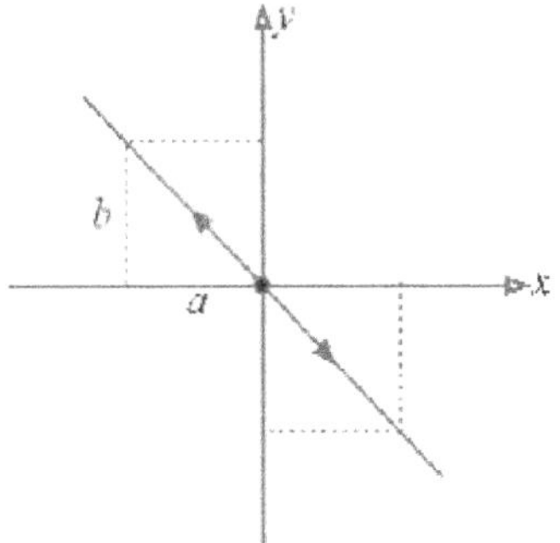

3. $\phi = \dfrac{\pi}{2}$

$$\boxed{\frac{x^2}{a^2} + \frac{y^2}{b^2} = 1}$$

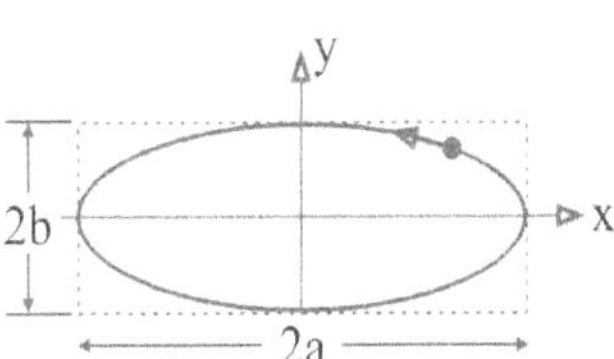

4. $\phi = \dfrac{\pi}{2}, a = b$

$$\boxed{x^2 + y^2 = a^2}$$

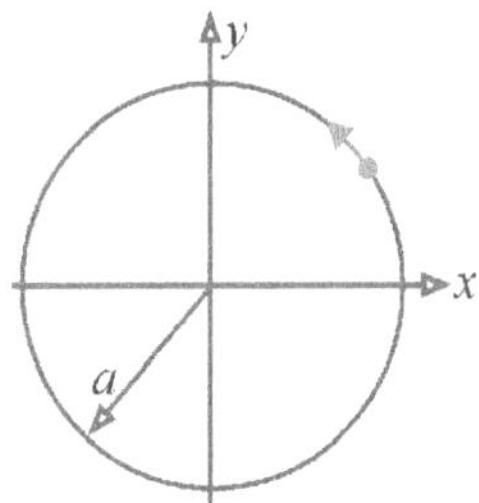

4.10 Damped Oscillations

Till now we have studied the free oscillations, in which energy of the oscillating body remain constant. But in practice medium in which body oscillates offers some resistance. Due to which energy of the oscillating body goes on decreasing, and so body finally stops oscillating. These oscillations are called damped oscillations. Let b be the damping coefficient, then damping force

$$F_v = -bv$$

For damped oscillator, restoring force

$$F = -(kx + bv)$$

or

$$m\frac{d^2x}{dt^2} = -\left(kx + b\frac{dx}{dt}\right)$$

or
$$m\frac{d^2x}{dt^2} + b\frac{dx}{dt} + kx = 0$$

or
$$\frac{d^2x}{dt^2} + \frac{b}{m}\frac{dx}{dt} + \frac{k}{m} = 0$$

The solution of this equation is

$$x = A_0 e^{\frac{-bt}{2m}} \sin\left(\omega_d t + \phi\right)$$

where $\omega_d = \sqrt{\dfrac{k}{m} - \left(\dfrac{b}{2m}\right)^2}$, it is called damped frequency.

If $b = 0$ (there is no damping), then $\omega' = \sqrt{\dfrac{k}{m}}$. If the damping constant is small but not

zero (so that $b \ll \sqrt{km}$), then $\omega' \simeq \omega$. The amplitude, which is $A_0 e^{-\frac{bt}{2m}}$, gradually decreases with time. The energy of the damped oscillation

$$E = \frac{1}{2}kA^2$$

$$E = \frac{1}{2}k\left(A_0 e^{\frac{-bt}{2m}}\right)^2$$

or
$$E = \frac{1}{2}kA_0^2 e^{\frac{-bt}{m}} = E_0 e^{\frac{-bt}{m}}$$

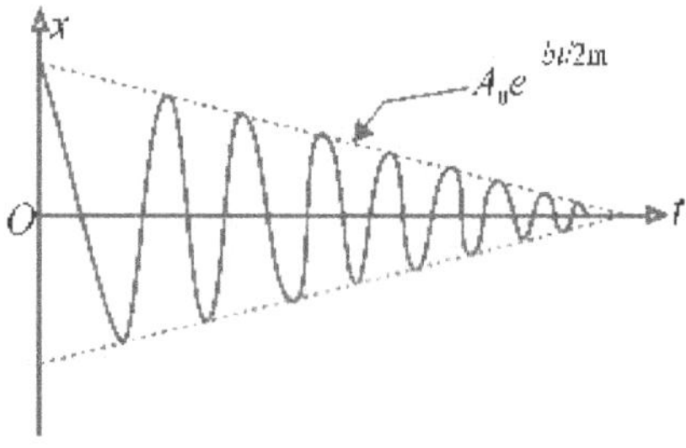

Fig. 4.84 Variation of amplitude with time

where $E_0 = \dfrac{1}{2}kA_0^2$, is the initial energy of the oscillator.

Forced oscillations and resonance

If the oscillations of a body to be continue, then the work is to be done by the periodic force. The motion is some what complicated for some time and after this the body oscillates with the frequency ω of the applied force. Such oscillations are called forced oscillations. Equation of motion for the motion can be written as

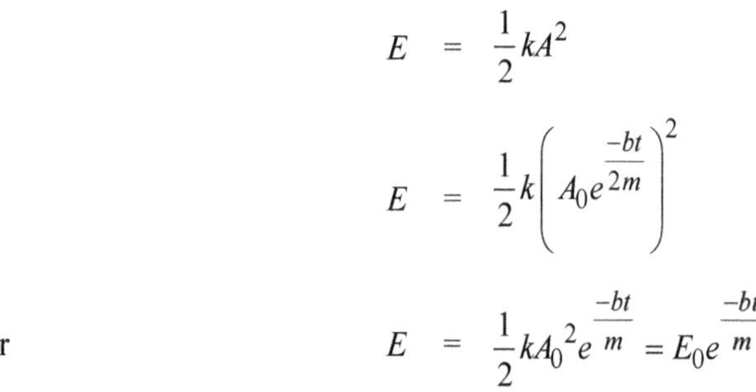

$$m\frac{d^2x}{dt^2} = -kx - b\frac{dx}{dt} + F_0 \sin \omega t$$

or
$$m\frac{d^2x}{dt^2} + b\frac{dx}{dt} + kx = F_0 \sin \omega t$$

The amplitude of oscillations is given by

$$A = \frac{\dfrac{F_0}{m}}{\sqrt{\left(\omega^2 - \omega_0^2\right)^2 + \left(\dfrac{b\omega}{m}\right)^2}},$$

where $\omega_0 = \sqrt{\dfrac{k}{m}}$

If we vary the angular frequency ω of the applied force, the amplitude of motion changes

and becomes maximum, when $\omega = \omega_d = \sqrt{\omega_0^2 - \left(\dfrac{b}{2m}\right)^2}$

This is the condition of resonance.

Ex. 43 Two identical simple pendulums each of length ℓ are connected by a weightless spring as shown in *Fig. 4.85*. The force constant of the spring is k. In equilibrium, the pendulums are vertical and the spring is horizontal and undeformed. Find the time period of small oscillation of the linked pendulums, when they are deflected from their equilibrium positions through equal displacements in the same vertical plane:
(a) in the same direction
(b) in opposite direction and released.

Sol.

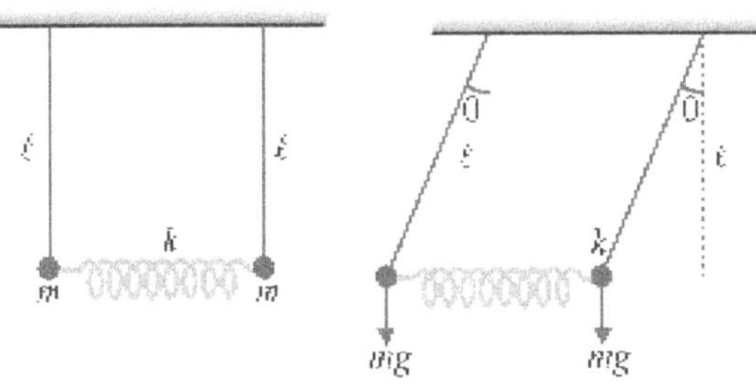

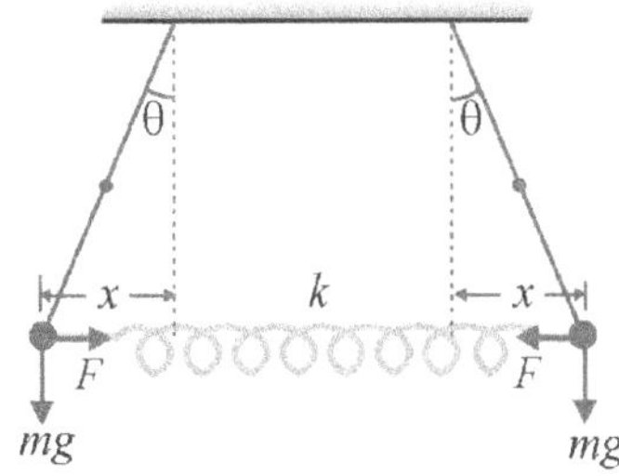

Fig. 4.85

(a) When both the pendulums are displaced in the same direction, there is no extension in the spring. Therefore the restoring torque on the bobs is due to their weight

$$\therefore \qquad \tau = -mg \times \ell \sin\theta$$

for small θ

$$\tau = -mg\ell\theta$$

and

$$\alpha = \frac{mg\ell}{I}(-\theta)$$

Compare with standard equation of SHM $\alpha = -\omega^2\theta$, we get

$$\omega = \sqrt{\frac{mg\ell}{I}}$$

and

$$T = \frac{2\pi}{\omega} = 2\pi\sqrt{\frac{I}{mg\ell}}$$

$$= 2\pi\sqrt{\frac{m\ell^2}{mg\ell}} = 2\pi\sqrt{\frac{\ell}{g}}$$

(b) Let each side of the pendulum is displaced by x, the total extension of the spring become 2x, where $x = \ell\sin\theta$. For small θ, $x = \ell\theta$.

$\therefore$ Force in the spring $F = k(2x) = 2k\ell\theta$

Restoring torque $\tau = -(mg \times \ell\sin\theta + 2k\ell\theta \times \ell\cos\theta)$

for small θ, $\sin\theta \simeq \theta$ and $\cos\theta = 1$

$$\therefore \qquad \tau = -(mg\ell\theta + 2k\ell^2\theta)$$

and

$$\alpha = \frac{\left(mg\ell + 2k\ell^2\right)}{I}(-\theta)$$

Compare with standard equation of SHM, $\alpha = -\omega^2\theta$ we get

$$\omega = \sqrt{\frac{mg\ell + 2k\ell^2}{I}}$$

and

$$T = \frac{2\pi}{\omega} = 2\pi\sqrt{\frac{I}{\left(mg\ell + 2k\ell^2\right)}}$$

$$= 2\pi\sqrt{\frac{m\ell^2}{mg\ell + 2k\ell^2}}$$

$$= 2\pi\sqrt{\frac{\ell}{\left(g + \dfrac{2k\ell}{m}\right)}} \qquad\qquad Ans.$$

Ex. 44 Two non-viscous, incompressible and immiscible liquids of densities ρ and $1.5\,\rho$ are poured into the two limbs of a circular tube of radius R and small cross-section kept fixed in a vertical plane as shown in figure. Each liquid occupies one-fourth the circumference of the tube.
(a) Find the angle θ that the radius vector to the interface makes with the vertical in equilibrium position.
(b) If the whole liquid is given a small displacement from its equilibrium position, show that the resultant oscillations are simple harmonic. Find the time period of these oscillations.

Sol.

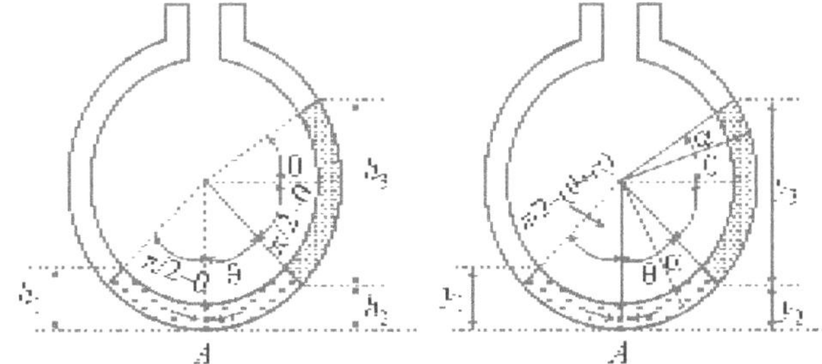

Fig. 4.86

(a) The pressure at A from both sides of liquid is equal

$$\therefore \qquad \rho_1 h_1 g = \rho_1 h_2 g + \rho_2 h_3 g$$

where

$$h_1 = R - R\sin\theta, \quad h_2 = R - R\cos\theta, \quad h_3 = R\cos\theta + R\sin\theta$$

and

$$\rho_1 = 1.5\rho, \quad \rho_2 = \rho$$

$$\therefore 1.5\rho\left(R - R\sin\theta\right) = 1.5\rho\left(R - R\cos\theta\right) + \rho\left(R\cos\theta + R\sin\theta\right)$$

or

$$0.5\cos\theta = 2.5\sin\theta$$

or

$$\theta = \tan^{-1}\left(\frac{1}{5}\right) = 11.3°$$

(b) When liquids displaced slightly, the unbalanced head of liquid causes the restoring force

$$\Delta P = (\rho_1 y_2 g + \rho_2 y_3 g) - (\rho_1 y_1 g)$$

where $\quad y_1 = R - R\sin(\theta + \alpha), \; y_2 = R - R\cos(\theta + \alpha)$

and $\quad y_3 = R\sin(\theta + \alpha) + R\cos(\theta + \alpha)$

$$\therefore \; \Delta P = 1.5\rho\left[R - R\cos(\theta + \alpha)\right]g$$

$$+\rho\left[R\sin(\theta + \alpha) + R\cos(\theta + \alpha)\right]g - 1.5\rho\left[R - R\sin(\theta + \alpha)\right]g$$

$$= \rho Rg\left[2.5\sin(\theta + \alpha) - 0.5\cos(\theta + \alpha)\right]$$

$$= \rho Rg\left[2.5(\sin\theta\cos\alpha + \cos\theta\sin\alpha) - 0.5(\cos\theta\cos\alpha - \sin\theta\sin\alpha)\right]$$

As $\tan\theta = \dfrac{1}{5}$, $\sin\theta = \dfrac{1}{\sqrt{26}}$ and $\cos\theta = \dfrac{5}{\sqrt{26}}$

for small α, $\cos\alpha = 1$, $\sin\alpha \simeq \alpha$

After substituting these value in above equation, we get

$$\Delta p = 2.55\,\rho Rg\alpha$$

$$= 2.55\rho g y \quad (R\alpha = y)$$

Restoring force $F = -\Delta p A$

$$= -2.55\rho g A y$$

and acc. $\quad a = \dfrac{F}{m}$

where m $\rightarrow$ mass of the liquid

$$m = \left(\dfrac{\pi R}{2}\right)A\rho + \left(\dfrac{\pi R}{2}\right)A \times 1.5\rho = 1.25\,\pi R A\rho$$

$\therefore \qquad a = \dfrac{-2.55\rho g A y}{1.25\,\pi R A\rho}$

$$= -2.04\left(\dfrac{g}{\pi R}\right)y$$

Now comparing with standard equation of SHM $a = -\omega^2 y$, we get

$$\omega = \sqrt{\dfrac{2.04g}{\pi R}}$$

and $\qquad T = \dfrac{2\pi}{\omega} = 2\pi\sqrt{\dfrac{\pi R}{2.04g}}$ $\qquad$ *Ans.*

Ex. 45 You are riding in an automobile of mass 3000 kg. Assuming that you are examining the oscillation characteristics of its suspension system. The suspension sags 15 cm when the entire automobile is placed on it. Also, the amplitude of oscillations decreases by 50% during one complete oscillation. Estimate the values of (a) the spring constant and (b) the damping constant b for the spring and shock absorbs supports 750 kg (g = 10 m/s²).

Sol.

(a) If k is the spring constant of each spring, then for four wheels
$4kx = mg$

or $\qquad k = \dfrac{mg}{4x} = \dfrac{3000 \times 10}{4 \times 0.15} = 5 \times 10^4 \; N/m$

$\qquad$ *Ans.*

(b) We know that $A' = A_0 e^{\frac{-bt}{2m}}$

For $\quad A' = \dfrac{A_0}{2}$, we have $\quad \dfrac{A_0}{2} = A_0 e^{\frac{-bt}{2m}}$

or $\qquad e^{\frac{bt}{2m}} = 2$

or $\qquad \dfrac{bt}{2m} = \ell n2$

or $\qquad b = \dfrac{2m\,\ell n2}{t}$

But $\qquad t = 2\pi\sqrt{\dfrac{m}{4k}} = 2 \times \dfrac{22}{7} \times \sqrt{\dfrac{3000}{4 \times 5 \times 10^4}}$

$$= \dfrac{44}{70}\sqrt{\dfrac{3}{2}} \; s$$

Hence $\qquad b = \dfrac{2 \times 750 \times 0.693}{\dfrac{44}{70}\sqrt{\dfrac{3}{2}}} = 1350.4 \; kg/s$

$\qquad$ *Ans.*

Ex. 46 A block possessing kinetic energy K collides head-on elastically with a stationary spring-blocks system and rebounds in opposite direction with kinetic energy K′. The masses of all the blocks are equal. Calculate the energy of oscillations of the spring blocks system.

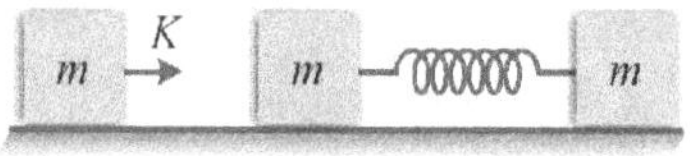

Fig. 4.87

Sol. If u is the speed of the block, then

$$\dfrac{1}{2}mu^2 = K \quad \text{or} \quad u = \sqrt{\dfrac{2k}{m}}.$$

The speed of block with which it rebounds, $u' = \sqrt{\dfrac{2k'}{m}}$

The maximum energy that can be stored in the spring will be the energy of oscillations. At the instant of maximum compression, let speed of each connected block is v. By conservation of momentum, we have

$$mu = m(-u') + 2mv$$

or $\quad m\sqrt{\dfrac{2k}{m}} = -m\sqrt{\dfrac{2k'}{m}} + 2mv$ $\qquad$ … (i)

For elastic collision,

$$K = K' + \dfrac{1}{2} \times 2m \times v^2 + E_{\text{oscillation}} \quad \text{… (ii)}$$

After solving above equations, we get

$$E_{\text{oscillation}} = \left[\dfrac{k - 3k' - 2\sqrt{kk'}}{2}\right] \qquad \textit{Ans.}$$

Review of formulae & Important Points

1. Differential equation

(a) Linear SHM :
$$F = -kx$$

$$\frac{d^2\vec{x}}{dt^2} + \frac{\vec{k}}{m} = a, \text{ here } k = \omega^2 m.$$

(b) Angular SHM :
$$\tau = -c\theta$$

$$\frac{d^2\vec{\theta}}{dt^2} + \frac{c}{I}\vec{\theta} = 0, \text{ here } c = \omega^2 I$$

2. Value of $\vec{x}$ or $\vec{\theta}$:

(i) $x = A\sin(\omega t + \phi_0); \; \theta = \theta_0 \sin(\omega t + \phi_0)$

(ii) $x = A\cos(\omega t + \phi_0)$

(iii) $x = A\sin\omega t + B\cos\omega t$. with amplitude $= \sqrt{A^2 + B^2}$

3. Time taken to travel from mean position to $\dfrac{A}{2}$ is $\dfrac{T}{12}$ and from $\dfrac{A}{2}$ to A will be $\dfrac{T}{6}$.

4. Velocity of the particle :

$$v = \omega A\cos(\omega t + \phi_0) = \omega\sqrt{A^2 - x^2}$$

$v_{max} = \omega A$, at mean position.
$v_{max} = 0$, at extreme positions.

5. Acceleration of the particle :

$$a = -\omega^2 A\sin(\omega t + \phi_0) = -\omega^2 x$$

$$\left|a_{max}\right| = \omega^2 A, \text{ at extreme positons}$$

$$\left|a_{min}\right| = 0, \text{ at mean position}$$

6. Energy of the particle in SHM :

$$K.E. = \frac{1}{2}m\omega^2 A^2\cos^2(\omega t + \phi_0) = \frac{1}{2}m\omega^2(A^2 - x^2)$$

$$P.E. = \frac{1}{2}m\omega^2 A^2\sin^2(\omega t + \phi_0) = \frac{1}{2}kx^2$$

Total mechanical energy

$$E = K.E. + P.E. = \frac{1}{2}m\omega^2 A^2 \text{ (constant)}$$

$$\therefore \frac{dE}{dt} = 0$$

7. At $x = \dfrac{A}{\sqrt{2}}$, K.E. of the oscillating particle is equal to its P.E.

8. Average K.E. of the period = Average P.E. = $\dfrac{1}{4}m\omega^2 A^2$.

9. Time period of simple pendulum

$$T = 2\pi\sqrt{\frac{\ell}{g}}$$

10. When point of suspension is accelerating, then

$$T = 2\pi\sqrt{\frac{\ell}{a_{net}}}$$

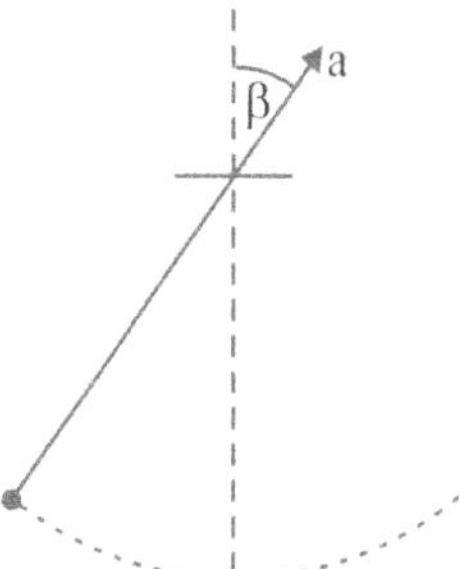

where $a_{net} = \sqrt{a^2 + g^2 + 2ag\cos\beta}$

11. Time period of a infinitely large pendulum

$$T = 2\pi\sqrt{\frac{R}{g}} = 84.6 \text{ minute}$$

12. Time period of a body oscillating in a tunnel dug along the diameter of the earth

$$T = 2\pi\sqrt{\frac{R}{g}}$$

13. Time period of a physical pendulum

$$T = 2\pi\sqrt{\frac{I}{mgd}}$$

14. Time period of mass – springs shown in figures,

$$T = 2\pi\sqrt{\frac{M}{k}}$$

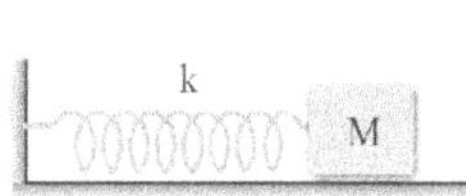

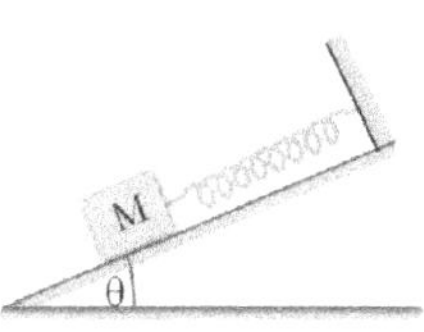

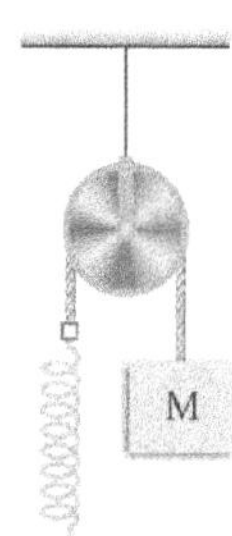

15. If m_s is the mass of the spring, then time period

$$T = 2\pi\sqrt{\frac{\left(M + \dfrac{m_s}{3}\right)}{k}}$$

16. Time period of torsional pendulum

$$T = 2\pi\sqrt{\frac{I}{c}}$$

17. **Time period of a floating body**

$$T = 2\pi\sqrt{\frac{M}{A\rho_\ell g}}$$

18. **Time period of coupled oscillator**

$$\mu = \left(\frac{m_1 m_2}{m_1 + m_2}\right)$$

$$T = 2\pi\sqrt{\frac{\mu}{k}}$$

19. **Springs in series :** $k \propto \dfrac{1}{\ell}$

$$\frac{1}{k} = \frac{1}{k_1} + \frac{1}{k_2} + ... + \frac{1}{k_n}$$

Springs in parallel : $k = k_1 + k_2 + ... + k_n$

20. Composition of two SHM^s of equal frequency in perpendicular directions.

$$x = a\sin\omega t$$

and $\qquad y = b\sin(\omega t + \phi)$

$$\frac{x^2}{a^2} + \frac{y^2}{b^2} - \frac{2xy}{ab}\cos\phi = \sin^2\phi$$

For $\phi = 0$ and π : straight line.

$$\phi = \frac{\pi}{2} \text{ : an ellipse}$$

$$\phi = \frac{\pi}{2}, \, a = b \text{ : a circle.}$$

21. **Damped oscillator :** Differential equation of damped oscillator

$$\frac{d^2 x}{dt^2} + \frac{b}{m}\frac{dx}{dt} + \frac{k}{m}x = 0$$

where $x = A_0 e^{-bt/2m}\sin(\omega_d t + \phi)$

$$\omega_d = \sqrt{\frac{k}{m} - \left(\frac{b}{2m}\right)^2}$$

22. Differential equation of forced oscillations

$$m\frac{d^2 x}{dt^2} + b\frac{dx}{dt} + kx = F_0\sin\omega t$$

$$A = \frac{F_0/m}{\sqrt{(\omega_0{}^2 - \omega_d{}^2)^2 + \left(\frac{b\omega}{m}\right)^2}}, \text{ where } \omega_0 = \sqrt{\frac{k}{m}}$$

SHM | **MCQ Type 1** | Exercise 4.1

Level -1

Only one option correct

1. A particle starts SHM from the mean position. Its amplitude is A and time period is T. At the time when its speed is half of the maximum speed, its displacement y is

   (a) $\dfrac{A}{2}$ (b) $\dfrac{A}{\sqrt{2}}$

   (c) $\dfrac{A\sqrt{3}}{2}$ (d) $\dfrac{2A}{\sqrt{3}}$

2. A particle is moving with constant angular velocity along the circumference of a circle. Which of the following statement is true?
   (a) The particle so moving executes SHM
   (b) The projection of the particle on any one of the diameters executes SHM
   (c) The projection of the particle on any of the diameters executes SHM
   (d) None of the above

3. Which of the following equation does not represent a simple harmonic motion

   (a) $y = a\sin\omega t$ (b) $y = a\cos\omega t$

   (c) $y = a\sin\omega t + b\cos\omega t$ (d) $y = a\tan\omega t$

4. A particle in SHM is described by the displacement function $x(t) = A\cos(\omega t + \theta)$. If the initial $(t = 0)$ position of the particle is 1 cm and its initial velocity is π cm/s. The angular frequency of the particle is π rad/s, then its amplitude is

   (a) 1 cm (b) $\sqrt{2}$ cm

   (c) 2 cm (d) 2.5 cm

5. A particle executing simple harmonic motion along y-axis has its motion described by the equation $y = A\sin(\omega t) + B$. The amplitude of the simple harmonic motion is
   (a) A (b) B
   (c) $A + B$ (d) $\sqrt{A + B}$

6. Two simple harmonic motions are represented by the equations $y_1 = 0.1\sin\left(100\pi t + \dfrac{\pi}{3}\right)$ and $y_2 = 0.1\cos\pi t$. The phase difference of the velocity of particle 1 with respect to the velocity of particle 2 is

   (a) $\dfrac{-\pi}{3}$ (b) $\dfrac{\pi}{6}$

   (c) $\dfrac{-\pi}{6}$ (d) $\dfrac{\pi}{3}$

7. A system exhibiting SHM must possess
   (a) inertia only
   (b) elasticity as well as inertia
   (c) elasticity, inertia and an external force
   (d) elasticity only

8. If $x = a\sin\left(\omega t + \dfrac{\pi}{6}\right)$ and $x' = a\cos\omega t$, then what is the phase difference between the two waves
   (a) $\pi/3$ (b) $\pi/6$
   (c) $\pi/2$ (d) π

9. If a simple pendulum oscillates with an amplitude of 50 mm and time period of 2 sec, then its maximum velocity is
   (a) 0.10 m/s (b) 0.15 m/s
   (c) 0.8 m/s (d) 0.26 m/s

10. The amplitude of a particle executing SHM with frequency of 60 Hz is 0.01 m. The maximum value of the acceleration of the particle is

    (a) $144\pi^2$ m/s^2 (b) 144 m/s^2

    (c) $\dfrac{144}{\pi^2}$ m/s^2 (d) $288\pi^2$ m/s^2

11. For a particle executing simple harmonic motion, which of the following statement is not correct ?
    (a) The total energy of the particle always remains the same.
    (b) The restoring force of always directed towards a fixed point.
    (c) The restoring force is maximum at the extreme positions.
    (d) The acceleration of the particle is maximum at the equilibrium position.

12. For a particle executing simple harmonic motion, the kinetic energy K is given by $K = K_0\cos^2\omega t$. The maximum value of potential energy is
    (a) K_0 (b) Zero

    (c) $\dfrac{K_0}{2}$ (d) Not obtainable

13. The potential energy of a particle with displacement x is $U(x)$. The motion is simple harmonic, when (k is a positive constant)

    (a) $U = \dfrac{1}{2}kx^2$ (b) $U = kx^3$

    (c) $U = k$ (d) $U = kx$

14. When a mass M is attached to the spring of force constant k, then the spring stretches by l. If the mass oscillates with amplitude l, what will be maximum potential energy stored in the spring

    (a) $\dfrac{kl}{2}$ (b) $2kl$

    (c) $\dfrac{1}{2}Mgl$ (d) Mgl

Answer Key	1	(c)	3	(d)	5	(a)	7	(b)	9	(b)	11	(d)	13	(a)
Sol. from page 343	2	(c)	4	(b)	6	(c)	8	(a)	10	(a)	12	(a)	14	(c)

15. A body executes simple harmonic motion. The potential energy (P.E.), the kinetic energy (K.E.) and total energy (T.E.) are measured as a function of displacement x. Which of the following statement is true?
    (a) P.E. is maximum when $x = 0$.
    (b) K.E. is maximum when $x = 0$.
    (c) T.E. is zero when $x = 0$.
    (d) K.E. is maximum when x is maximum.

16. If $< E >$ and $< U >$ denote the average kinetic and the average potential energies respectively of mass describing a simple harmonic motion, over one period, then the correct relation is
    (a) $< E > = < U >$
    (b) $< E > = 2 < U >$
    (c) $< E > = -2 < U >$
    (d) $< E > = - < U >$

17. A particle executes simple harmonic motion with a frequency f. The frequency with which its kinetic energy oscillates is
    (a) $f / 2$
    (b) f
    (c) $2f$
    (d) $4f$

18. A body is executing Simple Harmonic Motion. At a displacement x its potential energy is E_1 and at a displacement y its potential energy is E_2. The potential energy E at displacement $(x + y)$ is
    (a) $\sqrt{E} = \sqrt{E_1} - \sqrt{E_2}$
    (b) $\sqrt{E} = \sqrt{E_1} + \sqrt{E_2}$
    (c) $E = E_1 + E_2$
    (d) $E = E_1 - E_2$

19. A particle moves such that its acceleration a is given by $a = -bx$, where x is the displacement from equilibrium position and b is a constant. The period of oscillation is
    (a) $2\pi\sqrt{b}$
    (b) $\dfrac{2\pi}{\sqrt{b}}$
    (c) $\dfrac{2\pi}{b}$
    (d) $2\sqrt{\dfrac{\pi}{b}}$

20. To make the frequency double of an oscillator, we have to
    (a) double the mass
    (b) half the mass
    (c) quadruple the mass
    (d) reduce the mass to one-fourth

21. The period of a simple pendulum is doubled, when
    (a) its length is doubled.
    (b) the mass of the bob is doubled.
    (c) its length is made four times.
    (d) the mass of the bob and the length of the pendulum are doubled.

22. A simple pendulum is made of a body which is a hollow sphere containing mercury suspended by means of a wire. If a little mercury is drained off, the period of pendulum will

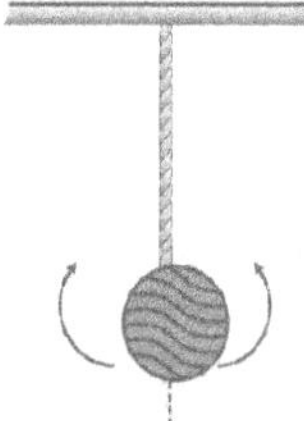

    (a) remain unchanged
    (b) increase
    (c) decrease
    (d) become erratic

23. A pendulum suspended from the ceiling of a train has a period T, when the train is at rest. When the train is accelerating with a uniform acceleration a, the period of oscillation will
    (a) increase
    (b) decrease
    (c) remain unaffected
    (d) become infinite

24. The mass and diameter of a planet are twice those of earth. The period of oscillation of pendulum on this planet will be (If it is a second's pendulum on earth)
    (a) $\dfrac{1}{\sqrt{2}}$ s
    (b) $2\sqrt{2}$ s
    (c) 2 s
    (d) $\dfrac{1}{2}$ s

25. A man measures the period of a simple pendulum inside a stationary lift and finds it to be T s. If the lift accelerates upwards with an acceleration g / 4, then the period of the pendulum will be

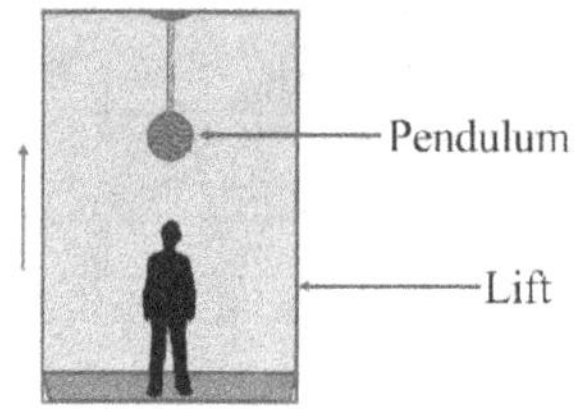

    (a) T
    (b) $\dfrac{T}{4}$
    (c) $\dfrac{2T}{\sqrt{5}}$
    (d) $2T\sqrt{5}$

26. A simple pendulum is executing simple harmonic motion with a time period T. If the length of the pendulum is increased by 21%, the percentage increase in the time period of the pendulum of increased length is
    (a) 10 %
    (b) 21 %
    (c) 30 %
    (d) 50 %

27. A chimpanzee swinging on a swing in a sitting position, stands up suddenly, the time period will
    (a) become infinite
    (b) remain same
    (c) increase
    (d) decrease

28. Length of a simple pendulum is l and its maximum angular displacement is θ, then its maximum K.E. is
    (a) $mgl \sin\theta$
    (b) $mgl(1+\sin\theta)$
    (c) $mgl(1+\cos\theta)$
    (d) $mgl(1-\cos\theta)$

29. Two bodies M and N of equal masses are suspended from two separate massless springs of force constants k_1 and k_2 respectively. If the two bodies oscillate vertically such that their maximum velocities are equal, the ratio of the amplitude M to that of N is
    (a) $\dfrac{k_1}{k_2}$
    (b) $\sqrt{\dfrac{k_1}{k_2}}$
    (c) $\dfrac{k_2}{k_1}$
    (d) $\sqrt{\dfrac{k_2}{k_1}}$

Answer Key	15	(b)	17	(c)	19	(b)	21	(c)	23	(b)	25	(c)	27	(d)	29	(d)
Sol. from page 343	16	(a)	18	(b)	20	(d)	22	(b)	24	(b)	26	(a)	28	(d)		

30. A block of mass m, attached to a spring of spring constant k, oscillates on a smooth horizontal table. The other end of the spring is fixed to a wall. The block has a speed v when the spring is at its natural length. Before coming to an instantaneous rest, if the block moves a distance x from the mean position, then

(a) $x = \sqrt{m/k}$
(b) $x = \dfrac{1}{v}\sqrt{m/k}$
(c) $x = v\sqrt{m/k}$
(d) $x = \sqrt{mv/k}$

31. A mass m attached to a spring oscillates every 2 sec. If the mass is increased by 2 kg, then time-period increases by 1 sec. The initial mass is
(a) 1.6 kg
(b) 3.9 kg
(c) 9.6 kg
(d) 12.6 kg

32. A mass m is suspended separately by two different springs of spring constant k_1 and k_2 gives the time-period t_1 and t_2 respectively. If same mass m is connected by both springs as shown in figure, then time-period t is given by the relation

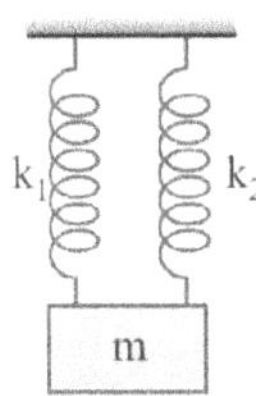

(a) $t = t_1 + t_2$
(b) $t = \dfrac{t_1.t_2}{t_1 + t_2}$
(c) $t^2 = t_1^2 + t_2^2$
(d) $t^{-2} = t_1^{-2} + t_2^{-2}$

33. A horizontal platform with an object placed on it is executing SHM in the vertical direction. The amplitude of oscillation is $3.92 \times 10^{-3} m$. What must be the least period of these oscillations, so that the object is not detached from the platform
(a) 0.1256 s
(b) 0.1356 s
(c) 0.1456 s
(d) 0.1556 s

34. A particle executes simple harmonic motion (amplitude = A) between $x = -A$ and $x = +A$. The time taken for it to go from 0 to $A/2$ is T_1 and to go from $A/2$ to A is T_2. Then
(a) $T_1 < T_2$
(b) $T_1 > T_2$
(c) $T_1 = T_2$
(d) $T_1 = 2T_2$

35. On a smooth inclined plane, a body of mass M is attached between two springs. The other ends of the springs are fixed to firm supports. If each spring has force constant k, the period of oscillation of the body (assuming the spring as massless) is

(a) $2\pi\left(\dfrac{m}{2k}\right)^{1/2}$
(b) $2\pi\left(\dfrac{2M}{k}\right)^{1/2}$
(c) $2\pi\dfrac{Mg\sin\theta}{2k}$
(d) $2\pi\left(\dfrac{2Mg}{k}\right)^{1/2}$

36. An ideal spring with spring-constant k is hung from the ceiling and a block of mass M is attached to its lower end. The mass is released with the spring initially unstretched. Then the maximum extension in the spring is
(a) $4\,Mg/k$
(b) $2\,Mg/k$
(c) Mg/k
(d) $Mg/2k$

37. Which of the following function represents a simple harmonic oscillation?
(a) $\sin\omega t - \cos\omega t$
(b) $\sin^2\omega t$
(c) $\sin\omega t + \sin 2\omega t$
(c) $\sin\omega t - \sin 2\omega t$

38. For a particle executing SHM the displacement x is given by $x = A\cos\omega t$. Identify the graph which represents the variation of potential energy (P.E.) as a function of time t and displacement x

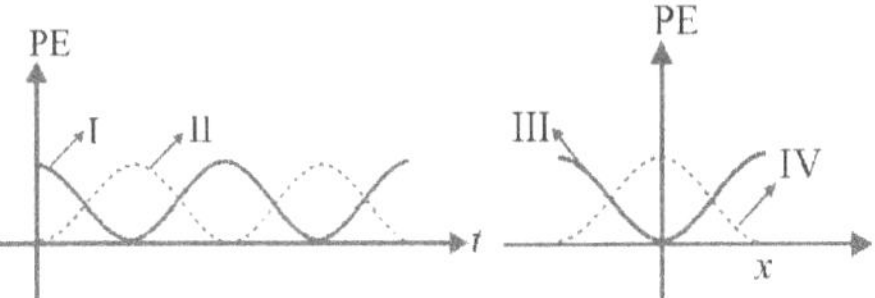

(a) I, III
(b) II, IV
(c) II, III
(d) I, IV

39. A particle of mass 0.3 kg is subjected to a force $F = -kx$ where $k = 15$ N/m . What will be the initial acceleration if it is released from a point 20 cm away from the origin
(a) 15 m/s²
(b) 10 m/s²
(c) 5 m/s²
(d) 3 m/s²

40. Starting from the origin a body oscillates simple harmonically with a period of 2 s. After what time will the kinetic energy be 75 % of its total energy :
(a) $\dfrac{1}{6}$ s
(b) $\dfrac{1}{4}$ s
(c) $\dfrac{1}{3}$ s
(d) $\dfrac{1}{12}$ s

41. A coin is placed on a horizontal plateform which undergoes vertical simple harmonic motion of angular frequency ω. The amplitude of oscillation is gradually increased. The coin will leave contact with the plateform for the first time
(a) at the mean position of the palteform.
(b) for an amplitude of $\dfrac{g}{\omega^2}$.
(c) for an amplitude of $\dfrac{g^2}{\omega^2}$.
(d) at the highest position of the plateform.

42. Which of the following relationships between the acceleration and displacement x of a particle involve SHM?
(a) $a = 2x$
(b) $a = 4x^2$
(c) $a = -5x$
(d) $a = -3x^2$

Answer Key	30	(c)	32	(d)	34	(a)	36	(b)	38	(a)	40	(a)	42	(c)
Sol. from page 343	31	(a)	33	(a)	35	(a)	37	(a)	39	(b)	41	(b)		

43. Given $x = 2.0 \cos 2\pi t$ for SHM, the time period of oscillation is
   (a)   1 s   (b)   2 s
   (c) 2π s   (d)   none of these

44. The acceleration of a particle undergoing SHM is graphed in figure. At point 2 the velocity of the particle :

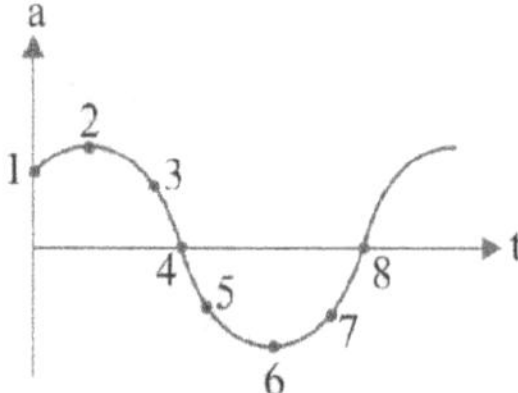

   (a)   zero   (b)   negative
   (c)   positive   (d)   none of these

45. The displacement vs time of a particle executing SHM is shown in figure. The initial phase ϕ

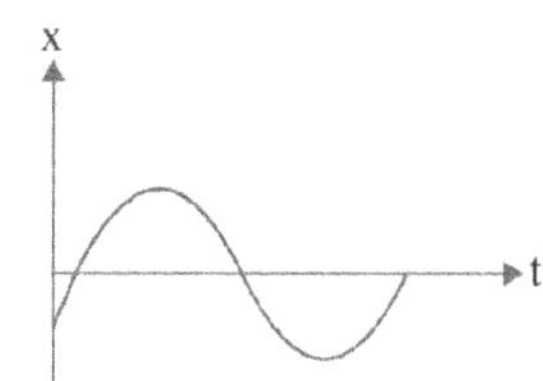

   (a) $-\pi < \phi < -\dfrac{\pi}{2}$ (b) $\pi < \phi < \dfrac{3\pi}{2}$

   (c) $-\dfrac{3\pi}{2} < \phi < -\pi$ (d) $\dfrac{\pi}{2} < \phi < \pi$

46. A graph of the square of the velocity against the square of the acceleration of a given simple harmonic motion is

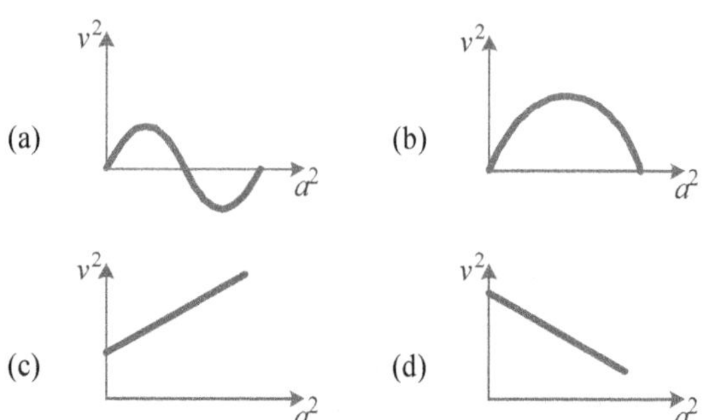

47. Two pendulums have time periods T and $5T/4$. They start SHM at the same time from the mean position. After how many oscillations of the smaller pendulum they will be again in the same phase
   (a)   5   (b)   4
   (c)   11   (d)   9

48. If the potential energy of a harmonic oscillator of mass 2 kg on its equilibrium position is 5 joules and the total energy is 9 joules when the amplitude is one meter, the period of the oscillator (in sec) is
   (a)   1.5   (b)   3.14
   (c)   6.28   (d)   4.67

49. A mass of 2.0 kg is put on a flat pan attached to a vertical spring fixed on the ground as shown in the figure. The mass of the spring and the pan is negligible. When pressed slightly and released the mass executes a simple harmonic motion. The spring constant is 200 N/m. What should be the minimum amplitude of the motion so that the mass gets detached from the pan (Take g = 10 m/s^2)

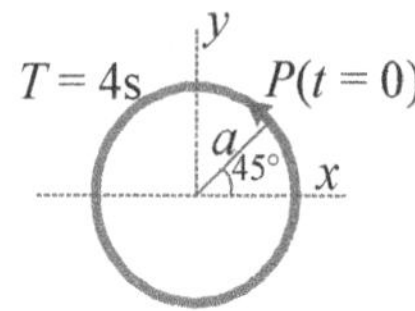

   (a)   8.0 cm

   (b)   10.0 cm

   (c)   Any value less than 12.0 cm

   (d)   4.0 cm

50. The following figure depict a circular motion. The radius of the circle, the period of revolution, the initial position and the sense of revolution are indicated on the figure.

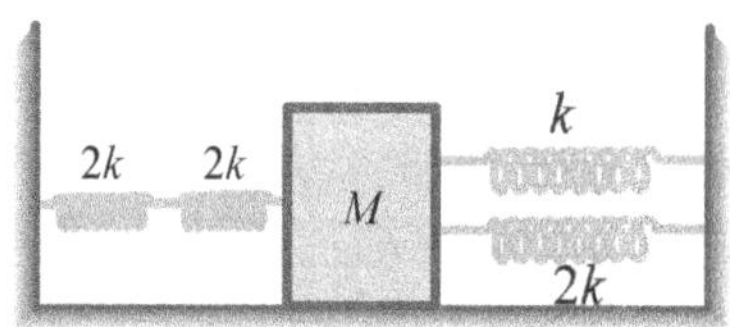

The simple harmonic motion of the x-projection of the radius vector of the rotating particle P can be shown as :

   (a) $x(t) = a \cos\left(\dfrac{2\pi t}{4} + \dfrac{\pi}{4}\right)$ (b) $x(t) = a \cos\left(\dfrac{\pi t}{4} + \dfrac{\pi}{4}\right)$

   (c) $x(t) = a \sin\left(\dfrac{2\pi t}{4} + \dfrac{\pi}{4}\right)$ (d) $x(t) = a \cos\left(\dfrac{\pi t}{3} + \dfrac{\pi}{2}\right)$

51. Four massless springs whose force constants are $2k$, $2k$, k and $2k$ respectively are attached to a mass M kept on a frictionless plane (as shown in figure). If the mass M is displaced in the horizontal direction, then the frequency of the system

   (a) $\dfrac{1}{2\pi}\sqrt{\dfrac{k}{4M}}$ (b) $\dfrac{1}{2\pi}\sqrt{\dfrac{4k}{M}}$

   (c) $\dfrac{1}{2\pi}\sqrt{\dfrac{k}{7M}}$ (d) $\dfrac{1}{2\pi}\sqrt{\dfrac{7k}{M}}$

52. A particle moves on the x-axis according to the law, $x = A \sin^2 \omega t$. The motion is simple harmonic
   (a)   with amplitude A (b)   with amplitude $A/2$
   (c)   with time period π/ω (d)   with time period $2\pi/\omega$

Answer Key	43	(a)	45	(a)	47	(a)	49	(b)	51	(b)
Sol. from page 343	44	(a)	46	(d)	48	(b)	50	(a)	52	(b)

Level -2

Only one option correct

1. A bent tube of uniform cross-section area A has a non-viscous liquid of density ρ. The mass of liquid in the tube is m. The time period of oscillation of the liquid is

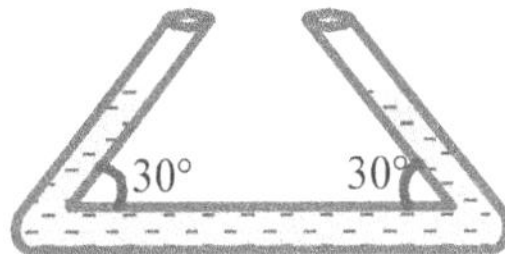

(a) $2\pi\sqrt{\dfrac{m}{\rho gA}}$

(b) $2\pi\sqrt{\dfrac{m}{2\rho gA}}$

(c) $2\pi\sqrt{\dfrac{2m}{\rho gA}}$

(d) none of these

2. Two blocks of masses m and $2m$ are connected to a massless spring of force constant k. the spring is stretched by x_0 and the blocks are made to oscillate on a smooth horizontal surface. The amplitude of motion of block of mass m is

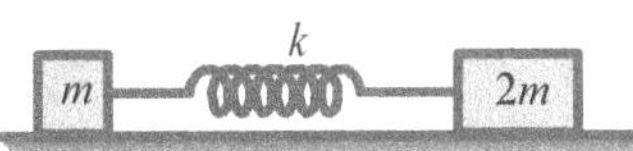

(a) $x_0/3$

(b) $2x_0/3$

(c) x_0

(d) $x_0/6$

3. A mass M is suspended from a light spring. An additional mass m added displaces the spring further by a distance x. Now the combined mass will oscillate on the spring with period

(a) $T = 2\pi\sqrt{\left(mg\,/\,x\left(M+m\right)\right)}$

(b) $T = 2\pi\sqrt{\left(\left(M+m\right)x\,/\,mg\right)}$

(c) $T = \left(\pi\,/\,2\right)\sqrt{\left(mg\,/\,x\left(M+m\right)\right)}$

(d) $T = 2\pi\sqrt{\left(\left(M+m\right)/\,mgx\right)}$

4. A particle at the end of a spring executes simple harmonic motion with a period t_1, while the corresponding period for another spring is t_2. If the period of oscillation with the two springs in series is T, then

(a) $T = t_1 + t_2$

(b) $T^2 = t_1^2 + t_2^2$

(c) $T^{-1} = t_1^{-1} + t_2^{-1}$

(d) $T^{-2} = t_1^{-2} + t_2^{-2}$

5. A mass M is suspended from a spring of negligible mass. The spring is pulled a little and then released so that the mass executes SHM of time period T. If the mass is increased by m, the time period becomes $5T/3$. Then the ratio of m/M is

(a) $\dfrac{5}{3}$

(b) $\dfrac{3}{5}$

(c) $\dfrac{25}{9}$

(d) $\dfrac{16}{9}$

6. Two masses m_1 and m_2 are suspended together by a massless spring of constant k. When the masses are in equilibrium, m_1 is removed without disturbing the system. The amplitude of oscillations is

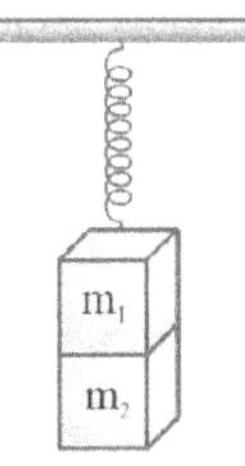

(a) $\dfrac{m_1 g}{k}$

(b) $\dfrac{m_2 g}{k}$

(c) $\dfrac{\left(m_1 + m_2\right)g}{k}$

(d) $\dfrac{\left(m_1 - m_2\right)g}{k}$

7. The displacement of a particle varies according to the relation $x = 4\left(\cos \pi t + \sin \pi t\right)$. The amplitude of the particle is

(a) 8

(b) -4

(c) 4

(d) $4\sqrt{2}$

8. A particle of mass m is executing oscillations about the origin on the x-axis. Its potential energy is $U\left(x\right) = k\left[x\right]^3$, where k is a positive constant. If the amplitude of oscillation is a, then its time period T is

(a) proportional to $\dfrac{1}{\sqrt{a}}$

(b) independent of a

(c) proportional to $\sqrt{a}$

(d) proportional to $a^{3/2}$

9. A cylindrical piston of mass M slides smoothly inside a long cylinder closed at one end, enclosing a certain mass of gas. The cylinder is kept with its axis horizontal. If the piston is disturbed from its equilibrium position, it oscillates simple harmonically. The period of oscillation will be

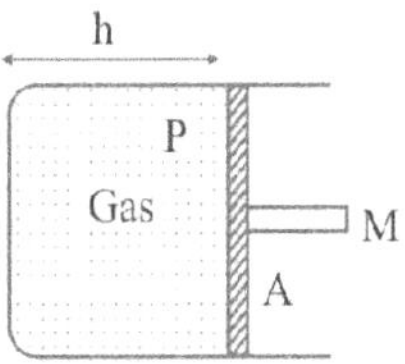

(a) $T = 2\pi\sqrt{\left(\dfrac{Mh}{PA}\right)}$

(b) $T = 2\pi\sqrt{\left(\dfrac{MA}{Ph}\right)}$

(c) $T = 2\pi\sqrt{\left(\dfrac{M}{PAh}\right)}$

(d) $T = 2\pi\sqrt{MPhA}$

Answer Key	1	(a)	3	(b)	5	(d)	7	(d)	9	(a)
Sol. from page 345	2	(b)	4	(b)	6	(a)	8	(a)		

10. A clock which keeps correct time at $20°C$, is subjected to $40°C$. If coefficient of linear expansion of the pendulum is $12 \times 10^{-6} / °C$. How much will it gain or loose in time

    (a) 10.3 s/day   (b) 20.6 s/day

    (c) 5 s/day   (d) 20 min./day

11. The period of oscillation of a simple pendulum of length L suspended from the roof of a vehicle which moves without friction down an inclined plane of inclination α, is given by

    (a) $2\pi\sqrt{\dfrac{L}{g\cos\alpha}}$ (b) $2\pi\sqrt{\dfrac{L}{g\sin\alpha}}$

    (c) $2\pi\sqrt{\dfrac{L}{g}}$ (d) $2\pi\sqrt{\dfrac{L}{g\tan\alpha}}$

12. The bob of a simple pendulum executes simple harmonic motion in water with a period t, while the period of oscillation of the bob is t_0 in air. Neglecting frictional force of water and given that the density of the bob is $(4/3)\times 1000\,\text{kg}/\text{m}^3$. What relationship between t and t_0 is true

    (a) $t = t_0$ (b) $t = t_0 / 2$

    (c) $t = 2t_0$ (d) $t = 4t_0$

13. A spring of force constant k is cut into two pieces such that one piece is double the length of the other. Then the long piece will have a force constant of

    (a) $(2/3)k$ (b) $(3/2)k$

    (c) $3k$ (d) $6k$

14. One end of a long metallic wire of length L is tied to the ceiling. The other end is tied to massless spring of spring constant k. A mass m hangs freely from the free end of the spring. The area of cross-section and Young's modulus of the wire are A and Y respectively. If the mass is slightly pulled down and released, it will oscillate with a time period T equal to

    (a) $2\pi\left(\dfrac{m}{k}\right)$ (b) $2\pi\left\{\dfrac{(YA+kL)m}{YAk}\right\}^{1/2}$

    (c) $2\pi\dfrac{mYA}{kL}$ (d) $2\pi\dfrac{mL}{YA}$

15. The displacement y of a particle executing periodic motion is given by $y = 4\cos^2(t/2)\sin(1000t)$. This expression may be considered to be a result of the superposition of independent harmonic motions

    (a) Two   (b) Three

    (c) Four   (d) Five

16. The function $\sin^2(\omega t)$ represents

    (a) a simple harmonic motion with a period $2\pi/\omega$.

    (b) a simple harmonic motion with a period π/ω.

    (c) a periodic but not simple harmonic motion with a period $2\pi/\omega$.

    (d) a periodic but not simple harmonic motion with a period π/ω.

17. A simple pendulum has time period T_1. The point of suspension is now moved upward according to equation $y = kt^2$ where $k = 1\,\text{m}/\text{s}^2$. If new time period is T_2, then ratio $\dfrac{T_1^2}{T_2^2}$ will be

    (a) $2/3$ (b) $5/6$

    (c) $6/5$ (d) $3/2$

18. A simple pendulum is hanging from a peg inserted in a vertical wall. Its bob is stretched in horizontal position from the wall and is left free to move. The bob hits on the wall the coefficient of restitution is $\dfrac{2}{\sqrt{5}}$. After how many collisions the amplitude of vibration will become less than $60°$

    (a) 6   (b) 3

    (c) 5   (d) 4

19. Two identical balls A and B each of mass 0.1 kg are attached to two identical massless springs. The spring mass system is constrained to move inside a rigid smooth pipe bent in the form of a circle as shown in the figure. The pipe is fixed in a horizontal plane. The centres of the balls can move in a circle of radius 0.06 m. Each spring has a natural length of 0.06π m and force constant $0.1\,\text{N}/\text{m}$. Initially both the balls are displaced by an angle $\theta = \pi/6$ radian with respect to the diameter PQ of the circle and released from rest. The frequency of oscillation of the ball B is

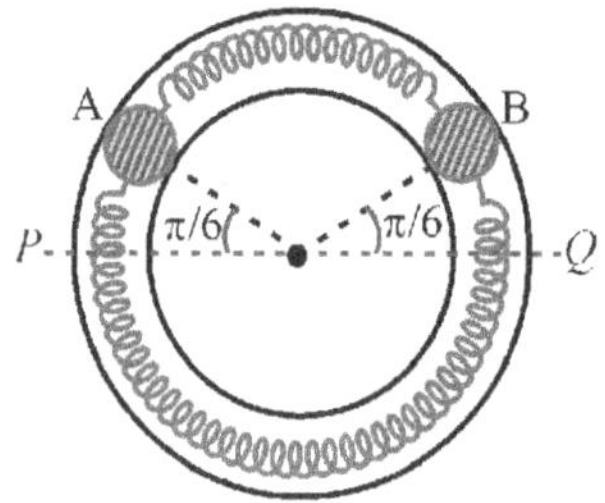

    (a) $\pi\,\text{Hz}$ (b) $\dfrac{1}{\pi}\,\text{Hz}$

    (c) $2\pi\,\text{Hz}$ (d) $\dfrac{1}{2\pi}\,\text{Hz}$

Answer Key	10	(a)	12	(c)	14	(b)	16	(d)	18	(b)
Sol. from page 345	11	(a)	13	(b)	15	(b)	17	(c)	19	(b)

20. One end of a spring of force constant k is fixed to a vertical wall and the other to a block of mass m resting on a smooth horizontal surface. There is another wall at a distance x_0 from the block. The spring is then compressed by $2x_0$ and released. The time taken to strike the wall is

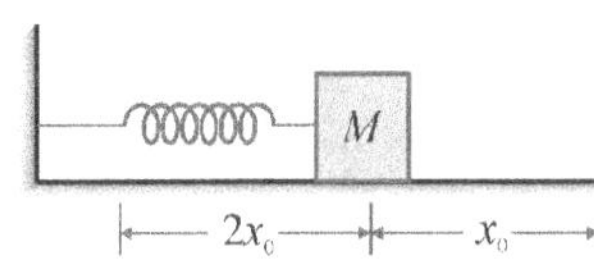

(a) $\dfrac{1}{6}\pi\sqrt{\dfrac{k}{m}}$

(b) $\sqrt{\dfrac{k}{m}}$

(c) $\dfrac{2\pi}{3}\sqrt{\dfrac{m}{k}}$

(d) $\dfrac{\pi}{4}\sqrt{\dfrac{k}{m}}$

21. A particle free to move along x - axis has potential energy given by $U(x) = k[1 - \exp(-x^2)]$ for $-\infty \le x \le +\infty$ where k is a positive constant of appropriate dimensions, then :
    (a) at points for away from origin the particle is in unstable equilibrium.
    (b) for any finite non-zero value of x, there is a force directed away from the origin.
    (c) if its total mechanical energy is $\dfrac{K}{2}$, it has minimum kinetic energy at the origin.
    (d) for small displacements from $x = 0$, the motion is simple harmonic.

22. A block P of mass m is placed on a smooth horizontal surface. A block Q of same mass is placed over the block P and the coefficient of static friction between them is μ_s. A spring of spring constant k is attached to block Q. The blocks are displaced together to a distance A and released. The upper block oscillates without slipping over the lower block. The maximum frictional force between the blocks is

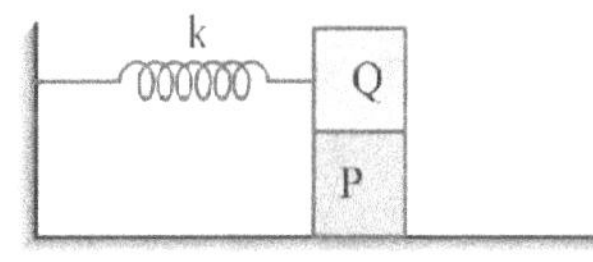

(a) zero

(b) kA

(c) $\dfrac{1}{2}kA$

(d) $\mu_s g$

23. A block of mass M is connected to a spring of force constant k and is placed on a smooth horizontal surface. The block is displaces and it compresses the spring by a. If a vertical wall is at a distance b $(b < a)$ from the mean position of the block, then the time period of motion of the block assuming elastic collision between block and the wall

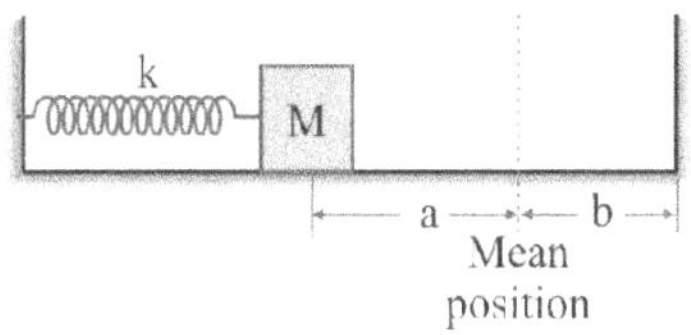

(a) $2\pi\sqrt{\dfrac{M}{k}}$

(b) $2\pi\dfrac{b}{a}\sqrt{\dfrac{M}{k}}$

(c) $[\pi + 4\pi\sin^{-1}\dfrac{b}{a}]\sqrt{\dfrac{M}{k}}$

(d) $[\pi + \sin^{-1}\dfrac{b}{a}]\sqrt{\dfrac{M}{k}}$

24. A block of mass M is connected to a spring of force constant k and is placed on a smooth horizontal surface. The block is displaces and compresses the spring by a. The block is left free to move from this position, when the block is at a distance $a/2$ from the mean position it collides elastically with an identical block. Time the oscillating block takes to reach from extreme to the mean position is :

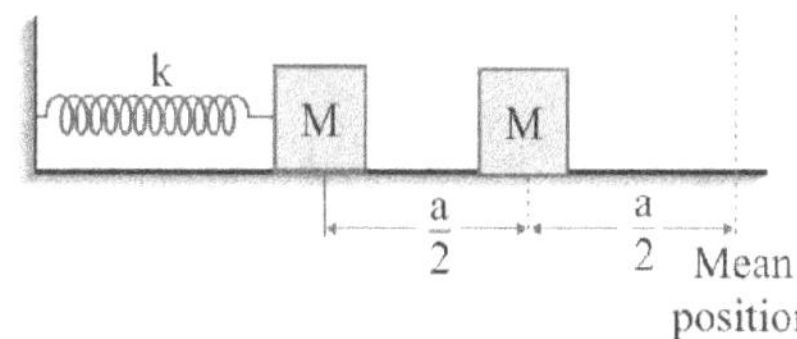

(a) $2\pi\sqrt{\dfrac{M}{k}}$

(b) $\pi\sqrt{\dfrac{M}{k}}$

(c) $\dfrac{5\pi}{6}\sqrt{\dfrac{M}{k}}$

(d) None

25. A highly rigid cubical block A of small mass M and side L is fixed rigidly onto another cubical block B of same dimensions and of **low modulus of rigidly** η such that lower face of A completely covers the upper face of B. The lower face of B is rigidly held on a horizontal surface. A small force F is applied perpendicular to one of the side face of A. After the force is withdrawn, block A executes small oscillations, the time period of which is given by :

(a) $2\pi\sqrt{M\eta L}$

(b) $2\pi\sqrt{\dfrac{M\eta}{L}}$

(c) $\dfrac{2\pi\sqrt{ML}}{\eta}$

(d) $2\pi\sqrt{\dfrac{M}{\eta L}}$

26. A cylinder of mass m and radius R is attached to massless spring-pulley system as shown in figure. The friction is sufficient to cause pure rolling of the cylinder. The time period of cylinder of small horizontal displacement is

(a) $2\pi\sqrt{\dfrac{m}{2k}}$

(b) $2\pi\sqrt{\dfrac{m}{k}}$

(c) $2\pi\sqrt{\dfrac{2m}{k}}$

(d) none of these

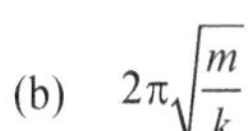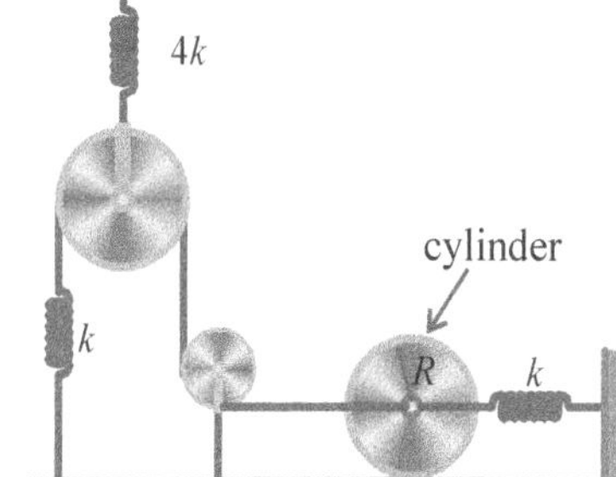

Answer Key	20	(c)	22	(c)	24	(c)	26	(b)
Sol. from page 345	21	(d)	23	(c)	25	(d)		

27. A man is swinging on a swing made of 2 ropes of equal length L and in direction perpendicular to the plane of paper. The time period of the small oscillations about the mean position is

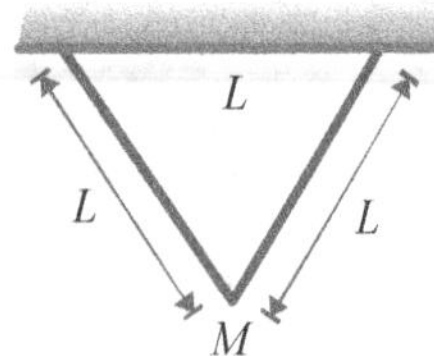

(a) $2\pi\sqrt{\dfrac{L}{2g}}$ (b) $2\pi\sqrt{\dfrac{\sqrt{3}L}{2g}}$

(c) $2\pi\sqrt{\dfrac{L}{2\sqrt{3}g}}$ (d) $\pi\sqrt{\dfrac{L}{g}}$

28. A particle performs SHM in a straight line. In the first second, starting from rest, it travels a distance a and in the next second it travels a distance b in the same direction. The amplitude of the SHM is

(a) $a - b$ (b) $\dfrac{2a - b}{3}$

(c) $\dfrac{2a^2}{3a - b}$ (d) none of these

29. In block-springs system is shown figure, all the spring and pulleys are massless. The time period of small vertical displacement of block is

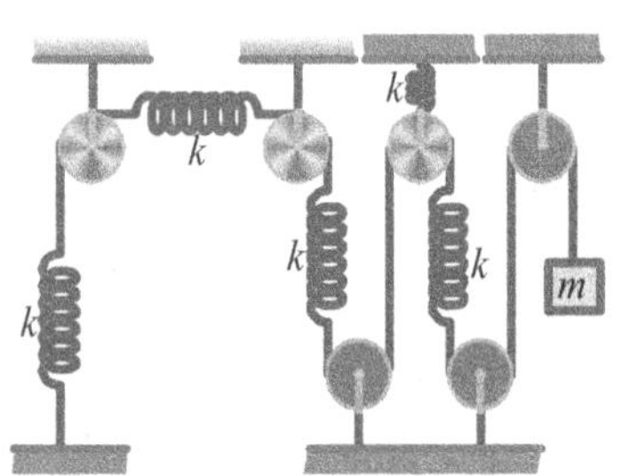

(a) $T = 2\pi\sqrt{\dfrac{m}{k}}$ (b) $T = 2\pi\sqrt{\dfrac{8m}{k}}$

(c) $T = 2\pi\sqrt{\dfrac{4m}{k}}$ (d) none of these

30. A small bob attached to a light inextensible thread of length l has a periodic time T when allowed to vibrate as a simple pendulum. The thread is now suspended from a fixed end O of a vertical rigid rod of length $\dfrac{3l}{4}$ (as in figure). If now the pendulum performs periodic oscillations in this arrangement, the periodic time will be

(a) $\dfrac{3T}{4}$

(b) $\dfrac{T}{2}$

(c) T

(d) $2T$

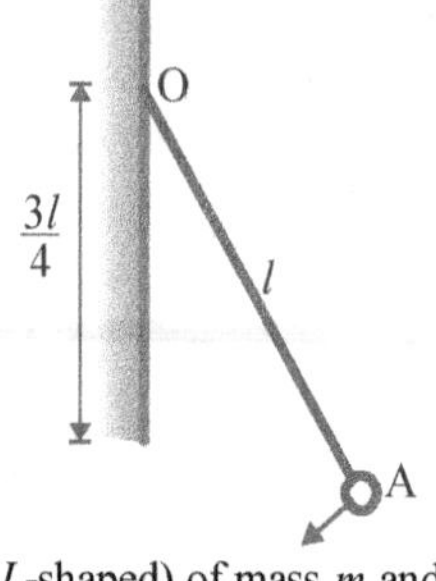

31. A system of two identical rods (L-shaped) of mass m and length l are resting on a peg P as shown in the figure. If the system is displaced in its plane by a small angle θ, find the period of oscillations

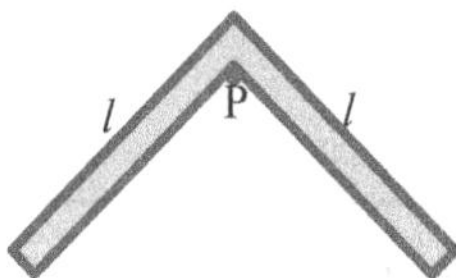

(a) $2\pi\sqrt{\dfrac{\sqrt{2}l}{3g}}$ (b) $2\pi\sqrt{\dfrac{2\sqrt{2}l}{3g}}$

(c) $2\pi\sqrt{\dfrac{2l}{3g}}$ (d) $3\pi\sqrt{\dfrac{l}{3g}}$

32. In the figure shown, the spring are connected to the rod at one end and at the midpoint. The rod is hinged at its lower end. Rotational SHM of the rod (Mass m, length L) will occur only if

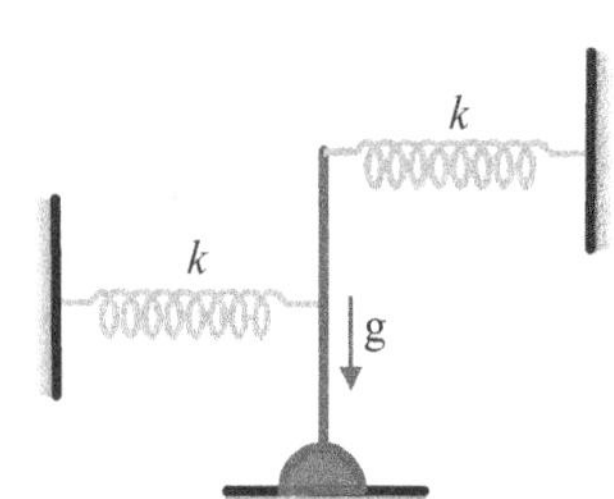

(a) $k > mg/3L$ (b) $k > 2mg/3L$
(c) $k > 2mg/5L$ (d) $k > 0$

33. Part of a simple harmonic motion is graphed in the figure, where y is the displacement from the mean position. The correct equation describing this S.H. M. is

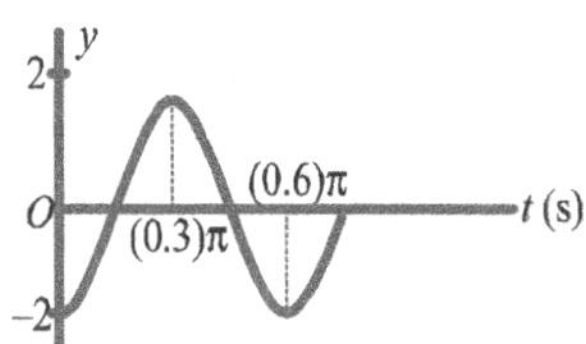

(a) $y = 4\cos(0.6t)$ (b) $y = 2\sin\left(\dfrac{10}{3}t - \dfrac{\pi}{2}\right)$

(c) $y = 4\sin\left(\dfrac{10}{3}t + \dfrac{\pi}{2}\right)$ (d) $y = 2\cos\left(\dfrac{10}{3}t + \dfrac{\pi}{2}\right)$

Answer Key	27	(b)	29	(b)	31	(b)	33	(b)
Sol. from page 345	28	(c)	30	(a)	32	(c)		

34. A uniform rod of length L and mass M is pivoted at the centre. Its two ends are attached to two springs of equal spring constants k. The springs are fixed to rigid supports as shown in the figure, and the rod is free to oscillate in the horizontal plane. The rod is gently pushed through a small angle θ in one direction and released. The frequency of oscillation is

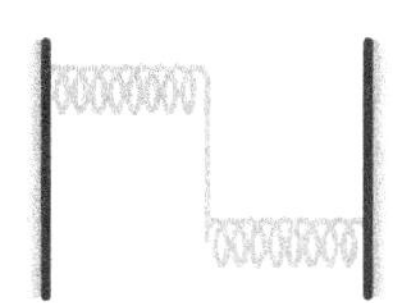

(a) $\dfrac{1}{2\pi}\sqrt{\dfrac{2k}{M}}$

(b) $\dfrac{1}{2\pi}\sqrt{\dfrac{k}{M}}$

(c) $\dfrac{1}{2\pi}\sqrt{\dfrac{6k}{M}}$

(d) $\dfrac{1}{2\pi}\sqrt{\dfrac{24k}{M}}$

35. On a smooth inclined plane, a body of mass M is attached between two springs. The other ends of the springs are fixed to firm supports. If each spring has force constant k, the period of oscillation of the body (assuming the springs as massless) is

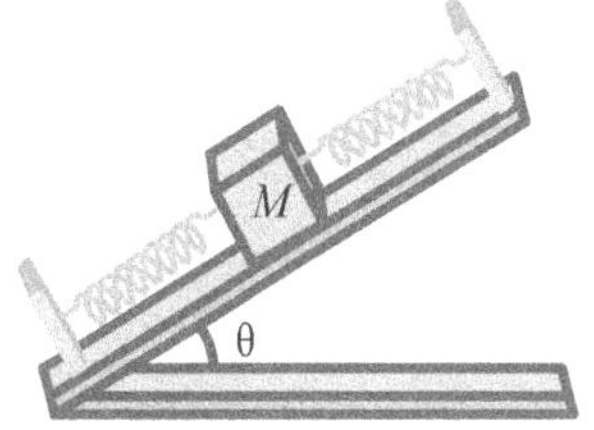

(a) $2\pi\left(\dfrac{M}{2k}\right)^{1/2}$

(b) $2\pi\left(\dfrac{2M}{k}\right)^{1/2}$

(c) $2\pi\dfrac{Mg\sin\theta}{2k}$

(d) $2\pi\left(\dfrac{2Mg}{k}\right)^{1/2}$

36. In the arrangement of block-springs system the block is displaced down slightly. The time period of oscillations is

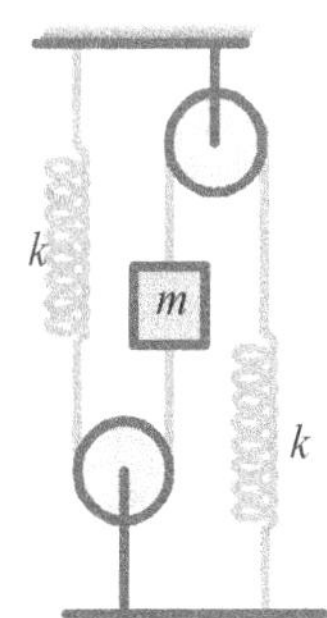

(a) $\sqrt{2}\,\pi\sqrt{\dfrac{m}{k}}$

(b) $2\pi\sqrt{\dfrac{m}{k}}$

(c) $\pi\sqrt{\dfrac{m}{2k}}$

(d) none of these

37. A block of mass m is connected with two ideal pulley and a massless spring of force constant k as shown in fig. The block is slightly displaced from its equilibrium position, its time period of oscillation is

(a) $2\pi\sqrt{\dfrac{m}{k}}$

(b) $4\pi\sqrt{\dfrac{m}{k}}$

(c) $6\pi\sqrt{\dfrac{m}{k}}$

(d) $8\pi\sqrt{\dfrac{m}{k}}$

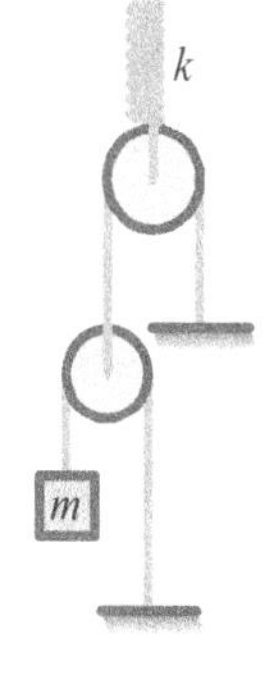

38. Three simple harmonic motions in the same direction having the same amplitude A and same period are superposed. If each differs in phase from the next by $45°$ then

(a) the resultant amplitude is $(1+\sqrt{3})A$

(b) the phase of the resultant motion relative to the first is $90°$

(c) the energy associated with the resulting motion is $(3+2\sqrt{2})$ times the energy associated with any single motion.

(d) the resulting motion is not simple harmonic.

39. The height of liquid column in a U tube is 0.3 meter. If the liquid in one of the limbs is depressed and then released, then the time period of liquid column will be

(a) 1.1 sec   (b) 19 sec   (c) 0.11 sec   (d) 2 sec

40. A horizontal rod of mass m and length L is pivoted smoothly at one end. The rod's other end is supported by a spring of force constant k. The rod is rotated (in vertical plane) by a small angle θ from its horizontal equilibrium position and released. The angular frequency of the subsequent simple harmonic motion is

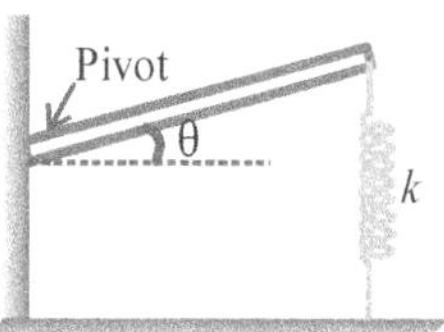

(a) $\sqrt{\dfrac{3k}{m}}$

(b) $\sqrt{\dfrac{k}{3m}}$

(c) $\sqrt{\dfrac{3k}{m}+\dfrac{3g}{2L}}$

(d) $\sqrt{\dfrac{k}{m}}$

Answer Key	**34**	(c)	**36**	(a)	**38**	(c)	**40**	(a)
Sol. from page 345	**35**	(a)	**37**	(d)	**39**	(a)		

41. A mass m is suspended from a spring of force constant k and just touches another identical spring fixed to the floor as shown in the figure. The time period of small oscillations is

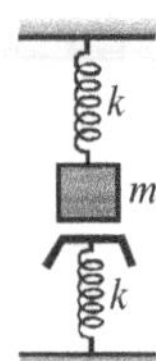

(a) $2\pi\sqrt{\dfrac{m}{k}}$

(b) $\pi\sqrt{\dfrac{m}{k}} + \pi\sqrt{\dfrac{m}{k/2}}$

(c) $\pi\sqrt{\dfrac{m}{3k/2}}$

(d) $\pi\sqrt{\dfrac{m}{k}} + \pi\sqrt{\dfrac{m}{2k}}$.

42. A massless rod is pivoted at point O. A string carrying a mass m at one end is attached to the point A on the rod.

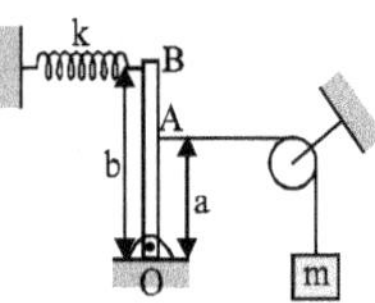

The period of small vertical oscillation of mass m around its equilibrium position is

(a) $T = 2\pi\dfrac{a}{b}\sqrt{\dfrac{m}{k}}$

(b) $T = \pi\dfrac{a}{b}\sqrt{\dfrac{m}{k}}$

(c) $T = 2\pi\dfrac{b}{a}\sqrt{\dfrac{m}{k}}$

(d) $T = \pi\dfrac{b}{a}\sqrt{\dfrac{m}{k}}$

43. When an oscillator completes 100 oscillations, its amplitude reduces to one third of its initial value A_0. Its amplitude at the end of 200 oscillations will be

(a) $A_0 / 8$

(b) $2A_0 / 3$

(c) $A_0 / 6$

(d) $A_0 / 9$

44. A block of mass m is suspended from a spring and executes vertical SHM of time period T as shown in figure.

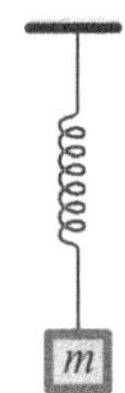

The amplitude of the SHM is A, spring is never in compressed state during the oscillation. The minimum force exerted by spring is never in compressed state during the oscillation. The minimum force exerted by spring on the block is

(a) $mg - \dfrac{4\pi^2}{T^2} mA$

(b) $mg + \dfrac{4\pi^2}{T^2} mA$

(c) $mg - \dfrac{\pi^2}{T^2} mA$

(d) $mg + \dfrac{\pi^2}{T^2} mA$

45. m_1 and m_2 are connected with a light inextensible string with m_1 lying on smooth table and m_2 hanging as shown in figure. m_1 is also connected to a light spring which is initially unstretched and the system is released from rest –

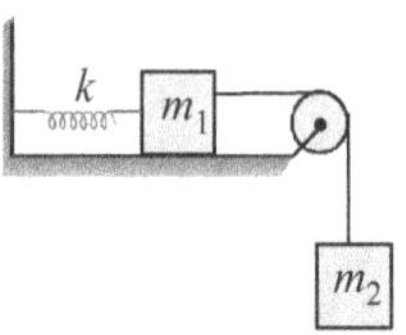

(a)   system performs SHM with angular frequency given by
$$\sqrt{\dfrac{k(m_1 + m_2)}{m_1 m_2}}$$

(b)   system performs SHM with angular frequency given by
$$\sqrt{\dfrac{k}{m_1 + m_2}}$$

(c)   tension in string will be 0 when the system is released.

(d)   maximum displacement of m_1 will be $\dfrac{m_2 g}{k}$

46. The bob in a simple pendulum of length ℓ is released at $t = 0$ from the position of small angular displacement θ. Linear displacement of the bob at any time t from the mean position is given by

(a) $\ell\theta\cos\sqrt{\dfrac{g}{\ell}}\, t$

(b) $\ell\sqrt{\dfrac{g}{\ell}}\, t\cos\theta$

(c) $\ell g \sin\theta$

(d) $\ell\theta\sin\sqrt{\dfrac{g}{\ell}}\, t$

47. A block of mass m, attached to a fixed position O on a smooth inclined wedge of mass M, oscillates with amplitude A and linear frequency f. The wedge is located on a rough horizontal surface. If the angle of the wedge is $60°$, then the force of friction acting on the wedge is given by (coefficient of static friction = μ)

(a) $\mu(M + m)g$

(b) $\dfrac{1}{2} m\omega^2 A \sin\omega t$

(c) $\mu(M + m)\omega^2 A \sin\omega t$

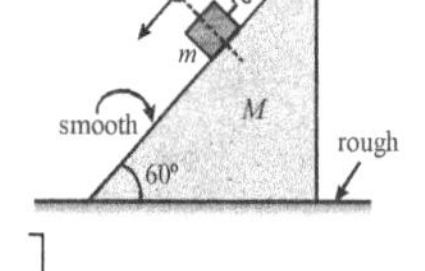

(d) $\mu\left[(M + m)g + \dfrac{\sqrt{3}}{2} m\omega^2 A \sin\omega t \right]$

48. A system is shown in the figure. The time period for small oscillations of the two blocks will be

(a) $2\pi\sqrt{\dfrac{3m}{k}}$

(b) $2\pi\sqrt{\dfrac{3m}{2k}}$

(c) $2\pi\sqrt{\dfrac{3m}{4k}}$

(d) $2\pi\sqrt{\dfrac{3m}{8k}}$

49. A uniform pole of length $2L$ is laid on a smooth horizontal table as shown in figure. The mass of pole is M and it is connected to a frictionless axis at O. A spring with force constant k is connected to the other end. The pole is displaced by a small angle θ from equilibrium position and released such that it performs small oscillations. Its frequency of oscillations

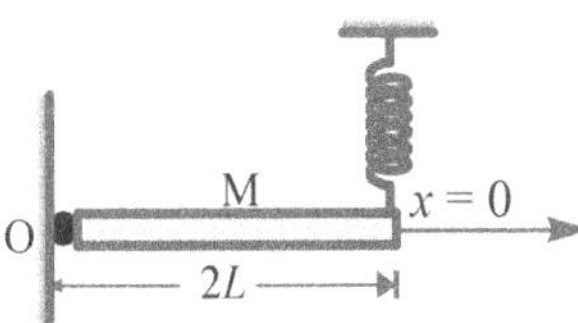

(a) $\omega = \sqrt{\dfrac{M}{3k}}$

(b) $\omega = \sqrt{\dfrac{k}{3M}}$

(c) $\omega = \sqrt{\dfrac{3k}{M}}$

(d) $\omega = \sqrt{\dfrac{k}{2M}}$

50. A U-tube is of non uniform cross-section. The area of cross-sections of two sides of tube are A and 2A (see fig.). It contains non-viscous liquid of mass m. The liquid is displaced slightly and free to oscillate. Its time period of oscillations is

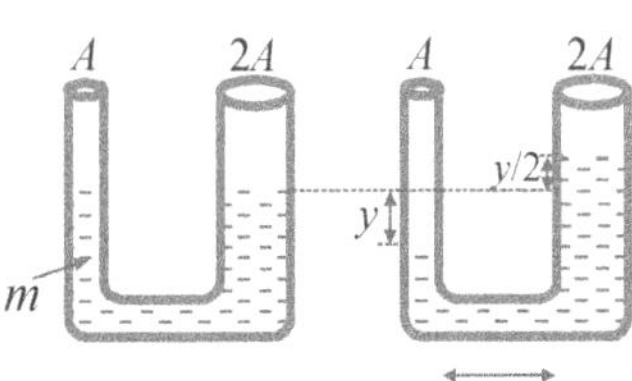

(a) $T = 2\pi\sqrt{\dfrac{m}{3\rho gA}}$

(b) $T = 2\pi\sqrt{\dfrac{m}{2\rho gA}}$

(c) $T = 2\pi\sqrt{\dfrac{m}{\rho gA}}$

(d) none of these

51. A ring of mass M and radius R is hanged from a point on the rim. The ring displaced slightly along its plane, and free to oscillate. The length of equivalent simple pendulum ℓ is

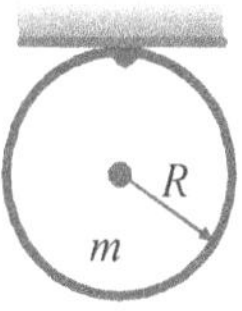

(a) $\ell = R$

(b) $\ell = 2R$

(c) $\ell = \sqrt{2}\,R$

(d) none of these

52. Two pendulum having lengths 1 m and 16 m are both provided small displacements in the same direction at the same instant. They will again be in phase at the mean position after the shorter pendulum completes

(a) $\dfrac{1}{4}$ th oscillation

(b) 4 oscillations

(c) 5 oscillations

(d) 16 oscillations

53. A charged particle is deflected by two mutually perpendicular oscillating electric fields such that the displacement of the particle due to each one of them is given by

$x = a \sin(\omega t)$ and $y = a \sin\left(\omega t + \dfrac{\pi}{6}\right)$ respectively. The trajectory followed by the charged particle is

(a) a circle with equation $x^2 + y^2 = a^2$

(b) a straight line with equation $y = \sqrt{3}\,x$

(c) an ellipse with equation $x^2 + y^2 - xy = \dfrac{3}{4}\,a^2$

(d) an ellipse with equation

$$x^2 + y^2 - \sqrt{3}\,xy = \dfrac{1}{4}\,a^2$$

54. Consider the following statements :

A body vibrating due to forced oscillation is acted upon by

1. a restoring force which is direct proportional to its displacement

2. a retarding force which is direct proportional to its velocity

3. an external periodic force of constant amplitude and frequency of these statements

(a) 1 and 2 are correct

(b) 2 and 3 are correct

(c) 1 and 3 are correct

(d) 1, 2 and 3 are correct

55. The angular frequency of motion whose equation is

$$4\dfrac{d^2 y}{dt^2} + 9y = 0 \text{ is (where } y \text{ is displacement and } t \text{ is time)}$$

(a) $\dfrac{9}{4}$

(b) $\dfrac{4}{9}$

(c) $\dfrac{3}{2}$

(d) $\dfrac{2}{3}$

Answer Key								
Sol. from page 345	**48**	(c)	**50**	(a)	**52**	(b)	**54**	(d)
	49	(c)	**51**	(b)	**53**	(d)	**55**	(c)

56. The displacement of a body *in* a one–dimensional motion is represented by the equation : $x\,(t) = 3\sin \pi t + 4\cos \pi t$.

    Which one of the following is the correct statement :

    (a) This equation represents SHM of amplitude 5 units and frequency 1 unit

    (b) This equation represent SHM of amplitude 5 units and frequency 2 units

    (c) This equation represent SHM of amplitude 5 units and frequency 1/2 units

    (d) This equation does not represent SHM

57. A particle slides back and forth between two inclined frictionless planes joined smoothly at the bottom. The time period of the motion

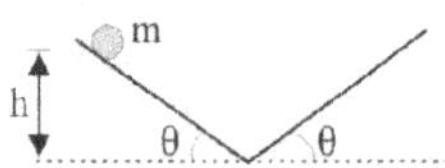

    (a) $\sqrt{\dfrac{2h}{g}}$ (b) $\dfrac{1}{\sin\theta}\sqrt{\dfrac{2h}{g}}$

    (c) $\sqrt{\dfrac{32h}{g}}\sin\theta$ (d) $\dfrac{4}{\sin\theta}\sqrt{\dfrac{2h}{g}}$

58. A rod of mass M and length L is hinged at its centre of mass so that it can rotate in a vertical plane. Two springs each of stiffness k are connected at its ends, as shown in the figure. The time period of SHM is

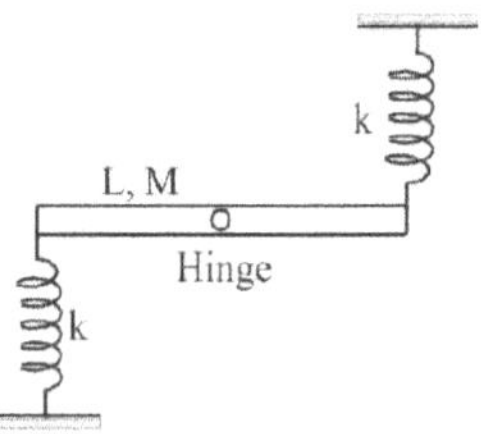

    (a) $2\pi\sqrt{\dfrac{M}{6k}}$ (b) $2\pi\sqrt{\dfrac{M}{3k}}$

    (c) $2\pi\sqrt{\dfrac{ML}{k}}$ (d) $\pi\sqrt{\dfrac{M}{6k}}$

59. Three identical massless springs each of force constant k are attached to a block of mass M with two massless pulleys as shown. The time period of vertical oscillations of the block is

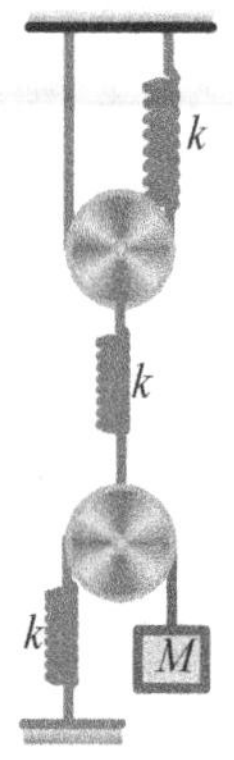

    (a) $2\pi\sqrt{\dfrac{6M}{k}}$ (b) $2\pi\sqrt{\dfrac{M}{6k}}$

    (c) $2\pi\sqrt{\dfrac{3M}{k}}$ (d) $2\pi\sqrt{\dfrac{M}{k}}$

60. A block of mass m is kept on smooth horizontal surface and connected with two springs as shown in figure. Initially springs are in their natural length. Time period of small horizontal oscillation of the block is :

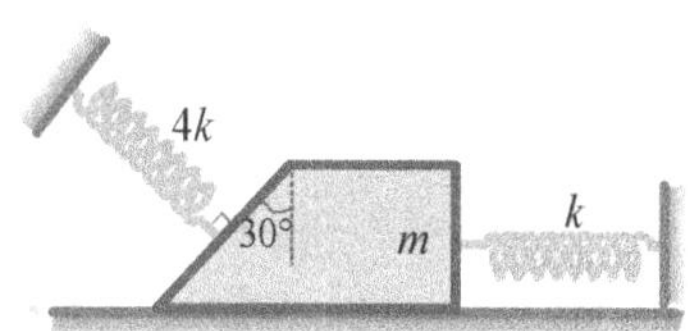

    (a) $2\pi\sqrt{\dfrac{m}{k}}$ (b) $2\pi\sqrt{\dfrac{m}{5k}}$

    (c) $\pi\sqrt{\dfrac{m}{k}}$ (d) $\left(\pi+\dfrac{2}{\sqrt{3}}\right)\sqrt{\dfrac{m}{k}}$

Answer Key	56	(c)	58	(a)	60	(c)
Sol. from page 345	57	(d)	59	(a)		

SHM — MCQ Type 2 — Exercise 4.2

Multiple options correct

1. Which of the following expressions represent simple harmonic motion

   (a) $x = A \sin(\omega t + \delta)$ (b) $x = B \cos(\omega t + \phi)$

   (c) $x = A \tan(\omega t + \phi)$ (d) $x = A \sin\omega t \cos\omega t$

2. A vertical mass-spring system executes simple harmonic oscillations with a period of 2 s. A quantity of this system which exhibits simple harmonic variation with a period of 1 s is
   (a) Velocity
   (b) Potential energy
   (c) Phase difference between acceleration and displacement
   (d) Difference between kinetic energy and potential energy

3. A linear harmonic oscillator of force constant 2×10^6 N/m and amplitude 0.01 m has a total mechanical energy of 160 joules. Its
   (a) Maximum potential energy is 100 J.
   (b) Maximum K.E. is 100 J
   (c) Maximum P.E. is 160 J.
   (d) Minimum P.E. is zero.

4. Two blocks A and B each of mass m are connected by a massless spring of natural length L and spring constant k. The blocks are initially resting on a smooth horizontal floor with the spring at its natural length as shown in figure. A third identical block C also of mass m moves on the floor with a speed v along the line joining A and B and collides with A. Then

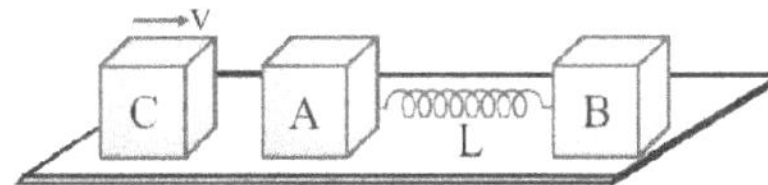

   (a) The kinetic energy of the A–B system at maximum compression of the spring is zero.
   (b) The kinetic energy of the A–B system at maximum compression of the spring is $mv^2/4$.
   (c) The maximum compression of the spring is $v\sqrt{m/k}$.
   (d) The maximum compression of the spring is $v\sqrt{m/2k}$

5. A simple pendulum of length L and mass (bob) M is oscillating in a plane about a vertical line between angular limits $-\phi$ and $+\phi$.

   For an angular displacement $\theta\,(|\theta| < \phi)$, the tension in the string and the velocity of the bob are T and v respectively. The following relations hold good under the above conditions

   (a) $T \cos\theta = Mg$

   (b) $T - Mg\cos\theta = \dfrac{Mv^2}{L}$

   (c) The magnitude of the tangential acceleration of the bob $|a_T| = g \sin\theta$

   (d) $T = Mg\cos\theta$

6. Three simple harmonic motions in the same direction having the same amplitude a and same period are superposed. If each differs in phase from the next by 45°, then

   (a) The resultant amplitude is $(1+\sqrt{2})a$.

   (b) The phase of the resultant motion relative to the first is 90°.

   (c) The energy associated with the resulting motion is $(3 + 2\sqrt{2})$ times the energy associated with any single motion.

   (d) The resulting motion is not simple harmonic.

7. The coordinates of a particle moving in a plane are given by $x(t) = a \cos(pt)$ and $y(t) = b \sin(pt)$ where a, b ($< a$) and p are positive constants of appropriate dimensions. Then :
   (a) the path of the particle is an ellipse.
   (b) the velocity and acceleration of the particle are normal to each other at $t = \dfrac{\pi}{2p}$
   (c) the acceleration of the particle is always directed towards the focus.
   (d) the distance travelled by the particle in time interval $t = 0$ to $t = \dfrac{\pi}{2p}$ is a.

8. A spring has natural length 40 cm and spring constant 500 N/m. A block of mass 1 kg is attached at one end of the spring and other end of the spring is attached to ceiling. The block released from the position, where the spring has length 45 cm.
   (a) the block will perform SHM of amplitude 5 cm.
   (b) the block will have maximum velocity $30\sqrt{5}$ cm/s.
   (c) the block will have maximum acceleration 15 m/s^2
   (d) the minimum potential energy of the spring will be zero.

9. A particle is executing SHM with amplitude A, time period T, maximum acceleration a_0 and maximum velocity v_0. Its starts from mean position at $t = 0$ and at time t, it has the displacement $A/2$, acceleration a and velocity v then
   (a) $t = T/12$ (b) $a = a_0/2$
   (c) $v = v_0/2$ (d) $t = T/8$

10. The amplitude of a particle executing SHM about O is 10 cm. Then
   (a) When the K.E. is 0.64 of its max. K.E. its displacement is 6 cm from O.
   (b) When the displacement is 5 cm from O its K.E. is 0.75 of its max. P.E.
   (c) Its total energy at any point is equal to its maximum K.E.
   (d) Its velocity is half the maximum velocity when its displacement is half the maximum displacement.

Answer Key	1	(a,b,d)	3	(b,c)	5	(b,c)	7	(a,b, c)	9	(a, b)
Sol. from page 352	2	(b, d)	4	(b,d)	6	(a,c)	8	(b, c)	10	(a, b, c)

11. The displacement of a particle varies according to the relation $x = 3\sin 100\,t + 8\cos^2 50t$. Which of the following is/are correct about this motion.
(a) The motion of the particle is not S.H.M.
(b) The amplitude of the S.H.M of the particle is 5 units
(c) The amplitude of the resultant S.H. M. is $\sqrt{73}$ units
(d) The maximum displacement of the particle from the origin is 9 units.

12. A system is oscillating with undamped simple harmonic motion. Then the
(a) average total energy per cycle of the motion is its maximum kinetic energy.
(b) average total energy per cycle of the motion is $\dfrac{1}{\sqrt{2}}$ times its maximum kinetic energy.
(c) root mean square velocity is $\dfrac{1}{\sqrt{2}}$ times its maximum velocity
(d) mean velocity is 1/2 of maximum velocity.

13. Function $x = A\sin^2\omega t + B\cos^2\omega t + C\sin\omega t\cos\omega t$ represents SHM
(a) For any value of A, B and C (except $C = 0$)
(b) If $A = B$; $C = 2B$, amplitude $= |B\sqrt{2}|$
(c) If $A = B$; $C = 2B$
(d) If $A = B$; $C = 0$,

14. The speed v of a particle moving along a straight line, when it is at a distance (x) from a fixed point of the line is given by $v^2 = 108 - 9x^2$ (all quantities are in cgs units)
(a) the motion is uniformly accelerated along the straight line
(b) the magnitude of the acceleration at a distance 3cm from the point is 27 cm/sec^2
(c) the motion is simple harmonic about the given fixed point
(d) the maximum displacement from the fixed point is 4 cm

15. A horizontal plank has a rectangular block placed on it. The plank starts oscillating vertically and simple harmonically with an amplitude of 40 cm. The block just loses contact with the plank when the latter is at momentary rest. Then
(a) the period of oscillation is $(2\pi/5)$
(b) the block weighs double its weight, when the plank is at one of the positions of momentary rest
(c) the block weighs 0.5 times its weight on the plank halfway up
(d) the block weighs 1.5 times its weight on the plank halfway down

16. A particle moves in the x-y plane according to the equation, $\vec{r} = (\hat{i} + 2\hat{j})A\cos\omega t$. The motion of the particle is
(a) on a straight line
(b) on an ellipse
(c) periodic
(d) simple harmonic

17. A 20 gm particle is subjected to two simple harmonic motions $x_1 = 2\sin 10\,t$, $x_2 = 4\sin(10t + \pi/3)$, where x_1 and x_2 are in metre and t is in sec.
(a) The displacement of the particle at $t = 0$ will be $2\sqrt{3}m$

(b) Maximum speed of the particle will be $20\sqrt{7}m/s$
(c) Magnitude of maximum acceleration of the particle will be $200\sqrt{7}m/s^2$
(d) Energy of the resultant motion will be 28 J

18. A particle of mass m is moving in a potential well, for which the potential energy is given by $U(x) = U_0\,(1 - \cos ax)$ where U_0 and a are constants. Then (for the small oscillations)
(a) the time period of small oscillations is $T = 2\pi\sqrt{\dfrac{m}{aU_o}}$
(b) the speed of the particle is maximum at $x = 0$
(c) the amplitude of oscillations is $\dfrac{\pi}{2a}$
(d) the time period of small oscillations is $T = 2\pi\sqrt{\dfrac{m}{a^2 U_o}}$

19. A particle is subjected to two simple harmonic motions along x and y directions according to, $x = 3\sin 100\,\pi t$; $y = 4\sin 100\pi t$.
(a) Motion of particle will be on ellipse traversing it in clockwise direction.
(b) Motion of particle will be on a straight line with slope 4/3.
(c) Motion will be a simple harmonic motion with amplitude 5.
(d) Phase difference between two motions is $\pi/2$.

20. The motion of simple pendulum in air is
(a) periodic
(b) oscillatory
(c) simple harmonic
(d) damped harmonic

21. Which of the following will change the time period as they are taken to moon?
(a) A simple pendulum
(b) A torsional pendulum
(c) A physical pendulum
(d) A spring -mass system

22. Which of the following quantities are always be negative in SHM?
(a) $\vec{a}.\vec{r}$
(b) $\vec{v}.\vec{r}$
(c) $\vec{F}.\vec{r}$
(d) $\vec{F}.\vec{a}$

23. In SHM :
(a) the minimum P.E. is equal to minimum K.E.
(b) the maximum P.E. is equal to maximum K.E.
(c) the maximum K.E is equal to total mechanical energy
(d) the maximum P.E. is equal to total mechanical energy

24. The energy of a particle executing simple harmonic motion is given by $E = Ax^2 + Bv^2$ where x is the displacement from mean position $x = 0$ and v is the velocity of the particle at x then choose the correct statement(s)
(a) amplitude of SHM. is $\sqrt{\dfrac{2E}{A}}$
(b) maximum velocity of the particle during S.H.M. is $\sqrt{\dfrac{E}{B}}$
(c) Time period of motion is $2\pi\sqrt{\dfrac{B}{A}}$
(d) displacement of the particle is proportional to the velocity of the particle.

Answer Key	11	(b, d)	13	(a, b, c)	15	(a, b, c, d)	17	(a, b, c, d)	19	(b, c)	21	(a, c)	23	(a, b, c, d)
Sol. from page 352	12	(a, c)	14	(b,c)	16	(a, c, d)	18	(b, c, d)	20	(a, b, d)	22	(a, c)	24	(b, c)

25. A block of mass m is kept on a horizontal platform of mass M. The platform is doing SHM in horizontal plane with angular frequency ω. There is no slipping between the block and the platform due to friction. Then

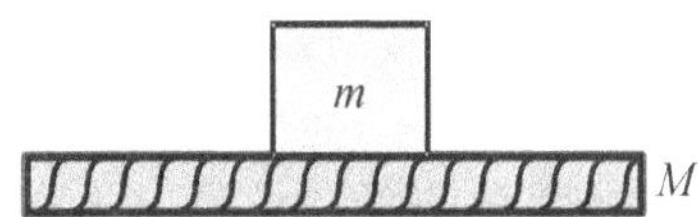

(a) the friction force on the block is directly proportional to the displacement of the platform from mean position.

(b) the contact force on the block is directly proportional to the displacement of the platform from mean position.

(c) the net contact force on the block is directly proportional to mass of block (m)

(d) the net contact force on the platform due to the block is directly proportional to mass of plank (M)

26. A particle executes simple harmonic motion between $x = -A$ and $x = +A$. The time taken for it to go from 0 to $A/2$ is T_1 and to go from $A/2$ to A is T_2, then

(a) $T_1 < T_2$ (b) $T_1 > T_2$

(c) $T_1 = T_2$ (d) $2T_1 = T_2$

Answer Key

Solution from page 23

	25	(a, c)	26	(a, d)						

SHM   Statement Questions   Exercise 4.3

Read the two statements carefully to mark the correct option out of the options given below:

(a) If both the statements are true and the **statement - 2** is the correct explanation of **statement - 1**.

(b) If both the statements are true but **statement - 2** is not the correct explanation of the **statement - 1**.

(c) If **statement - 1** true but **statement - 2** is false.

(d) If **statement - 1** is false but **statement - 2** is true.

1. *Statement- 1*
An oscillatory motion is necessarily periodic.
Statement- 2
A simple harmonic motion is necessarily oscillatory.

2. *Statement- 1*
The force acting on a particle moving along x-axis is $F = -k(x + v_0 t)$, where k is a constant.
Statement- 2
To an observer moving along x-axis with constant velocity v_0, it represents SHM.

3. *Statement- 1*
When a simple pendulum is made to oscillate on the surface of moon, its time period increases.
Statement- 2
Moon is much smaller as compared to earth.

4. *Statement- 1*
Pendulum clock can not be used in an earth satellite.
Statement- 2
The value of g in satellite is zero.

5. *Statement- 1*
If the amplitude of simple harmonic oscillator is doubled, its total energy becomes four times.
Statement- 2
The total energy is directly proportional to the square of amplitude of oscillations.

6. *Statement- 1*
The energy is increased because the amplitude is increased.
Statement- 2
The amplitude is increased because energy is increased.

7. *Statement- 1*
A particle executing simple harmonic motion comes to rest at the extreme positions .
Statement-2
The resultant force on the particle is zero at these positions.

8. *Statement- 1*
At extreme positions of a particle executing SHM, both velocity and acceleration are zero.
Statement- 2
In SHM, acceleration always acts towards mean position.

9. *Statement- 1*
Soldiers are asked to break steps while crossing the bridges.
Statement- 2
The frequency of marching may be equal to the natural frequency of bridge and lead to resonance which can break the bridge.

10. *Statement- 1*
The amplitude of an oscillating pendulum decreases gradually with time.
Statement- 2
The frequency of the pendulum decreases with time.

11. *Statement- 1*
In SHM, the the velocity is maximum when acceleration is minimum.
Statement- 2
Displacement and velocity of SHM differ in phase by $\dfrac{\pi}{2}$ rad.

12. *Statement - 1*
Consider motion for a mass spring system under gravity, motion of M is not a simple harmonic motion unless M is negligibly small.
Statement - 2
For SHM, acceleration must be proportional to the displacement and its directed towards the mean position.

Answer Key

Sol. from page 354

1	(d)	3	(b)	5	(a)	7	(c)	9	(a)	11	(b)
2	(a)	4	(c)	6	(c)	8	(d)	10	(c)	12	(d)

SHM — Passage & Matrix — Exercise 4.4

PASSAGES

Passage for (Q. 1 - 3) :

A uniform thin cylindrical disc of mass M and radius R is attached to two identical massless springs of spring constant k which are fixed to the wall as shown in the figure. The springs are attached to the axle of the disc symmetrically on either side at a distance d from its centre. The axle is massless and both the springs and the axle are in a horizontal plane. The unstretched length of each spring is L. The disc is initially at its equilibrium position with its centre of mass (CM) at a distance L from the wall. The disc rolls without slipping with velocity $\vec{v}_0 = v_0\hat{i}$. The coefficient of friction is μ.

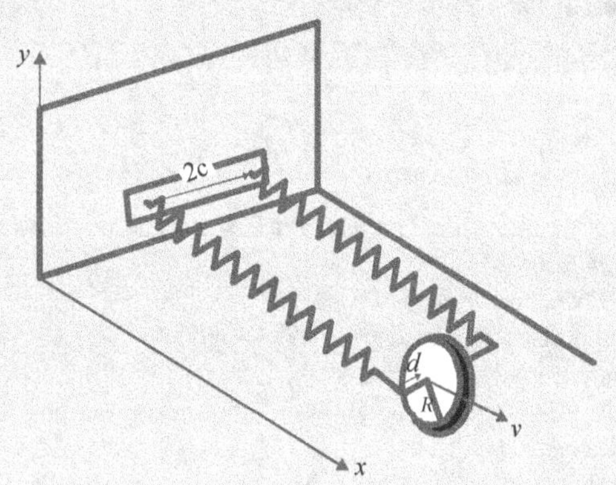

1. The net external force acting on the disc when its centre of mass is at displacement x with respect to its equilibrium position is
   (a) $-kx$
   (b) $-2kx$
   (c) $-\dfrac{2kx}{3}$
   (d) $-\dfrac{4kx}{3}$

2. The centre of mass of the disk undergoes simple harmonic motion with angular frequency ω equal to
   (a) $\sqrt{\dfrac{k}{M}}$
   (b) $\sqrt{\dfrac{2k}{M}}$
   (c) $\sqrt{\dfrac{2k}{3M}}$
   (d) $\sqrt{\dfrac{4k}{3M}}$

3. The maximum value of v_0 for which the disc will roll without slipping is
   (a) $\mu g\sqrt{\dfrac{M}{k}}$
   (b) $\mu g\sqrt{\dfrac{M}{2k}}$
   (c) $\mu g\sqrt{\dfrac{3M}{k}}$
   (d) $\mu g\sqrt{\dfrac{5M}{2k}}$

Passage for (Q. 4 - 6) :

For the damped oscillator shown in figure, $m = 250g$, $k = 85\dfrac{N}{m}$ and $b = 70$ g/s

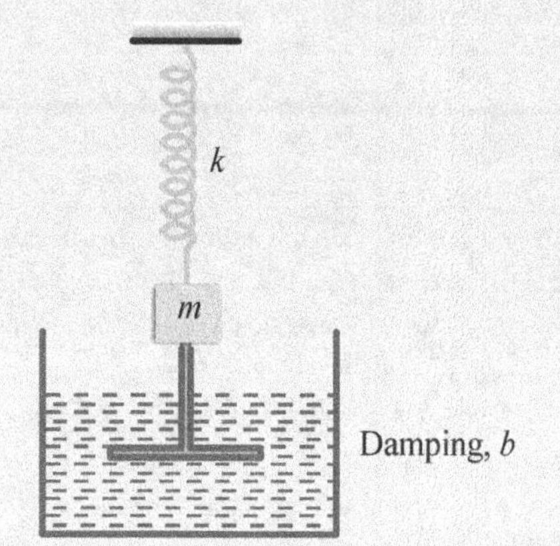

4. What is the period of motion?
   (a) 0.12 s
   (b) 0.34 s
   (c) 0.44 s
   (d) 0.60 s

5. How long does it take for the amplitude of the damped oscillations to drop to half its initial value?
   (a) 1s
   (b) 2.5 s
   (c) 5.0 s
   (d) 12 s

6. How long does it take for the mechanical energy to drop to one half its initial value?
   (a) 1 s
   (b) 5 s
   (c) 3 s
   (d) 2.5 s

Passage for (Q. 7 - 9) :

A spring of force constant 1200 N/m is mounted horizontally on a horizontal table. A mass of 3.0 kg is attached to the free end of the spring, pulled sideways to a distance of 2.0 cm and released.

7. What is the frequency of oscillation of mass?
   (a) 2 s^{-1}
   (b) 2.4 s^{-1}
   (c) 3.2 s^{-1}
   (d) 4.2 s^{-1}

8. What is the maximum acceleration of the mass?
   (a) 8 m/s^2
   (b) 3 m/s^2
   (c) 2 m/s^2
   (d) 12 m/s^2

9. What is the maximum speed of the mass?
   (a) 0.20 m/s
   (b) 0.40 m/s
   (c) 0.60 m/s
   (d) 0.80 m/s

Answer Key	1	(d)	3	(c)	5	(c)	7	(c)	9	(b)
Sol. from page 355	2	(d)	4	(b)	6	(d)	8	(a)		

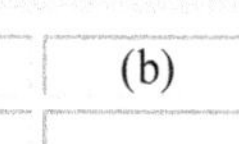

Passage for (Q. 10 - 12) :

A spring of force constant k = 1200 N/m is mounted horizontally on a horizontal table. A mass of 3.0 is attached to the free end of the spring, pulled sideways to a distance 2.0 cm and released , let us take the position of the mass, when the spring is unstretched, as $x = 0$, and the direction from left to right as the positive direction of x-axis. Give x as a function of time t for the oscillating mass, if at the moment we start the stop watch ($t = 0$), the mass is;

10. At the mean position :
    - (a) $x = 2 \sin 20\, t$
    - (b) $x = 2 \sin 10\, t$
    - (c) $x = 4\sin 20\, t$
    - (d) none of these

11. At the maximum stretched position
    - (a) $2 \cos 20\, t$
    - (b) $2 \sin 20\, t$
    - (c) $4 \cos 20\, t$
    - (d) none of these

12. At the maximum compressed position
    - (a) $2 \cos 20\, t$
    - (b) $-2\cos 20\, t$
    - (c) $-2 \sin 20\, t$
    - (d) none of these

Passage for (Q. 13 - 15) :

Two particles A and B are performing SHM along x and y-axis respectively with equal amplitude and frequency of 2 cm and 1 Hz respectively. Equilibrium positions of the particles A and B are at the co-ordinates (3cm, 0) and (0, 4 cm) respectively. At $t = 0$, B is at its equilibrium position and moving towards the origin, while A is nearest to the origin and moving away from the origin.

13. Equation of motion of particle A can be written as
    - (a) $x = (2\ \text{cm}) \cos 2\pi t$
    - (b) $x = (3\ \text{cm}) - (2\ \text{cm}) \cos 2\pi t$
    - (c) $x = (2\ \text{cm}) \sin 2\pi t$
    - (d) $x = (3\ \text{cm}) - (2\ \text{cm}) \sin 2\pi t$

14. Equation of motion of particle B can be written as
    - (a) $y = (2\ \text{cm}) \cos \sqrt{61}\ \text{cm}$
    - (b) $y = (4\ \text{cm}) - (2\ \text{cm}) \cos 2\pi t$
    - (c) $y = (2\ \text{cm}), \sin 2\pi t$
    - (d) $y = (4\text{cm}) - (2\ \text{cm}) \sin 2\pi t$

15. Minimum and maximum distance between A and B during the motion is
    - (a) $\sqrt{5}$ cm and $\sqrt{61}$ cm
    - (b) 3 cm and 7cm
    - (c) 1 cm and 5 cm
    - (d) 9cm and 16cm

Passage for (Q. 16 - 18) :

Two identical blocks P and Q have mass m each lie on a smooth horizontal surface as shown. They are attached to two identical springs (of spring constant k) initially unstretched. Now the left spring (attached with P) is compressed by $A/2$ and the right spring (attached with Q) is compressed by A. Both the blocks are then released from rest simultaneously.

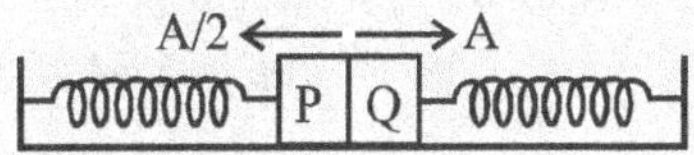

16. The speed of block P just before P and Q are about to collide for the first time
    - (a) $\sqrt{\dfrac{k}{m}}\ \dfrac{A}{2}$
    - (b) $\sqrt{\dfrac{k}{m}}\ A$
    - (c) $\sqrt{\dfrac{k}{4m}}\ A$
    - (d) None of these

17. The speed of block Q just before P and Q are about to collide for the first time
    - (a) $\sqrt{\dfrac{k}{m}}\ \dfrac{A}{2}$
    - (b) $\sqrt{\dfrac{k}{m}}\ A$
    - (c) $\sqrt{\dfrac{k}{4m}}\ A$
    - (d) None of these

18. After what time when they were released from rest, shall the blocks collide for the first time
    - (a) $\dfrac{\pi}{2}\ \sqrt{\dfrac{m}{k}}$
    - (b) $\pi\ \sqrt{\dfrac{m}{k}}$
    - (c) $\dfrac{\pi}{3}\ \sqrt{\dfrac{m}{k}}$
    - (d) None of these

Passage for (Q. 19 - 21) :

An oscillator consists of a block attached to a spring ($k = 400$ N/m). At some time t, the position (measured from the system's equilibrium location), velocity, and acceleration of the block are $x = 0.100\ m$, $v = -13.6$ m/s and $a = -123$ m/s^2. Calculate

19. The frequency of oscillation is :
    - (a) 2.38 Hz
    - (b) 3.32 Hz
    - (c) 5.58 Hz
    - (d) 6.68 Hz

20. The mass of the block is:
    - (a) 0.2×500 kg
    - (b) 0.325 kg
    - (c) 0.4×250 kg
    - (d) 0.500 kg

21. The amplitude of the motion
    - (a) 0.100 m
    - (b) 0.300 m
    - (c) 0.400 m.
    - (d) 0.500 m

Passage for (Q. 22 - 24) :

The pendulum in figure consists of a uniform disc with radius 10.0 cm and mass 500g attached to a uniform rod with length 500 mm and mass 270 g.

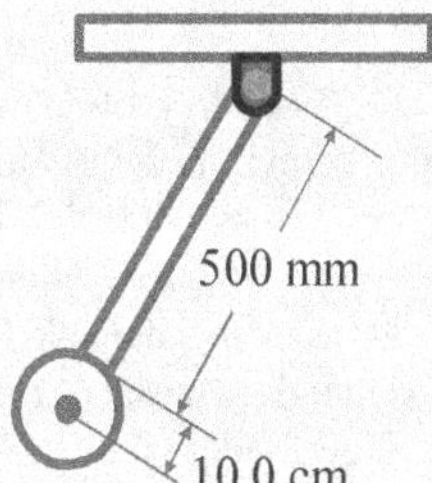

Answer Key	10	(a)	12	(b)	14	(d)	16	(a)	18	(a)	20	(b)
Sol. from page 355	11	(a)	13	(b)	15	(a)	17	(b)	19	(c)	21	(c)

22. The rotational inertia of the pendulum about the pivot point is
    (a) 0.102 kg-m^2 (b) 0.205 kg m^2
    (c) 0.305 kg-m^2 (d) 0.500 kg m^2
23. What is the distance between the pivot point and the centre of mass of the pendulum ?
    (a) 30.0 cm   (b) 35.6 cm
    (c) 47.7 cm   (d) 49.3 cm
24. The period of oscillation is
    (a) 1.50 s   (b) 2.0 s
    (c) 3.0 s   (d) 4.0 s

Passage for (Q. 25 - 27) :

A body of mass 100g hangs from a long spiral spring. When pulled down 10cm below its equilibrium position and released, it vibrate with a period of 2s.

25. The velocity of the body as it passes through equilibrium position is
    (a) 31.4 cm/s   (b) 35.4 cm/s
    (c) 40.0 cm/s   (d) 44.6 cm/s
26. The acceleration of the body when it is 5cm above the equilibrium position is
    (a) 43.9 cm/s^2 (b) 37.8 cm/s^2
    (c) 49.3 cm/s^2 (d) 54.6 cm/s^2
27. When it is moving upward, the time it takes to move from a point 5cm below its equilibrium position to a point 5cm above it is
    (a) 1 s   (b) 0.66 s
    (c) 0.45 s   (d) 0.33 s

Passage for (Q. 28 - 30) :

Two springs, each of unstreched length 0.2 m but having different force constants k_1 and k_2, are attached to opposite ends of a block of mass m on a level frictionless surface. The outer ends of the springs are now attached to two pins P_1 and P_2, 10 cm from the original positions of the ends of the springs. Let $k_1 = 1$N/m, $k_2 = 3$N/m, $m = 0.1$ kg

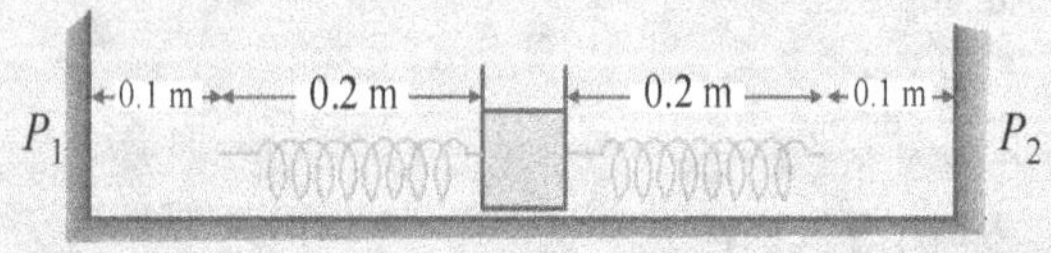

28. The length of the spring of force constants k_1 in its new equilibrium position, after the spring have been attached to the pins
    (a) 0.25 m   (b) 0.35 m
    (c) 0.40 m   (d) 0.30 m
29. The block slightly displaced from its new equilibrium position and released. Its time period of oscillations is approximately
    (a) 1 s   (b) 1.2 s
    (c) 2 s   (d) None of these
30. The block is oscillating with an amplitude 0.05m. At the instant it passes through its equilibrium position, a lump of putty of mass 0.1 kg is dropped vertically onto the block and sticks to it. The new amplitude of motion is
    (a) 3.53 cm   (b) 4.34 cm
    (c) 5.50 cm   (d) 6.67 cm

Passage for (Q. 31 - 33) :

A force F is applied on a spring block system as shown in fig.

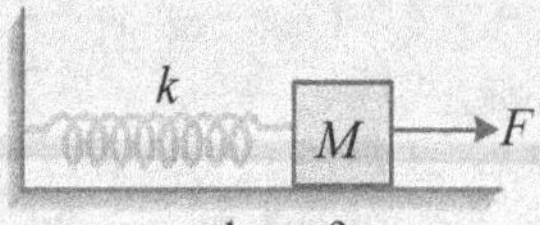

smooth surface

31. If F is constant, the amplitude of oscillation will be
    (a) $\dfrac{F}{k}$ (b) $\dfrac{F}{2k}$
    (c) $\dfrac{F}{3k}$ (d) $\dfrac{2F}{k}$
32. If $\vec{F} = \dfrac{k}{2}\vec{x}$ the time period of oscillation is
    (a) $2\pi\sqrt{\dfrac{m}{k}}$ (b) $2\pi\sqrt{\dfrac{2m}{k}}$
    (c) $2\pi\sqrt{\dfrac{m}{2k}}$ (d) $2\pi\sqrt{\dfrac{m}{3k}}$
33. If $\vec{F} = \dfrac{k}{2}\vec{x}$ and the block is given $v_u\hat{i}$ velocity at $x = 0$ then the time period and amplitude of oscillation is
    (a) $\sqrt{\dfrac{2m}{k}}v_u$ (b) $\sqrt{\dfrac{m}{k}}v_u$
    (c) $\sqrt{\dfrac{m}{2k}}v_u$ (d) none of these

Passage for (Q. 34 - 36) :

A 2 kg block hangs without vibrating at the bottom end of a spring with a force constant of 800 N/m. The top end of the spring is attached to the ceiling of an elevator car. The car is rising with an upward acceleration of 10 m/s^2. When the acceleration suddenly ceases at time $t = 0$, the car moves upward with constant speed. (g = 10 m/s^2)

34. What is the angular frequency of oscillation of the block after the acceleration ceases ?
    (a) $10\sqrt{2}$ rad / s   (b) 20 rad/s
    (c) $20\sqrt{2}$ rad / s   (d) 32 rad/s
35. The amplitude of the oscillation is
    (a) 7.5 cm   (b) 5 cm
    (c) 2.5 cm   (d) 1 cm
36. The initial phase angle observed by a rider in the elevator, taking downward direction to be positive and positive extreme position to have $\pi/2$ phase constant, is equal to
    (a) zero   (b) $\pi/2$ rad
    (c) π rad   (d) $3\pi/2$ rad

Answer Key	22	(b)	24	(a)	26	(c)	28	(b)	30	(a)	32	(b)	34	(b)	36	(b)
Sol. from page 355	23	(c)	25	(a)	27	(d)	29	(a)	31	(a)	33	(a)	35	(c)		

37. The graph plotted between phase angle (ϕ) and displacement of a particle from equilibrium position (y) is a sinusoidal curve as shown below. Then the best

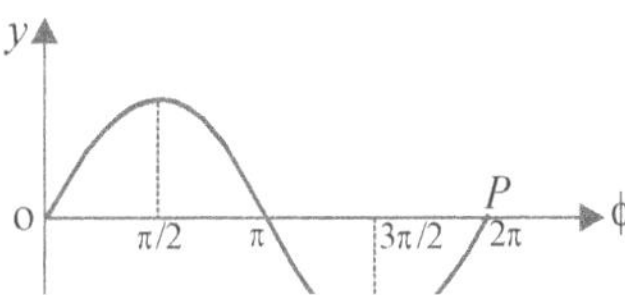

Column A		Column B
A. K.E versus phase angle curve	(p)	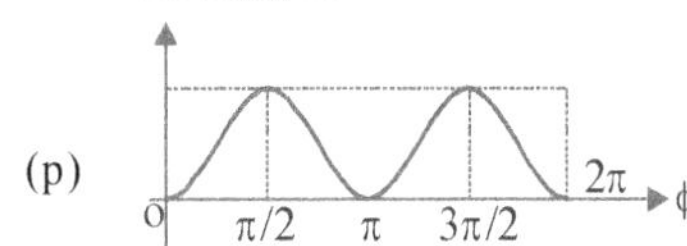
B. P.E. versus phase angle curve	(q)	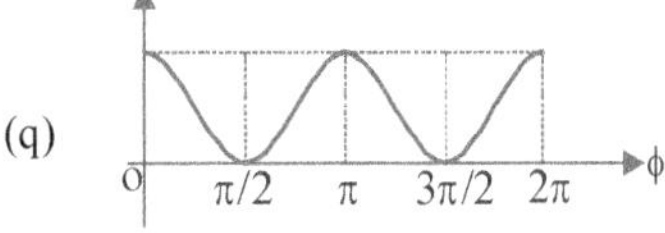
C. T.E. versus phase angle curve	(r)	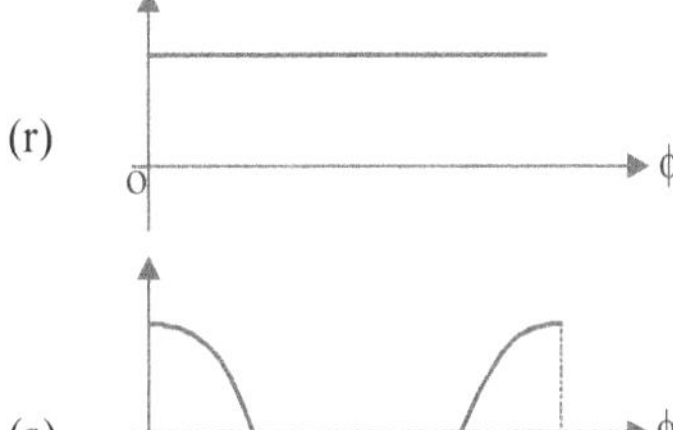
D. Velocity versus phase angle curve	(s)	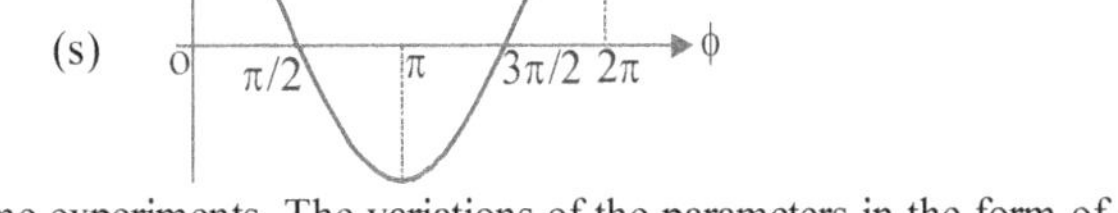

38. Column I gives a list of possible set of parameters measured in some experiments. The variations of the parameters in the form of graphs are shown in Column II. Match the set of parameters given in Column I with the graphs given in Column II

Column I		Column II
A. Potential energy of a simple pendulum (y-axis) as a function of displacement (x-axis)	(p)	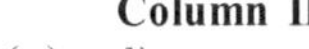
B. Displacement (y-axis) as a function of time (x-axis) for a one dimensional motion at zero or constant acceleration when the body is moving along the positive x-direction	(q)	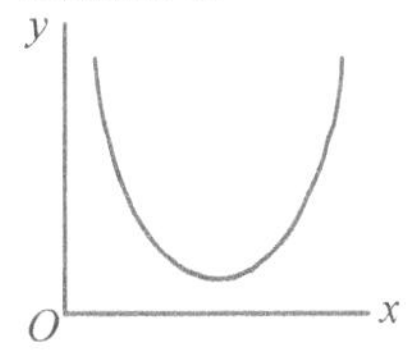
C. Range of a projectile (y-axis) as a function of its velocity (x-axis) when projected at a fixed angle	(r)	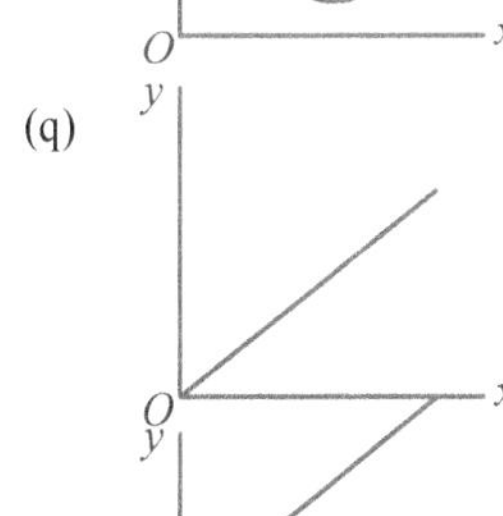
D. The square of the time period (y-axis) of a simple pendulum as a function of its length (x-axis)	(s)	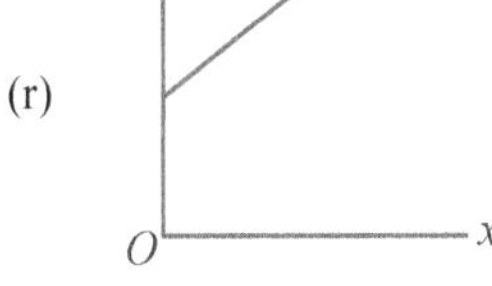

Answer Key

Sol. from page 355

37	A → (q); B → (p); C → (r); D → (s)	38	A → (p); B → (q, s); C → (s); D → (q)

39. Which of the following pairs are correctly matched ?

Column I		Column II	
A.	$\dfrac{d^2 y}{dt^2} = v^2 \dfrac{d^2 y}{dx^2}$	(p)	Resonant vibration
B.	$\dfrac{d^2 y}{dt^2} + \omega^2 y = 0$	(q)	Free vibration
C.	$\dfrac{d^2 y}{dt^2} + 2k \dfrac{dy}{dt} + \omega^2 y = 0$	(r)	Damped vibration
D.	$\dfrac{d^2 y}{dt^2} + 2k \dfrac{dy}{dt} + \omega^2 y = F \sin pt$	(s)	Forced vibration
		(t)	Progressive wave

40. Match **Column I** with **Column II** and select the correct answer using the codes given below :

Column I		Column II	
A.	Phase difference between acceleration and displacement in case of a particle executing SHM.	(p)	0
B.	Phase difference between any two points on a wave front	(q)	$\pi / 2$
C.	Phase difference between emf and current in an AC circuit containing pure inductance	(r)	π
D.	Phase difference between electric and magnetic fields in a plane sinusoidal electromagnetic wave propagating along positive direction of x–axis.	(s)	2π

41. A simple harmonic oscillator consists of a block attached to spring with $k = 200$ N/m. The block slides on a frictionless horizontal surface, with equilibrium point $x = 0$. A graph of the block's velocity v as a function of time t is shown. Correctly match the required information in the column I with the values given in the column II. (use $\pi^2 = 10$)

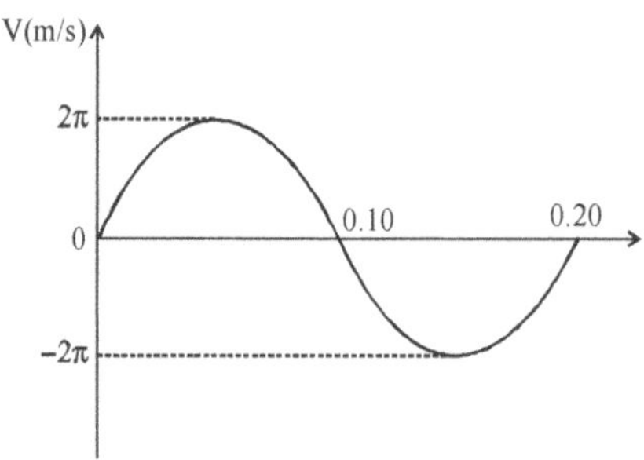

Column I		Column II	
A.	The block's mass in kg	(p)	-0.20
B.	The block's displacement at $t = 0$ in metres	(q)	-200
C.	The block's acceleration at $t = 0.10$ s in m/s²	(r)	0.20
D.	The block's maximum kinetic energy in joule	(s)	4.0

42. A particle of mass 2 kg is moving on a straight line under the action of force $F = (8 - 2x)$ N. The particle is released at rest from $x = 6$m. For the subsequent motion match the following (All the values in the column II are in their S.I. units)

Column I		Column II	
A.	Equilibrium position at x	(p)	$\pi/4$
B.	Amplitude of SHM is	(q)	$\pi/2$
C.	Time taken to go directly from $x = 2$ to $x = 4$	(r)	4
D.	Energy of SHM is	(s)	2

43. A small block of mass m is connected to one end of a massless rod. A spring of force constant k is attached to the other end of the rod. The rod is pivoted at P. The block is displaced slightly downward and left free to oscillate. For small angular displacement θ of the block, match the following columns :

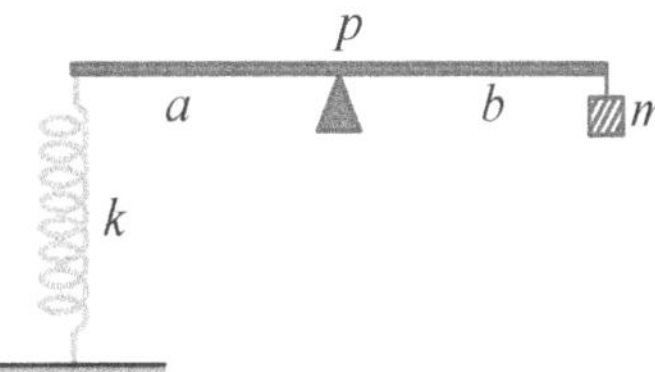

Column-I		Column-II	
A.	Restoring torque	(p)	$\dfrac{1}{2}k\,a^2\theta^2$
B.	Angular acceleration	(q)	$k\,a^2\theta$
C.	Energy of oscillations	(r)	$\dfrac{k\,a^2\theta}{m\,b^2}$
D.	Time period of oscillations	(s)	$2\pi\sqrt{\dfrac{b^2 m}{a^2 k}}$

44. A uniform plank of mass m, free to move in the horizontal direction, is placed on the top of a solid cylinder of mass $2m$ and radius R. The plank is attached to a fixed wall with the help of a light spring of force constant k. The plank is slightly displaced towards spring and released. There is no slipping anywhere. For any displacement x, amplitude x_0 and velocity v of the plank, match the columns :

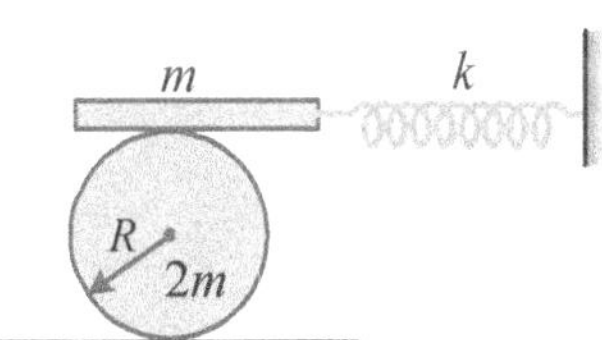

Column-I		Column-II	
A.	Restoring force on the plank	(p)	$\dfrac{1}{2}kx_0^2$
B.	Energy of oscillations of the system	(q)	kx
C.	Acceleration of the plank	(r)	$\dfrac{7}{8}mv^2 + \dfrac{1}{2}kx^2$
D.	Angular frequency	(s)	$\dfrac{4kx}{7m}$
		(t)	$\sqrt{4k/7m}$

45. A block of mass m is projected towards a spring with velocity v_0. The force constant of the spring is k. The block is projected from a distance ℓ from the free end of the spring. The collision between block and the wall is completely elastic. Match the following columns :

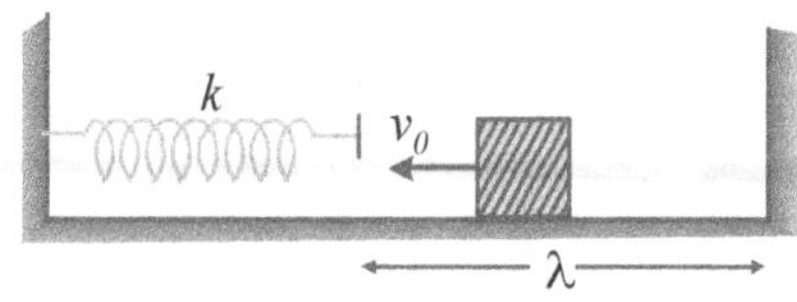

Column-I		**Column-II**	
A.	Maximum compression of the spring	(p)	$-\sqrt{\dfrac{kv_0^2}{m}}$
B.	Energy of oscillations of block	(q)	$\sqrt{\dfrac{mv_0^2}{k}}$
C.	Time period of oscillations	(r)	$\dfrac{1}{2}mv_0^2$
D.	Maximum acceleration of the block	(s)	$\left[\dfrac{2\ell}{v_0}+\pi\sqrt{\dfrac{m}{k}}\right]$

46. In the **column I**, a system is described in each option and corresponding time period is given in the **column II**. Suitably match them.

Column I		**Column II**	
A.	A simple pendulum of length 3ℓ oscillating with small amplitude in a lift moving down with retardation g/2.	(p)	$T=2\pi\sqrt{\dfrac{2\ell}{3g}}$
B.	Two springs of force constants k and 2k are connected to a mass as shown below	(q)	$T=2\pi\sqrt{\dfrac{\ell}{g}}$

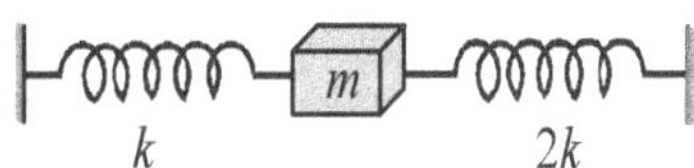

C.	The time period of small oscillation of a uniform rod of length ℓ smoothly hinged at one end. The rod oscillates in vertical plane.	(r)	$T=2\pi\sqrt{\dfrac{2\ell}{g}}$
D.	A cubical block of edge 2ℓ and specific density $\rho/2$ is in equilibrium with some volume inside water filled in a large fixed container. Neglect viscous forces and surface tension. The time period of small oscillations of the block in vertical direction.	(s)	$T=2\pi\sqrt{\dfrac{m}{3k}}$

47. Two blocks A and B of mass m and $2m$ connected by a light spring of spring constant k lie at rest on a fixed smooth horizontal surface. Initially the spring is unstressed. Now at time $t = 0$ both the blocks are imparted horizontal velocities towards each other of magnitudes $2u$ and u as shown in figure. In the subsequent motion, the only horizontal force acting on blocks is due to spring. Match the conditions in column I with the instants of time they occur as given in column II.

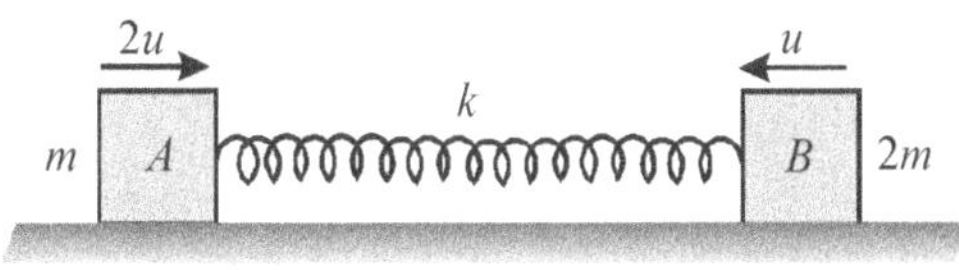

Smooth fixed horizontal surface

Column I		**Column II**
A.	The length of spring is least at time	(p) $\quad t = \dfrac{\pi}{2}\sqrt{\dfrac{2m}{3k}}$
B.	The length of spring is maximum at time	(q) $\quad t = \pi\sqrt{\dfrac{2m}{3k}}$
C.	The acceleration of both blocks is zero simultaneously at time	(r) $\quad t = \pi\sqrt{\dfrac{3m}{2k}}$
		(s) $\quad t = \dfrac{\pi}{2}\sqrt{\dfrac{3m}{2k}}$

48. **Column I** describes some situations in which a small object moves. **Column II** describes some characteristics of these motions. Match the situations in **Column I** with the characteristics in **Column II** and indicate your answer by darkening appropriate bubbles in 4×4 matrix given in the *ORS*.

Column I		**Column II**	
A.	The object moves on the x-axis under a conservative force in such a way that its "speed " and position" satisfy $v = c_1\sqrt{c_2 - x^2}$ where c_1 and c_2 are positive constants.	(p)	The object executes a simple harmonic motion.
B.	The object moves on the x-axis in such a way that its velocity and its displacement from the origin satisfy $v = -kx$, where k is a positive constant.	(q)	The object does not change its direction.
C.	The object is attached to one end of a mass-less spring of a given spring constant. The other end of the spring is attached to the ceiling of an elevator. Initially everything is at rest. The elevator starts going upwards with a constant acceleration a. The motion of the object is observed from the elevator during the period it maintains this acceleration.	(r)	The kinetic energy of the object keeps on decreasing.
D.	The object is projected from the earth's surface vertically upwards with a speed $2\sqrt{GM_e / R_e}$, where, M_e is the mass of the earth and R_e is the radius of the earth, Neglect forces from objects other than the earth.	(s)	The object can change its direction only once.

SHM — Subjective Integer Type   Exercise 4.5

Solution from page 359

1. Two linear simple harmonic motions of equal amplitudes and frequencies ω and 2ω are impressed on a particle along the axis of x and y respectively. If the initial phase difference between them is $\pi/2$, find the resultant path followed by the particle.

   Ans : resultant path followed by the particle is a parabola.

2. A block is kept on a horizontal table. The table is undergoing simple harmonic motion of frequency 3 Hz in a horizontal plane. The coefficient of static friction between the block and the table surface is 0.72, find the maximum amplitude of the table in which the block does not slip on the surface. ($g = 10$ m/s^2) :

   Ans : 2 cm.

3. 10^{-4} kg oxygen is contained in a non–conducting cylindrical vessel of cross–sectional area 29.15×10^{-5} m^2 and volume 10^{-3} m^3. It is closed by a frictionless non-conducting piston which is free to move in a vertical direction. If the piston is slightly depressed and then released, show that the piston will execute simple harmonic motion. Find its frequency. Ignore atmospheric pressure and take $C_p/C_v = 1.4$ for oxygen.   **Ans.** $1/\pi = 0.32$ /s.

4. A cubical body (side 0.1 m and mass 0.002 kg) float in water. It is pressed and then released, so that it oscillates vertically. Find the time period.   **Ans.** 28 m s.

5. A uniform rod is placed on two spinning wheels as shown in figure. The axes of the wheels are separated by a distance $\ell = \dfrac{50}{\pi^2} m$, the coefficient of friction between the rod and the wheels is $\mu = 0.1$. Demonstrate that in this case the rod performs harmonic oscillations. Find the period of these oscillations.

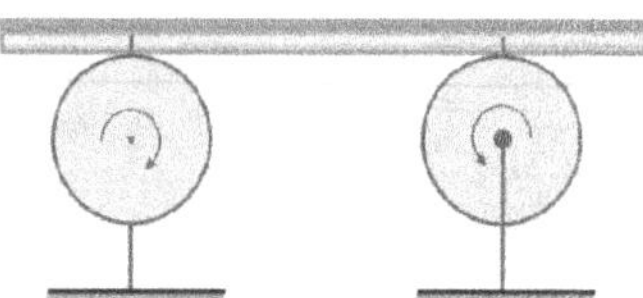

Ans. $T = \pi \sqrt{\dfrac{2\ell}{\mu g}} = 10 \ s$

SHM — Subjective   Exercise 4.6

Solution from page 360

1. Which of the following examples represent (nearly) simple harmonic motion and which represent periodic but not simple harmonic motion ?

   (i) The rotation of earth about its axis.

   (ii) Motion of an oscillating mercury column in a U–tube.

   (iii) Motion of a ball bearing inside a smooth curved bowl, when released from a point slightly above the lower most point.

   (iv) General vibrations of a polyatomic molecule about its equilibrium position.

   Ans. (i) Periodic but not simple harmonic. (ii) Simple harmonic.(iii) Simple harmonic.(iv) Periodic but not simple harmonic.

2. Which of the following relationships between the acceleration a and the displacement x of a particle involve simple harmonic motion ? (a) $a = 0.7 x$ (b) $a = -200 x^2$ (c) $a = -10 x$ (d) $a = 100 x^3$

   Ans. Only (c) represents S.H.M. because here $a \propto x$ and a acts in the opposition direction of x.

3. Answer the following questions :

   (a) Time period of a particle in SHM depends on the force constant k and mass m of the particle $T = 2\pi \sqrt{m/k}$. A simple pendulum executes SHM approximately. Why then is the time period of a pendulum independent of the mass of the pendulum ?

   (b) The motion of a simple pendulum is approximate simple harmonic for small angle of oscillations. For larger angles of oscillations, a more involved analysis shows that T is greater than $2\pi \sqrt{l/g}$. Think of a qualitative argument to appreciate this result.

   (c) A man with a wristwatch on his hand falls from the top of a tower. Does the watch give correct time during the free fall ?

   (d) What is the frequency of oscillation of a simple pendulum mounted in a cabin that is freely falling under gravity ?

   Ans.

   (a) $T = 2\pi \sqrt{g/l}$. Hence time period of a simple pendulum is independent of mass.

   (b) If θ is large, then $\sin \theta < \theta$, so that there is effective decrease in the value of g for large angles. Hence the time period, $T = 2\pi \sqrt{g/l}$ increases.

   (c) yes.

   (d) Inside a cabin falling freely under gravity, $g = 0$. Hence the frequency, $f = 1/2\pi \sqrt{g/l}$ of a simple pendulum mounted in the cabin will be zero.

4. Figure corresponds to two circular motions. The radius of the circle, the period of revolution, the initial position, and the sense of revolution (i.e. clockwise or anti–clockwise) are indicated on each figure. Obtain the corresponding simple harmonic motions of the x projection of the radius vector of the revolving particle P, in each case.

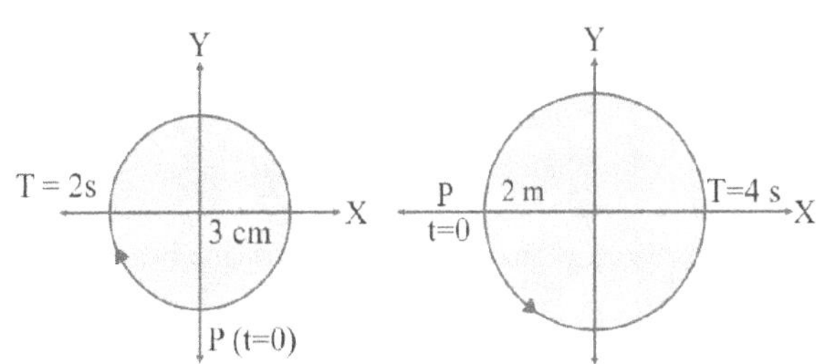

$$T = 2s \quad 3 \text{ cm} \quad P(t=0)$$

$$P \; t=0 \quad 2 \text{ m} \quad T=4 \text{ s}$$

$$\text{Ans : } x(t) = -3 \sin \pi t, \; x(t) = -2 \cos \frac{\pi t}{2}.$$

5. Plot the corresponding reference circle for each of the following simple harmonic motions. Indicate the initial $(t = 0)$ position of the particle, the radius of the circle, and the angular speed of the rotating particle. For simplicity, the sense of rotation may be fixed to be anticlockwise in every case : (x is in cm and t is in s).

(i) $\quad x = -2 \sin (3t + \frac{\pi}{3})$ $\qquad$ (ii) $x = \cos (\frac{\pi}{6} - t)$

(ii) $\quad x = 3 \sin (2\pi t + \frac{\pi}{4})$ $\qquad$ (iv) $x = 2 \cos \pi t$

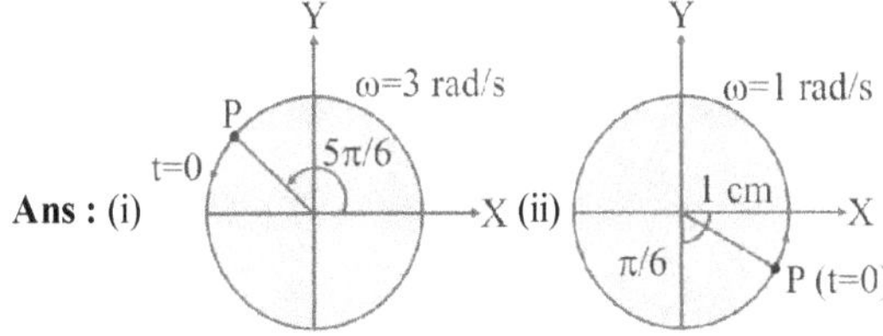

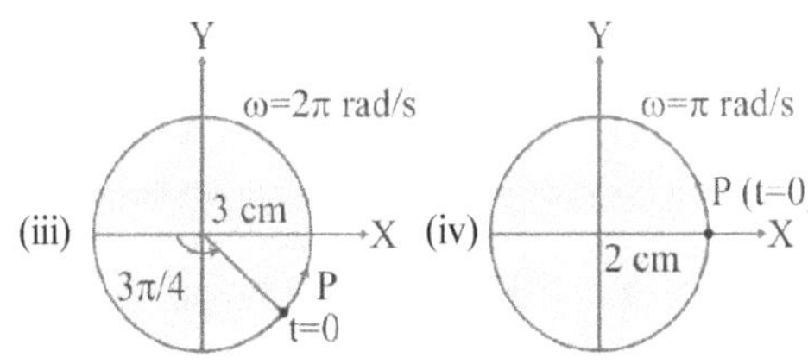

Ans : (i), (ii), (iii), (iv) reference circles as shown.

6. A particle in SHM is described by the displacement function,

$$x(t) = B \sin (\omega t + \alpha), \; \omega = \frac{2\pi}{T}.$$ If the initial $(t = 0)$ position of the particle is 1 cm and its initial velocity is π cm/s, what are its amplitude and initial phase angle ? The angular frequency of the particle is π/s. $\qquad$ **Ans :** $B = \sqrt{2}$ cm, $\frac{\pi}{4}$ or $\frac{5\pi}{4}$.

7. A body oscillates with SHM according to the equation $x = (5.0 \text{ m})$ $\cos [(2\pi \text{ rad/s}) \, t + \frac{\pi}{4}]$. At $t = 1.5 \; s$, calculate (a) displacement, (b) speed and (c) acceleration of the body.

$\qquad$ **Ans :** (a) -3.535 m (b) 22.22 m/s (c) 139.56 m/s^2.

8. A body of mass 0.1 kg is executing SHM according to the equation

$$y = 0.5 \cos (100 \, t + \frac{3\pi}{4}) \text{ metre.}$$ Find (i) the frequency of oscillation (ii) initial phase (iii) maximum velocity (iv) maximum acceleration and (v) total energy.

Ans : (i) $\frac{50}{\pi}$ Hz (ii) $\frac{3\pi}{4}$ rad (iii) 50 m/s (iv) 5000 m/s^2 (v) 125 J.

9. A point oscillates along the x axis according to the law $x = A \cos (\omega t - \frac{\pi}{4})$. Draw the approximate plots

(a) of displacement x, velocity projection v_x, and acceleration projection w_x as functions of time t ;

(b) velocity projection v_x and acceleration projection a_x as functions of the coordinate x.

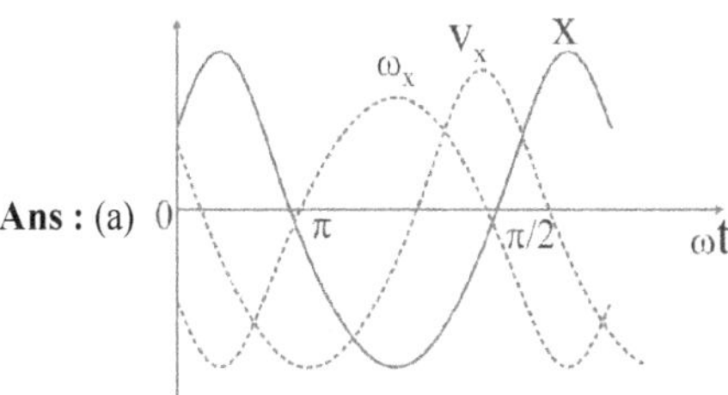

Ans : (a)

(b) $(v_x/A\omega)^2 + (x/A)^2 = 1$ and $a_x = -\omega^2 x.$

10. A point moves along the x axis according to the law $x = a \sin^2(\omega t - \pi/4)$. Find :

(a) the amplitude and period of oscillations; draw the plot $x \, (t)$;

(b) the velocity projection v_x as a function of the coordinate x; draw the plot $v_x \, (x)$.

Ans : (a) The amplitude is equal to a/2, and the period is $T = \pi/\omega$ (b) $v_x^2 = 4 \, \omega^2 x \, (a - x).$

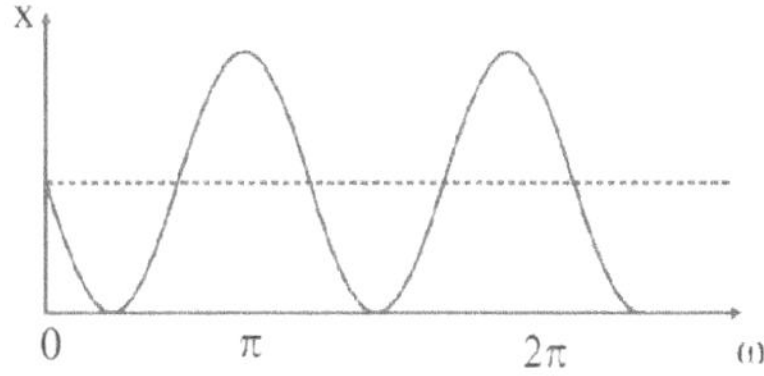

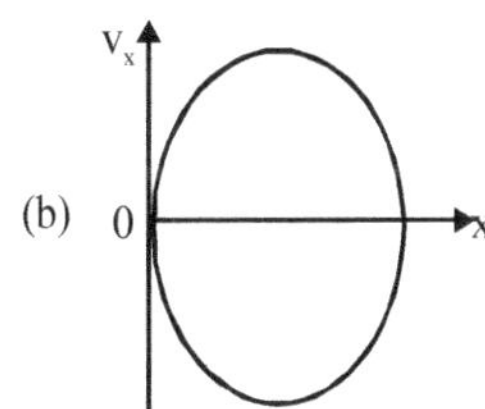

11. A particle performs harmonic oscillations along the x– axis about the equilibrium position $x = 0$. The oscillation frequency is $\omega = 4.00\ s^{-1}$. At a certain moment of time the particle has a coordinate $x_0 = 25.0$ cm and its velocity is equal to $v_{x_0} = 100$ cm/s. Find the coordinate x and the velocity v_x of the particle $t = 2.40$ s after that moment.

> **Ans :** $x = a \cos(\omega t + \alpha) = -29$ cm, $v_x = -81$ cm/s, where
>
> $a = \sqrt{x_0^2 + \left(v_{x_0}/\omega\right)^2}$, $\alpha = \tan^{-1}(-v_{x_0}/\omega x_0)$.

12. A particle of mass m is located in a unidimensional potential field where the potential energy of the particle depends on the coordinate x as $U(x) = U_0(1 - \cos ax)$; U_0 and a are constants. Find the period of small oscillations that the particle performs about the equilibrium position.   **Ans :** $T = 2\pi\sqrt{m/a^2 U_0}$

13. Determine the period of oscillations of mercury of mass $m = 200$ g poured into a bent tube whose right arm forms an angle $\theta = 30°$ with the vertical. The cross–sectional area of the tube is S = 0.50 cm^2. The viscosity of mercury to be neglected.

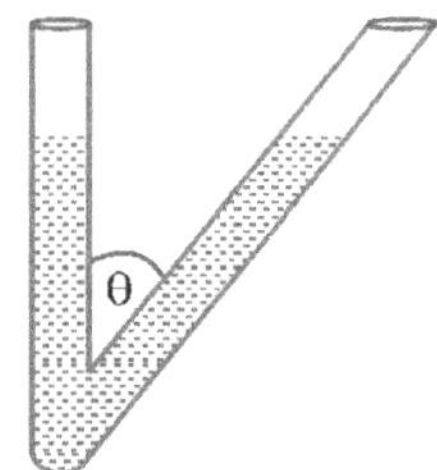

> **Ans :** $T = 2\pi\sqrt{m/S\rho g(1 + \cos\theta)} = 0.8\,s$

14. In the arrangement shown in figure the sleeve M of mass m = 0.20 kg is fixed between two identical springs whose combined stiffness is equal to $k = 20$ N/m. The sleeve can slide without friction over a horizontal bar AB. The arrangement rotates with a constant

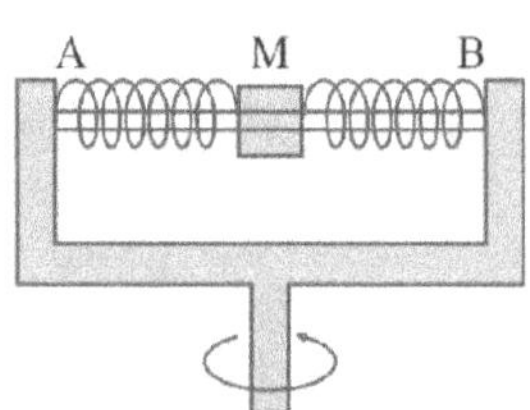

angular velocity $\omega = 4.4$ rad/s about a vertical axis passing through the middle of the bar. Find the period of small oscillations of the sleeve. At what values of ω will there be no oscillations of the sleeve.

> **Ans :** $T = 2\pi/\sqrt{\dfrac{k}{m} - \omega^2} = 0.7\,s$, $\omega \geq \sqrt{k/m} = 10\,rad/s$

15. Suppose that the two springs in figure have different spring constant k_1 and k_2. Show that the frequency f of oscillation of the block is then

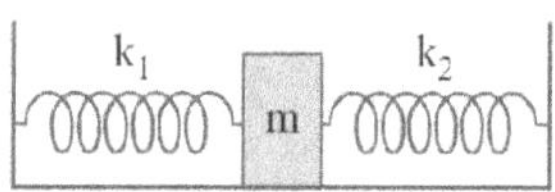

given by $f = \sqrt{f_1^2 + f_2^2}$, where f_1 and f_2 are the frequencies at which the block would oscillate if connected only to spring 1 or only to spring 2.

16. A uniform spring with unstretched length L and spring constant k is cut into two pieces of unstretched lengths L_1 and L_2, with $L_1 = nL_2$. What are the corresponding spring constants (a) k_1 and (b) k_2 in terms of n and k? If a block is attached to the original spring, it oscillates with frequency f. If the spring is replaced with the piece L_1 or L_2, the corresponding frequency is f_1 or f_2. Find (c) f_1 and (d) f_2 in terms of f.

> **Ans.** (a) $(n+1)k/n$; (b) $(n+1)k$; (c) $\sqrt{(n+1)/n}\,f$; (d) $\sqrt{(n+1)}\,f$.

17. A stick with length L oscillates as a physical pendulum, pivoted about point O in figure.

  (a) Derive an expression for the period of the pendulum in terms of L and x, the distance from the pivot point to the centre of mass of the pendulum.

  (b) For what value of x/L is the period a minimum ?

  (c) Show that if $L = 1.00$ m and g = 9.80 m/s^2, this minimum is 1.53 s.

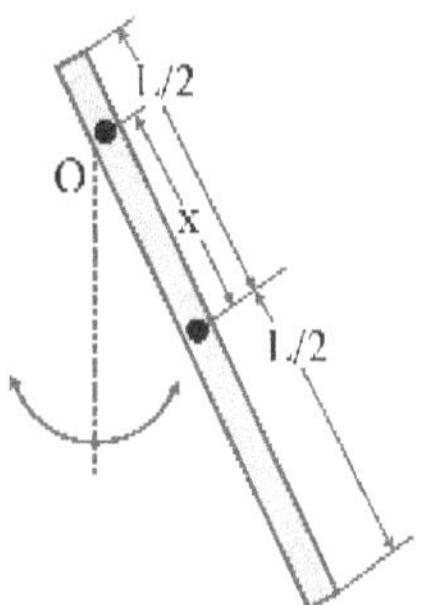

> **Ans.** (a) $2\pi\sqrt{\dfrac{\left(\dfrac{ML^2}{12} + mx^2\right)}{mgx}}$ (b) $\dfrac{x}{L} = \dfrac{1}{\sqrt{12}}$.

18. A point particle of mass 0.1 kg is executing SHM of amplitude 0.1 m. When the particle passes through the mean position, its kinetic energy is 8×10^{-3} J. Obtain the equation of motion of this particle if the initial phase of oscillation is 45° .

> **Ans :** $y = 0.1 \sin\left(4t + \dfrac{\pi}{4}\right)$.

19. A simple pendulum is made by attaching of a 1 kg bob to a 5 m copper wire of diameter 0.08 cm and it has certain period of oscillation. Next a 10 kg bob is substituted for 1 kg bob, calculate the change in the period if any. (Young's modulus of copper $= 12.4 \times 10^{10}$ N/m^2)   **Ans :** 4.486 s, 4.489 s, 0.003 s.

20. Two particles execute simple harmonic motion of same amplitude and frequency along the same straight line. They pass one another, when going in opposite directions, each time their displacement is half of their amplitude. What is the phase difference between them ? **Ans : 120°.**

21. Two light springs of force constants k_1 and k_2 and a block of mass m are in one line AB on a smooth horizontal table such that one end of each spring is fixed on rigid support and the other end is free as shown in figure. The distance CD between the free ends of springs is 60 cm. If the block moves along AB with a velocity 120 cm/s in between the springs, calculate the period of oscillation of block. ($k_1 = 1.8$ N/m, $k_2 = 3.2$ N/m, $m = 200$ g)

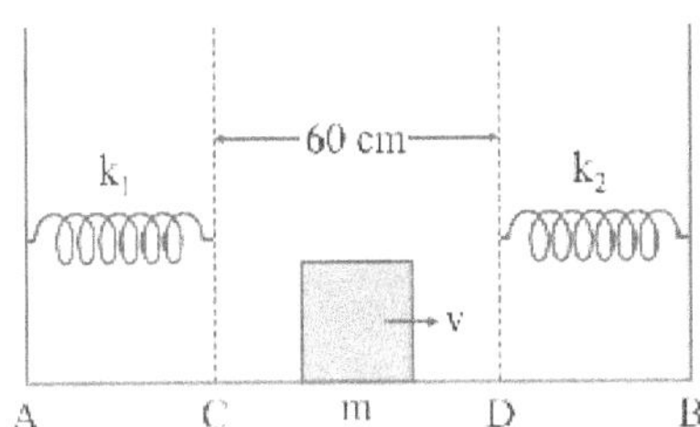

Ans : 2.83 s.

22. A block is resting on a piston which is moving vertically with simple harmonic motion of period 1.0 s. At what amplitude of motion will the block and piston separate ? What is the maximum velocity of the piston at this amplitude ?

Ans : 0.25 m, 1.57 m/s.

23. A solid sphere of radius R is floating in a liquid of density σ with half of its volume submerged. If the sphere is slightly pushed and released. It starts

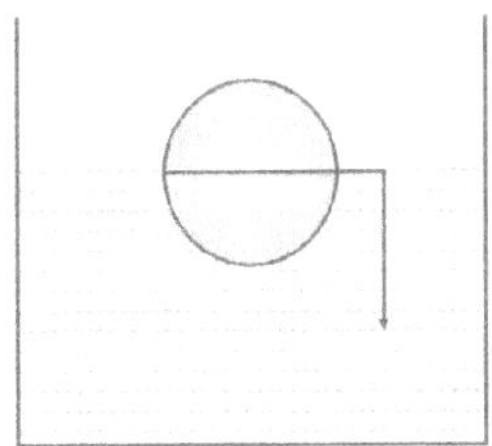

executing simple harmonic motion. Find the frequency of these oscillations.

$$\text{Ans : } f = \frac{1}{2\pi}\sqrt{\frac{3g}{2R}}.$$

24. A uniform cylinder of length L and mass M having cross–sectional area A is suspended, with its length vertical from a fixed point by a massless spring, such that it is half submerged in a liquid of density σ at equilibrium position. When the cylinder is given a small downward push and released it starts oscillating vertically with small amplitude. If the force constant of the spring is k, calculate the frequency of oscillations of cylinder.

$$\text{Ans : } f = \frac{1}{2\pi}\sqrt{\frac{k + A\sigma g}{M}}.$$

25. A horizontal spring-block system of mass M executes simple harmonic motion. When the block is passing through its equilibrium position, an object of mass m is put on it and the two move together. Find the new amplitude of vibration.

$$\text{Ans: } A\sqrt{\frac{M}{(M + m)}}$$

26. A long uniform rod of length L and mass M is free to rotate in a horizontal plane about a vertical axis through its one end O. A spring of force constant k is connected horizontally between one end of the rod and a fixed wall. When the rod is in equilibrium it is parallel to the wall

(a) What is the period of small oscillations resulting when the rod is rotated slightly and released.

(b) What will be the maximum speed of the displaced end of the rod if the amplitude of motion is θ_0 ?

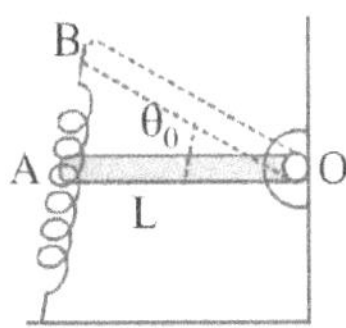

$$\text{Ans : } T = 2\pi\sqrt{\frac{M}{3K}}, \; L\theta_0\sqrt{\frac{3K}{M}}.$$

27. Springs of spring constants k, $2k$, $4k$, $8k$, ...,$2048\,k$,.... are connected in series. A mass m is attached to the lower end of the last spring and the system is allowed to oscillate. Calculate the time period of oscillations. $$\text{Ans : } T = 2\pi\sqrt{\frac{2m}{k}}.$$

28. Two masses m_1 and m_2 are suspended together by a massless spring of force constant k as shown in figure. When the masses are in equilibrium, m_1 is removed without disturbing the system. Find the angular frequency and amplitude of oscillation of mass m_2.

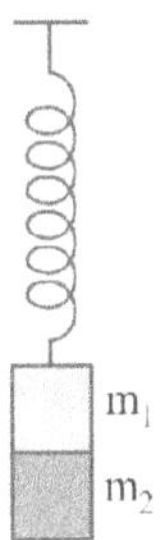

$$\text{Ans : } \omega = \sqrt{\frac{k}{m_2}}, \; A = \frac{m_1 g}{k}.$$

29. In the arrangement shown in figure pulleys are small and light and springs are ideal. k_1, k_2, k_3 and k_4 are force constants of the springs. Calculate period of small vertical oscillations of block of mass m.

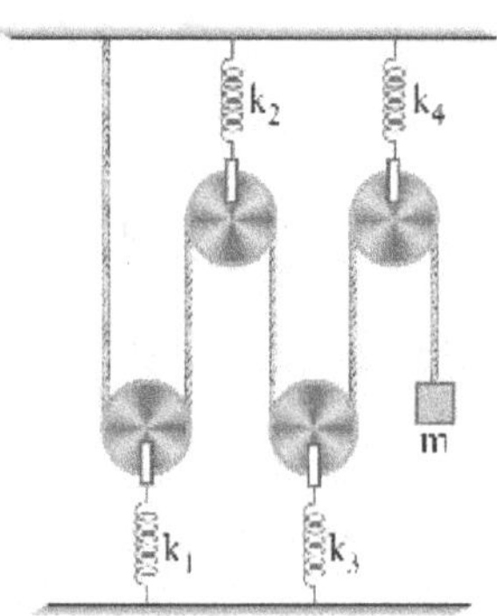

$$\text{Ans : } T = 4\pi\sqrt{m\left(\frac{1}{k_1}+\frac{1}{k_2}+\frac{1}{k_3}+\frac{1}{k_4}\right)}\,.$$

30. Figure shows a particle of mass m attached with four identical springs, each of length l. Initial tension in each spring is F_0. Neglecting gravity, calculate period of small oscillations of the particle along a line perpendicular to the plane of the figure.

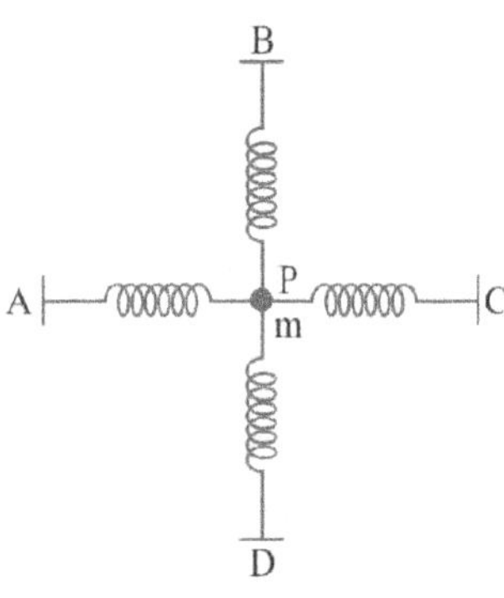

$$\text{Ans : } T = 2\pi\sqrt{\frac{ml}{4F_0}}\,.$$

31. A thin rod of length L and area of cross–section S is pivoted at its lower point P inside a stationary, homogeneous and non–viscous liquid. The rod is free to rotate in a vertical plane about a horizontal axis passing through P. The density d_1 of material of the rod is smaller than density d_2 of the liquid. The rod is displaced by a small angle θ from the equilibrium position and then released. Show that the motion of the rod is simple harmonic and determine its angular frequency in terms of given parameters.

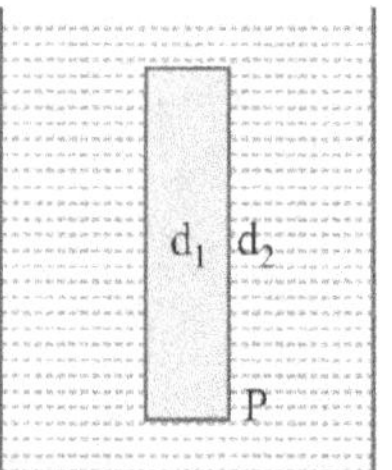

$$\text{Ans. } \omega = \sqrt{\frac{3g}{2L}\left(\frac{d_2-d_1}{d_1}\right)}\,.$$

32. In the arrangement shown in figure pulleys are small and massless and spring are also massless. Find the time period of small vertical oscillations of block of mass m.

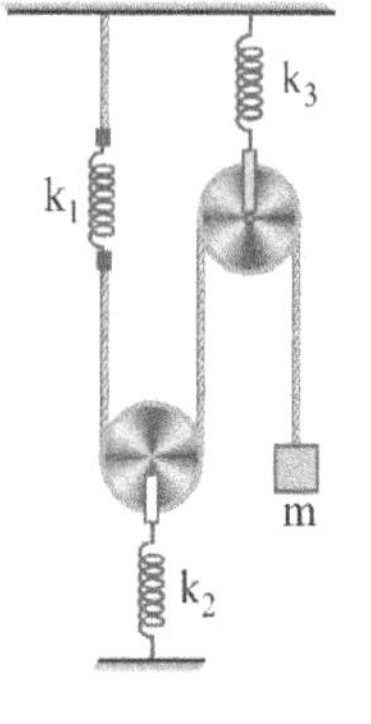 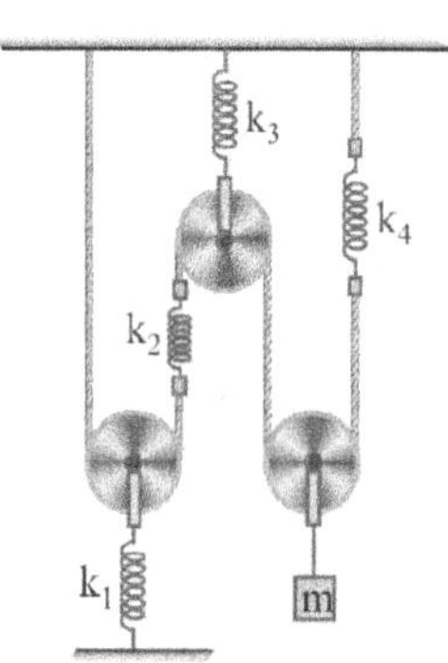

$$\textit{Ans.}\text{(i) } T = 2\pi\sqrt{m\left(\frac{1}{k_1}+\frac{4}{k_2}+\frac{4}{k_3}\right)}$$

$$\text{(ii) } T = 2\pi\sqrt{m\left(\frac{4}{k_1}+\frac{1}{4k_2}+\frac{4}{k_3}+\frac{1}{4k_4}\right)}$$

Hints & Solutions

1. (c) $\omega\sqrt{A^2 - y^2} = \dfrac{\omega A}{2}$

   or $y = \dfrac{\sqrt{3}}{2}A$

2. (c) The projection of the particle on any diameter varies sinusoidally, so it represents SHM.

3. (d) $y = a\tan\omega t$, has no practical periodicity, so it cannot represent SHM.

4. (b) Given, $1 = A\cos(\omega x_0 + \theta)$

   or $A\cos\theta = 1$ ... (i)

   Also velocity $v = \omega A\sin(\omega t + \theta)$

   or $\pi = \pi A\sin(\omega \times 0 + \theta)$

   or $A\sin\theta = 1$ ... (ii)

   Squaring equations (i) and (ii) and adding, we get

   $A = \sqrt{2}$

5. (a) In $y = A\sin\omega t + B$, the oscillating part is $A\sin\omega t$, so amplitude of motion is A.

6. (c) Given, $y_1 = 0.1\sin(100\pi t + \pi/3)$

   and $y_2 = 0.1\sin(\pi t + \pi/2)$

   so $\phi = \phi_1 - \phi_2 = \pi/3 - \pi/2 = -\pi/6$

7. (b) Elasticity brings the particle towards mean position and inertia needed to cross mean position.

8. (a) $x = a\sin(\omega t + \pi/6)$ and $x' = a\sin(\omega t + \pi/2)$

   $\therefore \quad \Delta\phi = \dfrac{\pi}{2} - \dfrac{\pi}{6} = \dfrac{\pi}{3}$

9. (b) $v_{max} = \omega A = \dfrac{2\pi}{T}A = \dfrac{2\pi}{2} \times 0.050$

   $= 0.15$ m/s.

10. (a) $a_{max} = \omega^2 A = (2\pi f)^2 A$

    $= (2\pi \times 60)^2 \times 0.01 = 144\pi^2$

11. (d) The acceleration of the particle at equilibrium position is zero.

12. (a) The maximum potential energy is equal to its maximum kinetic energy, so

    $U_{max} = K_{max} = K_0$.

13. (a) $F = -\dfrac{dU}{dx} = -\dfrac{d(1/2\,kx^2)}{dx} = -kx$, so represent SHM.

14. (c) Energy stored in the spring will be

    $= \dfrac{1}{2}kx^2 = \dfrac{1}{2}\left(\dfrac{Mg}{\ell}\right)\ell^2 = \dfrac{Mg\ell}{2}$.

15. (b) $K = \dfrac{1}{2}m\omega^2(A^2 - x^2)$

    $\therefore \quad K_{max} = \dfrac{1}{2}m\omega^2 A^2$, at $x = 0$.

16. (a) $E_{av} = U_{av} = \dfrac{1}{4}m\omega^2 A^2$

17. (c) $K = \dfrac{1}{2}m\omega^2 A^2\cos^2\omega t$

    $= \dfrac{1}{2}m\omega^2 A^2\left(\dfrac{1 + \cos 2\omega t}{2}\right)$

    $= \dfrac{1}{4}m\omega^2 A^2 + \dfrac{1}{4}m\omega^2 A^2\cos 2\omega t$

    Clearly frequency of kinetic energy is 2ω or $2f$.

18. (b) $E_1 = \dfrac{1}{2}kx^2$ and $E_2 = \dfrac{1}{2}ky^2$

    $\therefore x = \sqrt{2E_1/k}$ and $y = \sqrt{\dfrac{2E_1}{k}}$

    Now $E = \dfrac{1}{2}k(x + y)^2$

    or $\sqrt{\dfrac{2E}{k}} = x + y$

    or $\sqrt{\dfrac{2E}{k}} = \sqrt{\dfrac{2E_1}{k}} + \sqrt{\dfrac{2E_2}{k}}$

    or $\sqrt{E} = \sqrt{E_1} + \sqrt{E_2}$.

19. (b) $a = -bx$, on comparing with $a = -\omega^2 x$

    we get $\omega = \sqrt{b}$.

    $\therefore \quad T = \dfrac{2\pi}{\omega} = \dfrac{2\pi}{\sqrt{b}}$.

20. (d) As $\omega = \sqrt{\dfrac{k}{m}}$, so to make the frequency double the mass should be four times.

21. (c) As $T = 2\pi\sqrt{\dfrac{\ell}{g}}$, so time period becomes double when length becomes four times.

22. (b) When some mercury is drained off, the centre of gravity of the bob moves down and so length of the pendulum increases, which result increase in time period.

23. (b) In this case $T = 2\pi\sqrt{\dfrac{\ell}{\sqrt{a^2 + g^2}}}$, Clearly time period will decrease.

24. (b) $g = \dfrac{GM}{R^2}$. On the planet $g' = \dfrac{G(2M)}{(2R)^2} = \dfrac{g}{2}$.

    $T = 2\pi\sqrt{\ell/g}$ and $T' = 2\pi\sqrt{\ell/(g/2)} = \sqrt{2}\,T$

    $= \sqrt{2} \times 2 = 2\sqrt{2}$.

25. (c) $T = 2\pi\sqrt{\dfrac{\ell}{g}}$,

$$T' = 2\pi\sqrt{\dfrac{\ell}{g+a}} = 2\pi\sqrt{\dfrac{\ell}{\left(g+\dfrac{g}{4}\right)}} = \dfrac{2}{\sqrt{5}}T.$$

26. (a) $T = 2\pi\sqrt{\dfrac{\ell}{g}}$ and $T' = 2\pi\sqrt{\dfrac{1.21\ell}{g}} = 1.1\,T$

$$\therefore \dfrac{T'-T}{T}\times 100 = \dfrac{1.1T-T}{T}\times 100 = 10\%$$

27. (d) In the stand position, the centre of gravity of chimpanzee rises and so length of the pendulum and so time period decreases.

28. (d)

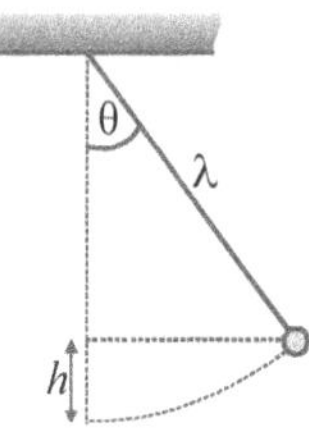

Maximum KE $=$ maximum PE
$\qquad\qquad = mgh$
$\qquad\qquad = mg\ell\,(1 - \cos\theta)$.

29. (d) $\qquad \omega_1 A_1 = \omega_2 A_2$

or $\qquad \sqrt{\dfrac{k_1}{m}}A_1 = \sqrt{\dfrac{k_2}{m}}A_2$

or $\qquad \dfrac{A_1}{A_2} = \sqrt{\dfrac{k_2}{k_1}}$.

30. (c) $\qquad \dfrac{1}{2}mv^2 = \dfrac{1}{2}kx^2$

$\therefore \qquad x = v\sqrt{\dfrac{m}{k}}$

31. (a) $2 = 2\pi\sqrt{\dfrac{m}{k}}$ and $2+1 = 2\pi\sqrt{\dfrac{m+2}{k}}$.

After solving, $m = 1.6$ kg

32. (d) $t_1 = 2\pi\sqrt{\dfrac{m}{k_1}}$, $t_2 = 2\pi\sqrt{\dfrac{m}{k_2}}$ and $t = 2\pi\sqrt{\dfrac{m}{(k_1+k_2)}}$

After solving above equations, we get

$$\dfrac{1}{t^2} = \dfrac{1}{t_1^2} + \dfrac{1}{t_2^2}$$

33. (a) The block can be detached from the platform, when it moves down. So

$$mg - N = ma$$
or $\qquad mg - 0 = m\omega^2 A$

$$\therefore \qquad \omega = \sqrt{\dfrac{g}{A}}$$

and $\qquad T = 2\pi\sqrt{\dfrac{A}{g}} = 2\pi\sqrt{\dfrac{3.92\times 10^{-3}}{g}}$

$\qquad\qquad = 0.1256$ s.

34. (a) $T_1 = \dfrac{T}{12}$ and $T_2 = \dfrac{T}{6}$.

Clearly $\qquad T_2 = 2T_1$

35. (a) The springs are in parallel,

so $\quad T = 2\pi\sqrt{\dfrac{m}{(k+k)}} = 2\pi\sqrt{\dfrac{m}{2k}}$

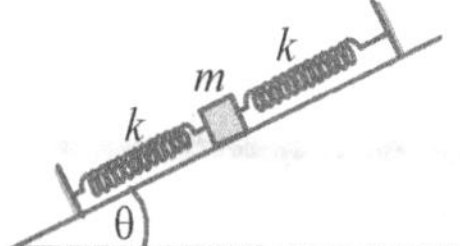

36. (b) $\qquad \dfrac{1}{2}kx^2 = Mgx$

or $\qquad x = \dfrac{2Mg}{k}$

37. (a) $\qquad x = \sin\omega t - \cos\omega t$

$\therefore \qquad \dfrac{d^2x}{dt^2} = -\omega^2(\sin\omega t - \cos\omega t)$

$\qquad\qquad = -\omega^2 x$. So it represents SHM.

38. (a) In $x = A\cos\omega t$, the particle starts oscillating from extreme position. So at $t = 0$, its potential energy is maximum.

39. (b) $\qquad a = \dfrac{F}{m} = \dfrac{kx}{m} = \dfrac{15\times 0.20}{0.3}$

$\qquad\qquad = 10$ m/s^2.

40. (a) $\dfrac{1}{2}m\omega^2 A^2\cos^2\omega t = \dfrac{3}{4}\times\dfrac{1}{2}m\omega^2 A^2$

or $\qquad \cos\omega t = \dfrac{\sqrt{3}}{2}$

or $\qquad \omega t = \dfrac{\pi}{6}$

or $\qquad t = \dfrac{\pi}{6\omega} = \dfrac{\pi\times T}{6\times 2\pi} = \dfrac{2}{12} = \dfrac{1}{6}$ s.

41. (b)

$$mg - N = ma$$
or $\qquad mg - 0 = m\times\omega^2 A$

$$\therefore \qquad A = \dfrac{g}{\omega^2}$$

42. (c) Acceleration should be like, $a = -kx$.

43. (a) $\omega = 2\pi$, $\therefore T = \dfrac{2\pi}{\omega} = \dfrac{2\pi}{2\pi} = 1$

44. (a) At point 2, the acceleration of the particle is maximum, which is at the extreme position. At extreme position, the velocity of the particle will be zero.

45. (a) For $\qquad x = (-A)$, we have

$$-A = A\sin(\omega\times 0 + \phi_0)$$

or $\qquad \phi_0 = -\dfrac{\pi}{2}$.

So for $x < (-A)$, $\phi_0 < (-\pi/2)$.

46. (d)
$$v^2 = \omega^2(A^2 - x^2) \qquad \ldots (i)$$
and
$$a^2 = (\omega^2 x)^2 = \omega^4 x^2 \qquad \ldots (ii)$$

From above equations, we have

$$v^2 = -\frac{a^2}{\omega^2} + \omega^2 A^2 \Rightarrow y = mx + c$$

It represents straight line with negative slope.

47. (a)
$$(n+1)T = n \times \frac{5T}{4}$$
or
$$n = 4$$
The number of oscillations of smaller pendulum $= n + 1 = 5$.

48. (b) The kinetic energy $= 9 - 5 = 4$ J.
$$E = \frac{1}{2}m\omega^2 A^2$$
or
$$4 = \frac{1}{2} \times 2 \times \omega^2 \times 1^2$$
or
$$\omega = 2 \text{ rad/s}$$

$$\therefore \quad T = \frac{2\pi}{\omega} = \frac{2\pi}{2} = 3.14 \text{ s}$$

49. (b)
$$mg - N = ma$$
or
$$mg - 0 = m\omega^2 A$$
or
$$A = \frac{g}{\omega^2} = \frac{g}{k/m}$$
$$= \frac{10}{200/2} = 0.1 \text{ m}$$

50. (a)

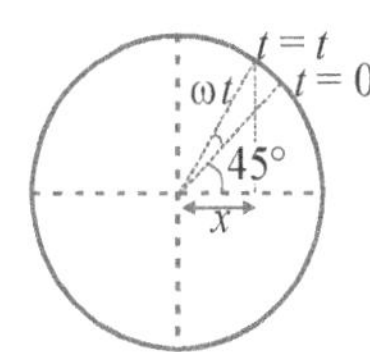

$$x = a\cos\left(\omega t + \frac{\pi}{4}\right)$$
or
$$x = a\cos\left(\frac{2\pi t}{4} + \frac{\pi}{4}\right)$$

51. (b) The equivalent system is shown in figure .

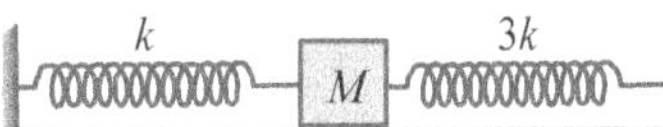

The equivalent force constant of which
$$k_e = k + 3k = 4k$$

$$\therefore \quad \omega = \sqrt{\frac{k_e}{m}} = \sqrt{\frac{4k}{m}} = 2\sqrt{\frac{k}{m}}$$

and
$$f = \frac{\omega}{2\pi} = \frac{2}{2\pi}\sqrt{\frac{k}{m}} = \frac{1}{\pi}\sqrt{\frac{k}{m}}.$$

52. (b)
$$x = A\sin^2\omega t = \frac{A(1 - \cos 2\omega t)}{2}$$
$$= \frac{A}{2} - \frac{A}{2}\cos 2\omega t$$

Clearly amplitude of motion is $A/2$.

Solutions EXERCISE 4.1 LEVEL -2

1. (a)

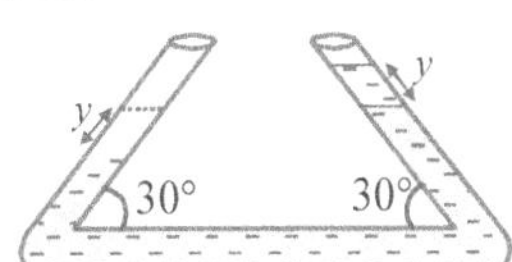

The restoring force
$$F = -(PA)$$
$$= -[\rho g(2y\sin 30°)]A$$
$$= \rho g A(-y)$$

$$\therefore \quad a = \frac{F}{m} = \frac{\rho g A}{m}$$

Thus
$$T = 2\pi\sqrt{\frac{m}{\rho g A}}$$

2. (b) If Δx_1 and Δx_2 are their respective amplitude of motion, then
$$m\Delta x_1 + 2m(-\Delta x_2) = 0 \qquad \ldots (i)$$
and
$$\Delta x_1 + \Delta x_2 = x_0 \qquad \ldots (ii)$$
After solving above equations, we get
$$\Delta x_1 = \frac{2x_0}{3}.$$

3. (b) The force constant, $k = \dfrac{mg}{x}$

$$\therefore \quad T = 2\pi\sqrt{\frac{(M+m)}{mg/x}} = 2\pi\sqrt{\frac{(M+m)x}{mg}}$$

4. (b)
$$t_1 = 2\pi\sqrt{\frac{m}{k_1}} \text{ and } t_2 = 2\pi\sqrt{\frac{m}{k_2}}.$$

In series $k_e = \dfrac{k_1 k_2}{k_1 + k_2}$,

$$\therefore \quad T = 2\pi\sqrt{\frac{m}{k_e}} = 2\pi\sqrt{\frac{m}{k_1 k_2 /(k_1 + k_2)}}$$

$$\therefore \quad k_1 = \frac{4\pi^2 m}{t_1^2} \text{ and } k_2 = \frac{4\pi^2 m}{t_2^2}$$

Also $T^2\left(\dfrac{k_1 k_2}{k_1 + k_2}\right) = 4\pi^2 m$

or $T^2\left[\dfrac{(4\pi^2 m/t_1^2)(4\pi^2 m/t_2^2)}{\dfrac{4\pi^2 m}{t_1^2} + \dfrac{4\pi^2 m}{t_2^2}}\right] = 4\pi^2 m$

or
$$T^2 = t_1^2 + t_2^2.$$

5. (d)
$$T = 2\pi\sqrt{\frac{M}{k}} \text{ and } \frac{5T}{3} = 2\pi\sqrt{\frac{M+m}{k}}$$

After simplifying above equations, we get
$$\frac{m}{M} = \frac{16}{9}$$

6. (a) When m_1 is removed, the unbalanced upward force is $= m_1 g$.

So amplitude of motion $= \dfrac{m_1 g}{k}$.

7. (d) In this case amplitude of motion

$$A = \sqrt{a^2 + b^2}$$
$$= \sqrt{4^2 + 4^2} = 4\sqrt{2}$$

8. (a) Given, $U = k|x|^3$; $\therefore$ $F = -\dfrac{dU}{dx} = -3k|x|^2$

For SHM, $\quad F = -ma = -m\omega^2 x$

From above, $\quad \omega = \sqrt{\dfrac{3kx}{m}}$,

$$\therefore \quad T = \dfrac{2\pi}{\omega} = 2\pi\sqrt{\dfrac{m}{3kx}} = 2\pi\sqrt{\dfrac{m}{3k(a\sin\omega t)}}$$

Clearly $\quad T \propto \dfrac{1}{\sqrt{a}}$.

9. (a) Volume of the gas $V = Ah$. Suppose piston is displaced slightly by x, then change in volume, $\Delta V = Ax$.
For isothermal process,
$$PV = \text{constant}$$
or $\quad P\Delta V + V\Delta P = 0$

or $\qquad \Delta P = -\dfrac{P\Delta V}{V}$

Restoring force, $F = (\Delta P)A$

$$= -\left(\dfrac{P\Delta V}{V}\right)A$$

$$= -\dfrac{P(Ax)A}{Ah}$$

Acceleration of the piston,

$$a = \left(\dfrac{PA}{Mh}\right)(-x)$$

$$\therefore \qquad T = 2\pi\sqrt{\dfrac{Mh}{PA}}$$

10. (a) We know that

$$\dfrac{\Delta T}{T} = \dfrac{\alpha\Delta t}{2}$$

$$\therefore \qquad \Delta T = \left(\dfrac{\alpha\Delta T}{2}\right)T$$

$$= \dfrac{(12\times 10^{-6})\times 20}{2}\times 24 \times 3600$$

$$= 10.36 \text{ s/day, loss}$$

11. (a) $\quad a_{net} = \sqrt{g^2 + (g\sin\alpha)^2 + 2g(g\sin\alpha)\cos(90° + \alpha)}$

$$= g\cos\alpha.$$

$$\therefore \quad T = 2\pi\sqrt{\dfrac{L}{g\cos\alpha}}.$$

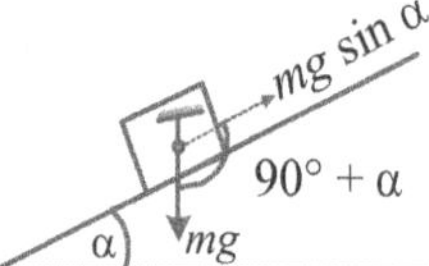

12. (c)

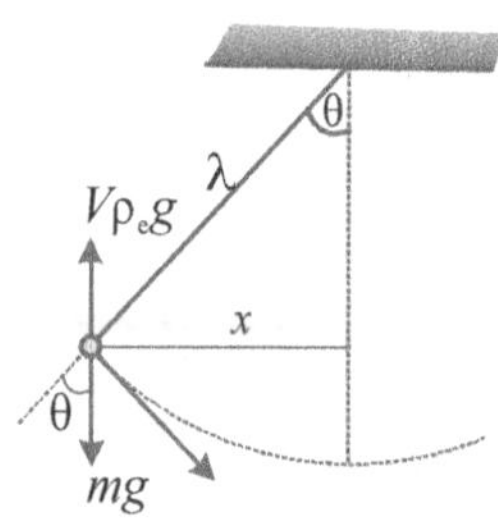

$$t_0 = 2\pi\sqrt{\dfrac{\ell}{g}}.$$

The restoring force in a liquid

$$F = -(mg - V\rho_e g)\sin\theta$$

$$= -\left(mg - \dfrac{m}{\left(\dfrac{4}{3}\times 1000\right)}\times 1000g\right)\left(\dfrac{x}{\ell}\right)$$

or $\quad a = \left(g - \dfrac{3g}{4}\right)\left(\dfrac{-x}{\ell}\right) = \dfrac{g}{4}\left(\dfrac{-x}{\ell}\right)$

$$\therefore \quad t = 2\pi\sqrt{\dfrac{\ell}{(g/4)}} = 2t_0.$$

13. (b) $\quad \ell_1 + \ell_2 = \ell$ and $\ell_1 = 2\ell_2$

$$\therefore \quad \ell_1 = \dfrac{2\ell}{3} \text{ and } \ell_2 = \dfrac{\ell}{3}$$

$$\therefore \quad k_1 = \dfrac{3k}{2} \text{ and } k_2 = 3k.$$

14. (b) The force constant of wire, $k' = \dfrac{Ay}{L}$.

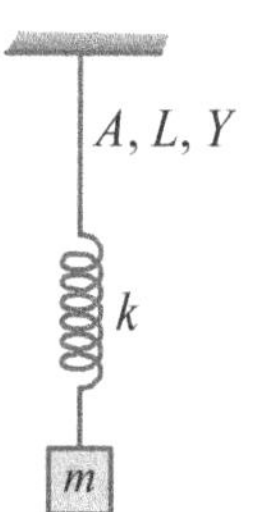

So effective force constant

$$k_e = \dfrac{kk'}{k+k'} = \dfrac{k\left(\dfrac{AY}{L}\right)}{k + \left(\dfrac{AY}{L}\right)}$$

$$\therefore \qquad T = 2\pi\sqrt{\dfrac{m}{k_e}} = 2\pi\sqrt{\dfrac{(YA + kL)m}{YAk}}$$

15. (b) $\quad y = 4\cos^2(t/2)\sin 1000t$

$$= 2[1 + \cos t]\sin 1000t$$

$$= 2\sin 1000t + 2\cos t\sin 1000t$$

$$= 2\sin 1000t + \sin(1000t + t) + \sin(1000t - t)$$

$$= 2\sin 1000t + \sin(1001t) + \sin(999t)$$

Clearly the given expression is the combination of three SHMs.

16. (d) $y = \sin^2 \omega t$

$$= \left[\frac{1 - \cos 2\omega t}{2}\right] = \frac{1}{2} - \frac{1}{2}\cos 2\omega t$$

The time period, $T = \dfrac{2\pi}{\omega'} = \dfrac{2\pi}{2\omega} = \dfrac{\pi}{\omega}$.

17. (c) Given, $y = kt^2$; $\therefore a = \dfrac{d^2 y}{dt^2} = 2k = 2 \times 1 = 2 \text{ m/s}^2$

Thus $T_1 = 2\pi\sqrt{\dfrac{\ell}{g}}$ and $T_2 = 2\pi\sqrt{\dfrac{\ell}{(g+2)}}$. For $g = 10$,

$$\frac{T_1^2}{T_2^2} = \frac{6}{5}.$$

18. (b) Velocity of bob just before collision, $u = \sqrt{2g\ell}$.

The velocity of wall just after collision becomes,

$$v = -eu$$
$$= e\sqrt{2g\ell}.$$

If h is the height attained after first collision, then

$$\frac{1}{2}m(e\sqrt{2g\ell})^2 = mgh$$

or $\qquad h = e^2 \ell$

Height attained after n^{th} collision

$$h_n = e^{2n}\ell$$

or $\qquad \ell(1 - \cos\theta) = e^{2n}\ell$

or $\qquad 1 - \cos\theta = \left(\dfrac{2}{\sqrt{5}}\right)^{2n}$

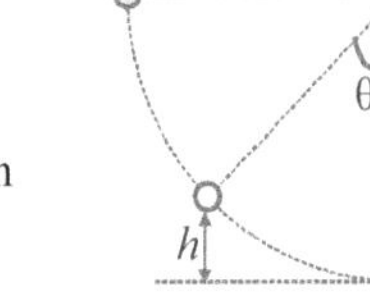

For $\theta < 60°$, $\left(\dfrac{4}{5}\right)^n < \dfrac{1}{2}$

$\Rightarrow \qquad n \simeq 3$

19. (b) The equivalent system is shown in figure.

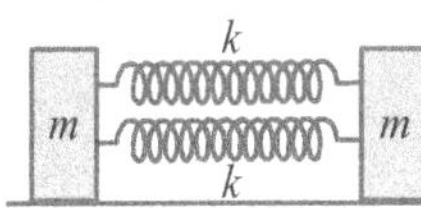

The reduced mass, $\mu = \dfrac{mm}{m+m} = \dfrac{m}{2}$

and $\qquad k_e = 2k.$

$\therefore \qquad \omega = \sqrt{\dfrac{k}{m}} = \sqrt{\dfrac{2k}{m/2}} = 2\sqrt{\dfrac{k}{m}}$

$$= 2\sqrt{\frac{0.1}{0.1}} = 2 \text{ rad/s}$$

or $\qquad f = \dfrac{\omega}{2\pi} = \dfrac{2}{2\pi} = \dfrac{1}{\pi} \text{ Hz}$

20. (c) Time period, $T = 2\pi\sqrt{\dfrac{M}{k}}$. The time taken

$$t = \frac{T}{4} + \frac{T}{12} = \frac{T}{3}$$
$$= \frac{2\pi}{3}\sqrt{\frac{M}{k}}.$$

21. (d) Given, $\qquad U = K\left[1 - e^{-x^2}\right]$

$\therefore \qquad F = -\dfrac{dU}{dx} = e^{-x^2} \times (-2x)$

For small value of x, $x^2 \to 0$, so $e^{-x^2} \to 1$.

$\therefore \quad F = -2x$, which represents SHM.

22. (c) The maximum frictional force occurs at extreme position,

where acceleration, $a = \omega^2 A = \dfrac{kA}{2m}$.

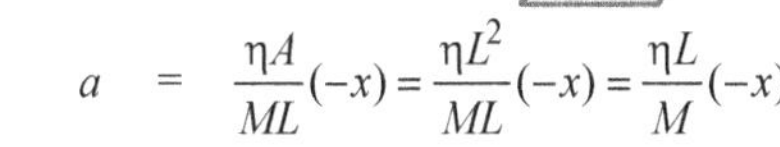

By Newton's second law,

$$kA - f = ma$$

or $\qquad kA - f = m\left(\dfrac{kA}{2m}\right)$

or $\qquad f = \dfrac{kA}{2}.$

23. (c) $T = 2\pi\sqrt{\dfrac{M}{k}}$; for displacement b,

$$b = a\sin\frac{2\pi}{T}t$$

$\therefore \qquad t = T\sin^{-1}\left(\dfrac{b}{a}\right).$

The time period of motion,

$$T' = 2\left(\frac{T}{4} + t\right) = \frac{T}{2} + 2t$$

$$= \pi\sqrt{\frac{M}{k}} + 2 \times T\sin^{-1}\left(\frac{b}{a}\right)$$

$$= \pi\sqrt{\frac{M}{k}} + 2 \times 2\pi\sqrt{\frac{M}{k}}\sin^{-1}\left(\frac{b}{a}\right)$$

$$= \left[\pi + 4\pi\sin^{-1}\left(\frac{b}{a}\right)\right]\sqrt{\frac{M}{k}}$$

24. (c) The time taken in first $a/2$ is $T/6$ and in next $a/2$ will be $T/4$. So

$$t = \frac{T}{6} + \frac{T}{4} = \frac{5}{12}T$$
$$= \frac{5}{12} \times 2\pi\sqrt{\frac{M}{k}} = \frac{5\pi}{6}\sqrt{\frac{M}{k}}.$$

25. (d) We know that $\quad \eta = \dfrac{f}{e} = \dfrac{F/A}{x/L}$

$\therefore \qquad F_{rest} = -\dfrac{\eta A}{L}(-x)$

acceleration , $\quad a = \dfrac{\eta A}{ML}(-x) = \dfrac{\eta L^2}{ML}(-x) = \dfrac{\eta L}{M}(-x)$

$\therefore \qquad T = 2\pi\sqrt{\dfrac{M}{\eta L}}$

26. **(b)** The equivalent system is :

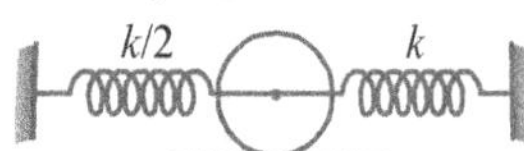

Total inertia of motion

$$= m + \frac{I}{R^2}$$

$$= m + \frac{mR^2}{2R^2} = \frac{3}{2}m$$

The equivalent force constant

$$k_e = k + k/2 = 3k/2$$

$$\therefore \quad T = 2\pi\sqrt{\frac{\text{total inertia}}{k_e}} = 2\pi\sqrt{\frac{3m/2}{3k/2}}$$

$$= 2\pi\sqrt{\frac{m}{k}}.$$

27. **(b)** The equivalent pendulum is shown in figure.

$$\therefore \quad T = 2\pi\sqrt{\frac{L\sin 60°}{g}}$$

$$= 2\pi\sqrt{\frac{\sqrt{3}L}{2g}}$$

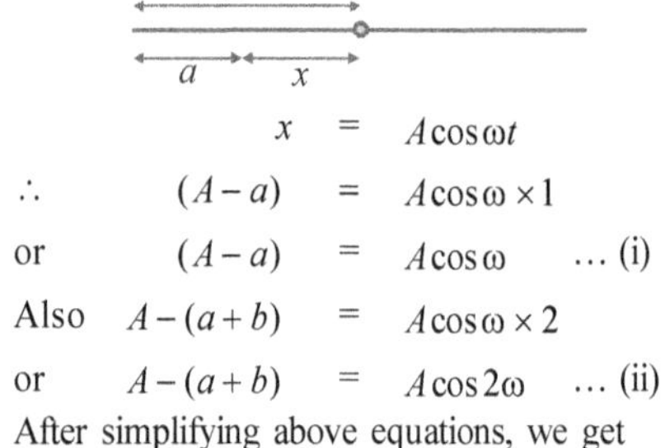

28. **(c)** When particle starts from mean position,

$$x = A\cos\omega t$$

$$\therefore \quad (A - a) = A\cos\omega \times 1$$

$$\text{or} \quad (A - a) = A\cos\omega \quad \ldots \text{(i)}$$

$$\text{Also} \quad A - (a + b) = A\cos\omega \times 2$$

$$\text{or} \quad A - (a + b) = A\cos 2\omega \quad \ldots \text{(ii)}$$

After simplifying above equations, we get

$$A = \left[\frac{2a^2}{3a - b}\right]$$

29. **(b)** The equivalent system is shown in figure. Thus equivalent force constant

$$\frac{1}{k_e} = \frac{1}{k} + \frac{1}{k} + \frac{1}{k} + \frac{4}{k} + \frac{1}{k}$$

$$\therefore \quad k_e = \frac{k}{8}$$

Time period $\quad T = 2\pi\sqrt{\frac{m}{k/8}} = 2\pi\sqrt{\frac{8m}{k}}$

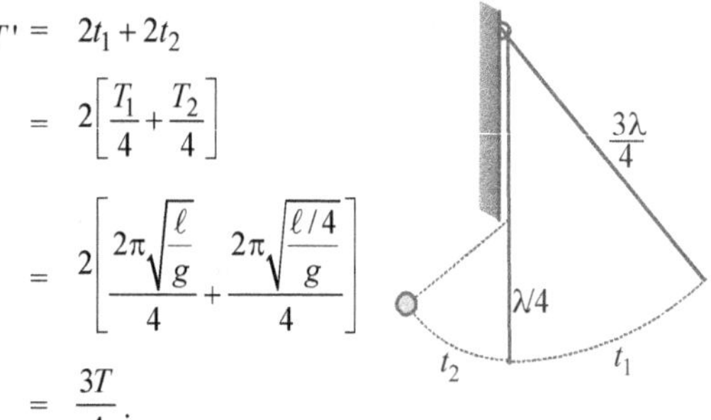

30. **(a)** The time period

$$T' = 2t_1 + 2t_2$$

$$= 2\left[\frac{T_1}{4} + \frac{T_2}{4}\right]$$

$$= 2\left[\frac{2\pi\sqrt{\frac{\ell}{g}}}{4} + \frac{2\pi\sqrt{\frac{\ell/4}{g}}}{4}\right]$$

$$= \frac{3T}{4}.$$

31. **(b)** The given rod system is equivalent to as shown in figure.

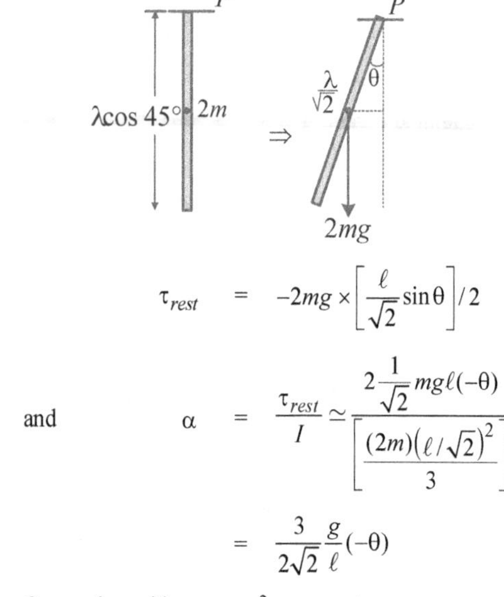

$$\tau_{rest} = -2mg \times \left[\frac{\ell}{\sqrt{2}}\sin\theta\right]/2$$

and $\quad \alpha = \frac{\tau_{rest}}{I} \simeq \dfrac{2\frac{1}{\sqrt{2}}mg\ell(-\theta)}{\left[\dfrac{(2m)(\ell/\sqrt{2})^2}{3}\right]}$

$$= \frac{3}{2\sqrt{2}}\frac{g}{\ell}(-\theta)$$

Comparing with $\alpha = -\omega^2\theta$, we get

$$\omega = \sqrt{\frac{3g}{2\sqrt{2}\ell}} \quad \text{and} \quad T = 2\pi\sqrt{\frac{2\sqrt{2}\ell}{3g}}.$$

32. **(c)** For small value of θ,

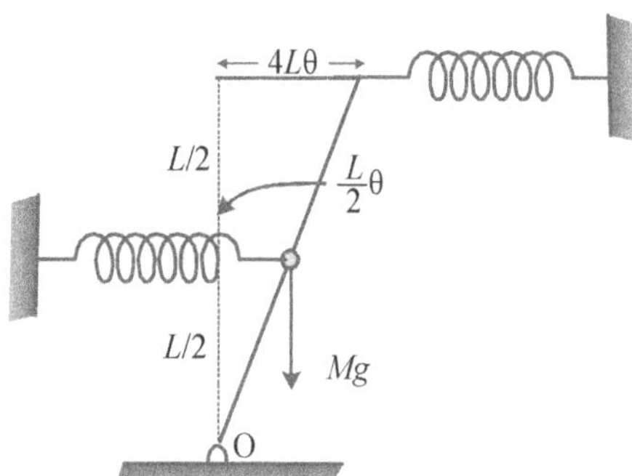

$$\tau_0 = -\left[k(L\theta)L + k(L\theta/2)\frac{L}{2} - Mg\frac{L}{2}\theta\right]$$

$$\text{or} \quad \tau_0 = -\left[5\frac{kL^2\theta}{4} - \frac{MgL\theta}{2}\right]$$

For angular SHM, $\tau_0 > 0$

$$\text{or} \quad \frac{5kL^2\theta}{4} - \frac{MgL\theta}{2} > 0$$

$$\text{or} \quad k > \left(\frac{2Mg}{5L}\right).$$

33. **(b)** From the figure, $\dfrac{T}{2} = 0.3\pi$, $\therefore T = 0.6\pi$

and $\quad \phi_0 = -\dfrac{\pi}{2}.$

Thus $\quad y = A\sin(\omega t + \phi_0)$

$$= 2\sin\left(\frac{2\pi}{0.6\pi}t + -\frac{\pi}{2}\right)$$

$$= 2\sin\left(\frac{10t}{3} - \frac{\pi}{3}\right).$$

34. **(c)**

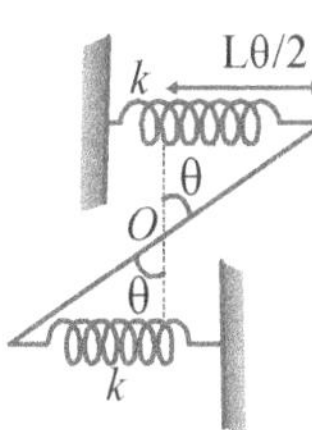

The restoring torque

$$\tau_0 = -\left[k\left(\frac{L\theta}{2}\right)\times\frac{L}{2}+k\left(\frac{L\theta}{2}\right)\frac{L}{2}\right]$$

$$= \frac{kL^2}{2}(-\theta)$$

$$\therefore\quad \alpha = \frac{\tau_0}{I}=\frac{kL^2}{2\left(\dfrac{ML^2}{12}\right)}(-\theta)$$

$$\therefore\quad \omega = \sqrt{\frac{6k}{M}}$$

35. **(a)** In the given device, both the springs are in parallel and so equivalent force constant

$$k_e = 2k.$$

The time period, $T = 2\pi\sqrt{\dfrac{M}{k_e}}=2\pi\sqrt{\dfrac{M}{2k}}$

36. **(a)** In this device, the springs are in parallel, and so

$$T = 2\pi\sqrt{\frac{m}{2k}}.$$

37. **(d)** When one displaces the block by y, the pulley A will go down by $y/2$. Accordingly the pulley B goes down by $y/4$. So spring will stretch by $y/4$.

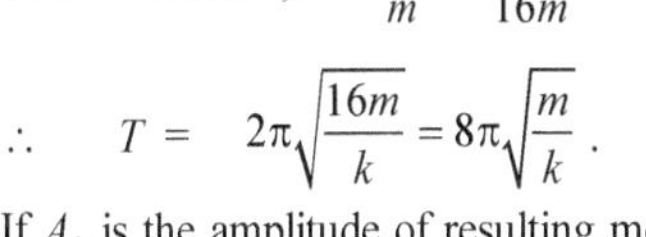

Thus $\quad\dfrac{ky}{4} = 2T_1$

and $\quad 2T = T_1$

$$\therefore\quad T = \frac{ky}{16}$$

The restoring force, $F=-T=-\dfrac{k}{16}y$

and acceleration, $a=\dfrac{F}{m}=\dfrac{k}{16m}(-y)$

$$\therefore\quad T = 2\pi\sqrt{\frac{16m}{k}}=8\pi\sqrt{\frac{m}{k}}.$$

38. **(c)** If A_0 is the amplitude of resulting motion, then

$$A_0 = \sqrt{2}A+A=A(\sqrt{2}+1)$$

The energy associated to any one SHM

$$E = \frac{1}{2}m\omega^2 A^2,$$

$$\therefore\quad E_0 = \frac{1}{2}m\omega^2[A(\sqrt{2}+1)]^2$$

$$= \frac{1}{2}m\omega^2 A^2[2+1+2\sqrt{2}]$$

$$= E[3+2\sqrt{2}].$$

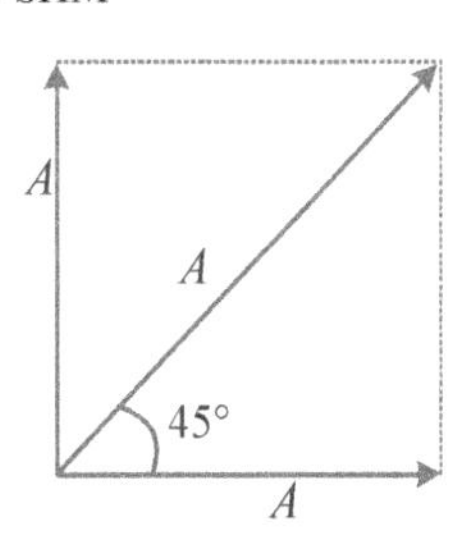

39. **(a)** The time period is given by

$$T = 2\pi\sqrt{\frac{\ell/2}{g}}=2\pi\sqrt{\frac{h}{g}}=2\pi\sqrt{\frac{0.3}{9.8}}$$

$$= 1.1\ \text{s}$$

40. **(a)**

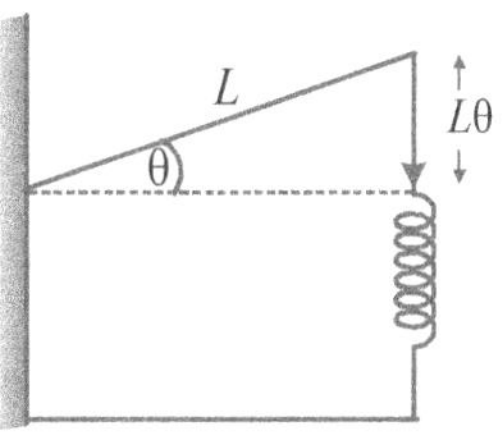

The restoring torque

$$\tau = -(kL\theta)\times L$$

$$\therefore\quad \alpha = \frac{\tau}{I}=\frac{kL^2}{\left(\dfrac{mL^2}{3}\right)}(-\theta)$$

On comparing with $\alpha=-\omega^2\theta$, we get

$$\omega = \sqrt{\frac{3k}{m}}.$$

41. **(d)** The half of the oscillation is completed with one spring and other half oscillation with two springs and so

$$T' = \left[\frac{T}{2}\right]_{\text{one spring}}+\left[\frac{T}{2}\right]_{\text{two springs in parallel}}$$

$$= \pi\sqrt{\frac{m}{k}}+\pi\sqrt{\frac{m}{2k}}.$$

42. **(a)** In this device, the restoring torque is constituted by spring force ($F=kb\theta$). So for small θ

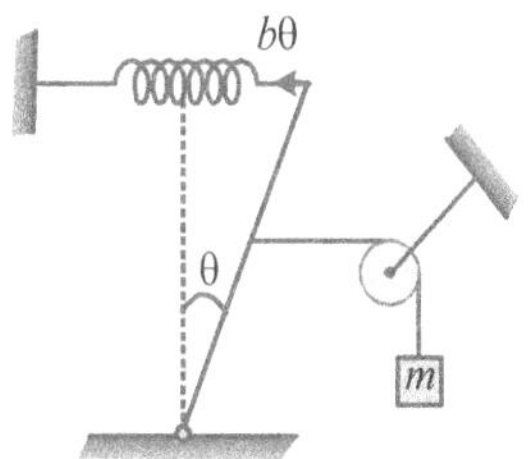

$$\tau_{\text{rest}} = -(kb\theta)\times b$$

and $\quad\alpha = \dfrac{\tau_{\text{rest}}}{I}=\dfrac{kb^2}{ma^2}(-\theta)$

On comparing with, $\alpha=-\omega^2\theta$, we get

$$\omega = \sqrt{\frac{kb^2}{ma^2}}\ \text{or}\ T=2\pi\sqrt{\frac{ma^2}{kb^2}}.$$

43. **(d)** If t be the time of 100 oscillations, then by

$$A = A_0 e^{-bt/2m}$$

or $\quad\dfrac{1}{3} = e^{-bt/2m}$

Again $\quad A = A_0 e^{-\frac{b\times 2t}{2m}}$

or $\quad A = A_0(e^{-bt/2m})^2=A_0\left(\dfrac{1}{3}\right)^2=\dfrac{A_0}{9}.$

44. **(a)** The minimum force will occur at the instant when block is at its lowest position and hang tendency downward motion.

So
$$mg - F = ma$$
or
$$F = mg - ma$$
$$= mg - m(\omega^2 A)$$
$$= mg - m \times \left(\frac{2\pi}{T}\right)^2 A$$
$$= mg - \frac{4\pi^2}{T^2} mA$$

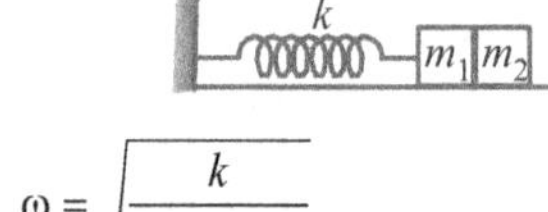

45. **(b)** The equivalent system is shown in figure.

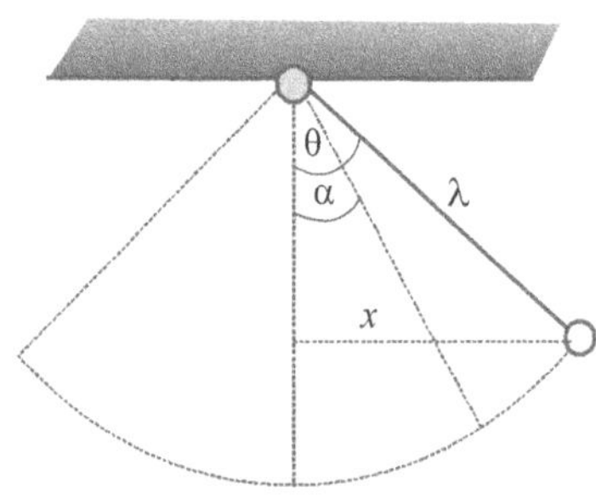

$$\therefore \; \omega = \sqrt{\frac{k}{(m_1 + m_2)}}$$

46. **(a)** The angle traverses by the thread starting from extreme position in time t is

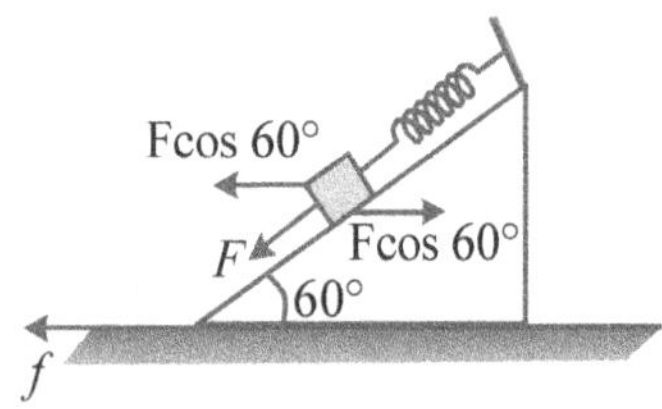

$$\alpha = \theta \cos \omega t .$$
$$\therefore \quad x = \ell\alpha = \ell\theta \cos \omega t$$
$$= \ell\theta \cos \sqrt{\frac{g}{\ell}} \; t.$$

47. **(b)** During the oscillation, the force exerted by the block along inclined plane

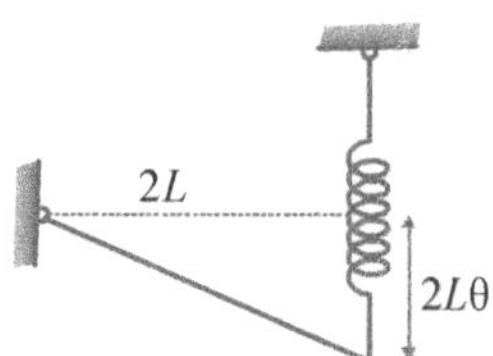

$$F = ma$$
$$= m(\omega^2 x)$$
$$= m\omega^2 A \sin \omega t$$

Horizontal component of this will cause frictional force, so
$$f = F \cos 60°$$
$$= [m\omega^2 A \sin \omega t] \cos 60°$$
$$= \frac{1}{2} m\omega^2 A \sin \omega t$$

48. **(c)** The reduced mass of the system
$$\mu = \frac{mm}{m + m} = \frac{m}{2}$$

and
$$k_e = \frac{k \times 2k}{k + 2k} = \frac{2k}{3}$$

Time period
$$T = 2\pi\sqrt{\frac{\mu}{k_e}} = 2\pi\sqrt{\frac{m/2}{2k/3}} = 2\pi\sqrt{\frac{3m}{4k}}$$

49. **(c)**

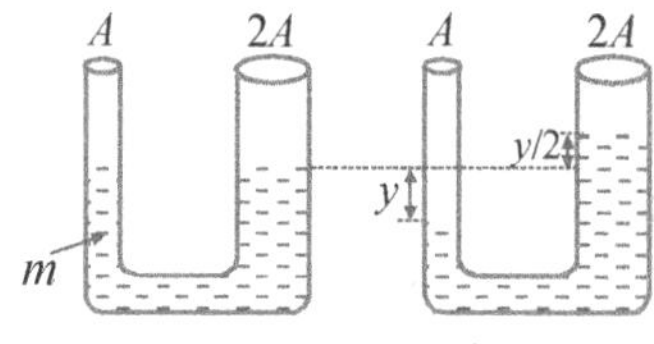

The restoring torque for small θ
$$\tau_{rest} = -[k(2L\theta) \times 2L]$$
and
$$\alpha = \frac{\tau_{rest}}{I}$$
$$= \frac{4kL^2}{\dfrac{M(2L)^2}{3}}(-\theta) = \frac{3k}{M}(-\theta)$$

On comparing with $\alpha = -\omega^2\theta$, we get
$$\omega = \sqrt{\frac{3k}{M}}.$$

50. **(a)**

Suppose the liquid in left side limb is displaced slightly by y, the liquid in right limb will increase by $y/2$. The restoring force
$$F = -PA$$
$$= -\rho g\left(\frac{3y}{2}\right) \times 2A = 3\rho gA(-y) .$$
$$a = \frac{F}{m} = 3\rho gA(-y)/m$$

On comparing with, $a = -\omega^2 y$, we get
$$\omega = \sqrt{\frac{3\rho gA}{m}} \text{ and } T = 2\pi\sqrt{\frac{m}{3\rho gA}}$$

51. **(b)** The restoring torque (for small displacement),
$$\tau_{rest} = -mg(R\theta)$$
$$\therefore \; \alpha = \frac{\tau_{rest}}{I} = \frac{mgR}{2mR^2}(-\theta) = \frac{g}{2R}$$
$$\therefore \; T = 2\pi\sqrt{\frac{2R}{g}}$$

The length of equivalent pendulum
$$\ell = 2R.$$

52. (b) $T_1 = 2\pi\sqrt{\dfrac{1}{g}}$ and $T_2 = 2\pi\sqrt{\dfrac{16}{g}} = 4T_1$

They will be again in phase, if shorter one complete one more oscillation, so

$$(n+1) \times T_1 \quad = \quad nT_2$$

or $\qquad (n+1) \times T_1 \quad = \quad n \times 4T_1$

$\therefore \qquad\qquad n \quad = \quad \dfrac{1}{3}$

and $\qquad n+1 \quad = \quad \dfrac{4}{3}$

For whole number multiply n and $(n+1)$ by 3, so we get 1 and 4.

53. (d) $\phi = \dfrac{\pi}{6}$. The equation of trajectory

$$\frac{x^2}{a^2} + \frac{y^2}{a^2} - \frac{2xy}{ab}\cos\frac{\pi}{6} = \sin^2\frac{\pi}{6}$$

or $\quad \dfrac{x^2}{a^2} + \dfrac{y^2}{a^2} - \dfrac{2xy}{ab} \times \dfrac{\sqrt{3}}{2} = \dfrac{1}{4}$

or $\quad x^2 + y^2 - \sqrt{3}xy = \dfrac{a^2}{4}$.

54. (d) The differential equation of forced oscillation is;

$$m\frac{d^2x}{dt^2} + b\frac{dx}{dt} + kx = F\sin\omega t$$

Clearly 1, 2, 3 all are correct.

55. (c) We can write

$$\frac{d^2y}{dt^2} + \frac{9}{4}y \quad = \quad 0$$

On comparing with $a = -\omega^2 y$, we get

$$\omega \quad = \quad \frac{3}{2}.$$

56. (c) Given, $\qquad x \quad = \quad 3\sin\pi t + 4\cos\omega t$

The general equation of SHM can be written as

$$x \quad = \quad A\sin(\omega t + \phi)$$

or $\qquad x \quad = \quad A\sin\omega t\cos\phi + A\cos\omega t\sin\phi$

On comparing two equations, we get

$A\sin\phi = 4$ and $A\cos\phi = 3$

$\therefore \qquad A^2 = 25$ and $A = 5$

So, $\qquad x \quad = \quad 5\sin(\pi t + \phi)$

Also $\qquad \omega \quad = \quad \pi$

or $\qquad f \quad = \quad \dfrac{\omega}{2\pi} = \dfrac{\pi}{2\pi} = \dfrac{1}{2}$ Hz.

57. (d) The time taken by particle to move down to bottom

$$t = \frac{1}{\sin\theta}\sqrt{\frac{2h}{g}}.$$

Thus $\qquad T \quad = \quad 4t = \dfrac{4}{\sin\theta}\sqrt{\dfrac{2h}{g}}$

58. (a) The restoring torque (for small θ)

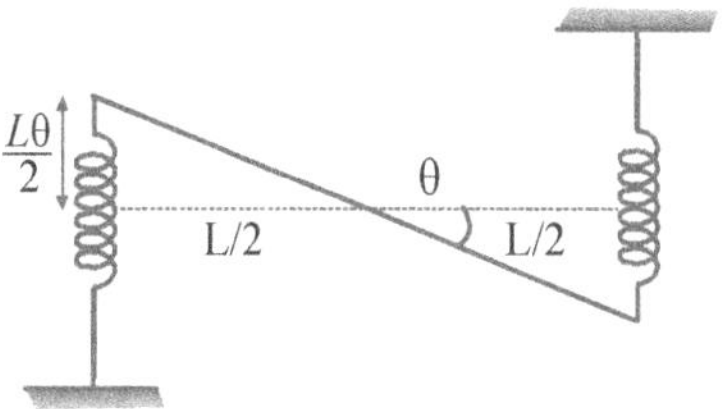

$$\tau_{\text{rest}} \quad = \quad -\left[\frac{kL\theta}{2} \times \frac{L}{2}\right] \times 2$$

$$= \quad \frac{kL^2}{2}(-\theta)$$

$\therefore \quad \alpha = \dfrac{\tau_{\text{rest}}}{I} = \dfrac{kL^2/2}{ML^2/12}(-\theta) = \dfrac{6k}{M}(-\theta)$

$\therefore \qquad\qquad T \quad = \quad 2\pi\sqrt{\dfrac{M}{6k}}$.

59. (a) The equivalent system is shown in figure.

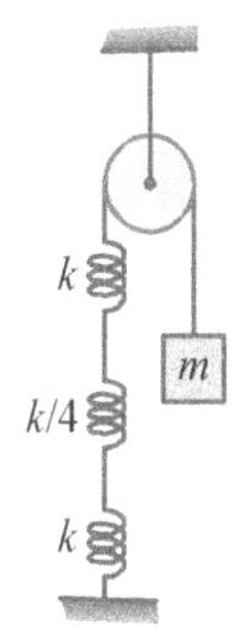

The equivalent force constant

$$\frac{1}{k_e} \quad = \quad \frac{1}{k} + \frac{1}{k/4} + \frac{1}{k}$$

or $\qquad k_e \quad = \quad k/6$

Thus $\qquad T \quad = \quad 2\pi\sqrt{\dfrac{M}{k/6}} = 2\pi\sqrt{\dfrac{6M}{k}}$.

60. (c) When block is displaced slightly by x slightly towards right then $x' = x\cos 30°$.

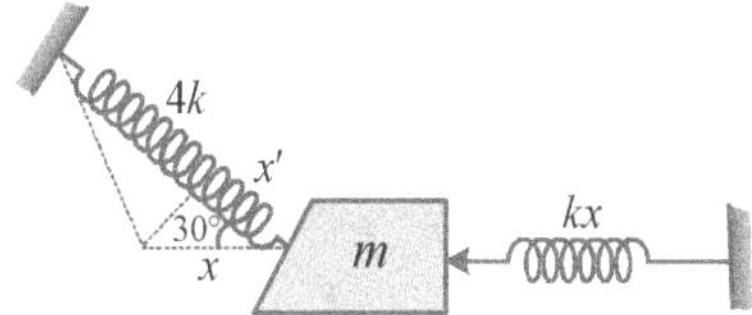

The restoring force

$$F \quad = \quad -(kx + 4kx'\cos 30°)$$

$$= \quad -[kx + 4k(x\cos 30°)\cos 30°]$$

$$= \quad -[kx + 3kx]$$

$$= \quad -4kx.$$

$$a \quad = \quad \frac{F}{m} = \frac{4k}{m}(-x)$$

On comparing with $a = -\omega^2 x$, we get

$$\omega = \sqrt{\frac{4k}{m}} \text{ and } T = 2\pi\sqrt{\frac{m}{4k}} = \pi\sqrt{\frac{m}{k}}.$$

Solutions EXERCISE 4.2

1. (a, b, d) $x = A\tan(\omega t + \phi)$ has no practical periodicity so it does not represent SHM or otherwise

$$\frac{dx}{dt} = \omega A \sec^2\theta, \text{ and so}$$

$$\frac{d^2x}{dt^2} \neq -kx.$$

2. (b, d)

$$U = \frac{1}{2}m\omega^2 A^2 \sin^2\omega t$$

$$= \frac{1}{2}m\omega^2 A^2 \left[\frac{1-\cos 2\omega t}{2}\right]$$

$$= \frac{1}{2}m\omega^2 A^2 - \frac{1}{4}m\omega^2 A^2 \cos 2\omega t$$

Clearly frequency of PE is 2ω and so time period of KE will be half the time period of oscillations.
Also difference of KE and PE

$$= \frac{1}{2}m\omega^2 A^2 (\cos^2\omega t - \sin^2\omega t)$$

$$= \frac{1}{2}m\omega^2 A^2 \cos 2\omega t.$$

3. (b, c) $KE_{max} = \frac{1}{2}mv_{max}^2 = \frac{1}{2}kA^2 = \frac{1}{2} \times 2 \times 10^6 \times (0.01)^2 = 100$ J

$PE_{max} = $ total energy $= 160$ J.

4. (b, d) After the collision the velocity of block A will be v. At the maximum compression, both the blocks have same velocity, so

$$mv + 0 = mv' + mv'$$

$$\Rightarrow \quad v' = \frac{v}{2}.$$

Kinetic energy of blocks

$$K = \frac{1}{2}mv'^2 + \frac{1}{2}mv'^2$$

$$= \frac{1}{2}m(v/2)^2 + \frac{1}{2}m(v/2)^2$$

$$= \frac{mv^2}{4}$$

If x be the maximum compression, then

$$\frac{1}{2}mv^2 + 0 = \frac{1}{2}mv'^2 + \frac{1}{2}mv'^2 + \frac{1}{2}kx_{max}^2$$

After substituting the values, we get

$$x_{max} = v\sqrt{\frac{m}{k}}.$$

5. (b, c)

$$T - Mg\cos\theta = \frac{Mv^2}{L}$$

$$a_T = \frac{F_t}{M}$$

$$= \frac{Mg\sin\theta}{M} = g\sin\theta$$

6. (a, c) The resultant amplitude

$$A = \sqrt{2}a + a = a(\sqrt{2}+1)$$

$$E = \frac{1}{2}m\omega^2 a^2$$

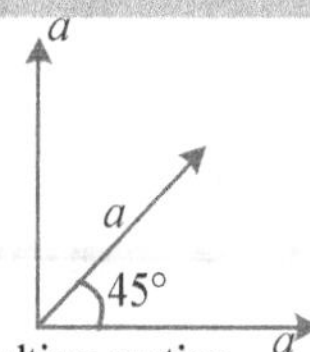

Energy associated with the resulting motion

$$E' = \frac{1}{2}m\omega^2 A^2 = \frac{1}{2}m\omega^2 [a(\sqrt{2}+1)]^2$$

$$= \frac{1}{2}m\omega^2 a^2 (3 + 2\sqrt{2}) = E(3 + 2\sqrt{2}).$$

7. (a, b, c) $x = a\cos pt = a\sin(pt + \pi/2)$ and $y = b\sin pt$
Thus for $\phi = \pi/2$, we have

$$\frac{x^2}{a^2} + \frac{y^2}{b^2} - \frac{2xy}{ab}\cos\frac{\pi}{2} = \sin^2\frac{\pi}{2}$$

or $\frac{x^2}{a^2} + \frac{y^2}{b^2} = 1 \Rightarrow$ ellipse

$$\vec{r} = \vec{x} + \vec{y}$$

$$= a\cos pt\,\hat{i} + b\sin pt\,\hat{j}$$

$$\vec{v} = \frac{d\vec{r}}{dt} = -ap\sin pt\,\hat{i} + bp\cos pt\,\hat{j}$$

$$\vec{a} = \frac{d^2\vec{r}}{dt^2}$$

$$= -ap^2\cos pt\,\hat{i} - bp^2\sin pt\,\hat{j}$$

$$= -p^2(a\cos pt\,\hat{i} + b\sin pt\,\hat{j})$$

$$= -p^2\vec{r}$$

It represents the acceleration is towards focus.
Also $\vec{v}.\vec{a} = 0$.

8. (b, c, d) The initial force in the spring

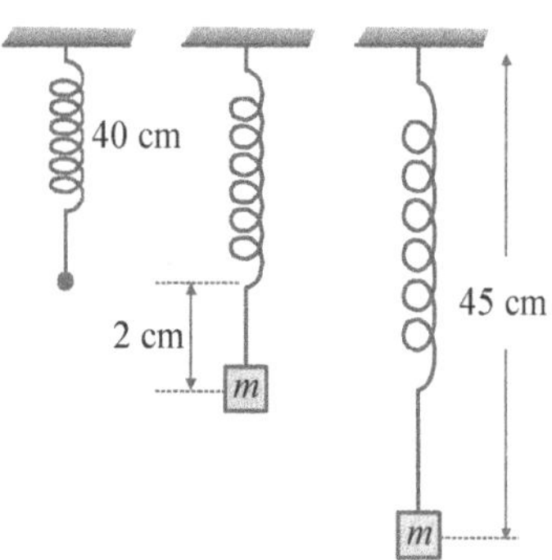

$F = ky = 500 \times 0.05 = 25$ N
The weight of the block $= 10$ N
For mean position,

$$k\,y_0 = mg$$

or $500\,y_0 = 1 \times 10 \Rightarrow y_0 = 2$ cm.

$\therefore \quad A = 3$ cm

Angular frequency

$$\omega = \sqrt{\frac{k}{m}} = \sqrt{\frac{500}{1}} = \sqrt{500}$$

$$v_{max} = \omega A = \sqrt{500} \times 3 = 30\sqrt{5}\ \text{m/s}$$

9. (a, b) At $x = \dfrac{A}{2}$

$$a = \frac{\omega^2 A}{2} = \frac{a_0}{2}.$$

Also $t = \dfrac{T}{12}$ (calculated earlier)

10. (a, b, c) $E = K_0 = U_0 = \dfrac{1}{2}kA^2 = \dfrac{1}{2}k(0.1)^2$

At $x = 0.06$, $U = \dfrac{1}{2}k(0.06)^2$

$$K = \frac{1}{2}k(0.1)^2 - \frac{1}{2}k(0.06)^2$$
$$= 0.64\, E.$$

$x = 0.05$, $U = \dfrac{1}{2}k(0.05)^2$

$\therefore \quad K = \dfrac{1}{2}k(0.1)^2 - \dfrac{1}{2}k(0.05)^2$
$$= 0.75\, E$$

11. (b, d) $x = 3\sin 100t + 4 \times 2\cos^2 50t$
$$= 3\sin 100t + 4(1 + \cos 100t)$$
$$= 4 + 3\sin 100t + 4\cos 100t$$
$$= 4 + 5\sin\left(100t + \frac{\pi}{4}\right)$$

Clearly, $A = 5$, the maximum displace from origin,
$$x = 4 + 5 = 9$$

12. (a, c) $k_{av} = U_{av} = \dfrac{1}{4}m\omega^2 A^2$

$\therefore \quad E = k_{av} + U_{av} = \dfrac{1}{2}m\omega^2 A^2$
$$= k_{max}$$

Root mean square velocity of $-v_{max}$ and v_{max} will be

$$\sqrt{\frac{v_{max}^2 + \left(-v_{max}\right)^2}{2}} = \frac{1}{\sqrt{2}}v_{max}$$

13. (a, b, c) The given equation is
$x = A\sin^2 \omega t + B\cos^2 \omega t + C\sin \omega t \cos \omega t$
Rearranging the equation in a meaningful form (for interpretation of SHM)

$$x = \frac{A}{2}(2\sin^2 \omega t) + \frac{B}{2}(2\cos^2 \omega t) + \frac{C}{2}(2\sin \omega t \cos \omega t)$$

$$= \frac{A}{2}[1 - \cos 2\omega t] + \frac{B}{2}[1 + \cos 2\omega t] + \frac{C}{2}[\sin 2\omega t]$$

(a) For $A = 0$ and $B = 0$, $x = \dfrac{C}{2}\sin(2\omega t)$

The above equation is that of SHM with amplitude $\dfrac{C}{2}$

and angular frequency 2ω. Thus option (a) is correct.

(b) If $A = B$ and $C = 2B$ then $x = B + B\sin 2\omega t$

This is equation of SHM. The mean position of the particle executing SHM is not at the origin.

Option (b) is correct. $[x = B = x' = b\sin 2\omega t]$

(c) $A = -B$, $C = 2B$; Therefore

$x = B\cos 2\omega t + B\sin 2\omega t$

Let $B = X\cos \phi = X\sin \phi$ then

$x = X\sin 2\omega t \cos \phi + X\cos 2\omega t \sin \phi$

This represents equation of SHM.

(d) $A = B$, $C = 0$ and $x = A$. This equation does not represents SHM.

14. (b, c) $v^2 = 108 - 9x^2$ or $v^2 = 9(12 - x^2)$

We can compare the above expression with y

$v = \omega\sqrt{A^2 - x^2}$, which is expression of velocity for SHM.

From this, we will get $\omega = 3$ and $A = \sqrt{12}$

SHM is not a uniformly accelerated motion.

Acceleration at a distance 3 cm from the mean position.

$q = \omega^2(3\text{cm}) = 27\ \text{cm}/\text{s}^2$.

Maximum displacement from the mean position

$= A = \sqrt{12}$.

15. (a, b, c, d)

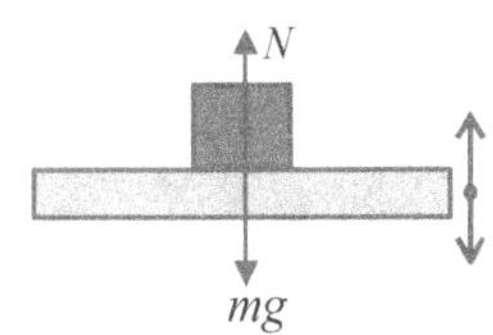

$mg - N = ma$

or $mg - 0 = m\omega^2 A$

$\therefore \quad \omega = \sqrt{\dfrac{g}{A}} = \sqrt{\dfrac{10}{0.40}} = 5\text{s}$

$$T = \frac{2\pi}{\omega} = \frac{2\pi}{5}\,\text{s}.$$

$a_{max} = \omega^2 A = 25 \times 0.4 = 10\ \text{m/s}^2 = g$

When plank moves in upward direction,

$N = m(g + a) = m(g + g) = 2mg$.

16. (a, c, d) $\vec{r} = A\cos \omega t\, \hat{i} + 2A\cos \omega t\, \hat{j}$

$\therefore \quad a = A$, $b = 2A$ and $\phi = 0$

Thus $\dfrac{x^2}{a^2} + \dfrac{y^2}{b^2} - \dfrac{2xy\cos 0}{ab} = \sin^2 0$

or $y = +\dfrac{b}{a}x = +2x$

It represents straight line.

17. **(a,b,c,d)** At $t = 0$, Displacement $x = x_1 + x_2 = 4\sin\dfrac{\pi}{3} = 2\sqrt{3}\,m$

Resulting amplitude

$$A = \sqrt{2^2 + 4^2 + 2(2)(4)\cos(\pi/3)}$$

$$= \sqrt{4 + 16 + 8} = \sqrt{28} = 2\sqrt{7}\,m$$

Maximum speed $= A\omega = 20\sqrt{7}$ m/s

Maximum acceleration $= A\omega^2 = 200\sqrt{7}\,m/s^2$

Energy of the motion $= \dfrac{1}{2}m\omega^2 A^2 = 28\,J$

18. **(b, c, d)** $\qquad U = U_0(1 - \cos ax)$

$\therefore \qquad F = -\dfrac{dU}{dx} = -aU_0\sin ax$

For small value of x, $\sin ax \simeq ax$

so $\qquad F = -aU_0 \times ax = a^2 U_0(-x)$

$\qquad acc = (a^2 U_0/m)(-x)$

On comparing with , $a = -\omega^2 x$, we get

$$\omega = \sqrt{\dfrac{a^2 U_0}{m}}$$

and $\qquad T = 2\pi\sqrt{\dfrac{m}{a^2 U_0}}$.

At $x = \dfrac{\pi}{2a}$. $\quad U = U_0\left[1 - \cos\left(a \times \dfrac{\pi}{2a}\right)\right] = U_0$

So amplitude of oscillation, $A = \dfrac{\pi}{2a}$.

19. **(b, c)** $\quad a = 3, b = 4, \phi = 0$

So $\qquad y = \dfrac{b}{a}x = \dfrac{4}{3}x$ (straight line)

$$A = \sqrt{a^2 + b^2} = 5$$

20. **(a, b, d)** The motion of simple pendulum in air is damped harmonic motion.

21. **(a, c)** At moon the value of acceleration due to gravity changes, so (a) and (c) will change.

22. **(a, c)** As $\vec{a}$ and $\vec{F}$ are opposite to $\vec{r}$ in SHM

so $\qquad \vec{a}.\vec{r} = ar\cos\pi = -ar$.

and $\qquad \vec{F}.\vec{r} = Fr\cos\pi = -Fr$.

23. **(a, b, c, d)** Explained in theory.

24. **(b, c)** Amplitude is obtained for $v = 0$

$\therefore$ Amplitude $= \sqrt{\dfrac{E}{A}}$

Maximum velocity is obtained for $x = 0$

$$v_{\max} = \sqrt{\dfrac{E}{B}}$$

$$v_{\max} = \text{amplitude} \times \omega$$

$\Rightarrow \qquad \omega = \sqrt{\dfrac{A}{B}} \Rightarrow T = 2\pi\sqrt{\dfrac{B}{A}}$

25. **(a, c)**

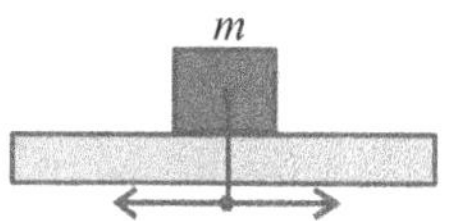

$$f = ma = m\omega^2 x$$

Contact force, $R = \sqrt{N^2 + f^2} = \sqrt{(mg)^2 + (m\omega^2 x)^2}$

$$\propto m$$

26. **(a, d)** $\quad T_1 = \dfrac{T}{12}$ and $T_2 = \dfrac{T}{6}$.

Solutions **EXERCISE-4.3**

1. **(d)** Damped oscillations are non-periodic.

2. **(a)** With respect to an observer, the force on the particle

$F = -k[x + (v_0 - v_0)t] = -kx$, so it represents SHM.

3. **(b)** At moon $T = 2\pi\sqrt{\dfrac{\ell}{(g/6)}}$, so time period increases. Second statement does not explain this.

4. **(c)** The effective value of gravity inside satellite is zero. The value of g is not zero in satellite.

5. **(a)** As $E \propto A^2$, $E' = 4E$.

6. **(c)** $E = \dfrac{1}{2}m\omega^2 A^2$; with increase in A, E must be increased. If E increases, A need not be increased, there may increase m or ω.

7. **(c)** The force at the extreme position is, $F = m\omega^2 A$.

8. **(d)** At extreme position, $a = \omega^2 A$ and $v = 0$.

9. **(a)** At resonance, the amplitude of oscillations become quite large.

10. **(c)** Due to air resistance, the energy of oscillating decreases and so amplitude decreases.

11. **(b)** $\qquad x = A\sin\omega t$

and $\qquad v = \omega A\cos\omega t = \omega A\sin(\omega t + \pi/2)$

12. **(d)** Mass of the block need not be small enough.

For SHM, $\qquad a = -\omega^2 x$.

Passage for (Q 1- 3) :

1. (d)

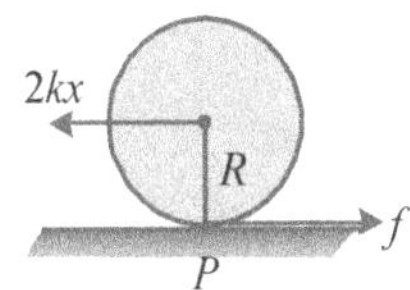

$$\alpha = \frac{\tau_p}{I} = \frac{2kx \times R}{\dfrac{3MR^2}{2}} = \frac{4kx}{3RM}$$

$$\therefore \quad a_{cm} = \alpha R = \frac{4kx}{3M}$$

Net force, $\quad \vec{F} = M\vec{a}_{cm} = -M\left(\frac{4k\vec{x}}{3M}\right)$

$$= -\frac{4kx}{3}.$$

2. (d) $\quad F_{net} = -\dfrac{4kx}{3}$

On comparing with $F = -M\omega^2 x$, we get

$$\omega = \sqrt{\frac{4k}{3M}}.$$

3. (c) $\dfrac{1}{2}Mv_0^2 + \dfrac{1}{2}\left(\dfrac{MR^2}{2}\right)\left(\dfrac{v_0}{R}\right)^2 = \dfrac{1}{2}(2k)x_{max}^2$

$$\Rightarrow \quad x_{max} = \sqrt{\frac{3}{4}\frac{Mv_0^2}{k}}.$$

The friction will have its maximum value at extreme position, and so

$$2kx_{max} - f_{max} = \frac{4k}{3}x_{max}$$

or $\quad f_{max} = \dfrac{2}{3}kx_{max}$

or $\quad \mu Mg = \dfrac{2}{3}k\sqrt{\dfrac{3}{4}\left(\dfrac{Mv_0^2}{k}\right)}$

or $\quad v_0 = \mu g\sqrt{\dfrac{3M}{k}}.$

Passage for (Q. 4 - 6) :

4. (b)

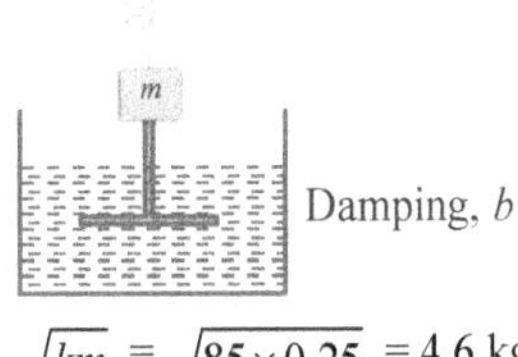

$$\sqrt{km} = \sqrt{85 \times 0.25} = 4.6 \text{ kg/s}$$

Given $b = 70$ g/s. As $b \ll \sqrt{km}$, so the period is approximately that of the undamped oscillator. Thus

$$T = 2\pi\sqrt{\frac{m}{k}} = 2\pi\sqrt{\frac{0.25}{85}} = 0.34 s.$$

5. (c) If A_o is the initial amplitude of motion, then

$$A_o e^{\frac{-bt}{2m}} = \frac{A_o}{2}$$

or $\quad e^{\frac{bt}{2m}} = 2$

or $\quad \dfrac{bt}{2m} = \ell n 2$

$$\therefore \quad t = \frac{2m\ell n2}{b} = \frac{2 \times 0.25\,\ell n2}{0.070}$$

$$= 5.0 \text{ s.} \qquad \textbf{\textit{Ans.}}$$

6. (d) We know that

$$E = E_o e^{\frac{-bt}{m}}$$

For $\quad E = \dfrac{E_o}{2};$

$$\frac{E_o}{2} = E_o e^{\frac{-bt}{m}}$$

or $\quad \dfrac{bt}{m} = \ell n2$

or $\quad t = \dfrac{m\ell n2}{b} = \dfrac{0.25 \times \ell n2}{0.070} = 2.5$ s.

Passage for (Q. 7 - 9) :

7. (c) $\quad f = \dfrac{1}{2\pi}\sqrt{\dfrac{k}{m}} = \dfrac{1}{2\pi}\sqrt{\dfrac{1200}{3}}$

$$= 3.2 \text{ s}^{-1}$$

8. (a) $\quad a_{max} = \omega^2 A = \dfrac{k}{m} \times A$

$$= \frac{1200}{3} \times 0.02 = 8 \text{ m/s}^2.$$

9. (b) $\quad v_{max} = \omega A = \sqrt{\dfrac{1200}{3}} \times 0.02 = 0.4$ m/s

Passage for (Q. 10 - 12) :

10. (a) $\quad \omega = \sqrt{\dfrac{k}{m}} = \sqrt{\dfrac{1200}{3}} = 20$ rad/s

At $t = 0$, $x = 0$, so $\phi_0 = 0$

$$\therefore \quad x = A\sin(\omega t + \phi_0) = 2\sin(20t)$$

11. (a) At $t = 0$, $x = A$, so $\phi_0 = \pi/2$

$$\therefore \quad x = 2\sin(20t + \pi/2) = 2\cos 20t$$

12. (b) At $t = 0$, $x = -A$, and so $\phi_0 = -\pi/2$

$$\therefore \quad x = 2\sin(20t - \pi/2) = -2\cos 20t$$

Passage for (Q. 13 - 15) :

13. (b)

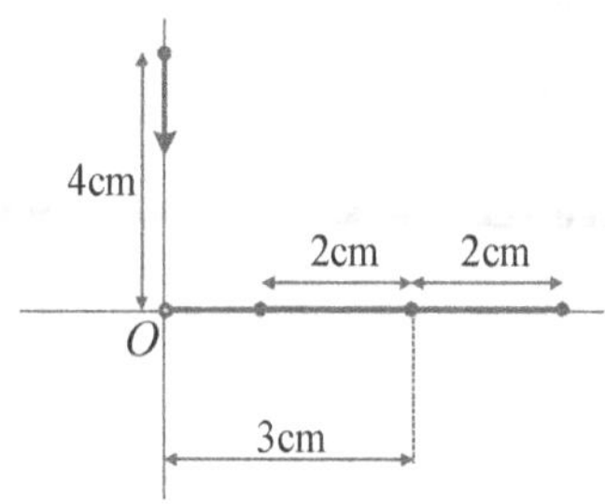

The particle is at left extreme ($T = 1$s)

$$\therefore \qquad -A = A\sin(\omega \times 0 + \phi_0)$$

or $\qquad \phi_0 = -\pi/2$

Thus $\qquad x = 3 + A\sin(\omega t + \phi_0)$

or $\qquad x = 3 + 2\sin\left(\dfrac{2\pi}{T}t - \dfrac{\pi}{2}\right)$

or $\qquad x = 3 - 2\cos(2\pi t)$.

14. (d) $\qquad 0 = A\sin(\omega \times 0 + \phi_0)$

or $\qquad \phi_0 = 0 \text{ or } \pi$

$$\therefore \qquad x = 4 + 2\sin\left(\dfrac{2\pi}{T}t + \pi\right)$$

or $\qquad x = 4 - 2\sin(2\pi t)$.

15. (a) The minimum distance will occur when particles are at extreme (near origin) position,

$$x_{\min} = \sqrt{2^2 + 1^2} = \sqrt{5} \text{ cm}$$

The maximum distance will occur when the particles are extreme (away from origin),

$$x_{\max} = \sqrt{5^2 + 6^2} = \sqrt{61} \text{ cm}$$

Passage for (Q. 16 - 18) :

16. (a) Just before collision, both P & Q arrive at their equilibrium position

$$v_P = \omega \frac{A}{2} = \sqrt{\frac{k}{m}}\frac{A}{2}$$

17. (b) Speed of Q just before collision is

$$v_Q = \omega A = \sqrt{\frac{k}{m}}\, A$$

18. (a) The block shall meet after time $t = \dfrac{T}{4}$, where T is time period of either isolated spring block system.

$$t = \frac{T}{4} = \frac{1}{4}2\pi\sqrt{\frac{m}{k}} = \frac{\pi}{2}\sqrt{\frac{m}{k}}$$

Passage for (Q. 19 - 21) :

19. (c) $\qquad$ 20. (b) and 21. (c)
The velocity

$$v = \omega\sqrt{A^2 - x^2}$$

or $\qquad -13.6 = \omega\sqrt{A^2 - 0.1^2}$ $\qquad$ ...(i)

and acceleration $a = -\omega^2 x$

or $\qquad -123 = -\omega^2 \times 0.1$ $\qquad$ ... (ii)
Solving equations (i) and (ii), we get

$$\omega = 35.1 \text{ rad/s or } f = 5.58 \text{ Hz}$$

and $\qquad A = 0.400$ m

Also $\qquad \omega = \sqrt{k/m}$

$$\therefore \qquad m = \frac{k}{\omega^2} = \frac{400}{(35.1)^2}$$

$$= 0.325 \text{ kg.}$$

Passage for (Q. 22 - 24) :

22. (b) Rotational inertia
$$I = I_{\text{rod}} + I_{\text{disc}}$$

$$= \frac{0.27(0.5)^2}{3} + \left[\frac{(0.5)(0.1)^2}{2} + 0.5 \times (0.5 + 0.1)^2\right]$$

$$= 0.205 \text{ kg -m}^2$$

23 (c) The distance of cm from pivot

$$d = \frac{m_1 y_1 + m_2 y_2}{m_1 + m_2}$$

$$= \frac{0.27 \times 0.25 + 0.50 \times 0.6}{0.27 + 0.50}$$

$$= 47.7 \text{ cm.}$$

24 (a) The time period of physical pendulum is given by

$$T = 2\pi\sqrt{\frac{I}{mgd}}$$

$$= 1.50 \text{ s}$$

Passage for (Q. 25 - 27) :

25. (a) $T = 2$s, $\therefore \omega = \dfrac{2\pi}{T} = \dfrac{2\pi}{2} = \pi$ rad/s

Velocity, $\qquad v = \omega A = \pi \times 0.1$

$$= 0.314 \text{ m/s}$$

26. (c) $\qquad a = \omega^2 x = \pi^2 \times 0.05$

$$= 0.493 \text{ m/s}^2$$

27. (d) The time taken is

$$t = 2 \times \frac{T}{12} = \frac{T}{6} = \frac{2}{6} = 0.33 \text{ s .}$$

Passage for (Q. 28 - 30) :

28. (b) If x_1 and x_2 are the extensions in the springs then

$$x_1 + x_2 = 0.2 \qquad \text{... (i)}$$

Also $\qquad k_1 x_1 = k_2 x_2$
or $\qquad 1 \times k_1 = 3\, k_2$ $\qquad$ ... (ii)
After solving equations (i) and (ii), we get

$$x_2 = 0.05 \text{ m}$$

and $\qquad x_1 = 0.15 \text{ m}$
Thus length of spring of force constant k_1 is

$$\ell_1 = 0.2 + 0.15 = 0.35 \text{ m.}$$

29. (a) The time period, $T = 2\pi\sqrt{\dfrac{m}{(k_1 + k_2)}}$

$$= 2\pi\sqrt{\frac{0.1}{(1+3)}} = 1 \text{ s .}$$

30. (a) The velocity of the block at equilibrium position

$$v = \omega A$$

$$= \sqrt{\frac{k_1 + k_2}{m}} \times A$$

$$= \sqrt{\frac{4}{0.1}} \times 0.05 = 0.316 \text{ m/s}$$

By conservation of momentum,

$$0.1 \times v = (0.1 + 0.1)v'$$

$$\therefore \quad v' = \frac{v}{2} = 0.158 \text{ m/s}$$

If A' is the new amplitude, then

$$\frac{1}{2}(0.2) \times (0.158)^2 = \frac{1}{2}(1+3)A'^2$$

or $\quad A' = 0.0353$ m

Passage for (Q. 31 - 33) :

31. (a) If A be the amplitude of motion, then

$$kA = F \text{ or } A = \frac{F}{k}.$$

32. (b) Time period, $\quad T = 2\pi\sqrt{\frac{m}{k/2}} = 2\pi\sqrt{\frac{2m}{k}}$

33. (a) If A' be the amplitude now, then

$$\frac{1}{2}(k/2)A'^2 = \frac{1}{2}mv_u^2$$

$$\therefore \quad A' = \sqrt{\frac{2m}{k}}\,v_u$$

Passage for (Q. 34 - 36) :

34. (b) The angular frequency

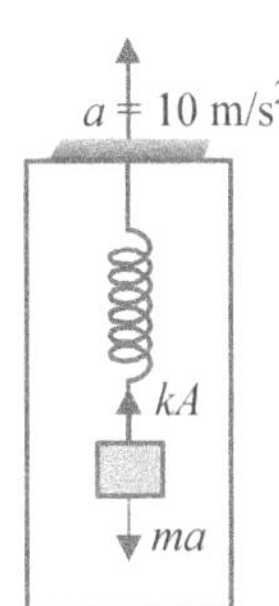

$$\omega = \sqrt{\frac{k}{m}} = \sqrt{\frac{800}{2}} = 20 \text{ rad/ s}$$

35. (c) In accelerated car, the pseudo force

$$F = ma = kA$$

or $\quad 2 \times 10 = 800\,A$

$\therefore \quad A = 2.5$ cm

36. (b) When the car's acceleration becomes zero, the present position of the block then becomes the extreme position and so,

$\phi = \pi/2$ rad.

37. **A → (q); B → (p); C → (r); D → (s)**

(A) At $\phi = 0$, K.E $= \frac{1}{2}m\omega^2 A^2 \cos^2\phi = \frac{1}{2}m\omega^2 A^2$ and always be positive.

(B) At $\phi = 0$, PE $= \frac{1}{2}m\omega^2 A^2 \sin^2\phi = 0$ and always be positive.

(C) T.E. in free oscillations remains constant.

(D) $v = \omega A \cos\phi$; At $\phi = 0$, $v_{max} = \omega A$ and varies sinusoidally.

38. **A → (p); B → (q, s); C → (s); D → (q)**

(A) Potential energy of simple pendulum

$$U = \frac{1}{2}m\omega^2 x^2 \text{ ; it is a parabola.}$$

(B) For zero acceleration, displacement

$s = vt$, so $s \propto t$ and for constant acceleration, $s = \frac{1}{2}at^2$; it is parabola.

(C) Range, $R = \dfrac{u^2 \sin 2\theta}{g}$; it is parabolic between R and u.

(D) $T = 2\pi\sqrt{\dfrac{\ell}{g}}$ or $T^2 \propto \ell$; it is a straight line.

39. **A → (t); B → (q); C → (r); D → (p, s)**
Theoritical

40. **A → (r); B → (p); C → (q); D → (s)**

(A) $x = A\sin\omega t$ and $a = -\omega^2 A\sin\omega t = \omega^2 A\sin(\omega t + \pi)$

$\therefore \quad \phi = \pi$ rad .

(B) All the particles on same wavefront are in the same phase.

$\therefore \quad \phi = 0$.

(C) $i = i_o \sin\omega t$ and $e = e_0 \sin(\omega t + \pi/2)$ $\therefore$ $\phi = \pi/2$

(D) $\phi = 0$ or 2π.

41. **(A) → r; (B) → p; (C) → q ; (D) → s**

$$v_m = A\omega \Rightarrow A = \frac{v_m}{\omega} = \frac{2\pi}{2\pi} \times (0.2) = 0.20\,m$$

$$T = 2\pi\sqrt{\frac{m}{k}} \Rightarrow m = \frac{T^2 k}{4\pi^2} = 0.2\,kg$$

At $t = 0.1$ sec, acc. is maximum $= -\omega^2 A = -200$ m/s^2

Maximum energy $= \frac{1}{2}mv_m^2 = 4$ J

or $\dfrac{1}{2}kA^2 = E_{max} = \dfrac{1}{2} \times 200 \times 0.04 = 4J = \dfrac{1}{2}v_m^2 = 4$ J

42. **A → (r); B → (s); C → (q); D → (r)**

(A) For equilibrium, $F = 8 - 2x = 0$

or $\quad x = 4\,m$

(B) From figure,

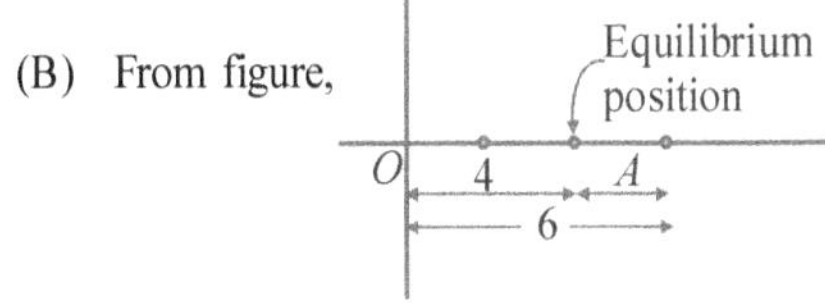

$A = 2\,m$

(C) Time taken from $x = 2$ to 4

or A to O is $\dfrac{T}{4}$, which differes in phase by $\dfrac{\pi}{2}$.

(D) Energy of SHM, $E = \displaystyle\int_4^6 F dx$

$$= \int_4^6 (8 - 2x)dx = \left|8x - x^2\right|_4^6$$

$$= 4 \text{ J.}$$

43. **A →(q); B → (r); C → (p);D → (s)**

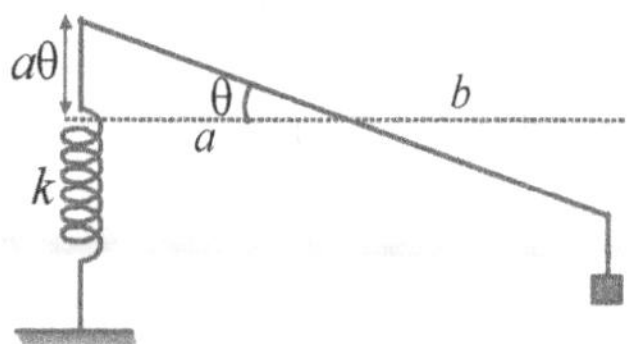

For small angle θ, the restoring torque

$$\tau = -(ka\theta) \times a = ka^2(-\theta)$$

$$\therefore \quad \alpha = \frac{\tau}{I} = \frac{ka^2}{mb^2}(-\theta)$$

On comparing with, $\alpha = -\omega^2\theta$, we get

$$\omega = \sqrt{\frac{ka^2}{mb^2}} \text{ and } T = 2\pi\frac{b}{a}\sqrt{\frac{m}{k}}.$$

Energy of oscillation, $E = \frac{1}{2}kA^2 = \frac{1}{2}k(a\theta)^2$.

44. **A → (q); B → (p, r); C → (s); D → (t)**

Suppose the plank is displaced by x. If some instant speed of plank is v, then speed of cylinder will be $v/2$. The total energy of the system.

$$E = \frac{1}{2}mv^2 + \frac{1}{2}kx^2 + \frac{1}{2}(2m)\left(\frac{v}{2}\right)^2 + \frac{1}{2}I\left(\frac{v/2}{R}\right)^2$$

$$= \frac{7}{8}mv^2 + \frac{1}{2}kx^2$$

For free oscillations, $\frac{dE}{dt} = 0$, after calculating we get

$$a = -4kx/7m$$

On comparing with $a = -\omega^2 x$, we get

$$\omega = \sqrt{\frac{4k}{7m}}.$$

45. **A → (q); B → (r); C → (s); D → (p)**

$$\frac{1}{2}kx_0^2 = \frac{1}{2}mv_0^2 \text{ or } x_0 = \sqrt{\frac{mv_0^2}{k}}$$

Time period,

$$T' = \left[2\frac{T}{4} + 2t\right]$$

$$= \left[\frac{2\pi}{2}\sqrt{\frac{m}{k}} + 2\frac{\ell_0}{v_0}\right]$$

Energy of oscillation $= \frac{1}{2}mv_0^2$.

46. **A→r; B→s; C→p; D→q**

(A) In frame of lift effective acceleration due to gravity is

$$g + \frac{g}{2} = \frac{3g}{2} \text{ downwards. } \therefore T = 2\pi\sqrt{\frac{2(3\ell)}{3g}}$$

(B) $T = 2\pi\sqrt{\frac{m}{k_{eff}}} = 2\pi\sqrt{\frac{m}{k+2k}} = 2\pi\sqrt{\frac{m}{3k}}.$

(C) $T = 2\pi\sqrt{\frac{I}{mgd}} = 2\pi\sqrt{\frac{\frac{m\ell^2}{3}}{mg\frac{\ell}{2}}} = 2\pi\sqrt{\frac{2\ell}{3g}}$

(D) $T = 2\pi\sqrt{\frac{m}{\rho A g}} = 2\pi\sqrt{\frac{(\rho/2)\,A\,(2\ell)}{\rho A g}} = 2\pi\sqrt{\frac{\ell}{g}}$

47. **A→p; B→r; C→q**

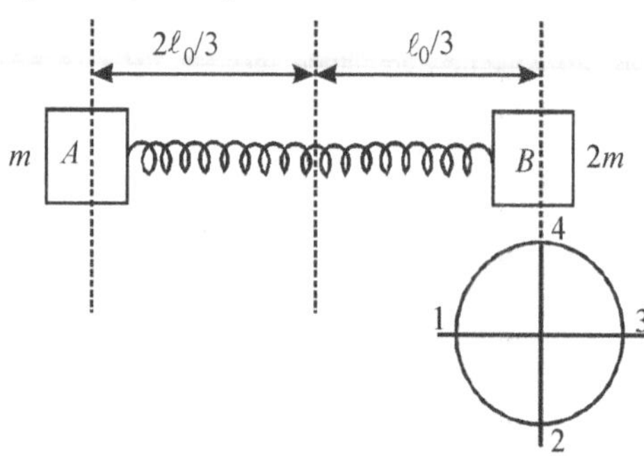

$$v_{CM} = \frac{2u \times m - u \times 2m}{3m} = 0 \text{ and } \omega = \sqrt{\frac{k}{\mu}} = \sqrt{\frac{k.3m}{m \times 2m}} = \sqrt{\frac{3k}{2m}}$$

(A) Spring is maximum compressed when phase of block B reaches position 1, and travels an angle

$$\frac{\pi}{2} \Rightarrow t = \frac{\pi}{2\omega} = \frac{\pi}{2}\sqrt{\frac{2m}{3k}}$$

(B) Spring is maximum elongated when phase of block B reaches position 3 and travels an angle

$$\frac{3\pi}{2} \Rightarrow t = \frac{3\pi}{2\omega} = \frac{3\pi}{2}\sqrt{\frac{2m}{3k}} = \pi\sqrt{\frac{3m}{2k}}$$

(C) Acceleration for both is zero when both pass their respective mean positions i.e. phase of B reaches position 2 and hence travels π angle

$$\Rightarrow t = \frac{\pi}{\omega} = \pi\sqrt{\frac{2m}{3k}}$$

48. **A→p ; B→q, r ; C→p ; D→q, r**

A → p

Reason : For a simple harmonic motion $v = a\sqrt{\omega^2 - x^2}$. On comparing it with $v = c_1\sqrt{c_2 - x^2}$ we find the two comparable.

B → q, r

Reason : $v = -kx$

when x is positive; v is $-$ ve, and as x decreases, v decreases. Therefore kinetic energy will decreases. When $x = 0$, $v = 0$. Therefore the object does not change its direction.

When x is negative, v is positive. But as x decreases in magnitude, v also decreases. Therefore kinetic energy decreases. When $x = 0$, $v = 0$. Therefore the object does not change its direction.

C → p

Reason : When $a = 0$, let the spring have an extension x. Then $kx = mg$.

When the elevator starts going upwards with a constant acceleration, as seen by the observer in the elevator, the object is at rest.

$\therefore \quad ma + mg = kx'$

$\Rightarrow \quad ma = k(x' - x)$ (Since a is constant)

D → q, r

The speed is $\sqrt{2}$ times the escape speed. Therefore the object will leave the earth. It will therefore not change the direction and its kinetic energy will keep on decreasing.

1. The given SHM^s may be represented as:
$$x = A \sin \omega t \qquad ...(i)$$
and
$$y = A \sin (2\omega t + \pi/2)$$
$$= A \cos 2\omega t$$
$$= A [1 - 2 \sin^2 \omega t] \qquad ...(ii)$$
From equations (i) and (ii), we have
$$y = A\left[1 - 2\frac{x^2}{A^2}\right]$$
or
$$y = A - \frac{2x^2}{A}$$

It shows a parabola.

2. For no slip on table
$$ma \leq f_{lim}$$
or
$$m\omega^2 A \leq \mu\, mg$$

$\therefore$
$$A_{max} = \frac{\mu g}{\omega^2}$$
$$= 0.02 \text{ m} \qquad \textit{Ans.}$$

3.
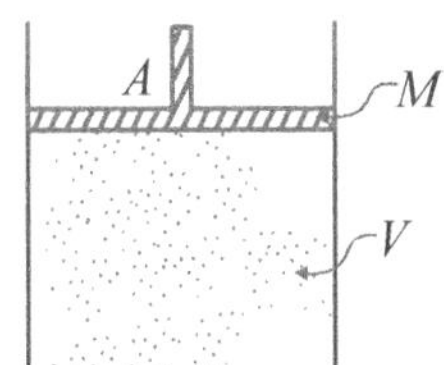

Given, Area of cross – section
$$A = 29.15 \times 10^{-5} \text{ m}^2$$
$$v = 10^{-3} \text{ m}^3$$
If M be the mass of the positon, then pressure
$$P = \frac{Mg}{A}$$

In non – conducting cylinder, the process will be adiabatic and so
$$PV^\gamma = \text{constant}$$
On differentiation, we have
$$P \times \gamma\, V^{\gamma-1} dV + V^\gamma dP = 0$$
$\therefore$
$$dP = -\gamma\frac{P}{V}(dV)$$
For small displacement (y) of the piston
$$dV = (Ay)$$
Restoring force, $F = (dP)A$
$$= -\gamma\frac{P}{V}(Ay)A$$
or
$$F = \frac{\gamma P}{V} A^2 (-y)$$
Acceleration of the piston
$$a = \frac{F}{M}$$
$$= \frac{\gamma P A^2}{VM}(-y)$$
Thus
$$T = 2\pi\sqrt{\frac{VM}{\gamma g A^2}}$$
As,
$$\frac{Mg}{A} = P,$$

$\therefore$
$$T = 2\pi\sqrt{\frac{V}{\gamma g A}}$$
$$= 2\pi\sqrt{\frac{10^{-3}}{1.4 \times 9.8 \times 29.15 \times 10^{-5}}}$$
$$= \pi$$
$\therefore$
$$f = \frac{1}{T} = \frac{1}{\pi}\, s^{-1} \qquad \textit{Ans.}$$

4. The time period is given by
$$T = 2\pi\sqrt{\frac{M}{A\rho g}}$$
$$= 2\pi\sqrt{\frac{0.002}{0.1^2 \times 1000 \times 9.8}}$$
$$= 0.028\ s \qquad \textit{Ans.}$$

5. When the rod is slightly displaced from its means position, then restoring force,

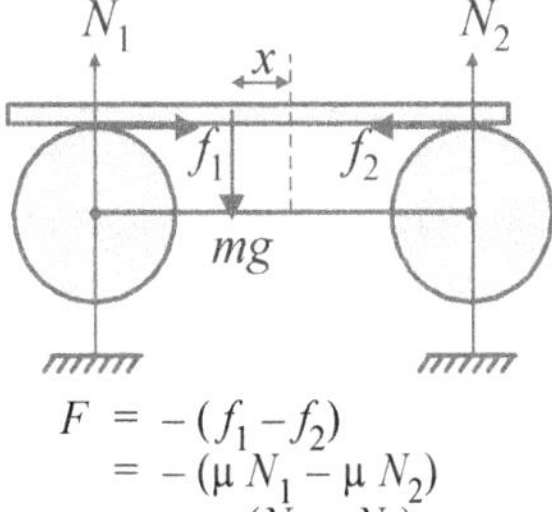

$$F = -(f_1 - f_2)$$
$$= -(\mu N_1 - \mu N_2)$$
$$= -\mu (N_1 - N_2)$$
For the vertical equilibrium of the rod, we have
$$N_1 + N_2 = mg \qquad ...(i)$$
and for rotational equilibrium, we have
$$mg (\ell/2 - x) - N_2\, \ell = 0 \qquad ...(ii)$$
$\therefore$
$$N_2 = \frac{mg}{\ell}(\ell/2 - x)$$
and
$$N_1 = mg - N_2$$
$$= mg - \frac{mg}{\ell}\left(\frac{\ell}{2} - x\right)$$
$$= \frac{mg}{\ell}\left[\frac{\ell}{2} + x\right]$$
Thus
$$F = \mu\left[\frac{mg}{\ell}\left(\frac{\ell}{2} + x\right) - \frac{mg}{\ell}\left(\frac{\ell}{2} - x\right)\right]$$
$$= -\mu\frac{mg}{\ell}(2x)$$
Acceleration of the rod
$$a = \frac{F}{m}$$
$$= \frac{2\mu g}{\ell}(-x)$$
Thus
$$T = 2\pi\sqrt{\frac{\ell}{2\mu g}}$$
$$= \pi\sqrt{\frac{2\ell}{\mu g}}. \qquad \textit{Ans.}$$

Solutions **EXERCISE-4.6**

1. Answer is the solution.
2. The standard equation of linear SHM is
$$a = -\omega^2 x$$
∴ only (c) represents equations of SHM
3. (b) The time period of large amplitude is given by
$$T = 2\pi\sqrt{\frac{\ell}{g}}\left(1+\frac{\theta^2}{16}\right)$$

Clearly T is given by $2\pi\sqrt{\dfrac{\ell}{g}}$

(c) The time period of wristwatch is
$$T = 2\pi\sqrt{\frac{m}{k}},$$
which is free from value of g, and so it will give correct time during free fall.

(d) Explanation is given in the answer.
4. In time t, the angle
$$\theta = \omega t$$
$$= \frac{2\pi}{T}t$$
$$= \frac{2\pi}{2}t$$
$$= \pi t$$
Thus, $-x = 3\sin\omega t$
or $x = -3\sin\pi t.$
Do the other part similarly.
5. Answer is the solution.
6. Given $x = B\sin(\omega t + \alpha)$
At $t = 0,$
            $x = 1$
∴ $1 = B\sin(0 + \alpha)$
or $B\sin\alpha = 1$ .... (i)

Also $v = \dfrac{dx}{dt} = \omega A\cos(\omega t + \alpha)$

At $t = 0,$ $v = \pi$
∴ $\pi = \pi A\cos(\omega \times 0 + \alpha)$
or $A\cos\alpha = 1$ ......(ii)

From equations (i) and (ii), we get
$$B = \sqrt{2}$$

and $\alpha = \dfrac{\pi}{4}$ or $\dfrac{5\pi}{4}$ **Ans.**

7. Given $x = 5\cos\left[2\pi t + \dfrac{\pi}{4}\right]$

∴ $v = \dfrac{dx}{dt}$
$$= -5\times 2\pi\sin\left[2\pi t + \frac{\pi}{4}\right]$$

and $a = \dfrac{dv}{dt}$
$$= -10\pi(2\pi)\cos\left[2\pi t + \frac{\pi}{4}\right]$$

After substituting $t = 1.5$ s, we get
$x = +3.535$ m,
$v = -22.22$ m/s,
$a = -139.56$ m/s^2.   **Ans.**

8. Given $y = 0.5\cos\left(100t + \dfrac{3\pi}{4}\right)$

On comparing with,
$$y = A\cos(\omega t + \phi_0), \text{ we have}$$
$A = 0.5,$
$\omega = 100$

and $\phi_0 = \dfrac{3\pi}{4}$

(i) $f = \dfrac{\omega}{2\pi} = \dfrac{100}{2\pi} = \dfrac{50}{\pi}Hz$

(ii) $\phi_0 = \dfrac{3\pi}{4}$

(iii) $v_{max} = \omega A$
$$= 100\times 0.5$$
$$= 50 \text{ m/s}$$

(iv) $a_{max} = \omega^2 A = 100^2\times 0.5 = 5000$ m/s^2

(v) $E = \dfrac{1}{2}m\omega^2 A^2$
$$= \frac{1}{2}\times 0.1\times(100)^2\times(0.5)^2 = 125 \text{ J.}\ \textbf{Ans.}$$

9. (a) Answer is the solution.

(b) Given $x = A\cos\left(\omega t - \dfrac{\pi}{4}\right)$ ...(i)

∴ $v_x = \dfrac{dx}{dt}$
$$= -\omega A\sin\left(\omega t - \frac{\pi}{4}\right)\quad ....(ii)$$

From above equations, we have
$$\cos\left(\omega t - \frac{\pi}{4}\right) = \frac{x}{A}$$
$$-\sin\left(\omega t - \frac{\pi}{4}\right) = \frac{v_x}{\omega A}$$

and squaring and adding, we get
$$\frac{x^2}{A^2} + \frac{v_x^2}{(\omega A)^2} = 1.\qquad \textbf{Ans.}$$

10. Given, $x = a\sin^2\left(\omega t - \dfrac{\pi}{4}\right)$
$$= a\left[\frac{1-\cos 2\left(\omega t - \frac{\pi}{4}\right)}{2}\right]$$
$$= \frac{a}{2} - \frac{a}{2}\cos\left(2\omega t - \frac{\pi}{2}\right)$$
$$= \frac{a}{2} - \frac{a}{2}\sin 2\omega t\qquad ...(i)$$

(a) Amplitude of oscillations

$$A = \frac{a}{2}$$

and $\omega' = 2\omega$

$\therefore \quad T = \frac{2\pi}{\omega'} = \frac{2\pi}{2\omega} = \frac{\pi}{\omega}$

(b) $v_x = \frac{dx}{dt} = -\frac{a}{2} \times 2\omega \cos 2\omega t$

$\quad = -\omega a \cos 2\omega t \qquad ....(ii)$

From equations (i) and (ii), we have

$$-\sin 2\omega t = (2x - a)/a$$

and $\cos 2\omega t = \dfrac{v_x}{\omega a}$

Squaring and adding, we have

$$\left(\frac{2x-a}{a^2}\right)^2 + \left(\frac{v_x}{\omega a}\right)^2 = 1 \qquad \textit{Ans.}$$

It represents an ellipse.

11. Suppose $x = a\cos(\omega t + \alpha)$

$\therefore \quad v_x = \dfrac{dx}{dt}$

$\quad = -\omega a \sin(\omega t + \alpha)$

Given, at $t = 0$,

$\quad x_0 = 25$ cm

and $v_{x_0} = 100$ cm/s

$\therefore \quad x_0 = a\cos\alpha \qquad ....(i)$

and $v_{x_0} = -\omega a \sin\alpha$

$\therefore \quad \dfrac{v_{x_0}}{\omega} = -a\sin\alpha \qquad ...(ii)$

From equations, (i) and (ii), we have

$$a = \sqrt{x_0^2 + \left(\frac{v_{x_0}}{\omega}\right)^2}$$

and $\tan\alpha = -\left(\dfrac{v_{x_0}}{\omega x_0}\right)$

After substituting the values, we get

$\quad x = -29$ cm

and $v_a = -81$ cm

12. Given $U = U_0(1 - \cos ax)$

$\therefore \quad F = -\dfrac{dU}{dx} = -U_0(0 + a\sin ax)$

$\quad = -U_0 a \sin(ax)$

For small x, $\sin(ax) \simeq ax$

$\therefore \quad F = -U_0 a^2 x$

Acceleration $= \dfrac{F}{m} = \dfrac{-U_0 a^2}{m}(-x)$

$\therefore \quad T = 2\pi\sqrt{\dfrac{m}{a^2 U_0}}$

13. Suppose mercury in left limb is depressed by y. The corresponding increase in length of mercury in right limb will be y. The vertical head of mercury

$$h = (y + y\cos\theta)$$

The restoring force $F = \qquad -PA$

$\quad = -(\rho gh)s$

$\quad = -\rho g s (1 + \cos\theta) y$

Acceleration $a = \dfrac{F}{m}$

$\quad = \dfrac{\rho gs}{m}(1 + \cos\theta)(-y)$

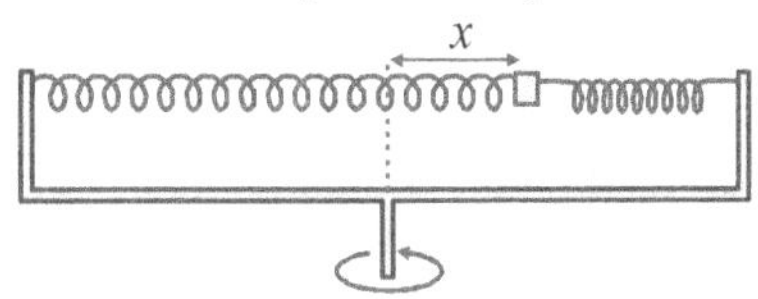

On comparing with $a = -\omega^2 y$,

we have $\omega = \sqrt{\dfrac{\rho gs(1 + \cos\theta)}{m}}$

$\therefore \quad T = \dfrac{2\pi}{\omega}$

$\quad = 2\pi\sqrt{\dfrac{m}{\rho gs(1 + \cos\theta)}} \qquad \textit{Ans.}$

14. Suppose the block is displaced slightly (x) from its mean position, then restoring force

$$F = -[\text{spring force} - \text{centrifugal force}]$$

$\quad = -[kx - m\omega^2 x]$

Acceleration of the block

$$a = \frac{F}{m}$$

$\quad = \left(\dfrac{k}{m} - \omega^2\right)(-x)$

$\therefore \quad T = \dfrac{2\pi}{\sqrt{\left(\dfrac{k}{m} - \omega^2\right)}}$

For no oscillations $kx - m\omega^2 x \le 0$

or $\quad \omega \ge \sqrt{k/m} \qquad \textit{Ans.}$

15. Given, $f_1 = \dfrac{1}{2\pi}\sqrt{\dfrac{k_1}{m}}$

and $f_2 = \dfrac{1}{2\pi}\sqrt{\dfrac{k_2}{m}}$

From above, $k_1 = 4\pi^2 m f_1^2$

and $k_2 = 4\pi^2 m f_2^2$

When block oscillates with the springs together,

$$f = \frac{1}{2\pi}\sqrt{\frac{k_1 + k_2}{m}}$$

$\quad = \dfrac{1}{2\pi}\sqrt{\dfrac{4\pi^2 m(f_1^2 + f_2^2)}{m}}$

$\therefore \quad f = \sqrt{f_1^2 + f_2^2} \qquad \textit{Ans.}$

16. Given, $L_1 + L_2 = L$

and $L_1 = nL_2$

From above, we get

$$L_1 = \frac{nL}{n+1}$$

and $$L_2 = \frac{L}{n+1}$$

Thus $$k_1 = \frac{(n+1)k}{n}$$

$$k_2 = (n+1)\,k$$

The frequency of original spring

$$f = \frac{1}{2\pi}\sqrt{\frac{k}{m}},$$

Also $$f_1 = \frac{1}{2\pi}\sqrt{\frac{k_1}{m}}$$

and $$f_2 = \frac{1}{2\pi}\sqrt{\frac{k_2}{m}}$$

$\therefore$ $$f_1 = \sqrt{\frac{(n+1)}{n}}\,f$$

and $$f_2 = \sqrt{(n+1)k}$$ ***Ans.***

17. (a) The restoring torque

$$\tau = [\,mg \times x \sin\theta\,]$$

For small angle θ,

$$\sin\theta \simeq \theta$$

$\therefore$ $$\tau = mgx\,(-\theta)$$

and $$a = \frac{\tau}{I}$$

$$= \frac{mgx}{I}(-\theta)$$

On comparing with standard equation of angular SHM,

$$\alpha = -\omega^2\,\theta,$$

we get $$\omega = \sqrt{\frac{mgx}{I}}$$

$\therefore$ $$T = 2\pi\sqrt{\frac{I}{mgx}}$$

For the case, $$I = \left(\frac{mL^2}{12} + mx^2\right)$$

$\therefore$ $$T = \sqrt{\frac{\left(\dfrac{mL^2}{12} + mx^2\right)}{mgx}}$$ ***Ans.***

(b) For T to be minimum,

$$\frac{dT}{dx} = 0,$$

or $$\frac{d}{dx}\frac{\left(\dfrac{mL^2}{12} + mx^2\right)^{1/2}}{(mgx)^{1/2}} = 0$$

After simplifying, we get

$$x = \frac{L}{\sqrt{12}}$$ ***Ans.***

(c) $$T_{min} = 2\pi\sqrt{\frac{\left(\dfrac{mL^2}{12} + \dfrac{mL^2}{12}\right)}{mg \times \dfrac{L}{\sqrt{12}}}}$$

$$= 2\pi\sqrt{\frac{\sqrt{12}}{6} \times \frac{L}{g}}$$

$$= 2\pi\sqrt{\frac{\sqrt{12} \times 1}{6 \times 9.8}}$$

$$= 1.53 \text{ s}$$ ***Ans.***

18. Given $$\frac{1}{2}m\omega^2 A^2 = 8 \times 10^{-3}$$

or $$\frac{1}{2} \times 0.1 \times \omega^2 \times 0.1^2 = 8 \times 10^{-3}$$

$\therefore$ $$\omega = 4 \text{ rad/s}$$

Thus $$y = A\sin(\omega t + \phi_0)$$

$$= 0.1\sin(4t + \frac{\pi}{4})$$

19. The area of cross – section of the wire

$$A = \frac{\pi}{4}d^2$$

$$= \frac{\pi}{4}(0.004 \times 10^{-2})^2$$

$$= 1.256 \times 10^{-7} \text{ m}^2$$

The change in length, $\Delta L = \dfrac{FL}{AY}$

For 1 kg bob $$\Delta L = \frac{(1 \times 9.8) \times 5}{1.256 \times 10^{-7} \times 12.4 \times 10^{10}}$$

$$= 3.15 \times 10^{-3} \text{ m}$$

For 10 kg bob, $\Delta L = 10(\Delta L)$

$$= 3.15 \times 10^{-2} \text{ m}$$

Thus $$T_1 = 2\pi\sqrt{\frac{(5 + 0.00315)}{9.8}}$$

$$= 4.486 \text{ s}$$

and $$T_2 = 2\pi\sqrt{\frac{5 + 0.0315}{9.8}}$$

$$= 4.489 \text{ s}$$ ***Ans.***

20. Suppose θ is the phase difference between them,

then $$x_1 = A \sin \omega t \qquad ...(i)$$

and $$x_2 = A \sin(\omega t + \phi) \qquad ...(ii)$$

Putting $x_1 = x_2$

$$= A/2 \text{ in the above equations, we get}$$

$$\frac{A}{2} = A \sin \omega t$$

or $$\sin \omega t = \frac{1}{2}$$

and $$\frac{A}{2} = A\,[\sin \omega t \cos \phi + \cos \omega t \sin \phi\,]$$

or $\qquad \dfrac{A}{2} = A\left[\dfrac{1}{2}\cos\phi + \sqrt{1 - \left(\dfrac{1}{2}\right)^2}\sin\phi\right]$

or $\quad 2\cos^2\phi - 2\cos\phi - 2 = 0$

$\therefore \qquad \cos\phi = 1 \quad$ or $\quad -1/2$

$\qquad \cos\phi = 1$ is not acceptable.

$\therefore \qquad \cos\phi = -\dfrac{1}{2}$

or $\qquad \phi = 120°$ **Ans.**

21. In the device the block remains in contact with first spring for half the time period. i.e. $\dfrac{T_1}{2}$. Similarly with the second spring it is $\dfrac{T_2}{2}$.

If t is the time of motion from C to D, then total time of motion

$$T = 2t + \dfrac{T_1}{2} + \dfrac{T_2}{2}$$

$$= 2 \times \dfrac{CD}{v} + \dfrac{1}{2}\left[2\pi\sqrt{\dfrac{m}{k_1}} + 2\pi\sqrt{\dfrac{m}{k_2}}\right]$$

$$= 2.83 \text{ s} \qquad \textbf{Ans.}$$

22. If A be the amplitude of motion, then maximum acceleration,

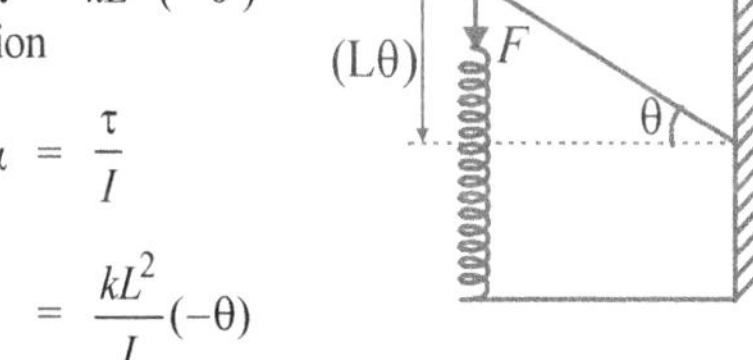

$$a = \omega^2 A$$

The block will separate from the piston when the piston moves downwards, so

$\qquad mg - N = ma$

$\therefore \qquad N = m(g - a)$

To leave contract, $N = 0$

$\therefore \qquad a = g$

or $\qquad \omega^2 A = g$

$\therefore \qquad A = \dfrac{g}{\omega^2} = \dfrac{g}{(2\pi/1)^2} = 0.25\ m$

Maximum velocity $\quad v_{max} = \omega A$

$$= \left(\dfrac{2\pi}{1}\right) \times 0.25\ \text{m} = 1.57\ \text{m/s} \qquad \textbf{Ans.}$$

23. For the floating sphere

$$Mg = \dfrac{V}{2}\sigma g$$

$$= \left(\dfrac{2}{3}\pi R^3\right)\sigma g$$

$\therefore \qquad M = \dfrac{2\pi R^3 \sigma}{3}$

The frequency of oscillations is given by

$$f = \dfrac{1}{2\pi}\sqrt{\dfrac{A\sigma g}{M}}$$

$$= \dfrac{1}{2\pi}\sqrt{\dfrac{(\pi R^2)\sigma g}{2\pi R^3 \sigma/3}} \qquad [\,A = \pi R^2\,]$$

$$= \dfrac{1}{2\pi}\sqrt{\dfrac{3g}{2R}}$$

24. See example 17.

25. If A is the initial amplitude of motion, then velocity of the block at mean position, then

$$v = \omega A$$

$$= \sqrt{\dfrac{k}{M}}\,A$$

Now by consevation of linear momentum, we have

$$Mv + 0 = (M + m)\,v'$$

$\therefore \qquad v' = \left[\dfrac{Mv}{M + m}\right]$

If A' be the new amplitude of motion, then

$$\dfrac{1}{2}(M + m)\left[\dfrac{Mv}{M + m}\right]^2 = \dfrac{1}{2}kA'^2$$

$$A' = \sqrt{\dfrac{M^2}{k(M + m)}}\,v$$

$$= \sqrt{\dfrac{M^2}{k(M + m)}} \times \sqrt{\dfrac{k}{M}}\,A$$

$$= \sqrt{\dfrac{M}{(M + m)}}\,A \qquad \textbf{Ans.}$$

The new frequency of vibration

$$f' = \dfrac{1}{2\pi}\sqrt{\dfrac{k}{M + m}} \qquad \textbf{Ans.}$$

26. If the rod is displaced through small angle θ, then extension in the spring will be $L\theta$. The force in the spring

$$F = k\,(L\theta)$$

Thus restoring torque

$$\tau = -F\,(L\cos\theta)$$

$$= -(kL\theta)\,(L\cos\theta)$$

For small θ, $\cos\theta = 1$

$\therefore \qquad \tau = kL^2\,(-\theta)$

Angular acceleration

$$\alpha = \dfrac{\tau}{I}$$

$$= \dfrac{kL^2}{I}(-\theta)$$

$\therefore \qquad T = 2\pi\sqrt{\dfrac{I}{kL^2}} = 2\pi\sqrt{\dfrac{ML^2}{3kL^2}}$

$$= 2\pi\sqrt{\dfrac{M}{3k}} \qquad \textbf{Ans.}$$

(b) The maximum speed

$$v_{max} = \omega A$$

$$= \sqrt{\dfrac{3k}{M}} \times L\theta_0$$

$$= L\theta_0\sqrt{\dfrac{3k}{M}} \qquad \textbf{Ans.}$$

27. The effective value of the spring constant

$$\dfrac{1}{k_e} = \dfrac{1}{k} + \dfrac{1}{2k} + \dfrac{1}{4k} + \dots\infty$$

or $\qquad \dfrac{1}{k_e} = \dfrac{1}{k}\left[1 + \dfrac{1}{2} + \dfrac{1}{4} + \dots\infty\right]$

$$= \frac{1}{k}\left[\frac{1}{1-\frac{1}{2}}\right]$$

$$= \frac{2}{k}$$

Thus $\qquad T = 2\pi\sqrt{\dfrac{m}{k_e}}$

$$= 2\pi\sqrt{\frac{2m}{k}} \qquad \textbf{\textit{Ans.}}$$

28. If F be the force is the spring, then for equilibrium

$$F - (m_1 + m_2)g = 0$$
$$\therefore \qquad F - m_2 g = m_1 g$$

when m_1 is removed the net force (restoring force) on the block, m_2,

$$F_{rest} = (F - m_2 g)$$
$$= m_1 g$$

$\therefore$ Amplitude $= \dfrac{m_1 g}{k}$

Angular frequency, $\omega = \sqrt{\dfrac{k}{m_2}}$ **_Ans._**

29. Each of the support spring of force constant k may be replaced by side spring of force constant $\dfrac{k}{4}$.

$$k_1/4$$
$$k_2/4 \quad \square\, m$$
$$k_3/4$$
$$k_4/4$$

The equivalent system is shown in figure. The equivalent force constant

$$\frac{1}{k_e} = \frac{1}{\frac{k_1}{4}} + \frac{1}{\frac{k_2}{4}} + \frac{1}{\frac{k_3}{4}} + \frac{1}{\frac{k_4}{4}}$$

or $\qquad \dfrac{1}{k_e} = 4\left[\dfrac{1}{k_1} + \dfrac{1}{k_2} + \dfrac{1}{k_3} + \dfrac{1}{k_4}\right]$

Time period

$$T = 2\pi\sqrt{\frac{m}{k_e}}$$

$$= 2\pi\sqrt{4m\left[\frac{1}{k_1} + \frac{1}{k_2} + \frac{1}{k_3} + \frac{1}{k_4}\right]} \qquad \textbf{\textit{Ans.}}$$

30. The force is the spring developed per unit of its length $= F_0/\ell$. If the particle is displaced down by y, then restoring force

$$= F = -4\left(\frac{F_0}{\ell} \times y\right).$$

The acceleration of the particle

$$a = \frac{4F_0}{m\ell}(-y).$$

Thus $\qquad T = 2\pi\sqrt{\dfrac{m\ell}{4F_0}}.$ **_Ans._**

31. The buoyant force on therod
$$F_b = Vd_2 g.$$
The restoring torque about p

$$\tau = -(F_b - mg)\frac{L}{2}\sin\theta$$

$$\tau = -(Vd_2 g - Vd_1 g)\times\frac{L}{2}\sin\theta$$

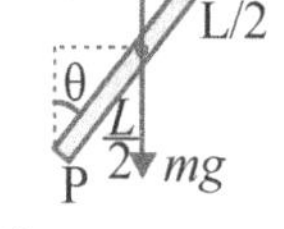

For small displacament θ, $\sin\theta \simeq \theta$,

$$\therefore \qquad \tau = -(d_2 - d_1)Vg\,\frac{L}{2}(\theta)$$

Angular frequency, $\omega = \sqrt{\dfrac{(d_2 - d_1)VgL}{2I}}$

$$= \sqrt{\frac{(d_2 - d_1)VgL}{2\frac{mL^2}{3}}}$$

$$= \sqrt{\frac{3}{2}\frac{(d_2 - d_1)VgL}{(Vd_1)L^2}}$$

$$= \sqrt{\frac{3g}{2L}\frac{(d_2 - d_1)}{d_1}} \qquad \textbf{\textit{Ans.}}$$

32. (i)   The equivalent force constant of the system

$$\frac{1}{k_e} = \frac{1}{k_1} + \frac{1}{\frac{k_2}{4}} + \frac{1}{\frac{k_3}{4}}$$

$$= \frac{1}{k_1} + \frac{4}{k_2} + \frac{4}{k_3}$$

Thus time period

$$T = 2\pi\sqrt{m\left[\frac{1}{k_1} + \frac{4}{k_2} + \frac{4}{k_3}\right]} \qquad \textbf{\textit{Ans.}}$$

(ii)   Solution similar to part (i)